# BEST BABY NAMES 2022

**Vermilion**
LONDON

This updated edition published in 2021
First published by Vermilion in 2012

1

Vermilion, an imprint of Ebury Publishing,
20 Vauxhall Bridge Road,
London SW1V 2SA

Vermilion is part of the Penguin Random House group of
companies whose addresses can be found at
global.penguinrandomhouse.com

Penguin
Random House
UK

Copyright © Applaud Media Ltd 2021

Siobhan Thomas has asserted her right to be identified as the author of
this Work in accordance with the Copyright, Designs and Patents Act 1988

www.penguin.co.uk

A CIP catalogue record for this book is available from the British Library

ISBN 9781785043857

Printed and bound in Great Britain by Clays Ltd, Elcograf S.p.A.

The authorised representative in the EEA is Penguin Random House
Ireland, Morrison Chambers, 32 Nassau Street, Dublin D02 YH68

Penguin Random House is committed to a sustainable future
for our business, our readers and our planet. This book is made
from Forest Stewardship Council® certified paper.

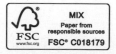

MIX
Paper from
responsible sources
FSC
www.fsc.org   FSC® C018179

# SIOBHAN THOMAS

# BEST BABY NAMES 2022

This book is dedicated to your new baby

# Contents

Acknowledgements                                          vi
Introduction                                               1
Using this Book                                            2

**Part 1 Finding the Right Name for Your Baby**            5
    Choosing the Perfect Name          6
    Useful Factors to Consider         13
    Common Hurdles                     20
    Quick Checks Before You Name Your Baby!   23

**Part 2 Inspiration**                                    31
    Naming Trends for 2021/22          32

**Part 3 Baby Names**                                     55
    Names for Baby Boys A–Z            57
    Names for Baby Girls A–Z           271

# Acknowledgements

Enormous thanks to Rosanne Rivers, a freelance writer, novelist and leader of writing workshops for young people. Her work was invaluable in compiling and editing the thousands of names in this book.

I would also like to thank James Macfarlane for giving me the opportunity to write this book and for his continuous encouragement and good humour from beginning to end.

Thanks, also, to James Brighton, Alan Jones and Annabel Freer for their assistance and input.

Finally I must thank Helen O'Shea and Dan Holt for their reviews of the manuscript and for their honest opinions and feedback. My mum, Pat, and my husband, Owen, also did their share of rereading – but more importantly I want to thank them, and Orla Goncalves, for all their help with the children, without which this book would never have been completed!

# Introduction

Congratulations! A new baby is on the way!

It is an incredibly amazing, exciting and life-changing time whether it's your first child or another in your ever-extending family. Suddenly, you are doing loads of planning in preparation for your new arrival. You may be rearranging your home or deciding which of the numerous items to buy to welcome your baby. There is so much to do and somehow you have to think of a good name as well. At first, it can seem a rather daunting responsibility as you want to find the very best name for them, but remember it can also be great fun. The wonderful thing about name-choosing is that it is not limited, not by income or space or anything at all. You are completely free to choose as many options and combinations as you like from the seemingly infinite number of names out there.

To choose a name for a brand new person is a uniquely special part of your preparations and a lovely experience to look back upon. By just relaxing and setting a little time aside, you can give your baby a very special gift that will really become as much a part of them in the future as the way they smile!

Naturally, you'll be keen to get it right so how are you going to decide the perfect name for them? The answers are in this book – which will help you on your baby-naming journey! Perhaps you like Hunter, Hassan, Arthur or Bailey or maybe Luna, Olivia or Florence. There are so many to consider that it can be confusing to work out how to begin. In the following pages are ways to start thinking about names, consider your ideas, any possible drawbacks and how to tackle them. You will also discover how and where to find inspiration, how to focus your choices, narrow them down to a shortlist and make that very final decision, arriving at the perfect baby name.

We hope to give you the confidence to plunge in, not worry too much and enjoy yourself. This experience may well become part of your earliest happy memories with your new baby. There is definitely a name out there that you will love and that you will be very happy to say and hear in the coming years. Sit back and let your imagination run wild as you begin to browse through this book. After all, you are very likely to be holding your brilliant final choice in your hands at this very moment!

## Using This Book

This book does not have to be read from beginning to end. In fact, that probably isn't the best way at all. It is designed for you to dip in anywhere by browsing or using the contents page. There are pointers and inspiration for everyone; couples and single parents who often like to involve siblings, wider family and close friends in helping to choose the perfect name. Stick markers in, make notes in the margins, highlight your favourites and cross out any names you want to veto. You might also be surprised how different a name can sound when you say it aloud.

**Part One** is a complete how-to guide on choosing baby names. It helps kick off the journey with ideas and suggestions on how and where to start. It helps in recognising various drawbacks with some names, how to come to agreement with your partner and how to cope with other people's opinions.

**Part Two** is all about inspiration. It offers famous names from categories such as film, sport, high achievers, fiction and many others. It is also reassuring to see a wide range of names, complete with a surname, written down and established as completely acceptable by the wider world.

Many people like to dive straight into page 51 and find out what the latest Top 100 most popular names are for England and Wales. While there will always be traditional names, and famous name trends, 2022 looks set to be more diverse than ever as new parents seek wider areas of inspiration. Everything from classical and traditional, mythological, fictional, the natural world to gender-neutral options is inspiration.

**Part Three** is the name section, with an alphabetical list of over nine thousand names from all over the world. It is in two sections – boys' names and girls' names with gender-neutral names in both sections. Each entry includes additional information on the origin, meaning, spelling and pronunciation of each name.

# PART ONE

# Finding the Right Name for Your Baby

# Choosing the Perfect Name

## What Makes a Good Name?

What makes a good name is hugely dependent on when and where. We can look back over the last century and recognise some of the baby names that were popular 100 years ago; however, many of our modern names would be completely alien to parents of that time. The same is true about all of us who have grown up in different countries and different cultures around the world. Apart from our generation and where we live, our own very individual life experiences will affect our attitudes towards certain names. The names of friends, family, film stars, heroes, bullies, private relationships or public personalities are all going to affect how we view any particular name.

Old-fashioned differences between our aspirations for girls and boys still influence our choice of names today. With girls' names, many parents still say that they are seeking something 'feminine', or 'pretty'. For boys, parents often say they are looking for a 'strong' name. Of course, that isn't to say that a girls' name can't be pretty and strong, or a boys' name can't be gentle without being weak. There are also plenty of names that are widely used for both genders, which may well support a recent trend for names that are gender neutral.

In some cultures, such as Greek Orthodox, the name of a new baby is often determined by the father's name; having a 'Junior' in the family has long been associated with Americans too, but it has become much less popular there in recent years as parents seek out more unique names. Elsewhere names are determined by a whole host of factors: a baby girl, born at the end of the week to Ghanaian parents, might be called 'Afia', which means 'born on a Friday'; many Native American names are drawn from nature (direct translations include Rainbow and Butterfly); and African cultures often draw on their aspirations for their children, using names such as 'Prosperity' or 'Beautiful'.

In the UK we have been experimenting with new ideas for some time. In 2011, there was a raging debate on the baby forums when the Beckhams named their daughter 'Harper Seven' and when Beyoncé and Jay-Z called their baby girl 'Blue Ivy Carter'. Some people loved these unique and audacious choices for names, while others disagreed, saying that they were too self-consciously unusual. However, five years later when Jamie and Jools Oliver named their baby son River Rocket it hardly created a murmur. Indeed some public speculation was supportive along the lines that the names probably had relevance as the River Cafe is where Jamie Oliver had his big break into TV. Rocket was fine as it is either aspirational or a salad, appropriately for a chef.

If you do not want anything too off the wall and want to be sure of a name that will be considered 'good' and already in circulation for your baby's generation, you can look at the Top 100 currently most popular baby names on pages 51–3. The names parents are choosing are becoming ever more diverse. The latest figures from the Office for National Statistics (ONS) show that 40% of girls and 50% of boys have a name in the top 100. This may be due to a number of factors including the desire for unique names, the influence of a more international popular culture and a growth in the number of babies born to international-born parents living in the UK. Many parents have said how they thought they had made an unusual choice only to find out later that it appeared surprisingly high on the popularity lists.

In recent decades the UK has become more cosmopolitan and people today are no longer surprised by unfamiliar names. With names from many countries, cultures and languages with several spelling options, unusual and unique names themselves have become more acceptable and far less of a social risk than in Granny's time. The emergence of the young royals into parenthood has created a renewed interest in the royal family and the names they choose for their babies. The Duke and Duchess of Cambridge named their babies George, Charlotte and Louis while Meghan and Harry chose Archie and Lilibet, all popular choices in the UK. Celebrities in the music, TV and film worlds are often pioneers in naming creativity which has encouraged more parents to be bold in their choices. For example: Hart, True, Stormi and Chicago may soon start to appear as popular choices.

## When to Choose a Name

For those who have had their children's names ready and waiting before their babies were even conceived, the pressure is off – unless you change your mind, of course! In theory, there is no rush – you have nine months to consider your baby's name. You'd think that this would be long enough, but it isn't always! Lots of people find that their baby is in their arms before they have made up their mind. In fact, there are many parents who have their name options finalised well ahead of baby's arrival, only to find that they change their mind after meeting their newborn. There is no need to panic if you aren't ready to name the baby straight away. It is perfectly acceptable to give yourselves a little time with your new arrival to consider what name you are going to give them. Don't feel under pressure from your friends and family who absolutely need to know what to write in the new baby card, or the grandparents who just have to have the name to tell their friends. This is your baby, and you'll do it in your own good time! Cuddle them, talk to them, try out your shortlist (and any others that come to mind) and you'll soon find a name that feels right for your baby. However, do keep in mind that in the UK parents are legally obliged to register their child's name before they are six weeks old. But this should give you plenty of time to decide!

---

## Registering Your Baby

**Birth Registration Overview**

All births in England, Wales and Northern Ireland must be registered within 42 days of the child being born. You should do this by making an appointment at the local register office in the area where the baby was born or at the hospital before the mother leaves. The hospital will tell you if you can register the birth there. If you can't register the birth in the area where the baby was born, you can go to another register office and they will send your details to the correct office.

The child's surname is usually that of either the mother or the father but, in cases where the parents are unmarried and the father does not attend the registration, it is possible to give the child an alternative surname. The government website (see link below) will provide full details. There are also directions to the appropriate registration districts for those outside the above geographical areas.

www.gov.uk/register-birth

---

## How to Choose a Name

Start the process with an open mind. If you're raising the baby with a partner, you'll both need to give proper consideration to one another's suggestions. It is helpful saying names aloud to one another; a name you like might not work on paper for your partner, but when they hear it spoken it might sound more appealing – of course it may also sound less appealing, so be prepared for that too! Respect one another's opinions on names. Avoid setting your heart on just one name too early; try to be flexible and listen to your partner's suggestions and objections. A name that sounds perfect to you may have been the name of the bully at your partner's primary school, and these associations can be hard to let go of.

It's OK to be experimental. Don't feel silly suggesting or trying out names that are a bit more adventurous than people may expect. If David Bowie's alter ego Ziggy Stardust was your teenage idol and you fancy bringing the name back into your life, see what it sounds like! You never know – your partner may approve!

If you find that you have lots of name possibilities, then a list will help you to keep track of your ideas. It is particularly useful if you start considering names early on in your pregnancy. You may find that your attitude to some of them changes over time, and when you look back at the list a couple of months down the line you may be surprised at what you initially wrote down!

Another good way to make your mind up on a name is to imagine its use in different situations. Consider whether a name appeals to you when used on a toddler and when used on an adult. Can you imagine it being accepted in both the playground and the boardroom? Perhaps some names are more Mercury Prize than Nobel Prize, or more stuntman than clergyman. Of course, everyone's opinions on this will differ, but thinking about names in this way might make a difference to your preferences.

## Naming Babies after Other People

### Going Double-Barrelled
**Girls' names are more commonly hyphenated than boys' names, but there are still lots of possibilities for both sexes. Rose and May are popular second names for girls**

('Anna-Rose', 'Lily-May'); Lee and James are quite common in double-barrelled boys' names ('Tommy-Lee', 'Tyler-James'). Other combinations that work well include 'Emily-Grace', 'Mia-Louise', 'Thomas-Jay' and 'Alfie-Joe'.

It's a creative way of making a name more interesting or to modernise an older name that you want to use. Hyphenating a double-barrelled name isn't strictly necessary but without it people may confuse the second half of the name for a middle name. Experiment with combinations, but avoid hyphenating names with lots of syllables and stick to just two names!

Taking things on a step from name association, some babies are named directly after a family member. In some families it is tradition to name a baby after the father, or grandfather; in other cases, children may be named after a recently deceased member of the family. Sometimes people choose the name of an aunt, uncle or other person who they particularly looked up to or got on with, or who they feel was a significant influence on them while growing up. Of course, the delivery of a baby can be very special and emotional, so there have been babies who were named after the person who delivered them!

## Other Ideas for Inspiration

Once you know you're having a baby, regardless of how important it is to you to find a name quickly, start paying more attention to the names that are spoken around you every day. It is a good way to pick up new ideas, to gauge the popularity of a name, to hear different pronunciations and nicknames, and sometimes it can help to dispel your existing feelings towards a name. For example, a name you always associated with a miserable elderly aunt might actually be the name of that pretty, cheerful and well-spoken newsreader you like – suddenly the name is more appealing. Likewise, a name you think is a little unusual may actually be coming back into fashion again.

Listen out for parents talking to (and sometimes shouting at!) their children out and about.

Here are some ideas for finding a completely random list of names to inspire you.

- Credits at the end of television programmes and films
- Names of the players in televised sports
- Authors' names on book spines along a bookshelf – at home, the library or a bookshop
- Birth, death and marriage announcements in local or national newspapers
- Names of journalists and the people who feature in newspaper and magazine articles

If you are a keen reader, cast your eyes back over your bookshelf and remind yourself of the various character names that featured in them. Or see our list of suggested names from well-known literature in our Inspiration Lists (see pages 31–50).

You can also use the book in conjunction with the babynames.co.uk website. Here you can set up an account and save names to a shortlist that you can come back to as and when you like. You can also find further information on the current popularity of names, as well as suggestions for inspiration, including a random names generator. There is a huge community of mums and mums-to-be there, and discussions take place night and day on the subject of baby names. You can have a go at anonymously bouncing ideas off other people who are in the same boat as you, especially if you have decided not to divulge your potential baby names to friends and family.

When you're done with taking this naming business seriously, you can always try the 'Are you feeling lucky?' approach with this book. Choose a page at random and get your partner to point to a name with their eyes covered. OK, this isn't an altogether serious suggestion but you never know, it might find you a winner!

# Useful Factors to Consider

## Personal Associations with Names

As already discussed, people's attitudes and opinions on different names vary hugely. Your favourite name might provoke quite unexpected reactions when suggested to your partner or family. The strong, on-trend choice that you have in mind for your son is old-fashioned and dull according to your best friend. People can catch you unawares with their disapproval, insinuating that your choice of baby name is trashy, tacky or has other unattractive connotations.

Opinions on names are formed by naming trends and personal associations, i.e., who you know (or know of) with that name. You may not even be able to recall where you have heard that name; it may have been in a film, a news article or a distant connection, such as a friend of a friend that you have heard about but never met. You may have formed an opinion on it as a result of this very vague association. Sometimes we form an opinion on a name based on its stereotypical image – perhaps you associate a certain name with the age-old 'blonde bimbo' persona, or maybe you think of another name as being 'posh' – appropriate only for the kind of character Hugh Grant plays in a romantic comedy film.

Often, however, our connections with a name are much stronger than this. If you grew up knowing a person, or there is someone frequently in the public eye – a celebrity or politician – then you may find that they are the first person to enter your mind when you hear it. Your impression of this person is likely to shape your attitude towards that name. Cameron is a unisex name that has been popular in the name charts for many years, and may previously have owed its popularity to celebrities such as Cameron Diaz. Since 2010, however, when David Cameron became Prime Minister of the United Kingdom, the name has had a more political connotation.

Another example is names of pets. For those who have never owned a pet or had much contact with one it might sound rather silly, but if you grew up with a spaniel called Tom or a moggy named Megan, the thought of the name on your newborn baby might seem like calling your child Spot or Patch!

Some of our personal associations with names can be more negative. When you put a name to your partner and they say 'no' because of a girl they didn't like at primary school, put yourself in their shoes before you get frustrated. Childhood relationships can leave emotions etched into our memories forever, and nearly all of us can recall the name of the school bully. Unless someone else with that name has become known to you later in life, your personal feelings towards it are likely to be negative and you probably won't want it for your baby. Other common associations with names that can put you off using them for your child can be names of ex-partners, or people you work with. Even if these are people you like and get on with, it can often just seem unsuitable to take their name and use it on your child.

Popularity of a name also influences our attitudes towards it. There are notable trend cycles with names, and some names are seen as old-fashioned because they were more popular among our grandparents' and great-grandparents' generations than they are now. There are some names that haven't been fashionable for several generations, such as Winifred or Walter. For many people, the more popular a name is, the more attractive it is – to a point. People can also be deterred by a very popular name. They may prefer to avoid their child having to be known by their first name together with their last initial to differentiate them from the other children in their class with the same name – for example, 'Oliver T' or 'Olivia T' (both very popular names in recent years). Teachers often have the added problem that they know so many children that they find it hard to find a name they like that they don't already associate with another child! See the popularity charts (pages 51–53) for more information on what is popular now and has been in recent years.

## A Name that Works with the Child's Surname

Your baby's surname will affect the suitability of his or her first name. Some combinations just won't sound right to your ears. Try saying first names out loud with your last name – it is surprising how different a name sounds once it is paired with a surname. As with nearly every aspect of choosing your baby's name, it is pretty subjective as to what sounds 'good'.

Sometimes parents choose alliterative names such as Emma Edwards or Sebastian Summers. There are numerous celebrity examples of alliterative names: Janet Jackson, Lucy Liu and Lennox Lewis to name just a few. These are fine if you are naming your first child, but if you go on to have several more and want to continue the theme you could find the naming process becomes more and more challenging!

While it is a subjective matter, there are also some things you might want to avoid when pairing a name with a surname.

- **Rhyming:** Most people would choose to avoid a first name that rhymes with their second name – such as 'Carys Harris' or 'Mark Clark'. Such a name might be amusing, and even attractively quirky – particularly if you imagine them on a musician or artist – but what if you put these names on a troubled teenager who lacks confidence in their own self-image? Even in the wild world of celebrities you don't find many examples of rhyming names. Jack Black is an example but he was born Thomas Jacob Black. It might be better to let your child adopt a stage name when they start frequenting the red carpets and in the meantime maybe opt for something a little less rock n' roll, just in case they grow up to be an accountant.
- **Famous names:** In general, people tend to steer clear of giving their child the same first and second name as famous people. So if your surname is Brand, the names Jo or Russell are likely to be put into the 'No' list pretty quickly. This is especially the case if the person is famous for all the wrong reasons, such as Fred West or Myra Hindley.
- **Common pairings:** If you have a common surname, think carefully about the first name you choose. A name that is very popular combined with a common surname might mean that your son or daughter shares his or her name with a classmate or friend!
- **Very long names:** If your child is going to have a double-barrelled surname, then you might want to steer clear of double-barrelled or very long first names to keep the potential mockery in the future to a minimum – and to give the poor child a chance to learn to spell it!

Unless you have the time or inclination to think about the issue of pairing a first name with a surname, you needn't get too consumed with the subject. It can sometimes be easy to overthink these things. The important thing is that you choose a first name for your baby that *you* like. Provided it sounds like a pretty good fit with the second name, doesn't have any glaringly obvious rhymes or innuendos and the initials don't spell out an obscenity, then the combination of names will be perfectly acceptable.

## Spelling Variations

The name you give your baby, how it is spelt and how it is pronounced is entirely down to you. If you want to call your baby 'James', but spell it 'Jaymes', that is your decision and nobody can stop you.

The subject of name spellings can provoke a hot debate. It is understandable that some people decide to alter a traditional spelling of a name in order to make it more unique or more interesting, but at the same time you should consider what issues this might present in the future. Is it likely to result in misspellings, mispronunciations and questioning over its origin for the rest of the child's life?

While new spellings can be ridiculed for their simplification of traditional names, old-fashioned spellings are criticised sometimes for being confusing (particularly Gaelic names from Irish or Scottish traditions). Names such as 'Ciaran' are familiar to many of us, but when written down, the spelling can surprise people. More extreme examples of tricky Gaelic names include 'Fionnghuala' or 'Aoife' – but many people enjoy having a less obvious name spelling. And perhaps it is more widely accepted when your unusual name has a cultural tradition that you can explain to other people, so that you cannot be accused of having a 'made-up' name.

If the difficult original spellings of popular names are an issue for you, then you may choose to use an anglicised or phonetic spelling; 'Neve', for example, is becoming an increasingly popular spelling of the classic Irish name 'Niamh'. Consider your reasons for simplifying a name, though. We live in an ever-more diverse society, where names from different cultures are being introduced all the time. The assumption that a name that is a little unusual or hard to spell will cause significant problems for that child growing up might be exaggerated. Perhaps we should assume a greater level of intelligence and acceptance on the part of others!

## Pronunciation Variations

Pronunciation of names can vary, and some people have strong views as to the correct way to pronounce certain names. Differences may simply be the result of different accents and dialects, or even different nationalities – for example 'Tanya' where some people pronounce it '*Tarn*-yah' and others pronounce it '*Tan*-yah'. Even if the pronunciation of a name does seem obvious to you, it is worth double-checking, just to make sure you haven't misunderstood it. That might sound unlikely but it does happen. In her teens, writer Caitlin Moran changed her name from 'Catherine' to 'Caitlin' after seeing the name in a Jilly Cooper novel. She believed at the time that the correct pronunciation was '*Cat*-lin' and continues to pronounce it that way today – she says it has caused confusion for people all of her adult life!

If you are in any doubt whatsoever, do some quick checks on your prospective name before making it final. Ensure you know what the popular or original spelling of that name is, and how it is commonly pronounced – regardless of whether or not you intend to follow suit.

## Names that Work with Twins and Other Siblings

There are no rules when it comes to what you can and can't call children based on the names of their siblings. For some people it is important that their children's names complement one another, while other people don't give it much thought. When people talk about finding names that work they usually just mean that they *sound OK*.

However, as with pairing first names with surnames, there are some general dos and don'ts when it comes to drawing the line between endearing and eccentric, or amusing and absurd. Again, this is down to personal opinion.

- **Themes:** You may decide that a theme would work for your family. Perhaps flower names like Rose and Daisy or names that start with the same letter like Jack and James. Of course, the more children you have, the harder it becomes to continue with a theme, so consider what you will do if in the future you extend your family.
- **Rhyming:** Rhyming your children's names with each other may sound sweet to you at first, but could become cloying in the future so think carefully about choosing names that rhyme. If you are totally against rhyming names, make sure to consider how your children's names might be shortened. For example, if you have decided on naming your twins Matilda and William, they could well end up being Tilly and Willy or Tilly and Billy.
- **Suitability:** Many names are categorised by people as traditional or modern, simple or fussy, popular or unusual. If your first two children have names that clearly fall into such a category, it might be unfair to give the third child something totally different. Imagine the protest from your youngest child after being named 'Tallulah-Belle', when her sisters are named Ellie and Clare.

- **Combinations:** Consider whether your choices of sibling names match any famous partnerships or celebrity couples such as 'Brad and Angelina', fashion labels such as 'Florence and Fred' at Tesco or fictional television duos such as 'Charlie and Lola'. This isn't to say that you should avoid these well-known associations, but it is better for you to have thought them through ahead of time rather than have them brought to your attention by other people after the baby (or babies) have been born and named.

## Middle Names

There are no rules as to how many names you can give your child. The most common format in the UK is a first name, which is used for everyday purposes, and a second name (or middle name), which is used less frequently. Second or third names are most commonly used on official documents or registration forms and sometimes they are abbreviated to their first initial in signatures, for example 'Siobhan E. Thomas'. If your child falls out of love with their first name then they may choose to use their second name in its place and it is a common port of call for those who do change their first name.

# Common Hurdles

## Disagreeing with Other People

While opinions will always be divided to some extent, it is easy to predict whether certain names, or types of names, will be accepted as 'good' names by the majority of people. Names that have remained popular through generations, such as William or Elizabeth, will come in for little criticism.

Unusual names, such as 'Blade' or 'Cruz', are more controversial and often meet more resistance from friends, family and the wider public.

When it comes to pleasing other people, what you must bear in mind is that once the baby has been born, their previous opinions on the name will really matter very little to them. The subject of names is much more divisive before the baby's arrival. As soon as people get to know your child, most of them will forget their earlier associations; the name will become the baby's – not the name of a character in *EastEnders*, a famous footballer or the lady who works in the post office. While it may take friends and family some time to get used to, they'll soon associate the name with your baby and in no time at all it will stop feeling strange to them and start to feel treasured – it will become part of your child. Many a grandparent has been heard to say 'I wasn't sure about it at first but now I love it!'

Ultimately, the name of a baby is down to his or her parents. It can be fun talking through name ideas with your best friend or your mum, but if you want to be open about your baby's name ahead of their arrival, be prepared for other people's reactions. If you think that negative comments will knock the wind out of your sails, keep the names to yourself. Perhaps think twice before publicising your shortlist too widely.

## Disagreeing with Your Partner

With a bit of luck, you and your partner may find that you agree on a name, or a list of names, quite easily. But what happens when you don't?

If you feel that your partner is repeatedly rejecting your suggestions of names then perhaps you need to think about changing your approach. Firstly, consider exactly how you make your suggestions. Launching into a list of names at eleven o'clock at night, pouncing on them as they walk in the door from work or informing them in no uncertain terms that Trixabelle is the perfect name for your daughter is more than likely going to get you a 'no'. Pick your moment – everyone has times when they are more open to discussing these things. You must also allow your partner time to consider a name. You may have been thinking about it all day and imagining it in wooden letters on the nursery room door, but they will need time to process and digest it too. So don't expect an immediate response; just ask them to consider it in their own time.

Also, try to find out what it is about certain names that your partner doesn't like. Are you repeatedly offering names with tricky Gaelic spellings that he thinks will make life hard for the child? Are you only coming up with long-winded, double-barrelled names that she thinks are too fussy? Understanding your partner's reasons for rejecting a name will help you to find one that you both like.

If there is a name that you really love, and your partner refuses to agree to it, don't push them too hard on the subject. You can't (or at least you shouldn't) force someone into agreeing to a name for their baby. If you are both going to be bringing this child up then it is important that you do things in agreement as much as possible from Day 1, and your baby's name is the best place to start. It may be the case that you need to go back to the drawing board, but sometimes it can be possible to persuade your partner into thinking of the name more favourably. Avoid getting into an argument, but let them know that a name is a strong contender for you and that you would really like them to consider it seriously before writing it off alto-gether. If they have particular negative associations with

that name then you could attempt to override these associations by pointing out other, more appealing people or
characters that have this name. For example, if your partner dismisses the name Harry because of Harry Potter,
point out that not all Harrys are associated with wizardry
and wearing small round glasses – prior to Mr Potter the
best-known Harry on screen was 'Dirty Harry', a different
image altogether! So if you want to be more persuasive do
a bit more research on the name you like and see whether
you think the meaning, history or popularity of the name
might help your partner to see it in a different light.

The powers of persuasion must be allowed to work both
ways, of course! It is easy to become preoccupied with con-
vincing your partner to accept a name that you are in love
with. However, you need to be open-minded to their suggestions too. If there is a name that they would really like
for your baby then don't rule it out immediately. Keep it on
your shortlist and give it a chance to grow on you – you may
be surprised at how your feelings change, given some time.

# Quick Checks Before You Name Your Baby!

Once you have fallen in love with a name you can become
blinkered to its downsides – if it has any. There are some
key points that are worth checking in order to establish
certain associations or drawbacks to the name. If you find
any, it doesn't mean that you should discard it; it's just better to know these things ahead of time. If Angelina is the
name you have settled on, wouldn't you rather you were
already aware of the fictional world of Angelina Ballerina
before your baby girl gets given three stuffed tutu-wearing
mice as new baby presents?

## Nicknames and Shortenings

As they grow up, the child's name might evolve if they, or others, decide to use it differently. These changes can be a result of shortenings, nicknames or simply differences in pronunciation. It is worth considering the obvious possibilities with a name from the outset, so if the familiar form 'Jimmy' from 'James' really bothers you then you can either choose to avoid the name altogether or make a point of explaining to other people that you would prefer his full name used as much as possible. Of course, this might work with close relations, but be realistic about how much influence you are going to have over playground and sporting friendships in the future.

Changes to names come about in different ways. Names are often shortened and there are some very obvious examples such as 'Dan' from 'Daniel' or 'Liz' from 'Elizabeth'. Many names have a familiar form such as 'Bill' from 'William' or 'Maggie' from 'Margaret'. Of course, you may actually prefer some of these diminutives to their longer originals, so you can bypass the lengthy alternative altogether. For many years 'Max' has been much more popular than 'Maxwell', as has Charlie over Charles. Other names have less obvious, or less frequently used, shortened forms. It is quite common for names of more than one syllable to be shortened informally to just the one syllable, especially by close friends and family. You might hear 'Lucy' affectionately shortened to 'Luce', or 'Siobhan' to 'Shiv'. You can usually be sure that these nicknames weren't the driving factor for choosing that name in the first place. They wouldn't offend most parents but it is still worth giving a thought to how a name might be shortened in the future by other people.

Nicknames aren't always the result of shortening a name or using its familiar form, and consequently they can be hard to predict. We all know of people who live with a nickname that forever prompts the question 'Why?' and the answer is often long-winded, nonsensical or ridiculous. In some cases, nobody knows how the nickname came about. Sometimes a name may originate from a story about that person (John 'Two Jags' Prescott), or from an aspect of their personality, hobby or job (David 'Golden Balls' Beckham). In these incidences all you can do is hope that if your child gets such a nickname, it is tasteful and in good humour. Many people have nicknames that are short-lived, used for a period of their lives such as their time at college or university, or used only by their work colleagues or teammates in the sport that they play. You do come across people who have lived by their nickname for so long that few people actually know their real name any more, but in most cases people grow out of their nicknames in the long run – often to their relief!

Sometimes a nickname can result from the modification of a person's first name, surname or both, which is another reason to try out name ideas with the surname. Say the name over a few times and make sure you don't think that there are any glaringly obvious innuendos, spoonerisms or jokes to be had – such as the English football player Fitz Hall who is known by his nickname as 'One Size'. The use of someone's surname, or a variant of their surname, as their nickname is a phenomenon particularly associated with team sports such as football – Paul Gascoigne's nickname 'Gazza' being one of the most famous examples. This tends to be more common among boys.

Once you have considered the obvious potential for nicknames, don't get bogged down with the idea that there may be some horrific double meaning or pet form of the name; if you can't think of it now, the chances are most other people won't either. And if your child does end up with a nickname that you don't approve of, it will probably have been unavoidable – do you think Scarlett Johansson's parents could have seen 'Scar-Jo' coming?

## Check out Common Associations

You will probably have already thought of any obvious celebrity namesakes – for example, there are few women of childbearing age in the UK who haven't heard of the Hollywood actress Angelina Jolie. But in the case of Angelina Ballerina, dancing mice aren't necessarily going to be at the forefront of your mind, unless you already have (or spend time with) young children. Arduous research into popular children's television culture won't be required; just ask a friend who has children whether they think the name is popular or has any associations for them. You might also want to run the name through a quick search on the Internet just to see who is attracting attention at the moment with that name – particularly with your surname. The latest D-list celebrity hitting the headlines for a drunken gaffe is unlikely to affect your decision to use a name (nobody will remember them this time next year) but you might like to know if there are any public figures out there (good or bad) with that name.

Of course, it's not just people (or mice) that you want to look out for when it comes to names. Popular names are used as brand names for all sorts of products and services, for example Jessica nail varnish and George clothing at Asda. If you work in a beauty salon and shop at Asda then these names might lose some appeal, or it might be what gave you the idea in the first place! Remember that associations don't just fall into 'good' and 'bad' categories; some of these associations (even strong ones) will have no impact on our personal preferences for a name.

## Consider the Initials

Most children in the UK are given at least one middle name and the English language has over 1,000 three-letter words, so there are plenty of name combinations that will spell out a real word when the initials are written down. More often than not these are unremarkable – S.I.T., H.A.T. and so on. At best they can be amusing, but in some rare cases initials can spell out a swear word or a slang term for something inappropriate (you can use your own imagination for examples of these!).

Also consider the first initial(s) together with the surname, as mistakes can occasionally happen in this way too – for example, it might not take the school children long to notice that 'Caleb Oliver Ward' could be abbreviated to 'C.O.Ward' or 'Una Grace Lee' to 'U.G.Lee'!

It is quite common to give your child the same first initial as their siblings or parents but remember that this can lead to confusion when it comes to mail sent to your address. Even if the middle initial differs, a lot of mail is sent to 'S. Thomas' without the Mr/Mrs prefix or sometimes with an incorrect title. Generally this would be a minor thing to niggle about when the postman arrives but it could also lead to embarrassing situations or arguments when people open the wrong mail!

### Coordinated Names

For those parents who are really coordinated, you might want to take into account the first names of everyone else in the family. But how a name works with both siblings' and parents' names should still be a consideration – you might not want to be signing off your Christmas cards next year 'from Pat, Rick & Baby Patrick' but until you consider the name alongside your names this kind of mistake can easily go unnoticed.

## Is There a Joke to be Had?

When it comes to ensuring that your child's name is not going to make for an easy target, you have to accept that there is no such thing as a 'bully-proof' name. Bullies are innovative and if they are going to bully a person they will seek out something about that person to pick on. However, you can certainly do your child a favour by avoiding a name that has an obvious joke 'built in'. Look out for:

- **Double meanings:** Ben Dover, Harry Pits, Amanda Hugenkiss, Hugh Jass … if you're a lover of *The Simpsons* you will be familiar with all these gag names that Bart Simpson gets the bartender, Moe, to call out. It's an old joke but spare a second to check that when you say your child's names aloud there is no suggestion of an alternative word or expression in there.
- **Silly spoonerisms:** Some names can also fall into the trap of *spoonerism*, where a joke is made by swapping corresponding consonants or vowels of the first and last name around – 'Kelly Smith' would become 'Smelly Kith', 'Mary Hegg' would become 'Hairy Megg' and so on. These are easy to spot when you think about them and might make a name worth ruling out if you think the spoonerism is likely to be used offensively.
- **Awkward anagrams:** Let's face it, it really isn't the end of the world if your baby's name can be rearranged to spell 'This Moaner' (Erin Thomas), but it is quite interesting. There are a number of free anagram checkers online so it is easy to find out what anagrams could be made of their potential name(s) if you would like to know.
- **Rhyming slang:** The use of rhyming slang comes and goes and there are many people who are unfamiliar with this use of replacing words or phrases with other

(unrelated) rhyming words. A couple of popular terms use people's names and consequently you should definitely avoid naming your child 'Ruby Murray' (curry) or 'Pete Tong' (wrong).

Finally, it's best to avoid your child's name becoming the joke of the class by steering clear of the plain ridiculous. You know how much our society likes to make fun of one another. Celebrities may get away with naming their children 'Jermajesty' (Jermaine Jackson), 'Blue Angel' (The Edge, U2) or Pilot Inspektor (Jason Lee) – and there is possibly even an argument for having to differentiate the child so that they stand out from their parents' glittering star status – but in your average classroom 'Denim' and 'Diezel' (Toni Braxton's children) are going to stand out like a sore thumb. There is a lot to be said for being different, but draw a line between *unusual* and *absurd*.

# PART TWO

# Inspiration

# Naming Trends for 2021/22

There is no accurate way to predict the name charts – popularity of certain names is often generated by recent events and media coverage of high-profile people. Award-winners, musicians, Netflix characters, reality stars, novelists, book characters, royal babies, sports medal winners – all can bring a name back into fashion, inspire new trends, or even stop it becoming popular!

While traditional names remain as popular as ever, we have also seen a rise in the quest for unique names, with unusual spelling variations. As the world becomes ever-more globally connected, parents are choosing names from around the world and country origin is no boundary. There is a rise in names also inspired by geographical place names such as Sienna and Florence as people travel more and more. Gender-neutral names such as Sam and Charlie have always been popular but now seem to be a more conscious choice, as are names inspired by nature such as Sky, Willow and Bay.

## Gender-neutral names

| | |
|---|---|
| Milo | Avery |
| Bailey | Drew |
| Jasper | Storm |
| Noah | Charlie |
| Billie | River |
| Arlo | Bobbie |
| Sam | Ashley |
| Sky | Kelsey |
| Campbell | Alex |
| Robin/Robyn | Ryan |

## Natural world

Names inspired by nature continue to be popular, perhaps ever more so as we become more concerned about the planet. Many nature names are also gender-neutral, reflecting today's modern parenting values.

## Natural world names

| Boys | Girls |
|------|-------|
| Robin | Willow |
| Bay | Flora |
| Flint | Hazel |
| Forrest | Cove |
| Rio | Saffron |
| Sky | Olive |
| Tiger | Ivy |
| Wolfie | Juniper |

# Recent high achievers

The primary reason for choosing a name is that you like it, but finding out that it is associated with one or more successful people in the world is always going to be pleasing! Whether or not you think you might be about to raise the next prize-winning physicist, musician, actor or literary prize winner doesn't matter – a name that has positive associations is bound to make you feel good about your choice.

*Girls*
Greta Thunberg (*Time* Person of the Year 2019)
Arlo Parks (Breakthrough Artist, Brit Awards 2021)
Bernadine Evaristo and Margaret Atwood (Winners of the Booker Prize 2019)
Louise Glück (Nobel Prize for Literature, 2020)
Hollie Doyle (The Sunday Times Sportswoman of the Year 2020)
Chloé Zhao (Best Director, Oscars 2021)
Emerald Lilly Fennell (Oscar for Best Original Screenplay 2021)

*Boys*
Abiy Ahmed (Nobel Peace Prize 2019)
Daniel Kaluuya (Best Supporting Actor, Oscars, 2021)
Douglas Stuart (Winner Booker Prize, 2020)
Kyle Soller (Best Actor, Olivier Awards 2019)

Michael Kiwanuka (Mercury Prize, 2020)
Lewis Hamilton (BBC Sports Personality of the Year 2020)
Colson Whitehead (Pulitzer Prize for Fiction 2020)

# Popular culture

The names of actors, musicians, models, writers and television stars are part of our everyday conversations and this is often reflected in the most popular baby name charts. Luna and Robyn are big risers, perhaps inspired by the JK Rowling characters in the Harry Potter and Cormoran Strike books and screen adaptations. Margot is a big climber, perhaps inspired by Margot Robbie and Margo from *Despicable Me*. Hunter and Grayson have become more popular for boys, perhaps inspired by Hunter Parrish or the character in *Eastenders* and Grayson Dolan or Grayson Perry. The popularity of Alexa has fallen, probably due to the popularity of voice recognition technology.

The real change here has been in the rise in popularity of social media influencers, who many of us follow on a daily basis, whether via Instagram, Twitter, Youtube or reality television shows and vlogs. Will we see a rise in the popularity of names such as Buzz, Buddy and Max (Giovanna and Tom Fletcher) or Rosie and Paul (Sam Faiers)?

Young actors and celebrities might also inspire baby names. Milo and Millie are very popular and this might be influenced by Milo Parker and Millie Bobby Brown.

## Actors

*Boys*
Chris Evans
Donald Glover
Zac Efron

*Girls*
Viola Davis
Alicia Vikander
Brie Larson

Rami Malek
Ryan Gosling
Jamie Foxx
Daniel Kaluuya
Eddie Redmayne
Ben Wishaw
Kit Harrington
Aziz Ansari
Benedict Cumberbatch
Paul Mescal
Babou Ceesay
Idris Elba
Regé-Jean Page
Rory Kinnear
Mark Rylance
Sam Tutty
Tom Hiddleston
Charlie Stemp
Ralph Fiennes
Joel Montague
Trevor Dion Nicholas

Scarlett Johansson
Halle Berry
Dakota Johnson
Octavia Spencer
Saoirse Una Ronan
Vanessa Kirby
Jodie Comer
Thandiwe Newton
Annie Murphy
Phoebe Dynevor
Sofia Vergara
Daisy Edgar-Jones
Natalie Dormer
Anne-Marie Duff
Noma Dumezweni
Imelda Staunton
Denise Gough
Katherine McPhee
Carrie Hope Fletcher
Billie Piper
Sheridan Smith

## Child actors

*Boys*
Milo Parker
Finn Wolfhard
Caleb McLaughlin
Joel Dawson
Angus Imrie
Louis Serkis
Bleu Landau
Noah Jupe

*Girls*
Millie Bobby Brown
Landry Bender
Mackenzie Foy
Pixie Davies
Skai Jackson
Ramona Marquez
Dafne Keen
Tisha Martin

## Comedians

*Boys*
Jack Whitehall
Jay Pharoah
Dara O Briain
Noel Fielding
James Acaster
Josh Widdicombe

*Girls*
Shappi Khorsandi
Amy Poehler
Phoebe Waller-Bridge
Tina Fey
Gina Yashere
Tiffany Haddish

Romesh Ranganathan
Sacha Baron Cohen

Rachel Brosnahan
Rosie Jones

## Fashion

*Boys*
Tyson Beckford
Zac Posen
Presley Walker Gerber
Marc Jacobs
Erdem Moralioglu
David Gandy
Lucky Blue Smith
Toby Huntington-Whiteley

*Girls*
Kendall Jenner
Paloma Elsesser
Gigi Hadid
Stella McCartney
Kaia Gerber
Coco Chanel
Noah Carlos
Cara Delevingne

## Reality television

*Boys*
Spencer Matthews
Karamo Brown
Antoni Porowski
Rylan Clark-Neal
Mark Wright
Ollie Locke
Marvin Humes
Scott Disick

*Girls*
Sam Faiers
Nadiya Hussain
Binky Felstead
Georgia Toffolo
Millie Mackintosh
Rochelle Humes
Megan McKenna
Khloe Kardashian

## Social media

*Boys*
Kurtis Conner
Eugene Lee Yang
Cody Ko
Brooklyn Beckham
Noel Miller
Nickelson Wooster
Louis Cole
Joe Wicks

*Girls*
Addison Rae
Alexa Chung
Haley Pham
Avery Ovard
Estee Lalonde
Iskra Lawrence
Emily Canham
Charli and Dixie D'Amelio

## Celebrity Babies

*Boys*
Miles Theodore Stephens (John Legend & Chrissy Teigen)

Romeo Alejandro David (Alec Baldwin & Hilaria Thomas)
River Rocket (Jamie & Jools Oliver)
Hart (Miranda Kerr & Evan Spiegel)
Ennis Howard (Kirsten Dunst & Jesse Plemons)
Buzz, Buddy and Max (Giovanna and Tom Fletcher)
Beckett (Michael Phelps & Nicole Johnson)
Francisco (Lin-Manuel Miranda & Vanessa Nadal)

*Girls*
Marvel Jane (Pete Wentz & Meagan Camper)
True (Khloe Kardashian & Tristan Thompson)
Dream (Rob Kardashian & Blac Chyna)
Stormi Webster (Kylie Jenner & Travis Scott)
James (Ryan Reynolds & Blake Lively)
Dusty Rose (Adam Levine & Behati Prinsloo)
Story (Aaron Paul & Lauren Parsckian)
Apple (Gywneth Paltrow & Chris Martin)

## Visual artists

*Boys*
Damien Hirst
Leonardo da Vinci
Jack Vettriano
Vincent van Gogh
Antony Gormley
Grayson Perry
Anish Kapoor
Chris Ofili

*Girls*
Chantal Joffe
Georgia O'Keeffe
Beryl Cook
Barbara Hepworth
Marlene Dumas
Tamara de Lempicka
Francine van Hove
Rachel Whiteread

# FICTIONAL NAMES

We continue to be inspired by characters from our favourite books and films. Disney films evoke happy memories from our own childhoods, and the more recent films have provided fresh names to consider. And whether you love Harry Potter or Game of Thrones (or both!) there are some wonderful, creative names to choose from these books and films. Luna is now in the top 50 list for girls. Classic and contemporary children's books are also a rich source of name inspiration.

## Disney film characters

| Boys | Girls |
|---|---|
| Mickey | Belle |
| Donald | Ariel |
| Kristoff | Minnie |
| Flynn | Anna |
| Olaf | Elsa |
| Eric | Jasmine |
| Jack | Tiana |
| Georgie | Aurora |

## Star Wars characters

| Boys | Girls |
|---|---|
| Han Solo | Leia Organa |
| Anakin Skywalker | Padmé Amidala |
| Luke Skywalker | Rey |
| Kylo Ren | Qi'ra |
| Lando Calrissian | Mara Jade |
| Finn | Maz Kanata |
| Mace Windu | Shmi Skywalker |
| Tobias Beckett | Jyn Erso |

## Marvel characters

| Boys | Girls |
|---|---|
| Loki Laufeyson | Hope Pym |
| Peter Quill | Peggy Carter |
| Clint Barton | Wanda Maximoff |
| Tony Stark | Natasha Romanoff |
| Thor Odinson | Virginia Potts |
| Bruce Banner | Maria Hill |
| Scott Lang | Jane Foster |
| Steve Rogers | Carol Danvers |

## Game of Thrones

| Boys | Girls |
|---|---|
| Robb Stark | Arya Stark |
| Ned Stark | Catelyn Stark |
| Brandon Stark | Sansa Stark |
| Jon Snow | Cersei Lannister |

| | |
|---|---|
| Jaime Lannister | Lysa Arryn |
| Theon Greyjoy | Daenerys Targaryen |
| Stannis Baratheon | Brienne of Tarth |
| Joffrey Baratheon | Margaery Tyrell |

## Hunger Games

| *Boys* | *Girls* |
|---|---|
| Peeta Mellark | Katniss Everdeen |
| Gale Hawthorne | Primrose ("Prim") Everdeen |
| Haymitch Abernathy | Effie Glimmer |
| Coriolanus Snow | Rue |
| Finnick | Johanna |
| Cato | Lucy Gray |

## Harry Potter

| *Boys* | *Girls* |
|---|---|
| Ron Weasley | Ginny Weasley |
| Albus Dumbledore | Luna Lovegood |
| Sirius Black | Fleur Delacour |
| Cedric Diggory | Cho Chang |
| Fred Weasley | Hermione Granger |
| George Weasley | Lavender Brown |
| Arthur Weasley | Lily Potter |
| Frank Longbottom | Minerva McGonagall |

## Contempory fiction characters

| *Boys* | *Girls* |
|---|---|
| Charles Wallace | Alice Liddel |
| Max (*Where the Wild Things Are*) | Violet Baudelaire |
| Edmund Pevensie | Arrietty Clock |
| Klaus Baudelaire | Lyra Belacqua |
| Greg Heffley | Meg Wallace |
| Alex Rider | Becky Thatcher |
| Jack (*Grandpa's Great Escape*) | Petrova Fossil |
| Atticus Finch | Roberta (Bobbie) Waterbury |

## Shakespeare play characters

| *Boys* | *Girls* |
|---|---|
| Benedick | Miranda |

| | |
|---|---|
| Cassio | Ophelia |
| Romeo | Olivia |
| Lysander | Cordelia |
| Edgar | Beatrice |
| Antonio | Juliet |
| Orsino | Desdemona |
| Mark | Hermia |

## Classic fiction characters

| *Boys* | *Girls* |
|---|---|
| Arthur Huntingdon | Elinor Dashwood |
| Edward Rochester | Lydia Bennet |
| Edgar Linton | Fanny Price |
| Oliver Twist | Harriet Smith |
| Fitzwilliam Darcy | Adele Varens |
| Charles Bingley | Agnes Grey |
| George Knightley | Clara Peggotty |
| Edwin Drood | Rosa Bud |

# MUSICAL NAMES

Music is a rich source of name inspiration, from musical terms to classic and contemporary musicians. You could choose the name of your favourite artist (Bowie, Dolly), from a song title (Isabel) or a musical term (Allegra), for example.

## Musical terms

| *Boys* | *Girls* |
|---|---|
| Largo | Aria |
| Forte | Harmony |
| Lieder | Allegra |
| Opus | Chanson |
| Fife | Calypso |
| Reed | Piper |
| Solo | Viola |
| Bene | Chhaya |

## Classical musicians

*Boys*
Johann Sebastian Bach
Wolfgang Amadeus Mozart
Frederic Chopin
Benjamin Britten
Hans Zimmer
Alfie Boe
Andrea Bocelli
Sheku Kanneh-Mason

*Girls*
Renée Fleming
Clara Butt
Nicola Benedetti
Sarah Chang
Vanessa-Mae Vanakorn Nicholson
Kathleen Ferrier
Jessye Norman
Laura Wright

## Musical theatre characters

*Boys*
Alexander Hamilton
Evan Hansen
Emmett Forrest
Oliver Twist
Fiyero Tiggular
Joseph
Danny Zuko
Simba

*Girls*
Cosette
Elle Woods
Miss Adelaide
Carlotta Giudicelli
Annie Warbucks
Inez Stubbs
Velma Kelly
Nala

## Pop music

*Boys*
George Ezra
Olly Murs
Justin Bieber
Zayn Malik
Harry Styles
Adam Levine
Ed Sheeran
Matthew Healy

*Girls*
Billie Eilish
Ellie Goulding
Selena Gomez
Ariana Grande
Jess Glynne
Taylor Swift
Fleur East
Rae Morris

## Dance and RnB

*Boys*
Taio Cruz
Kendrick Lamar
Pharrell Williams
Aloe Blacc

*Girls*
Rita Ora
Missy Elliott
Beyonce
Iggy Izalea

| | |
|---|---|
| Sean Combs | Alicia Keys |
| Frank Ocean | Maya Jane Coles |
| Calvin Harris | Lisa Lashes |
| Richie Hawtin | Jorja Smith |

## Rock and indie

| *Boys* | *Girls* |
|---|---|
| Van McCann | Alecia Moore (Pink) |
| Robby Takac | Avril Lavigne |
| Chester Bennington | Arlo Parks |
| Gerard Way | Gwen Stefani |
| Ricky Wilson | Ellie Rowsell |
| Noel Gallagher | Nadine Shah |
| Chad Kroeger | Shirley Manson |
| Alex Turner | Phillipa (Pip) Brown |

## Soul

| *Boys* | *Girls* |
|---|---|
| Bruno Mars | Emeli Sande |
| Elton John | Paloma Faith |
| Marvin Gaye | Toni Braxton |
| Jason Mraz | Jill Scott |
| Otis Redding | Aretha Franklin |
| Usher Raymond IV | Jennifer Hudson |
| Levi Stubbs | Etta James |
| George Michael | Joss Stone |

## Jazz

| *Boys* | *Girls* |
|---|---|
| Jack Savoretti | Esperanza Spalding |
| Sonny Rollins | Ella Fitzgerald |
| Jools Holland | Eva Cassidy |
| Gregory Porter | Norah Jones |
| Jamie Cullum | Sade Adu |
| Louis Armstrong | Billie Holiday |
| Michael Bublé | Diana Krall |
| Chet Baker | Nina Simone |

# Sport and dance

We all have favourite sports that we watch or play. Whether you are into tennis, football, athletics, skiing or only watch once every four years when the Olympics occurs, the international world of sports is a rich inspiration for names.

*Boys*
Eden Hazard
Dane Coles
Maro Itoje
Mason Crane
Rafael Nadal
Max Whitlock
Geraint Thomas
Marcel Hirscher

*Girls*
Jeannie Longo
Marta Vieira da Silva
Melanie Behringer
Ada Hegerberg
Nikita Parris
Rochelle Clark
Simone Biles
Carly Patterson

## Olympic greats

*Boys*
Usain Bolt
Bradley Wiggins
Steve Redgrave
Paavo Nurmi
Nikolai Andrianov
Mark Spitz
Sebastian Coe
Daley Thompson

*Girls*
Jessica Ennis-Hill
Laura Trott
Katherine Grainger
Jayne Torvill
Birgit Fischer
Larisa Latynina
Tanni Grey-Thompson
Kelly Holmes

## Dance

*Girls*
Isadora Duncan
Sofia Boutella
Shriya Saran
Otlile Mabuse
Katya Jones
Misty Copeland
Tamara Rojo
Ginger Rogers

*Boys*
Gorka Marquez
Kevin Clifton
Sergei Polunin
Carlos Acosta
Matthew Morrison
Ashley Banjo
Fred Astaire
Joaquin Cortés

# History-makers

Your baby will have a wonderful impact on your world, but there are some babies that go on to change the world. Here are some of the people who have inspired us all.

| *Boys* | *Girls* |
|---|---|
| Barack Obama | Ada Lovelace |
| Martin Luther King | Virginia Woolf |
| Nelson Mandela | Mary Wollstonecraft |
| Simon Bolivar | Emmeline Pankhurst |
| Guy Fawkes | Indira Ghandi |
| Oskar Schindler | Harriet Tubman |
| Bill Gates | Rosa Parks |
| Thomas Jefferson | Margaret Thatcher |

# Mythological names

Greek and Roman names continue to inspire us; they are not common in the most popular names lists, but will be recognisable and your child might enjoy reading about their namesake one day!

## Greek gods

| *Boys* | *Girls* |
|---|---|
| Hermes | Artemis |
| Zeus | Hera |
| Chronos | Athena |
| Hades | Demeter |
| Ares | Nyx |
| Phanes | Eirene |
| Poseidon | Hestia |
| Dionysus | Hemera |

## Roman gods

| *Boys* | *Girls* |
|---|---|
| Jupiter | Juno |
| Sol | Venus |
| Liber | Diana |

| | |
|---|---|
| Neptune | Vesta |
| Cupid | Ceres |
| Sancus | Luna |
| Saturn | Fortuna |
| Mars | Veritas |

## Names from the Bible

| *Boys* | *Girls* |
|---|---|
| David | Eve |
| Zachariah | Esther |
| Luke | Tamar |
| Abraham | Judith |
| Ethan | Leah |
| Isaac | Naomi |
| Reuben | Zelda |
| Solomon | Delilah |

## Names from the Quran

| *Boys* | *Girls* |
|---|---|
| Darim | Aisha |
| Bashir | Daneen |
| Kaamil | Jahida |
| Ghalib | Lafiza |
| Nahid | Omera |
| Taheem | Reyah |
| Madani | Tahira |
| Habib | Zahra |

# TRADITIONAL NAMES BY COUNTRY

You are not restricted to choosing a name from your own or your child's birth country. It could be that you lived in another country, or had a memorable holiday there. With many babies having parents from different countries, you could choose a name that works in both too. Names inspired by places, such as a city or state, have become more popular too, such as Savannah and Austin.

## Place names

| *Boys* | *Girls* |
|---|---|
| Brooklyn | Siena |
| Paris | Bristol |
| Phoenix | Chelsea |
| Austin | Savannah |
| Caspian | Dakota |
| Hamilton | Jordan |
| Jackson | Florence |
| Lincoln | Carmel |

## England

| *Boys* | *Girls* |
|---|---|
| Harold | Mavis |
| Percy | Mabel |
| Horace | Ethel |
| Alfred | Doris |
| Cyril | Dolly |
| Herbert | Edie |
| Reginald | Winifred |
| Bernard | Geraldine |

## Nicknames

| *Boys* | *Girls* |
|---|---|
| Spike | Blue |
| Sonny | Honey |
| Buster | Angel |
| Buddy | Bee |
| Jonty | Star |
| Ace | Bonnie |
| Skipper | Rosie |
| Rex | Betsy |

# UK royal names

William and Catherine have three children: Prince George Alexander Louis, Princess Charlotte Elizabeth Diana, and the latest addition, Prince Louis Arthur Charles.

The British monarchy has been riding a wave of international popularity and media interest for the past few years. Meghan and Harry have two children: Archie Harrison and Lilibet Diana.

| *Boys* | *Girls* |
|---|---|
| William | Meghan |
| Harry | Charlotte |
| Archie | Catherine |
| Charles | Elizabeth/Lilibet |
| George | Victoria |
| Louis | Beatrice |
| Alfred | Diana |
| Andrew | Eugenie |

## International Royal names

| *Boys* | *Girls* |
|---|---|
| Daniel (Sweden) | Silvia (Sweden) |
| Harald (Norway) | Madeleine (Sweden) |
| Albert (Monaco) | Estelle (Sweden) |
| Philipp (Liechtenstein) | Ingrid (Norway) |
| Hans-Adam (Liechtenstein) | Caroline (Monaco) |
| Alois (Liechtenstein) | Stephanie (Monaco) |
| Frederik (Denmark) | Tatjana (Liechtenstein) |
| Hussein (Jordan) | Margrethe (Denmark) |

## Ireland

| *Boys* | *Girls* |
|---|---|
| Seamus | Niamh |
| Connor | Orlagh |
| Ronan | Roisin |
| Patrick | Ciara |
| Oisin | Saoirse |
| Sean | Grace |
| Daniel | Aoife |
| Jack | Clodagh |

## Wales

| *Boys* | *Girls* |
|---|---|
| Bryn | Anwen |

| | |
|---|---|
| Gethin | Ffion |
| Idris | Sian |
| Ceri | Tegan |
| Evan | Carys |
| Owen | Rhiannon |
| Tristan | Lowri |
| Rhodri | Angharad |

## Scotland

| *Boys* | *Girls* |
|---|---|
| Cameron | Isla |
| Logan | Iona |
| Donald | Fiona |
| Douglas | Mackenzie |
| Gordon | Moire |
| Alisdair | Elspeth |
| Clyde | Flora |
| Alexander | Morven |

## United States of America

| *Boys* | *Girls* |
|---|---|
| Tyler | Madison |
| Kyle | Emma |
| Jackson | Ensley |
| Lincoln | Madelyn |
| Caden | Harper |
| Logan | Avery |
| Ashton | Skylar |
| Carter | Ava |

## France

| *Boys* | *Girls* |
|---|---|
| Etienne | Alice |
| Paul | Anaïs |
| Armand | Chloé |
| Yanis | Camille |
| Gabriel | Manon |
| Mathis | Jeanne |
| Louis | Louise |
| Enzo | Lea |

## Italy

| Boys | Girls |
|------|-------|
| *Boys* | *Girls* |
| Matteo | Anna |
| Alessandro | Maria |
| Luca | Rosa |
| Lorenzo | Giovanna |
| Luigi | Sofia |
| Antoni | Alessia |
| Marco | Chiara |
| Stefano | Antonia |

## Spain

| Boys | Girls |
|------|-------|
| *Boys* | *Girls* |
| Javier | Lucia |
| Mario | Martina |
| Carlos | Maria |
| Matias | Sofia |
| Alejandro | Paula |
| Sebastian | Ana |
| Hugo | Carla |
| Pablo | Gabriela |

## The Netherlands

| Boys | Girls |
|------|-------|
| *Boys* | *Girls* |
| Levi | Saar |
| Luuk | Mila |
| Stijn | Sanne |
| Daan | Anouk |
| Sem | Eva |
| Bram | Lotte |
| Lars | Isa |
| Markus | Lieke |

## Greece

| Boys | Girls |
|------|-------|
| *Boys* | *Girls* |
| Christos | Eleni |
| Nikolaos | Katerina |
| Ioannis | Dimitra |
| Panagiotis | Sophia |
| Vasileios | Angeliki |

Adonis
Homer
Quinn

Cassia
Anastasia
Athena

# Russia

*Boys*
Maxim
Ivan
Alexandr
Dmitry
Mikhail
Nikolas
Daniil
Vladimir

*Girls*
Anastasia
Daria
Polina
Zoya
Viktoria
Alissa
Tatiana
Mischa

# Sweden

*Boys*
William
Oscar
Liam
Elias
Isak
Axel
Ludvig
Nils

*Girls*
Ella
Ebba
Lilly
Astrid
Saga
Alicia
Freja
Maja

# Germany

*Boys*
Leon
Lucas
Finn
Jonas
Maximilian
Elias
Moritz
Emil

*Girls*
Leonie
Lena
Hannah
Mila
Mia
Johanna
Mathilda
Greta

# Top 100 Boys Girls, 2019 England and Wales

| Rank | Boys Name | Change in Rank | Rank | Girls Name | Change in Rank |
|---|---|---|---|---|---|
| 1 | OLIVER | – | 1 | OLIVIA | – |
| 2 | GEORGE | – | 2 | AMELIA | – |
| 3 | NOAH | ↗ | 3 | ISLA | ↗ |
| 4 | ARTHUR | ↗ | 4 | AVA | ↘ |
| 5 | HARRY | ↘ | 5 | MIA | ↗ |
| 6 | LEO | – | 6 | ISABELLA | ↗ |
| 7 | MUHAMMAD | ↗ | 7 | SOPHIA | ↗ |
| 8 | JACK | ↘ | 8 | GRACE | ↗ |
| 9 | CHARLIE | ↗ | 9 | LILY | ↗ |
| 10 | OSCAR | ↘ | 10 | FREYA | ↗ |
| 11 | JACOB | – | 11 | EMILY | ↘ |
| 12 | HENRY | ↗ | 12 | IVY | ↗ |
| 13 | THOMAS | ↘ | 13 | ELLA | ↘ |
| 14 | FREDDIE | ↗ | 14 | ROSIE | ↗ |
| 15 | ALFIE | – | 15 | EVIE | ↗ |
| 16 | THEO | ↗ | 15 | FLORENCE | – |
| 17 | WILLIAM | ↘ | 17 | POPPY | ↘ |
| 18 | THEODORE | ↗ | 18 | CHARLOTTE | ↘ |
| 19 | ARCHIE | ↘ | 19 | WILLOW | ↗ |
| 20 | JOSHUA | ↘ | 20 | EVELYN | ↘ |
| 21 | ALEXANDER | ↗ | 21 | ELSIE | ↗ |
| 22 | JAMES | ↘ | 22 | PHOEBE | ↘ |
| 23 | ISAAC | ↘ | 23 | SOPHIE | ↘ |
| 24 | EDWARD | – | 24 | SIENNA | ↘ |
| 25 | LUCAS | ↗ | 25 | ALICE | ↘ |
| 26 | TOMMY | ↗ | 26 | SOFIA | ↗ |
| 27 | FINLEY | ↗ | 27 | RUBY | ↗ |
| 28 | MAX | ↗ | 28 | ISABELLE | ↘ |
| 29 | LOGAN | ↘ | 29 | HARPER | ↘ |
| 30 | ETHAN | ↘ | 30 | MATILDA | ↗ |
| 31 | MOHAMMED | ↗ | 31 | DAISY | ↘ |
| 32 | TEDDY | ↗ | 32 | EMILIA | ↗ |
| 33 | BENJAMIN | ↗ | 33 | JESSICA | ↘ |
| 34 | ARLO | ↗ | 34 | MAYA | ↗ |
| 34 | JOSEPH | ↘ | 35 | EVA | ↘ |
| 34 | SEBASTIAN | ↘ | 36 | LUNA | ↗ |

| | | | | | |
|---|---|---|---|---|---|
| 37 | HARRISON | ↘ | 37 | MILLIE | ↗ |
| 38 | ELIJAH | ↗ | 38 | ELIZA | ↗ |
| 39 | ADAM | ↘ | 39 | CHLOE | ↘ |
| 40 | DANIEL | ↘ | 40 | MAISIE | ↗ |
| 41 | SAMUEL | ↘ | 41 | PENELOPE | ↗ |
| 42 | LOUIE | ↗ | 42 | ARIA | – |
| 43 | MASON | ↘ | 43 | ESME | ↘ |
| 44 | REUBEN | ↘ | 44 | SCARLETT | ↘ |
| 45 | ALBIE | ↗ | 45 | IMOGEN | ↘ |
| 46 | RORY | ↗ | 46 | THEA | ↗ |
| 47 | JAXON | ↘ | 47 | ADA | ↗ |
| 48 | HUGO | ↗ | 48 | LAYLA | ↘ |
| 49 | LUCA | ↗ | 49 | HARRIET | ↘ |
| 50 | ZACHARY | ↗ | 50 | MILA | ↘ |
| 51 | REGGIE | ↘ | 51 | VIOLET | ↗ |
| 52 | HUNTER | ↘ | 52 | ELEANOR | ↘ |
| 53 | LOUIS | ↗ | 53 | BELLA | ↗ |
| 54 | DYLAN | ↘ | 54 | ERIN | ↘ |
| 55 | ALBERT | – | 55 | ELIZABETH | ↘ |
| 56 | DAVID | ↘ | 56 | ROSE | ↘ |
| 57 | JUDE | ↘ | 56 | MOLLY | ↗ |
| 58 | FRANKIE | ↗ | 58 | HALLIE | ↗ |
| 59 | ROMAN | ↗ | 59 | EMMA | ↘ |
| 60 | EZRA | ↘ | 60 | LOLA | ↘ |
| 61 | TOBY | ↘ | 61 | LUCY | – |
| 62 | RILEY | ↘ | 62 | BONNIE | ↗ |
| 63 | CARTER | ↘ | 63 | ELLIE | ↘ |
| 64 | RONNIE | ↗ | 64 | NANCY | – |
| 65 | FREDERICK | – | 65 | ROBYN | ↗ |
| 66 | GABRIEL | ↘ | 66 | ZARA | ↗ |
| 67 | STANLEY | ↗ | 67 | LOTTIE | ↘ |
| 68 | BOBBY | ↗ | 68 | HANNAH | ↘ |
| 69 | JESSE | ↗ | 69 | MARIA | ↘ |
| 70 | MICHAEL | ↗ | 70 | AURORA | ↘ |
| 71 | ELLIOT | ↘ | 71 | ARABELLA | ↗ |
| 72 | GRAYSON | ↗ | 72 | HOLLY | ↘ |
| 73 | MOHAMMAD | ↘ | 73 | JASMINE | ↗ |
| 74 | LIAM | ↗ | 74 | GRACIE | ↘ |
| 75 | JENSEN | ↘ | 75 | GEORGIA | ↘ |
| 76 | ELLIS | ↗ | 76 | DELILAH | ↗ |
| 77 | HARLEY | ↘ | 77 | DARCIE | ↗ |

| 78 | HARVEY | – | 78 | ORLA | ↗ |
| 79 | JAYDEN | ↘ | 79 | AMBER | ↘ |
| 80 | JAKE | ↘ | 80 | AMELIE | – |
| 81 | RALPH | ↗ | 81 | IRIS | ↗ |
| 82 | ROWAN | ↗ | 82 | ANNA | ↗ |
| 83 | ELLIOTT | ↗ | 82 | ABIGAIL | ↘ |
| 84 | JASPER | ↗ | 84 | AYLA | ↗ |
| 85 | OLLIE | ↗ | 85 | MARYAM | ↘ |
| 86 | CHARLES | ↘ | 86 | LILLY | ↘ |
| 86 | FINN | ↘ | 87 | ANNABELLE | ↘ |
| 88 | FELIX | ↗ | 88 | SARA | ↗ |
| 89 | CALEB | ↘ | 89 | EDITH | ↗ |
| 90 | CHESTER | ↗ | 90 | BEATRICE | ↘ |
| 91 | JACKSON | ↘ | 91 | CLARA | ↘ |
| 92 | HUDSON | ↗ | 92 | SUMMER | ↘ |
| 93 | LEON | ↗ | 93 | HEIDI | ↘ |
| 94 | IBRAHIM | ↗ | 94 | MARGOT | ↗ |
| 95 | RYAN | ↘ | 95 | MARTHA | ↘ |
| 96 | BLAKE | ↘ | 96 | ZOE | – |
| 97 | ALFRED | ↗ | 97 | LARA | ↗ |
| 98 | OAKLEY | ↗ | 98 | LYLA | ↘ |
| 99 | MATTHEW | ↘ | 98 | MABEL | ↗ |
| 100 | LUKE | ↘ | 100 | FELICITY | – |

# PART THREE

# Baby Names

# Names for Baby Boys A–Z

# Names For Baby Boys A–Z

# A

## Aadyha

**Meaning:** Security
**Origin:** Arabic
**Pronunciation:** AH maan
**Description:** Amaan is an alternative spelling of the name Aman. It is a popular name in both English- and Arabic-speaking countries, and is a name that appears in the Quran.
**Alternative spellings:** Aman

## Aahil

**Meaning:** Prince
**Origin:** Arabic
**Pronunciation:** AH hill
**Description:** Aahil is an Arabic word meaning 'prince.' Although it translates to prince, it generally refers to a king or ruler who presides over multiple nations and countries.
**Alternative spellings:** Ahil, Ahel, Aahel

## Aaran

**Meaning:** Strong mountain
**Origin:** Hebrew
**Pronunciation:** AH ran
**Description:** Aaran is a Hebrew name derived from the Egyptian name Aharan and was the name given to the older brother of Moses.
**Alternative spellings:** Aarin, Aaryn, Arran

## Aarav

**Meaning:** Peaceful
**Origin:** Sanskrit
**Pronunciation:** AH raav
**Description:** This name originates from the Indian word 'rav', which means 'calm' or 'peaceful.' More specifically, it means 'rustling sound' or 'melodious music,' to describe a person who is at peace with himself.
**Alternative spellings:** Arav, Araav

## Aariz

**Meaning:** Respectable
**Origin:** Arabic
**Pronunciation:** AH riz
**Description:** Aariz is of Arabic origin and has many meanings. It is most commonly understood to mean 'respectable' and 'intelligent man'.
**Alternative spellings:** Ariz, Arris

## Aaron

**Meaning:** Strong mountain
**Origin:** Hebrew
**Pronunciation:** AIR ron
**Description:** As well as being a biblical name borne by the brother of Moses, the origin of Aaron could be linked to Egypt. Widely popular since the 1990s, it is the name of well-known figures Aaron Carter (singer) and Aaron Lennon (footballer).

**Alternative spellings:** Aaran, Aron, Arran, Arron, Arun

## Aarush
**Meaning:** First ray of sun
**Origin:** Sanskrit
**Pronunciation:** ah ROOSH
**Description:** Aarush is Sanskrit in origin. It is derived from a Hindi word that means 'first ray of the sun'.
**Alternative spellings:** Aaroosh, Arush

## Aaryan
**Meaning:** From Hadria
**Origin:** Latin
**Pronunciation:** ar REE an
**Description:** This name comes from the Latin name Hadrianus, hence the meaning 'from Hadria'. The name Hadrianus has belonged to six popes and also several early Christian saints and martyrs.
**Alternative spellings:** Aarian, Aryan

## Aayan
**Meaning:** Era
**Origin:** Arabic
**Pronunciation:** UH yan
**Description:** Aayan is an alternative spelling of the name Ayan. Consequently it also means 'era' or its various synonyms. It is a name that is frequently mentioned in the Quran and thus is extremely popular in Muslim communities.
**Alternative spellings:** Ayan

## Abbas
**Meaning:** Austere; lion
**Origin:** Hebrew

**Pronunciation:** AH bas
**Description:** A male name of Arabic origin, which means 'lion' or 'austere' and is favoured by Muslim parents. Abbas was the name of the prophet Muhammad's uncle and ancestor of the Abbasid caliphs who formerly ruled the Islamic world.
**Alternative spellings:** Abas

## Abdirahman
**Meaning:** Servant to the merciful
**Origin:** Arabic
**Pronunciation:** AB DEE rah man
**Description:** Abdirahman is thought to be a variant of the Arabic name Abdulrahman, meaning 'servant to the merciful.' It is built from the Arabic words '*abd*,' '*al*' and '*rahman*.' It is also sometimes found as a surname.
**Alternative spellings:** Abdulrahman, Abdur-Rahman, Abdurahman, Abdurrahman

## Abdul
**Meaning:** Servant of Allah
**Origin:** Arabic
**Pronunciation:** AB dul
**Description:** Abdul is of Arabic origin and is the shortened form of Abdullah. Abdul means 'servant' and is commonly used together with its longer form, Abdullah. Also used as a surname.
**Alternative spellings:** Abdal, Abdel

## Abdullah
**Meaning:** Servant of Allah
**Origin:** Arabic
**Pronunciation:** ab DUL ah

**A**

**Description:** This name, popular with Muslim parents, means 'God's servant'. One of the most popular names in the Islamic world, it is believed to be the name of the father of the prophet Muhammad.
**Alternative spellings:** Abd-Allah, Abdallah

## Abdullahi

**Meaning:** Allah's servant
**Origin:** Arabic
**Pronunciation:** AB dul ah hee
**Description:** Abdullahi is an Arabic boys' name, and means 'Allah's servant.' It is a variant of the more commonly used name Abdullah.

## Abdur

**Meaning:** Servant
**Origin:** Arabic
**Pronunciation:** AB dur
**Description:** Abdur is a variant of the Arabic name Abdul, which is short for Abdullah, meaning 'servant.' It is commonly followed by a second Muslim theophoric (God-invoking) name, such as Rahman or Razzaq, to make Abdul Rahman or Abdul Razzaq.

## Abe

**Meaning:** Father
**Origin:** Hebrew
**Pronunciation:** AIB
**Description:** Abe is a Jewish name thought of as a shortened form of Abraham. It could also be from the Aramaic word *'abba'*, meaning 'father'.
**Alternative spellings:** Aabe, Aybe

## Abel

**Meaning:** Breath; vapour
**Origin:** Hebrew
**Pronunciation:** AY bull
**Description:** In the Bible, Abel is the youngest son of Adam and Eve. As the story goes, he was murdered by his jealous brother Cain. This name is especially popular in Spain.
**Alternative spellings:** Abal, Aybel

## Abid

**Meaning:** God's follower
**Origin:** Arabic
**Pronunciation:** AH bid
**Description:** Abid is the masculine version of the feminine name Abida, meaning God's follower.
**Alternative spellings:** Abbid

## Abida

**Meaning:** God's follower
**Origin:** Hebrew
**Pronunciation:** AB ee dah
**Description:** This name comes from two separate origins depending on the gender of the bearer. The masculine version of the name is of Hebrew origin while the feminine version is Arabic and said to mean 'God's follower'.
**Alternative spellings:** Abbida, Abeeda

## Abir

**Meaning:** Fragrance
**Origin:** Arabic
**Pronunciation:** A BIR
**Description:** Abir is an Arabic name found on both boys and girls. Abir is also the name of a dye found in India.
**Alternative spellings:** Abeer

## Abner

**Meaning:** Father of light
**Origin:** Hebrew
**Pronunciation:** AB ner
**Description:** Abner is a biblical name meaning 'father of light'. The name was borne by the leader of King Saul's army and relative to the king himself. Abner is now fairly uncommon.
**Alternative spellings:** Abna, Abnur

## Abraham

**Meaning:** Father of many nations
**Origin:** Hebrew
**Pronunciation:** AY bruh ham
**Description:** Abraham is a biblical name, borne by a man of great faith who was given a child aged 100. It is also heavily linked to Abraham Lincoln, the 16th president of America.
**Alternative spellings:** Abrahim, Ibrahim

## Abram

**Meaning:** Father of many nations
**Origin:** Hebrew
**Pronunciation:** AY bram
**Description:** Abram is another variant of the name Abraham, meaning 'father of many nations'. It is often shortened to Bram and is also used as a surname.
**Alternative spellings:** Abbram, Abriam

## Absalom

**Meaning:** Father of peace
**Origin:** Hebrew
**Pronunciation:** AB sa lom
**Description:** Absalom is a biblical name that means 'father of peace'. It is believed to be the name of the third son of King David but isn't very commonly used due to its relationship with grief within the Bible.
**Alternative spellings:** Abshalom, Absolom, Absolon

## Abu

**Meaning:** Father
**Origin:** Arabic
**Pronunciation:** AH boo
**Description:** Abu is a name that has both African and Arabic roots. The name was brought into the limelight in Western culture by the Disney film *Aladdin*, in which it is the name of Aladdin's monkey.
**Alternative spellings:** Abbu, Aboo

## Abubakar

**Meaning:** Father of the Camel
**Origin:** Arabic
**Pronunciation:** ABU baak err
**Description:** Abubakar is a popular name in the Muslim world as it was the name of one of the sahabas of the Holy Prophet. The name is composed of two words, 'abu' meaning 'father' and 'bakr' meaning 'young camel'. Abu Bakr as-Siddiq was the closest companion of the prophet Muhammad. In naming their children Abubakar, Muslims show their respect to the Holy Prophet. It is also the name of Pahang's royal mosque in Malaysia.
**Alternative spellings:** Abu-Bakr, Abubakr

## Acacus
**Meaning:** Mountain
**Origin:** Greek
**Pronunciation:** AH ka cus
**Description:** Acacus is an uncommon name of Greek origin. In Greek mythology, Acacus was a king of Acacesium in Arcadia. It is said that he raised Hermes, an Olympian god and the son of Zeus.
**Alternative spellings:** Acakus, Akacus, Akakus

## Ace
**Meaning:** Number one
**Origin:** Latin
**Pronunciation:** AYS
**Description:** Ace is a word commonly used to describe an expert, coming from the notion of being 'number one'. An ace is also one of the most powerful cards to hold in many card games. It has now become a popular name.
**Alternative spellings:** Ase, Ayce

## Acheron
**Meaning:** River of woe
**Origin:** Greek
**Pronunciation:** AYK er on
**Description:** In Greek mythology, Acheron was the name of a river bordering Hades, the Greek Underworld. Originally Acheron was the son of Demeter and was punished for helping the Titans by being cast into the Underworld, where he turned into the river.
**Alternative spellings:** Akeron, Akheron

## Achilles
**Meaning:** Unknown
**Origin:** Greek

**A**

**Pronunciation:** a KIL ees
**Description:** In Greek mythology the warrior Achilles was made invincible by being dipped into the River Styx by his goddess mother. However, his mother held on to his heel so this part of his body was able to be harmed, hence the phrase to have an 'Achilles heel'.
**Alternative spellings:** Achiles, Akilles

## Actaeon
**Meaning:** Herdsman
**Origin:** Greek
**Pronunciation:** AK tay on
**Description:** In Greek mythology, Actaeon was a huntsman who saw the goddess Artemis naked and as a result was turned into a stag and torn to pieces by his own dogs.
**Alternative spellings:** Aktaeon, Aktaion

## Adair
**Meaning:** Rich owner of spears
**Origin:** English
**Pronunciation:** ad DARE
**Description:** Derived from the English name Edgar meaning 'rich owner of spears'. It can also be used as a girls' name but is more usually used for boys.
**Alternative spellings:** Adare

## Adam
**Meaning:** Red earth
**Origin:** Hebrew
**Pronunciation:** AD dum
**Description:** A very popular modern name with biblical roots. According to the Bible, Adam is the name of the first man on Earth. The name derives from the word

'*adama*', which means earth in Hebrew.
**Alternative spellings:** Aadam, Adem

## Addison

**Meaning:** Son of Adam
**Origin:** English
**Pronunciation:** AD iss on
**Description:** The name Addison would have originally been given as a surname, meaning 'son of Adam'. Although the name is technically masculine, it has evolved into a unisex given name.
**Alternative spellings:** Addisonne, Adison

## Aden

**Meaning:** Full of fire
**Origin:** Gaelic
**Pronunciation:** Ay den
**Description:** A respelling of Aiden, which itself is a modern variant of Aodh. Aden is a unisex name as well as the place name of a city in South Yemen.
**Alternative spellings:** Aedan, Aidan, Aiden, Aodh, Ayden

## Adil

**Meaning:** Just; righteous; fair
**Origin:** Arabic
**Pronunciation:** AH deel
**Description:** Adil, meaning just, righteous or fair, is fairly uncommon in Britain, but may be more popular in the Middle East due to its Arabic origins.
**Alternative spellings:** Adeel, Adill

## Adina

See entry in 'Names for Baby Girls A–Z'

## Aditya

**Meaning:** Belonging to Aditi
**Origin:** Sanskrit
**Pronunciation:** a DEET ya
**Description:** In Hindu legend the name Aditya belonged to one of Aditi's 33 children. The word Aditya also refers to the sun. It is most commonly used in English- and Hindi-speaking countries.
**Alternative spellings:** Adeetya, Adityah

## Adlai

**Meaning:** God is just
**Origin:** Hebrew
**Pronunciation:** AD lye
**Description:** Adlai is a concentrated version of the Hebrew name Adaliah and carries the meaning 'God is just'. It is borne by a minor figure in the Bible.
**Alternative spellings:** Addlai, Adlye

## Adnan

**Meaning:** Settler
**Origin:** Arabic
**Pronunciation:** AD nan
**Description:** The name Adnan gets its meaning from the story of Adnan, a descendant of Ishmael who settled in the Arabian Peninsula.
**Alternative spellings:** Addnan

## Adrian

**Meaning:** From Hadria
**Origin:** Latin
**Pronunciation:** AY dri uhn
**Description:** Adrian means 'from Hadria'. Hadria is a town in northern Italy, which also gave its name to the Adriatic Sea.

**Alternative spellings:** Adrean, Adrien

# Adriel
**Meaning:** Of God's flock
**Origin:** Hebrew
**Pronunciation:** AY dree el
**Description:** Adriel is a name of biblical origin meaning 'of God's flock' or a follower of God. It has been more recently associated with angels and in particular the Angel of Death.
**Alternative spellings:** Adriell

# Advik
**Meaning:** Unique
**Origin:** Sanskrit
**Pronunciation:** AAD viik
**Description:** Advik is a Indian boys' Sanskrit name meaning 'unique'.
**Alternative spellings:** Aadvik

# Adyan
**Meaning:** Son of Ad
**Origin:** Muslim
**Pronunciation:** AD yan
**Description:** Adyan is a rare Muslim name derived from one of the prophets of Islam.
**Alternative spellings:** Adian, Adyann

# Ahad
**Meaning:** Servant of the only one
**Origin:** Arabic
**Pronunciation:** AH had
**Description:** Al-Ahad is one of the names of God in the Quran and is a common name in the Arabic world. Ahad is often used

following Abdul, which means 'servant of Allah'.
**Alternative spellings:** Ahed

# Ahmad
**Meaning:** Highly commendable
**Origin:** Arabic
**Pronunciation:** AH med
**Description:** Ahmad is a shortened version of the popular baby name Muhammad. It is of Arabic origin and is said to mean 'highly commendable'. Ahmed is an alternative of this name and is also extremely popular.

# Ahmed
**Meaning:** Worthy of praise
**Origin:** Arabic
**Pronunciation:** AH med
**Description:** Ahmed is one of the names given to the prophet Muhammad. It is popular with Muslim parents as a variant of Muhammad, one of the most commonly found boys' names in the world.
**Alternative spellings:** Achmad, Achmat, Achmed, Achmet, Ahmad, Ahmat, Ahmeed, Ahmet

# Ahyan
**Meaning:** Era
**Origin:** Arabic
**Pronunciation:** AYE an
**Description:** Ahyan is a variant spelling of the name Ayan, which is an Arabic name. The name covers a variety of words that all have similar meanings i.e. time, era, epoch. As it features heavily in the Quran it is extremely popular among Muslim families.

## Ai
See entry in 'Names for Baby Girls A–Z'

## Aiden
**Meaning:** Full of Fire
**Origin:** Gaelic
**Pronunciation:** AY den
**Description:** This name can be traced to both Gaelic and Celtic origin. The translation of both origins relates to fire, to be full of fire or bright with fire.
**Alternative spellings:** Aidan, Ayden

## Ailsa
See entry in 'Names for Baby Girls A–Z'

## AJ
**Meaning:** No meaning
**Origin:** English
**Pronunciation:** AYE jay
**Description:** AJ is a modern English invention composed of two letters and as such, has no real meaning. It is pronounced like the two letters as well. Although AJ is usually initials for two separate names, it is sometimes used as a given name as well.
**Alternative spellings:** Ajay

## Ajax
**Meaning:** Name of Greek hero
**Origin:** Greek
**Pronunciation:** AY jaks
**Description:** Ajax is the name of two Greek heroes, Ajax the Great, who was the cousin of Achilles, and Ajax the Lesser, who was a leader during the Trojan War.
**Alternative spellings:** Ajaks

## Ajay
**Meaning:** Invincible
**Origin:** Sanskrit
**Pronunciation:** AY jay
**Description:** Ajay is a popular Indian name for boys. It originates from the Sanskrit word for 'invincible' and can also be considered a phonetically spelt variation of the initials 'A' and 'J'.
**Alternative spellings:** A.J.

## Akash
**Meaning:** Open air
**Origin:** Sanskrit
**Pronunciation:** a KASH
**Description:** Akash is a boys' given name derived from the Hindi term 'Akasha', meaning 'open air'. In Hindu philosophy there are five basic elements that make up the human body – Akash is one of these.
**Alternative spellings:** Akaash, Akkash

## Akito
**Meaning:** Bright person
**Origin:** Japanese
**Pronunciation:** ah KEE to
**Description:** Akito is a Japanese boys' name composed of the elements of '*aki*' meaning 'bright' and '*to*' meaning 'person'.

## Akram
**Meaning:** Noblest
**Origin:** Arabic
**Pronunciation:** AK ram
**Description:** Akram is a common Muslim name and surname. Like many Islamic names, it owes its history to the prophet

Muhammad, and it is said to mean 'noblest'. The name's popularity has risen due to international Pakistan cricketer Wasim Akram.

## Akshara

**Meaning:** Unchangeable
**Origin:** Sanskrit
**Pronunciation:** ak SHA rah
**Description:** A unisex name said to mean 'unchangeable'. Popular in India, this versatile name is a favourite among Indian parents.
**Alternative spellings:** Akhshara, Aksara

## Akshay

**Meaning:** Eternal
**Origin:** Sanskrit
**Pronunciation:** AHK shay
**Description:** Akshay is a boys' given name of Sanskrit origin, meaning 'eternal'. It is a rare variant of the Hindi name 'Akash'.
**Alternative spellings:** Akshaay, Akshai

## Alaa

**Meaning:** Servant of Allah
**Origin:** Arabic
**Pronunciation:** ah LAH
**Description:** This name can be used for both girls and boys. It is often used as a shortened version of Aladdin and is said to mean 'servant of Allah'. Alaa is often given as a name by Muslim parents.
**Alternative spellings:** Ala, Allaa

## Alan

**Meaning:** Rock
**Origin:** Gaelic
**Pronunciation:** A lun
**Description:** Alan is of Celtic origin, with the uncertain derivation probably being from a word meaning 'rock'. It is also a river running through Wales. It was introduced to England by followers of William the Conqueror.
**Alternative spellings:** Allan, Allen

## Aland

**Meaning:** Precious
**Origin:** Gaelic
**Pronunciation:** AH land
**Description:** Aland is a variant of the name Alan. This name is uncommon in England but can be found more often in Wales. It is also the name given to a series of islands in the Baltic Sea.
**Alternative spellings:** Alland, Allund, Alund

## Alastair

**Meaning:** Defender of man
**Origin:** Gaelic
**Pronunciation:** AL is ter
**Description:** Alastair is the Gaelic equivalent of the masculine name Alexander, and both are said to mean 'defender of man'. This is a more popular variant of the Scottish name Alasdair.
**Alternative spellings:** Alasdair, Alaster, Alisdair, Alistair, Alister

## Albert

**Meaning:** Noble; bright; famous
**Origin:** German
**Pronunciation:** AL burt
**Description:** A popular name among European royal families. It became popular in Britain in the late 19th century, thanks to

Queen Victoria's husband Prince Albert.
**Alternative spellings:** Alburt, Allbert

## Alberto
**Meaning:** Noble
**Origin:** Italian
**Pronunciation:** al BEHR tow
**Description:** Alberto is the Italian, Portuguese and Spanish form of Albert. It is particularly popular in Italy and is the name of Alberto Aquilani, an Italian footballer.
**Alternative spellings:** Albert, Albertio

## Albie
**Meaning:** From Alba
**Origin:** Latin
**Pronunciation:** AL bee
**Description:** Albie is a variant of the Latin boys' name Alban.
**Alternative spellings:** Alby, Albye

## Aldrin
**Meaning:** Old and wise ruler
**Origin:** English
**Pronunciation:** AL drin
**Description:** Aldrin is an English name meaning 'old and wise ruler'. It is also the last name of famous astronaut, Buzz Aldrin, who was one of the first people to land on the moon.

## Alec
**Meaning:** Defender of man
**Origin:** Greek
**Pronunciation:** A lik
**Description:** Alec is a shortened form of Alexander, originating

from the UK. 'A smart Alec' is also a derogatory term for someone attempting to be clever.
**Alternative spellings:** Alek, Alic, Alick, Alik

## Aled
**Meaning:** Defender of man; child
**Origin:** Welsh
**Pronunciation:** A led
**Description:** This name is thought to derive from the more common name Alexander. It is believed that people named Aled are very affectionate and take huge pride in their appearance. As well as 'defender of man', Aled could also mean 'child'.
**Alternative spellings:** Aledd

## Alejandro
**Meaning:** Defender of man
**Origin:** Greek/Spanish
**Pronunciation:** al ay HAHN droh
**Description:** Alejandro is a Mediterranean variant of the Greek name Alexander predominantly found in Greece and Spain. It has been a popular name for many years.
**Alternative spellings:** Alehandro, Aleyandro

## Alessandro
**Meaning:** Defender of man
**Origin:** Italian
**Pronunciation:** al les SAHN dro
**Description:** Another variant of the Greek name Alexander, Alessandro is particularly popular in Italy.
**Alternative spellings:** Aleksandro, Alexandro, Alexandru, Alexsandro,

Aliksandro, Alisandro, Alissandro, Alixandro, Alyxandro

## Alessio
**Meaning:** Defender of man
**Origin:** Italian
**Pronunciation:** a LESS see oh
**Description:** Alessio is a popular Italian boys' name and a variant of the Greek name Alexander.
**Alternative spellings:** Alecio, Allecio, Elessio

## Alexander
**Meaning:** Defender of man
**Origin:** Greek
**Pronunciations:** AL eks ahn duh; al eks AHN duh
**Description:** From the Latin form of the Greek name Alexandros, which means 'to defend' and 'man warrior'. Alexander became very popular in the post-classical period and means 'defender of man'. Usage is largely derived from the fame of Alexander the Great, King of Macedon.
**Alternative spellings:** Aleksander, Alessander, Alexsander, Aliksander, Alisander, Alissander, Alixander, Alyxander

## Alexandre
**Meaning:** Defender of man
**Origin:** French
**Pronunciation:** Alex ON druh
**Description:** This unisex name is the French form of the Greek name Alexander. However, more emphasis is put on the middle 'a', which is pronounced 'o'. Commonly used in countries across the world, this name has been extremely popular for many years.

**Alternative spellings:** Aleksandre, Alessandre, Alexsandre, Aliksandre, Alisandre, Alissandre, Alixandre, Alyxandre

## Alexandros
**Meaning:** Defender of man
**Origin:** Greek
**Pronunciation:** al ex HAHN dros
**Description:** Alexandros is another variant of the Greek name Alexander. It is popular in the Mediterranean as an exotic twist on the traditional Greek boys' name.
**Alternative spellings:** Alexendros, Alyxandros

## Alexandru
**Meaning:** Defender of man
**Origin:** Greek/Spanish
**Pronunciation:** al ex HAHN dru
**Description:** Alexandru is a Greek and Spanish boys' name that is another Mediterranean variant of the Greek name Alexander and the Greek/Spanish name Alejandro. It is more commonly seen as a surname.
**Alternative spellings:** Aleksandro, Alessandro, Alexandro, Alexsandro, Aliksandro, Alisandro, Alissandro, Alixandro, Alyxandro

## Alexis
See entry in 'Names for Baby Girls A–Z'

## Alexus
**Meaning:** Defender of man; helper
**Origin:** Greek
**Pronunciation:** ah LEX us
**Description:** A modern variant of the name Alexis. Lexus is a pet form of this name as well as being a name in its own right.

**Alternative spellings:** Aleksus, Alexis, Alexsus

## Alf
**Meaning:** Elf
**Origin:** Norse
**Pronunciation:** ALF
**Description:** Alf is derived from the Old Norse word '*álf*', meaning 'elf'. It is often the short form of names such as Alfie or Alfred, but can stand as a first name on its own as well.

## Alfie
**Meaning:** Elf counsel
**Origin:** English
**Pronunciation:** AL fee
**Description:** Pet form of Alfred, proving to be a popular name in recent years. This might be to do with the remake of cult film *Alfie*, starring Jude Law.
**Alternative spellings:** Alfi, Allfie

## Alfonso
**Meaning:** Noble; brave
**Origin:** German
**Pronunciation:** AL phon SO
**Description:** Alfonso is a variation of the name Alphons, and is composed of the elements of '*apal*' meaning '*noble*' and '*funs*' meaning 'brave'.
**Alternative spellings:** Alphonso

## Alfred
**Meaning:** Elf counsel
**Origin:** English
**Pronunciation:** AL fred
**Description:** A relatively common name before the Norman Conquest of Britain, Alfred was borne by Alfred the Great. It is an example of an Old English name that

spread impressively over Europe. Nowadays, its pet form, Alfie, is more popular.
**Alternative spellings:** Alfrid, Allfred, Alvred

## Alger
**Meaning:** Elf spear
**Origin:** English
**Pronunciation:** AL ga
**Description:** Alger is a transferred surname of Old English origin that means 'elf spear'. Also a shortened version of the name Algernon.
**Alternative spellings:** Alga, Algar, Algare

## Algernon
**Meaning:** With a moustache; elf spear
**Origin:** French
**Pronunciation:** AL ger non
**Description:** Algernon was originally a Norman nickname given to those with a moustache as the Normans were generally clean-shaven. Alger also means 'elf spear' in Old English so the meaning of Algernon could be similar. It is quite a rare name nowadays.
**Alternative spellings:** Alganon, Algarnon

## Ali
**Meaning:** Sublime
**Origin:** Arabic
**Pronunciation:** AH lee
**Description:** According to Islamic belief, Ali was the name of Muhammad's cousin who married his daughter Fatima. Ali is also a shortened form of female names like Alice and Alison.

**Alternative spellings:** Ahlee, Aly

## Alison
See entry in 'Names for Baby Girls A–Z'

## Alix
See entry in 'Names for Baby Girls A–Z'

## Alpha
**Meaning:** Strongest
**Origin:** Greek
**Pronunciation:** AL fuh
**Description:** An unusual name given to boys, Alpha is also the first letter of the Greek alphabet. It is sometimes used as a word to describe the strongest male in a pack of animals.
**Alternative spellings:** Alfa

## Alvin
**Meaning:** Elf friend
**Origin:** English
**Pronunciation:** AL vin
**Description:** As this name derives from an Old English origin meaning 'elf' or 'magical being', it has many magical connotations.
**Alternative spellings:** Alfin, Alven, Alvyn, Elvin

## Alyaan
**Meaning:** Supreme
**Origin:** Sanskrit
**Pronunciation:** AL yaan
**Description:** Alyaan is a Sanskrit Indian boys' name meaning 'supreme' or 'exalted'. It is also often spelt Alyan.
**Alternative spellings:** Alyan

## Amal
**Meaning:** Hard-working
**Origin:** Hebrew
**Pronunciation:** ah MAHL
**Description:** This name has Hebrew origins and therefore has many meanings. Most famous from the protagonist of Gian Carlo Menotti's opera, *Amahl and the Night Visitors.*
**Alternative spellings:** Ahmal, Amel

## Aman
**Meaning:** Security
**Origin:** Arabic
**Pronunciation:** AH maan
**Description:** This name is mostly used in Arabic- and English-speaking countries. In East Malaysia there is a town called Sri Aman, which is the trade centre for timber, rubber and pepper.
**Alternative spellings:** Arman, Eman

## Amani
**Meaning:** Desires
**Origin:** Arabic
**Pronunciation:** ah MAH ne
**Description:** In Arabic-speaking countries Amani is used as a male name, but in Swahili-speaking countries it has also been taken up as a feminine name.
**Alternative spellings:** Ahmani

## Amar
**Meaning:** Immortal
**Origin:** Sanskrit
**Pronunciation:** AH mar
**Description:** Amar is an Indian name and comes from the Sanskrit word for 'immortal'. Similar names include Amare, Amari and Ammar.
**Alternative spellings:** Ammar

## Amarachi
See entry in 'Names for Baby Girls A–Z'

## Amarah
**Meaning:** God's grace
**Origin:** African
**Pronunciation:** ah MAR ah
**Description:** A spelling variant of the shortened form of Amarachi, Amara. It could also derive from an Arabic word meaning 'eternal' or 'unfading'. It is most commonly used by Muslim parents and is a unisex name.
**Alternative spellings:** Amara, Ammara

## Amari
**Meaning:** Prince
**Origin:** Arabic
**Pronunciation:** ah MARH ee
**Description:** Used as both a girls' and a boys' name, the name Amari could have been inspired by the feminine Arabic name Amira, which means 'princess'. The name is mostly found in America and is favoured by African-American parents.
**Alternative spellings:** Amarie

## Ambrose
**Meaning:** Immortal
**Origin:** Greek
**Pronunciation:** AM broze
**Description:** Ambrose is a name borne by a 4th-century bishop of Milan. It derives from the Greek word *'ambrose'*, meaning 'immortal'. It is more common in Ireland than England or the USA.
**Alternative spellings:** Ambroze

## Ameen
**Meaning:** Truthful
**Origin:** Arabic
**Pronunciation:** ah MEEN
**Description:** A variant of the Arabic name Amin. A popular name in Muslim communities.
**Alternative spellings:** Amin

## Ameer
**Meaning:** Prince
**Origin:** Arabic
**Pronunciation:** ah MAR
**Description:** Ameer is a variant of the popular boys' name Amir. The origins of the name can be found in both the Muslim and Jewish religions, and it can mean 'prince' or 'treetop'.
**Alternative spellings:** Ameir, Amer, Amir, Emeer, Emir

## Amos
**Meaning:** Born of God
**Origin:** Hebrew
**Pronunciation:** AI muhs
**Description:** Amos is a name of Hebrew origin, meaning 'to carry, born of God'. It has biblical references in the 'book of Amos'. The name was once very popular in America but is now rarely used.
**Alternative spellings:** Amoss, Emos

## Amrit
**Meaning:** Nectar of immortals
**Origin:** Sanskrit
**Pronunciation:** AM rit
**Description:** Amrit is a unisex name often used by Hindu parents. It is of Sanskrit origin and is found in the Vedic epics to refer to a physical object that gives immortality.
**Alternative spellings:** Amreet

## Anakin

**Meaning:** No meaning
**Origin:** English
**Pronunciation:** ANA kin
**Description:** Anakin is a modern invented name, most famously the name of Anakin Skywalker, the antagonist in the Star Wars franchise.

## Anas

See entry in 'Names for Baby Girls A–Z'

## Anders

**Meaning:** Different
**Origin:** Scandinavian
**Pronunciation:** AN ders
**Description:** Anders is the Scandinavian variant of Andrew.

## Andre

**Meaning:** Manliness
**Origin:** Greek
**Pronunciation:** AN drey
**Description:** A French form of the Greek name Andrew.
**Alternative spellings:** Andrei

## Andreas

**Meaning:** Manliness
**Origin:** Greek
**Pronunciation:** an DREY as
**Description:** Andreas is the New Testament Greek form of Andrew. Like its feminine equivalent, it comes from the word *'andreia'*, meaning 'manliness' or 'virility'.
**Alternative spellings:** Andreass, Andreyas

## Andrei

**Meaning:** Warrior
**Origin:** Greek
**Pronunciation:** AN drey

**Description:** Andrei is the Bulgarian, Moldovan, Russian or Romanian form of Andrew.
**Alternative spellings:** Andrej, Andres, Andrey

## Andrew

**Meaning:** Manliness
**Origin:** Greek
**Pronunciation:** AN droo
**Description:** The name Andrew has long been popular in the English-speaking world, especially in Scotland.
**Alternative spellings:** Andru

## Andy

**Meaning:** Manliness
**Origin:** Greek
**Pronunciation:** AN dee
**Description:** Originally a pet form of Andrew, Andy is now a name in its own right. It is used as both a boys' and a girls' name, although its spelling variant Andi is specifically feminine.
**Alternative spellings:** Andi, Andie

## Anees

**Meaning:** Friendly
**Origin:** Arabic
**Pronunciation:** a NEES
**Description:** Anees is a name of Arabic origin, meaning 'friendly'.
**Alternative spellings:** Aanees, Ahnees

## Aneurin

**Meaning:** Pure
**Origin:** Welsh
**Pronunciation:** AN yur in
**Description:** Aneurin is a mistranscription of the name Aneirin; a scribal mistake in the 17th century has made this variant the far

more common version of the name today.

**Alternative spellings:** Aneirin

## Angel

**Meaning:** Messenger of God
**Origin:** Greek
**Pronunciation:** AYN gel
**Description:** A common Spanish name from the Greek *'angelos'*, meaning 'messenger'. New Testament Greek suggests a more specific definition of 'messenger of God'.
**Alternative spellings:** Aingel, Ayngel

## Angelo

**Meaning:** Messenger of God
**Origin:** Italian
**Pronunciation:** AN jeh lo
**Description:** Angelo is Italian in origin and is a variation of Angel, which means 'messenger of God'. It is more common in America and may be used as a tribute to Michelangelo, the famous artist.
**Alternative spellings:** Angello, Angeloh

## Angus

**Meaning:** One; choice
**Origin:** Gaelic
**Pronunciation:** ANG gus
**Description:** Anglicised form of the Scottish name Aonghas, meaning 'one' or 'choice'.
**Alternative spellings:** Aonghas, Aonghus

## Anis

**Meaning:** Friendly; pure
**Origin:** Arabic/Greek
**Pronunciation:** Ah nees

**Description:** Anis is an Arabic boys' name popular in Tunisia, meaning 'friendly'. It is also popular in Greece as a girls' name, meaning 'pure' or 'holy'.
**Alternative spellings:** Anais, Anees, Annis

## Anish

**Meaning:** Supreme
**Origin:** Sanskrit
**Pronunciation:** a NEESH
**Description:** Anish is derived from Sanskrit. Meaning 'supreme' in Hindi, the name is sometimes applied to both Krishna and Vishnu. It is also the name of a river in Russia.
**Alternative spellings:** Aneesh, Annish

## Ansh

**Meaning:** Portion
**Origin:** Indian
**Pronunciation:** AAN sh
**Description:** Ansh is an Indian boys' name meaning 'portion'. Other variations include Aansh, Aanshi and Aanush, although they all have different meanings.
**Alternative spellings:** Aansh

## Anton

**Meaning:** Priceless
**Origin:** Latin
**Pronunciation:** an TON
**Description:** Anton is a shortened form of Anthony. The name is of Old Roman origins and shares the same meaning. Anton is also popular in Scandinavian countries and Russia.

## Anthony

**Meaning:** Protector
**Origin:** Latin

**A**

**Pronunciation:** AN ton ee; AN thon ee
**Description:** An Old Roman name of uncertain origin. It could derive from Antonius, a popular Latin name that itself is thought to have spawned from Adonis, an ancient Greek. A common shortening of this name is Tony.
**Alternative spellings:** Anthoni, Antoni, Antony

## Antoine
**Meaning:** Beyond praise
**Origin:** French
**Pronunciation:** AHN twahn
**Description:** Antoine is a boys' name meaning 'beyond praise'. It is the French form of Anthony and was very popular in France in the early 1990s.
**Alternative spellings:** Anthony, Antwone

## Antonio
**Meaning:** Protector
**Origin:** Spanish
**Pronunciation:** an TONE ee oh
**Description:** Antonio is a variation of the Roman family name Antonius. Often this name is shortened to Tony and is used mainly in English- and Spanish-speaking countries, especially America.
**Alternative spellings:** Anthonio

## Anusha
See entry in 'Names for Baby Girls A–Z'

## Anwar
**Meaning:** Bright
**Origin:** Arabic
**Pronunciation:** AN war

**Description:** Anwar is an uncommon name of Arabic origin, meaning 'bright' or 'clear'.
**Alternative spellings:** Aanwar, Anwaar

## Apollo
**Meaning:** Destroy
**Origin:** Greek
**Pronunciation:** a POL oh
**Description:** In Greek mythology, Apollo was the god of medicine, the sun, dancing, music and poetry. He was the sun of Zeus and Leto and his twin sister was Artemis. He is recognised as one of the most important and complex Olympian deities.
**Alternative spellings:** Apolo, Appollo, Appolo

## Aqeel
**Meaning:** Wise
**Origin:** Arabic
**Pronunciation:** AH keel
**Description:** Aqeel is an uncommon name of Arabic origin, meaning 'wise'. Aqeel ibn Abi Talib was a cousin of the prophet Muhammad.
**Alternative spellings:** Akeel, Aqel

## Aqib
**Meaning:** Successor
**Origin:** Arabic
**Pronunciation:** AH kib
**Description:** Aqib is an uncommon name of Arabic origin, meaning 'successor'.
**Alternative spellings:** Akib, Aqeeb

## Aran
**Meaning:** Mountain of strength

**Origin:** Hebrew
**Pronunciation:** AH ran
**Description:** Aran has Hebrew roots and means 'mountain of strength'. It is variation of the biblical name Aaron, and therefore has a similar meaning to it.
**Alternative spellings:** Arann, Araan

## Aras

**Meaning:** Eagle
**Origin:** Lithuanian
**Pronunciation:** AH ras
**Description:** Aras is a Lithuanian name meaning 'eagle'. It is most likely influenced by the Old German word '*arn*' and the Old Norse word '*örn*', both of which mean 'eagle'. A related name is Arnold, which has a similar meaning of 'eagle power'.
**Alternative spellings:** Araas

## Archer

**Meaning:** Bowman
**Origin:** English
**Pronunciation:** AR cher
**Description:** Archer is a common surname in England, though it can be used as a given name. It is derived from the Middle English word '*archere*' and was given as an occupational name for skilled bowmen in the 14th century.
**Alternative spellings:** Archere, Archier

## Archibald

**Meaning:** Courageous
**Origin:** German
**Pronunciation:** ARCH i bold

**Description:** Archibald is of Old German origin, but has made its way to Britain and is extremely popular in Scotland. Its shortened version, Archie, is even more popular.
**Alternative spellings:** Archibold

## Archie

**Meaning:** Courageous
**Origin:** German
**Pronunciation:** AR chee
**Description:** Short for Archibald but now given as a name in its own right. Currently a very popular name in Britain.
**Alternative spellings:** Archi, Archy

## Arda

**Meaning:** Bronze
**Origin:** Hebrew
**Pronunciation:** AR dah
**Description:** Arda is a unisex name that comes from the Hebrew word for 'bronze'. It could also be a variant of the unisex name Arden, said to mean 'great forest'.
**Alternative spellings:** Ardah, Arder

## Areeb

**Meaning:** Helpful; skilful
**Origin:** Arabic
**Pronunciation:** a REEB
**Description:** Areeb is an Arabic boys' name meaning 'helpful' or 'skilful'.
**Alternative spellings:** Ahreeb

## Arham

**Meaning:** Compassion
**Origin:** Arabic
**Pronunciation:** ARR haam
**Description:** Arham is an Arabic male name meaning 'mercy' or

'compassion'. Variations of the name include Erhem, Arhem, Ar-hamme and Arhamm.
Alternative spellings: Erhem, Arhem, Arhamme, Arhamm

## Ari
**Meaning:** Lion; eagle
**Origin:** Hebrew
**Pronunciation:** AH ree
**Description:** Ari is a Hebrew boys' name meaning 'lion' or 'eagle'. It is the shortened version of the ancient Greek name Aristides and the more common Greek name Ariel.
**Alternative spellings:** Aree, Arri

## Aria
**Meaning:** Lion
**Origin:** Hebrew
**Pronunciation:** AHR ee ah
**Description:** Aria has various origins and meanings. It could come from the Italian word for 'air' although in Hebrew its meaning is said to be 'lion'. It is unisex, but is more common in the Middle East as a masculine name.
**Alternative spellings:** Ariha

## Arian
**Meaning:** Silver
**Origin:** Welsh
**Pronunciation:** AIR ee an
**Description:** Most predominantly found in Wales, Arian is a Welsh name derived from the Greek name Arion. The meaning of the name Arian is said to be associated with the element silver.
**Alternative spellings:** Arion, Aryan

## Ariel

**A**

**Meaning:** God's lion
**Origin:** Hebrew
**Pronunciation:** AR ee el; AIR ee al
**Description:** This unisex name widely increased in popularity after Shakespeare's play *The Tempest* was performed.
**Alternative spellings:** Arial

## Arif
**Meaning:** Knowledgeable
**Origin:** Arabic
**Pronunciation:** a REEF
**Description:** Arif is a common boys' name in the Arabic world. It means 'smart, widely knowledgeable and wise'.
**Alternative spellings:** Aarif, Aref

## Aris
**Meaning:** War
**Origin:** Greek
**Pronunciation:** AIR ees
**Description:** Aris is an alternative spelling of the Greek name Ares, who was the god of war.
**Alternative spellings:** Ares

## Ariyan
**Meaning:** Noble
**Origin:** Indian
**Pronunciation:** AREE yan
**Description:** Ariyan is most likely a different spelling of the Indo-Iranian name Aryan, which means 'noble'. In fact, the word is actually used as a designation and ethnic label for the Indic people of the Vedic period.
**Alternative spellings:** Arian

## Arjan
**Meaning:** From Hadrian
**Origin:** Dutch

**Pronunciation:** AR jaan
**Description:** Arjan is a Dutch version of the name Adrian, meaning 'from Hadria'. Arjan is also an Indian name, but the Punjabi version is pronounced differently.
**Alternative spellings:** Arjun

## Arley

**Meaning:** Heap of stones; hare wood
**Origin:** English
**Pronunciation:** ARR lee
**Description:** Arley is a variation of the name Harley, which is an English name meaning 'heap of stones' or 'hare wood'. It is most likely a modern invention, although it does have roots in a traditional name.
**Alternative spellings:** Arlie

## Arlo

**Meaning:** Fortified hill
**Origin:** English
**Pronunciation:** AHR loh
**Description:** Arlo is a variation on the Old English '*harlow*', which means 'fortified hill'. It has been modified into the modern form Arlo over the years. In Spain Arlo means 'bayberry'.

## Armaan

**Meaning:** Goal; longing
**Origin:** Persian
**Pronunciation:** AR mon
**Description:** Armaan is a Hindi/ Urdu name of Persian origin. Its original meaning is thought to be 'goal'; however it was confused in translation and it now means 'longing' or 'wishing' in Hindi. It is used frequently in the Punjabi region of India for both Hindu and Sikh males.

**Alternative spellings:** Arman, Armon

## Arman

**Meaning:** Soldier
**Origin:** Israeli
**Pronunciation:** ARR maan
**Description:** Arman is the Israeli version of the German name Armand, which means 'soldier'. Both names are actually related to Herman, which means 'army man'.
**Alternative spellings:** Armaan

## Armand

**Meaning:** Soldier
**Origin:** German
**Pronunciation:** ARR maand
**Description:** Armand is a German name meaning 'soldier'. It is also related to Herman, which has the similar meaning of 'army man'.

## Armani

**Meaning:** Free
**Origin:** Italian
**Pronunciation:** ah MAR nee
**Description:** Armani is an Italian surname that is said to mean 'free'. The success of the Italian designer Giorgio Armani has led to the use of Armani as a first name, given to both boys and girls.
**Alternative spellings:** Armaani, Armanie

## Arnav

**Meaning:** Ocean water
**Origin:** Sanskrit
**Pronunciation:** Arh NAHV
**Description:** Arnav is a variation of the name Arnava and

shares its meaning of 'ocean water'. Arnav is a popular name in Arabic-speaking countries and it is one of the most commonly found Muslim boys' names in America.
**Alternative spellings:** Ahnav, Arhnav

## Arnie
**Meaning:** Ruler; strong as an eagle
**Origin:** German
**Pronunciation:** ARN ee
**Description:** Arnie is the diminutive of the German name Arnold, meaning 'ruler' or 'strong as an eagle'. It is derived from the elements of *'arn'* meaning 'eagle' and *'wald'* meaning 'power'. It died out as an English name after the Middle Ages but was revived in the 19th century.
**Alternative spellings:** Arnee

## Arnold
**Meaning:** Powerful eagle
**Origin:** German
**Pronunciation:** AR nold
**Description:** Arnold is a Frankish name derived from the words for 'eagle' and 'ruler'.
**Alternative spellings:** Arnald

## Aronas
**Meaning:** Unknown
**Origin:** English
**Pronunciation:** eh ROW nah
**Description:** Aronas is most likely a contemporary invention, and as such has no real meaning. The closest name to Aronas is the girls' name Arona, which is a Maori name meaning 'colourful'.

## Arooj
**Meaning:** Unknown
**Origin:** Persian
**Pronunciation:** ah ROOGE
**Description:** Arooj is a very unusual name and there is not much documentation on it. It is found used as a unisex name, but the variant Urooj is usually masculine. It originates from the Middle East and is possibly a Persian name.
**Alternative spellings:** Urooj

## Arran
**Meaning:** Strong mountain
**Origin:** Hebrew
**Pronunciation:** AH run
**Description:** Arran could be seen as a variation of Aaron, meaning 'strong mountain'. However, Arran could also originate from the Scottish Isle of Arran.
**Alternative spellings:** Aaran, Aaron, Aron, Arron, Arun

## Arthur
**Meaning:** Bear; stone
**Origin:** Gaelic
**Pronunciation:** AR thur
**Description:** The origin of this name is unclear, but it may come from the Celtic word *'artos'*, which means 'bear' or the Irish word *'art'* for stone. The name is strongly associated with King Arthur.
**Alternative spellings:** Arther, Arthor, Arthur

## Arun
**Meaning:** Dawn sky
**Origin:** Sanskrit
**Pronunciation:** AH roon
**Description:** Arun originates from a Sanskrit word referring to

a reddish-brown colour, which is associated with the sky at dawn.
**Alternative spellings:** Ahrun, Aroon

## Arvin
**Meaning:** People's friend
**Origin:** English
**Pronunciation:** AR vin
**Description:** Arvin is an uncommon boys' name of English and Old German origin. It means 'people's friend', and is also a city in California and a type of plant.
**Alternative spellings:** Aarvin, Arvyn

## Arya
See entry in 'Names for Baby Girls A–Z'

## Aryaan
**Meaning:** Illustrious
**Origin:** Sanskrit
**Pronunciation:** air ee AHN
**Description:** Aryaan is derived from the Indian word for 'illustrious' and the Sanskrit word for 'gentleman'. It is an uncommon name in England.
**Alternative spellings:** Aaryan, Arryan

## Asa
**Meaning:** Faithful
**Origin:** Hebrew
**Pronunciation:** AY sah
**Description:** Asa can be found in the Bible as the name of a king of Judah. He was renowned for his faithfulness and the meanings associated with the name stem from this.
**Alternative spellings:** Esa, Isa

## Asad
**Meaning:** Lion
**Origin:** Arabic
**Pronunciation:** a SAAD
**Description:** Asad is one of many Arabic boys' names meaning 'lion'. Assad is the more common spelling in English, though Asad is the more accurate transliteration.
**Alternative spellings:** Assad

## Asaph
**Meaning:** Collector
**Origin:** Hebrew
**Pronunciation:** AY saff
**Description:** Asaph is a name that features in the Bible and for that reason is sometimes considered a religious name.
**Alternative spellings:** Aisaph, Asaff, Aysaph

## Ash
**Meaning:** Ash tree clearing
**Origin:** English
**Pronunciation:** AH sh
**Description:** Ash is a short form of the common unisex name Ashley, meaning 'ash tree clearing'. Although it is often used as a nickname, it can also be a name on its own.

## Asha
See entry in 'Names for Baby Girls A–Z'

## Ashby
**Meaning:** From the ash tree
**Origin:** English
**Pronunciation:** ash BEE
**Description:** Ashby was originally an Anglo-Saxon last name and is connected to the tribe of the

same name. It was given to a group of people who once lived in a dwelling near an ash tree, hence the meaning of the name. This follows the contemporary trend of using last names as first names.

## Achden

**Meaning:** Belonging to Ashton
**Origin:** English
**Pronunciation:** ash DEN
**Description:** Ashden was originally a surname referring to people who came from Ashton, a place in England.
**Alternative spellings:** Ashdon

## Asher

**Meaning:** Fortunate
**Origin:** Hebrew
**Pronunciation:** ASH er
**Description:** A biblical name borne by one of the sons of Jacob who was promised a life of abundance and blessing. Often shortened to Ash.
**Alternative spellings:** Asha, Ashah

## Ashley

**Meaning:** Field of ash
**Origin:** English
**Pronunciation:** ASH lee
**Description:** Ashley was originally a male name but is now unisex, most commonly used for girls. It comes from an English surname referring to a 'field of ash'. However, 'ash' is a type of tree and the 'ley' suffix suggests 'wood', so it could also mean 'ash wood/tree'.
**Alternative spellings:** Ashlee, Ashleigh

## Ashton

**Meaning:** Ash tree settlement
**Origin:** English
**Pronunciation:** ASH tun
**Description:** Originally a surname, Ashton was used as the name of ash tree settlements. Now Ashton is a popular boys' name, possibly due to the fame of model and actor Ashton Kutcher.
**Alternative spellings:** Ashtan, Ashtun

## Ashwin

**Meaning:** Calendar month
**Origin:** Sanskrit
**Pronunciation:** ASH win
**Description:** Ashwin is said to derive from Ashvin, the name of the seventh month on the Hindu calendar. It is most predominantly found in Hindi-speaking countries.
**Alternative spellings:** Ashvin

## Asim

**Meaning:** Protector
**Origin:** Arabic
**Pronunciation:** a SEEM
**Description:** Asim is a popular Arabic boys' name meaning 'protector, guardian and defender'.
**Alternative spellings:** Aseem, Azim

## Aspen

**Meaning:** Aspen tree
**Origin:** English
**Pronunciation:** ASS pen
**Description:** Aspen is a unisex name that has derived from the aspen tree, known by its delicate leaves and white bark. As

a given name, Aspen is found predominantly in America.
**Alternative spellings:** Aspun

## Aston
**Meaning:** Ash tree settlement
**Origin:** English
**Pronunciation:** ASS tun
**Description:** The unisex name Aston comes from an Old English place name meaning 'east town settlement with an ash tree'. It may owe its increase of use as a first name to the popularity of the English sports car, the Aston Martin.
**Alternative spellings:** Astan, Asten, Astun

## Astor
**Meaning:** Thunder god
**Origin:** Scandinavian
**Pronunciation:** AS ter
**Description:** Astor is a Scandinavian derived from the elements of '*as*' meaning 'God' and '*tor*' meaning 'thunder'.
**Alternative spellings:** Aster

## Atif
**Meaning:** Compassionate
**Origin:** Arabic
**Pronunciation:** a TEEF
**Description:** Atif is a boys' given name of Arabic origin, meaning 'compassionate' or 'sympathetic'.
**Alternative spellings:** Ateef, Atiff

## Atlas
**Meaning:** Not enduring
**Origin:** Greek
**Pronunciation:** AT lass
**Description:** In Greek mythology, Atlas was one of the primordial Titans. He was a giant forced to hold up the heavens on his shoulders as punishment from Zeus.
**Alternative spellings:** Atlass, Atlus

## Atticus
**Meaning:** Man of Attica
**Origin:** Latin
**Pronunciation:** AT a kuss
**Description:** Atticus is a name from ancient Greece, meaning 'man of Attica or 'a man from Athens'. The name's popularity has risen considerably in recent years, possibly due to the enduring appeal of Harper Lee's novel, *To Kill a Mockingbird*.
**Alternative spellings:** Aticus, Attikas

## Aubrey
**Meaning:** Elfin
**Origin:** German
**Pronunciation:** AW bree
**Description:** Aubrey comes from the Germanic name Alberic, which means 'elfin king'. It is now popular as a girls' name due to its similarity to the popular name Audrey.
**Alternative spellings:** Aubree, Aubrie, Awbrey

## Audley
**Meaning:** From the old meadow
**Origin:** English
**Pronunciation:** ODD lee
**Description:** Audley is a surname originally derived from the placename Audley, in Staffordshire. This follows the contemporary trend of using last names as first names.

## August

**Meaning:** Eighth month of the year
**Origin:** English
**Pronunciation:** AUH gust
**Description:** August is a boys' name that comes from the English word of the same spelling and refers to the eighth month of the year. Like June and May, these are popular contemporary name choices for parents who want to name their child something a bit more modern.

## Auguste

**Meaning:** Great; magnificent
**Origin:** Latin
**Pronunciation:** ohg USTE
**Description:** Derived from the name Augustus, the name comes from the Latin word *augere* meaning 'great' or 'magnificent' and was a title given to Roman emperors.
**Alternative spellings:** August

## Augustus

**Meaning:** To increase
**Origin:** Latin
**Pronunciation:** or GUSS tuss
**Description:** Augustus is a Latin name taken from the word *augere*, meaning 'to increase'. It was borne by the Emperor Augustus in 27 BC. It is after him that the calendar month of August was named.
**Alternative spellings:** Augustuss, Orgustus

## Aurelio

**Meaning:** Golden
**Origin:** Italian
**Pronunciation:** or EL ee OH
**Description:** Aurelio is the Italian version of the name Aurelius, derived from the Latin word *aureus* meaning 'golden' or 'gilded'.

## Austen

**Meaning:** Great
**Origin:** Latin
**Pronunciation:** AU sten
**Description:** Austen is a variant of the Latin names Augustine and Augustus – meaning 'great' or 'magnificent'. Despite sounding similar, it is not to be confused with the American unisex name of similar spelling, Austin, which has risen in popularity since the Austin Powers movies.
**Alternative spellings:** Austin, Austyn

## Austin

**Meaning:** Great; magnificent
**Origin:** Latin
**Pronunciation:** OSS tin
**Description:** Austin is a unisex name particularly popular in America.
**Alternative spellings:** Orstin, Ostin

## Avery

**Meaning:** Elf counsel
**Origin:** English
**Pronunciation:** AYE ver ee
**Description:** Avery is an English name meaning 'elf counsel'. The name is a variation of Alfred, which is composed of 'alf' meaning 'elf' and 'fred' meaning 'counsel'. It used to be a surname, but is now widely used as a given name for both boys and girls.

**A**

## Avi

**Meaning:** Father of many nations
**Origin:** Hebrew
**Pronunciation:** AH vee
**Description:** Avi is a boys' name very common in the Jewish state of Israel. It is a shortened variant of the well-known biblical name Abraham.
**Alternative spellings:** Ave, Avy

## Awais

**Meaning:** Gifted
**Origin:** Arabic
**Pronunciation:** AH ways
**Description:** Awais is a masculine Arabic name said to mean 'gifted'. It is extremely unusual in Britain and its use in other parts of the world is scarce too.
**Alternative spellings:** Ahwais, Aways

## Axel

**Meaning:** Father of peace
**Origin:** Hebrew
**Pronunciation:** AK suhl
**Description:** Axel, which is Hebrew in origin, is a common name in Scandinavia, central Europe and America. Axel Witsel is a Belgian international footballer and Axl Rose (a slight variant of Axel) is the lead singer of rock band Guns N' Roses.
**Alternative spellings:** Aksel, Axell, Axil, Axill, Axl

## Ayaan

**Meaning:** Good luck
**Origin:** African
**Pronunciation:** ie YAHN
**Description:** Ayaan is a word used in the Quran said to refer to good luck and destiny. Someone who is experiencing particularly good luck may be referred to in Somalia as an 'ayaan'. Now it is used as a unisex name.
**Alternative spellings:** Ayahn, Iyaan

## Ayaz

**Meaning:** Respected
**Origin:** Arabic
**Pronunciation:** AY yaz
**Description:** Ayaz is an uncommon Arabic boys' name that is more commonly seen as a surname. The name is derived from the city of Ayask in Iran.
**Alternative spellings:** Ayaaz

## Ayden

**Meaning:** Full of fire
**Origin:** Gaelic
**Pronunciation:** AY den
**Description:** This variant of the name Aiden has become popular since 2001 in line with other misspellings of old names. Unlike Aiden, Ayden can be used as a girls' name.
**Alternative spellings:** Aden, Aedan, Aidan, Aiden, Aodh, Aydan

## Ayman

**Meaning:** Lucky
**Origin:** Arabic
**Pronunciation:** EYE mun
**Description:** Derived from the Arabic for 'right', this name

literally means 'he who is on the right-hand side', meaning a moral or lucky person. Another variation of the name is Aymeen; however both versions are uncommon names today.
**Alternative spellings:** Aiman, Aymaan

## Ayomide
See entry in 'Names for Baby Girls A–Z'

## Ayub
**Meaning:** Prophet of God
**Origin:** Hebrew
**Pronunciation:** AY yoob
**Description:** The origin and meaning of this name are hard to trace; however Ayub is thought to be a Muslim variant of the Hebrew name 'Job', the name of a character in the Bible.
**Alternative spellings:** Ayoob, Ayuub

## Ayush
**Meaning:** Long life
**Origin:** Sanskrit
**Pronunciation:** AH yush
**Description:** Because of its meaning, Ayush is used as a given name in the hope that it will bring prosperity.
**Alternative spellings:** Aiyush

## Azaan
**Meaning:** Power
**Origin:** Hebrew
**Pronunciation:** ah ZAHN
**Description:** Azaan is a spelling variation of Azan, which is Hebrew in origin and can be found in the Old Testament.
**Alternative spellings:** Azan, Azahn

## Azariah
**Meaning:** Yaweh has helped
**Origin:** Hebrew
**Pronunciation:** az AIR ee ah
**Description:** Azariah is a Hebrew name meaning 'Yaweh Has Helped'. It was the name of many an Old Testament character in the Bible.

## Azlan
**Meaning:** Lion
**Origin:** English
**Pronunciation:** AZ laan
**Description:** Azlan is most likely a variation of the name Aslan, which is a Turkish name meaning 'lion'. That is why the author C. S. Lewis used it to name the lion protagonist of the Chronicles of Narnia.
**Alternative spellings:** Azlaan

## Azriel
**Meaning:** Helper of God
**Origin:** Hebrew
**Pronunciation:** az ree ELL
**Description:** Azriel is a variant of the Hebrew name Azreal, who is an archangel in many religions. Although it is predominatnly found as a boys' name it is also sometimes used as a girls' name.
**Alternative spellings:** Asriel, Azreel, Azryel

# B

## Bacchus

**Meaning:** Grapevine
**Origin:** Latin
**Pronunciation:** BAK uss
**Description:** The uncommon name Bacchus is the Latin name for the Greek god Dionysus who was the god of the grape harvest, winemaking, wine and of ritual madness.
**Alternative spellings:** Bachus, Bakhus

## Baha

**Meaning:** Splendour
**Origin:** Arabic
**Pronunciation:** BA ha
**Description:** Baha is predominantly found as a boys' name, but is also used for girls. This could be to do with its associations of splendour and beauty. Baha could also be seen as a variant of the Spanish girls' name Baja, meaning 'lower'.
**Alternative spellings:** Bahah

## Baker

**Meaning:** Person who bakes
**Origin:** English
**Pronunciation:** BAKE er
**Description:** Baker, like Taylor and Hunter, is an occupational name given to people who baked for a living. It derives from the English vocabulary word of the same spelling and meaning.

## Bailey

**Meaning:** Bailiff
**Origin:** English
**Pronunciation:** BAY lee
**Description:** Originally a surname given to those who lived near a bailey, Bailey is now predominantly used as a unisex first name. The name prevails among girls in America and boys in the UK.
**Alternative spellings:** Bailee, Baileigh, Bailie, Baylee, Bayleigh, Bayley, Baylie

## Balius

**Meaning:** Dappled
**Origin:** Greek
**Pronunciation:** BAH li uss
**Description:** In Greek mythology, Balius was one of two immortal horses (the other being Xanthus) sired by Zeus.
**Alternative spellings:** Balios, Ballius

## Barack

**Meaning:** Blessed
**Origin:** Hebrew
**Pronunciation:** bah RAHK
**Description:** Barack is a boys' given name of Hebrew origin, meaning 'blessed'. It is an anglicisation of the Hebrew 'Baruch' and is borne by former US president Barack Hussein Obama.
**Alternative spellings:** Barach, Baruch

## Baran

**Meaning:** Noble warrior; ram; rain
**Origin:** Various
**Pronunciation:** bah RAHN
**Description:** Baran has various origins and meanings. In Russian, the name means 'ram,' the Gaelic meaning is 'noble warrior' and the Turkish meaning is 'rain'. It is also closely related to the name Baron.

## Bardo

**Meaning:** Water; bright wolf
**Origin:** Tibetan; German
**Pronunciation:** BAR doh
**Description:** Bardo is found in both Tibetan and German cultures although it means different things in each. In Tibet, the name means 'water', while in German, Bardo is most likely a short form of the name Bardolph, meaning 'bright wolf'.

## Barkley

**Meaning:** No meaning
**Origin:** English
**Pronunciation:** BARK lee
**Description:** Barkley is most likely a modern invention, and as such does not have a meaning. It may be connected to the names Berkeley and Barclay. Barkley is also an English surname, borne by many famous sportspeople.
**Alternative spellings:** Barklee

## Barnabas

**Meaning:** Son of consolation
**Origin:** Aramaic
**Pronunciation:** BAR nah bus
**Description:** The name Barnabas is quite popular in Britain and is often shortened to Barney. St Barnabas was a Jewish Cypriot and early Christian missionary who gave all his property to the Church.
**Alternative spellings:** Barnabus, Barnubus

## Barnaby

**Meaning:** Son of consolation
**Origin:** Aramaic
**Pronunciation:** BAR na bee
**Description:** Barnaby shares its meaning of 'son of consolation' with Barnabas. It is an alternative to the popular name.
**Alternative spellings:** Barnabi

## Barney

**Meaning:** Son of consolation
**Origin:** Aramaic
**Pronunciation:** BAR nee
**Description:** Originally the pet form of Barnabas or Barnaby, Barney is now a name in its own right.
**Alternative spellings:** Barni, Barny

## Baron

**Meaning:** Title of nobility
**Origin:** English
**Pronunciation:** BARE on
**Description:** Baron is taken from the English vocabulary name of the same spelling and meaning, and it is a title often given to members of nobility.

## Barry

**Meaning:** Fair-haired
**Origin:** Gaelic
**Pronunciation:** BA ree
**Description:** Barry is an anglicised form of the Irish name Barra, which comes from 'Fionnbarr'.
**Alternative spellings:** Barri, Barrie

## Bart

**Meaning:** Farmer's son
**Origin:** Aramaic
**Pronunciation:** BART
**Description:** Bart is short for both Barton and Bartholomew. It was made famous by the success of American cartoon show *The Simpsons,* where Bart is one of the Simpson children.
**Alternative spellings:** Barte

B

## Bartholomew

**Meaning:** Son of Talmai
**Origin:** Hebrew
**Pronunciation:** bar THOL o mew
**Description:** Bartholomew is a name of Hebrew origin. There are several saints named Bartholomew, although the apostle is the most famous. The name is often shortened to Bart.
**Alternative spellings:** Bartholomew, Bartolowmew

## Bartlomiej

**Meaning:** Farmer's son
**Origin:** Hebrew
**Pronunciation:** bart lo MEY
**Description:** Bartlomiej is a Polish variation of the masculine name Bartholomew.
**Alternative spellings:** Bartholomew

## Bartosz

**Meaning:** Son of Talmai
**Origin:** Polish
**Pronunciation:** BART ozz
**Description:** Bartosz is the Polish form of the name Bartholomew. Bartholomew is a boys' name of Greek origin. There are several saints named Bartholomew, although the apostle is the most famous. The name is often shortened to Bart, popularised by Bart Simpson of the TV cartoon *The Simpsons*.

## Basil

**Meaning:** Royal; kingly
**Origin:** Greek
**Pronunciation:** BA zil
**Description:** Basil, despite it being the name of a herb, is actually derived from the Greek name Vassilios, meaning 'royal' or 'kingly'. Basil Rathbone was a famous British actor with this name.

## Baxter

**Meaning:** Baker
**Origin:** English
**Pronunciation:** BAKS ter
**Description:** Baxter is a name derived from the Old English word for 'baker'. It was popular throughout the late 19th century and early 20th century, but the name has a certain modern ring to it that makes it a popular choice for contemporary babies.

See entry in 'Names for Baby Girls A–Z'

## Bear

**Meaning:** Animal
**Origin:** English
**Pronunciation:** BEH ar
**Description:** The name bear most likely comes from the animal of the same name, and is usually used as a nickname. Edward Michael Grylls is better known as 'Bear Grylls,' and is a famous British adventurer and television presenter.

## Beau

**Meaning:** Beautiful
**Origin:** French
**Pronunciation:** BOH
**Description:** Beau has had a surge in popularity recently. It originates from France and like Belle, its feminine counterpart, means 'beautiful'. It can sometimes be used as a girls' name too.
**Alternative spellings:** Bo, Bow

## Beck

**Meaning:** Dweller near the brook
**Origin:** English
**Pronunciation:** BECK
**Description:** Beck is an uncommon boys' given name of English origin, meaning 'dweller near the brook'. It is a common surname in Scandinavian countries.
**Alternative spellings:** Bec, Bekk

## Beckett

**Meaning:** Bee Cottage
**Origin:** English
**Pronunciation:** BECK ett
**Description:** Beckett is a variation of the name Becket, an English; Irish name meaning 'bee cottage'. It is a name that has been popular in recent years and is the name of many celebrity babies.
**Alternative spellings:** Becket

## Bellerophon

**Meaning:** Great hero
**Origin:** Greek
**Pronunciation:** behl LEH ro fon
**Description:** In Greek mythology, Bellerophon was a great hero of monster slaying.
**Alternative spellings:** Bellerofon, Bellerophos

## Ben

**Meaning:** Son of my sorrow
**Origin:** Hebrew
**Pronunciation:** BEN
**Description:** Ben can be short for Benjamin, Benedict or Bennett as well as being a first name in its own right.
**Alternative spellings:** Benn

## Benas

**Meaning:** Son of my sorrow
**Origin:** Hebrew
**Pronunciation:** BEN ass
**Description:** Benas is an uncommon, exotic variant of the old Hebrew name Benjamin. It is more common in Hispanic regions.
**Alternative spellings:** Benass, Bennas

## Benedict

**Meaning:** Blessed
**Origin:** Latin
**Pronunciation:** BEN ee dikt
**Description:** The name Benedict is mainly used in English-speaking countries. This name is very common among popes and was also the name of the saint who inspired the Catholic monastic order, the Order of St Benedict.
**Alternative spellings:** Benedikt, Benedyct

## Benicio

**Meaning:** Blessed
**Origin:** Spanish
**Pronunciation:** ben EE see oh
**Description:** Benicio is a Spanish boys' name meaning 'blessed'. It is the Spanish version of the name Benedict, and as such shares the same meaning. Benicio del Toro is a famous Puerto Rican actor.

## Benjamin

**Meaning:** Son of my sorrow
**Origin:** Hebrew
**Pronunciation:** BEN jah min
**Description:** A biblical name borne by the youngest of the

12 sons of Jacob. In the Bible, Benjamin's mother Rachel died giving birth to him. In her last moments she named him Benoni, meaning 'son of my sorrow'. His father did not wish him to bear such an ill-omened name, and renamed him Benyamin.
**Alternative spellings:** Benjaman, Benyamin

## Bennett
**Meaning:** Blessed
**Origin:** Latin
**Pronunciation:** BEN et
**Description:** Bennett is derived from the Latin word '*benedict*'. Today it is more commonly found as a surname.
**Alternative spellings:** Bennet

## Benny
**Meaning:** Son of my right hand
**Origin:** Hebrew
**Pronunciation:** BEN ee
**Description:** Benny is a name of Hebrew origin, meaning 'son of my right hand'. It is a common nickname for children named Benjamin, and a variant of the nickname Ben.
**Alternative spellings:** Benni, Bennie

## Benson
**Meaning:** Son of Ben
**Origin:** English
**Pronunciation:** ben SON
**Description:** Benson was originally an English surname meaning 'son of Ben'. In recent years, it has also become a popular first name.
**Alternative spellings:** Bensen

## Bentley
**Meaning:** Bent grass meadow
**Origin:** English
**Pronunciation:** BENT lee
**Description:** The name Bentley has passed down the generations from Old England. It is a place name in many counties across England, appearing in Suffolk, Essex, Derbyshire, Warwickshire and Hampshire. It is most commonly known due to the famous English car company of the same name.

## Benton
**Meaning:** Town in the bent grass
**Origin:** English
**Pronunciation:** ben TUN
**Description:** Benton was originally an English surname referring to people who lived in a 'town in the bent grass'. This follows the contemporary trend of using last names as first names.

## Berat
**Meaning:** Letters patent
**Origin:** Turkish
**Pronunciation:** beer AAT
**Description:** It is not entirely known what this Turkish name means, but it most likely means 'letters patent', which is an open document issued by a monarch or government granting an office, right, monopoly, title or status to a person.

## Berlin
**Meaning:** Boardline
**Origin:** German
**Pronunciation:** ber LIN
**Description:** Berlin is an edgy baby name coming from the

capital city of Germany. Berlin is the largest city in Germany and, like Camden and Brooklyn, is part of the trend of using place names as baby names.

## Bernard

**Meaning:** Brave bear
**Origin:** German
**Pronunciation:** BER nard
**Description:** Bernard is an old-fashioned name of German origin. Meaning 'strong, brave bear', the name was one of the most popular in the English-speaking world in the early 20th century; however, it is far less common in recent years.
**Alternative spellings:** Barnard, Bearnard, Bernd, Burnard

## Bertie

**Meaning:** Noble; famous; bright
**Origin:** German
**Pronunciation:** BUR tee
**Description:** Bertie is commonly a nickname for those given the birth name Albert or Bertram, but it has recently found its way into popularity as a name in its own right. Bertie Ahern was the taoiseach of Ireland for 10 years.
**Alternative spellings:** Bertee

## Bertrand

**Meaning:** Bright raven; bright shield
**Origin:** German
**Pronunciation:** BURT rand
**Description:** Bertrand is a German name derived from the elements of '*berht*' meaning 'bright' and '*hramn*' meaning 'raven' or '*rand*' meaning 'shield.' Bertrand Russell was a famous British philosopher.

## Bilal

**Meaning:** Refreshing
**Origin:** Arabic
**Pronunciation:** BIH lal
**Description:** The name Bilal is the Arabic form of Billy. It is thought that the first convert of the prophet Muhammad was a slave who went by the name of Bilal. He then went on to become the very first high priest and treasurer of the muslim Empire.
**Alternative spellings:** Billal

## Bill

**Meaning:** Seeking protection
**Origin:** German
**Pronunciation:** BILL
**Description:** Bill is a shortened form of the popular name William, but is also a name in its own right.
**Alternative spellings:** Bil

## Billie

**Meaning:** Seeking protection
**Origin:** German
**Pronunciation:** BIL ee
**Description:** Billie also originates as a pet form of the name William. Although the name is unisex, this particular spelling is favoured for girls.
**Alternative spellings:** Billi, Billy

## Billy

**Meaning:** Seeking protection
**Origin:** German
**Pronunciation:** BILL ee
**Description:** The most masculine spelling of the shortened form of William.
**Alternative spellings:** Billi, Billie

## Bishop

**Meaning:** Priest
**Origin:** English
**Pronunciation:** BISH up
**Description:** Bishop is originally an English occupational name given to religious priests. While it is usually used as a last name, it has also become a first name in recent years.

## Bjorn

**Meaning:** Bear
**Origin:** Swedish
**Pronunciation:** BY urn
**Description:** Bjorn is a Swedish boys' name that means 'bear'. Note that the 'j' is not pronounced. It is also one of the more common Swedish names.

## Blake

**Meaning:** Black; white
**Origin:** English
**Pronunciation:** BLAYK
**Description:** Interestingly, Blake has two meanings that are opposite to one another. The Old English words for black and white are both linked to this name and it was often given as a nickname for someone with very bright or very dark hair.
**Alternative spellings:** Blaike, Blayke

## Blakely

**Meaning:** Dark wood
**Origin:** English
**Pronunciation:** BLAKE lee
**Description:** Blakely was originally an English last name referring to people who lived next to a dark wood or clearing.

This follows the contemporary trend of using last names as first names.

## Blythe

See entry in 'Names for Baby Girls A–Z'

## Bob

**Meaning:** Bright fame
**Origin:** German
**Pronunciation:** BOB
**Description:** Bob is an altered short form of Robert, meaning 'bright fame'.

## Bobbie

**Meaning:** Bright fame
**Origin:** English
**Pronunciation:** BOB ee
**Description:** Bobbie can be used as both a boys' and girls' name. It is a more modern variant of the English shortened name Bob, which derives from Robert.
**Alternative spellings:** Bobbee, Bobbey, Bobby

## Bodhi

**Meaning:** Wise
**Origin:** Sanskrit
**Pronunciation:** BOHD ee
**Description:** Bodhi is an uncommon name of Sanskrit origin, meaning 'wise', 'enlightening' or 'knowledge'. In Buddhism, it is the word given to the understanding possessed by a Buddha.
**Alternative spellings:** Bodhee, Bodhie

## Bogdan

**Meaning:** Gift from God
**Origin:** Russian
**Pronunciation:** BOG daan

**Description:** Bogdan is of Russian and Ukrainian origins, meaning 'gift from God'.
**Alternative spellings:** Bogdon

## Boreades
**Meaning:** Son of Boreas
**Origin:** Greek
**Pronunciation:** bo READ ees
**Description:** In Greek mythology, the Boreades were three giant sons of Boreas (the north wind) and Khione (goddess of snow).
**Alternative spellings:** Boreads, Boredes

## Boris
**Meaning:** Glorious in battle
**Origin:** Russian
**Pronunciation:** BOH riss
**Description:** Originally thought to come from the Russian '*bogoris*' meaning 'small', the name Boris is now considered a short form of the Russian name Borislav, meaning 'glorious in battle'.
**Alternative spellings:** Borris, Boriss, Borys

## Bosco
**Meaning:** Forest
**Origin:** Italian
**Pronunciation:** BOSS koh
**Description:** Bosco is an Italian boys' name meaning 'forest' or 'from the woods'. It is taken from the Latin word '*boscus*' meaning 'shrub' or 'undergrowth'.

## Bowden
**Meaning:** Curved hill
**Origin:** English
**Pronunciation:** BOW den

**Description:** Bowden is an English surname made from the Old English words '*boga*' meaning 'bow' and '*dùn*' meaning 'hill' – together they mean a hill that is curved. This follows the contemporary trend of using last names as first names.
**Alternative spellings:** Bowdon

## Bowie
**Meaning:** Blond
**Origin:** Scottish
**Pronunciation:** BOW ee
**Description:** Bowie is a Scottish boys' name meaning 'blond'. It was made popular in recent years due to the glam rock star, David Bowie.
**Alternative spellings:** Bowee

## Bracken
**Meaning:** Descendant of Breacain
**Origin:** Gaelic
**Pronunciation:** BRAH ken
**Description:** Bracken is a unisex name derived from the Gaelic surname Breacain. The surname was originally given to the descendants of the clan that Saint Breacain belonged to. Bracken is also the name for a fern.
**Alternative spellings:** Bracain, Braken

## Brad
**Meaning:** Broad wood clearing
**Origin:** English
**Pronunciation:** BRAD
**Description:** The name Brad came about as a shortened form of the name Bradley, but is now a first name in its own right.
**Alternative spellings:** Bradd

## Braden

**Meaning:** Salmon
**Origin:** Gaelic
**Pronunciation:** BRAY den
**Description:** Braden is a popular boys' name in America and Canada in recent years. It derives from the Irish surname O'Bradan, which is the Gaelic word for 'salmon'. There are over 20 variants of the name, all of which are increasingly popular.
**Alternative spellings:** Bradin, Bradyn, Braedan, Braiden, Brayden

## Bradley

**Meaning:** Broad wood clearing
**Origin:** English
**Pronunciation:** BRAD lee
**Description:** Bradley was originally used as a place name that meant 'broad wood clearing'. It then became a surname before being transferred to a forename.
**Alternative spellings:** Bradlee, Bradly

## Brady

**Meaning:** Descendant of Brádach
**Origin:** Irish
**Pronunciation:** BRAY dee
**Description:** Brady is originally an Irish surname meaning 'descendant of Bradach'. However, in contemporary usage, it is not uncommon to see it used as a given name as well.
**Alternative spellings:** Bradee

## Brandon

**Meaning:** Gorse hill
**Origin:** English
**Pronunciation:** BRAN den
**Description:** Brandon was originally used as a surname that combined the Old English words for a broom or gorse *(brom)* and a hill *(dun)*. It may also be considered a variant of Brendan.
**Alternative spellings:** Brandan, Branden, Brandun, Brandyn

## Braxton

**Meaning:** Bracca's town
**Origin:** English
**Pronunciation:** BRAKS ten
**Description:** Braxton was originally an English surname from the Old English, referring to a place name 'Bracca's town'. The 'tun' part of the name refers to 'town' while the first part of the name is the name of the town itself.

## Breckin

**Meaning:** Freckled
**Origin:** Irish
**Pronunciation:** breck IN
**Description:** Breckin is a variant spelling of the Irish name Breckin, meaning 'freckled'. Breckin Meyer is a famous American actor with this name.
**Alternative spellings:** Breccan

## Brendan

**Meaning:** Prince
**Origin:** Gaelic
**Pronunciation:** BREN dan
**Description:** Brendan derives from the Old Irish name Breannain. It is widely used in Ireland in homage to St Brendan, known as 'the voyager'.
**Alternative spellings:** Brenden, Brendon

## Brennan

**Meaning:** Teardrop

**Origin:** Gaelic
**Pronunciation:** BREN ann
**Description:** Brennan is a name for boys and girls that rose to popularity in the 1990s. It is of Irish and Gaelic origin and means 'teardrop'.
**Alternative spellings:** Brenan, Brennen, Brennon, Brenyn

## Brent

**Meaning:** From a high place
**Origin:** English
**Pronunciation:** brent
**Description:** Brent is an English last name referring to someone who came from a high place or a steep hill. It also indicates people who lived in a place called Brent. This follows the contemporary trend of using last names as first names.

## Brett

**Meaning:** Inhabitant of Britain
**Origin:** English
**Pronunciation:** BRET
**Description:** Brett is a very popular boys' name in America and Canada. It is common as both a surname and a given name.
**Alternative spellings:** Bret, Brette, Brit

## Brian

**Meaning:** Strength
**Origin:** Gaelic
**Pronunciation:** BRY un
**Description:** Brian is a Gaelic name popular in Britain and Ireland. It is often spelt Bryan.
**Alternative spellings:** Brien, Brion, Bryan

## Brody

**Meaning:** Muddy place
**Origin:** Gaelic

**B**

**Pronunciation:** BROH dee
**Description:** The meaning for this name originates from the Celtic word 'brothaigh'. It was used as a surname for those who lived by muddy places and over time it has transferred into a forename.
**Alternative spellings:** Brodi, Brodie

## Brogan

**Meaning:** Shoe
**Origin:** Gaelic
**Pronunciation:** BRO gun
**Description:** Brogan is a unisex name that was originally an Irish surname. Brogan is Gaelic in origin and is said to be derived from the word 'brog', which means 'shoe'.
**Alternative spellings:** Brogun

## Brook

See entry in 'Names for Baby Girls A–Z'

## Brooks

**Meaning:** Of the brook
**Origin:** English
**Pronunciation:** BRUK ss
**Description:** Brooks is an English boys' name meaning 'of the brook,' referring to a small stream.

## Brooklyn

**Meaning:** Stream
**Origin:** English
**Pronunciation:** BRUK lin
**Description:** Brooklyn derives from the name of a borough in New York. It is very popular due to its combination of two well-loved names: Brooke and Lynn. The name is very popular in the USA and Canada.

**Alternative spellings:** Brooklin, Brooklynn

## Bruce
**Meaning:** Unknown
**Origin:** Gaelic
**Pronunciation:** BROOS
**Description:** The name Bruce was originally a Scottish surname, notably belonging to Robert Bruce, a Scottish king in the 14th century.
**Alternative spellings:** Brooce, Bruse

## Bruno
**Meaning:** Brown
**Origin:** German
**Pronunciation:** BRU no
**Description:** Bruno started life as a name given to upper-class families in the Middle Ages in Germany. It has been long established in America and may have been introduced to Britain from there.
**Alternative spellings:** Broono, Brunoh

## Bryan
**Meaning:** High; noble
**Origin:** Gaelic
**Pronunciation:** BRY un
**Description:** Bryan is an alternative spelling of the popular Gaelic name Brian. It has long been the name associated with Brian Boru the Irish warrior king.
**Alternative spellings:** Brian

## Bryce
**Meaning:** Of Britain
**Origin:** Scottish
**Pronunciation:** BRI-se
**Description:** Bryce is a popular boys' name of Scottish origin, meaning 'of Britain'. It is common as both a surname and a given name. Bryce Canyon, America is one of the most breathtaking natural geological sites in the world.
**Alternative spellings:** Brice, Bryse

## Bryn
**Meaning:** Hill
**Origin:** Greek
**Pronunciation:** BREN, BRIN
**Description:** Bryn was originally a Welsh place name describing a dwelling next to a hill. It was then adopted into a unisex first name.
**Alternative spellings:** Bren, Brenne, Brin

## Bryson
**Meaning:** Son of Brice
**Origin:** English
**Pronunciation:** BRY son
**Description:** Bryson is an English boys' name meaning 'son of Brice,' where Brice is a Scottish surname.
**Alternative spellings:** Brysen

## Buddy
**Meaning:** Brother
**Origin:** English
**Pronunciation:** BUD dee
**Description:** Buddy is an uncommon boys' name, often shortened to Bud. Buddy is often used as a word signifying friendship or for a loved pet.
**Alternative spellings:** Buddey, Buddie

## Burhan
**Meaning:** Proof
**Origin:** Arabic
**Pronunciation:** BUR hahn

**Description:** Burhan is an uncommon Arabic name meaning 'proof'. It is an epithet of the prophet Muhammad. The name is somewhat popular in Turkey.
**Alternative spellings:** Buran, Burhaan

## Burt

**Meaning:** Bright; glorious
**Origin:** English
**Pronunciation:** burt
**Description:** Burt is a name derived from the Old English '*beorht*' meaning 'bright' or 'glorious'. Burt Reynolds and Burt Lancaster were two famous actors with this name.
**Alternative spellings:** Bert

## Buster

**Meaning:** A person who breaks things
**Origin:** English
**Pronunciation:** BUS tar
**Description:** The name Buster was originally a nickname meaning 'a person who broke things', from the word 'bust'. Buster Keaton was an American actor and director from the silent film era who made the name popular.

## Byron

**Meaning:** Cattle shed
**Origin:** English
**Pronunciation:** BY ron
**Description:** This name originates from the surname of those who lived near cattle sheds or those who worked there, but was slowly adopted as a first name.
**Alternative spellings:** Biron, Byrun

# C

## Cade

**Meaning:** Barrel maker
**Origin:** English
**Pronunciation:** KADE
**Description:** Cade is an Old English surname said to refer to a barrel maker. It has now been adopted as a unisex name.
**Alternative spellings:** Caid, Cayde, Kade, Kayd

## Caden

**Meaning:** Son; spirit of battle
**Origin:** Gaelic
**Pronunciation:** KAY den
**Description:** This name is mainly used in English-speaking countries, where it is thought to mean 'son'. It also has Welsh origins, where it is said to mean 'spirit of battle'. For this reason it is common among Welsh families.
**Alternative spellings:** Cadon, Caiden, Caidon, Cayden, Caydon, Kaden, Kadon, Kaiden, Kaidon, Kayden, Kaydon

## Cadmus

**Meaning:** Alphabet
**Origin:** Greek

B
C

**Pronunciation:** CAD mus
**Description:** In Greek mythology, Cadmus was the son of Agenor and the brother of Europa. He went on to found the city of Thebes. He was credited with the introduction of the Phoenician alphabet.
**Alternative spellings:** Cadmos, Kadmos, Kadmus

## Caelan

**Meaning:** Slender
**Origin:** Gaelic
**Pronunciation:** Kay laahn
**Description:** Caelan is a name of Gaelic origin. Its meaning is debated but some agree that it means 'slender'. It is an uncommon name in England but is more widely used in Ireland. Although it is most commonly found as a name for boys, it is in fact unisex.
**Alternative spellings:** Caolan, Caylan, Kaelan, Kaolan, Kaylan

## Cai

**Meaning:** Rejoice
**Origin:** English
**Pronunciation:** KY
**Description:** Cai is an alternative spelling of the Scandinavian name Kai, which means 'rejoice'. It has become common in recent years for parents to slightly change the spelling of a name to suit their own choice.
**Alternative spellings:** Kai

## Cain

**Meaning:** Spear
**Origin:** Hebrew
**Pronunciation:** KAYN
**Description:** Cain can be traced to several origins. In the Bible it was the name of the first son of Adam and Eve, who killed his own brother, and it means 'a spear'. However, in Wales Cain is a girls' name that means 'full of beauty'.
**Alternative spellings:** Caine, Kain, Kane, Kayne

## Caio

**Meaning:** Happy
**Origin:** Latin
**Pronunciation:** CAY o
**Description:** Caio is an exotic boys' name meaning happy. It is a variant of the Welsh name Caeo and the Latin name Caius. It is more commonly seen as a surname.
**Alternative spellings:** Cayo, Kaio

## Cairo

**Meaning:** Victorious
**Origin:** Arabic
**Pronunciation:** KY ro
**Description:** Cairo is the place name of Egypt's capital city and it means 'victorious'. It is therefore a fitting name for a child conceived or born in Egypt.
**Alternative spellings:** Kairo, Kyro

## Cairon

**Meaning:** Victorious
**Origin:** Arabic
**Pronunciation:** KY ron
**Description:** This name derives from the city of Cairo. Cairo was originally given as a name to those who resided in the city; however, over time the name has developed into Cairon. The name could also be seen as a variant of the name Kieran.

Alternative spellings: Kairon, Kyron

## Calchas
Meaning: Bronze man
Origin: Greek
Pronunciation: KAHL kas
Description: In Greek mythology, Calchas was a seer with a gift of interpreting the flight of birds and the entrails of the enemy during the tide of battle.
Alternative spellings: Calchus, Calkas

## Caleb
Meaning: Dog; loyal
Origin: Hebrew
Pronunciation: KAY leb
Description: Caleb is a biblical name meaning 'dog'. It is also considered to mean 'loyal' or 'whole-hearted', depending on how the Hebrew is translated. Caleb was the name of one of Moses' followers on the journey to the Promised Land.
Alternative spellings: Kaleb, Kayleb

## Callan
Meaning: Rock
Origin: Gaelic
Pronunciation: KAL an
Description: Callan is an uncommon boys' name of Gaelic origin. A British TV series by the name of *Callan* caused the name's popularity to rise in the 1970s.
Alternative spellings: Caelan, Calan, Caolan, Callen

## Calum
Meaning: Peace
Origin: Latin

Pronunciation: KAL lum
Description: This name is very popular among followers of the Christian faith due to the symbolism of a dove, peace and the Holy Spirit. It also became popular due to St Columba, who was an influential Irish missionary in the 16th century.
Alternative spellings: Callum, Kallum, Kalum

## Calvin
Meaning: Bald
Origin: French
Pronunciation: CAL vin
Description: Originally a French surname, Calvin meant 'little bald one' from the diminutive *'calve'*. The name's popularity in modern times is largely due to the success of designer fashion label Calvin Klein.
Alternative spellings: Kalvin

## Camden
Meaning: Enclosed valley
Origin: English
Pronunciation: KAM den
Description: Camden is most likely an Old English surname meaning 'enclosed valley'. It is also a borough in north-west London, and as such is part of the trend where place names also double as given names.

## Cameron
Meaning: Crooked nose
Origin: Gaelic
Pronunciation: KAM er uhn
Description: Cameron is a name of Scottish origin. It is a quite common surname, but has become

C

increasingly popular as a first name for both boys and girls.

**Alternative spellings:** Camron, Kameron, Kamran, Kamron

## Camille

See entry in 'Names for Baby Girls A–Z'

## Campbell

**Meaning:** Crooked mouth
**Origin:** Gaelic
**Pronunciation:** CAM bell
**Description:** Campbell is a common Scottish, English and American surname. Recently the name has become a popular given name in America for both boys and girls.
**Alternative spellings:** Campbel, Kampbell

## Carey

**Meaning:** Dark
**Origin:** Irish
**Pronunciation:** care EE
**Description:** Carey was originally an Irish surname taken from the Old Irish adjective 'ciar' meaning 'dark' or 'black'. This follows the contemporary trend of using last names as first names.

## Carl

**Meaning:** Free man
**Origin:** English
**Pronunciation:** KARL
**Description:** Carl derives from the Old English word 'ceorl' meaning 'free man'. It is also the German form of Charles.
**Alternative spellings:** Karl

## Carlo

**Meaning:** Free man
**Origin:** Spanish
**Pronunciation:** CAR lo
**Description:** Carlo is a shortened version of Carlos, a popular Spanish boys' name. Originating from the German name Charles, its Italian form, Carlo, has remained popular in the last century.
**Alternative spellings:** Carloh, Carlow

## Carlos

**Meaning:** Free man
**Origin:** Spanish
**Pronunciation:** KARH lohs
**Description:** Carlos is the Spanish equivalent of the English name Charles.
**Alternative spellings:** Karlos

## Carlton

**Meaning:** Free peasant settlement
**Origin:** English
**Pronunciation:** KARL ton
**Description:** Carlton is an American and English boys' name that was popular in the early 20th century.
**Alternative spellings:** Karlton

## Carmel

See entry in 'Names for Baby Girls A–Z'

## Carson

**Meaning:** Carr's son
**Origin:** English
**Pronunciation:** CAR sun
**Description:** Carson would originally have been a surname given to someone who hailed from a marshy area, or whose father had lived there. It has

developed into a first name throughout history, but is rare in the UK today.
**Alternative spellings:** Karson

## Carter
**Meaning:** Cart transporter
**Origin:** English
**Pronunciation:** CAR ter
**Description:** Carter was originally used as a surname for those who transported goods in a cart. It is now used as both a first name and a surname.
**Alternative spellings:** Carta, Karter

## Carwyn
**Meaning:** Love; fair; blessed
**Origin:** Welsh
**Pronunciation:** CAR win
**Description:** Carwyn is a Welsh boys' name meaning 'love, fair and blessed'. It is the masculine form of Carwen.
**Alternative spellings:** Caerwyn, Carwin, Corwyn

## Casey
**Meaning:** Alert
**Origin:** English
**Pronunciation:** CAY see
**Description:** The name Casey derives from the Gaelic name Cathasaigh. It also comes from the folk hero 'Casey' Jones, who died while saving the lives of passengers on board the *Cannonball Express*. His name comes from his birth town, Cayce, Kentucky.
**Alternative spellings:** Casie, Cayce, Caycie, Caysie, Kacey, Kaci, Kacie, Kacy, Kasey, Kasie, Kaycee, Kaycie, Kaysie

## Cash
**Meaning:** Cash
**Origin:** English
**Pronunciation:** CASH
**Description:** Cash is an uncommon English name meaning 'cash' or 'profit'. It is more recognised as a surname, borne by famous singer Johnny Cash.
**Alternative spellings:** Cassh, Kash

## Caspar
**Meaning:** Treasurer
**Origin:** Persian
**Pronunciation:** CAS par
**Description:** Caspar is a Dutch form of the name Jaspar. In Christian belief it was borne by one of the three wise men who visited Christ.
**Alternative spellings:** Casper, Kacper, Kaspar, Kasper

## Caspian
**Meaning:** Sea
**Origin:** English
**Pronunciation:** KAS pee an
**Description:** The Caspian Sea is a landlocked sea in north-west Asia, which was named after the ancient Caspians who used to live on its shore.
**Alternative spellings:** Caspean, Kasspian

## Cassidy
**Meaning:** Curly
**Origin:** Gaelic
**Pronunciation:** CASS id ee
**Description:** Cassidy comes from the Gaelic surname O'Caiside. It can be seen as both a boys' and a girls' name.
**Alternative spellings:** Cassidey, Cassidi, Cassidie

## Cassius

**Meaning:** Hollow
**Origin:** Latin
**Pronunciation:** cass EE us
**Description:** Cassius is a name that is likely to be of Latin origin, and may have been a Roman clan. There is also the suggestion that the name may have come from the Shakespeare character Caius Cassius. Cassius Clay was the birth name of heavyweight boxing champion of the world Muhammad Ali.
**Alternative spellings:** Kassius

## Castiel

**Meaning:** Speed of God; God is my anger
**Origin:** Hebrew
**Pronunciation:** cast EE el
**Description:** Castiel is most likely a variation of the name Cassiel, who is an angel found in the Bible. Cassiel is one of the Seven Archangels, and the name means 'speed of God' or 'God is my anger'.
**Alternative spellings:** Kastiel

## Cavan

**Meaning:** Handsome
**Origin:** Gaelic
**Pronunciation:** CA van
**Description:** Cavan is an uncommon boys' name of Irish and Gaelic origin, meaning 'handsome'. Cavan is also the name of a town in Ireland.
**Alternative spellings:** Cavann, Cavyn

## Cayson

**Meaning:** No meaning
**Origin:** American
**Pronunciation:** CAY sun
**Description:** Cayson is most likely a modern, American invented name and as such has no meaning. It can be a combination of the names Casey and Jason, or a variation of Cason.
**Alternative spellings:** Cason, Kason

## Cecil

**Meaning:** Blind
**Origin:** Latin
**Pronunciation:** see SIL
**Description:** Cecil comes from the name Cecilius, which is derivted from the Latin word '*caecus*' meaning 'blind'.

## Cedric

**Meaning:** Bounty
**Origin:** Celtic
**Pronunciation:** SED rick
**Description:** Cedric is a Celtic name that was created by Scottish writer Sir Walter Scott for his novel, *Ivanhoe*. It is a Celtic name meaning 'bounty'. It was also made popular by J.K. Rowling, who named one of her more memorable characters Cedric Diggory.
**Alternative spellings:** Cedrick

## Celyn

See entry in 'Names for Baby Girls A–Z'

## Chace

**Meaning:** Huntsman
**Origin:** English
**Pronunciation:** chAYce
**Description:** Chace is an Old English surname given as an occupational name for huntsman. As a given name it was uncommon

but in recent years it has become popular in America.
**Alternative spellings:** Chas, Chayce, Chayse

## Chad
**Meaning:** Unknown
**Origin:** English
**Pronunciation:** CHAD
**Description:** The name Chad is a respelling of the Old English name Ceadda. Its meaning is unknown; however, it is the name of an African country so could be good for someone with African roots.
**Alternative spellings:** Chadd

## Chaim
**Meaning:** Life
**Origin:** Hebrew
**Pronunciation:** CHAIM
**Description:** Chaim is a common name for Jewish boys. It is a variant of the Hebrew name Chayyim, which is derived from the Hebrew word for 'life'. It was believed that giving a baby this name would help the baby to remain healthy.
**Alternative spellings:** Chayim, Chayyim

## Chance
**Meaning:** Chance; opportunity
**Origin:** English
**Pronunciation:** CHANSE
**Description:** Chance derives from the English vocabulary word 'chance' meaning 'opportunity' or 'luck'. It is also a derivation of Chauncey, a French name that means 'chancellor'. It can be used for girls or boys.
**Alternative spellings:** Chanse

## Chandler
**Meaning:** Candle seller
**Origin:** French
**Pronunciation:** CHAND ler
**Description:** Chandler originated as a surname for those who made or sold candles and derives from the Old French word 'chandele'. The name is associated with one of the characters in the hit TV sitcom *Friends*.
**Alternative spellings:** Chandla, Chandlar

## Channing
**Meaning:** People of Cana; wolf cub
**Origin:** English
**Pronunciation:** CHANN ing
**Description:** Channing is an English name meaning either 'people of Cana' or 'wolf cub'. It has become a popular modern name due to actor Channing Tatum.
See entry in 'Names for Baby Girls A–Z'

## Charles
**Meaning:** Free man
**Origin:** German
**Pronunciation:** CHARLZ
**Description:** From the Germanic word 'karl', which means 'free man'. Charles was a popular name in the 17th century, thanks to its royal usage during that time.
**Alternative spellings:** Charls

## Charlie
**Meaning:** Free man
**Origin:** German
**Pronunciation:** CHAR lee
**Description:** Pet form of Charles and Charlotte, now commonly

C

given as an independent name to both boys and girls.

**Alternative spellings:** Charlee, Charleigh, Charley, Charli, Charly

## Charon
**Meaning:** Fierce brightness
**Origin:** Greek
**Pronunciation:** KARE on
**Description:** In Greek mythology, Charon was the boatman over the River Styx who carried the dead into the Underworld.
**Alternative spellings:** Charron, Karon

## Chase
**Meaning:** Hunter
**Origin:** French
**Pronunciation:** CHAY ce
**Description:** While more popular as a boys name, it has also been given to girls. It would originally have been a given surname for a hunter in France or England. It is particularly popular in the US.

## Che
**Meaning:** Argentine speech interjection
**Origin:** Spanish
**Pronunciation:** CHE
**Description:** Che was most likely made popular by Che Guevara (he was actually born Ernesto Guevara, and 'Che' was his nickname), the Argentine revolutionary. The word 'che' is actually an Argentine speech interjection, similar to 'bro' in English. Che Guevara often used the word, and that was how he got his famous nickname.

## Chester
**Meaning:** Fort
**Origin:** Latin
**Pronunciation:** CHES ter
**Description:** Chester was originally an English surname, derived from the name of the city Chester. The city's name originates from the Latin word for 'fort', due to its connections with Hadrian's Wall.
**Alternative spellings:** Chesta, Chestar

## Chevy
**Meaning:** Knight
**Origin:** French
**Pronunciation:** CHEV ee
**Description:** Chevy is a shortening of the French word 'chevalier' meaning 'knight'. Chevy Chase is an American comedian with this name.

## Chris
**Meaning:** Follower of Christ
**Origin:** Greek
**Pronunciation:** KRIS
**Description:** Chris is a short form of Christopher, Christophe, Christine and other similar names, as well as being a male name in its own right.
**Alternative spellings:** Chriss, Kris

## Christian
**Meaning:** Follower of Christ
**Origin:** Latin
**Pronunciation:** KRIS ti an
**Description:** Christian is a unisex name that literally means 'follower of Christ'. Incidentally, the name 'Christ' is a translation of the Hebrew term 'messiah', meaning 'anointed'.

**Alternative spellings:** Christian, Christien, Cristian, Kristian, Krystian

## Christophe
**Meaning:** Follower of Christ
**Origin:** Greek
**Pronunciation:** KRIS toff
**Description.** Christophe is the French form of the Greek name Christopher, meaning 'bearer or follower of Christ'. Christophe is also seen as a surname.
**Alternative spellings:** Christoff, Kristophe

## Christopher
**Meaning:** Follower of Christ
**Origin:** Greek
**Pronunciation:** KRIS toff ur
**Description:** Popular among early Christians who wanted to honour Christ with a personal link, Christopher is a name that largely rose in popularity in the 16th century.
**Alternative spellings:** Christofer, Christophar, Kristopher

## Cian
**Meaning:** Ancient
**Origin:** Gaelic
**Pronunciation:** KEE ann
**Description:** In Irish mythology the name Cian was borne by a son-in-law of Brian Boru, and also by the ancient and influential clan who were known as the Cianachta. The name is still popular in Ireland and other parts of the world today.
**Alternative spellings:** Kean, Kian

## Ciaran
**Meaning:** Dark-haired
**Origin:** Gaelic
**Pronunciation:** KEER rahn

**Description:** The name Ciaran derives from the Irish word *'ciar,'* which means 'black' or 'dark' and can be linked back to Ciar, son of Fergus, King of Ulster.
**Alternative spellings:** Keiran, Keiron, Kieran, Kieren, Kieron, Kiran

## Cillian
**Meaning:** Fiesty
**Origin:** Gaelic
**Pronunciation:** KILL yan
**Description:** Cillian is a Gaelic boys' name, possibly a variation of Killian. Both names are said to have originated with meanings associated with war, but as a given name we would assume the meaning of Cillian to be 'feisty'.
**Alternative spellings:** Cillyan, Killian

## Clark
**Meaning:** Clerk
**Origin:** English
**Pronunciation:** CLARK
**Description:** Clark is a name originally given to someone with the occupation of a clerk, which in the Middle Ages was a holy man with the ability to read and write.
**Alternative spellings:** Clarke

## Clay
**Meaning:** Clay
**Origin:** English
**Pronunciation:** CLAY
**Description:** Clay may have originated as a surname used for those who lived in areas known to contain clay soils. It is also the shortened form of the name Clayton.
**Alternative spellings:** Cley, Klay

**C**

## Clayton

**Meaning:** Clay settlement
**Origin:** English
**Pronunciation:** CLAY ton
**Description:** Like Clay, Clayton originated as a surname for those who lived near clay soils. It is still a very common surname but is also a very popular first name choice especially in the US.
**Alternative spellings:** Claiton, Cleyton, Klayton

## Clement

**Meaning:** Merciful; gentle
**Origin:** English
**Pronunciation:** kle MENT
**Description:** Clement is the English form of the Latin name Clemens, which means 'merciful' and 'gentle'. It is also related to the English vocabulary word 'clemency,' also meaning 'merciful'. This was the name of 14 different popes.

## Clint

**Meaning:** Town on a hilltop
**Origin:** English
**Pronunciation:** clint
**Description:** Clint is a shortened version of the name Clinton, meaning 'town on a hilltop'. Clint Eastwood is a famous American actor with this name.

## Clive

**Meaning:** Lives near a cliff
**Origin:** English
**Pronunciation:** clive
**Description:** Clive is an English baby name that was originally given to people who lived near or on a cliff. Clive Owen is a famous British actor with this name.

## Clyde

**Meaning:** From the banks of the River Clyde
**Origin:** Scottish
**Pronunciation:** cul LYDE
**Description:** Clyde was originally a Scottish surname to refer to people who lived near the banks of the River Clyde. The name of the river is taken from the Gaelic 'cluaidh', although the meaning of this is unclear.

## Coby

**Meaning:** Supplanter
**Origin:** English
**Pronunciation:** coh BEE
**Description:** Coby is a modern construction, and was probably originally a nickname for those named Jacob. This means that Coby has the same meaning as Jacob, which is 'supplanter'.
**Alternative spellings:** Cobie, Cobee, Kobe

## Cody

**Meaning:** Obliging
**Origin:** Gaelic
**Pronunciation:** KOH dee
**Description:** The origin of the name Cody can be traced back to Gaelic surnames, specifically MacOda, which has become abbreviated and Americanised, and then translated from a surname to a first name. It is said to mean 'obliging' and can be used for both girls and boys.
**Alternative spellings:** Codey, Codie, Kody

## Coen

**Meaning:** Brave
**Origin:** Dutch

**Pronunciation:** KOE en
**Description:** Coen is a Germanic variant of the name Conrad. It is most common in the Netherlands.
**Alternative spellings:** Coewn, Cohen, Kohen

## Cohen

**Meaning:** Priest
**Origin:** Hebrew
**Pronunciation:** KOE en
**Description:** Cohen originates from the Hebrew name Kohen, borne by a priest and the brother of Moses in Jewish belief. It could also be the anglicised version of the Old Irish surname Cadhan.
**Alternative spellings:** Coen, Koen, Kohen

## Colby

**Meaning:** Settlement
**Origin:** English
**Pronunciation:** KOHL bee
**Description:** Colby was originally a surname derived from an Old English place name. As a first name it has increased in popularity over the past 20 years.
**Alternative spellings:** Colbey, Colbi, Colbie, Kolby

## Cole

**Meaning:** Dark
**Origin:** English
**Pronunciation:** COLE
**Description:** Cole is an English surname that has been transferred into a given name. It is taken from the Old English word 'cola', meaning 'dark complexion'. Other sources suggest the name to be a short form of the surname Coleman.

**Alternative spellings:** Cohl

## Colin

**Meaning:** Young creature
**Origin:** Gaelic
**Pronunciation:** COLL in; CO lin
**Description:** Colin is a Gaelic name meaning 'young creature', but may also be considered a pet form of Nicholas.
**Alternative spellings:** Collin, Kolin

## Colton

**Meaning:** From the coal or dark town
**Origin:** English
**Pronunciation:** COHL ton
**Description:** Colton is an English name meaning 'from the coal or dark town'. The 'coal' in the name is what most likely gave the name its meaning.
**Alternative spellings:** Kolton

## Conall

**Meaning:** Strong wolf
**Origin:** Gaelic
**Pronunciation:** KON al
**Description:** Conall is a Scottish and Irish boys' name associated with the early chieftains and warriors of Ireland.
**Alternative spellings:** Conal, Connal, Connell

## Conan

**Meaning:** Little wolf; little hound
**Origin:** Irish
**Pronunciation:** COH nan
**Description:** Conan is an Irish name that maeans 'little wolf' or 'little hound.' The name comes from the Gaelic element of 'cú', meaning 'wolf' or 'hound'. Conan

O'Brien is a famous American talk show host.

## Connor
**Meaning:** Lover of hounds
**Origin:** Gaelic
**Pronunciation:** CON nor
**Description:** Taken from the Gaelic name Conchobhar, Connor has become increasingly popular outside of Ireland and has many variants. It is also derived from the Irish name Conaire, which can be found in Irish legends.
**Alternative spellings:** Conner, Conor, Konner, Konnor

## Conrad
**Meaning:** Bold counsel
**Origin:** German
**Pronunciation:** KON rad
**Description:** Conrad is the usual English spelling of German name Konrad. It is often seen as a surname and means 'brave', 'counsel' or 'ruler'. It is often abbreviated to Kurt in Britain.
**Alternative spellings:** Konrad

## Constantine
**Meaning:** Steadfast
**Origin:** Latin
**Pronunciation:** KON stan teen
**Description:** Constantine was originally a boys' name but is now a unisex name. It shares the same Latin roots as the word 'constant' and means 'steadfast'.
**Alternative spellings:** Constanteen, Konstanteen, Konstantine

## Cooper
**Meaning:** Barrel maker
**Origin:** English
**Pronunciation:** COO pur
**Description:** Before being adapted to a given name, Cooper was originally an occupational surname for one who made and sold barrels and tubs. It is still a common surname but is slowly becoming popular as a first name too.
**Alternative spellings:** Couper

## Corban
**Meaning:** Gift to God
**Origin:** Hebrew
**Pronunciation:** KOR ban
**Description:** Corban is a variant of the Hebrew name Korban, meaning a 'blessing from God dedicated back to God'. The name can be found within Jewish communities but is rare elsewhere.
**Alternative spellings:** Corben, Corbin, Korbin

## Corben
**Meaning:** Dark-haired
**Origin:** Gaelic
**Pronunciation:** CORE bin
**Description:** Corben derives from the Old French name Corbin, which means 'raven-coloured' or 'black-haired'.
**Alternative spellings:** Corbin, Corbyn, Korbin

## Corey
**Meaning:** Spear
**Origin:** Gaelic
**Pronunciation:** COR ee
**Description:** The name Corey is of disputed origin. It could derive from the Gaelic word *'coire'*, meaning 'seething pool', 'cauldron' or 'hollow'. It may also be an anglicised version of

Corra, meaning 'spear'. It is a unisex name.
**Alternative spellings:** Coree, Corie, Cory, Koree, Korey, Kory

## Corin
**Meaning:** Spear
**Origin:** Latin
**Pronunciation:** KOR in
**Description:** Corin is an uncommon Latin name meaning 'spear'. The story of Corin descends from the Sabine name Quirinus, a Roman god of war.
**Alternative spellings:** Coren, Corrin, Korin

## Cormac
**Meaning:** Cart driver
**Origin:** Gaelic
**Pronunciation:** KOR mac
**Description:** Cormac is thought to have derived from a Gaelic word to describe a horseman or cart driver. It is a popular name in Ireland and America.
**Alternative spellings:** Cormack, Kormac, Kormack

## Cosmo
**Meaning:** Harmony; order; beauty
**Origin:** Italian
**Pronunciation:** COS mo
**Description:** Cosmo is a boys' name of Italian and Greek origin, meaning 'order, harmony and beauty'. The name came to Britain with the arrival of the Duke of Gordon in the 17th century.
**Alternative spellings:** Cosimo, Cosme, Kosmo

## Craig
**Meaning:** Rock
**Origin:** Gaelic
**Pronunciation:** krAYG
**Description:** Craig comes from the Gaelic word *'creag'*, meaning 'rock'.
**Alternative spellings:** Craeg, Kraig

## Creon
**Meaning:** Heir to the throne
**Origin:** Greek
**Pronunciation:** KREE on
**Description:** In Greek mythology, Creon was the ruler of Thebes in the legend of Oedipus.
**Alternative spellings:** Creonn, Kreon

## Cristiano
**Meaning:** Follower of Christ
**Origin:** Latin
**Pronunciation:** cris tee AH no
**Description:** Cristiano is a boys' given name of Latin origin, popular in Italian- and Portuguese-speaking countries. The meaning of the name is 'follower of Christ'.
**Alternative spellings:** Christian, Cristian, Kristiano

## Cruz
**Meaning:** Cross
**Origin:** Spanish
**Pronunciation:** KROOZE
**Description:** Cruz is a unisex name that derives from the Spanish word for 'cross'. It has connotations of the cross of crucifixion and religion. It is better known as a boys' name.
**Alternative spellings:** Crooz, Cruise, Cruze, Kruise, Kruz, Kruze

## Curtis
**Meaning:** Courteous
**Origin:** French

**C**

**Pronunciation:** CUR tiss
**Description:** Curtis derives from the word 'courteous' and was given as a nickname in the Middle Ages.
**Alternative spellings:** Kurtis

## Cyprian

**Meaning:** Cypriot
**Origin:** Greek
**Pronunciation:** SEE pree ahn
**Description:** Cyprian is an uncommon name of Greek origin. It is from the Greek word *'kyprios'*, meaning 'the Cypriot'.

**Alternative spellings:** Ciprian, Siprian

## Cyrus

**Meaning:** Throne
**Origin:** Persian
**Pronunciation:** SI russ
**Description:** Cyrus comes from the Persian word for 'throne'. Its meaning may come from the many Persian kings who took this name. It is popular in America.
**Alternative spellings:** Cyruss, Sirus

# D

## Daedalus

**Meaning:** Cunning worker
**Origin:** Greek
**Pronunciation:** DAY dah lus
**Description:** In Greek mythology, Daedalus was a skilled craftsman and artisan. He was the father of Icarus. In modern English the word Daedalus has been used extensively in the video-game industry.
**Alternative spellings:** Daedelus, Daydalus, Daydelus

## Dafydd

**Meaning:** Beloved
**Origin:** Hebrew
**Pronunciation:** DAV ith
**Description:** Dafydd is the Welsh form of the Hebrew name David. The name Dafydd has religious tendencies as David features prominently in the Bible.
**Alternative spellings:** David

## Dainton

**Meaning:** From Dainton
**Origin:** English
**Pronunciation:** DAIN ton
**Description:** Dainton is an unusual name in Britain, despite its origins as an English place name.
**Alternative spellings:** Daintan, Daynton

## Dale

**Meaning:** Valley dweller
**Origin:** English
**Pronunciation:** DAIL
**Description:** Dale was originally a surname given to those local to a dale or valley. Now it is used as a given name.
**Alternative spellings:** Dail, Dayle

## Dallas

**Meaning:** Skilled
**Origin:** Irish
**Pronunciation:** DAAL as

**Description:** Dallas is an Irish name meaning 'skilled,' and it is also the name of a city in Texas. This name is part of the growing trend of names taken from places.

## Dalton

**Meaning:** From the valley
**Origin:** English
**Pronunciation:** DOLL ton
**Description:** Dalton is an Old English name meaning 'from the valley town'. There are many locations dotted across England with this name. In the last 20 years Dalton has become a popular name for boys in America.
**Alternative spellings:** Dallton, Dalten, Delton

## Damian

**Meaning:** To tame
**Origin:** Greek
**Pronunciation:** DAY me en
**Description:** Damian derives from the Greek name Damianos. The name has religious connotations as St Damian is said to be the patron saint of physicians.
**Alternative spellings:** Damien, Damion, Daymian

## Damon

**Meaning:** To tame
**Origin:** Greek
**Pronunciation:** DAY mon
**Description:** Damon is a derivative of *'daman'*, meaning 'to tame' or 'subdue'.
**Alternative spellings:** Daimon, Daymon

## Dan

**Meaning:** God is my judge
**Origin:** Hebrew
**Pronunciation:** DAN
**Description:** Dan is the shortened version of Daniel, a common name in the English-speaking world. Daniel was mentioned often in the Bible and is of Hebrew origin.
**Alternative spellings:** Dann

## Dana

**Meaning:** Fertility; from Denmark
**Origin:** Gaelic
**Pronunciation:** DAY na
**Description:** Although Dana is used for both boys and girls, the masculine and feminine forms have separate origins. Dana in the feminine form comes from Gaelic origin and in Irish mythology was the name of the goddess of fertility. As a boys' name it means 'from Denmark'.
**Alternative spellings:** Danah, Dayna

## Dane

**Meaning:** From Denmark
**Origin:** English
**Pronunciation:** DAYN
**Description:** Dane is an English boys' name originally used to signify Danish ancestry. More recently the name has lost its Danish origins to become a name in itself.
**Alternative spellings:** Dain, Daine, Dayne

## Daniel

**Meaning:** God is my judge
**Origin:** Hebrew
**Pronunciation:** DAN yule
**Description:** Daniel is a biblical name borne by the prophet, whose story is told in the Book

**D**

of Daniel. His story was a favourite tale in the Middle Ages and was often represented in miracle plays.
**Alternative spellings:** Danial, Daniyal, Danyaal, Danyal, Danyel, Danyl

## Danielius
**Meaning:** God is my judge
**Origin:** Hebrew
**Pronunciation:** dan ee EL ee us
**Description:** Danielius is a Greek variant of Daniel, which is a very common name in the English-speaking world. Daniel was mentioned frequently in the Bible and is of Hebrew origin.
**Alternative spellings:** Danielios

## Danny
**Meaning:** God is my judge
**Origin:** Hebrew
**Pronunciation:** DAN nee
**Description:** Originally a pet form of Daniel, Danny is now used as a first name in its own right.
**Alternative spellings:** Dannie

## Dante
**Meaning:** Enduring
**Origin:** Spanish
**Pronunciation:** DAHN tay
**Description:** A historical name most associated with Dante Alighieri, the author of *The Divine Comedy*. He is considered one of the greatest poets of all time. Dante can be used as a shortened version of Durante. The name is mainly used in Italy today.
**Alternative spellings:** Dantay

## Danyl
**Meaning:** God is my judge
**Origin:** Hebrew
**Pronunciation:** DAN il
**Description:** Danyl is a modern and shortened variant of the Hebrew name Daniel. Much like Danyaal, it took the phonetic spelling of the name.
**Alternative spellings:** Danil, Danyll

## Dara
**Meaning:** Oak tree
**Origin:** Gaelic
**Pronunciation:** DAH ruh
**Description:** Dara is a boys' name originating in Ireland and recently has become popular in both America and Ireland.
**Alternative spellings:** Daire, Darragh

## Darcy
**Meaning:** From Arcy
**Origin:** English
**Pronunciation:** DAR see
**Description:** Darcy is a unisex name created from the surname d'Arcy. The name Darcy became well established in England during the Middle Ages. Now, the name has links with Jane Austen's *Pride and Prejudice*, in which Mr Darcy is a main character.
**Alternative spellings:** Darcey, Darci, Darcie

## Darin
**Meaning:** Dwelling by a hill
**Origin:** English
**Pronunciation:** DARE en
**Description:** Often thought of as a variation of the name Darren, Darin is also a name in its own right. Darin is an Old English surname that could mean 'dwelling by

a hill'. It is pronounced differently to Darren.
**Alternative spellings:** Darein

## Darius
**Meaning:** Guardian
**Origin:** Persian
**Pronunciation:** DAH ree us
**Description:** Darius is a name of Persian origin and was borne by the king of the Persians in the 6th century BC.
**Alternative spellings:** Daryus

## Darragh
**Meaning:** Dark oak
**Origin:** Gaelic
**Pronunciation:** DAH ruh
**Description:** Darragh is a boys' name from Ireland. In America it is more commonly seen as a surname rather than a given name.
**Alternative spellings:** Daire, Dara

## Darrell
**Meaning:** From Airelle
**Origin:** French
**Pronunciation:** dare ELL
**Description:** Darrell is a French name taken from the Norman-French 'd'Airelle', referring to a person who came from the French town of Airelle.
**Alternative spellings:** Daryl, Darryl, Daryll, Darryll, Darrel

## Darren
**Meaning:** Great
**Origin:** Gaelic
**Pronunciation:** DA ren
**Description:** The origins of Darren are somewhat blurred – it is thought to come from the Gaelic surname meaning 'great', but it is also linked to a Welsh mountain named Moel Darren.
**Alternative spellings:** Darran, Darrin, Darryn

**D**

## Darsh
**Meaning:** Lord Krishna; moonlight
**Origin:** Sanskrit
**Pronunciation:** DARSH
**Description:** Darsh is an Indian Gujarati boys' name that has the meanings 'Lord Krishna' and 'moonlight'.
**Alternative spellings:** Daarsh

## Darwin
**Meaning:** Dear friend
**Origin:** English
**Pronunciation:** DAR win
**Description:** Darwin comes from the surname used in Old English, derived from the personal name 'Deorwine'. It is famously linked to Charles Darwin, who was responsible for the theory of evolution. The name is gathering popularity as a given name.
**Alternative spellings:** Darwinn

## Dashiell
**Meaning:** Unknown
**Origin:** French
**Pronunciation:** Dash EEL
**Description:** It is thought that this name is the anglicised form of the French family name de Chiel, but there is no documented meaning of the name. Samuel Dashiell Hammett was a famous American novelist in the 1930s and 40s, and the name is found most often in America.
**Alternative spellings:** Dashiel

## Dave

**Meaning:** Darling
**Origin:** Hebrew
**Pronunciation:** DAYV
**Description:** Dave is a shortened form of the biblical name David but is also a name in its own right.
**Alternative spellings:** Daive, Dayv

## David

**Meaning:** Darling
**Origin:** Hebrew
**Pronunciation:** DAY vid
**Description:** A biblical name borne by King David of Israel, who killed the giant Goliath with a slingshot before his rise to power. David is a very popular name in English-speaking countries.
**Alternative spellings:** Daivid, Davide

## Davis

**Meaning:** Son of David
**Origin:** Welsh
**Pronunciation:** day VIS
**Description:** Davis is more common as a surname but it is also a popular choice for first names. It is taken from the Welsh 'Dafydd', which when anglicised becomes David. Davis refers to people whose fathers were called David.

## Dawood

**Meaning:** Beloved
**Origin:** Hebrew
**Pronunciation:** DA wood
**Description:** Dawood is an uncommon name of Hebrew origin, meaning 'beloved'.
**Alternative spellings:** Dawud, Duwood

## Dawson

**Meaning:** Son of David
**Origin:** English
**Pronunciation:** DAW son
**Description:** Most commonly a surname, Dawson is an English boys' name that has risen in popularity as a first name over the last 10 years in America and England.
**Alternative spellings:** Dayson, Dowson

## Dawud

**Meaning:** Darling
**Origin:** Hebrew
**Pronunciation:** dah WOOD
**Description:** Dawud is the Arabic variant of the Hebrew name David. It is rarely found in Britain but would make a nice alternative to the popular name David.
**Alternative spellings:** Dahwud, Dawood

## Dax

**Meaning:** Town in France
**Origin:** French
**Pronunciation:** DAAX
**Description:** Dax is a French name taken from a town in south-western France from before the Roman occupation.

## Dayton

**Meaning:** Day's settlement
**Origin:** English
**Pronunciation:** DAY ton
**Description:** Dayton is an uncommon English boys' name. Its popularity has increased in America in recent years. It is also the name of a city in Ohio, America.

**Alternative spellings:** Daytan, Dayten

## Deacon

**Meaning:** Messenger
**Origin:** Greek
**Pronunciation:** DEE kan
**Description:** Thought to have derived directly from the name for a cleric in the Christian church who is not yet a priest or minister. It is a common surname in Britain and is now also used as a first name.
**Alternative spellings:** Deacon, Deecon

## Dean

**Meaning:** Valley; church official
**Origin:** English
**Pronunciation:** DEEN
**Description:** Dean comes from the Old English word *'denu'*, which would have been given as a surname to those who lived near a valley. It is also an occupational name for a church, university or group supervisor. Now it is commonly used as a first name.
**Alternative spellings:** Deen, Deyn

## Declan

**Meaning:** Endowed with goodness
**Origin:** English
**Pronunciation:** DEK lin
**Description:** Declan is the anglicised version of the Irish name Deaglan. It is thought that an Irish saint had this name.
**Alternative spellings:** Declin, Deklan

## Demetrius

**Meaning:** Follower of Demeter

**Origin:** Greek
**Pronunciation:** de MEE tree uhs
**Description:** Demetrius is a Greek name meaning 'follower of Demeter'. Demeter is the goddess of the harvest. The name Demetrius appears in a number of William Shakespeare's plays, including *A Midsummer Night's Dream*.
**Alternative spellings:** Dametrius, Demetris, Dimetrius

## Dennis

**Meaning:** Servant of Dionysus
**Origin:** Greek
**Pronunciation:** DEN niss
**Description:** Dennis comes from the name of the Greek god of revelry, Dionysus. As such, the name connotes a person who is amiable and very social. Denny and Den are short forms of this name.
**Alternative spellings:** Denis

## Denny

**Meaning:** The Dane's village; servant of Dionysus
**Origin:** English
**Pronunciation:** DEN nee
**Description:** Denny is a variant of the Scandinavian name Denby and the English name Dennis. In most cases Denny is likely to be a shortened version of Dennis.
**Alternative spellings:** Denney

## Denver

**Meaning:** Dane crossing
**Origin:** English
**Pronunciation:** DEN ver
**Description:** Denver was originally used as a surname for those located near Denver in Norfolk. It is also the capital of Colorado,

**D**

USA. Denver is now used as a given name as well as a surname.
**Alternative spellings:** Denvar

## Denzel
**Meaning:** From Denzell
**Origin:** English
**Pronunciation:** DEN zell
**Description:** Denzell is a Cornish village that provides the root of the name Denzel.
**Alternative spellings:** Denzell, Denzil

## Derek
**Meaning:** Ruler
**Origin:** German
**Pronunciation:** DER ick
**Description:** Derek derives from the Germanic name Theoderic, which means 'ruler of people'. The name arrived on British shores in the 1400s and gained traction in the 19th century.
**Alternative spellings:** Dereck, Derick, Derik, Derrek

## Desmond
**Meaning:** From South Munster
**Origin:** Gaelic
**Pronunciation:** DEZ muhnd
**Description:** Desmond is a common Irish name, which is commonly shortened to Des.
**Alternative spellings:** Desmund, Dezmond

## Dev
**Meaning:** God-like
**Origin:** Sanskrit
**Pronunciation:** DEHV
**Description:** The name Dev is commonly used as a shortened version of several longer names including Devlin, Devin and Devan. Dev is a name often favoured by Indian parents.
**Alternative spellings:** Dehv

## Devon
**Meaning:** From Devon
**Origin:** English
**Pronunciation:** DEH vun
**Description:** Devon is a unisex name that derives from the place name of Devon in southwest England. Originally it was used for those born in Devon, but it is now becoming a popular name countrywide and in America.
**Alternative spellings:** Devone, Devun

## Dewi
**Meaning:** Beloved
**Origin:** Welsh
**Pronunciation:** DOO ee
**Description:** Dewi is a modern variation of the name Dewey, which is thought to have been derived from the name David.
**Alternative spellings:** Dewey, Dewie

## Dexter
**Meaning:** Right-handed; prosperous
**Origin:** Latin
**Pronunciation:** DEX ter
**Description:** As well as a name, Dexter is also a Latin word meaning 'right-handed'. As a given name it also means 'prosperous'.
**Alternative spellings:** Deckster

## Dhruv
**Meaning:** North Star
**Origin:** Sanskrit

**Pronunciation:** DROOHV
**Description:** In Hindu belief
Druhv was the name of an often-
ignored second son of a king. He
prayed to the god Vishnu, who
turned him into the North Star
so that he would never again be
ignored.
**Alternative spellings:** Dhruve
Droov

## Diego
**Meaning:** Supplanter
**Origin:** Spanish
**Pronunciation:** dee AY go
**Description:** Diego is a Spanish
boys' name that is said to be a
variant of the name James. It is a
fairly unusual name in Britain but
popular in Spain and America.
**Alternative spellings:** Diaygo

## Digby
**Meaning:** Dyke; ditch; farm; town
**Origin:** English
**Pronunciation:** dig BEE
**Description:** Digby is both a given
name and a surname. The name
comes from the name of an English town, which comes from a
combination of the Old English 'dic'
meaning 'dyke' or 'ditch' and the
Old Norse 'byr', meaning 'farm or
'town'.

## Digory
**Meaning:** Lost one
**Origin:** French
**Pronunciation:** dig OR ee
**Description:** Digory is a variation
of Diggory, a French name that
means 'lost one'. Digory Kirke is
a fictional character in C. S. Lewis'
Chronicles of Narnia books.

**Alternative spellings:** Diggory

## Dilan
**Meaning:** Sea
**Origin:** English
**Pronunciation:** dill EN
**Description:** Dilan is an alterna-
tive spelling of the name Dylan. In
Welsh mythology Dylan was the
god of the sea, accidentally slain
by his uncle Govannon.
**Alternative spellings:** Dhilan,
Dylan, Dillon

## Dillan
**Meaning:** Sea; loyal
**Origin:** Gaelic
**Pronunciation:** DIL un
**Description:** Dillan is an alterna-
tive spelling of the name Dylan. It
could either come from the Gaelic
god of the sea, Dylan, or from the
Gaelic name Dillon, which is said
to mean 'loyal'.
**Alternative spellings:** Dillon,
Dylan

## Dimitri
**Meaning:** Earth mother
**Origin:** Greek
**Pronunciation:** dee MEE tree
**Description:** Dimitri is a name
of Greek origin, meaning 'earth
mother'. It is the Slavic version
of Demetrius and one of the
most popular boys' names in
Russia.
**Alternative spellings:** Dimitrie,
Dimitry

## Diomedes
**Meaning:** God-like cunning
**Origin:** Greek
**Pronunciation:** di o MEED ez

**D**

**Description:** In Greek mythology, Diomedes was a hero who fought in the Trojan War.
**Alternative spellings:** Diomeedes, Dyomedes

## Dion
**Meaning:** Servant of Dionysus
**Origin:** Greek
**Pronunciation:** DYE on
**Description:** Dion is a unisex name derived from the name of the Greek god of revelry, Dionysus. Dione is a specifically feminine form of the name, while Deon is the spelling more often used for boys.
**Alternative spellings:** Deon, Dione, Dionne

## Dionysus
**Meaning:** Grapevine
**Origin:** Greek
**Pronunciation:** dye on EYE suss
**Description:** In Greek mythology, Dionysus was the god of the grape harvest, winemaking, wine and of ritual madness. Its Latin form is Bacchus.
**Alternative spellings:** Dionisus, Dyonisus

## Diya
See entry in 'Names for Baby Girls A–Z'

## Dominic
**Meaning:** Lord
**Origin:** Latin
**Pronunciation:** DOM in ik
**Description:** Dominic comes from the Latin name Dominicus, derived from the word for 'lord'. Dominic is a popular Roman Catholic name

in honour of St Dominic and the name has grown in popularity since the 1970s.
**Alternative spellings:** Domenic, Dominik

## Diyan
**Meaning:** Lamp
**Origin:** Indian
**Pronunciation:** DEE yaan
**Description:** Diyan is an Indian boys' name meaning 'lamp' or 'bright light'.
**Alternative spellings:** Diyaan

## Domas
**Meaning:** Twin
**Origin:** Dutch
**Pronunciation:** doh MAS
**Description:** Domas is the Dutch version of the name Thomas, meaning 'twin'. In the New Testament, the name was borne by one of Christ's 12 Apostles, referred to as Thomas, called Didymus. Didymos is the Greek word for 'twin', and the name is the Greek form of an Aramaic byname meaning 'twin'.
**Alternative spellings:** Thomas

## Dominykas
**Meaning:** Lord
**Origin:** Lithuanian
**Pronunciation:** dom IN ikas
**Description:** Dominykas is the Lithuanian version of the name Dominic. Dominic comes from the Late Latin name Dominicus, derived from the word for 'lord'. A popular Roman Catholic name in honour of St Dominic, the name has grown in popularity since the 1970s.
**Alternative spellings:** Dominic

## Dominique

See entry in 'Names for Baby Girls A–Z'

## Don

**Meaning:** World ruler
**Origin:** Gaelic
**Pronunciation:** DON
**Description:** The name Don came about as the shortened form of Donald; however it is a name in its own right.
**Alternative spellings:** Donn

## Donald

**Meaning:** World ruler
**Origin:** Gaelic
**Pronunciation:** DON ald
**Description:** Donald is the anglicised form of the Scottish name Domhnall, which is formed from the words meaning 'world' and 'rule'. The 'd' at the end of the name Donald comes from an English misinterpretation fuelled by German names such as 'Ronald'.
**Alternative spellings:** Donalde, Donold

## Donovan

**Meaning:** Brown-haired chieftain
**Origin:** Gaelic
**Pronunciation:** DON na vun
**Description:** Donovan is an Irish and Gaelic name that is popular for boys in America. The meaning of the name implies 'dark- or brown-haired chieftain'.
**Alternative spellings:** Donavan, Donavon, Donevon, Donoven

## Dorian

**Meaning:** Member of the Greek tribe
**Origin:** Greek
**Pronunciation:** daw REE an
**Description:** Dorian was first used, and made popular, by Oscar Wilde's famous novel, *The Picture of Dorian Gray*. Wilde most likely took the name from an ancient Greek tribe called the Dorians.

## Dougie

**Meaning:** Black river
**Origin:** Gaelic
**Pronunciation:** DUG less
**Description:** Dougie is a nickname that has become used as a first name in recent years. It is an abbreviated version of the name Douglas, which means 'black river' and was the name given to two powerful Scottish clans.

## Douglas

**Meaning:** Black river
**Origin:** Gaelic
**Pronunciation:** DUG less
**Description:** Originally used both as a first and surname, the name Douglas was actually given to females in the 17th century, but it is used exclusively as a male name today. It is very popular in Scotland.
**Alternative spellings:** Douglass, Dougless

## Drew

**Meaning:** Manliness
**Origin:** Greek
**Pronunciation:** DROO
**Description:** Drew is primarily a short form of the Greek name Andrew.
**Alternative spellings:** Dru

## Drey

**Meaning:** No meaning
**Origin:** English

**D**

119

**Pronunciation:** drey
**Description:** Drey is a modern invented name and, because of this, has no meaning attached to it.
**Alternative spellings:** Dray

## Duke
**Meaning:** Leader
**Origin:** English
**Pronunciation:** duke
**Description:** Duke is originally a title for the English nobility, derived from the Latin '*dux*' meaning 'leader'. It is now a common given name for boys. Duke Ellington was a famous American composer and originator of big-band jazz.

## Duncan
**Meaning:** Brown chief
**Origin:** Gaelic
**Pronunciation:** DUN cun
**Description:** Duncan is an anglicised form of the Gaelic name Donnchadh. It was considered to be a royal name in early Scotland.
**Alternative spellings:** Duncun, Dunkan

## Dustin
**Meaning:** Thor's stone
**Origin:** English
**Pronunciation:** DUST inn
**Description:** Dustin is an English surname that was originally taken from a Norman surname, Torsten. It is composed of the elements of '*thor*' and '*stone*'.

## Dusty
**Meaning:** Full of dust
**Origin:** American

**Pronunciation:** dust EE
**Description:** Dusty is an American name taken from the English vocabulary word of the same spelling and meaning. It is a rather contemporary name and not often found outside of America.

## Dwayne
**Meaning:** Dark
**Origin:** Gaelic
**Pronunciation:** DWAYN
**Description:** Dwayne is a name of Gaelic origin, meaning 'dark' or 'black'.
**Alternative spellings:** Duwayne, Dwayn

## Dwight
**Meaning:** God of wine
**Origin:** English
**Pronunciation:** dwy ITE
**Description:** Dwight is an English name that comes from the medieval name Diot, which in turn is a diminutive of Dionysia, the feminine form of Dionysus. Therefore, it shares the same meaning as Dionysus, who was the Greek god of wine.

## Dyfan
**Meaning:** To tame; subdue
**Origin:** Welsh
**Pronunciation:** DIE fan
**Description:** Dyfan is the Welsh form of the Greek name Damon. The name is a derivative of '*daman*', meaning 'to tame' or 'subdue'. Dyfan is also the name of a Welsh saint, although he is a highly obscure figure who is often mistaken with Sain Deruvian.

# E

## Eamon
**Meaning:** Wealthy protector
**Origin:** Irish
**Pronunciation:** AYE mon
**Description:** Eamon is a variant of the name Eamonn and the Irish version of the name Edmund. It is composed of two Old English words - '$\bar{e}ad$' ('prosperity, riches') and '$mund$' ('protector').
**Alternative spellings:** Eamonn

## Earl
**Meaning:** Warrior; nobleman
**Origin:** English
**Pronunciation:** ERL
**Description:** The name Earl comes from the title of an earl. An earl is a British peer ranking below a marquess and above a viscount.
**Alternative spellings:** Earle, Erle, Urle

## Easton
**Meaning:** Town in the east
**Origin:** English
**Pronunciation:** east TUN
**Description:** Easton was originally a surname but has now become a popular choice for a first name. It is composed of the Old English words '$east$' meaning the direction, and '$ton$' meaning town, giving its meaning of 'town in the east'.

## Eben
**Meaning:** Stone
**Origin:** Hebrew
**Pronunciation:** EE ben
**Description:** Eben is a shortened variant of the Jewish name Ebenezer.
**Alternative spellings:** Eauben, Ebenn, Eeben

## Edan
**Meaning:** Little fire
**Origin:** Gaelic
**Pronunciation:** EE dan
**Description:** Edan is an uncommon name of Gaelic origin. The more common English variant is Aidan, but Edan has become popular in recent years.
**Alternative spellings:** Eden, Edun

## Eddie
**Meaning:** Guardian of prosperity
**Origin:** English
**Pronunciation:** Eh DEE
**Description:** Eddie came about as a pet form of names beginning with Ed, such as Edward and Edwina. It is now used as a unisex name in its own right. It is a very common first name.
**Alternative spellings:** Eddi, Eddy

## Eden
See entry in 'Names for Baby Girls A–Z'

## Edgar
**Meaning:** Rich owner of spears
**Origin:** English
**Pronunciation:** ED gar
**Description:** The name Edgar is derived from the Old English

name Eadgar. The name was borne by an English king and St Edgar the Peaceful.
**Alternative spellings:** Edger

## Edison
**Meaning:** Son of Edward
**Origin:** English
**Pronunciation:** ED ih sun
**Description:** Edison was the surname of famous American inventor Thomas Edison, and has since become a given name across the world. In English it literally means 'son of Edward'.
**Alternative spellings:** Adison, Eddison, Edisson

## Edmund
**Meaning:** Guardian of prosperity
**Origin:** English
**Pronunciation:** ED mund
**Description:** The name Edmund derives from two elements of the Old English language: *'ead'*, meaning 'riches', and *'mund'*, which means 'protection'.
**Alternative spellings:** Edmond, Edmunde

## Eduard
**Meaning:** Guardian of prosperity
**Origin:** English
**Pronunciation:** ED wood
**Description:** Eduard is an alternative spelling of the name Edward. Derived from Old English *'ead'* (meaning 'prosperity') and *'weard'* (meaning 'guard'), Edward is one of the most perennially popular of all Old English names. Edward was the name of three Anglo-Saxon kings and eight kings of England. Edward the Confessor, penultimate

Anglo-Saxon king of England, had a reign marked by peace and prosperity.
**Alternative spellings:** Edward, Eduardo

## Edwin
**Meaning:** Lucky
**Origin:** English
**Pronunciation:** ED win
**Description:** The name Edwin is Old English in origin and is said to mean 'lucky'.
**Alternative spellings:** Edwen, Edwinn

## Eesa
**Meaning:** Salvation
**Origin:** Hebrew
**Pronunciation:** EE sa
**Description:** Eesa is a name that is considered possibly the true name of Jesus Christ. It has become increasingly popular in the UK in recent years.
**Alternative spellings:** Eisa

## Efan
**Meaning:** God is gracious
**Origin:** Welsh
**Pronunciation:** EF fan
**Description:** Efan is a variant of the Welsh name Evan, which in turn is the Welsh form of the English name John. Efan is uncommon as a given name in England. Efan was the nickname given to Efangwu 'Efan' Ekoku, an English-born Nigerian footballer.
**Alternative spellings:** Evan

## Efe
**Meaning:** Older brother
**Origin:** Turkish
**Pronunciation:** EH fee

**Description:** Efe is an uncommon Turkish boys' name, which means 'older brother'. It is also a shortened variant of the Nigerian boys' name Efetobore.
**Alternative spellings:** Efee, Effe

## Ehsan

**Meaning:** Perfection; excellence
**Origin:** Arabic
**Pronunciation:** ee SHAAN
**Description:** Ehsan is an Arabic boys' name meaning 'perfection' or 'excellence'. It is actually a religious term, referring to a Muslim's responsibility to obtain perfection in worship. It is one of the three dimensions of the Islamic religion.

## Eisa

**Meaning:** Jesus
**Origin:** Arabic
**Pronunciation:** EYE sah
**Description:** Eisa is the Arabic form for Jesus. It is also a feminine name in Scandinavian countries, and the female version of Eisa means 'glowing embers' in Old Norse.
**Alternative spellings:** Eesa

## Eli

**Meaning:** Jehovah is good
**Origin:** Hebrew
**Pronunciation:** EE ly
**Description:** Shortened form of Elijah, a Hebrew prophet who ascended into heaven in a blazing chariot.
**Alternative spellings:** Ely

## Elia

**Meaning:** Jehovah is good
**Origin:** Hebrew
**Pronunciation:** EH le ah
**Description:** Elia is a unisex name that comes from the same root as the Hebrew name Elijah, which means 'Jehovah is good'.
**Alternative spellings:** Elea, Eliah

E

## Elias

**Meaning:** The Lord is my God
**Origin:** Hebrew
**Pronunciation:** ee LYE us
**Description:** Elias is a Biblical name, and was originally used for followers of the Christian religion. While it has not been a traditionally popular name, it is now growing in popularity.
**Alternative spellings:** Elyas

## Elijah

**Meaning:** Jehovah is good
**Origin:** Hebrew
**Pronunciation:** eh LY jah
**Description:** Elijah was a Hebrew prophet who ascended to heaven in a blazing chariot.
**Alternative spellings:** Elija, Elijeh

## Elio

**Meaning:** Sun
**Origin:** Greek
**Pronunciation:** el EE oh
**Description:** Elio is a variation of the Greek name Helios. In Greek mythology, Helios was the god of the sun who rode his chariot across the sky each day.

## Eliot

**Meaning:** My God is the Lord
**Origin:** Hebrew
**Pronunciation:** ell EE ott

**Description:** Eliot, a variation of the more common Elliot, is a unisex given name as well as a surname. It comes from the same Hebrew roots as Elias or Elijah.
**Alternative spellings:** Elliot, Elliott

## Elisha
See entry in 'Names for Baby Girls A–Z'

## Ellis
**Meaning:** Jehovah is good
**Origin:** Hebrew
**Pronunciation:** ELL iss
**Description:** Ellis derives from a medieval version of Elias. Often used as a transferred surname, Ellis has enjoyed good stints of popularity as a unisex name.
**Alternative spellings:** Eliss, Elliss

## Ellison
**Meaning:** My God is the Lord
**Origin:** English
**Pronunciation:** ell ISS sun
**Description:** Ellison is the English variation of the name Ellis, and they share the same meaning, which is 'my God is the lord'. It is also both a surname and a unisex given name.
**Alternative spellings:** Elison

## Elvis
**Meaning:** Unknown
**Origin:** English
**Pronunciation:** EL viss
**Description:** The name Elvis is famously borne by Elvis Presley, supposed founder of rock and roll. 2010 was the first year

the name did not appear in the top 1,000 baby names in the US since 1954.
**Alternative spellings:** Ellvis, Elviss

## Elwood
**Meaning:** Elder tree forest
**Origin:** English
**Pronunciation:** ed WUWD
**Description:** Elwood is an English name and surname that means 'elder tree forest' in Old English and comes from a place name.

## Eman
**Meaning:** Faith
**Origin:** Arabic
**Pronunciation:** EE man
**Description:** Eman is a unisex name of separate origins. It can be a variant of the unisex name Iman, which is of Arabic origin and is said to mean 'faith'. Alternatively, the name could be a short form of the male name Emmanuel.
**Alternative spellings:** Eeman, Emaan, Iman

## Emanuel
**Meaning:** God is with us
**Origin:** Hebrew
**Pronunciation:** ih MAN you uhl
**Description:** Emanuel is a popular boys' name meaning 'God is with us'. It is a variant of the Hebrew name Emmanuel.
**Alternative spellings:** Emanual, Emanuele, Imanuel

## Emerson
**Meaning:** Son of Emery
**Origin:** English
**Pronunciation:** EM er sun

**Description:** Emerson is an Old English boys' name literally meaning 'Emery's son'. While quite uncommon as a given name, Emerson is more common as a surname in England and America.
**Alternative spellings:** Emersson, Emmerson

## Emil

**Meaning:** Enthusiastic
**Origin:** Latin
**Pronunciation:** AY mul
**Description:** Emil is said to be of Latin origin and is derived from the Roman surname Aemilius. It is said to mean 'enthusiastic'.
**Alternative spellings:** Amil, Emile

## Emile

**Meaning:** Eager
**Origin:** Latin
**Pronunciation:** em EEL
**Description:** Emile is an uncommon boys' name originating from the Latin name Emil. Emile is considered to be the French version of the name.
**Alternative spellings:** Emil

## Emilio

**Meaning:** Imitating
**Origin:** Latin
**Pronunciation:** eh MEE li O
**Description:** This name is most commonly found in Italian-, Portuguese- and Spanish-speaking countries. It comes from the Latin element *'aemulus'*, which means 'imitating'.
**Alternative spellings:** Emelio, Emileo

## Emilis

**Meaning:** Enthusiastic
**Origin:** Lithuanian
**Pronunciation:** ey MIL us
**Description:** Emilis is the Lithuanian form of the name Emil, meaning 'enthusiastic'. Emil (and Emilis) is said to be of Latin origin and is derived from the Roman surname Aemilius.

## Emir

**Meaning:** Ruler
**Origin:** Arabic
**Pronunciation:** eh MEER
**Description:** Emir is a variation of the name Amir, meaning 'ruler'. It was a name that would originally have been given to rulers of Arabic caliphates, which are areas containing an Islamic steward who is a leader of a Muslim community.
**Alternative spellings:** Amir

## Emmanuel

**Meaning:** God is with us
**Origin:** Hebrew
**Pronunciation:** ih MAN you uhl
**Description:** Also spelt Emanuel, in Hebrew this name means 'God is with us'. It is sometimes shortened to the Spanish version Manuel or Manny. In Christianity Emmanuel is sometimes used as a name for Jesus.
**Alternative spellings:** Emanuel

## Emmett

**Meaning:** Universal
**Origin:** English
**Pronunciation:** EHM eht
**Description:** Emmett is the English masculine version of Emma, which is a German name meaning 'universal'. The element of *'ermen'* means 'whole' or

'universal' in German. It also has Hebrew roots and also means 'truth'.

**Alternative spellings:** Emet, Emmet, Emett

## Emory

**Meaning:** House strength; industrious leader

**Origin:** German

**Pronunciation:** em ORR ee

**Description:** Emory has Old German origins and means 'house strength' and 'industrious leader'. Historically it was a last name, but has become a first name in the modern age.

**Alternative spellings:** Emre, Emery

## Emre

**Meaning:** Friend

**Origin:** Turkish

**Pronunciation:** EM ree

**Description:** Emre is a Turkish boys' name meaning 'friend'. Related names include Emra, Emrah and Emreh.

**Alternative spellings:** Emory, Emery

## Emrys

**Meaning:** Immortal

**Origin:** Welsh

**Pronunciation:** EHM rees

**Description:** Emrys is the Welsh form of the Greek name Ambrose. Ambrose, meaning 'immortal,' is a name borne by a 4th-century bishop of Milan. The name is generally more common in Ireland than England or the USA.

## Enes

**Meaning:** Human being

**Origin:** Turkish

**Pronunciation:** EH nes

**Description:** Enes is an uncommon name of Turkish origin, meaning 'human being'.

**Alternative spellings:** Ehnes, Enees

## Enoch

**Meaning:** Dedicated

**Origin:** Hebrew

**Pronunciation:** EE nuk

**Description:** Enoch means 'trained and vowed', 'dedicated and profound'. The name was popular in the early 20th century but has been less common since.

**Alternative spellings:** Enock

## Enrico

**Meaning:** Home ruler

**Origin:** Italian

**Pronunciation:** ehn REE ko

**Description:** Enrico is a name of German and Italian origin, meaning 'home ruler'. It is regarded as the Italian form of Henry.

**Alternative spellings:** Enriko, Enrique

## Enrique

**Meaning:** Home ruler

**Origin:** Spanish

**Pronunciation:** en REE kay

**Description:** Enrique is a popular boys' name meaning 'home ruler'. It is the Spanish variant of the name Henry.

**Alternative spellings:** Enricay, Enrikay

## Enzo

**Meaning:** Ruler of the home

**Origin:** Italian

**Pronunciation:** EN zo

**Description:** Enzo could be considered the shortened form of many Italian names ending with

'enzo', such as Lorenzo. The name could also be the Italian variant of the name Henry, in which case it means 'ruler of the home'.
**Alternative spellings:** Enso, Enzoh

## Eoghan
**Meaning:** Born of yew; youth
**Origin:** Gaelic
**Pronunciation:** YEW en
**Description:** Eoghan is an old Irish name meaning 'born of yew; youth'. Anglicised variants of the name include Owen.
**Alternative spellings:** Euan, Ewan, Owen

## Eoin
**Meaning:** God is gracious
**Origin:** Hebrew
**Pronunciation:** OH en
**Description:** Eoin is a Gaelic variant of John, meaning 'God is gracious'. Eoin is derived specifically from the Latin Johan, where the 'j' was pronounced 'y'.
**Alternative spellings:** Eohin

## Ephraim
**Meaning:** Fruitful
**Origin:** Hebrew
**Pronunciation:** EF ram
**Description:** Ephraim is a popular name for Jewish boys but remains uncommon in the wider UK population. It is of Hebrew origin and is said to mean 'fruitful'.
**Alternative spellings:** Efraim, Efrayim, Efrem

## Eren
**Meaning:** Saint; holy person
**Origin:** Turkish
**Pronunciation:** eh REN

**Description:** Eren is a Turkish name meaning 'saint' or 'holy person'. It is also likely to be related to the girls' name Erin, which means Eren can be used for both boys and girls as a name choice.

## Eric
**Meaning:** Eternal ruler
**Origin:** Norse
**Pronunciation:** EH rik
**Description:** The name Eric is of Old Norse origin. It consists of the words *'ei'* and *'rikr'* and its meaning is 'eternal ruler'. As a given name, Eric arrived on British shores over 1,000 years ago before the Norman Conquest of Britain.
**Alternative spellings:** Erick, Erik, Eryk

## Ernest
**Meaning:** Sincere
**Origin:** German
**Pronunciation:** ER nest
**Description:** The name Ernest derives from the Old German word *'eornost'* meaning 'serious battle'. The name first spread to England from mainland Europe in the 18th century. The spelling 'Earnest' comes from the modern English adjective of the same spelling, meaning 'sincere'.
**Alternative spellings:** Earnest

## Ernie
**Meaning:** Serious
**Origin:** German
**Pronunciation:** ER nee
**Description:** Ernie is a variant of the German name Ernest. It was

E

quite popular as a given name in the early 20th century but is now uncommon.
**Alternative spellings:** Erne, Erno

## Errol
**Meaning:** Warrior; nobleman
**Origin:** Scottish
**Pronunciation:** ERE rol
**Description:** Errol is the Scottish version of the name Earl, meaning 'warrior' or 'nobleman'. Errol Flynn was a famous Australian-born actor who had this name.

## Erwin
**Meaning:** Army friend
**Origin:** German
**Pronunciation:** err WIN
**Description:** Erwin is a German name derived from the Old German elements of '*heri*' meaning 'army' and '*wini*' meaning 'friend'.
**Alternative spellings:** Irwin

## Esa
**Meaning:** Faithful
**Origin:** Hebrew
**Pronunciation:** ESS ah
**Description:** This unisex name has several spelling variations. The name appears in the Bible several times but is mostly known as the name of the third king of Judah, who ruled for 40 years.
**Alternative spellings:** Asa, Isa

## Eshaan
**Meaning:** Worthy
**Origin:** Arabic
**Pronunciation:** esh AAN
**Description:** Eshaan is an uncommon Arabic boys' name meaning 'one who is worthy' or 'one who is in Allah's grace'.
**Alternative spellings:** Eshaann, Eshan

## Eshan
**Meaning:** Another name for Lord Shiva
**Origin:** Indian
**Pronunciation:** EE shan
**Description:** Eshan is one of the many names of the Hindu god, Lord Shiva. He is one of three major deities in the Hindu religion and is known as 'the Destroyer,' although he is both benevolent and fearsome at the same time.
**Alternative spellings:** Eeshan, Eshaan

## Esme
See entry in 'Names for Baby Girls A–Z'

## Essa
See entry in 'Names for Baby Girls A–Z'

## Eteocles
**Meaning:** Truly glorious
**Origin:** Greek
**Pronunciation:** e TEE o kleez
**Description:** In Greek mythology, Eteocles was the son of Oedipus, who became a king of Thebes.
**Alternative spellings:** Eteokles, Eteucles

## Ethan
**Meaning:** Firm; long-lived
**Origin:** Hebrew
**Pronunciation:** EE than
**Description:** The name Ethan is seen in the Bible. It was popular

in the US in the 18th century following the fame of Ethan Allen, leader of a Vermont patriot group in the American Revolution.
**Alternative spellings:** Ethen, Ethun

## Etienne
**Meaning:** Crown
**Origin:** French
**Pronunciation:** ETT ee en
**Description:** Etienne is the French variant of Stephen, meaning 'crown'.
**Alternative spellings:** Eitan, Etien, Ettenne

## Euan
**Meaning:** Born from the yew
**Origin:** Greek
**Pronunciation:** YUH wen
**Description:** Scottish form of the name Eugene. Euan is Celtic for 'born from the yew'.
**Alternative spellings:** Eoghan, Ewan, Ewen

## Eugene
**Meaning:** Wellborn; noble
**Origin:** Greek
**Pronunciation:** YUH jeen
**Description:** Greek in origin; the common shortened form of Eugene is Gene.
**Alternative spellings:** Eugen

## Eurus
**Meaning:** The east wind
**Origin:** Greek
**Pronunciation:** YOO ros
**Description:** Eurus (sometimes spelt Euros) is a Greek name that means 'the east wind'. In Greek myth, Eurus is one of the Anemoi, who were the wind gods; each was responsible for a different direction in which the wind blew. Eurus was associated with autumn, and was found near the palace of the sun god, Helios.
**Alternative spellings:** Euros

## Evan
**Meaning:** God is gracious
**Origin:** Hebrew
**Pronunciation:** EH van
**Description:** Evan may be considered an anglicised form of the Welsh Iefan, which itself came from Ieuan. These are forms of John and mean 'God is gracious'.
**Alternative spellings:** Evun

## Everly
See entry in 'Names for Baby Girls A–Z'

## Everson
**Meaning:** Son of Everard
**Origin:** English
**Pronunciation:** ever SUN
**Description:** Everson was originally an English name referring to people who were the 'son of Everard'. This follows the contemporary trend of using last names as first names.

## Ewan
**Meaning:** Born from the yew
**Origin:** Gaelic
**Pronunciation:** YOO an
**Description:** Ewan is the anglicised form of Eoghan, or Eugene.
**Alternative spellings:** Euan, Ewan

## Eyad
**Meaning:** Support; might; strength
**Origin:** Arabic

E

**Pronunciation:** EE yad
**Description:** Eyad is an Arabic boys' name that means 'support,' 'might' and 'strength'.
**Alternative spellings:** Eyaad

## Ezekiel

**Meaning:** God will provide strength
**Origin:** Hebrew
**Pronunciation:** ee ZEE kyul
**Description:** Ezekiel was the name of a prophet in the Old Testament.

It is Hebrew in origin and is said to mean 'God will provide strength'.
**Alternative spellings:** Ezekial

## Ezra

**Meaning:** Helpful
**Origin:** Hebrew
**Pronunciation:** AIRZ ra
**Description:** The name Ezra comes from the Hebrew for 'helpful'. It was popular in the 17th century but is now uncommon.
**Alternative spellings:** Esra, Ezrah

# F

## Fabian

**Meaning:** Bean grower
**Origin:** Latin
**Pronunciation:** FAY bee en
**Description:** The name Fabian comes from the Latin surname Fabianus, which is generally held to refer to a family of bean growers. Several Roman emperors have been called this, as well as a total of 16 saints. This is a very popular name over the whole of Europe.
**Alternative spellings:** Fabien, Fabiun

## Fabio

**Meaning:** Bean grower
**Origin:** Latin
**Pronunciation:** FAB ee oh
**Description:** Fabio is the Spanish equivalent of the name Fabian.
**Alternative spellings:** Fabeo, Fabyo

## Fabrice

**Meaning:** Craftsman
**Origin:** French
**Pronunciation:** fab REECE
**Description:** Fabrice is a French name derived from the Roman Fabricius, meaning 'craftsman' or someone who worked with their hands.

## Fahad

**Meaning:** Panther
**Origin:** Arabic
**Pronunciation:** fah HAHD
**Description:** Fahad is said to mean 'panther', the connotations of which are of stealth, courage and grace. It is most commonly found in Islamic communities.
**Alternative spellings:** Fahd

## Faheem

**Meaning:** Mastermind
**Origin:** Arabic
**Pronunciation:** fah HEEM

**Description:** Faheem is an Arabic boys' name, which literally means 'to mastermind'. Faheem hence means 'one who understands with ease and is greatly blessed with wisdom'.
**Alternative spellings:** Fahim

## Faisal

**Meaning:** Resolute
**Origin:** Arabic
**Pronunciation:** FAY saal
**Description:** Faisal is an Arabic name that means 'resolute'. King Faisal of Saudi Arabia ruled for over 10 years.
**Alternative spellings:** Faysal, Feisal

## Faiz

**Meaning:** Successful
**Origin:** Arabic
**Pronunciation:** FAH eez
**Description:** Faiz is an uncommon name of Arabic origin, meaning 'successful' or 'victorious'.
**Alternative spellings:** Faez, Fahiz

## Faizaan

**Meaning:** Generosity; abundance; benefit
**Origin:** Arabic
**Pronunciation:** FAY zaan
**Description:** Faizaan is an uncommon Arabic boys' name meaning 'generosity', 'abundance' or 'benefit'.
**Alternative spellings:** Fayzaan

## Falak

**Meaning:** Star
**Origin:** Arabic
**Pronunciation:** FAL AK
**Description:** Falak is a unisex name of Arabic origins, meaning 'star'. It is favoured by Muslim parents and often given as a baby name because of its bright meaning.
**Alternative spellings:** Falach, Falack

## Farhaan

**Meaning:** Happiness; euphoria
**Origin:** Arabic
**Pronunciation:** FAR haan
**Description:** Farhaan is an Arabic boys' name. The name is said to mean 'happiness' and 'euphoria'.
**Alternative spellings:** Farhan, Farhann

## Farhad

**Meaning:** Happiness
**Origin:** Persian
**Pronunciation:** FAR haad
**Description:** Farhad was the protagonist of an ancient series of Persian poems depicting his failed attempt to woo Armenian Princess Shirin away from Khosrau II. Its meaning makes it the perfect name for a very happy baby boy.
**Alternative spellings:** Fahad

## Faris

**Meaning:** Stone
**Origin:** Greek
**Pronunciation:** fair IS
**Description:** As well as being a variant of the name Farris, this name is also the Middle English version of the more traditional name Peter.
**Alternative spellings:** Fariss, Farris

## Faruq

**Meaning:** One who can distinguish the truth

**Origin:** Arabic
**Pronunciation:** fah RUK
**Description:** Faruq is an alternative spelling to the Arabic name Farouk. It means 'one who can distinguish right from wrong; truth from a lie'.
**Alternative spellings:** Farouk, Farouq

## Fateh
**Meaning:** Conqueror
**Origin:** Arabic
**Pronunciation:** FAH tey
**Description:** Fateh is an Arabic name meaning 'conqueror'.
**Alternative spellings:** Fatih

## Faunus
**Meaning:** Horned god
**Origin:** Latin
**Pronunciation:** fa UH nus
**Description:** According to ancient Roman myth, Faunus was the horned god of the forest, plains and field.
**Alternative spellings:** Fanus, Faunas

## Federico
**Meaning:** Peaceful ruler
**Origin:** Spanish
**Pronunciation:** fed er EE co
**Description:** Federico is a Mediterranean boys' name meaning 'peaceful ruler'. It is the Spanish and Italian variant of the German name Frederick.
**Alternative spellings:** Frederico

## Felipe
**Meaning:** Friend of horses
**Origin:** Spanish
**Pronunciation:** FEL eep

**Description:** Felipe is the Spanish version of the name Philip, which means 'friend of horses'. Felipe is a name that is popular in Brazil.
**Alternative spellings:** Philip

## Felix
**Meaning:** Happy; fortunate
**Origin:** Latin
**Pronunciation:** FEE liks
**Description:** Felix is a Latin name meaning 'happy and fortunate'. It managed to penetrate Western culture largely thanks to its positive undertones.
**Alternative spellings:** Felicks, Felics

## Fenton
**Meaning:** Settlement on the marsh
**Origin:** English
**Pronunciation:** FEN ton
**Description:** Fenton is an English surname meaning 'settlement on the marsh'. Though uncommon, it is sometimes used as a boys' given name.
**Alternative spellings:** Fennton, Fentonn, Fentton

## Fergus
**Meaning:** Man of force
**Origin:** Gaelic
**Pronunciation:** FUR gus
**Description:** Fergus is a name of Gaelic origin, and has been popular in both Ireland and Scotland for many years. It is said to mean 'man of force,' and was the name given to an Irish prince who crossed the sea to settle in Argyll, Scotland. It is once again proving popular across the UK.

## Fernando

**Meaning:** Intelligent
**Origin:** Spanish
**Pronunciation:** fehr NAN doh
**Description:** Fernando is a boys' given name of Spanish origin, meaning 'intelligent' and 'brave'. It is a popular name in Spain.
**Alternative spellings:** Fernandho, Fernandoh

## Fernley

**Meaning:** Fern field
**Origin:** English
**Pronunciation:** fern LEE
**Description:** Fernley is an Old English name meaning 'fern field' or 'fern meadow'. This is a name that follows the historical trend of using place names as first names.

## Filip

**Meaning:** Lover of horses
**Origin:** Greek
**Pronunciation:** FIL ip
**Description:** Filip is a Polish variation of the Greek name Phillip. The use of the version spelt Filip is unusual in Britain with Phillip being the more prominent version.
**Alternative spellings:** Philip, Phillip

## Finbar

**Meaning:** Fair-haired
**Origin:** Irish
**Pronunciation:** fin BAR
**Description:** Finbar is derived from the Old Irish word *'fionn-bharr'* meaning 'fair-haired'. The shortened, anglicised version of the name is Barry.

**Alternative spellings:** Finbarr, Finbarre, Finnbar

## Finch

**Meaning:** Bird
**Origin:** English
**Pronunciation:** finch
**Description:** Finch comes from the bird of the same name. In the Middle Ages, these birds were often caught and sold as songbirds or to cook them, so the name may be an occupational name referring to the people who captured the birds.

## Finley

**Meaning:** Fair-haired courageous one
**Origin:** Gaelic
**Pronunciation:** FIN lee
**Description:** Finley is a variant of the Gaelic name Finlay, which is an Irish surname meaning 'fair-haired courageous one'.
**Alternative spellings:** Findlay, Finlay, Fyndlay, Fynley

## Finn

**Meaning:** Fair-haired
**Origin:** Gaelic
**Pronunciation:** FIN
**Description:** Finn, an Irish boys' name, is derived from the Gaelic word *'fionn'* meaning 'fair'.
**Alternative spellings:** Fin, Phin

## Finnian

**Meaning:** Fair
**Origin:** Gaelic
**Pronunciation:** FINN i an
**Description:** Finnian is an uncommon boys' name of Irish and Gaelic origin meaning 'fair'. It is a variant of the more popular spelling, Finian.

**F**

**Alternative spellings:** Finian, Finyan, Phinnian

## Fintan
**Meaning:** Little fair one
**Origin:** Gaelic
**Pronunciation:** FIN tan
**Description:** Fintan is an uncommon Irish boys' name of Gaelic origin. It means 'little fair one'.
**Alternative spellings:** Finton, Fintun

## Fionn
**Meaning:** Fair
**Origin:** Gaelic
**Pronunciation:** FYE on
**Description:** Fionn is a variant of the Gaelic boys' name Finbar. The name is understood to mean 'white or fair hair; fair'.
**Alternative spellings:** Ffion, Fion, Fyon

## Fisher
**Meaning:** One who fishes
**Origin:** English
**Pronunciation:** fish ER
**Description:** Fisher was an English occupational surname given to those who fished for a living. Like Taylor and Hunter, these occupational names are very popular modern baby name choices.

## Fletcher
**Meaning:** Arrow maker
**Origin:** English
**Pronunciation:** FLETCH er
**Description:** The name Fletcher first came into use as a surname in England in the Middle Ages, used to describe a maker of arrows. This is because the Old French word *'fletch'* means 'arrow'.
**Alternative spellings:** Fletcha

## Florian
**Meaning:** Blooming; flowering
**Origin:** Latin
**Pronunciation:** floor EE an
**Description:** Florian is a Latin name that comes from the Roman name Florianus. The prefix 'flōs' suggests the blooming or flowering of plants.
**Alternative spellings:** Florien

## Flynn
**Meaning:** Red-haired
**Origin:** Gaelic
**Pronunciation:** FLIN
**Description:** Flynn is a unisex name and also a common surname, first recorded in 1255. It is popular in Ireland.
**Alternative spellings:** Flinn, Flinne, Flyn

## Ford
**Meaning:** Someone who lives near a ford
**Origin:** English
**Pronunciation:** ford
**Description:** Ford is an old English surname that refers to someone who lived near a ford. It is now better known as a famous American car manufacturer.

## Forrest
**Meaning:** Forest
**Origin:** English
**Pronunciation:** FAWR est
**Description:** Forrest is from an English surname meaning 'forest,' which belonged to someone who

lived near a forest. The world's most famous Forrest is perhaps Forrest Gump, played by Tom Hanks in the 1994 movie of the same name.
**Alternative spellings:** Forest

## Foster
**Meaning:** Forester
**Origin:** English
**Pronunciation:** fos TUR
**Description:** Foster is an old English occupational name that refers to someone who keeps the forest. Like Taylor or Hunter, Foster can now be used as a first name choice.

## Fox
**Meaning:** Animal of the same name
**Origin:** English
**Pronunciation:** fahks
**Description:** Fox is most likely from the English word of the same meaning, referring to the animal. It can also be used as a nickname or a surname, such as George Fox, the founder of the Quakers.

## Fran
See entry in 'Names for Baby Girls A–Z'

## Francesco
**Meaning:** Free man
**Origin:** Italian
**Pronunciation:** fran CHESS co
**Description:** Francesco is the most common boys' name in Italy. It has seen a rise in popularity in England in recent years. It is the Italian variant of the French name Francis. The name means 'free man'.

**Alternative spellings:** Franchesco, Franchesko

## Francis
**Meaning:** From France
**Origin:** Latin
**Pronunciation:** FRAN sis
**Description:** The name Francis derives from an Italian nickname for someone from France. History suggests that St Francis of Assisi is the original bearer of this name. He was originally baptised Giovanni but was renamed by his father when he returned from France.
**Alternative spellings:** Franciss, Fransis

## Francisco
**Meaning:** Free man
**Origin:** Latin
**Pronunciation:** fran CEES co
**Description:** Francisco is a name of Latin origin. It has seen a rise in popularity in England in recent years. It is the Spanish variant of the French name Francis. The name means 'free man'.
**Alternative spellings:** Francesco, Franchesco, Franchesko

## Franciszek
**Meaning:** From France
**Origin:** Latin
**Pronunciation:** FRAN cee shek
**Description:** This Polish variation of the name Francis is rare in Britain but popular in Poland.
**Alternative spellings:** Franciszeck

## Franco
**Meaning:** Name of German tribe
**Origin:** Italian
**Pronunciation:** FRANC oh

**Description:** Franco is a common Italian surname and given name. It is closely related to the name Frank, which refers to the old Germanic tribe called the Franks, who invaded modern-day France.
**Alternative spellings:** Franko

## Frank
**Meaning:** Spear; sincere
**Origin:** German
**Pronunciation:** FRANK
**Description:** Frank is an English form of the French name 'Francois', from the German tribe the Franks. The name was first derived from the German for 'spear' or 'javelin'. As an English vocabulary word, Frank also has the meaning of 'sincere'.
**Alternative spellings:** Franke

## Frankie
**Meaning:** He who is free
**Origin:** French
**Pronunciation:** FRAN kee
**Description:** Frankie is most usually the pet form of one of the masculine French names, either Frank or Francis – both of which share the meaning 'He who is free'.
**Alternative spellings:** Franky

## Franklin
**Meaning:** Liberated
**Origin:** English
**Pronunciation:** FRAN klen
**Description:** The name Franklin comes from an Old English word meaning 'liberated'. In medieval England a franklin was a man who owned his own portion of land but was not a man of gentility. Franklin owes its use as a first name to American Benjamin Franklin, as people named their children in honour of him.
**Alternative spellings:** Franklen, Franklyn

## Fraser
**Meaning:** Unknown
**Origin:** English
**Pronunciation:** FRAY zer
**Description:** Fraser is a Scottish surname transferred into a given name. It is ultimately derived from the Norman place name and is of uncertain meaning.
**Alternative spellings:** Frasier, Frazer

## Frazer
**Meaning:** Of the forest men
**Origin:** French
**Pronunciation:** fr aa SHER
**Description:** Frazer is a variant of the male name Fraser. There is also a possible Old English meaning belonging to the name and it is that of 'curly hair'. Although the name is close to the French word '*fraise*' meaning strawberry, it is not believed to have any association.
**Alternative spellings:** Fraiser

## Fred
**Meaning:** Peaceful ruler
**Origin:** English
**Pronunciation:** FRED
**Description:** A short form of Alfred and Frederick, now given as a first name in its own right.
**Alternative spellings:** Fread

## Freddie
**Meaning:** Peaceful ruler
**Origin:** German

**Pronunciation:** FRED dee
**Description:** A pet form of Frederick, Fred and occasionally Frederica, the name Freddie is now seen as a unisex given name.
**Alternative spellings:** Freddi, Freddy

## Frederick
**Meaning:** Peaceful ruler
**Origin:** German

**Pronunciation:** FRED ur rik
**Description:** Frederic is of Old German origin and is comprised of the words for 'peace' and 'ruler'. The name failed following its Norman introduction, but was resurrected in the 18th century.
**Alternative spellings:** Frederic, Frederik, Fredric, Fredrick, Fredrik

# G

## Gabriel
**Meaning:** Strength from God
**Origin:** Hebrew
**Pronunciation:** GAY bree uhl
**Description:** A biblical name borne by archangel Gabriel, who according to the Old Testament appeared to Daniel after he was thrown into the lion's den. In the New Testament, Gabriel announced Christ's immaculate conception to Mary.
**Alternative spellings:** Gabrial

## Gael
**Meaning:** Irishman
**Origin:** Gaelic
**Pronunciation:** GUY el
**Description:** Gael is a Gaelic name that refers to a group of people from a Celtric tribe and, as such, means 'Irishman'.

## Gage
**Meaning:** Oath
**Origin:** French
**Pronunciation:** GAY ge

**Description:** Gage is a French name created in the 14th century that means 'oath' or 'pledge'. It was a surname originally but has become a first name in modern times.

## Gale
**Meaning:** Father of exaltation
**Origin:** Hebrew
**Pronunciation:** GAYL
**Description:** Gale, the male form of the girls' name Gail, is a character in the hugely popular *Hunger Games*, book and film, and because of that may be a popular choice for boys.
**Alternative spellings:** Gael

## Gareth
**Meaning:** Gentle
**Origin:** Welsh
**Pronunciation:** GA reth
**Description:** Gareth was first seen in the 15th century in Malory's Morte d'Arthur tales and is said to mean 'gentle'.
**Alternative spellings:** Garreth

## Garrett

**Meaning:** Spear strength
**Origin:** German
**Pronunciation:** GARE ett
**Description:** Garrett is a name that is derived from the German elements of '*gēr*' meaning 'spear' and 'hard' or 'strong'. While it is usually found as a surname in the UK, it is a popular given name choice in the US.
**Alternative spellings:** Garret

## Gary

**Meaning:** Spear
**Origin:** German
**Pronunciation:** GA ree
**Description:** Gary was originally a surname that derived from the Old English word '*gar*' meaning 'spear'.
**Alternative spellings:** Garey, Garry

## Gavin

**Meaning:** White hawk
**Origin:** Welsh
**Pronunciation:** GAV en
**Description:** Gavin is a popular British boys' name derived from the Welsh name Gawain, meaning 'white hawk'.
**Alternative spellings:** Gavan, Gaven, Gavyn

## Gene

**Meaning:** Noble
**Origin:** Greek
**Pronunciation:** JEEN
**Description:** Gene is a unisex name derived from the masculine name Eugene.
**Alternative spellings:** Gine, Jean

## George

**Meaning:** Farmer
**Origin:** Greek
**Pronunciation:** JORJ
**Description:** St George is the patron saint of England, and is well known from the legend of St George and the dragon. Popularity was bolstered in the 18th century when George I became king of England.
**Alternative spellings:** Jeorge, Jorge

## Georgie

**Meaning:** Farmer
**Origin:** Greek
**Pronunciation:** JORGE ee
**Description:** Georgie is used as a pet name for the names George, Georgina and Georgiana. The names are commonly associated with knighthood and chivalry due to heavy use of the name in legends associated with dragons.
**Alternative spellings:** Georgi, Georgy, Jorgie, Jorgy

## Gerard

**Meaning:** Strength of the spear
**Origin:** German
**Pronunciation:** JEH rard
**Description:** Gerard is a boys' given name of German origin, popular in English-speaking countries. The name means 'strength of the spear'.
**Alternative spellings:** Geraud, Gerrard, Jerard

## Gethin

**Meaning:** Dark
**Origin:** Welsh
**Pronunciation:** GETH in
**Description:** A Welsh name that would have originally been given as a surname, but eventually developed into a first name. Welsh names went out of popularity until

the 19th century, and Gethin has been popular since.

## Gian

**Meaning:** God is gracious
**Origin:** Hebrew
**Pronunciation:** Jee ahn
**Description:** Gian is a unisex name of Hebrew and Italian origin. It is commonly used as the shortened form of Giovanni or other names starting with Gian-.
**Alternative spellings:** Giann, Jian

## Gianluca

**Meaning:** John Luke
**Origin:** Italian
**Pronunciation:** jee an LEW ka
**Description:** Gianluca is an Italian boys' name that translates into English as 'John Luke'. It is the shortened version of Giovanni Luca.
**Alternative spellings:** Gianluka

## Gianni

**Meaning:** God is gracious
**Origin:** Hebrew
**Pronunciation:** jee AN nee
**Description:** Gianni is a name of Hebrew and Italian origin. It is a variant of the name Giovanni, which means 'God is gracious'.
**Alternative spellings:** Giani, Jianni

## Gibson

**Meaning:** Son of Gib
**Origin:** Scottish
**Pronunciation:** GIB sun
**Description:** Gibson is a Scottish name and refers to someone who was the son of Gib (or Gilbert).

## Gideon

**Meaning:** Mighty warrior
**Origin:** Greek
**Pronunciation:** Gid EE On
**Description:** This name derives from the transcription of Gidon in Hebrew, which means 'mighty warrior'. The name is also in the Old Testament and belongs to an Israelite judge. For this reason it is seen as a very biblical name.
**Alternative spellings:** Gidion

## Gilbert

**Meaning:** Bright promise
**Origin:** French
**Pronunciation:** GILL bert
**Description:** Gilbert is the English variant of the French name of the same spelling. The French pronunciation has a soft 'g' making it sound like 'Jilber'. It was popular at the beginning of the 20th century but is far less common in recent years.
**Alternative spellings:** Gilburt, Guilbert

## Giles

**Meaning:** Small goat
**Origin:** Greek
**Pronunciation:** JYE ulls
**Description:** Giles is a common surname in England, and was once a relatively popular given name. It refers to goatskin from which ancient shields were made.
**Alternative spellings:** Gilles, Gyles, Jiles, Jyles

## Giorgio

**Meaning:** Farmer
**Origin:** Greek

**G**

**Pronunciation:** JIYOR jiyo
**Description:** Giorgio is a boys' given name of Greek and Italian origin. It is a variant of the Greek name George, meaning 'farmer'.
**Alternative spellings:** Georgio, Giorgi

## Giovanni
**Meaning:** God is gracious
**Origin:** Italian
**Pronunciation:** GEE oh VAR nee
**Description:** Giovanni is the Italian form of the name John, which means 'God is gracious'.
**Alternative spellings:** Giovani, Giovannie

## Glen
**Meaning:** Valley
**Origin:** Gaelic
**Pronunciation:** GLEN
**Description:** Glen is a boys' name coined from the Scottish word '*glen*', meaning 'valley'.
**Alternative spellings:** Glenn

## Glyn
**Meaning:** Valley
**Origin:** Welsh
**Pronunciation:** GLIN
**Description:** Taken from the Welsh word '*glyn*', meaning 'valley', this boys' name is mostly found in Wales.
**Alternative spellings:** Glin, Glynn

## Gordon
**Meaning:** Place name; hill
**Origin:** Scottish, English
**Pronunciation:** GORE dun
**Description:** Thought to be derived from one of a number of place names, including Gordon in Berwickshire.
**Alternative spellings:** Gordan, Gorden

## Gracie
See entry in 'Names for Baby Girls A–Z'

## Gracjan
**Meaning:** Grace
**Origin:** Polish
**Pronunciation:** GRAY shan
**Description:** Gracjan is an uncommon Polish boys' name meaning 'grace'.
**Alternative spellings:** Gracian, Graczan

## Grady
**Meaning:** Noble
**Origin:** Irish
**Pronunciation:** GRAY dee
**Description:** Grady is a name of Irish origin and comes from the Irish word '*gráda*' meaning 'noble'. This name is a popular given name choice in the US.

## Graham
**Meaning:** Gravel homestead
**Origin:** English
**Pronunciation:** GRAY am
**Description:** The name Graham is of Scottish origin, and was originally a surname. It is thought to have been related to Grantham, Lincolnshire.
**Alternative spellings:** Grayham, Greham

## Grayson
**Meaning:** Son of grey-haired man
**Origin:** English
**Pronunciation:** GRAY sun

**Description:** Grayson is an increasingly popular boys' name of Old English origin. The name, and similar variants such as Carson, have seen a surge of popularity in America over the last 20 years.
**Alternative spellings:** Graysen, Greyson

## Greg
**Meaning:** Watchful
**Origin:** Greek
**Pronunciation:** greg
**Description:** Greg is a short form of the name Gregory, a Greek name that means 'watchful' or 'alert'. Both names come from the Latin name Grēgorios.
**Alternative spellings:** Gregg

## Gregor
**Meaning:** Vigilant
**Origin:** Greek
**Pronunciation:** GREY gor
**Description:** Gregor is a variant of the popular Greek name Gregory. Gregor is widely used as a surname but is less common as a given name in recent years.
**Alternative spellings:** Greger, Grigor, Grygor

## Gregory
**Meaning:** Sentry
**Origin:** Greek
**Pronunciation:** GREG ger ree
**Description:** Gregory comes from a Greek word meaning 'sentry'. It was introduced to England by St Gregory the Great and has been a popular boys' name since the Norman Conquest.
**Alternative spellings:** Gregorey, Gregorie

## Greyson
**Meaning:** Son of a grey-haired man
**Origin:** English
**Pronunciation:** GRAY sun
**Description:** Greyson is a variation of the name Grayson. The name has Old English roots, and as the name itself suggests, the meaning refers to a man who is the 'son of a grey-haired man'.
**Alternative spellings:** Grayson

## Griff
**Meaning:** Lord; prince
**Origin:** English
**Pronunciation:** Griff
**Description:** Griff is a variation, and the English form of the Welsh name Gruffudd, meaning 'lord' or 'prince'. It can also be a nickname for the names Griffin and Griffith.

## Griffith
**Meaning:** Lord; strong fighter
**Origin:** Welsh
**Pronunciation:** GRIH fith
**Description:** Griffith is a name of Welsh origin meaning lord, strong fighter or strong leader.
**Alternative spellings:** Griffeth, Gruffudd, Gruffydd

## Gruffydd
**Meaning:** Lord
**Origin:** Welsh
**Pronunciation:** gruf FITH
**Description:** Gruffydd is the old Welsh form of the name Griffith. Both are considered to be equally standard forms of the same name. Unlike Griffith, Gruffydd is very uncommon in recent years.
**Alternative spellings:** Griffith

**G**

## Guillermo

**Meaning:** Protection
**Origin:** Spanish
**Pronunciation:** GEE eyre mo
**Description:** Guillermo is the Spanish version of the name William, and as such shares the same meaning of 'protection'. Guillermo del Toro is a famous Mexican film director.

## Gunnar

**Meaning:** Fighter; soldier; warrior
**Origin:** Nordic
**Pronunciation:** GOON ar
**Description:** Gunnar is a popular Nordic first name composed of the elements of *gunnr* meaning 'war' and *arr* meaning 'warrior'.
**Alternative spellings:** Gunar

## Gus

**Meaning:** Strong choice
**Origin:** Gaelic
**Pronunciation:** GUS
**Description:** Gus is often a diminutive for names such as Angus, August, Augustine or Augustus. However, it can also be a stand-alone name that is derived from the Old Irish word *gusmhar* or *gusair* meaning 'strength' or 'force' and *gusto* meaning 'choice'.

## Guto

**Meaning:** Lord; prince
**Origin:** Welsh
**Pronunciation:** gi TAW
**Description:** Guto is the diminutive of the Welsh name Gruffudd. The name is derived from two Welsh elements – the first part is of uncertain meaning, but 'udd' means 'lord' or 'prince'. It was a common name among medieval Welsh royalty.

## Guy

**Meaning:** Guide
**Origin:** French
**Pronunciation:** GAI
**Description:** The name Guy derives from the French word for 'guide', *guider*. It is also British slang for a man.

## Gwion

**Meaning:** Anger
**Origin:** Welsh
**Pronunciation:** GWUY on
**Description:** Gwion is an uncommon Welsh name derived from the Welsh boys' name Gavin.
**Alternative spellings:** Gawion, Gwain

# H

## Haaris

**Meaning:** Vigilant guard
**Origin:** Arabic
**Pronunciation:** haah REES
**Description:** Haaris, not to be mistaken for the English Harris, is a masculine name of Arabic origin. It is a variant form of the name Haris and both are said to mean 'vigilant guard'.
**Alternative spellings:** Haahris

## Habib

**Meaning:** Beloved one

**Origin:** Arabic
**Pronunciation:** ha BEEB
**Description:** Habib is the masculine version of the Arabic name Habiba. Habib can also be considered a shortened form of the name Habibullah.
**Alternative spellings:** Habeeb

# Hadi

**Meaning:** True direction
**Origin:** Arabic
**Pronunciation:** HAH dee
**Description:** Hadi is a masculine name of Arabic origin and it is said to mean 'true direction'.
**Alternative spellings:** Hadie, Haydi

# Hadley

**Meaning:** Heather meadow
**Origin:** English
**Pronunciation:** HAD ley
**Description:** Hadley is an uncommon given name but a popular surname. It is of Old English origin meaning 'heather meadow'.
**Alternative spellings:** Hadlee, Hadleigh, Hadli, Hadlie, Hadly

# Haidar

**Meaning:** Lion
**Origin:** Arabic
**Pronunciation:** HAY dar
**Description:** Haidar is an uncommon Arabic boys' name meaning 'lion'.
**Alternative spellings:** Haider, Haydar, Hyder

# Haider

**Meaning:** Lion
**Origin:** Arabic
**Pronunciation:** HAY dar

**Description:** Haidar is an uncommon Arabic boys' name meaning 'lion'.
**Alternative spellings:** Hayder

# Hakeem

**Meaning:** Wise
**Origin:** Arabic
**Pronunciation:** hah KEEM
**Description:** Hakeem is a common Arabic boys' name meaning 'wise' or 'intelligent'.
**Alternative spellings:** Hakim

# Hammand

**Meaning:** Praiseworthy
**Origin:** Arabic
**Pronunciation:** HAH mad
**Description:** Hammad is an uncommon Arabic boys' name that is a variant of the Arabic name Mohammed, after the prophet Muhammad.
**Alternative spellings:** Hamad

# Hamid

**Meaning:** Praiseworthy
**Origin:** Arabic
**Pronunciation:** HAH meed
**Description:** Hamid is a common Arabic surname and is sometimes used as a given name for baby boys. When spelt with an additional 'a' (Haamid), the name takes on a new meaning as 'praiser (of God)'.
**Alternative spellings:** Haamid, Hammad, Hameed, Hammid

# Hamish

**Meaning:** Supplanter
**Origin:** Gaelic
**Pronunciation:** HAY mish
**Description:** Hamish is a name deriving from the Gaelic name Seamus and is the Scottish

**H**

equivalent of the English name James. Hamish can be seen as a surname or a given name.
**Alternative spellings:** Hamishe, Hammish

# Hamza
**Meaning:** Steadfast
**Origin:** Arabic
**Pronunciation:** HAM zuh
**Description:** It is possible that this name derives from the Arabic word *'hamuza'*, which means 'strong'. This name was used by one of Muhammad's uncles and is favoured by Muslim parents. Hamza is also a letter in the Arabic alphabet.
**Alternative spellings:** Hamzah

# Hank
**Meaning:** Home ruler
**Origin:** English
**Pronunciation:** HANK
**Description:** Hank is a diminutive form of the name Henry, but has been a rather uncommon name in the UK and is more commonly found in the United States.

# Hansel
**Meaning:** God is gracious
**Origin:** German
**Pronunciation:** han SELL
**Description:** Hansel is a variation of the German name Hans, meaning 'God is gracious'. It is also found in the popular Brothers Grimm children's story, 'Hansel and Gretel', about a pair of siblings captured by an evil witch who wants to eat them.

# Hansen
**Meaning:** Son of Hans
**Origin:** Scandinavian
**Pronunciation:** han SON
**Description:** Hansen is a popular surname in Scandinavian countries, particularly Denmark, and means 'son of Hans'. This follows the contemporary trend of using last names as first names.
**Alternative spellings:** Hanson

# Hao
**Meaning:** The good
**Origin:** Chinese
**Pronunciation:** HOW
**Description:** Hao is an uncommon boys' given name of Chinese origin, meaning 'the good'. The name can be spelt in a variety of ways but all are uncommon in English-speaking countries.
**Alternative spellings:** Hao, Hau, Hauo

# Hari
**Meaning:** Colour
**Origin:** Sanskrit
**Pronunciation:** Hah ree
**Description:** Hari is considered a unisex name and has the bright meaning of 'colour'. The name is sometimes used as an alternative to Vishnu and Krishna. Hari could also be considered a respelling of the popular boys' name Harry, meaning 'ruler of the home'.
**Alternative spellings:** Harie, Harri, Harrie, Harry

# Haris
**Meaning:** Son of Harry
**Origin:** English
**Pronunciation:** HA ris
**Description:** Haris would have been a name originally given to someone whose father was called

Harry. It is an alternative spelling to Harris, and would have been a surname before it became a first name.
**Alternative spellings:** Harris

## Harlan
**Meaning:** From the hare's land
**Origin:** English
**Pronunciation:** HAAR lahn
**Description:** Harlan is an English name meaning 'from the hare's land'.
**Alternative spellings:** Harlen

## Harley
**Meaning:** Clearing of stones
**Origin:** English
**Pronunciation:** HAR lee
**Description:** Harley was originally a surname but was transferred to a boys' first name. Harley has recently become a popular name for girls, too.
**Alternative spellings:** Harlee, Harli, Harlie, Harly

## Harlow
**Meaning:** Rocky hill
**Origin:** English
**Pronunciation:** HAR low
**Description:** Harlow was originally given as a surname to those who lived near a rocky hill. Due to the trend for surnames as first names, Harlow is now found as a unisex given name.
**Alternative spellings:** Hahlow, Harlo

## Harman
**Meaning:** Grey man
**Origin:** English
**Pronunciation:** HAR man
**Description:** Harman is a known surname in America and England but a less popular given name. It is of Old English origin meaning 'grey man', where it is believed to have derived from Hardman.
**Alternative spellings:** Harmann, Harmen, Harmon, Harmonn

## Harold
**Meaning:** Army leader
**Origin:** Norse
**Pronunciation:** HA rold
**Description:** Harold is an Old English name ultimately of Scandinavian origin, from the Old Norse name 'Haraldr'. Harold is often shortened to the popular boys' name Harry.
**Alternative spellings:** Harald, Harrold

## Haroon
**Meaning:** Strong mountain
**Origin:** Hebrew
**Pronunciation:** HAH roon
**Description:** Haroon is a phonetic variation of the name Haroun. It is thought that both of these names mean 'strong mountain'.
**Alternative spellings:** Haroone, Haroun

## Harper
See entry in 'Names for Baby Girls A–Z'

## Harri
**Meaning:** Home ruler
**Origin:** German
**Pronunciation:** hah REE
**Description:** Modern spelling of the name Harry. Harry started as a nickname for Henry but became a name in it own right. A popular

**H**

145

name in modern times, its usage has increased from 2001 potentially due to the popularity of J.K. Rowling's fictional wizard Harry Potter.
**Alternative spellings:** Harry

## Harrison
**Meaning:** Son of Harry
**Origin:** English
**Pronunciation:** HAH risson
**Description:** Harrison originated as a surname, meaning 'son of Harry'.
**Alternative spellings:** Harrison, Harrysson

## Harris
**Meaning:** Son of Harry
**Origin:** English
**Pronunciation:** HA ris
**Description:** Harris is an English name that would have been given to someone whose father was called Harry. It was previously interchangeable with Harrison, but both have now become names in their own right. It is more commonly seen as a surname.
**Alternative spellings:** Haris

## Harry
**Meaning:** Ruler of the home
**Origin:** German
**Pronunciation:** HAH ree
**Description:** Harry originated as a pet form of Henry, but has long since been a name in its own right. Since the publication of J.K. Rowling's first Harry Potter book in 1997, the name has grown in popularity.
**Alternative spellings:** Hari, Harie, Harri, Harrie

## Harun
**Meaning:** Strong mountain
**Origin:** Arabic
**Pronunciation:** hah ROON
**Description:** The name Harun is Arabic in origin and thought to be linked with the Hebrew name Aaron. It may have the meaning 'strong mountain'.
**Alternative spellings:** Haaron, Haarun, Haron

## Harvey
**Meaning:** Battleworthy
**Origin:** English
**Pronunciation:** HAR vee
**Description:** Originally a surname, Harvey is gaining popularity as a first name.
**Alternative spellings:** Harvay, Harvi, Harvie, Harvy

## Hasan
**Meaning:** Good; beautiful
**Origin:** Arabic
**Pronunciation:** ha SAN
**Description:** Hasan is an Arabic name meaning 'good' or 'beautiful'. There are, in fact, two different spellings of Hasan although both have similar meanings – Hasan is the more common name, while Hassaan is the variation.
**Alternative spellings:** Hassan, Hassaan

## Haseeb
**Meaning:** Respected
**Origin:** Arabic
**Pronunciation:** hah SEEB
**Description:** Haseeb is generally taken to mean 'respected' and is a popular name in Pakistan.
**Alternative spellings:** Hasibe, Hazeeb

## Hashim

**Meaning:** Force for good
**Origin:** Arabic
**Pronunciation:** ha SHEEM
**Description:** Hashim is a commonly found family name in the Middle East, but is also used as a given name. Hashim was the title given to the great-grandfather of the prophet Muhammad.
**Alternative spellings:** Hasheem, Hashime

## Hashir

**Meaning:** Collector
**Origin:** Arabic
**Pronunciation:** hah SHEER
**Description:** Hashir is a common Arabic surname. The name Hashir is another name for the prophet Muhammad or 'one who collects or gathers'.
**Alternative spellings:** Hasheer, Hashiir

## Hasnain

**Meaning:** Handsome
**Origin:** Arabic
**Pronunciation:** HAS na IYN
**Description:** Hasnain was developed as a mixture of the Arabic names Hussain and Hassan. Generally the name Hasnain means 'handsome one'.
**Alternative spellings:** Hasnane

## Hassan

**Meaning:** Handsome
**Origin:** Arabic
**Pronunciation:** HAH san
**Description:** Hassan is a popular boys' name in Arabic culture and is said to mean 'handsome'. Hasani is a Swahili variant of this name.
**Alternative spellings:** Hasan, Hasani

## Hayden

**Meaning:** Hedged valley
**Origin:** English
**Pronunciation:** HAY den
**Description:** A unisex name that means 'hedged valley'. In German, the meaning of the name is 'pagan'.
**Alternative spellings:** Haiden, Haydn, Heydan, Haydon, Heydon

## Haytham

**Meaning:** Young eagle
**Origin:** Arabic
**Pronunciation:** HAY tham
**Description:** Haytham is an uncommon boys' given name of Arabic origin, meaning 'young eagle' or 'lion'.
**Alternative spellings:** Haaytham, Haythaam

## Hazem

**Meaning:** Firm; resolute
**Origin:** Arabic
**Pronunciation:** HAZ um
**Description:** Hazem is an Arabic boys' name meaning 'firm' or 'resolute'. It is both a surname and a given name in Arabic countries.
**Alternative spellings:** Hazm, Hazim

## Heath

**Meaning:** Heath; place
**Origin:** English
**Pronunciation:** Hee th
**Description:** Originally used as a surname for those who lived near a heath, the word has now become a well-loved first name for both boys and girls.

**H**

**Alternative spellings:** Heathe, Hethe

# Heathcliff
**Meaning:** From the heath cliff
**Origin:** English
**Pronunciation:** heeth CLIFF
**Description:** Heathcliff is an English place name referring to someone who is 'from the heath cliff'. Of course, Heathcliff is also a character in Emily Brontë's novel, *Wuthering Heights*.

# Hector
**Meaning:** Anchor
**Origin:** Greek
**Pronunciation:** HEK tor
**Description:** Latinised form of the Greek Hektor, this name is popular as both a first name and surname. In Greek legend Hector was a Trojan champion killed by Achilles during the Trojan War.
**Alternative spellings:** Hecktor, Hektor

# Helios
**Meaning:** Sun
**Origin:** Greek
**Pronunciation:** HEE lee os
**Description:** Helios is a name of Greek origin. In Greek mythology, Helios was the god of the sun who rode his chariot across the sky each day.
**Alternative spellings:** Helius, Hellios

# Hemi
**Meaning:** God is gracious
**Origin:** Maori
**Pronunciation:** hemmy
**Description:** Hemi is of Maori origins and means 'God is gracious'.

It is the Maori version of James, and therefore shares the same meaning.
**Alternative spellings:** Hemy, Hemmy

# Henderson
**Meaning:** Son of Henry
**Origin:** Scottish
**Pronunciation:** hen DER sun
**Description:** Henderson was originally a Scottish last name meaning 'son of Henry'. This is a very common last name in Scotland. This follows the contemporary trend of using last names as first names.

# Hendrix
**Meaning:** Home ruler
**Origin:** Dutch
**Pronunciation:** hen DRICKS
**Description:** Hendrix is the Dutch version of the name Henry, meaning 'home ruler'. Comprised of 'haim' (home) and 'ric' (power; ruler), Henry is a German name adopted by Normans who introduced it to Britain. The name was borne by numerous British kings including Henry VIII in the Tudor period.
**Alternative spellings:** Hendricks, Henryk

# Henley
**Meaning:** High wood
**Origin:** English
**Pronunciation:** HEN lee
**Description:** The name Henley originated as a place name and then a surname. It is made up of the Old English words *'heah'* meaning 'high' and *'lea'* meaning 'clearing'. It is part of the growing

trend to use surnames as unisex first names.

**Alternative spellings:** Henlay, Henlee, Henleigh

## Henry

**Meaning:** Ruler of the home
**Origin:** German
**Pronunciation:** HEN ree
**Description:** Henry is a German name adopted by Normans who introduced it to Britain. It quickly became a favoured royal name and was most notoriously borne by King Henry VIII.
**Alternative spellings:** Henrey, Henri, Henrie

## Henryk

**Meaning:** Home ruler
**Origin:** Polish
**Pronunciation:** hen RICK
**Description:** Henryk is the Polish form of the name Henry, which is originally a German name meaning 'home ruler'. Comprised of haim (home) and ric (power; ruler), Henry is a German name adopted by Normans who introduced it to Britain. A more common spelling variation of this name is Henrick.
**Alternative spellings:** Hendrix, Hendricks

## Hephaestus

**Meaning:** He who shines by day
**Origin:** Greek
**Pronunciation:** heh FYE stuss
**Description:** In Greek mythology, Hephaestus was the god of technology, blacksmiths, craftsmen and fire.
**Alternative spellings:** Hephaestos, Hephastus, Hephestus

## Heracles

**Meaning:** Glory of Hera
**Origin:** Greek
**Pronunciation:** HER ah kleez
**Description:** In Greek mythology, Heracles was a divine hero and the son of Zeus.
**Alternative spellings:** Heraclus, Herakles, Hercules

## Herb

**Meaning:** Bright warrior
**Origin:** German
**Pronunciation:** herb
**Description:** Herb is a German name and a shortened form of Herbert, so the name shares the same meaning of 'bright warrior'. It can also refer to the English vocabulary word of the same name.

## Herbert

**Meaning:** Famous soldier
**Origin:** German
**Pronunciation:** HER bert
**Description:** The name Herbert is derived from the Germanic words *'hari'* and *'berht'* meaning 'soldier'.
**Alternative spellings:** Herburt

## Herbie

**Meaning:** Famous soldier
**Origin:** German
**Pronunciation:** HER bee
**Description:** Herbie is the pet form of the masculine name Herbert. It became popular in the 19th century when it became fashionable to adopt aristocratic surnames as given names.
**Alternative spellings:** Herbi, Herby

## Hercules

**Meaning:** Glory of Hera
**Origin:** Latin

**H**

**Pronunciation:** HERK yoo lees
**Description:** Hercules is the Roman name for the Greek demigod Heracles.
**Alternative spellings:** Heracles, Heraclus, Herakles

## Hermes

**Meaning:** Travel
**Origin:** Greek
**Pronunciation:** HER meez
**Description:** In Greek mythology, Hermes was the god of travellers, shepherds, literature and commerce.
**Alternative spellings:** Hermees, Hermeez

## Heston

**Meaning:** From Heston
**Origin:** English
**Pronunciation:** HES ton
**Description:** Heston is an English surname and occasional given name. It literally means 'from Heston', which is a borough of London.
**Alternative spellings:** Hesston, Hestan, Hestonn

## Hippolytus

**Meaning:** Loosener of horses
**Origin:** Greek
**Pronunciation:** hee POL ee tus
**Description:** In Greek mythology, Hippolytus was cursed by his own father, Theseus, and subsequently was dragged under the ocean's waves by horses.
**Alternative spellings:** Hippolitus

## Hira

**Meaning:** Diamond
**Origin:** Sanskrit
**Pronunciation:** HIH rar; HIH rah

**Description:** The name Hira can be used for both boys and girls and comes from an old Sanskrit word said to mean 'diamond'. The masculine form is pronounced 'hih-rar' whereas the feminine form is pronounced 'hih-ra'.
**Alternative spellings:** Hirah, Hirra

## Hirohi

**Meaning:** Abundant benevolence
**Origin:** Japanese
**Pronunciation:** hee RO hee
**Description:** This Japanese name can be written using the character 'hiro', which means 'abundant', and 'hito', meaning 'benevolence'. We can therefore take the name to mean 'abundant benevolence'.
**Alternative spellings:** Hirohie

## Hiroki

**Meaning:** Wide trees
**Origin:** Japanese
**Pronunciation:** hee RO key
**Description:** Hiroki can be written using the Japanese character 'hiro' when it means 'large and wide' with 'ki', meaning 'woods' – to mean 'large woods'. It is also possible to write it 'hiro' for 'abundance' and 'ki' for 'radiance' – to mean 'abundant radiance'.
**Alternative spellings:** Hirokie

## Hiromi

**Meaning:** Abundant beauty
**Origin:** Japanese
**Pronunciation:** hi row mee
**Description:** Hiromi is a unisex name often found in Japan. It consists of the characters 'hiro', meaning 'abundance', and 'mi', meaning 'beauty'.

**Alternative spellings:** Hiromie, Hiromy

## Hiromitsu
**Meaning:** Large light
**Origin:** Japanese
**Pronunciation:** hee ROW mee tsoo
**Description:** The name Hiromitsu is made up of the Japanese characters *'hiro'* and *'mitsu'*. *'Hiro'* can either mean 'wide and large' or 'abundance', while *'mitsu'* could mean 'ray of light' or 'support'.
**Alternative spellings:** Hiromittsu

## Hisham
**Meaning:** Generous
**Origin:** Arabic
**Pronunciation:** HE sham
**Description:** Hisham is an Arabic boys' name and a variant of Hicham. It is uncommon in English-speaking countries but is quite popular in Morocco.
**Alternative spellings:** Hicham, Hishaam

## Honor
See entry in 'Names for Baby Girls A–Z'

## Horatius
**Meaning:** Hour
**Origin:** Latin
**Pronunciation:** hoh RAY tee us
**Description:** Horatius is an uncommon name of Latin origin.
**Alternative spellings:** Horatios, Horaytius

## Howard
**Meaning:** Garden worker
**Origin:** French
**Pronunciation:** HOW ard
**Description:** Howard originated as an aristocratic surname and became popular as a first name in the 19th century. It is thought to derive from the French for 'worker with a hoe'.
**Alternative spellings:** Haward, Howerd

## Hubert
**Meaning:** Clever
**Origin:** German
**Pronunciation:** HUGH burt
**Description:** Although Hubert was a common name in the Middle Ages, it has since diminished in popularity. It is of Old German origin from a word that means 'clever'.
**Alternative spellings:** Huebert, Hughbert

## Hudson
**Meaning:** Son of Hugh
**Origin:** English
**Pronunciation:** HUD sun
**Description:** Hudson was originally an Old English surname meaning 'son of Hugh'. It has since been adapted as a first name for boys.
**Alternative spellings:** Hudsonne, Hudsun

## Huey
**Meaning:** Mind; spirit; heart
**Origin:** German
**Pronunciation:** HEW ee
**Description:** Huey is an uncommon boys' given name of German origin, meaning 'mind', 'heart' or 'spirit'. It is a variant of Hugh.
**Alternative spellings:** Hew, Hughey

**H**

## Hugh

**Meaning:** Mind; spirit; heart
**Origin:** German
**Pronunciation:** HEW
**Description:** The name Hugh derives from the Old French name Hugues. It has been widely used since the Middle Ages and is the name of various saints.
**Alternative spellings:** Hue, Huw

## Hugo

**Meaning:** Mind; spirit; heart
**Origin:** German
**Pronunciation:** HEW go
**Description:** Hugo is a Latin diminutive form of the name Hugh. It first emerged as a given name in the 19th century.
**Alternative spellings:** Hugoe

## Humphrey

**Meaning:** Peaceful warrior
**Origin:** German
**Pronunciation:** HUM free
**Description:** Humphrey is a common surname and an uncommon given name of Old German origin.
**Alternative spellings:** Humfrey, Humfry, Humphry

## Humza

**Meaning:** Steadfast
**Origin:** Arabic
**Pronunciation:** HUM za
**Description:** Humza is a variant of the popular Arabic boys' name Hamza. Hamza ibn Abd al-Muttalib was one of the prophet Muhammad's uncles, known for his strength and bravery in battle.
**Alternative spellings:** Hamza, Humzaa

## Hunter

**Meaning:** Hunter
**Origin:** English
**Pronunciation:** HUN tur
**Description:** Hunter comes literally from the English noun. It was originally a surname, given to a family who hunted as a profession, but like a lot of surnames it has been taken up as a boys' name. In its original usage as a first name it was specifically a masculine name, but it has now become popular as a name for both girls and boys.

## Huntley

**Meaning:** From the hunter's meadow
**Origin:** English
**Pronunciation:** hunt LEE
**Description:** Huntley was originally an English surname composed of the Old English elements of '*hunt*' and '*leah*' meaning 'wood' or 'clearing'. This follows the contemporary trend of using last names as first names.

## Husnain

**Meaning:** Good
**Origin:** Arabic
**Pronunciation:** hus NAYN
**Description:** Husnain is a Persian alternative spelling and variant of the popular Arabic boys' name Hussein. It is a diminutive of Hassan, meaning 'good', 'handsome' or 'beautiful'.
**Alternative spellings:** Husnein, Hussnain, Hussnein

## Hussein

**Meaning:** Handsome
**Origin:** Arabic
**Pronunciation:** hu SAYN

**Description:** Hussein is one of the many variations of the name Hassan. All are of the same Arabic origin, and share meanings of 'worthy' and 'handsome'.
**Alternative spellings:** Husain, Husayn, Husein, Huseyin, Hussain

## Huxley
**Meaning:** Hugh's meadow
**Origin:** English
**Pronunciation:** hux LEE
**Description:** Huxley is an English male name meaning 'Hugh's meadow'.
**Alternative spellings:** Huxlee

## Huzaifah
**Meaning:** Small sheep

**Origin:** Arabic
**Pronunciation:** huz EYE fah
**Description:** Huzaifah is an uncommon Arabic boys' name and a modern variant of Huthaifah, meaning 'small sheep'. Huzaifah Ibn Al-Yaman was a companion of the prophet Muhammad.
**Alternative spellings:** Hudhayfah, Huthaifah, Huzaifa

## Hylas
**Meaning:** Companion
**Origin:** Greek
**Pronunciation:** HI lass
**Description:** In Greek mythology, Hylas served as a companion of Heracles.
**Alternative spellings:** Hilas, Hylass

**H**

**I**

# I

## Ian
**Meaning:** God is gracious
**Origin:** Gaelic
**Pronunciation:** EE en
**Description:** Ian originated as the Scottish form of John and is sometimes found spelt Iain, especially in Scotland.
**Alternative spellings:** Ean, Iain

## Ianis
**Meaning:** God is gracious
**Origin:** Greek
**Pronunciation:** YAN iss
**Description:** Ianis is a variant spelling of the name Yannis, meaning 'God is gracious'. Both are variants of the popular boys name John.
**Alternative spellings:** Yannis

## Iasus
**Meaning:** Fire bringer
**Origin:** Greek
**Pronunciation:** EYE ah suss
**Description:** In Greek mythology, Iasus was a king of Argos.
**Alternative spellings:** Iaisos, Iasos

## Ibraheem
**Meaning:** Father of nations
**Origin:** Arabic
**Pronunciation:** ib ra HEEM
**Description:** Ibraheem, a variant of Ibrahim, is the Arabic form of the Hebrew name Abraham.
**Alternative spellings:** Abraham, Ibrahim, Ibrahime

## Icarus
**Meaning:** He follows

**Origin:** Greek
**Pronunciation:** IK ah rus
**Description:** In Greek mythology, Icarus attempted to escape from King Minos by flying to safety with wings made by his father. Icarus flew too close to the sun, melting the wax that held the wings together, and he fell into the ocean.
**Alternative spellings:** Icaros, Ikarus

## Idris

**Meaning:** Fiery leader
**Origin:** Welsh
**Pronunciation:** ID riss
**Description:** Idris was the name given to a giant in Welsh legend who was said to have an observatory on Cader Idris. The giant had a feisty nature and so the name carries these connotations.
**Alternative spellings:** Idrees, Idreez, Idriss, Idriz

## Iestyn

**Meaning:** Righteous
**Origin:** Latin
**Pronunciation:** YES tin
**Description:** Iestyn is a popular name in Wales derived from the Latin word for 'righteous'. The name could also be considered a Welsh variation on the name Justin, which means 'just'.
**Alternative spellings:** Iestin

## Ieuan

**Meaning:** God is gracious
**Origin:** Welsh
**Pronunciation:** YUGH yan
**Description:** Ieuan is the Welsh version of the popular boys' name John. It is a very uncommon name, even in Wales. It is a unique alternative to Ewan and Ian.

## Ifan

**Meaning:** God is gracious
**Origin:** Welsh
**Pronunciation:** EEF an
**Description:** Ifan is the Welsh variant of the name John, more widely found in its anglicised form Evan. Ifan can also be found as a surname.
**Alternative spellings:** Ifanne

## Iggy

**Meaning:** Fire
**Origin:** Latin
**Pronunciation:** igg EE
**Description:** Iggy is a name derived from the Latin word '*ignis*' meaning 'fire'. It is sometimes a shortened form of Ignatius.
**Alternative spellings:** Iggie

## Igor

**Meaning:** Warrior
**Origin:** Scandinavian
**Pronunciation:** EYE gore
**Description:** The name Igor derives from the English name George and is very common in Polish-, German- and Russian-speaking countries. It can also be considered a variation of the Irish, Welsh and Scottish name Ivor.
**Alternative spellings:** Egor

## Ihsan

**Meaning:** Perfection
**Origin:** Arabic
**Pronunciation:** ih SAHN
**Description:** In Islamic belief the concept of ihsan is to take your inner faith and project it into the world by performing deeds and

154

duties. The word Ihsan is also found in Hindu belief where it can refer to the third eye of the deity Shiva. As a baby name it means 'perfection'.
**Alternative spellings:** Isaan, Isan

## Ike
**Meaning:** Laughter
**Origin:** English
**Pronunciation:** IYKE
**Description:** Ike is the shortened version of the name Isaac, and as such, shares the same meaning of 'laughter'.

## Ikram
**Meaning:** Honour
**Origin:** Arabic
**Pronunciation:** ih KRAM
**Description:** Although the name Ikram is unisex, the masculine version is usually spelt Ikraam. The name comes from an Arabic word meaning 'honour' and is mainly found used by Muslim parents.
**Alternative spellings:** Ickram, Ikraam

## Ilias
**Meaning:** The Lord is my God
**Origin:** Hebrew
**Pronunciation:** IH lee as
**Description:** Ilias is an uncommon name of Hebrew and Arabic origin. It is a variant of Ilyas and Elijah. The name is somewhat popular in Greece.
**Alternative spellings:** Elijah, Ilyas

## Illyrius
**Meaning:** Cyclops
**Origin:** Greek
**Pronunciation:** ill LYE ree us

**Description:** In Greek mythology, Illyrius was the son of the cyclops Polyphemus.
**Alternative spellings:** Illirius, Illiryus

## Imad
**Meaning:** Pillar
**Origin:** Arabic
**Pronunciation:** EE mahd; IH mad
**Description:** Imad is an uncommon boys' given name of Arabic origin. The name generally refers to Allah being a pillar or source of great strength.
**Alternative spellings:** Ihmad, Imaad

## Imam
**Meaning:** Leader
**Origin:** Arabic
**Pronunciation:** EE mam
**Description:** The word imam refers to a leader within the Islamic faith. It could refer to someone claiming to be descended from Muhammad or to a leader of a Muslim community.
**Alternative spellings:** Emam, Imaam

## Iman
**Meaning:** Faith
**Origin:** Arabic
**Pronunciation:** EE man
**Description:** The name Iman came about as a shortened form of the name Immanuel, itself a variant of the name Emmanuel. The names carry separate meanings although they are both related to faith. Iman originated as a boys' name but is now often found on girls.
**Alternative spellings:** Eman, Imaan

I

## Imran

**Meaning:** Glorious nation
**Origin:** Arabic
**Pronunciation:** EEM ran
**Description:** This name is a spelling variation from the Hebrew name Amran. The name also derives from the Quran, where the grandfather of Jesus is noted to be called Imran.
**Alternative spellings:** Amran, Imaran

## Indiana

**Meaning:** India
**Origin:** English
**Pronunciation:** in dee AHR nah; in dee ANN ah
**Description:** Indiana is an elaboration on the feminine name India. However, Indiana is the name of the male character from the Indiana Jones franchise.
**Alternative spellings:** Indianah, Indyana

## Inigo

**Meaning:** Unknowing
**Origin:** Spanish
**Pronunciation:** EE ne go
**Description:** Inigo is a boys' name popular in Spain. The name is derived from Ignatius, which is thought to come from the Roman name Egnatius, meaning 'unknowing' in Latin.
**Alternative spellings:** Eneko, Inego, Ingo

## Ioan

**Meaning:** Gift from God
**Origin:** Welsh
**Pronunciation:** yo AN
**Description:** Ioan is the Welsh version of the popular baby name John. It has been popular in Wales for many years, although has only recently become popular in other countries.

## Iolo

**Meaning:** Handsome lord
**Origin:** Welsh
**Pronunciation:** eye OH lo
**Description:** Iolo is the diminutive of Iorwerth, a Welsh boys' name meaning 'handsome lord'. This name is sometimes used as a Welsh form of Edward.
**Alternative spellings:** Iolyn, Iorwerth

## Iona

See entry in 'Names for Baby Girls A–Z'

## Iosif

**Meaning:** God shall add another son
**Origin:** Romanian
**Pronunciation:** yo SEEF
**Description:** Iosif is the Russian, Romanian and Greek form of the biblical name Joseph. The name itself means 'God shall add another son'. It was an important biblical name, although it was uncommon in Britain until the mid-17th century.
**Alternative spellings:** Yosif, Yousif

## Irfan

**Meaning:** Wisdom
**Origin:** Arabic
**Pronunciation:** EER fahn
**Description:** Irfan is an uncommon boys' given name of Arabic origin, meaning 'wisdom' or 'wise one'.
**Alternative spellings:** Irfahn, Irrfan

## Isaac

**Meaning:** To laugh
**Origin:** Hebrew
**Pronunciation:** EYE zak
**Description:** Isaac is a biblical name borne by the son of Abraham, who was close to being sacrificed by his father. Instead, a ram was sacrificed, as Abraham had proven his devotion to God.
**Alternative spellings:** Isaak, Isack, Issac, Izaak

## Isha

**Meaning:** The Lord
**Origin:** Sanskrit
**Pronunciation:** Ee Shaa
**Description:** Isha can be used as a girls' or boys' name and is often found in India. As a feminine name it means 'woman' and is the name of the goddess Durga, whereas in the male form it means 'the Lord'.
**Alternative spellings:** Esha, Ishah

## Ishaan

**Meaning:** Guardian of the sun
**Origin:** Sanskrit
**Pronunciation:** ee sh AAAN
**Description:** This male name is predominantly used in Indian speaking countries. It is also a variation of the name Ishan, which can also be spelt Isan. Within the Hindu tradition Ishan is the guardian of the North East and is often associated with Lord Shiva. The Indian meaning of this name is 'guardian of the sun'.
**Alternative spellings:** Ishan

## Ishaaq

**Meaning:** To laugh
**Origin:** Muslim
**Pronunciation:** ee SHAACK
**Description:** Ishaaq is the Muslim version of the biblical name Isaac, meaning 'to laugh'. Isaac is a biblical name borne by the son of Abraham, who was close to being sacrificed by his father until God changed his mind. Instead, a ram was sacrificed, as Abraham had proven his devotion.
**Alternative spellings:** Isaac, Issac

## Ishan

**Meaning:** The Lord Vishnu; sun guardian
**Origin:** Sanskrit
**Pronunciation:** ee SHAN
**Description:** Ishan is an increasingly popular Hindi boys' name of Sanskrit origin and the male form of the name Ishana.
**Alternative spellings:** Eshaan, Ishaan

## Ishaq

**Meaning:** To laugh
**Origin:** Hebrew
**Pronunciation:** EES hak
**Description:** Ishaq is the Arabic variant of the Hebrew name Isaac, which is said to mean 'to laugh'.
**Alternative spellings:** Ishak

## Isaiah

**Meaning:** Salvation of the Lord
**Origin:** Aramaic
**Pronunciation:** eye ZYE ah
**Description:** Isaiah is a biblical name, and was the name given to one of the sons of Amos. It has slowly been growing in popularity in recent years.
**Alternative spellings:** Issaiah, Isaia

## Ismaeel

**Meaning:** God will hear
**Origin:** Hebrew
**Pronunciation:** ees ma EHL
**Description:** Ismaeel is a variant of the Arabic name Ishmael, which is of Hebrew origin and means 'God will hear'. It is often seen as religious as Ishmael is said to have built the temple of Kaaba in Mecca.
**Alternative spellings:** Ishmaeel, Ishmael, Ishmail, Ismael, Ismail

## Israel

**Meaning:** God will conquer
**Origin:** Hebrew
**Pronunciation:** IZ rale
**Description:** Israel is used in the Bible as the name of the land of Israel, and is now the name of a state in the Middle East tracing its roots back to this biblical land. It is now used as a unisex given name.
**Alternative spellings:** Israelle, Israil

## Issa

**Meaning:** Salvation
**Origin:** African
**Pronunciation:** Ess ah
**Description:** Issa is a variant of the African name Essa, meaning 'salvation' or 'protection'. It is a unisex name.
**Alternative spellings:** Essa, Essah

## Ivan

**Meaning:** God is gracious
**Origin:** Hebrew
**Pronunciation:** EYE van
**Description:** Ivan is the Slavic version of the English name John. Widely used in Russia, it was the name of many rulers, including the infamous 'Ivan the Terrible'.
**Alternative spellings:** Eivan

## Ivo

**Meaning:** Yew
**Origin:** French
**Pronunciation:** EE voh
**Description:** Ivo is an uncommon name of French and German origin. It is a form of the French name Yves.
**Alternative spellings:** Ivoh, Yvo

## Ivor

**Meaning:** Bow warrior; archer
**Origin:** Norse
**Pronunciation:** EYE vor
**Description:** Ivor is an Old Norse name that is made up of the elements 'yr' meaning 'bow' and 'arr' meaning 'warrior'. Together, it creates the name's meaning of 'bow warrior'. It was brought to Britain by Scandinavian settlers in the Middle Ages.
**Alternative spellings:** Ivorr

## Iwan

**Meaning:** God is gracious
**Origin:** Welsh
**Pronunciation:** EE wan
**Description:** Iwan is the Welsh variation of Ivan, which itself comes from the Hebrew name John. Iwan is quite an unusual name as its variants Evan or Ivan are more popular.
**Alternative spellings:** Ewan, Iwun

## Izaan

**Meaning:** Obedience
**Origin:** Arabic
**Pronunciation:** IZ aan
**Description:** Izaan is an uncommon Arabic name for boys meaning 'obedience' and 'disciplined'.
**Alternative spellings:** Izan, Izzan

# J

## Jac
**Meaning:** God is gracious
**Origin:** Hebrew
**Pronunciation:** jak
**Description:** Jac is an alternative spelling of the popular baby name Jack, which itself was a pet form of John. Whilst Jac is not a common version of the spelling, it has grown in popularity in the UK.
**Alternative spellings:** Jack

## Jace
**Meaning:** Healer
**Origin:** Greek
**Pronunciation:** JAYSS
**Description:** Jace is a name of Greek origin. The name is increasingly popular as a modern variant form of Jason, which has been in vogue in recent years, along with its counterpart, Jase.
**Alternative spellings:** Jase, Jayce

## Jack
**Meaning:** God is gracious
**Origin:** Hebrew
**Pronunciation:** JAK
**Description:** Jack was originally a pet form of John, but is now a well-established given name in its own right. It is also sometimes used as an informal pet form of James, perhaps influenced by the French form Jacques. It has been an extremely popular boys' name in England and Wales since 1995.
**Alternative spellings:** Jak, Jac

## Jackson
**Meaning:** Son of Jack
**Origin:** English
**Pronunciation:** JAX sun
**Description:** Jackson originated as a surname, which meant 'son of Jack', but is now used as a first name in its own right.
**Alternative spellings:** Jakson, Jaxon

## Jacob
**Meaning:** Supplanter
**Origin:** Hebrew
**Pronunciation:** JAY cobb
**Description:** From the Hebrew name Yaakov. Jacob is a biblical name borne by the cunning son of Isaac and Rebecca. The name has experienced a recent popularity boost due to the character Jacob in the successful Twilight franchise.
**Alternative spellings:** Jacub, Jakob, Jakub

## Jacobi
**Meaning:** Supplanter
**Origin:** Hebrew
**Pronunciation:** jah COH bee
**Description:** Jacobi is the Ashkenazic Jewish version of the name Jacob and as such, shares the same meaning of 'supplanter'.
**Alternative spellings:** Jacoby

## Jacques
**Meaning:** He who supplants
**Origin:** French
**Pronunciation:** ZHA hk
**Description:** Jacques is a popular French name and the French variant of James. It is derived from the Latin name Iacobus, which is now commonly referred to as Jacob.

**Alternative spellings:** Jacque, Jaq, Jaques

## Jad

**Meaning:** Benevolent
**Origin:** Arabic
**Pronunciation:** jad
**Description:** Jad is an Arabic boys' name meaning 'benevolent'. It is also the short form of the name Jadallah.
**Alternative spellings:** Jaad

## Jadon

**Meaning:** Thankful
**Origin:** Hebrew
**Pronunciation:** JAY don
**Description:** Jadon is a common boys' name that has become increasingly popular in America. The name has many variant forms, all originally more common as surnames, which in recent years have been used as given names.
**Alternative spellings:** Jaden, Jaeden, Jaedon, Jaidin, Jaidon, Jaydan, Jayden, Jaydon

## Jago

**Meaning:** Supplanter
**Origin:** Cornish
**Pronunciation:** jay GOH
**Description:** Jago is the Cornish version of the name Jacob. From the Hebrew Yaakov, Jacob was borne by the biblical father of twelve sons, who gave their names to the 12 tribes of Israel. Son of Isaac and Rebecca and twin brother of Esae, Jacob was the cunning younger twin who tricked his brother into trading his inheritance for a bowl of soup. He later tricked his blind, dying father into blessing him instead of Esau.
**Alternative spellings:** Jaygo

## Jaheim

**Meaning:** Raised up
**Origin:** Hebrew
**Pronunciation:** yah HEEM
**Description:** Jaheim is a name of Hebrew origin, meaning 'raised up'. The name is somewhat popular in America.
**Alternative spellings:** Jahaim, Jaheem

## Jai

**Meaning:** Champion
**Origin:** Sanskrit
**Pronunciation:** JAY
**Description:** Jai could be the short form of names such as Jaimal, but it is also a name in its own right. Although its meaning is 'champion' when used as a given name, it changes into 'chatty' when used as a pet name.
**Alternative spellings:** Jay

## Jaiden

**Meaning:** Champion
**Origin:** Greek
**Pronunciation:** JAY den
**Description:** The name Jaiden is thought to be a fairly modern creation, perhaps a combination of the names Hayden and Jai, meaning 'champion'. Although there is a similar Hebrew name, Jadon, there is not thought to be any relation between this and the modern name Jaiden, which only became popular in about the late 1990s.
**Alternative spellings:** Jadan, Jaden, Jadon, Jaidan, Jaidon, Jaydan, Jayden, Jaydon

## Jak

**Meaning:** Gracious is the Lord
**Origin:** Hebrew
**Pronunciation:** jak
**Description:** Jak is a spelling variant of the name Jack, which is derived as a pet form of the name John. John is Hebrew in origin and means 'gracious is the Lord'. Jak is the more unusual spelling of the name, and the version Jack has been one of the most popular names in Britain for quite some time.
**Alternative spellings:** Jac, Jack

## Jake

**Meaning:** God is gracious
**Origin:** Hebrew
**Pronunciation:** JAYK
**Description:** Jake is a variant of the name Jack but also a name in its own right. The name re-turned to fashion in the 1990s and may be used as a short form for Jacob.
**Alternative spellings:** Jaike, Jayk

## Jakob

**Meaning:** He who grasps the heel
**Origin:** Hebrew
**Pronunciation:** yah KUB
**Description:** Jakob, also seen spelt Jakub, can be seen as a Czech, Polish or Slovakian take on the Hebrew name Jacob. The Hebrew translation of the name Jacob is 'he who grasps the heel'. In the Bible, Jacob was an ancestor of the tribes of Israel.
**Alternative spellings:** Jacob, Jakub

## Jalen

**Meaning:** No meaning
**Origin:** American
**Pronunciation:** JAY len
**Description:** Jalen is a modern American invention and, for this reason, has no meaning attached to it.
**Alternative spellings:** Jalan, Jalon, Jaylen, Jaylan, Jaylon

## Jamal

**Meaning:** Handsome
**Origin:** Arabic
**Pronunciation:** ja MAHL
**Description:** Jamal is often found as a surname as well as a given name. It has associations with male beauty.
**Alternative spellings:** Jamaal, Jamall, Jameel, Jamel, Jamil

## James

**Meaning:** Supplanter
**Origin:** English
**Pronunciation:** JAY mes
**Description:** The English form of the name borne in the New Testa-ment by two of Christ's disciples, James son of Zebedee and James son of Alphaeus. James is a royal name in Britain associated with James I of Scotland.
**Alternative spellings:** Jaimes, Jaymes

## Jamie

**Meaning:** Supplanter
**Origin:** Hebrew
**Pronunciation:** JAY mee
**Description:** Originally a pet form of James; Jamie is now a common given name for both boys and girls.
**Alternative spellings:** Jaime, Jaimey, Jaimi, Jaimie, Jaimy, Jamey, Jaymey, Jaymi, Jaymie

**J**

## Jan

**Meaning:** Gift from God
**Origin:** Scandinavian
**Pronunciation:** jan; yan
**Description:** Jan has been a popular name across Scandinavia for many years, and is said to mean 'Gift from God' it could possibly originally derive from a Hebrew name. It is also a common nickname for women with the name Janet for example. Jan Molby is a former footballer.
**Alternative spellings:** Jann

## Jared

**Meaning:** He descends
**Origin:** Hebrew
**Pronunciation:** JAH red
**Description:** Jared is a biblical name, taken from the Old Testament. He was a descendant of Adam, and lived for many years.

## Jarvis

**Meaning:** Spear man
**Origin:** English
**Pronunciation:** JAAR vis
**Description:** Jarvis is the English form of the German last name Gervais, which in turn comes from the uncommon name Gervasius. The meaning of the names is derived from the Germanic element of 'ger,' meaning 'spear'.

## Javier

**Meaning:** The new house
**Origin:** Spanish
**Pronunciation:** HAV yer
**Description:** Javier is the Spanish form of the name Xavier. Both names come from the Catholic saint, Francis de Xavier, where Xavier is his birthplace. The place name comes from the word 'etxaberri,' which in Basque means 'new house'.
**Alternative spellings:** Xavier

## Jason

**Meaning:** Healer
**Origin:** Greek
**Pronunciation:** JAY sun
**Description:** Jason comes from the Greek name Iason, borne by the mythological hero and leader of the Argonauts. The name comes from the Greek word 'iasthai', meaning 'to heal'.
**Alternative spellings:** Jaison, Jayson

## Jasper

**Meaning:** Treasurer
**Origin:** Persian
**Pronunciation:** JASS per
**Description:** Jasper is the modern English form of Casper, the name of one of the three wise men (or Magi) who brought gifts to Jesus Christ at his birth.
**Alternative spellings:** Jaspar

## Jawad

**Meaning:** Generous
**Origin:** Arabic
**Pronunciation:** jah WAHD
**Description:** Jawad is an Arabic word meaning 'open-handed' or 'generous'. It can also be used as a name, though it is uncommon. Jawad is said to be one of the names used to describe Muhammad. It is also the name of a town in India.
**Alternative spellings:** Jahwad, Jawaad, Jawahd

## Jax

**Meaning:** Son of Jack
**Origin:** English
**Pronunciation:** JACKS
**Description:** Jax is a modern shortened form of the English name Jackson, which literally means 'son of Jack'. It is often given as a nickname to boys named Jack.
**Alternative spellings:** Jacks, Jaxx

## Jaxon

**Meaning:** Son of Jack
**Origin:** English
**Pronunciation:** JAX sun
**Description:** The name Jaxon can be seen as a variant of the name Jason or a variant spelling of the name Jackson.
**Alternative spellings:** Jackson, Jakson, Jaxson, Jaxxson

## Jay

**Meaning:** Victory
**Origin:** Sanskrit
**Pronunciation:** JAY
**Description:** Jay is an Indian name meaning 'victory' in Sanskrit. It can also be seen as a shortened form of names beginning with J, like Jason. Although it is most commonly found as a boys' name, it is unisex.
**Alternative spellings:** Jai

## Jaya

**Meaning:** Victory
**Origin:** Sanskrit
**Pronunciation:** JAY ah
**Description:** Jaya is a unisex name originating from a Sanskrit word meaning 'victorious'. In Hindu belief Jaya is one of the gatekeepers of the domain of the god Vishnu.
**Alternative spellings:** Jaia

## Jayce

**Meaning:** Healer
**Origin:** Greek
**Pronunciation:** jays
**Description:** Jayce is a different spelling of the name Jace, which in turn is a shortened form of the Greek name Jason. The name comes from the Greek name Iason, borne by the mythological hero and leader of the Argonauts, who sailed to Colchis to discover the golden fleece. Jason fell in love with sorceress Medea during this adventure, but was later killed by a timber beam falling from his ship the *Argo*. The name comes from the Greek word '*iasthai*,' meaning 'to heal'.
**Alternative spellings:** Jaice, Jays

## Jayden

**Meaning:** Thankful
**Origin:** Hebrew
**Pronunciation:** JAY den
**Description:** Jayden is a very popular boys' name in America and originates from the Hebrew name Jadon.
**Alternative spellings:** Jadan, Jaden, Jadon, Jaidan, Jaiden, Jaidon, Jaydan, Jaydon

## Jaylan

**Meaning:** Calm
**Origin:** Hebrew
**Pronunciation:** JAY lan
**Description:** Jaylan is a unisex name that has seen increased popularity in America in recent years. It is a modern variant of Jaylen, which descends from Jalon who was a descendant of Judah.

**J**

163

**Alternative spellings:** Jaelan, Jaelon, Jailan, Jalan, Jaylen, Jaylon

## Jean
See entry in 'Names for Baby Girls A–Z'

## Jed
**Meaning:** Loved by God
**Origin:** Hebrew
**Pronunciation:** JED
**Description:** The name Jed was originally used as a pet form of the name Jedidiah. This name is first seen in the Bible and derives from the element of *'yahew'*, which means 'beloved'.
**Alternative spellings:** Jedd

## Jedidiah
**Meaning:** Beloved of Yahweh
**Origin:** Hebrew
**Pronunciation:** jed I DIE ya
**Description:** Jedidiah is a Hebrew name, derived from the name Yedidyah, meaning 'beloved of Yahweh'. In the Old Testament, this was a name given by God to Solomon, who is King David's second son.

## Jeevan
**Meaning:** Life; bringer of life
**Origin:** Indian
**Pronunciation:** jee VAAN
**Description:** Jeevan is a male Indian given name meaning 'life' or 'bringer of life'. It comes from the Sanskrit language but is most often a Punjabi name.
**Alternative spellings:** Jevan

## Jeffrey
**Meaning:** God's peace

**Origin:** English
**Pronunciation:** JEFF rey
**Description:** Jeffrey is a common English boys' name. The name Geoffrey is the precursor to Jeffrey, from the German word *Gottfried* meaning 'God's peace'.
**Alternative spellings:** Geoffrey, Jeffery, Jeffory, Jefrey, Jeffry

## Jem
**Meaning:** He who supplants
**Origin:** English
**Pronunciation:** JEM
**Description:** Jem is an uncommon boys' name, often used as a nickname for James or Jeremy. It is a variant of the Hebrew name James, meaning 'he who supplants'.
**Alternative spellings:** Gem, Jemm

## Jensen
**Meaning:** Son of Johannes
**Origin:** Scandinavian
**Pronunciation:** JEN son
**Description:** The name Jensen has Scandinavian roots and is said to mean 'son of Jens'. It could also be the Scandinavian version of the surname Johnson. Jensen is part of a group of surnames growing popular as first names.
**Alternative spellings:** Jenson, Jensun

## Jenson
**Meaning:** Son of Jan
**Origin:** Scandinavian
**Pronunciation:** jen SUN
**Description:** Jenson is an unusual name, it that is hard to find much history of its usage. It can be traced back to Scandinavia, and is thought to be a variation

on the name Janson, which literally means 'son of Jan'. It is rare as
a first name, but does occur as a
boys' name, although more commonly it is a surname.
**Alternative spellings:** Jensen

# Jeremiah
**Meaning:** Appointed by God
**Origin:** Hebrew
**Pronunciation:** jer eh MY yah
**Description:** Jeremiah has biblical
associations as the name of the
prophet Jeremiah. He wrote the
Book of Jeremiah and it is also
believed that he wrote the Book of
Lamentations.
**Alternative spellings:** Jeremia,
Jerimiah

# Jeremy
**Meaning:** Appointed by God
**Origin:** Hebrew
**Pronunciation:** JEH ruh me
**Description:** Jeremy is an angli-
cised form of the biblical name
Jeremiah. The name Jeremy may
be seen in the Authorised Version
of the New Testament.
**Alternative spellings:** Jeremey,
Jeremie

# Jermaine
See entry in 'Names for Baby Girls
A–Z'

# Jerome
**Meaning:** Sacred name
**Origin:** Greek
**Pronunciation:** jeh ROME
**Description:** The name Jerome
comes from the biblical word
'*hieros*', which means 'holy' or
'sacred', and also the word '*onoma*',
which means 'name'.

**Alternative spellings:** Gerome,
Jerrome

# Jerry
**Meaning:** Spear ruler
**Origin:** English
**Pronunciation:** JEH ree
**Description:** Jerry is a unisex given
name of Old English origin. It is the
modern diminutive form of Gerald.
**Alternative spellings:** Gerri,
Gerrie, Gerry, Jerri, Jerrie

# Jess
See entry in 'Names for Baby Girls
A–Z'

# Jesse
**Meaning:** Gift
**Origin:** Hebrew
**Pronunciation:** JESS ee
**Description:** Jesse is a unisex
name originally borne by the father of King David, meaning 'gift'
in Hebrew. The more common
spelling of 'Jesse' is used for boys;
however Jessie is sometimes seen.
**Alternative spellings:** Jessie

# Jethro
**Meaning:** Pre-eminence
**Origin:** Hebrew
**Pronunciation:** JETH ro
**Description:** Jethro is an uncom-
mon name of Hebrew origin,
meaning 'pre-eminence'.
**Alternative spellings:** Jethroe,
Jethrow

# Jett
**Meaning:** Black gemstone
**Origin:** English
**Pronunciation:** JET
**Description:** Jett is a common
surname in America and has

**J**

recently become a more popular given name in English-speaking countries.
**Alternative spellings:** Jet

## Jibril
**Meaning:** Angel
**Origin:** Arabic
**Pronunciation:** jib RIL
**Description:** Jibril is an uncommon Arabic boys' given name. In Abrahamic religions, Gabriel (transliterated in Arabic as Jibril) is an angel who typically serves as a messenger to humans from God.
**Alternative spellings:** Gibral, Jibra'il

## Jim
**Meaning:** Supplanter
**Origin:** Hebrew
**Pronunciation:** JIM
**Description:** Jim is a shortened form of James and is now seen as a name in its own right.
**Alternative spellings:** Jym

## Jimmy
**Meaning:** Supplanter
**Origin:** Hebrew
**Pronunciation:** JIM ee
**Description:** Jimmy is a pet form of either James or Jim.
**Alternative spellings:** Jimmi, Jimmie

## Joachim
**Meaning:** Established by God
**Origin:** Hebrew
**Pronunciation:** wa KEEM
**Description:** Comes from the Hebrew name Johoiachin. Joaquin is a common modern spelling variant of this name. It was believed that Joachim was

the name of the Virgin Mary's father in medieval Catholic tradition.
**Alternative spellings:** Jachim, Joaquin

## Joan
See entry in 'Names for Baby Girls A–Z'.

## Joao
**Meaning:** God has given
**Origin:** Portuguese
**Pronunciation:** zh WOW
**Description:** Joao is the Portuguese form of the common boys' name John, which means 'God has given'. The name is a prominent one in the Bible and is of great importance to early Christianity, since it was borne by many saints. It is also the name of 23 popes.

## Jobey
**Meaning:** Persecuted
**Origin:** Hebrew
**Pronunciation:** joe BEE
**Description:** Jobey is a Hebrew name meaning 'persecuted' and is also a variation of the name Joby. This name can also be used for girls.
**Alternative spellings:** Joby

## Jocelyn
See entry in 'Names for Baby Girls A–Z'.

## Jody
**Meaning:** From Judea
**Origin:** English
**Pronunciation:** JO dee
**Description:** Jody is a unisex name evolving from numerous

other names such as George, Jude and Joseph. It is thought to mean 'from Judea' as it is similar to the name Jude.
**Alternative spellings:** Jodi, Jodie

## Joe
**Meaning:** The Lord gave more
**Origin:** Hebrew
**Pronunciation:** JO
**Description:** Joe is the shortened form of the Hebrew name Joseph, but is now a given name in its own right.

## Joel
**Meaning:** One true God
**Origin:** Hebrew
**Pronunciation:** JOLE
**Description:** Joel is a biblical name borne by one of King David's 'mighty men', and a prophet in the 8th century BC. Largely popular as a Jewish name, Joel has enjoyed success across the English-speaking world.
**Alternative spellings:** Jole

## Joey
**Meaning:** The Lord gave more
**Origin:** Hebrew
**Pronunciation:** JO ee
**Description:** Joey is a pct form of Joe or Joseph, as well as an independent given name. It is also the name of a baby kangaroo.
**Alternative spellings:** Joeiy

## Johann
**Meaning:** God is gracious
**Origin:** Hebrew
**Pronunciation:** YO hahn
**Description:** Johann is a name of Hebrew origin, meaning 'God is

gracious'. It is the German form of Johan, which is derived from John.
**Alternative spellings:** Johan, Johanne

## John
**Meaning:** God is gracious
**Origin:** Hebrew
**Pronunciation:** JON
**Description:** The name John was of great importance in early Christianity. It was borne by John the Baptist and John the Apostle. The name was also borne by many saints and by 23 popes. In its various forms in different languages, it has been the most perennially popular of all Christian names.
**Alternative spellings:** Jon, Jonne

## Johnathan
**Meaning:** Gift of God
**Origin:** Hebrew
**Pronunciation:** JON er thun
**Description:** Johnathan is a variant of the popular boys' name Jonathan. Both are of Hebrew origin and have strong links with the Bible. Jonathan was the son of King Saul and was noted for his manliness, generosity and unselfishness.
**Alternative spellings:** Jonathan, Jonathon, Jonothon

## Johnny
**Meaning:** God is gracious
**Origin:** Hebrew
**Pronunciation:** JON nee
**Description:** Johnny originally came about as a pet form of the name John; however it is now

**J**

found as a given name in its own right.
**Alternative spellings:** Johnni, Johnnie, Jonni, Jonnie, Jonny

## Jokubas
**Meaning:** Supplanter
**Origin:** Lithuanian
**Pronunciation:** jok OO bas
**Description:** Jokubas is the Lithuanian version of the name Jacob. The name means 'supplanter' and is from the Hebrew, Yaakov. Jacob was borne by the biblical father of 12 sons, who gave their names to the 12 tribes of Israel. Son of Isaac and Rebecca and twin brother of Esae, Jacob was the cunning younger twin who tricked his brother into trading his inheritance for a bowl of soup. He later tricked his blind, dying father into blessing him instead of Esau.

## Jolyon
**Meaning:** Youthful; soft-haired
**Origin:** Latin
**Pronunciation:** jolee ON
**Description:** Jolyon is a variation of the names Julian and Julien, and as such shares the same meaning of 'youthful' and 'soft-haired'.

## Jon
**Meaning:** Gracious Lord
**Origin:** Hebrew
**Pronunciation:** jon
**Description:** Jon was the shortened form of the Latin Johannes, before it became John. John is a Hebrew name meaning 'Gracious Lord'. Although the version spelt John is more popular in modern times, both of the spellings can be found in Britain and the name

in general is and has been one of the most popular boys' names for many years.
**Alternative spellings:** John

## Jonah
**Meaning:** Peace
**Origin:** Hebrew
**Pronunciation:** JOE nah
**Description:** The name Jonah features in the Bible in the legendary tale of Jonah and the whale. Yonah is the original form of this name and influences how it is pronounced in some languages.
**Alternative spellings:** Jona, Yonah

## Jonas
**Meaning:** Peace
**Origin:** Hebrew
**Pronunciation:** YOH nas
**Description:** Jonas is the Greek variation of the Hebrew name Jonah, seen in the Old Testament. It can also be found as a surname.
**Alternative spellings:** Jonass, Jonasse

## Jonty
**Meaning:** Gift of God
**Origin:** Hebrew
**Pronunciation:** JON tay
**Description:** Jonty is an American variant of Jonte, which is derived from the Hebrew name Jonathan. It is often given as a nickname to boys named Jonathan but has recently become a stand-alone name.
**Alternative spellings:** Johntay, Jonte, Jontey

## Jordan
**Meaning:** Flowing down
**Origin:** Hebrew
**Pronunciation:** JOR den

**Description:** The unisex name Jordan was originally given to children baptised using the holy water from the River Jordan. It is also the name of a country.
**Alternative spellings:** Jorden, Jordon, Jordun, Jordyn

## Jorge
**Meaning:** Farmer
**Origin:** Greek
**Pronunciation:** JORJ
**Description:** Jorge is a phonetically spelt variation of the popular name George, meaning 'farmer'. The variant Jorge is more widely found in Europe but is gaining popularity in the UK.
**Alternative spellings:** George, Jeorge

## Jose
**Meaning:** The Lord gave more
**Origin:** Hebrew
**Pronunciation:** ho ZAY
**Description:** Jose is the Spanish form of the Hebrew name Joseph, which means 'the Lord gave more'.
**Alternative spellings:** Josay

## Joseph
**Meaning:** The Lord gave more
**Origin:** Hebrew
**Pronunciation:** JO zeff
**Description:** English form of the biblical Hebrew name Yosef, meaning 'the Lord gave more', often in reference to having another son. This was borne by the favourite son of Jacob in the Bible. The name is still very popular today.
**Alternative spellings:** Josef, Joseff, Josif, Joszef, Jozef

## Josh
**Meaning:** God is salvation
**Origin:** Hebrew
**Pronunciation:** JOSH
**Description:** Josh originally came about as a pet name of Joshua but is now found as a given name in its own right.
**Alternative spellings:** Joshe

## Joshua
**Meaning:** God is salvation
**Origin:** Hebrew
**Pronunciation:** JOH shoo ah
**Description:** Borne in the Bible by the Israelite leader who took command of the Children of Israel after the death of Moses. The name enjoyed a great surge of popularity in the 1990s.
**Alternative spellings:** Jeshua

## Jovan
**Meaning:** The supreme God
**Origin:** Latin
**Pronunciation:** JO vahn
**Description:** Jovan is a boys' name of Latin origin that originated from the Roman supreme deity, Jupiter. It is popular in Serbia as the equivalent to the English name John.
**Alternative spellings:** Jovon, Jovun

## Jowan
**Meaning:** God has given
**Origin:** Cornish
**Pronunciation:** joh WAAN
**Description:** Jowan is the Cornish version of the common boys' name John. It is a prominent biblical name meaning 'God has given,' and is used many times in the Bible. It is also the name of many saints and 23 popes.

J

## Juan

**Meaning:** God is gracious
**Origin:** Spanish
**Pronunciation:** WAHN
**Description:** Juan is the Spanish variant of the Hebrew name John. It is a very popular name in Spain and in Spanish-speaking communities worldwide.
**Alternative spellings:** Huon, Juwan

## Judah

**Meaning:** Praised
**Origin:** Hebrew
**Pronunciation:** joo DAH
**Description:** In the Bible, Judah was the fourth of Jacob's 12 sons. The name is rising in popularity in recent years. The Greek form of the name is Judas and is very rarely used due to the infamy of the betrayer Judas Iscariot.
**Alternative spellings:** Juda, Yudah

## Jude

**Meaning:** Praise
**Origin:** Greek
**Pronunciation:** JOODE
**Description:** Jude is a short form of Judas, and is used in the Bible to distinguish between the Judas who betrayed Christ and other men of that name.
**Alternative spellings:** Jeude, Jood

## Jules

See entry in 'Names for Baby Girls A–Z'

## Julian

**Meaning:** Bearded youth
**Origin:** Latin
**Pronunciation:** JOO lee un
**Description:** Julian is derived from the Latin name 'Julius'.
**Alternative spellings:** Juliun, Julyan

## Julio

**Meaning:** Bearded youth
**Origin:** Greek
**Pronunciation:** HOO lee oh; JOO lee oh
**Description:** Julio is a Spanish form of Julius, introduced to the English-speaking world by Hispanic settlers in the US.
**Alternative spellings:** Julioh

## Julius

**Meaning:** Bearded youth
**Origin:** Latin
**Pronunciation:** JOO lee us
**Description:** Julius is a Roman family name notably borne by Julius Caesar.
**Alternative spellings:** Julyus, Yulius

## Junaid

**Meaning:** Warrior; soldier; shield
**Origin:** Arabic
**Pronunciation:** yun AID
**Description:** This name derives from the Urdu word meaning 'warrior' or 'fighter'; however, it is also believed that the name comes from the Arabic word *jund* 'meaning 'solider' or 'shield'.Either way, the name hasconnotations of strength and fighting.
**Alternative spellings:** Junade, Junaide

## Junior

**Meaning:** Son
**Origin:** English
**Pronunciation:** JOO ni uh

**Description:** Junior is a nickname used to distinguish a son from his father. It is of recent coinage as a given name and exists mostly in the United States.
**Alternative spellings:** Gunior, Juniur

## Jupiter
**Meaning:** Father god
**Origin:** Latin
**Pronunciation:** JOOP it er
**Description:** In Roman mythology, Jupiter was the king of the gods – the Latinised version of the original Greek god Zeus. It is also the name of the fifth planet from the sun and the largest planet within the solar system.
**Alternative spellings:** Joopiter, Jupyter

## Justin
**Meaning:** Fair, righteous
**Origin:** Latin
**Pronunciation:** JUS tin
**Description:** Justin is an English form of the Latin name Justinus, from 'Justus'. It was a name borne by several early saints.
**Alternative spellings:** Justen, Justinn

# K

## Kabir
**Meaning:** The Great
**Origin:** Arabic
**Pronunciation:** kah BEER
**Description:** Kabir is a common boy's name originating from the Arabic Al-Kabir, which means 'The Great' – the 37th name of God in Islam. Kabir was a mystic poet and saint of India whose writings have greatly influenced the Bhakti movement.
**Alternative spellings:** Kaabir, Kabeer

## Kade
**Meaning:** Round
**Origin:** English
**Pronunciation:** Kayd
**Description:** Kade is a different spelling of the name Cade, which comes from an Old English surname meaning 'round'.
**Alternative spellings:** Cade

## Kaden
**Meaning:** Son; spirit of battle
**Origin:** Gaelic
**Pronunciation:** KAY den
**Description:** Kaden is the popular anglicised form of Kaiden. Kaiden is Celtic in origin and is said to mean 'warrior'.
**Alternative spellings:** Caden, Cadon, Caiden, Caidon, Cayden, Caydon, Kadan, Kaden, Kaedan, Kaeden, Kaidan, Kaydan Kayden

## Kaede
See entry in 'Names for Baby Girls A–Z'

## Kaelan
**Meaning:** Slender
**Origin:** Gaelic
**Pronunciation:** KAY lan
**Description:** Kaelan is a unisex name of Gaelic origin. Its meaning is debated but some agree that it

means 'slender'. It is most commonly used for boys.
**Alternative spellings:** Caelan, Caolan, Caylan, Kaolan, Kaylan

## Kai
**Meaning:** The sea
**Origin:** Hawaiian
**Pronunciation:** KY
**Description:** Kai is a Hawaiian word meaning 'the sea'. The Welsh version of this name means 'keeper of the keys'. It has recently become more popular as a baby name in Britain.
**Alternative spellings:** Ky, Kye

## Kain
**Meaning:** Acquire
**Origin:** Hebrew
**Pronunciation:** KAYN
**Description:** Kain is an uncommon given name but a popular surname. It is a variant of Kenan, which is a Hebrew name meaning 'acquire'. It could also be considered a variant of the Gaelic name Kane.
**Alternative spellings:** Caine, Cane, Kaine, Kane, Kayne

## Kaine
**Meaning:** Spear
**Origin:** Gaelic
**Pronunciation:** KAYN
**Description:** Kaine is a variant form of the masculine Gaelic name Kane. It could also be considered a variant of the Hebrew name Cain.
**Alternative spellings:** Caine, Cane, Kaine, Kane, Kayne

## Kairo
**Meaning:** Victorious
**Origin:** Arabic
**Pronunciation:** KYE ro

**Description:** Kairo is an uncommon Arabic boys' name and is a variant of Cairo, which is also the capital of Egypt and the oldest city in the Arabic world. It is derived from 'al Qahir', which is the Arabic name of the planet Mars.
**Alternative spellings:** Cairo, Kyro

## Kairon
**Meaning:** Dark-haired
**Origin:** Gaelic
**Pronunciation:** KYE ron
**Description:** Kairon is a less popular variant of the Irish name Kieran, although the two are pronounced differently. It is also an uncommon Indian name, named after a small Indian village.
**Alternative spellings:** Kyron

## Kaiser
**Meaning:** Emperor
**Origin:** German
**Pronunciation:** KAI sur
**Description:** Kaiser is the German word for 'emperor' and refers to the title that the ruler holds. This is an unusual boys' name choice and could be a good option for more adventurous parents.

## Kaison
**Meaning:** No meaning
**Origin:** American
**Pronunciation:** KAI sun
**Description:** Kaison is an invented, modern name and as such has no meaning. It can also be spelt in a variety of different ways.
**Alternative spellings:** Kayson, Kason, Cayson, Cason

## Kajus

**Meaning:** Rejoice
**Origin:** Latin
**Pronunciation:** KAH ee us
**Description:** Kajus is a variant of the Roman surname Caius, related to the Latin term *'guadere'*, meaning 'Aelto rejoices'. The name also features in the Bible, belonging to a saint.
**Alternative spellings:** Caius, Cajus, Kaius

## Kaleb

**Meaning:** Dog
**Origin:** Hebrew
**Pronunciation:** KAY leb
**Description:** Kaleb is an alternative spelling of Caleb. It is a biblical name that means 'dog'. Caleb was one of Moses' followers, and the change to add a K at the start of the name would have been a modern construction.
**Alternative spellings:** Caleb

## Kaleem

**Meaning:** Lecturer
**Origin:** Arabic
**Pronunciation:** kah LEEM
**Description:** Kaleem is an uncommon name of Arabic origin, meaning 'lecturer'.
**Alternative spellings:** Caleem, Kahleem

## Kalen

**Meaning:** Slender
**Origin:** Gaelic
**Pronunciation:** KAY len
**Description:** Kalen is an uncommon name of Gaelic origin, meaning 'slender' or 'uncertain'.
**Alternative spellings:** Caelan, Kaelen

## Kamar

**Meaning:** The moon
**Origin:** Arabic
**Pronunciation:** KAH maar
**Description:** Kamar is an Arabic boys' name meaning 'the moon'. This name is not to be confused with Kumar, which has a different meaning.
**Alternative spellings:** Qamar

## Kamil

**Meaning:** Sacrifice
**Origin:** Arabic
**Pronunciation:** kah MEAL
**Description:** The name Kamil derives from the name Camillus, which means 'altar server'. It is most popular in Arabic-, Polish- and Czech-speaking countries.
**Alternative spellings:** Camil, Kamill

## Kamile

**Meaning:** Sacrifice
**Origin:** Italian
**Pronunciation:** kah MEEL
**Description:** Kamile is the Polish variant of the French Camille, a name used for both boys and girls that originates from Roman mythology.
**Alternative spellings:** Camile, Camille, Kamille

## Kamran

**Meaning:** Crooked nose
**Origin:** Gaelic
**Pronunciation:** CAM ren
**Description:** Kamran is one of the many spelling variations for the name Cameron. This spelling also has a Persian meaning, which is 'prosperous'.

**K**

**Alternative spellings:** Cameron, Camron, Kameron, Kamron

## Kane
**Meaning:** Battle; a spear
**Origin:** Hebrew
**Pronunciation:** KAYN
**Description:** The name Kane is a variation of Cain. In the Bible, Cain killed his brother, Abel. In English the name Cane derived from the medieval word for 'cane' or 'reed'.
**Alternative spellings:** Caine, Cane, Kaine

## Kaoru
**Meaning:** Fragrant
**Origin:** Japanese
**Pronunciation:** Kah o roo
**Description:** This name can most commonly be found in Japan and is written using only one Japanese character meaning 'fragrant'. It can be adopted as both a girls' and a boys' name.
**Alternative spellings:** Kaoruh, Kayoru

## Karam
**Meaning:** Generous
**Origin:** Arabic
**Pronunciation:** KAH raam
**Description:** This Arabic name is most commonly used for boys, but can be found as a girls' name. The name is thought to have derived from the name Karim, which can also be spelt Kareem.
**Alternative spellings:** Karaam, Kharam

## Karan
**Meaning:** Ear
**Origin:** Sanskrit
**Pronunciation:** kar AHN

**Description:** Karan is an old Indian name that has been transliterated from Sanskrit as meaning 'ear'. It is also the name of a town in Mali.
**Alternative spellings:** Kaaran, Karaan

## Karim
**Meaning:** Generous
**Origin:** Arabic
**Pronunciation:** kah REEM
**Description:** Karim is a popular name among Muslim families, thought to mean 'generous'.
**Alternative spellings:** Kareem, Kareme

## Karl
**Meaning:** Free man
**Origin:** German
**Pronunciation:** KARL
**Description:** Karl is a German variant of the English name Charles. It is also a variant spelling of the name Carl.
**Alternative spellings:** Carl

## Karol
**Meaning:** Free man
**Origin:** Latin
**Pronunciation:** KA rawl
**Description:** The name Karol comes from Carolus, the Latin form of Charles. The form Karol is rarely found in Britain.
**Alternative spellings:** Carol

## Karson
**Meaning:** Carr's son
**Origin:** English
**Pronunciation:** karr SUN
**Description:** Karson is a variation of the English name Carson. It was originally a surname given to someone who hailed

from a marshy area, or whose father had lived there. It has developed into a first name throughout history, but is rare in the UK today.
**Alternative spellings:** Carson

## Karter
**Meaning:** Cart transporter
**Origin:** English
**Pronunciation:** kar TUR
**Description:** Kartor is a modern, variant spelling of the English name Carter. Carter is taken from the surname originally given to those who transported goods in a cart. The use of the letter K breathes fresh life into the traditional name.
**Alternative spellings:** Carter

## Kasey
**Meaning:** Vigilant guard
**Origin:** Gaelic
**Pronunciation:** KAY see
**Description:** Kasey is a spelling variant of the names Casey and Kaci. It derives from the Gaelic name Cathasaigh and is popular in America and Ireland.
**Alternative spellings:** Casey, Casie, Cayce, Caycie, Caysie, Kacey, Kaci, Kacie, Kacy, Kasie, Kaycee, Kaycie, Kaysie

## Kasim
**Meaning:** Divided
**Origin:** Arabic
**Pronunciation:** kah SEEM
**Description:** Kasim is an alternative spelling of the Arabic boys' name Kassim. It is more common as a surname but has increased in popularity as a given name in recent years.

**Alternative spellings:** Kaseem, Kassim

## Kason
**Meaning:** No meaning
**Origin:** American
**Pronunciation:** kay SUN
**Description:** Kason is a different version of the name Kayson. Both names are modern American inventions and as such have no real meaning.
**Alternative spellings:** Kayson, Cason, Cayson

## Kasper
**Meaning:** Treasurer
**Origin:** Persian
**Pronunciation:** KASS per
**Description:** Kasper is a popular Danish name of Persian origin, meaning 'treasurer'.
**Alternative spellings:** Caspar, Casper, Kacper, Kaspar

## Kay
See entry in 'Names for Baby Girls A–Z'

## Kaya
See entry in 'Names for Baby Girls A–Z'

## Kayan
**Meaning:** High status
**Origin:** Persian
**Pronunciation:** kai YAAN
**Description:** Kayan is a Persian name meaning 'high status,' referring to someone who is important. It also has Indian connections, and in Hindi the name means 'name of a dynasty of King Kaikobad'.
**Alternative spellings:** Cayan

## Kayd

**Meaning:** Barrel maker
**Origin:** English
**Pronunciation:** KAYD
**Description:** Kayd is a modern variant of the name Cade, said to refer to a barrel maker. It is now used as a unisex name. Kayd may also be found used as an abbreviation of the masculine name Kaden, which is Celtic in origin and means 'warrior'.
**Alternative spellings:** Cade, Caid, Cayde, Kayd

## Kaylan

**Meaning:** Slender
**Origin:** Gaelic
**Pronunciation:** KAY lan
**Description:** Kaylan is a modernised and American version of the Gaelic name Caelan. Though previously uncommon, the name has increased in popularity in recent years as a given name for both boys and girls.
**Alternative spellings:** Caelan, Caolan, Caylan, Kaelan, Kaolan

## Kaylum

**Meaning:** Peace
**Origin:** Latin
**Pronunciation:** KAY lum
**Description:** Kaylum could be a variation of the name Calum, which comes from the Latin word '*columba*', meaning 'dove'. It is a very popular name in Britain, especially in Scotland.
**Alternative spellings:** Caylum

## Kayson

**Meaning:** Healer
**Origin:** Greek
**Pronunciation:** KAY sun
**Description:** Kayson is a name of Greek origin. It is a modern coinage thought to be based on the name Jason, which has become popular in recent years.
**Alternative spellings:** Cayson, Kasen, Kason

## Kazumi

**Meaning:** Beautiful harmony
**Origin:** Japanese
**Pronunciation:** Ka zoo mee
**Description:** This Japanese name is written using the characters of '*kazu*', meaning 'peace and harmony', along with '*mi*', which means 'beautiful'. It is most commonly found in Japan and can be used for both boys and girls.
**Alternative spellings:** Kazumie

## Kazuo

**Meaning:** First born
**Origin:** Japanese
**Pronunciation:** ka ZOO oh
**Description:** This Japanese name means 'first born', so is most commonly given to sons who are born first in the family.
**Alternative spellings:** Kazuoh, Kazzuo

## Keagan

**Meaning:** Fiery
**Origin:** Irish
**Pronunciation:** KEE gan
**Description:** Keagan is an Irish baby name that has connotations of fire and therefore means 'fiery'. This name would be ideal for a little redheaded baby.
**Alternative spellings:** Keegan

## Keane

**Meaning:** Ancient

**Origin:** Gaelic
**Pronunciation:** KEEN
**Description:** Keane is the pet form of the name Keenan, but is also used in its own right. Both are Gaelic in origin and are said to mean 'ancient'.
**Alternative spellings:** Kean, Keene

## Keanu

**Meaning:** Cool breeze from the mountains
**Origin:** Hawaiian
**Pronunciation:** ki AH nu
**Description:** Keanu is a Hawaiian name meaning 'cool breeze blowing down from the mountains'.
**Alternative spellings:** Kearnu

## Keaton

**Meaning:** Kite town
**Origin:** English
**Pronunciation:** KEE ton
**Description:** Keaton is of Old English origin, meaning 'shed' or 'kite town'. It is more commonly found as a surname.
**Alternative spellings:** Keeton, Keyton

## Keegan

**Meaning:** Fiery
**Origin:** Irish
**Pronunciation:** KEE gan
**Description:** Keegan is a variant spelling of the Irish name Keagan, and shares the same meaning of 'fiery'.
**Alternative spellings:** Keagan

## Keelan

**Meaning:** Graceful
**Origin:** Gaelic
**Pronunciation:** Key lan

**Description:** Keelan is the unisex version of the Gaelic name Keeley. Depending on which origin is taken, Keelan could mean 'graceful' or 'slender'.
**Alternative spellings:** Ceelan, Keylan

## Keenan

**Meaning:** Ancient
**Origin:** Gaelic
**Pronunciation:** KEE nan
**Description:** Keenan, a name that means 'ancient' or 'distant', is a more anglicised version of the Irish name Cian. Keenan is more commonly found as a surname.
**Alternative spellings:** Keenen, Keenon, Kenan

## Kei

**Meaning:** Joyful
**Origin:** Japanese
**Pronunciation:** KAY i
**Description:** Kei is a unisex name more commonly found on boys. This name was originally a pet form of the name Keiko; however, over time it has transferred into a forename in its own right.
**Alternative spellings:** Kehi

## Keir

**Meaning:** Dark-haired
**Origin:** Gaelic
**Pronunciation:** KEE er
**Description:** Keir is an uncommon boys' name of Gaelic origin. The meanings vary and include 'dusky', 'dark-haired', 'dark-skinned' and 'swarthy'.
**Alternative spellings:** Keer, Keirr

## Keith

**Meaning:** Woodland

**K**

**Origin:** Gaelic
**Pronunciation:** KEETH
**Description:** Keith is a commonly found surname, especially in Scotland, where it is considered to be aristocratic. It is also a popular given name for boys.
**Alternative spellings:** Keeth, Keyth

## Kelly

See entry in 'Names for Baby Girls A–Z'

## Kelsey

**Meaning:** Victorious ship
**Origin:** English
**Pronunciation:** KEL see
**Description:** The name Kelsey comes from the Old English word *'ceolsige',* which means 'victorious ship'. It was originally used as a surname but is now a unisex given name.
**Alternative spellings:** Kelsea, Kelsi, Kelsie, Kelsy

## Kelvin

**Meaning:** Narrow water
**Origin:** Gaelic
**Pronunciation:** KEHL vin
**Description:** Kelvin is a Gaelic boys' name meaning 'narrow water'. It is also a scientific unit for temperature, named after Scottish physicist William Thomson, Lord Kelvin, who created the measurement.
**Alternative spellings:** Calvin

## Kendrick

**Meaning:** Keen power; summit; son of Henry
**Origin:** English
**Pronunciation:** KEN drik

**Description:** Kendrick is an English surname that means 'keen power'. It is also an Old Welsh and Scottish given name where it means 'summit' and 'son of Henry' respectively.
**Alternative spellings:** Kendric, Kendrik

## Kennedy

**Meaning:** Leader
**Origin:** Gaelic
**Pronunciation:** KEH na dee
**Description:** Kennedy derives from the Gaelic element of *'ceann',* meaning 'head'. It was most likely first used as a nickname for a clan leader, before transferring to a surname. It is now a given name for both boys and girls.
**Alternative spellings:** Kenedy, Kennedey, Kennedi, Kennedie

## Kenneth

**Meaning:** Fire born; handsome
**Origin:** Gaelic
**Pronunciation:** KEN neth
**Description:** Kenneth is a popular boys' name of Gaelic origin. Kenneth derives from the Gaelic *'coinneach',* which means 'handsome', and it also means 'fire born'. Often shortened to Ken or Kenny, the name was at its highest popularity in the early 20th century and is less common since.
**Alternative spellings:** Keneth, Kennith

## Kenny

**Meaning:** Handsome
**Origin:** Gaelic
**Pronunciation:** KEH nee

**Description:** Kenny is the abbreviated form of the name Kenneth. Kenny is often found as a surname as well as a boys' first name.
**Alternative spellings:** Kennie

# Kent
**Meaning:** Border
**Origin:** English
**Pronunciation:** KENT
**Description:** Originally a surname, Kent is also a county in England. It has recently gained popularity as a boys' given name.
**Alternative spellings:** Kente

# Kenzie
**Meaning:** The fairest
**Origin:** Gaelic
**Pronunciation:** KEN zee
**Description:** Kenzie is a unisex name and is a shortened form of Mackenzie, which derives from the Gaelic surname McKenzie, originally MacCoinneach. The meaning of the name varies. For a girl it is said to mean 'the fairest' yet for a boy it means 'handsome one'.
**Alternative spellings:** Kenzee, Kenzi, Kenzy

# Kenzo
**Meaning:** Wise
**Origin:** Japanese
**Pronunciation:** KEN zo
**Description:** The name Kenzou is built from the Japanese characters for 'intelligent; wise' (*ken*) and 'three' (*zou*). The name is usually transcribed in English as Kenzo.
**Alternative spellings:** Kenzou

# Keon
**Meaning:** God is gracious

**Origin:** Gaelic
**Pronunciation:** KEE on
**Description:** Keon is a boys' name of Gaelic and Hebrew origins. It is a variant of Ewan, from John, meaning 'God is gracious'. It has risen in popularity in recent years.
**Alternative spellings:** Kion, Kyon

# Kerem
**Meaning:** Vineyard
**Origin:** Hebrew
**Pronunciation:** KER ehm
**Description:** Kerem is a unisex name of Hebrew origin, meaning 'vineyard'. It is thought to be derived from Jeremy.
**Alternative spellings:** Karim, Kereem, Kerim

# Kerry
See entry in 'Names for Baby Girls A–Z'

# Keston
**Meaning:** Area in London
**Origin:** English
**Pronunciation:** kes TUN
**Description:** Keston is a place name, specifically a town in the London Borough of Bromley and on the border of Greater London and Kent.
**Alternative spellings:** Kestin, Kesten

# Kevin
**Meaning:** Beloved
**Origin:** Gaelic
**Pronunciation:** KEH vin
**Description:** Kevin is an anglicised version of the Gaelic name Caoimhin. It is a popular name worldwide, but has fallen from the top 100 boys' names in the UK.

**K**

**Alternative spellings:** Keven, Kevyn

## Keyaan
**Meaning:** Kingly
**Origin:** Arabic
**Pronunciation:** keh YAHN
**Description:** Keyaan seems to be a masculine name of Arabic origin. Its meaning is believed to be 'kingly'.
**Alternative spellings:** Keyahn, Keyarn

## Keyan
**Meaning:** God is gracious
**Origin:** Gaelic
**Pronunciation:** kee YAN
**Description:** Keyan is a variation of the Gaelic name Kiyan, meaning 'God is gracious'. The names are in turn a variant of Ewan, from John, which means they all share the same meaning.
**Alternative spellings:** Kiyan

## Khalid
**Meaning:** Immortal; eternal
**Origin:** Arabic
**Pronunciation:** KAH leed
**Description:** Khalid is a popular name among the Arabic community and is said to mean 'immortal' or 'undying'. It has grown in popularity in the UK in recent years.

## Khalil
**Meaning:** Friend
**Origin:** Arabic
**Pronunciation:** kah LEEL
**Description:** Khalil is an Arabic name meaning 'friend'. It is rare in the UK.
**Alternative spellings:** Kalil, Khaleel

## Kian
**Meaning:** Ancient
**Origin:** Gaelic
**Pronunciation:** KI an
**Description:** Kian is the anglicised version of Cian.
**Alternative spellings:** Cian, Kean

## Killian
**Meaning:** Feisty
**Origin:** Gaelic
**Pronunciation:** KILL yan
**Description:** Killian is an alternate spelling of the Gaelic name Cillian. Both names are said to have originated with meanings associated with war, but as a given name we would assume the meaning of Cillian to be 'feisty'
**Alternative spellings:** Cillian

## Kim
See entry in 'Names for Baby Girls A–Z'

## Kimberley
See entry in 'Names for Baby Girls A–Z'

## King
**Meaning:** Leader
**Origin:** English
**Pronunciation:** king
**Description:** King can be both a given name and a surname, and is derived from the English word of the same spelling and means 'head' or 'leader'. The word itself comes from the Old English word *cyning* meaning 'tribal leader'.

## Kingsley
**Meaning:** King's meadow
**Origin:** English

**Pronunciation:** KINGS lee
**Description:** Kingsley was originally given as a surname to those who cared for the king's land. It has evolved into a first name and is very popular in the US.
**Alternative spellings:** Kingslee, Kingsleigh

## Kingston

**Meaning:** King's town
**Origin:** English
**Pronunciation:** KINGS tun
**Description:** Kingston is an uncommon name of English origin, meaning 'King's town' after the Jamaican city.
**Alternative spellings:** Kingstun

## Kip

**Meaning:** Bearer of Christ
**Origin:** English
**Pronunciation:** kip
**Description:** Kip, like Kit, is a shortened version of Christopher and as such, shares the same meaning of 'bearer of Christ'.

## Kiran

**Meaning:** Beam of light
**Origin:** Sanskrit
**Pronunciation:** KEE ran
**Description:** Kiran is a unisex name of Sanksrit origin, said to mean 'beam of light'. It could also be considered a spelling variant of the Gaelic name Kieran.
**Alternative spellings:** Ciaran, Keiran, Keiron, Kieran, Kieron

## Kieron

**Meaning:** Dark one
**Origin:** Gaelic
**Pronunciation:** KIER ron

**Description:** This name is mainly used in English-speaking countries such as America, Canada, England and Australia. This spelling is a variant of the English and Irish name Kieran. There is also a Hindi variation of this name, which is spelt Kiran. In Hindi it means 'beam of light'.
**Alternative spellings:** Kieran

## Kishan

**Meaning:** Krishna
**Origin:** Sanskrit
**Pronunciation:** kee SHAAN
**Description:** Kishan is an uncommon boys' name of Sanskrit origin. It is a modern form of Krishna, the name of a Hindu deity believed to be an incarnation of the god Vishnu.
**Alternative spellings:** Keeshan, Kishaan

## Kit

**Meaning:** Follower of Christ
**Origin:** Greek
**Pronunciation:** KIT
**Description:** Kit is an abbreviation of the name Christopher, meaning 'follower or bearer of Christ'. It is especially popular in America.
**Alternative spellings:** Kitt

## Kiva

See entry in 'Names for Baby Girls A–Z'

## Kiyan

**Meaning:** God is gracious
**Origin:** Gaelic
**Pronunciation:** KEE yan
**Description:** Kiyan is a boys' name of Gaelic and Hebrew origins. It is a variant of Ewan, from John,

**K**

meaning 'God is gracious'. It has risen in popularity in recent years.
**Alternative spellings:** Kean, Keon, Kian, Kion

## Klay
**Meaning:** Clay
**Origin:** English
**Pronunciation:** CAH lay
**Description:** Klay is a different spelling of the name Clay. Clay is a name that either exists as a shortened form of Clayton, a transferred surname or a name given to somebody who lived on clay soils.
**Alternative spellings:** Clay

## Knox
**Meaning:** Round hill
**Origin:** English
**Pronunciation:** NOX
**Description:** Knox is an unusual boys' name of Old English origin, where it originally meant 'hill with a rounded peak'.
**Alternative spellings:** Nox

## Kobe
**Meaning:** Supplanter
**Origin:** Hebrew
**Pronunciation:** koh BEE
**Description:** Kobe is a rather uncommon baby name and is likely to be a diminutive form of the name Jacob. A famous bearer of the name is Kobe Bryant, LA Lakers basketball player – although his parents chose Kobe due to the Japanese beef.
**Alternative spellings:** Kobi, Kobie, Koby, Cobe, Coby

## Kodi
**Meaning:** Helpful
**Origin:** Gaelic
**Pronunciation:** KOH dee
**Description:** Kodi is a modern variant of the common Gaelic name Cody, meaning 'helpful'. It can be used for girls and boys.
**Alternative spellings:** Codey, Codie, Cody, Kody

## Kofi
**Meaning:** Born on Friday
**Origin:** Ghanaian
**Pronunciation:** KOH fi
**Description:** Kofi is a Ghanaian boys' name signifying birth on a Friday.
**Alternative spellings:** Kofey, Kofii, Kofy

## Kohen
**Meaning:** Priest
**Origin:** Hebrew
**Pronunciation:** koe EN
**Description:** Kohen is an alternative spelling of the name Cohen, which is borne by a priest and the brother of Moses in Jewish belief. It could also be the anglicised version of the Old Irish surname Cadhan.
**Alternative spellings:** Cohen

## Kole
**Meaning:** Dark
**Origin:** English
**Pronunciation:** kole
**Description:** Kole is a variation of the common boys' name Cole, which is an English surname that was transferred into a given name. It is taken from the Old English word 'cola,' meaning 'dark complexion'. Other sources suggest the name to be a short form of the name Coleman.
**Alternative spellings:** Cole

## Konrad

**Meaning:** Bold counsel
**Origin:** German
**Pronunciation:** KON rad
**Description:** Konrad is a German name meaning 'brave', 'counsel' or 'ruler', often seen just as 'bold counsel'.
**Alternative spellings:** Conrad

## Korenl

**Meaning:** Horn
**Origin:** English
**Pronunciation:** corn EL
**Description:** Kornel is most likely a modern respelling of the traditional name Cornel, which is a diminutive of Cornelius. The name means 'horn', because it comes from the Latin element of '*cornu*'. The respelling injects an element of fresh modernity into the name.
**Alternative spellings:** Cornel

## Korey

**Meaning:** Spear
**Origin:** Norse
**Pronunciation:** KOR ree
**Description:** The name Korey is a variant of Cory, a given name common for both boys and girls in America. It comes from a surname that was possibly either derived from the Gaelic '*corra*', meaning 'spear', Old Norse given name Kori (meaning 'the chosen one') or from 'ravine' in Gaelic, 'hollow' in Irish, 'seething pool' in Scots, or 'horn' in French.
**Alternative spellings:** Coree, Corey, Corie, Cory, Koree, Kory

## Kostas

**Meaning:** Constant; steadfast
**Origin:** Greek
**Pronunciation:** kos TAS
**Description:** Kostas is a short form of the Greek name Konstantinos. The name is the Greek version of the name Constantine and means 'constant' or 'steadfast'.
**Alternative spellings:** Costas

## Krishan

**Meaning:** Black
**Origin:** Sanskrit
**Pronunciation:** KRISH an
**Description:** Krishan is a variant of the name Krishna. The spelling of the Hindu god Krishna varies from region to region. The name is said to derive from a Sanskrit word meaning 'black'.
**Alternative spellings:** Krishaan, Krishann

## Krishna

**Meaning:** Deity
**Origin:** Sanskrit
**Pronunciation:** KRISH naa
**Description:** Krishna is the name of a Hindu deity believed to be an incarnation of the god Vishnu.
**Alternative spellings:** Krishnah

## Kristian

**Meaning:** Follower of Christ
**Origin:** Latin
**Pronunciation:** KRIS ti en
**Description:** Kristian is the Scandinavian version of the name Christian. It is unisex and means 'follower of Christ'.
**Alternative spellings:** Christian, Christien, Cristian, Krystian

## Krzysztof

**Meaning:** Bearer of Christ

**K**

**Origin:** Polish
**Pronunciation:** kriss TOFF
**Description:** Krzysztof is the Polish version of the name Christoph, meaning 'bearer of Christ'. The roots of the name come from the Greek words '*christo*' referring to Christ, and 'phero' meaning to bear or carry. Early Christians used this as a metaphorical name to express how they always carry Christ in their hearts.
**Alternative spellings:** Kristophe, Christophe

## Ksawery

**Meaning:** The new house
**Origin:** Polish
**Pronunciation:** ksa VE ri
**Description:** Ksawery is the Polish version of the name Xavier, which in turn is a Hispanicised version of the Basque place name '*etcheberria*,' meaning 'the new house'.

## Kuba

**Meaning:** Supplanter
**Origin:** Polish
**Pronunciation:** kuw BAH
**Description:** Kuba may sound like Cuba (as in the Caribbean island), but it is actually a Polish diminutive of the Hebrew name Jacob, and as such shares the same meaning with it.
**Alternative spellings:** Cuba

## Kunal

**Meaning:** Lotus
**Origin:** Sanskrit
**Pronunciation:** koo NAL
**Description:** Kunal has several meanings in Sanskrit including

'lotus', 'bird with beautiful eyes' and 'one with beautiful eyes'.
**Alternative spellings:** Kunall

## Kurt

**Meaning:** Courageous
**Origin:** German
**Pronunciation:** KURT
**Description:** Kurt is a boys' name popular in America. It is a variant of Conrad, which is of Old German origin.
**Alternative spellings:** Curt, Kert

## Kurtis

**Meaning:** Considerate
**Origin:** French
**Pronunciation:** KER tiss
**Description:** Kurtis is a spelling variation of the name Curtis. Both names come from the word 'courteous'.
**Alternative spellings:** Curtis

## Kush

**Meaning:** Son of Lord Rama
**Origin:** Sanskrit
**Pronunciation:** KUSH
**Description:** Kush is a variant of Kusha, who was one of the twin sons of Lord Rama in Hindu mythology. It is an uncommon name in English-speaking countries as Kush is the name given to a strain of cannabis.
**Alternative spellings:** Koosh, Kuush

## Kyan

**Meaning:** Little king
**Origin:** English
**Pronunciation:** KYE un
**Description:** Kyan is a modern variation of the name Ryan and is especially popular in America.

**Alternative spellings:** Kyanne

# Kye
**Meaning:** Key keeper
**Origin:** Welsh
**Pronunciation:** KY
**Description:** Kye is the phonetically anglicised version of the Welsh name Kai, meaning 'keeper of the keys'. The name Kai also originates from Hawaii, where it means 'ocean'.
**Alternative spellings:** Kai, Ky

# Kylan
**Meaning:** Narrow water
**Origin:** Gaelic
**Pronunciation:** KI lan
**Description:** Kylan derives from an Irish place name, referring to a place where water becomes very narrow. It is also a variant of the name Kyle.
**Alternative spellings:** Kylanne, Kylon

# Kyle
**Meaning:** Narrow water
**Origin:** Gaelic
**Pronunciation:** KY all
**Description:** Kyle is derived from a term that means a narrow channel between two land masses.
**Alternative spellings:** Kyill

# Kylo
**Meaning:** No meaning
**Origin:** English
**Pronunciation:** KY loh
**Description:** Kylo is an invented name and as such, there is no meaning. It has grown in popularity in recent times due to the Star Wars character, Kylo Ren, played by actor Adam Driver in the film *Star Wars: The Force Awakens*.

# Kymani
**Meaning:** Adventurous traveller
**Origin:** Jamaican
**Pronunciation:** ki MAN ee
**Description:** Kymani, often written Ky-Mani, is a Jamaican boys' name. It literally means an 'adventurous traveller'.
**Alternative spellings:** Kymanee, Kymanie, Kymany

# Kyran
**Meaning:** Black
**Origin:** Gaelic
**Pronunciation:** keer AN
**Description:** Kyran is a Gaelic name that has been popular for many years, although you may recognise the alternative spelling of Keiran.
**Alternative spellings:** Keiran

# Kyron
**Meaning:** Master
**Origin:** Greek
**Pronunciation:** KYE ron
**Description:** The name Kyron derives from the Greek legend of Chiron the centaur. It is thought that the name inspired the modern name Tyrone, used widely in the UK and US. Kyron is mainly found in Europe and Russia. It could also be considered a variant spelling of the Gaelic name Kairon.
**Alternative spellings:** Kairon

**K**

# L

## Lacey
See entry in 'Names for Baby Girls A–Z'

## Lachlan
**Meaning:** Viking settler
**Origin:** Gaelic
**Pronunciation:** LAHK lin
**Description:** Lachlan is a Gaelic name originally used in Scotland as a name for the settling Vikings. It then spread to Canada and Australia, where it is particularly popular.
**Alternative spellings:** Laclan, Laklan, Lochlan

## Laertes
**Meaning:** Avenger
**Origin:** Greek
**Pronunciation:** Lye ER teez
**Description:** In Greek mythology, Laertes was the king of the Cephallenians and father of Odysseus. In Shakespeare's *Hamlet*, Laertes is the brother of Ophelia.
**Alternative spellings:** Laertees, Layertees

## Laith
**Meaning:** Lion
**Origin:** Arabic
**Pronunciation:** LAYTH
**Description:** Laith is an uncommon Arabic boys' name that means 'lion', 'strong' or 'brave'. It is more commonly seen as a surname in the Arabic world.
**Alternative spellings:** Laithe, Lathe, Layth

## Lance
**Meaning:** Land
**Origin:** French
**Pronunciation:** LANCE
**Description:** Lance is a popular boys' name of French origin, derived from the Old German name Lanzo, meaning 'land'.
**Alternative spellings:** Lanse, Lantz

## Lando
**Meaning:** Famous throughout the land
**Origin:** Italian
**Pronunciation:** lan DOH
**Description:** Lando is an Italian variation of the name Roland, meaning 'famous throughout the land'. Lando Calrissian is a character in the Star Wars franchise.

## Landon
**Meaning:** Long hill
**Origin:** English
**Pronunciation:** LAN don
**Description:** Landon is a boys' name of English origin that means 'long hill'. It is a variant of Langdon.
**Alternative spellings:** Landan, Landen

## Laney
See entry in 'Names for Baby Girls A–Z'

## Landry
**Meaning:** Land ruler
**Origin:** English
**Pronunciation:** LAN dree

**Description:** Landry is a name with English and French origins and means 'ruler'. It was imported into Britain by the Normans.
**Alternative spellings:** Landrey

## Larry

**Meaning:** Man from Laurentum
**Origin:** Latin
**Pronunciation:** LAIR ee
**Description:** Larry is a shortened version of the name Laurence, meaning 'man from Laurentum'. Both names come from the name Laurentius.

## Larson

**Meaning:** Son of Lars
**Origin:** Scandinavian
**Pronunciation:** LAAR sun
**Description:** Larson is a Scandinavian surname meaning 'son of Lars'. Lars comes from the Roman name Laurentius. This follows the contemporary trend of using last names as first names.

## Laurel

**Meaning:** Laurel
**Origin:** English
**Pronunciation:** LOH rul
**Description:** Originally Laurel was a feminine name, deriving from the Old English laurel tree. Recently the name has picked up popularity as a boys' name, possibly due to the fame of the comedy duo Laurel and Hardy.
**Alternative spellings:** Loral

## Laurence

**Meaning:** From Laurentum
**Origin:** Latin
**Pronunciation:** LOR rents

**Description:** Laurence originates from the Roman name Laurentius. It can be found as a male English name and a French feminine name.
**Alternative spellings:** Laurince, Laurynce, Lawrence, Lorence

## Laurie

**Meaning:** Victory
**Origin:** Latin
**Pronunciation:** LAW ree
**Description:** The name Laurie can be used as a unisex name, as it was originally a shortened version of the names Laura and Laurence. It is now used as a name in its own right and is seen to mean 'victory'.
**Alternative spellings:** Lauri, Laury, Lawrie, Lowry

## Lawrence

**Meaning:** Crowned with a laurel
**Origin:** French
**Pronunciation:** LOR rents
**Description:** The anglicised form of Laurence, brought to Britain during the Norman Conquest.
**Alternative spellings:** Laurence, Laurince, Laurynce, Lorence

## Lawson

**Meaning:** Son of Lawrence
**Origin:** English
**Pronunciation:** LAW sun
**Description:** Lawson is part of a group of surnames that have been adapted as a boys' given name.
**Alternative spellings:** Lawsonne, Lorson

## Layson

**Meaning:** Crowned with a laurel
**Origin:** English
**Pronunciation:** LAAY sun

L

**Description:** Layson most likely came from the name Law, as in Lawrence and as such shares the meaning of 'crowned with a laurel'. It is found as a surname but it can also be used as a given name.

## Layton
**Meaning:** Leek settlement
**Origin:** English
**Pronunciation:** LAY tun
**Description:** Layton is a modern adaption of the Old English surname Leighton, which refers to 'a settlement with leeks growing'.
**Alternative spellings:** Laiton, Leighton, Leyton, Lleyton

## Lazarus
**Meaning:** God has helped
**Origin:** Hebrew
**Pronunciation:** laaz AH rus
**Description:** Lazarus is a Hebrew surname and given name meaning 'God has helped'. He was also a figure in the Bible who was brought back from the dead by Jesus.

## Leandro
**Meaning:** Lion man
**Origin:** Spanish
**Pronunciation:** lee ANN droh
**Description:** Leander is the Spanish version of the Greek name Leander, which comes from the Greek elements of 'leon' meaning 'lion' and 'aner' meaning 'man'. In Greek mythology, Leander fell in love with Hero, a priestess of Aphrodite who lived in a tower in Sestos. Every night Leander would swim across the Hellespont to be with her.
**Alternative spellings:** Leander

## Ledley
**Meaning:** Living near a field or stream
**Origin:** English
**Pronunciation:** led LEE
**Description:** Ledley is a place name that referred to people who lived near a physical feature such as a field or stream. Although more common as a surname, it can be used as a given name as well.

## Lee
**Meaning:** Wood; clearing
**Origin:** English
**Pronunciation:** LEE
**Description:** The name Lee comes from the Old English word 'lea' meaning 'clearing' or 'meadow'. It is a unisex name.
**Alternative spellings:** Lei, Leigh

## Leland
**Meaning:** Land lying fallow
**Origin:** English
**Pronunciation:** Lee lund
**Description:** Leland is an Old English surname, sometimes given as a unisex given name. It has risen in popularity as a given name in the last five years.
**Alternative spellings:** Leeland, Leelund

## Lennie
**Meaning:** Brave lion
**Origin:** English
**Pronunciation:** LEN nee
**Description:** Lennie is a variant of the Old German name Leonard, meaning 'brave lion'.
**Alternative spellings:** Lenney, Lenni, Lenny

## Lennon

**Meaning:** Dearest
**Origin:** English
**Pronunciation:** LEN on
**Description:** Lennon is a commonly found surname that has been adopted as a given name for boys. Popularity of this name is highly likely to be linked with the fame of the Beatles star John Lennon.
**Alternative spellings:** Lenon

## Lennox

**Meaning:** Field on River Leven
**Origin:** Gaelic
**Pronunciation:** Len KNOCKS
**Description:** Lennox is a name made from the Scottish *'ach'*, meaning 'field', and *'llyfn'*, meaning 'smooth' or 'docile'. It was originally given as a surname for those living by the River Leven.
**Alternative spellings:** Lennux, Lenox, Lenux

## Lenny

**Meaning:** Brave Lion
**Origin:** German
**Pronunciation:** len NEE
**Description:** Lenny is an abbreviated version of the German name Leonard. St. Leonard is the patron saint of peasants and horses.

## Leo

**Meaning:** Lion
**Origin:** Latin
**Pronunciation:** LEE oh
**Description:** From the Latin for 'lion'. It is borne by numerous Christian saints and is most commonly found as the pet name for Leonardo.
**Alternative spellings:** Leoh, Lio

## Leon

**Meaning:** Lion
**Origin:** Latin
**Pronunciation:** LEE on
**Description:** Leon is a derivative of Leo, the Latin personal name meaning 'lion'.
**Alternative spellings:** Leeon

## Leonard

**Meaning:** Brave lion
**Origin:** German
**Pronunciation:** LEN ard
**Description:** Leonard is an Old French name, comprised of German elements to mean 'brave lion'. A French saint named Leonard lived in the 5th century and was the patron of peasants and horses.
**Alternative spellings:** Lenard, Leonerd

## Leonardo

**Meaning:** Brave lion
**Origin:** German
**Pronunciation:** lee on ARDdough
**Description:** Leonardo is an elongation of the German name Leonard, despite the two names having different pronunciations of the *'leo'* element.
**Alternative spellings:** Lionardo

## Leonidas

**Meaning:** Strong
**Origin:** Greek
**Pronunciation:** lee on EYE dass
**Description:** Leonidas was borne by the legendary King of Sparta who is said to have held off the entire Persian army with only 300 of his guard. To this day the name carries connotations of bravery and strength.
**Alternative spellings:** Leonydas, Lionidas

L

## Leopold

**Meaning:** Bold people
**Origin:** German
**Pronunciation:** lee UH pold
**Description:** Leopold is a name of German origin. The name comes from the German words *'liut'* meaning 'people' and *'bold'* meaning 'brave'. Then *'liut'* was altered to the Latin *'leo'*.
**Alternative spellings:** Leopolde, Leupold

## Leroy

**Meaning:** The king
**Origin:** French
**Pronunciation:** LEE roy
**Description:** Leroy is a French name that was popular in English-speaking countries in the early 20th century, though its popularity has decreased in recent years. The meaning of Leroy is 'the king', from the French phrase *'Le roi'*.
**Alternative spellings:** Leeroy, Leroi

## Leslie

**Meaning:** Holly garden
**Origin:** Gaelic
**Pronunciation:** LEZ lee
**Description:** Leslie derives from the Scottish surname, meaning 'garden of holly'. It is also used as a unisex given name.
**Alternative spellings:** Leslee, Lesley, Lesli, Lesly

## Levi

**Meaning:** Allied
**Origin:** Hebrew
**Pronunciation:** LEE vye
**Description:** Levi could be a shortened version of the name Levon. Levi is also a brand of jeans and so the forename may be derived from this. It is unisex but more commonly found on boys.
**Alternative spellings:** Leevi

## Levin

**Meaning:** Dear friend
**Origin:** German
**Pronunciation:** LEH vin
**Description:** Levin is a modern German version of the Old German name Leobwin or Liebwin, meaning 'dear friend'. An English variation of this name is Lewin.

## Levison

**Meaning:** Son of Levy
**Origin:** Hebrew
**Pronunciation:** leh VEE sun
**Description:** Levison is traditionally a Jewish last name meaning 'son of Levy'. It is rarely used as a first name but could be an adventurous choice for parents looking for something more unusual.

## Levy

**Meaning:** Joining
**Origin:** Hebrew
**Pronunciation:** lev EE
**Description:** Levy is a Hebrew surname meaning 'joining'. It is also a surname found in Scotland and is a shortened form of Donlevy, meaning 'brown mountain'.
**Alternative spellings:** Levi

## Lewis

**Meaning:** Famous warrior
**Origin:** French
**Pronunciation:** LOO iss
**Description:** Lewis first appeared as an English form of the French

name Louis. It could have also derived from the surname Lewis.
**Alternative spellings:** Lewys, Loui, Louie, Louis, Luis

## Lewys
**Meaning:** Famed warrior
**Origin:** Welsh
**Pronunciation:** LOO is
**Description:** Lewys is the Welsh variant of the English name Lewis, which is the anglicisation of the French name Louis, meaning 'renowned fighter'. It is a popular name in Wales but the spelling is uncommon elsewhere.
**Alternative spellings:** Lewis, Loui, Louie, Louis, Luis

## Leyton
**Meaning:** Meadow settlement
**Origin:** English
**Pronunciation:** lay TON
**Description:** The name Leyton is a variant of the Old English name Leighton, which has been used as a first name since the early 1800s. Can also be spelt Lleyton or Layton. It is found as both first name and surname, but currently isn't found very often as either.
**Alternative spellings:** Layton

## Lex
**Meaning:** Defender of man
**Origin:** Greek
**Pronunciation:** LEX
**Description:** Lex is a shortened form of the Greek name Alexander, meaning 'defender of man'. It is a common boys' name in the Netherlands. Lex Luthor is the fictional nemesis of Superman.
**Alternative spellings:** Lecks, Lexx

## Lexus
**Meaning:** Law
**Origin:** Latin
**Pronunciation:** LEX us
**Description:** Lexus derives from the Latin word for 'law' and is now used as a unisex forename.
**Alternative spellings:** Lexsus, Lexuss

## Liam
**Meaning:** Protection
**Origin:** German
**Pronunciation:** LEE uhm
**Description:** Liam was originally a shortened version of the name William, but is now a name in its own right.
**Alternative spellings:** Lyam

## Liev
**Meaning:** Lion
**Origin:** Russian
**Pronunciation:** lee EHV
**Description:** Liev is the Russian form of Leo, and means 'lion'. Liev Schreiber is a famous American actor with this name.

## Lincoln
**Meaning:** Lake settlement
**Origin:** English
**Pronunciation:** LINK on
**Description:** This name is derived from the city of Lincoln in England, and has now become a very popular forename. It is also found as a surname.
**Alternative spellings:** Lincon

## Linden
**Meaning:** Lime tree hill
**Origin:** German
**Pronunciation:** LIN den

**L**

**Description:** Linden is a name of German origin. Linden can also be a variant of the name Lyndon. The linden tree is a deciduous tree known as a 'lime' tree in British English, though not related to the citrus tree of the same name.
**Alternative spellings:** Lindan, Lindon, Lyndan, Lyndon

## Linus
**Meaning:** Flax
**Origin:** Greek
**Pronunciation:** LYE nus
**Description:** In Greek mythology Linus is the musician son of Apollo. This is an uncommon boys' name.
**Alternative spellings:** Linas, Linnus

## Lleyton
**Meaning:** Leek settlement
**Origin:** English
**Pronunciation:** LEY ton
**Description:** Lleyton is a modern variant of the Old English name Leighton, which literally means 'leek or meadow settlement'.
**Alternative spellings:** Laiton, Layton, Leighton, Leyton

## Lloyd
**Meaning:** Grey
**Origin:** Welsh
**Pronunciation:** LOYD
**Description:** Lloyd is the transferred use of a Welsh surname that originates from a nickname meaning 'grey-haired'.
**Alternative spellings:** Loyd, Loyde

## Lochlan
**Meaning:** Viking settler
**Origin:** Gaelic
**Pronunciation:** LOK lahn

**Description:** Lochlan comes from the Gaelic name Lochlann, a term used in the Highlands for 'Viking settlers'.
**Alternative spellings:** Lochlann, Lockan Locklan

## Lockie
**Meaning:** From the land of the lakes
**Origin:** Scottish
**Pronunciation:** lock EE
**Description:** Lockie is a Scottish name meaning 'from the land of the lakes,' thought to have been used originally for Norse immigrants.
**Alternative spellings:** Locky

## Logan
**Meaning:** Hollow
**Origin:** Gaelic
**Pronunciation:** LO gun
**Description:** Logan is a Scottish surname that has now transferred into a forename for both girls and boys. It is popular in Canada and New Zealand.
**Alternative spellings:** Logun

## Loki
**Meaning:** Mischievous
**Origin:** Norse
**Pronunciation:** LOCK ee
**Description:** Loki is an uncommon boys' name of Old Norse origin. In the Old Norse mythology, Loki was the mischievous troublemaker in the Norse pantheon of gods.
**Alternative spellings:** Lokee, Lokey Lokie

## Lorcan
**Meaning:** Little fierce one
**Origin:** Gaelic
**Pronunciation:** LOR ken

**Description:** Lorcan is an uncommon name of Irish and Gaelic origin, meaning 'little fierce one'. It is sometimes equated with Laurence, though Lorcan is a name in its own right. The name is growing in popularity in Ireland in recent years.
**Alternative spellings:** Lorccn, Lorkan, Lorken

## Lorenzo

**Meaning:** Crowned with a laurel
**Origin:** Latin
**Pronunciation:** lor EN zoh
**Description:** Lorenzo is an Italian version of the English name Lawrence. It was originally a name given to a person from the Roman city Laurentum. It is a fairly uncommon name in the UK, but more popular in the US.

## Louie

**Meaning:** Famed warrior
**Origin:** French
**Pronunciation:** LOO ee
**Description:** Louie is the English variation of the French name Louis, meaning 'renowned or famed warrior'.
**Alternative spellings:** Lewis, Lewys, Loui, Louis, Luis

## Louis

**Meaning:** Famed warrior
**Origin:** French
**Pronunciation:** LOO ee; LOO is
**Description:** Louis was a very common name among French royals and noblemen. The name was borne by 16 French kings up to the French Revolution.
**Alternative spellings:** Lewis, Lewys, Loui, Louie, Luis

## Lowell

**Meaning:** Wolf cub
**Origin:** French
**Pronunciation:** loh UHL
**Description:** The name Lowell is an Old French name meaning 'wolf cub'. It is also the name of a city in the American state of Massachusetts.

## Lowen

**Meaning:** Joyful
**Origin:** Cornish
**Pronunciation:** loh WEN
**Description:** Lowen is a Cornish name that comes from a modern Cornish vocabulary word meaning 'joyful'. It is quite a rare name, even in the Cornish language.

## Luc

**Meaning:** From Lucanus
**Origin:** Greek
**Pronunciation:** LUKE
**Description:** Luc is a variant of the Greek boys' name Luke, meaning 'from Lucanus'. The spelling Luc is common in French- and Dutch-speaking regions and is rarely seen in English-speaking regions.
**Alternative spellings:** Louke, Luke

## Luca

**Meaning:** From Lucanus
**Origin:** Greek
**Pronunciation:** LOO cuh
**Description:** Luca is the Italian equivalent of the Greek name Luke and is extremely popular as a boys' name in Italy. It can also be spelt with a 'k', in which case its origin becomes Russian.
**Alternative spellings:** Louka, Lucca, Luka

L

## Lucas

**Meaning:** From Lucanus
**Origin:** Greek
**Pronunciation:** LOO cuhs
**Description:** Lucas derives from the Greek name Loukas, meaning 'from Lucanus'. Lucas is an extremely popular name in Australia, America, Brazil, Canada, France and Germany.
**Alternative spellings:** Loukas, Lucas, Lucus, Lukas, Lukus

## Lucien

**Meaning:** Light
**Origin:** Latin
**Pronunciation:** LOO shen; LOO see en
**Description:** Lucien is the French variant of the Latin boys' name Lucian, meaning 'light'. The name has recently had an upsurge in popularity.
**Alternative spellings:** Lucian, Lucjan

## Lucius

**Meaning:** Light
**Origin:** Latin
**Pronunciation:** LOO shuss
**Description:** Lucius is a Greek name of Latin origin. It is derived from the Latin word *'lux'* meaning 'light'. Lucio is the Italian, Spanish and Portuguese translation of the name.
**Alternative spellings:** Lucio, Lucios

## Luis

**Meaning:** Famed warrior
**Origin:** Spanish
**Pronunciation:** LOO ees
**Description:** Luis is the Spanish variation of the French name Louis. The spelling is rarely found in Britain.
**Alternative spellings:** Lewis, Lewys, Loui, Louie, Louis

## Luka

**Meaning:** From Lucanus
**Origin:** Russian
**Pronunciation:** loo KA
**Description:** Luka could be considered a spelling variant of the Italian name Luca but is also a Russian name in its own right.
**Alternative spellings:** Louka, Luca, Lucca

## Lukasz

**Meaning:** From Lucanus
**Origin:** Greek
**Pronunciation:** LOO kash
**Description:** Lukasz is a Polish variant of the Greek boys' name Luke.
**Alternative spellings:** Lukaj, Lukash

## Luke

**Meaning:** From Lucanus
**Origin:** Greek
**Pronunciation:** LUKE
**Description:** Luke is the Middle English form of the Greek name Loukas. The third gospel in the New Testament has been ascribed to Luke, which may have helped its popularity.
**Alternative spellings:** Louke, Luc

## Luqman

**Meaning:** Wise
**Origin:** Arabic
**Pronunciation:** LUK mahn
**Description:** The name Luqman is found in early Arabic and Turkish literature and also features in the

Quran. It carries the meaning of 'wise one'.
**Alternative spellings:** Lukman, Lukmahn, Luqmahn

## Lyle
**Meaning:** Island
**Origin:** English
**Pronunciation:** lie YAl
**Description:** Lyle is an English surname derived from the French word *l'isle*, meaning 'island'.

## Lyndon
**Meaning:** Lime tree hill
**Origin:** English
**Pronunciation:** LIN don
**Description:** Lyndon is the name of an area of Leicestershire. It most likely started as a family name for those from Lyndon, then became a boys' first name.
**Alternative spellings:** Lindan, Linden, Lindon, Lyndan

# M

## Mac
**Meaning:** Son of
**Origin:** Gaelic
**Pronunciation:** MAK
**Description:** Mac is a common first element in Scottish and Irish surnames. It is also often used as a nickname for given names such as MacKenzie.
**Alternative spellings:** Mack, Mak

## Macaulay
**Meaning:** Son of righteousness
**Origin:** Scottish
**Pronunciation:** mac ALL lay
**Description:** Macaulay, sometimes written as MacAulay, is a Scottish boys' name meaning 'son of righteousness'. It is a surname as well as a first name.
**Alternative spellings:** MacAulay, McAulay

## Maciej
**Meaning:** Gift from God
**Origin:** Hebrew
**Pronunciation:** MAH chey

**Description:** Maciej is the Polish variant of Matthew or Matthias, both of which mean 'gift from God'.
**Alternative spellings:** Maciaj

## Mackenzie
**Meaning:** The fairest
**Origin:** Gaelic
**Pronunciation:** ma KEN zee
**Description:** Mackenzie derives from the Gaelic surname McKenzie, originally MacCoinneach. The meaning of the name varies. For a girl it is said to mean 'the fairest' yet as a boys' name it means 'handsome one'.
**Alternative spellings:** Mackenzi, Mackenzy, Makenzie, Mckenzi, Mckenzie, Mckenzy

## Maddox
**Meaning:** Generous
**Origin:** Welsh
**Pronunciation:** MAH docks
**Description:** It is thought that the boys' name Maddox came from the Welsh surname Maddocks, which

L
M

means 'descendant of Maddock'. Now the name carries the meaning of 'generous'.
**Alternative spellings:** Maddocks, Madox

## Madison

**Meaning:** Matthew's son
**Origin:** English
**Pronunciation:** MADD isson
**Description:** The name Madison started life as a surname, meaning 'son of Mad'. Mad was used as a pet form of Matthew in the Middle Ages. Although it has masculine roots, it is now a unisex name.
**Alternative spellings:** Maddison, Madisyn, Madyson

## Mads

**Meaning:** Gift from God
**Origin:** Scandinavian
**Pronunciation:** mads
**Description:** Mads is the Scandinavian version of the name Matthew, and shares the same meaning of 'gift from God'. Mads Mikkelsen is a famous Danish actor with this name.

## Magnus

**Meaning:** Great
**Origin:** Latin
**Pronunciation:** MAG nus
**Description:** Magnus is considered a royal name in Norway and Denmark and is often found in Germany and Scotland.
**Alternative spellings:** Magnes, Magnuss

## Magor

**Meaning:** Council spear

**Origin:** German
**Pronunciation:** MAH goor
**Description:** Magor comes from the Old German name Malger, meaning 'council spear'. The name arrived in England in 1066, after the Norman Conquest.

## Mahad

**Meaning:** The one who is great
**Origin:** Arabic
**Pronunciation:** mah HAD
**Description:** Mahad is an Arabic name meaning 'the one who is great'.
**Alternative spellings:** Maahad, Mahaad, Mahhad

## Mahdi

**Meaning:** Guided by Allah
**Origin:** Arabic
**Pronunciation:** MAH dee
**Description:** Mahdi is an Arabic name, often favoured by Muslim parents due to its meaning of 'guided by Allah'.
**Alternative spellings:** Madi

## Mahir

**Meaning:** Talented
**Origin:** Arabic
**Pronunciation:** ma HEER
**Description:** Mahir is an Arabic name popular in Turkey.
**Alternative spellings:** Maheer

## Mahmoud

**Meaning:** Praiseworthy
**Origin:** Arabic
**Pronunciation:** mah MOOD
**Description:** Mahmoud is an Arabic name meaning 'praiseworthy'.
**Alternative spellings:** Mahmud

## Maison

**Meaning:** One who works with stone
**Origin:** English
**Pronunciation:** may SUN
**Description:** The name Maison is a modern spelling variant of the name Mason. It can be a boys' or girls' name and be used as a first name or surname. The original spelling has been around since the Middle Ages, but this variant is very modern and fairly uncommon.
**Alternative spellings:** Mason, Mayson

## Maiwand

**Meaning:** Name of a village in Afghanistan
**Origin:** Afghan
**Pronunciation:** mai WAND
**Description:** Maiwand is actually a place name, referring to a village in Afghanistan. It is notable for the 1880 Battle of Maiwand.

## Major

**Meaning:** Greater; military rank
**Origin:** Latin
**Pronunciation:** may JOOR
**Description:** Major is a Latin name meaning 'greater'. It is also a military rank, given to officers in higher positions.

## Maksim

**Meaning:** The greatest
**Origin:** Russian
**Pronunciation:** MACK sim
**Description:** Maksim is the Russian form of the name Maxim, meaning 'the greatest'. Both names come from the name Maximus, which had Roman origins. However, this form of the name is most commonly used in Slavic countries.
**Alternative spellings:** Maxim

## Maksymillian

**Meaning:** The greatest
**Origin:** Latin
**Pronunciation:** mac CEE mil ee an
**Description:** Maksymilian is an alternative spelling of the Latin name Maximilian, which means 'greatest'. It is likely to be a name that hails from Eastern Europe. The name Maximilian was created when Fredrick the Third, the German Emperor, combined the names Scipio Aemilianus and Quintus Fabius Maximus to name his son; they were both Roman generals.
**Alternative spellings:** Maximilian

## Malachy

**Meaning:** My messenger
**Origin:** English
**Pronunciation:** MAL a kye
**Description:** From the Hebrew name Malachi, who was a prophet and the writer of the final book in the Old Testament. The name has risen greatly in popularity in recent years.
**Alternative spellings:** Malachey, Malachi, Malakai, Malaki

## Malak

**Meaning:** Angel
**Origin:** Arabic
**Pronunciation:** MAH lak
**Description:** Malak is the name of an archangel in Islamic belief and the name still carries that meaning.

**M**

It is a unisex name more often found on boys.
**Alternative spellings:** Malach

## Malcolm
**Meaning:** Devotee of St Columba
**Origin:** Gaelic
**Pronunciation:** MAL kum
**Description:** Malcolm derives from the Gaelic name 'Mael Coluim', meaning 'devotee of St Columba'. St Columba was a popular 6th-century Irish monk.
**Alternative spellings:** Malcom

## Malik
**Meaning:** King
**Origin:** Arabic
**Pronunciation:** MAL ik
**Description:** Malik comes from the Arabic word for 'king'. It has risen in popularity since its use by African-American activist Malcolm X, who took the Islamic name El-Hajj Malik El-Shabazz.
**Alternative spellings:** Malic, Malick

## Manal
See entry in 'Names for Baby Girls A–Z'

## Manraj
**Meaning:** The heart's king
**Origin:** Punjabi
**Pronunciation:** man RAJ
**Description:** The name Manraj has its origins in the Punjabi language. It is used largely in English and Indian as both a given name and a surname. The meaning of Manraj is 'heart's king'.
**Alternative spellings:** Maanraj, Manraaj

## Manson
**Meaning:** Son of Magnus
**Origin:** Scottish
**Pronunciation:** man SUN
**Description:** Manson is a Scottish surname meaning 'son of Magnus' and is most often found in the far north-east of the country. This is a very common last name in Scotland. This follows the contemporary trend of using last names as first names.

## Manu
**Meaning:** Wisdom
**Origin:** Sanskrit
**Pronunciation:** man OO
**Description:** Manu, when translated from Sanskrit, means 'wisdom'. It is also the name of the progenitor of mankind in the Hindu religion.

## Manuel
**Meaning:** God is with us
**Origin:** Hebrew
**Pronunciation:** mah noo EL
**Description:** Manuel is a name of Hebrew origin, meaning 'God is with us'. It is the Spanish and Portuguese form of Immanuel.
**Alternative spellings:** Manwell

## Manveer
**Meaning:** Brave-minded
**Origin:** Punjabi
**Pronunciation:** man VEER
**Description:** Manveer is a common boys' name meaning 'brave-minded'. It has its origins in the Punjabi language. Manveer is a variant form of the Indian name Manvir.
**Alternative spellings:** Maanveer, Manvir

## Marc

**Meaning:** From the god Mars
**Origin:** Latin
**Pronunciation:** MARK
**Description:** Marc is the French form of the name Mark, and this spelling is becoming increasingly popular around the globe. It is most likely derived from the name of the Roman god of war, Mars.
**Alternative spellings:** Mark

## Marcel

**Meaning:** From the god Mars
**Origin:** Latin
**Pronunciation:** MAR sell
**Description:** The name Marcel derives from the Latin name Marcellus, itself derived from the name of the Roman god of war, Mars. This name was also borne by many popes and saints. Forms of this name include the Spanish variant Marcelo and the French version Marceau.
**Alternative spellings:** Marcell, Marrcel

## Marco

**Meaning:** From the god Mars
**Origin:** Latin
**Pronunciation:** MAR koh
**Description:** Marco is the Italian, Spanish and Portuguese form of the name Mark. This name was commonly used among the Romans and given to boys who were born in March, as this is the month of the god Mars.
**Alternative spellings:** Marcoh, Marko

## Marcus

**Meaning:** From the god Mars
**Origin:** Latin
**Pronunciation:** MAR kus
**Description:** The name Marcus, like Marcel and Marco, is derived from the name of the Roman god of war, Mars. It may have typically been given to boys born in March.
**Alternative spellings:** Markus

## Marek

**Meaning:** Dedicated to Mars
**Origin:** Latin
**Pronunciation:** MAR ik
**Description:** Marek is a popular Czech, Polish and Slovak name, the equivalent of Mark in English. Marek is of Latin origin and means 'dedicated to Mars'.
**Alternative spellings:** Marec, Mareck, Marik

## Mario

**Meaning:** God of war; male
**Origin:** Italian
**Pronunciation:** MAH ryo
**Description:** Mario is the Italian form of the name Marius, which either comes from Mars, the name of the Roman God of war, or the Latin root *maris*, meaning 'male'. A popular Mario is the hero of the Nintendo video game, Super Mario Bros.

## Mark

**Meaning:** From the god Mars
**Origin:** Latin
**Pronunciation:** MARK
**Description:** The name Mark derived from the Roman god of war, Mars. According to Arthurian legend, King Mark was the aged ruler of Cornwall, whose name may be derived from the Celtic word *'march'*, meaning 'horse'.
**Alternative spellings:** Marc

**M**

## Marley

**Meaning:** Forest of joy
**Origin:** English
**Pronunciation:** MAHr ley
**Description:** Marley is an Old English surname, which has now been transferred to a unisex given name.
**Alternative spellings:** Marlee, Marli, Marlie, Marly

## Marlon

**Meaning:** Little hawk
**Origin:** English
**Pronunciation:** MAR lon
**Description:** Marlon is a unisex name of English origin, meaning 'little hawk'. The name gained popularity in the 1900s, perhaps due to the fame of actor Marlon Brando.
**Alternative spellings:** Marlan, Marlen, Marlonn

## Marlow

**Meaning:** Driftwood
**Origin:** English
**Pronunciation:** mar LOW
**Description:** Marlow is an Old English name meaning 'driftwood'. It was also a place name in England and was given as a surname to people who lived in the area.
**Alternative spellings:** Marlowe

## Marsh

**Meaning:** Marsh
**Origin:** English
**Pronunciation:** MARSH
**Description:** The name Marsh was originally a surname adopted by those who lived on marshy ground. The name may also be thought of as a short form of the German name Marshall, meaning 'horse worker'.
**Alternative spellings:** Marshe

## Marshall

**Meaning:** Horse worker
**Origin:** German
**Pronunciation:** MAR shawl
**Description:** Marshall is a transferred surname, ultimately derived from the German for 'horse servant'. It is now a popular first name.
**Alternative spellings:** Marshal, Marshell

## Martin

**Meaning:** From the god Mars
**Origin:** Latin
**Pronunciation:** MAR tin
**Description:** The name Martin is derived from the Latin name Martinus, originally attributed to the Roman god of war, Mars.
**Alternative spellings:** Martinn

## Marty

**Meaning:** God of War
**Origin:** Latin
**Pronunciation:** MAR tee
**Description:** Marty is a short form of the name Martin. Both names are derived from the Latin name Martinus, originally attributed to the Roman god of war, Mars.

## Marvin

**Meaning:** Sea friend
**Origin:** Welsh
**Pronunciation:** MAR vin
**Description:** Marvin is a popular boys' name of Welsh origin and is a variant of Mervin. It is common as both a given name and as a surname. Its popularity has fallen since the middle of the 20th century.
**Alternative spellings:** Marven, Marvin, Marvyn

## Marwan

**Meaning:** Solid stone
**Origin:** Arabic
**Pronunciation:** MAR wan
**Description:** Marwan is a name of Arabic origin, meaning 'solid stone'. It is common in some Arabic states such as Egypt, Lebanon and Tunisia.
**Alternative spellings:** Marwon

## Mason

**Meaning:** Stoneworker
**Origin:** French
**Pronunciation:** MAY son
**Description:** This name has been around since the Middle Ages. It used to be given as a surname to those who worked with stone but has now transferred into a unisex given name.
**Alternative spellings:** Maison, Mayson

## Massimo

**Meaning:** The greatest
**Origin:** Latin
**Pronunciation:** MA see mo
**Description:** Massimo is a name of Latin origin, meaning 'the greatest'. It is the Italian form of Maximus.
**Alternative spellings:** Masimo, Massimoh

## Matas

**Meaning:** Gift from God
**Origin:** Hebrew
**Pronunciation:** MA tas
**Description:** Matas appears to be a variant of the name Matthew, coming from northern Europe. It is very popular in Britain, whereas Matas is usually found on the continent.
**Alternative spellings:** Mathas, Mattas

## Matei

**Meaning:** Gift of God
**Origin:** Bulgarian
**Pronunciation:** MAH tei
**Description:** Matei is the Bulgarian form of the name Matthew, meaning 'gift of God'. Mattew was the author of the first gospel in the New Testament and was a Christian evangelist.

## Mateo

**Meaning:** Gift of God
**Origin:** Spanish
**Pronunciation:** mah TEE oh
**Description:** Mateo is the Spanish form of the name Matthew, which in turn is the English form of the name of the Christian evangelist and author of the first gospel in the New Testament. The name is a form of the Hebrew name Mattathia, which means 'a gift from God'.
**Alternative spellings:** Matteo

## Mateusz

**Meaning:** Gift from God
**Origin:** Hebrew
**Pronunciation:** MA tee oosh
**Description:** Mateusz is derived from the biblical name Matthew and is used commonly in the Polish language.
**Alternative spellings:** Mateuzs

## Mathis

**Meaning:** Gift of God
**Origin:** French
**Pronunciation:** math US
**Description:** Mathis is the French version of the name Matthew, and as such shares the same meaning of 'gift of God'.

**M**

## Matthew

**Meaning:** Gift from God
**Origin:** Hebrew
**Pronunciation:** MATH yoo
**Description:** Matthew is the English form of the name of the Christian evangelist, author of the first gospel in the New Testament. It derives from the Hebrew name Mattathia, meaning 'gift from God'.
**Alternative spellings:** Mathew

## Matthias

**Meaning:** Gift of God
**Origin:** Greek
**Pronunciation:** ma THYE us
**Description:** Matthias is a name of German, Greek and Hebrew origin. The name is used across Europe in a variety of variant forms as both a given name and a surname. In the Christian Bible, Matthias was the disciple selected to replace Judas as an apostle.
**Alternative spellings:** Mathias, Mathyas

## Maurice

**Meaning:** One From Mauritania
**Origin:** Latin
**Pronunciation:** MORE us
**Description:** Maurice is a Latin name, derived from the words 'mauritius' or 'mauricius' and refers to a person who is from Mauritania, which corresponds to modern-day Morocco.

## Maverick

**Meaning:** Independent
**Origin:** English
**Pronunciation:** mav ER rik
**Description:** Maverick is a name whose meaning is derived from the English word of the same spelling, meaning 'independent'. It was first used in the 1950s Western TV series of the same name.
**Alternative spellings:** Maverik

## Max

**Meaning:** The greatest
**Origin:** Latin
**Pronunciation:** MAKS
**Description:** Max is a short form of Maximillian and to a lesser extent Maxwell, but it is now often found as a name in its own right.
**Alternative spellings:** Maks

## Maxim

**Meaning:** The greatest
**Origin:** Latin
**Pronunciation:** MACK sim
**Description:** This Russian name derives from Maksim, a variation of the name Maximus. This name had Roman origins and is most commonly used in Slavic-speaking countries.
**Alternative spellings:** Maksim, Maxsim

## Maxime

**Meaning:** The greatest
**Origin:** Latin
**Pronunciation:** mahk SEEM
**Description:** Maxime is a name of Latin origin, meaning 'the greatest'. It is the French form of Maximus.
**Alternative spellings:** Macsime, Maksime, Maxeem

## Maximilian

**Meaning:** The greatest
**Origin:** Latin
**Pronunciation:** MAC cee MIL ee an
**Description:** Derived from the Latin word *'maximus'*, meaning 'greatest'. The name was invented

by German emperor Frederick the Third, by combining the surnames of Roman generals Scipio Aemilianus and Quintus Fabius Maximus to name his son. The name is popular in German-speaking countries.
**Alternative spellings:** Maximillian, Maxymilian

## Maximus

**Meaning:** The greatest
**Origin:** Latin
**Pronunciation:** MAX i muus
**Description:** Maximus is a variant of the name Maxim. The name was borne by a variety of saints and was very popular among early Christians.
**Alternative spellings:** Maksimus, Maxymus

## Maxwell

**Meaning:** Mac's well
**Origin:** English
**Pronunciation:** MAKS wel
**Description:** Maxwell comes from a Scottish surname meaning 'well belonging to Mac'.
**Alternative spellings:** Macswell, Makswell, Maxwel

## McKenzie

**Meaning:** Fair One
**Origin:** Gaelic
**Pronunciation:** ma KEN zee
**Description:** This can also be spelt as Mackenzie. This name can be applied to both boys and girls, with the meaning varying between 'the fairest' for a girl, or 'son of the fair one' for a boy. It originated from the Gaelic surname 'Mac Coinnich'.
**Alternative spellings:** Mackenzie

## McKinley

**Meaning:** Son of fair hero
**Origin:** Scottish
**Pronunciation:** mac KIN lee
**Description:** McKinley is a Scottish surname meaning 'son of fair hero'. This follows the contemporary trend of using last names as first names.
**Alternative spellings:** MacKinley

## Md

**Meaning:** Praiseworthy
**Origin:** Arabic
**Pronunciation:** EM dee
**Description:** Md is an uncommon Arabic boys' name that is a much shortened variant of the Arabic name Muhammad, named after the prophet.

## Mehdi

**Meaning:** Rightly guided
**Origin:** Arabic
**Pronunciation:** MEHH dee
**Description:** A variant of the Arabic name Madhi, meaning 'rightly guided'.
**Alternative spellings:** Mehdie, Mehdy

## Mehmet

**Meaning:** Praiseworthy
**Origin:** Arabic
**Pronunciation:** meh MET
**Description:** Mehmet is an Arabic boys' name and a variant of the old Turkish name Mehmed, which is derived from the prophet Muhammad. Mehmed II was Sultan of the Ottoman Empire and a national hero in Turkey. He conquered Constantinople and brought an end to the Byzantine Empire. His name and its variants

**M**

are among the most popular boys' names in Turkey.

**Alternative spellings:** Mehmed, Mehmett, Mehmud

# Mekhi

**Meaning:** Who is like God?
**Origin:** Hawaiian
**Pronunciation:** MEH kay
**Description:** Mekhi is an increasingly popular name of Hawaiian and Hebrew origin. It is a modern variant of the popular Hebrew name Michael. The name transliterates as the question 'who is like God?'
**Alternative spellings:** Mechi, Mekhai

# Meleager

**Meaning:** Burning fire
**Origin:** Greek
**Pronunciation:** mel EE ah gar
**Description:** In Greek mythology, Meleager was a fierce warrior, second only to Heracles in his abilities.
**Alternative spellings:** Meleaeger, Meleger

# Melvin

**Meaning:** Bad town
**Origin:** English
**Pronunciation:** MEL vin
**Description:** Melvin is a boys' given name of English and French origin. It is probably derived from the surname Melville, from the French for 'bad town'.
**Alternative spellings:** Melven

# Memphis

**Meaning:** Place in United States
**Origin:** English
**Pronunciation:** MEM fiss
**Description:** Memphis is a place name, more specifically a city in the American state of Tennessee. Like Brooklyn and Paris, this is a trendy place name that would be a good choice for adventurous parents.

# Menelaus

**Meaning:** Hero
**Origin:** Greek
**Pronunciation:** men uh LAOW us
**Description:** In Greek mythology, Menelaus was a legendary king of Mycenaean Sparta and the husband of Helen of Troy. He was a hero of the Trojan war.
**Alternative spellings:** Menelaos, Menelyos

# Mercury

**Meaning:** Merchandise
**Origin:** Latin
**Pronunciation:** MEHR cure ree
**Description:** In Roman mythology, Mercury was a messenger who wore winged sandals. He was the god of trade, thieves and travel. It is also the name of the closest planet to the sun in the solar system.
**Alternative spellings:** Mercuri, Murcury

# Merrick

**Meaning:** Dark-skinned; Moorish
**Origin:** Latin
**Pronunciation:** MEH rick
**Description:** More commonly found as a surname and often associated with Joseph Merrick (the Elephant Man), Merrick as a first name is thought to have come from the name Maurice, which has Latin roots.
**Alternative spellings:** Merrick

## Micah

**Meaning:** Who is like God?
**Origin:** Hebrew
**Pronunciation:** MY kah
**Description:** The name Micah is a variation of the name Michael and therefore carries biblical associations. Micah wrote the book prophesising the breakdown of Jerusalem. The original spelling of the name Micah is actually Micaiah.
**Alternative spellings:** Mica

## Michael

**Meaning:** Who is like God?
**Origin:** Hebrew
**Pronunciation:** MY cal
**Description:** Michael is a biblical name borne by an archangel protector of the Hebrews, regarded as a Catholic saint. The name was also borne by a Persian prince mentioned in the Book of Daniel. Michael has been a relentlessly popular name since the early 20th century.
**Alternative spellings:** Micael, Micel, Michel, Michul, Mikal, Mikael, Mikail, Mikhail

## Mick

**Meaning:** Who is like god?
**Origin:** English
**Pronunciation:** mick
**Description:** Mick is a shortened version of Michael and as such, shares the same meaning of 'who is like God?'. Mick Jagger is the lead singer of the Rolling Stones.

## Miguel

**Meaning:** Who is like God?
**Origin:** Hebrew
**Pronunciation:** mee GHEL
**Description:** Miguel is the Spanish form of the name Michael.

**Alternative spellings:** Migel

## Mike

**Meaning:** Who is like God?
**Origin:** Hebrew
**Pronunciation:** MYK
**Description:** A common short form of the Hebrew name Michael, now given as a first name in its own right.
**Alternative spellings:** Myke

## Mikel

**Meaning:** Who is like God?
**Origin:** Hebrew
**Pronunciation:** MEE kel
**Description:** Mikel is an uncommon name of Hebrew origin. It is a modern American-English variant of Michael, meaning 'who is like God?'
**Alternative spellings:** Mikil

## Mikey

**Meaning:** Who is like God?
**Origin:** Hebrew
**Pronunciation:** MY kee
**Description:** The name Mikey is a variant of Micah and also Michael. It is often used as a pet form for Michael or Mick.
**Alternative spellings:** Mikie, Mykey, Myki, Mykie

## Mikolaj

**Meaning:** Victory of the people
**Origin:** Greek
**Pronunciation:** Mee CO low
**Description:** Although this name derives from Old Greek it is mainly used in Polish- and Russian-speaking countries. It is a form of the English and French name Nicholas.
**Alternative spellings:** Mickolaj

**M**

## Milan

**Meaning:** Loving
**Origin:** Slavic
**Pronunciation:** mih LAN
**Description:** Milan was originally a name of Slavic origin, meaning 'loving'. However it is also the name of a major Italian city, and is given to both boys and girls after the city of Milan.
**Alternative spellings:** Milanne, Millan

## Miles

**Meaning:** Mild and merciful
**Origin:** Latin
**Pronunciation:** MY ulls
**Description:** Miles is thought to have come from the Latin name Milo, meaning 'mild and merciful'. It could also have come into usage as a shortened form of Michael.
**Alternative spellings:** Myels, Myles

## Miller

**Meaning:** Grain mill worker
**Origin:** English
**Pronunciation:** MIH ler
**Description:** Miller is an English surname given to a person working in a grain mill. It had been adapted as a first name by the 19th century, although it has never been particularly common.
**Alternative spellings:** Miler

## Milo

**Meaning:** Mild and merciful
**Origin:** Latin
**Pronunciation:** MY lo
**Description:** Milo is a Roman name, meaning 'mild and merciful'. It could also be a shortened form of Miles.

**Alternative spellings:** Miloh, Mylo, Myloh

## Milosz

**Meaning:** Lover of glory
**Origin:** Czech
**Pronunciation:** MEE los
**Description:** Milosz, the pet form of Miloslav, is the Polish variant of the Czech name Milos. It is common as both a given name for boys and as a surname.
**Alternative spellings:** Meelos, Milos

## Minako

See entry in 'Names for Baby Girls A–Z'

## Miran

**Meaning:** Peace; World
**Origin:** Slavic
**Pronunciation:** MEER an
**Description:** Miran is a Slavic name derived from the element of '*miru,*' meaning 'peace' or 'world'. This is quite an unusual name, but would be a good choice for parents looking for somthing more unusual.

## Mischa

See entry in 'Names for Baby Girls A–Z'

## Mitch

**Meaning:** Who is like God?
**Origin:** English
**Pronunciation:** mitch
**Description:** Mitch is derived from Mitchell, which in turn is a variant of Michael and as such, shares the same meaning of 'Who is like God?'.

## Mitchell
**Meaning:** Who is like God?
**Origin:** Hebrew
**Pronunciation:** MITCH ell
**Description:** The forename Mitchell has been transferred from a common surname that derived from Michel (a medieval alternative of Michael)
**Alternative spellings:** Mitchel, Mitchull

## Mohammed
**Meaning:** Worthy of glory and praise
**Origin:** Arabic
**Pronunciation:** moh HAM mad; moh HAM med
**Description:** Mohammed and its spelling variants are some of the most frequently used boys' names in the world. It is popular with Muslim parents as it is the name of the prophet Muhammad.
**Alternative spellings:** Mohamad, Mohamed, Mohammad, Mohammod, Muhammad, Muhamed Muhammed, Muhamad

## Mohsin
**Meaning:** Charitable
**Origin:** Arabic
**Pronunciation:** moh SEEN
**Description:** Mohsin is an Arabic name said to mean 'charitable' or 'beneficial'.
**Alternative spellings:** Muhsin

## Moise
**Meaning:** Delivered from the water
**Origin:** Romanian
**Pronunciation:** MOO ise
**Description:** Moise is the Romanian spelling of the name Moses and as such, shares the same name meaning. Moses is the name of the Biblical character in the Old Testament, who leads the Israelites out of Egypt.

## Mona
See entry in 'Names for Baby Girls A–Z'

## Montague
**Meaning:** Pointed hill
**Origin:** French
**Pronunciation:** MON tay gu
**Description:** Montague is a name of French origin, meaning 'pointed hill'. It was common as a given name in the 19th century. It is also the name of a number of cities in America and Canada.
**Alternative spellings:** Montagew, Montagu

## Montgomery
**Meaning:** Gomeric's hill
**Origin:** French
**Pronunciation:** mont GOM err ree
**Description:** Montgomery was originally a surname that gradually transformed into a first name over time. Mainly used in English-speaking countries, this name has fallen out of popular use.
**Alternative spellings:** Montgomerey

## Monty
**Meaning:** Pointed hill
**Origin:** French
**Pronunciation:** mont EE
**Description:** Monty is a short form of the name Montague, a name of French origin, meaning 'pointed hill'. It was common as a given name in the 19th century.

**M**

# Morgan

**Meaning:** Great circle
**Origin:** Welsh
**Pronunciation:** MOR gun
**Description:** The name Morgan derives from the Old Welsh masculine name Morcant, which can mean 'bright or great sea' or 'great circle'.
**Alternative spellings:** Morgann, Morganne

# Morris

**Meaning:** Dark-skinned
**Origin:** English
**Pronunciation:** MORE us
**Description:** Morris is derived from the Latin Mauritius, meaning Moorish and referring to the Moors, a group of Arabic people who had dark colouring.
**Alternative spellings:** Morriss, Moris

# Morrison

**Meaning:** Son of Morris
**Origin:** English
**Pronunciation:** moriss SUN
**Description:** Morrison is an English surname meaning 'son of Morris'. This follows the contemporary trend of using last names as first names.

# Moses

**Meaning:** Delivered from the water
**Origin:** Hebrew
**Pronunciation:** MOZ es
**Description:** Moses is a biblical name associated with the famous story in the Old Testament, where he was abandoned as a baby but grows up to lead the Israelites out of Egypt and to the Promised Land, as well as receiving the Ten Commandments from God.

# Moshe

**Meaning:** Taken from the water
**Origin:** Hebrew
**Pronunciation:** mo SHEH
**Description:** Moshe is the original Hebrew name for Moses. Due to their biblical use the names are often said to mean 'taken from the water' because of the story of Moses.
**Alternative spellings:** Mosh

# Murray

**Meaning:** Lord and master
**Origin:** Gaelic
**Pronunciation:** MUH ree
**Description:** Murray is a boys' name of Gaelic origin, meaning 'lord and master'. It is one of the most common surnames in the world, and was once common as a given name.
**Alternative spellings:** Murrey, Murry

# Muriel

**Meaning:** Sea; bright
**Origin:** Celtic
**Pronunciation:** MUR ee AL
**Description:** Muriel is a Celtic name that was originally spelt Muirgheal. The name is composed of *muir* meaning 'sea,' and *gheal* meaning 'bright'.

# Murphy

**Meaning:** Sea warrior
**Origin:** Irish
**Pronunciation:** MUR fee
**Description:** Murphy is an Irish surname that was originally spelt Murchadh. Composed of the elements 'muir' meaning 'sea' and 'cath' meaning 'battle'. Although it was originally a surname it is now a popular choice for a first name.
**Alternative spellings:** Murphee

## Musa

**Meaning:** Taken from the water
**Origin:** Hebrew
**Pronunciation:** MOO sa
**Description:** The name Musa is the Arabic version of the biblical name Moses. It is mainly used in Turkish-, Arabic- and Hebrew-speaking countries. Although the name is technically masculine, it can also be found used for girls.
**Alternative spellings:** Musah

## Musab

**Meaning:** Undefeatable
**Origin:** Arabic
**Pronunciation:** mu SAAB
**Description:** Musab is an uncommon name, said to mean 'undefeatable'. In Islamic belief, Musab was the name of a sahabah, a companion of the prophet Muhammad.
**Alternative spellings:** Musabe, Mussab

## Mustafa

**Meaning:** Lordly
**Origin:** Arabic
**Pronunciation:** MOO staf fa
**Description:** The name Mustafa derives from the same word in Arabic to mean 'chosen'. The name is popular within Muslim families as Mustafa was often used as one of the names for the prophet Muhammad.
**Alternative spellings:** Mustafah

## Myles

**Meaning:** Fighter
**Origin:** German
**Pronunciation:** my ULZZ
**Description:** Myles is a variation of the name Milon, which is Germanic in origin. It is also a variation of Miles, which was brought over to England via the means of the Norman Conquest. However, there is also a Latin version in which it may have derived, Milo, which means soldier.
**Alternative spellings:** Miles

## Myron

**Meaning:** Sweet oil; perfume
**Origin:** Greek
**Pronunciation:** my RON
**Description:** Myron was used originally to honour the Greek sculptor of the same name and means 'sweet oil' or 'perfume' in Ancient Greek. This name is more popular in the United States but has declined in popularity since the 1960s.
**Alternative spellings:** Miron

**M**
**N**

# N

## Nabeel

**Meaning:** Noble
**Origin:** Arabic
**Pronunciation:** nah BEEL
**Description:** Nabeel is a masculine name of Arabic origin and it is said to mean 'noble'.
**Alternative spellings:** Nabeal, Nabel, Nabil

## Nadeem

**Meaning:** Life of the party
**Origin:** Arabic
**Pronunciation:** nah DEEM

**Description:** Nadeem is an Arabic name meaning 'life of the party', referring to a friend or companion that you would like to wine and dine with.

## Nana
See entry in 'Names for Baby Girls A–Z'

## Napoleon
**Meaning:** Lion of Naples
**Origin:** Italian
**Pronunciation:** nap OH lee ON
**Description:** Napoleon is an Italian name meaning 'lion of Naples'. It is derived from the elements of '*Napoli*' meaning 'Naples' and '*leone*' meaning 'lion'.

## Narcissus
**Meaning:** Sleep
**Origin:** Greek
**Pronunciation:** nar SISS suss
**Description:** Narcissus is an uncommon name of Greek origin. In Greek mythology, Narcissus fell in love with his own reflection in a pool, and there he remained, mesmerised, until he turned into a flower – the narcissus, commonly known in English as a daffodil.
**Alternative spellings:** Narkissos, Narssisus

## Nat
See entry in 'Names for Baby Girls A–Z'

## Natan
**Meaning:** God has given
**Origin:** Hebrew
**Pronunciation:** NEE tan
**Description:** Natan is a variant of the name Nathan and is very popular in Russian- and Spanish-speaking countries. It is seen in the Bible as belonging to a prophet who overthrew King David.
**Alternative spellings:** Naytan

## Nate
**Meaning:** God has given
**Origin:** Hebrew
**Pronunciation:** NAYT
**Description:** Nate is a short form of Nathan or Nathaniel, but it is now given as a first name in its own right.
**Alternative spellings:** Nayte

## Nathan
**Meaning:** God has given
**Origin:** Hebrew
**Pronunciation:** NAYTH ann
**Description:** Nathan is considered a biblical name as it is the name of a prophet who overthrew King David. It can also be a shortened form of Nathaniel or Jonathan.
**Alternative spellings:** Nathen

## Nathanial
**Meaning:** God has given
**Origin:** Hebrew
**Pronunciation:** Na THAN yel
**Description:** Nathanial is derived from Nathan, both of which are Hebrew in origin and are said to mean 'God has given'. Nathanial was the first name of an apostle, but he was referred to as his surname Bartholomew. Nathaniel is less commonly found than Nathan but is becoming increasingly popular.
**Alternative spellings:** Nathaneal, Nathaniel, Nathanyal

## Ned
**Meaning:** Wealthy guardian
**Origin:** English

**Pronunciation:** NED
**Description:** Ned is a pet form of Edward, but also a name in its own right.

## Nehemiah
**Meaning:** Comforter
**Origin:** Hebrew
**Pronunciation:** nee ah MYE ah
**Description:** Nehemiah is a name of Hebrew origin. In the Hebrew Bible he is the central figure of the Book of Nehemiah. The name has risen in popularity in America in recent years.
**Alternative spellings:** Nahumiah, Nehemia, Nehumiah

## Neil
**Meaning:** Champion
**Origin:** Gaelic
**Pronunciation:** NEEL
**Description:** The name Neil comes from the Irish name Niall, the origin of which is disputed. Possible meanings are 'cloud', 'passionate' and 'champion'.
**Alternative spellings:** Neal, Neel, Neill

## Nelson
**Meaning:** Son of Neil
**Origin:** English
**Pronunciation:** NEL sun
**Description:** Nelson has been a common name for boys for many centuries. It is also one of the most common surnames in the English-speaking world.
**Alternative spellings:** Nellson, Nelsen, Nelsun

## Neo
**Meaning:** Gift; new
**Origin:** African, English

**Pronunciation:** NEE oh
**Description:** The name Neo can be found in several countries. It could originate from the English word 'new' or the African word meaning 'gift'.
**Alternative spellings:** Neoh, Neyo

## Neptune
**Meaning:** God of the sea
**Origin:** Latin
**Pronunciation:** NEP tune
**Description:** In Roman mythology, Neptune was the Roman god of water, the sea and religion. Neptune is also the name of a planet in the solar system.
**Alternative spellings:** Neptoone

## Nessus
**Meaning:** Centaur
**Origin:** Greek
**Pronunciation:** NESS us
**Description:** In Greek mythology, Nessus was a famous centaur who was killed by Heracles, and whose tainted blood in turn killed Heracles.
**Alternative spellings:** Nessos, Nessuss

## Nestor
**Meaning:** Return
**Origin:** Greek
**Pronunciation:** NES tor
**Description:** Nestor appeared in Homer's epic poem *The Odyssey*, where, despite his old age, he is noted for his bravery and oratorical ability.
**Alternative spellings:** Nesstor, Nestur

## Neville
**Meaning:** New village
**Origin:** French

**N**

**Pronunciation:** neh VILLE
**Description:** Neville is a French name meaning 'new village'. Originally a surname, it has been used as a first name since the 19th century.

## Niall

**Meaning:** Champion; cloud; passionate
**Origin:** Gaelic
**Pronunciation:** NY al
**Description:** Niall is the Irish root of the English name Neil. Niall's origin is somewhat disputed; as well as 'champion', it could mean 'cloud' or 'passionate'.
**Alternative spellings:** Nial, Nihal, Nyle

## Niam

**Meaning:** Happiness; comfort
**Origin:** Arabic
**Pronunciation:** nah EEM
**Description:** Niam is a variation of the boys' name, Naeem, meaning 'happiness' or 'comfort' in Arabic. However, it is also a Hebrew name and in that language, the name means 'pleasant'.
**Alternative spellings:** Naeem

## Nicholas

**Meaning:** Victory of the people
**Origin:** Greek
**Pronunciation:** NI cuh lus
**Description:** Nicholas comes from the Greek name Nikolaos, derived from the words for 'victory' and 'people'. Nicholas was a 4th-century bishop who brought gifts to children around Christmas time and earned the name of St Nicholas.
**Alternative spellings:** Nicolas, Nikolas

## Nick

**Meaning:** Victory of the people
**Origin:** Greek
**Pronunciation:** NIK
**Description:** Nick is a shortened form of Nicholas, but it is now given as a name in its own right.
**Alternative spellings:** Nic, Nik

## Nicky

**Meaning:** Victory of the people
**Origin:** Greek, English
**Pronunciation:** NIK ee
**Description:** Nicky is a unisex name of Greek and English origin. It is a shortened variant of the Greek name Nicholas, meaning 'victory of the people'.
**Alternative spellings:** Nickee, Nicki, Nickie

## Nico

**Meaning:** Victory of the people
**Origin:** Greek
**Pronunciation:** NICK oh
**Description:** Nico can be considered a shortened form of the name Nicholas and is often seen in Europe as a given name in its own right.
**Alternative spellings:** Nicoh, Niko

## Nicol

**Meaning:** Victory of the people
**Origin:** Greek
**Pronunciation:** nih KOL
**Description:** Nicol is a rare unisex variant of the masculine name Nicholas.
**Alternative spellings:** Nicoll

## Nihal

**Meaning:** Joyous
**Origin:** Arabic
**Pronunciation:** nih HAHL

**Description:** Nihal is a unisex Arabic name. It could also be considered a spelling variant of the Irish name Niall.
**Alternative spellings:** Niall, Nihall

## Nikhil
**Meaning:** Whole
**Origin:** Sanskrit
**Pronunciation:** nih KEEL
**Description:** Nikhil is a boys' name, meaning 'whole'. It is often found in India.
**Alternative spellings:** Nichil, Nikhill

## Nikita
**Meaning:** Undefeated
**Origin:** Russian
**Pronunciation:** nee KEE ath
**Description:** In its original Russian form Nikita is a masculine name said to mean 'undefeated'. It has since been found in many languages used as a unisex or a feminine name.
**Alternative spellings:** Nichita, Nicita, Nikitah

## Nikko
**Meaning:** Victory
**Origin:** English
**Pronunciation:** nee KOH
**Description:** Nikko is a version of the Greek name Nike meaning 'victory'. It is also the basis of the common name Nicholas.
**Alternative spellings:** Niko

## Niko
**Meaning:** Victory of the people
**Origin:** Greek
**Pronunciation:** nee KOH
**Description:** Niko is a variation of the name Nico, which itself is a variation of Nicholas. It can be presumed to share the same meaning as Nicholas, which is 'victory of the people'.
**Alternative spellings:** Nikko

## Nikolai
**Meaning:** Victory of the people
**Origin:** Greek
**Pronunciation:** NIK oh lye
**Description:** Nikolai is a Slavic variant of the boys' name Nicholas, of Greek origin, meaning 'victory of the people'.
**Alternative spellings:** Nicholai, Nicholi, Nikolay, Nikoli

## Nikodem
**Meaning:** Conquerer of the people
**Origin:** Slavik
**Pronunciation:** ni KO dem
**Description:** Nikodem is a name that has been popular in Poland for many years, and has now begun to rise in popularity in the UK. It is likely to be an alternative spelling of the name Nikodemus. It means 'conqueror of the people' or 'people's conqueror'.

## Nile
**Meaning:** Champion; cloud; passionate
**Origin:** English
**Pronunciation:** nay AL
**Description:** Nile is a variation of the name Niall, which is the Irish root of the English name Neil. The origin of Niall is somewhat disputed - as well as 'champion', it could mean 'cloud' or 'passionate'. It can also refer to the Nile River in Egypt.
**Alternative spellings:** Niall

**N**

## Noah

**Meaning:** Rest
**Origin:** Hebrew
**Pronunciation:** NO uh
**Description:** Noah is the biblical character who built an ark to save two animals of every species from God's flood. It is currently experiencing a burst of popularity.
**Alternative spellings:** Noa

## Noel

**Meaning:** Birthday of Christ
**Origin:** French
**Pronunciation:** NO ell
**Description:** Noel is a unisex name that comes from a French word meaning 'birthday'. The word now has associations with Christ's birthday, Christmas Day. The spelling Noelle is favoured for girls.
**Alternative spellings:** Nowell

## Nojus

**Meaning:** Rest
**Origin:** Hebrew
**Pronunciation:** NO jus
**Description:** There is not much known about the origin of this name; however it is thought to derive from the biblical name Noah.
**Alternative spellings:** Nojius

## Noran

See entry in 'Names for Baby Girls A–Z'

## Norbert

**Meaning:** Bright north
**Origin:** German
**Pronunciation:** NOR bert
**Description:** Norbert is an old-fashioned name of German origin, meaning 'bright north' or 'famous north'.
**Alternative spellings:** Norburt

## Norman

**Meaning:** North man
**Origin:** English
**Pronunciation:** nor MAN
**Description:** Common among the English before the Norman invasion in 1066, it gained in popularity afterwards. Although originally a surname, it is also a popular choice as a given name.

## Norton

**Meaning:** North settlement
**Origin:** English
**Pronunciation:** NOR tun
**Description:** Norton is most commonly found as a surname. It was originally given to those who lived in places dubbed 'Norton', meaning 'north town'. It is not frequently seen as a given name.
**Alternative spellings:** Norten

# O

## Oakley

**Meaning:** Oak wood
**Origin:** English
**Pronunciation:** OKE lee

**Description:** Oakley came about as a surname, given to those who lived in places near to a wood full of oak trees. The name is part of

a growing trend to give children surnames as first names.
**Alternative spellings:** Oaklee, Oakleigh

## Ocean
**Meaning:** The ocean
**Origin:** English
**Pronunciation:** OH shun
**Description:** Ocean is a name that comes from the noun in the English language to refer to a very large expanse of sea. It is a modern name and can be found on both boys and girls.
**Alternative spellings:** Oshun

## Octavius
**Meaning:** Eighth
**Origin:** Latin
**Pronunciation:** oc TAY vee us
**Description:** From the Latin word *'octavus'*, meaning 'eighth'. It was the family name of the Roman Emperor Augustus before he changed his name.
**Alternative spellings:** Octayvius

## Odysseus
**Meaning:** Full of wrath
**Origin:** Greek
**Pronunciation:** oh DIH see us
**Description:** Odysseus is the protagonist in Homer's epic poem *The Odyssey*.
**Alternative spellings:** Odisseus, Odyseus

## Odin
**Meaning:** Inspiration; rage; frenzy
**Origin:** Norse
**Pronunciation:** oh DIN
**Description:** Odin is an Old Norse name derived from the Norse word *'óðr'* meaning 'inpiration,' 'rage' or

'frenzy'. In Norse mythology, Odin was the highest of the gods and resided in Valhalla, where warriors went after death.

## Oisin
**Meaning:** Tiny deer
**Origin:** Gaelic
**Pronunciation:** OH sheen
**Description:** Oisin is a reopening of the name Ossain, which in Irish legend is the son of Finn and means 'tiny deer'.
**Alternative spellings:** Osain, Ossain

## Ola
See entry in 'Names for Baby Girls A–Z'

## Olaf
**Meaning:** Descendant of an ancestor
**Origin:** Norse
**Pronunciation:** OH laugh
**Description:** The name Olaf originates from the Old Norse word *'anleifr'*, meaning 'descendant of an ancestor'.
**Alternative spellings:** Ollaf

## Olan
**Meaning:** Name of a saint
**Origin:** Irish
**Pronunciation:** oh LAHN
**Description:** Olan is the name of an Irish saint who is the patron saint of the parish of Aghabullogue, a village in Cork.

## Ole
**Meaning:** Ancestor
**Origin:** Norse
**Pronunciation:** OH lee
**Description:** Ole is of Norse origin, meaning 'ancestor'. It is

O

popular in Danish- and Norwegian-speaking countries.
**Alternative spellings:** Olee, Olley, Ollie

## Oliver
**Meaning:** Olive
**Origin:** Latin
**Pronunciation:** OH lih ver
**Description:** The name Oliver has many origins. It is the masculine form of Olive, derived from the fruit that grows on olive trees. Alternately it could be connected with the Old Norse '*oleifr*', meaning 'ancestral relic'.
**Alternative spellings:** Olifer

## Olivier
**Meaning:** Olive tree
**Origin:** Latin
**Pronunciation:** oh lih VE ay
**Description:** Olivier is a name that was given to medieval ruler Charlemagne's closest companions. It is said that Olivier was thoughtful and cautious, and the name derives from the Latin for 'olive tree'. A common name in France, it is rarer in the UK.
**Alternative spellings:** Oliwier

## Ollie
**Meaning:** Olive
**Origin:** Greek
**Pronunciation:** OLL lee
**Description:** A shortened form of Oliver or Olive; Ollie is often seen as a name in its own right. It is technically a unisex name, but more often used for boys.
**Alternative spellings:** Oli, Olie, Olli, Olly, Oly

## Omar
**Meaning:** Long life

**Origin:** Arabic, Hebrew
**Pronunciation:** OH mar
**Description:** Omar is of both Arabic and Hebrew origin. It can be found in the Bible as the name of the son of Esau.
**Alternative spellings:** Omah, Omarr, Omer

## Omari
**Meaning:** Long life
**Origin:** Arabic
**Pronunciation:** oh MAR ee
**Description:** Omari is a unisex variation on the masculine name Omar, meaning 'long life'.
**Alternative spellings:** Omarie, Omary

## Ophion
**Meaning:** Ruler
**Origin:** Greek
**Pronunciation:** OH fi on
**Description:** In Greek mythology, Ophion ruled the world with Eurynome before the two of them were cast down by the Titans.
**Alternative spellings:** Ofion, Opheon

## Oren
**Meaning:** Pine; ash
**Origin:** Hebrew
**Pronunciation:** oh REN
**Description:** Oren is a Hebrew boys' name meaning 'pine' or 'ash'. He was a character in the Book of Characters, one of the last books of the Bible. He was one of six sons of Jerahmeel.

## Orestes
**Meaning:** Mountain
**Origin:** Greek
**Pronunciation:** Oh REH stehs

**Description:** An uncommon name of Greek origin, Orestes is derived from the Greek word *'oros'*, meaning 'mountain'.
**Alternative spellings:** Orestis, Orestus, Orestys

## Orin
**Meaning:** Pale
**Origin:** Gaelic, Hebrew
**Pronunciation:** OH rin
**Description:** Orin is an uncommon boys' name of Gaelic and Hebrew origins. It is a variant of *oran* (Gaelic, meaning pale) and *oren* (Hebrew, meaning pine tree).
**Alternative spellings:** Oran, Oren

## Orion
**Meaning:** Hunter
**Origin:** Greek
**Pronunciation:** oh RYE on
**Description:** Orion is an uncommon given name for boys. Orion was a mighty hunter, the son of Poseidon, who was turned into a constellation.
**Alternative spellings:** Oryon

## Orlando
**Meaning:** Famous land
**Origin:** German
**Pronunciation:** or LAN doe
**Description:** The name Orlando is the Italian version of the Old German name Roland, meaning 'famous land'.
**Alternative spellings:** Orhlando, Orlandoh

## Orpheus
**Meaning:** Darkness
**Origin:** Greek
**Pronunciation:** OR fee us

**Description:** In Greek mythology, Orpheus was a legendary poet and musician.
**Alternative spellings:** Orfeus, Orpheos

## Orson
**Meaning:** Bear
**Origin:** French
**Pronunciation:** OR sun
**Description:** Orson comes from the French nickname for 'bear'.
**Alternative spellings:** Orsonne

## Oscar
**Meaning:** Divine spear
**Origin:** English
**Pronunciation:** OSS car
**Description:** The name Oscar was originally used in James Macpherson's poems, which inspired Napoleon to name his godson Oskar. This is how the former king of Sweden came to have an English name.
**Alternative spellings:** Oscah, Oska, Oskar

## Osian
**Meaning:** Poet
**Origin:** Welsh
**Pronunciation:** OSH an
**Description:** Osian is a Welsh name that would have derived from the legendary poet Oisin.

## Oskar
**Meaning:** Lover of deer
**Origin:** Greek
**Pronunciation:** os KAHR
**Description:** Oskar is the Scandinavian version of Oscar. Its history can be traced back to usage in poems about the past of Scotland, written in the 1700s. Napoleon named his godson after the

**O**

character, who went on to become the king of Sweden. In 1895 Oscar Wilde was tried for homosexuality and as a result the popularity of the name Oscar dwindled, but it is now a very popular name, especially in America.
**Alternative spellings:** Oscar

## Oslo
**Meaning:** Capital of Norway
**Origin:** English
**Pronunciation:** os LOW
**Description:** Oslo is taken directly from the name of the capital of Norway. Like London and Paris, this name follows the trend of using place names for baby names.

## Osman
**Meaning:** Servant of God
**Origin:** Arabic
**Pronunciation:** OZ man
**Description:** Osman is a version of the male Arabic given name Uthman. The name was first used in Persia and was then adopted by Turkish, Bosnian, Indian and Pakistani communities, among others.
**Alternative spellings:** Osmann, Usman

## Otis
**Meaning:** Prosperity and fortune
**Origin:** German
**Pronunciation:** OH tiss
**Description:** Otis comes from the German male name Oda, meaning 'prosperity and fortune'.
**Alternative spellings:** Oatis, Otiss

## Otto
**Meaning:** Wealthy
**Origin:** German
**Pronunciation:** OTT oh; AW to

**Description:** The German name Otto is traditionally pronounced 'aw-to' but has been anglicised to 'otto'.
**Alternative spellings:** Autto, Otoh

## Owain
**Meaning:** Born of the yew tree
**Origin:** Gaelic
**Pronunciation:** OH wen
**Description:** The name Owain is thought to be a variation of the Greek name Eugene. However, it may derive from the name Eoghan, meaning 'lamb'.
**Alternative spellings:** Owaine, Owayn

## Owais
**Meaning:** Little wolf
**Origin:** Arabic
**Pronunciation:** oh-WAI
**Description:** Owais is an ancient Arabic name meaning 'little wolf'. It is formed from the Arabic word '*aws*', meaning wolf.
**Alternative spellings:** Uwais, Ouways, Ouweis.

## Owen
**Meaning:** Well born
**Origin:** Gaelic
**Pronunciation:** OH win
**Description:** The name Owen could be a transferred use of the surname or an anglicised version of the Gaelic name Owain.
**Alternative spellings:** Owin

## Ozzy
**Meaning:** No meaning
**Origin:** English
**Pronunciation:** ozz EE
**Description:** Ozzy is a short form of names such as Osvaldo

and Osborne. A famous English Ozzy is Ozzy Osbourne, who was the lead singer for

the heavy metal band, Black Sabbath.
**Alternative spellings:** Ozzie

# P

## Pablo
**Meaning:** Humble
**Origin:** Spanish
**Pronunciation:** PAHB low
**Description:** The name Pablo has most certainly been popularised by the fame of the artist Pablo Picasso, to whom it owes its introduction to Britain and America. It is especially popular in Spain.
**Alternative spellings:** Pabloh

## Paddy
**Meaning:** Patrician
**Origin:** Gaelic
**Pronunciation:** PAH dee
**Description:** The name Paddy first came about as a shortened version of the name Patrick, but is now a name in its own right. It arose in Ulster in the 17th century.
**Alternative spellings:** Paddi, Paddie

## Paolo
**Meaning:** Small
**Origin:** Latin
**Pronunciation:** POW low
**Description:** Paolo is a name of Italian and Latin origin, meaning 'small' or 'humble'. It is a popular name in Italy.
**Alternative spellings:** Powlo

## Paris
See entry in 'Names for Baby Girls A–Z'

## Parker
**Meaning:** Gamekeeper
**Origin:** English
**Pronunciation:** PAR ka
**Description:** Parker was originally a surname given to gamekeepers in the Middle Ages. It is now being used as a first name and is predominantly American.
**Alternative spellings:** Parcer

## Pascal
**Meaning:** Associated with Passover/Easter
**Origin:** Latin
**Pronunciation:** pass CAL
**Description:** Pascal is a name that is taken from the Latin word '*paschalis*' or '*pashalis*', meaning 'associated with Passover or Easter'. This name is often given to baby boys born on Easter Day.
**Alternative spellings:** Pascale, Pasqual

## Patrick
**Meaning:** Noble
**Origin:** Gaelic
**Pronunciation:** PAT rik
**Description:** Although the name Patrick derives from the Latin '*patricius*', a title given to distinguish a nobleman, it is considered a Gaelic name. Patrick is the name of the patron saint of Ireland.
**Alternative spellings:** Patrik, Patryck

O

P

## Paul

**Meaning:** Modest
**Origin:** Latin
**Pronunciation:** PAWL
**Description:** Paul comes from the Latin name Paulus, originally a Roman nickname meaning 'small' or 'modest'.
**Alternative spellings:** Paull, Pawel

## Pavel

**Meaning:** Small; little
**Origin:** Slavic
**Pronunciation:** pah VEL
**Description:** Pavel is a common name found in Slavic countries and it means 'small' or 'little'.
**Alternative spellings:** Pavell

## Pavish

**Meaning:** Bright
**Origin:** Hindi
**Pronunciation:** PAH vish
**Description:** Although there is some argument about the meaning of this name, Pavish is an Indian/Hindu name most likely meaning 'bright'.

## Payton

**Meaning:** Town of peacocks
**Origin:** Old English
**Pronunciation:** PAY tun
**Description:** Payton is a unisex name of separate origins. Some believe it derives from the name Patrick, meaning 'noble'. It is also said to be made up of the two Old English elements of *'pawa'*, meaning 'peacock', and *'tun'*, meaning 'town'. This would make the meaning of the name 'town of peacocks'.
**Alternative spellings:** Peyton

## Pedro

**Meaning:** Rock
**Origin:** Spanish
**Pronunciation:** PED roh
**Description:** Pedro is the Spanish variant of the name Peter.
**Alternative spellings:** Pedroh

## Peleus

**Meaning:** Man of Pelion
**Origin:** Greek
**Pronunciation:** PEL ee us
**Description:** In Greek mythology, Peleus was the father of Achilles and a brave warrior who fought alongside Heracles.
**Alternative spellings:** Peleos

## Percy

**Meaning:** Pierce valley
**Origin:** French
**Pronunciation:** PUR see
**Description:** Percy is a name of French origin, meaning 'pierce valley'. In medieval times, Percy was used as a nickname for Piers or Percival.
**Alternative spellings:** Percee, Perci, Percie

## Perry

**Meaning:** Proximity to a pear tree
**Origin:** English
**Pronunciation:** PEH ree
**Description:** The name Perry derives from an Old English surname originally given to those who lived near a pear tree. Originally a masculine name, it is now unisex.
**Alternative spellings:** Perri, Perrie

## Pete

**Meaning:** Rock
**Origin:** Greek

**Pronunciation:** PEET
**Description:** Although rarely seen as a given name in its own right, Pete is a popular pet name for those named Peter.
**Alternative spellings:** Peet, Peit

## Peter

**Meaning:** Rock
**Origin:** Greek
**Pronunciation:** PEE tuh
**Description:** Peter is the English form of the most well known of Christ's apostles. The name means 'rock' and has been in constant use since the Middle Ages.
**Alternative spellings:** Peeta, Peita, Peta

## Pharrell

**Meaning:** Descendant of the valorous man
**Origin:** American
**Pronunciation:** FAH rel
**Description:** Pharell is a modern American name for boys.
**Alternative spellings:** Farrell, Farryll, Pharryl

## Phil

**Meaning:** Lover of horses
**Origin:** Greek
**Pronunciation:** FILL
**Description:** Phil is a unisex name that first came about as a shortened form for the names Philip, Philippa or Phyliss. It is usually a pet name, but is sometimes a name in its own right.
**Alternative spellings:** Phill

## Philip

**Meaning:** Lover of horses
**Origin:** Greek
**Pronunciation:** FIL lip

**Description:** Philip comes from the Greek name Philippos, comprised of words meaning 'to love' and 'horse'. It has been popular since the classical period.
**Alternative spellings:** Philipe, Phillip, Phillipe

## Phoebus

**Meaning:** Bright
**Origin:** Greek
**Pronunciation:** FEE bus
**Description:** In Greek mythology, Phoebus was one of the names given to Apollo, the son of Zeus.
**Alternative spellings:** Foebus, Phoebos

## Phoenix

**Meaning:** Mythological bird
**Origin:** Greek
**Pronunciation:** FEE niks
**Description:** Phoenix as a given name comes from the mythological bird, said to die by fire, then rise from its own ashes. It is often found as a surname.
**Alternative spellings:** Fenix, Foenix, Phenix, Pheoinx

## Pierce

**Meaning:** Rock
**Origin:** Greek, English
**Pronunciation:** PEERS
**Description:** Pierce is an uncommon name of Greek and English origin.
**Alternative spellings:** Pearce, Peirs, Piers

## Pierre

**Meaning:** Rock
**Origin:** French
**Pronunciation:** pee AIR

P

**Description:** The French variant of Peter.
**Alternative spellings:** Piere, Pierr

## Piotr
**Meaning:** Rock
**Origin:** Greek
**Pronunciation:** PEA otr
**Description:** Piotr is a variation on Peter and is most commonly found in Slavic- and Polish-speaking countries.
**Alternative spellings:** Piotra, Piotre, Pietro

## Pietro
**Meaning:** Stone; rock
**Origin:** Italy
**Pronunciation:** PEE et roh
**Description:** Piertro is the Italian version of the popular name Peter, and shares the same meaning of 'stone' or 'rock'.
**Alternative spellings:** Peter

## Piper
**Meaning:** Pipe player
**Origin:** English
**Pronunciation:** PIPE er
**Description:** Piper was originally a surname given to those whose father played the pipe. It is now a unisex first name.
**Alternative spellings:** Pypa, Pyper

## Poseidon
**Meaning:** God of the sea
**Origin:** Greek
**Pronunciation:** Poss EYE don
**Description:** In Greek mythology, Poseidon was the god of the sea.
**Alternative spellings:** Poseydon

## Pranav
**Meaning:** Praise
**Origin:** Sanskrit
**Pronunciation:** PRA nav
**Description:** Pranav comes from the Sanskrit word for 'symbol'. It is a common name for Indian boys.
**Alternative spellings:** Praanav, Pranaav, Prannav

## Prateek
**Meaning:** Image or symbol of God
**Origin:** Sanskrit
**Pronunciation:** prah TEEK
**Description:** Prateek is a Sanskrit name meaning 'image of symbol of God'.
**Alternative spellings:** Pratik

## Presley
**Meaning:** Priest's meadow
**Origin:** English
**Pronunciation:** PRES ley
**Description:** Presley is a name of Old English origin, meaning 'priest's meadow'. Originally a surname, it has become a somewhat common given name.
**Alternative spellings:** Preslee, Presleigh, Presli, Preslie, Presly

## Preston
**Meaning:** Priest's town
**Origin:** English
**Pronunciation:** PRES tun
**Description:** Preston is the name of a town in Lancashire and would have been given as a surname to those who lived there. The word originates from the Old English 'preost', meaning 'priest', and 'tun', meaning 'town'. It is now found as a given name.

**Alternative spellings:** Prestan, Presten, Prestun

# Prince
**Meaning:** Prince
**Origin:** Latin
**Pronunciation:** PRINSE
**Description:** As well as being a royal title, Prince would have been given as a surname to those who worked in the prince's household. The name has had a surge in popularity as a first name since the fame of 80s singer Prince.
**Alternative spellings:** Prynce

# Prisha
See entry in 'Names for Baby Girls A–Z'

# Q

## Qasim
**Meaning:** Generous; selfless
**Origin:** Arabic
**Pronunciation:** KAH sim
**Description:** Qasim derives from the Arabic word *'qasama'*, meaning 'to share' or 'portion'. It now carries the meaning of 'selfless' or 'generous'.
**Alternative spellings:** Quasim

## Quentin
**Meaning:** Fifth born
**Origin:** Latin
**Pronunciation:** KWEN tin
**Description:** Quentin derives from the Latin name Quintinus, meaning 'fifth'.
**Alternative spellings:** Quenton, Quintin, Quinton

## Quest
**Meaning:** Voyage of discovery
**Origin:** English
**Pronunciation:** KWEST
**Description:** Quest is a fairly modern name, often given as a baby name for a boy. It comes from the English word for a 'voyage of discovery'.
**Alternative spellings:** Qwest

## Quincy
**Meaning:** Fifth born
**Origin:** Latin
**Pronunciation:** KWIN see
**Description:** Quincy derives from the Latin name Quintinus and means 'fifth'. It can also be a shortened form of the name Quentin.
**Alternative spellings:** Quency, Quincey, Quinci, Quincie

## Quinn
**Meaning:** Descendant of Cuinn
**Origin:** Gaelic
**Pronunciation:** KWIN
**Description:** Traditionally, Quinn was used as a surname for the son of Cuinn. It transferred into a male given name and is now used for both boys and girls.
**Alternative spellings:** Quin, Quinne, Qwin

P

Q

223

# R

## Raees
**Meaning:** Chief
**Origin:** Arabic
**Pronunciation:** RACE
**Description:** Raees is an uncommon variant of the Arabic name Rais, meaning 'chief' or 'leader'. It is a title used by the rulers of Muslim states in the Middle East and South Asia.
**Alternative spellings:** Race, Raees, Rais

## Rafael
**Meaning:** God has healed
**Origin:** Hebrew
**Pronunciation:** RAH fy elle
**Description:** Rafael is a variant of the biblical name Raphael. The name is made up of the elements of *'rapha'*, meaning 'to heal', and *'el'*, which means 'God'.
**Alternative spellings:** Rafaell, Rafaelle, Raffael, Raphael, Raphaell

## Rafal
**Meaning:** God has healed
**Origin:** Hebrew
**Pronunciation:** RAF al
**Description:** Rafal is the Polish variant of the Hebrew name Raphael, meaning 'God has healed'.
**Alternative spellings:** Rafel, Raffal, Raphal

## Rafe
**Meaning:** Wolf
**Origin:** Norse
**Pronunciation:** RAYF
**Description:** Rafe is a variant of the name Ralph, which comes from the Norse word for 'wolf'. It was popular in the 17th century but Ralph is now the preferred form. Rafe could also be seen as a shortened form of the name Rafael.
**Alternative spellings:** Raife, Rayfe

## Rafferty
**Meaning:** One who will prosper
**Origin:** Gaelic
**Pronunciation:** RAF er tee
**Description:** The name Rafferty originally came about as an Irish surname, meaning 'prosperous'. It was then transferred into a boys' given name.
**Alternative spellings:** Rafertey, Raferti, Rafertie, Raferty, Raffertey, Rafferti, Raffertie

## Rafi
**Meaning:** Holding high; servant of the exalted one
**Origin:** Arabic
**Pronunciation:** RA fi
**Description:** Rafi is a name used by Muslims, Jews and Christians of Armenian origin. The word Rafi is of Arabic origin, and its meaning is 'holding high' or 'servant of the exalted one'.
**Alternative spellings:** Rafee, Raffi, Raffy

## Raheem
**Meaning:** Kind-hearted
**Origin:** Arabic
**Pronunciation:** rah HEEM
**Description:** Raheem is a phonetic spelling variant of the Arabic name Rahim, meaning 'kind-hearted'. It is also the shortened form of

Abdurrahim, meaning 'servant of the merciful'.
**Alternative spellings:** Rahim, Rahime

## Rahim
**Meaning:** Compassionate
**Origin:** Arabic
**Pronunciation:** ra HEEM
**Description:** Rahim is an Arabic name meaning 'compassionate'. It is one of the most popular names in Afghanistan. In Islam, Rahim is one of the 99 attribute names of Allah.
**Alternative spellings:** Raheem, Rahiem

## Rahman
**Meaning:** The compassionate; the most gracious
**Origin:** Arabic
**Pronunciation:** RAH mahn
**Description:** This name usually forms part of a compound, such as Abdur Rahman, 'servant of God'.

## Raihan
**Meaning:** Sweet basil
**Origin:** Arabic
**Pronunciation:** ray HAN
**Description:** Raihan is considered to mean 'sweet basil'. It is not commonly found in Britain.
**Alternative spellings:** Rayhan

## Raja
**Meaning:** Optimism
**Origin:** Arabic
**Pronunciation:** rah-JUH
**Description:** This Arabic name is considered unisex, but the feminine and masculine forms are often pronounced differently. For girls it is pronounced

'rah-jah', whereas for boys it is 'rah-juh'.
**Alternative spellings:** Raija, Raijah, Rajah

## Rajan
**Meaning:** The radiant king
**Origin:** Sanskrit
**Pronunciation:** RA jan
**Description:** Rajan is a name of Hindi and Sanskrit origin, meaning 'the radiant king'. It can also be of Arabic origin, meaning 'anticipation'.
**Alternative spellings:** Raajan, Rajaan

## Rajveer
**Meaning:** The hero of the land; kingdom's warrior
**Origin:** Punjabi
**Pronunciation:** RAJ veer
**Description:** Rajveer is a somewhat common Punjabi name. It means 'the hero of the land; kingdom's warrior'.
**Alternative spellings:** Rajvir

## Ralf
**Meaning:** Wolf counsel
**Origin:** English
**Pronunciation:** RALF
**Description:** Ralf is a variant of the Old English name Ralph, meaning 'wolf counsel'. It was very common in the early 20th century but is now less popular.
**Alternative spellings:** Ralfe, Ralph, Ralphe

## Ralphie
**Meaning:** Wolf counsel
**Origin:** English
**Pronunciation:** RALF ee

R

225

**Description:** Ralphie is a variant of the Old English name Ralph, meaning 'wolf counsel'. It was very common in the early 20th century but its usage has declined.
**Alternative spellings:** Ralphee, Ralphi, Ralphy

## Ramla
See entry in 'Names for Baby Girls A–Z'

## Rana
See entry in 'Names for Baby Girls A–Z'

## Randall
**Meaning:** Wolf shield
**Origin:** Norse
**Pronunciation:** RAN dul
**Description:** Randall is a mainly US vernacular form of the Norse name Randolf.
**Alternative spellings:** Randalle, Randell

## Randolf
**Meaning:** Wolf shield
**Origin:** Norse
**Pronunciation:** RAN dulf
**Description:** Randolf is a Norman name derived from the Old Norse name Rannulfr. This name is comprised of elements meaning 'wolf' and 'shield'. It is also seen as a surname.
**Alternative spellings:** Randolph

## Randy
**Meaning:** Wolf shield
**Origin:** Norse
**Pronunciation:** RAN dee
**Description:** Most common in the US and Australia, Randy is a pet form of Randolf, Randall or Andrew, and it is also a name used for girls. It is also seen as a given name in its own right.
**Alternative spellings:** Randey, Randi, Randie

## Ranveer
**Meaning:** Hero of the battle
**Origin:** Indian
**Pronunciation:** ran VEE er
**Description:** Ranveer is an Indian male name meaning 'hero of the battle'. The popular Bollywood actor, Ranveer Singh, has contributed to the popularity of this name. See entry in 'Names for Baby Girls A–Z'

## Rashid
**Meaning:** Rightly guided
**Origin:** Arabic
**Pronunciation:** rash EED
**Description:** Rashid is a common Arabic boys' name meaning 'rightly guided'. It can be spelt in many different ways and is one of 99 names of Allah.
**Alternative spellings:** Raashid, Rachid, Rashed, Rachid, Rasheed

## Rastus
**Meaning:** To love
**Origin:** German
**Pronunciation:** RAS tus
**Description:** Rastus is a name found in the New Testament. It is also a short form of the Greek name Erastus, derived from the word *'eran'*, meaning 'to love'.
**Alternative spellings:** Rastuss

## Raul
**Meaning:** Wolf counsel
**Origin:** Norse

**Pronunciation:** rah OOL
**Description:** Raul is the Spanish version of the masculine name Ralph.
**Alternative spellings:** Raoul, Raull

## Ravi
**Meaning:** Sun
**Origin:** Sanskrit
**Pronunciation:** RA vi
**Description:** In ancient Hindu mythology, Ravi is the Hindu god of the sun.
**Alternative spellings:** Ravee, Ravvi

## Ray
**Meaning:** Decision protector
**Origin:** German
**Pronunciation:** RAY
**Description:** Ray is a shortened form of Raymond, but is also given as a name in its own right. Although Ray is a specifically masculine name, many of its spelling variants are favoured for girls.
**Alternative spellings:** Rae, Rai, Raye

## Rayan
**Meaning:** Gates to heaven
**Origin:** Sanskrit
**Pronunciation:** RY han
**Description:** Rayan is a unisex name that is said to refer to the gates of heaven in Islamic belief. Rayan is also a title used in India to distinguish those in power. As well as having Arabic roots, Rayan has origins in the Persian language where it is said to derive from the name Rayhan.
**Alternative spellings:** Raiyan, Rayann, Rayanne

## Rayhan
**Meaning:** Fragranced herb
**Origin:** Persian
**Pronunciation:** RY hahn
**Description:** Rayhan is a Persian name that features in the Quran. It could also be considered a spelling variant of the Sanskrit name Rayan.
**Alternative spellings:** Raihan, Rayhaan, Rehan, Rihan

## Raylan
**Meaning:** No meaning
**Origin:** American
**Pronunciation:** RAY laan
**Description:** Raylan is a modern baby name that was invented in America. As such, it has no meaning but it would be a great choice for parents looking for something interesting and unique.

## Rayyan
**Meaning:** Gate of paradise; splendour
**Origin:** Arabic
**Pronunciation:** ray YAN
**Description:** Rayyan is an Arabic boys' name and is said to be one of the gates of paradise, especially for those who have fasted throughout their lives.
**Alternative spellings:** Rayan
See entry in 'Names for Baby Girls A–Z'

## Raymond
**Meaning:** Decision protector
**Origin:** French
**Pronunciation:** RAY mund
**Description:** Raymond comes from the Old French name Raimund and was introduced to Britain by the Normans.
**Alternative spellings:** Raimond, Raymund

**R**

## Razzaq

**Meaning:** The provider
**Origin:** Muslim
**Pronunciation:** ra ZAK
**Description:** Razzaq is a name that usually forms a compound, such as Abdur Razzaq, meaning 'servant of the all-provider'.

## Reece

**Meaning:** Enthusiasm
**Origin:** Welsh
**Pronunciation:** reese
**Description:** An anglicised spelling of Rhys, the name Reece is now widespread outside Wales, among girls as well as boys. The name means 'enthusiasm'.
**Alternative spellings:** Rhys

## Reed

**Meaning:** Red-haired
**Origin:** Scottish
**Pronunciation:** reed
**Description:** Reed is an Old English surname meaning 'red' and is usually given to people with red hair.
**Alternative spellings:** Reid
See entry in 'Names for Baby Girls A–Z'

## Reese

See entry in 'Names for Baby Girls A–Z'

## Regan

See entry in 'Names for Baby Girls A–Z'

## Reggie

**Meaning:** Queen
**Origin:** Latin
**Pronunciation:** RED jee
**Description:** Reggie derives from the traditional boys' name Reginald. Reginald could be derived from the German name Reginwald, or from the Latin word *'regina'*, meaning 'queen'.
**Alternative spellings:** Reggi, Reggy

## Reginald

**Meaning:** Queen
**Origin:** Latin
**Pronunciation:** REG in old
**Description:** Reginald could derive from the German name Reginwald, or from the Latin word *'regina'*, meaning 'queen'. It was very popular in the early 20th century but has recently fallen from favour.
**Alternative spellings:** Regienald, Reginold

## Rehaan

**Meaning:** Sweet-scented
**Origin:** Arabic
**Pronunciation:** RAY han
**Description:** Rehaan is a variant of the popular Arabic name Rehan. Rehan features in the Quran and is said to mean 'sweet-scented'.
**Alternative spellings:** Reehan, Rehan

## Reign

**Meaning:** To rule
**Origin:** English
**Pronunciation:** rayn
**Description:** Reign come from the English vocabulary word meaning 'to rule' or to 'hold royal office,' and is a unique name choice.

## Reiss

**Meaning:** Twig
**Origin:** German

**Pronunciation:** REESE; RICE
**Description:** Reiss is a German surname of Old German origin, sometimes used as a given name. It is most commonly used by Ashkenazic Jewish people as an occupational name for a rice dealer or as an ornamental name from the Old German word *'Reis'*, meaning 'twig' or 'branch'.
**Alternative spellings:** Reis, Ryce

## Remi

**Meaning:** From Rheims
**Origin:** French
**Pronunciation:** reh ME
**Description:** The name Remi derives from the French town Rheims and would have originally been given to those who lived in the town. There was also a French saint who bore the name Remi.
**Alternative spellings:** Remy

## Rene

See Renee in 'Names for Baby Girls A–Z'

## Reon

**Meaning:** King
**Origin:** Gaelic
**Pronunciation:** RE on
**Description:** Reon is a rare variant of the boys' name Ryan, which is of Gaelic origin and means 'king'.
**Alternative spellings:** Rion, Ryon

## Reuben

**Meaning:** Behold; a son
**Origin:** Hebrew
**Pronunciation:** ROO ben
**Description:** Reuben is a biblical name borne by one of Jacob's 12 sons, and hence a name of one of the 12 tribes of Israel.
**Alternative spellings:** Reuban, Ruben

## Rex

**Meaning:** King
**Origin:** Latin
**Pronunciation:** REKS
**Description:** Rex is the Latin word for 'king' and it first came to exist as a given name in the 19th century.
**Alternative spellings:** Reks

## Reyan

**Meaning:** Door of heaven
**Origin:** Indian
**Pronunciation:** REE yan
**Description:** Reyan is a variant spelling of the name Riyan, an Indian boys' name meaning 'door of heaven'.
**Alternative spellings:** Riaan, Riyan

## Reyansh

**Meaning:** Ray of light
**Origin:** Hindi
**Pronunciation:** rey AANSH
**Description:** Reyansh is a Hindi boys' name meaning 'ray of light'. It is also used as an alternative name for the Hindu god, Lord Vishnu.

**R**

## Rhett

**Meaning:** Advice; counsel
**Origin:** Dutch
**Pronunciation:** reh ETT
**Description:** Rhett was a Dutch surname and anglicised form of de Raedt, where the Middle Dutch word *'raet'* means 'advice' or 'counsel'. It was brought to the United States by Dutch settlers in

the 1600s, particularly the South Carolina region. One of the main characters in *Gone with the Wind* is Rhett Butler.

# Rian

**Meaning:** Little king
**Origin:** Gaelic
**Pronunciation:** RIY an
**Description:** Rian is the anglicised spelling of the Irish name Ryan.
**Alternative spellings:** Ryan

# Ricardo

**Meaning:** Powerful
**Origin:** German
**Pronunciation:** ree KAR doh
**Description:** Ricardo is a variation of the German name Richard, meaning 'powerful'. It is often found in Italy.
**Alternative spellings:** Ricardoh, Rikardo

# Rich

**Meaning:** Powerful
**Origin:** German
**Pronunciation:** RITCH
**Description:** Rich is a shortened version of the German name Richard. It is now a given name in its own right. Rich also means 'wealthy' in English.
**Alternative spellings:** Ritch

# Richard

**Meaning:** Powerful
**Origin:** German
**Pronunciation:** RICH urd
**Description:** Proving to be an enduringly popular given name, Richard is of Frankish origin and was introduced to the UK by the Normans. The name is particularly associated with Richard I, who earned the nickname 'lionheart'.
**Alternative spellings:** Richarde, Ritchard

# Richie

**Meaning:** Powerful
**Origin:** German
**Pronunciation:** RITCH ee
**Description:** Richie is a shortened variant of the popular Old German name, Richard, meaning 'strong power'.
**Alternative spellings:** Richee, Richi, Richy, Ritchee, Ritchi, Ritchie, Ritchy

# Rick

**Meaning:** Powerful
**Origin:** German
**Pronunciation:** RIK
**Description:** Rick is a shortened form of Richard and sometimes Frederick. It is now seen as a name in its own right.
**Alternative spellings:** Rik

# Ricky

**Meaning:** Powerful
**Origin:** German
**Pronunciation:** RIK ee
**Description:** Ricky is a pet form of Richard and sometimes Frederick. It is now seen as a name in its own right and is regarded as a unisex name.
**Alternative spellings:** Ricki, Rickie, Riki, Rikie, Riky

# Rico

**Meaning:** Ruler of the home; powerful
**Origin:** Italian
**Pronunciation:** REE ko

**Description:** Rico originated as a pet name for Enrico and Ricardo. Enrico means 'ruler of the home' while Ricardo is a form of Richard, meaning 'powerful'.
**Alternative spellings:** Reeco, Ricoh

## Ridwan
**Meaning:** Merciful
**Origin:** Arabic
**Pronunciation:** rihd WAN
**Description:** Ridwan derives from the name of the keeper of the gates of heaven in Islamic belief. Connotations of the name are those of goodwill and mercifulness.
**Alternative spellings:** Riddwan

## Riley
**Meaning:** Unknown
**Origin:** Irish
**Pronunciation:** rye LEE
**Description:** Riley is most likely a respelling of the Irish surname, Reilley, from an Irish personal name Raghallach. It is unknown what this name means, however. It can also be a unisex English name meaning 'rye wood'.
**Alternative spellings:** Reilly, Riley, Ryleigh

## Ringo
**Meaning:** No meaning
**Origin:** English
**Pronunciation:** ring GOH
**Description:** Ringo is actually an invented nickname specifically for Ringo Starr, one of the members of The Beatles. Originally called Richard Starkey, Ringo was given this moniker for all the rings he wore.

## Rio
**Meaning:** River
**Origin:** Spanish
**Pronunciation:** REE o
**Description:** Rio is a fairly modern unisex name derived from the Spanish word for 'river'. It is also linked to major Brazilian city Rio de Janeiro, which directly translates to 'river of January'.
**Alternative spellings:** Reo, Rioh

## Rishi
**Meaning:** Wise
**Origin:** Sanskrit
**Pronunciation:** RIH shee
**Description:** The name Rishi derives from the seer said to reveal Vedic hymns when in a state of higher consciousness, called 'The Rishi'. The meaning of the name is therefore 'wise'.
**Alternative spellings:** Rhishi, Rishie

## River
**Meaning:** River
**Origin:** English
**Pronunciation:** RIH vuh
**Description:** River is a fairly modern name, borne out of the so-called 'flower power' era in the 1960s. It is considered unisex.
**Alternative spellings:** Riva, Ryver

## Riyad
**Meaning:** Meadows; gardens
**Origin:** Arabic
**Pronunciation:** ree AD
**Description:** Riyad is an Arabic boys' name meaning 'meadows' or 'garden'.
**Alternative spellings:** Riad

**R**

## Roan

**Meaning:** Red-haired
**Origin:** Gaelic
**Pronunciation:** ro UN
**Description:** Roan is a modern variation on the masculine Gaelic name Rowan. Its Gaelic meaning is 'red-haired,' and although it used to be specifically a boys' name it can now be found used for girls. However, its most common feminine form is spelt Rowanne.
**Alternative spellings:** Rohan, Rowan

## Robbie

**Meaning:** Bright Fame
**Origin:** German
**Pronunciation:** rob BIE
**Description:** Robbie is a nickname usually given to someone with the name Robert, although it has become popular as a given name in recent years. The name Robert was introduced into the UK by the Normans and has remained popular ever since.

## Robert

**Meaning:** Bright fame
**Origin:** German
**Pronunciation:** ROB ert
**Description:** Introduced to Britain by the Normans, Robert has since remained in the spotlight as a popular first name. It is often shortened to Bob.
**Alternative spellings:** Roburt

## Roberto

**Meaning:** Bright fame
**Origin:** German
**Pronunciation:** rob ER tow
**Description:** Roberto is a variant of Robert, a name of Old German origin meaning 'bright fame'. It is a common name in Italian-, Portuguese- and Spanish-speaking countries.
**Alternative spellings:** Roburto

## Robin

**Meaning:** Bright fame
**Origin:** German
**Pronunciation:** ROB in
**Description:** Robin used to exist as a pet form of Robert, but has since gained credence as a given name for both boys and girls. It is also the English vocabulary name for the red-chested songbird seen around Christmas time.
**Alternative spellings:** Robinn, Robyn

## Robson

**Meaning:** Son of Robert
**Origin:** English
**Pronunciation:** ROB son
**Description:** Robson is an English name derived from the German name Robert. Though commonly a surname, it is occasionally used as a given name.
**Alternative spellings:** Robsen, Robsun

## Rocco

**Meaning:** Battle cry
**Origin:** German
**Pronunciation:** ROCK o
**Description:** Rocco is predominantly used within the Italian language and derives from the German name Rochbert, which is no longer in use.
**Alternative spellings:** Roccoh, Rocko

## Rocket

**Meaning:** Spacecraft; herb
**Origin:** English
**Pronunciation:** rock ETT
**Description:** Taken from the English word of the same meanings, Rocket can either refer to the spacecraft or the herb used in cooking. Jamie Oliver and Pharrell Williams both chose this name for their sons.
**Alternative spellings:** Rockett

## Rocky

**Meaning:** Rest
**Origin:** Italian
**Pronunciation:** ROH kee
**Description:** Rocky is derived from the name Rock, which itself is the anglicised form of the name Roch. Roch carries the meaning of 'rest'. Rocky is also an English word meaning 'rough' or 'many rocks'.
**Alternative spellings:** Rocki, Rockie

## Roderick

**Meaning:** Famous ruler
**Origin:** German
**Pronunciation:** rod ERR rick
**Description:** Roderick is a German name composed of '*hrōþ*', meaning 'glory' and '*rīks*', meaning 'ruler'. A common shortened version of this name is Roddy.
**Alternative spellings:** Roderik

## Rodin

**Meaning:** Unknown
**Origin:** French
**Pronunciation:** ro DAN
**Description:** Rodin is actually a French surname most attributed to the great French sculptor, August Rodin, who created *The Thinker*.

In terms of meaning, however, it is unknown.

## Rodney

**Meaning:** Hroda's Island
**Origin:** English
**Pronunciation:** RAWD nee
**Description:** Rodney was originally a surname derived from a place name, Hroda's Island. It is now a popular first name choice for baby boys.

## Rodrigo

**Meaning:** Ruled with fame
**Origin:** German
**Pronunciation:** roh DREE goh
**Description:** Rodrigo is the Spanish version of the German name Roderick, meaning 'ruled with fame'.
**Alternative spellings:** Roderigo, Rodrigoh

## Rogan

**Meaning:** Red-haired
**Origin:** Irish
**Pronunciation:** ROH gan
**Description:** Rogan is an Irish baby name meaning 'red-haired'. Like the other Irish; Gaelic baby names starting with 'ro,' this name would be idea for a red-headed baby boy.

## Roger

**Meaning:** Famous spear
**Origin:** German
**Pronunciation:** ROD jer
**Description:** Roger was one of the most popular boys' names during the medieval period.
**Alternative spellings:** Rodger

## Rohin

**Meaning:** Rising

**Origin:** Indian
**Pronunciation:** row HIN
**Description:** Rohin is a common Hindu/Indian name meaning 'rising'.

## Roland

**Meaning:** Famous country
**Origin:** German
**Pronunciation:** ROH lund
**Description:** Roland is a name of French and German origin, meaning 'famous country'.
**Alternative spellings:** Rolland, Rowland

## Roma

See entry in 'Names for Baby Girls A–Z'

## Roman

**Meaning:** Citizen of Rome
**Origin:** Latin
**Pronunciation:** ROH mun
**Description:** The name Roman derives from the Latin word referring to the citizens of Rome. The Romans are associated with power, pride and strength and the given name shares these connotations.
**Alternative spellings:** Romann

## Romario

**Meaning:** Pilgrim to Rome
**Origin:** Italian
**Pronunciation:** ro MAR io
**Description:** Romario is a variant of the Italian name Romeo. It is often used as a nickname in Portuguese- and Spanish-speaking countries.
**Alternative spellings:** Romarioh, Romarrio

## Rome

**Meaning:** Capital city of Italy
**Origin:** English
**Pronunciation:** rome
**Description:** Rome is most famously the capital city of Italy, and is derived from the Latin word '*roma*'. It follows the trend where certain place names are used as baby names, such as India or Paris.

## Romeo

**Meaning:** Pilgrim to Rome
**Origin:** Italian
**Pronunciation:** RO me oh; ro MAY oh
**Description:** Romeo is most famous for being the name of the hero in Shakespeare's play *Romeo and Juliet*. Because of this it has connotations of love. It derives from the Italian city of Rome.
**Alternative spellings:** Romio, Romyo

## Ronald

**Meaning:** Open-minded
**Origin:** Norse
**Pronunciation:** RON uld
**Description:** Ronald is predominantly found in Scotland, especially in the form Ranald. The name is of Norse origin and was brought over by raiding Vikings.
**Alternative spellings:** Ronold, Ronuld

## Ronan

**Meaning:** Little seal
**Origin:** Gaelic
**Pronunciation:** ROW nan
**Description:** Ronan was first made popular by the ancient king of Leinster, who was tricked into killing his own son. The meaning of this name comes from the Irish name Ron, meaning 'seal'.

**Alternative spellings:** Rohnan, Rownan

## Ronnie
**Meaning:** Open-minded
**Origin:** Norse
**Pronunciation:** RON ee
**Description:** This unisex name is a spelling variant of the feminine name Ronni or the masculine name Ronny.
**Alternative spellings:** Ronni, Ronny

## Ronny
**Meaning:** Open-minded
**Origin:** Norse
**Pronunciation:** RON knee
**Description:** Ronny is considered unisex although this spelling is often reserved for boys. Originally a shortened form of Ronald, it is now used as a given name in its own right.
**Alternative spellings:** Ronney, Ronni, Ronnie

## Rory
**Meaning:** Red-haired king
**Origin:** Gaelic
**Pronunciation:** RAW ree
**Description:** Rory derives from the Gaelic words meaning 'red' and 'king'. Although it is technically masculine it is becoming popular as a girls' name.
**Alternative spellings:** Roari, Roary, Rori, Rorie

## Roscoe
**Meaning:** Doe wood
**Origin:** Norse
**Pronunciation:** ross COE
**Description:** Roscoe has Norse origins, and is derived from a place name that meant 'doe wood'

in Old Norse. It was especially popular in the 1880s but has steadily declined in use over the years.
**Alternative spellings:** Rosco

## Roshan
See entry in 'Names for Baby Girls A–Z.'

## Ross
**Meaning:** Headland
**Origin:** Gaelic
**Pronunciation:** ROSS
**Description:** Ross may be thought of as a transferred surname, but the word itself comes from the Gaelic term *'ros'* meaning 'headland'.
**Alternative spellings:** Rosse

## Roy
**Meaning:** Red
**Origin:** Gaelic
**Pronunciation:** ROY
**Description:** Roy originates from Scotland, where it means 'red'. It has since been reinterpreted in some places to mean 'king', from Old French.
**Alternative spellings:** Roi, Roye

## Ruairi
**Meaning:** Red-haired king
**Origin:** Gaelic
**Pronunciation:** ROO ry
**Description:** Ruairi is a name of Goidelic (Irish and Scottish Gaelic) origin. It translates as 'red-haired king'. Historically, it has also been anglicised as Roderick. Its equivalent in the Welsh language is Rhodri, also meaning 'red'-haired king.
**Alternative spellings:** Rhodri, Ruairidh, Ruari, Ruaridh

**R**

## Ruan

**Meaning:** Little red one
**Origin:** Gaelic
**Pronunciation:** ROO an
**Description:** Ruan comes from the Gaelic word for 'red', *'ruadh'*. The other form, from the tree, comes from a Norse word for the European plant. This word refers to the red leaves and berries of the rowan tree.
**Alternative spellings:** Rooan, Ruwan

## Rudi

**Meaning:** Famous wolf
**Origin:** German
**Pronunciation:** roo DEE
**Description:** Although this name is predominantly used in its female form it is actually unisex and comes from the name Rudolph. The name is mostly used in German-, Hungarian- and Spanish-speaking countries although it is occasionally seen in Britain too. There are several spelling variations of this name including Rudie and Rudy.
**Alternative spellings:** Rudie, Rudy

## Rudra

**Meaning:** The roarer
**Origin:** Hindi
**Pronunciation:** roo DRAH
**Description:** Rudra is a Hindu/Indian name that, directly translated, means 'the roarer'. It is also a deity in the Hindu religion who is associated with wind or storm and the hunt.
**Alternative spellings:** Rudrah

## Rufus

**Meaning:** Red-haired
**Origin:** Latin
**Pronunciation:** ROO fuhs
**Description:** Rufus comes from the Latin nickname meaning 'red-haired'.
**Alternative spellings:** Ruffus

## Rupert

**Meaning:** Bright fame
**Origin:** German
**Pronunciation:** ROO pert
**Description:** Rupert is a German form of Robert, and means 'bright fame'.
**Alternative spellings:** Rupurt

## Russ

**Meaning:** Little red one
**Origin:** French
**Pronunciation:** RUSS
**Description:** Russ is a short form of Russell, and may be taken to merely mean 'red' or 'little red one' from the Old French word *'rous'*.
**Alternative spellings:** Rus

## Russell

**Meaning:** Little red one
**Origin:** French
**Pronunciation:** RUSS el
**Description:** Russell, like Roan, means 'red-haired', yet is derived from an Old French nickname.
**Alternative spellings:** Rusel, Russel

## Ryder

**Meaning:** One who rides
**Origin:** English
**Pronunciation:** RI der
**Description:** Ryder is a name of Old English origin. The name was given as an occupational name for horseback riders in

medieval times. It is more common as a surname but has recently become popular as a given name.
**Alternative spellings:** Rider, Rydar

## Ryker
**Meaning:** Rich
**Origin:** Dutch
**Pronunciation:** RYE ker
**Description:** Ryker (and its related name, Riker) is the Dutch form of the name Richard, or Rich. The meaning of the name is also 'rich,' as in wealthy. There is a prison called Riker's Island in New York City, so parents may want to be careful with this name.
**Alternative spellings:** Riker

# S

## Saad
**Meaning:** Happy;
**Origin:** Arabic
**Pronunciation:** saa HD
**Description:** Saad is mainly used in Arabic- and Hebrew-speaking countries. It is also a variant of the name Sayid, which carries many meanings including 'happy'.
**Alternative spellings:** Saahd

## Sacha
**Meaning:** Defender of man
**Origin:** Greek
**Pronunciation:** SA sha
**Description:** Sacha is a name of Russian and Greek origin. It is a diminutive of Alexander, meaning 'defender of man'.
**Alternative spellings:** Sascha, Sasha

## Sachin
**Meaning:** Essence; existence
**Origin:** Sanskrit
**Pronunciation:** SA chin
**Description:** Sachin is a name of Sanskrit origin, meaning 'essence' or 'existence'. The name is an alternative name for the god Shiva.
**Alternative spellings:** Sachen, Sashin

## Saeed
**Meaning:** Happy; mister
**Origin:** Arabic
**Pronunciation:** say EED
**Description:** Saeed is a name of Arabic origin, meaning 'happy'. It is a variant of Said.
**Alternative spellings:** Saaed, Said, Sayed, Syed

## Safwan
**Meaning:** Purity
**Origin:** Arabic
**Pronunciation:** sahf WAHN
**Description:** Safwan is a masculine name of Arabic origin, the meaning of the name is said to be 'purity'.
**Alternative spellings:** Safwann, Sahfwan, Saphwan

## Sahar
**Meaning:** Vigilant; moon
**Origin:** Arabic

R

S

**Pronunciation:** SAH hahr
**Description:** Sahar is a unisex name, which in Arabic means 'vigilant', or in Hebrew can mean 'moon'.
**Alternative spellings:** Sarhar

## Sahib

**Meaning:** Master
**Origin:** Arabic
**Pronunciation:** SAH ib
**Description:** Sahib was used in India as a mark of respect. It is said to mean 'master'.
**Alternative spellings:** Sahibb

## Sahil

**Meaning:** Sea shore
**Origin:** Hindi
**Pronunciation:** sah HIl
**Description:** Sahil is a male Hindu name derived from the Indian word for 'sea shore,' which in turn is borrowed from the Arabic.

## Sai

**Meaning:** Paint
**Origin:** Japanese
**Pronunciation:** sai
**Description:** Sai is a Japanese boys' name meaning 'paint'. It is also an Indian name, although in Hindi it has a different meaning.

## Saif

**Meaning:** Sword
**Origin:** Arabic
**Pronunciation:** say EEF
**Description:** Saif comes from the Arabic word meaning 'curved sword'. This sword is an important Arabic symbol.
**Alternative spellings:** Sayf

## Sailor

**Meaning:** A crew member of a ship or boat
**Origin:** English
**Pronunciation:** SAY lor
**Description:** Traditionally an occupational surname for someone who worked aboard a boat. Slowly it is becoming popular as a given name for boys.
**Alternative spellings:** Saylor

## Salahuddin

**Meaning:** Righteous of religion
**Origin:** Arabic
**Pronunciation:** salah HOO din
**Description:** Salahuddin is a variation of the name Salah Al-Din, an Arabic name meaning 'righteous of religion'. It is comprised of two Arabic words, '*salah*', meaning 'righteousness' and '*din*,' meaning 'religion'.

## Salman

**Meaning:** Uppermost point
**Origin:** Arabic
**Pronunciation:** sal MAAN
**Description:** The name Salman, which derives from the name Solomon, is commonly used in Arabic- and Turkish-speaking countries. Other meanings of this name include 'healthy' and 'safe'.
**Alternative spellings:** Salmaan, Zalman

## Sam

**Meaning:** God has listened
**Origin:** Hebrew
**Pronunciation:** SAM
**Description:** Short form of Samuel, and less frequently Samson. Sam is also short for the girls'

name Samantha, and for Arabic names Samir and Samira.

## Sameer
**Meaning:** Lively in conversation
**Origin:** Arabic
**Pronunciation:** SAH meer
**Description:** Sameer is a masculine name of Arabic origin and is said to refer to 'the one with lively conversation'.
**Alternative spellings:** Samir

## Sami
**Meaning:** Elevated status
**Origin:** Arabic
**Pronunciation:** SAH mee
**Description:** Sami is a unisex name that comes from the Arabic element of '*sami*'.
**Alternative spellings:** Samie, Sammey, Sammi, Sammie, Sammy, Samy

## Sammy
**Meaning:** God has listened
**Origin:** Hebrew
**Pronunciation:** SA me
**Description:** Sammy is the pet form of both the masculine Samuel and the feminine Samantha. It may be used as a name in its own right as well.
**Alternative spellings:** Sami, Samie, Sammey, Sammi, Sammie, Samy

## Samson
**Meaning:** Sun
**Origin:** Hebrew
**Pronunciation:** SAM sun
**Description:** Samson is Hebrew in origin and comes from the biblical story of Samson and Delilah.
**Alternative spellings:** Samsen, Samsun

## Samuel
**Meaning:** God has listened
**Origin:** Hebrew
**Pronunciation:** SAM yule
**Description:** Samuel is a biblical name meaning 'he (God) has hearkened'.
**Alternative spellings:** Samual, Samuell

## Sanchit
**Meaning:** Collection
**Origin:** Indian
**Pronunciation:** san CHIT
**Description:** Sanchit is an Indian boys' name meaning 'collection' or 'accumulated', as in to have a large number of things.

## Sandeep
**Meaning:** Lighted lamp
**Origin:** Indian
**Pronunciation:** san DEEP
**Description:** Sandeep is a very common Indian boys' name meaning 'lighted lamp'. It is most likely taken from the Sanskrit '*saṃdīpa*'.
**Alternative spellings:** Sundeep

## Sandro
**Meaning:** Defender of man
**Origin:** Italian
**Pronunciation:** saan DROH
**Description:** Sandro is a shortened version of the name Alexander or Alessandro, and as such shares the same meaning of 'defender of man'.

## Sandy
**Meaning:** Defender of man
**Origin:** Greek
**Pronunciation:** SAN dee

S

**Description:** Sandy is a unisex name and pet form of either 'Alexander' or 'Alexandra'.
**Alternative spellings:** Sandie

## Sanjay
**Meaning:** Triumphant; victor
**Origin:** Sanskrit
**Pronunciation:** saan JAY
**Description:** Sanjay is a common Indian boys' name meaning 'triumphant' or 'victor'.

## Santana
**Meaning:** Saintlike; Saint Ana
**Origin:** Spanish
**Pronunciation:** saan TAN UH
**Description:** Santana is a unisex name and is the condensed form of Saint Ana. Carlos Santana is a famous Mexian rock musician.

## Santiago
**Meaning:** St James
**Origin:** Spanish
**Pronunciation:** san tee AH go
**Description:** Santiago comes from a combination of 'saint' and 'Diego'. St Diego is the patron saint of Spain. It is rare in Britain but popular in Europe.

## Santino
**Meaning:** The saints
**Origin:** Spanish
**Pronunciation:** san TEE no
**Description:** Santino is a variant of the Spanish boys' name Santos, meaning 'the saints'.
**Alternative spellings:** Santeeno, Santinoh

## Sanvir
**Meaning:** Strong; brave
**Origin:** Indian
**Pronunciation:** saan VEER
**Description:** Sanvir is an Indian boys' name meaning 'strong' and 'brave'.
**Alternative spellings:** Sanveer

## Sasha
**Meaning:** Defender of man
**Origin:** Greek
**Pronunciation:** SASH a
**Description:** An English respelling of Greek names Alexander and Alexandra. It can be used for both boys and girls.
**Alternative spellings:** Sacha

## Saul
**Meaning:** The child we asked for
**Origin:** Hebrew
**Pronunciation:** SAHL
**Description:** Saul originates from the Hebrew meaning 'the child we asked for'. It can be found in the Bible as the name of the first king of Israel and came into popular usage in the 17th century.
**Alternative spellings:** Saaul

## Sawyer
**Meaning:** Sawer of wood
**Origin:** English
**Pronunciation:** SAW yar
**Description:** Sawyer was originally an occupational surname meaning 'sawer of wood' or 'woodcutter'. It was the name of the main character in Mark Twain's *The Adventures of Tom Sawyer*.

## Saxon
**Meaning:** Swordsman
**Origin:** English
**Pronunciation:** sax ON
**Description:** Saxon was a surname taken from the Saxons,

who were a Germanic tribe. The name comes from the Germanic word '*sahs*' meaning 'knife'.

## Scott
**Meaning:** Painted warrior
**Origin:** English
**Pronunciation:** SCOT
**Description:** Scott is a popular name, which historically was a surname and is still a common last name today. It means 'painted warrior'.
**Alternative spellings:** Scot

## Seamus
**Meaning:** Supplanter
**Origin:** Gaelic
**Pronunciation:** SHAY mus
**Description:** Seamus is an Irish name and a variant of the Hebrew name James, meaning 'he who supplants'. Seamus is a common name for Irish families living in America.
**Alternative spellings:** Shamus, Sheamus, Seumas

## Sean
**Meaning:** God is gracious
**Origin:** Gaelic
**Pronunciation:** SHAWN
**Description:** Sean is the anglicised spelling of the name Eoin, which is the Irish equivalent of John. The name means 'God is gracious'.
**Alternative spellings:** Sêan, Shaun, Shawn, Sion

## Seb
**Meaning:** Revered
**Origin:** Greek
**Pronunciation:** SEB

**Description:** Seb is a diminutive of the Greek boys' given name Sebastian.
**Alternative spellings:** Sebb

## Sebastian
**Meaning:** Revered
**Origin:** Latin
**Pronunciation:** seb ASS ti an
**Description:** Sebastian is an over popular name that means 'revered'. It comes from the Latin name Sebastos, which was the Greek translation of the title Augustus used for Roman emperors.
**Alternative spellings:** Sebastien

## Seeley
**Meaning:** Blessed; silly
**Origin:** French
**Pronunciation:** see LEE
**Description:** Seeley is an Old French name meaning 'blessed'. It is also connected to the German word '*selig*', which forms the basis of the English word for 'silly'.
**Alternative spellings:** Sealey, Seely, Seelyee

## Selby
**Meaning:** Willow farm
**Origin:** English
**Pronunciation:** sell BEE
**Description:** Derived from an English surname meaning 'willow farm' in Old Norse, Selby is now also a prominent given name choice.
**Alternative spellings:**

## Selwyn
**Meaning:** Prosperous friend
**Origin:** English
**Pronunciation:** SEL win

S

**Description:** Selwyn is an Anglo-Saxon name meaning 'prosperous friend'. It is uncommon and can also be a surname.
**Alternative spellings:** Selwin

## Sergio
**Meaning:** Servant
**Origin:** Latin
**Pronunciation:** SEHR gee o
**Description:** Sergio is a name of Latin origin, meaning 'servant'.
**Alternative spellings:** Sergeo

## Seth
**Meaning:** Appointed
**Origin:** Hebrew
**Pronunciation:** SETH
**Description:** Seth is Hebrew in origin, and means 'appointed'.

## Seymour
**Meaning:** St-Maur
**Origin:** French
**Pronunciation:** SEE moor
**Description:** Seymour comes from the name Saint-Maur, which is a settlement in Normandy, France. It is considered a British name.
**Alternative spellings:** Seamor, Seamore, Seamour, Seymore

## Shaan
See entry in 'Names for Baby Girls A–Z'

## Shae
**Meaning:** Full of majesty
**Origin:** Gaelic
**Pronunciation:** shey
**Description:** Shae is a variant of the name Shea, which is Irish in origin and means 'full of majesty'. It can be given to baby girls or

boys. There are lots of variations in the spelling of this name: Shae is an anglicised version and is often a shortened version of Seamus.
**Alternative spellings:** Shea, Shay

## Shah
**Meaning:** King
**Origin:** Persian
**Pronunciation:** SHAH
**Description:** Shah is the title of the ruler of certain Asian countries and derives from the Persian word meaning 'king'. It is a common name in Iran.
**Alternative spellings:** Sha, Shaah

## Shane
**Meaning:** God is gracious
**Origin:** Hebrew
**Pronunciation:** SHE yn
**Description:** Shane is a masculine name derived from the Irish name Sean, which itself is derived from the Hebrew name John.
**Alternative spellings:** Shaine, Shayne

## Shannon
See entry in 'Names for Baby Girls A–Z'

## Shayaan
**Meaning:** Intelligent
**Origin:** Muslim
**Pronunciation:** shy AAN
**Description:** Shayaan is a Muslim boys' name meaning 'intelligent'. A similar girls' name is Shayan, although that is a variation of the Native American name Cheyeene.
**Alternative spellings:** Shayan

## Shayan

**Meaning:** Deserving; worthy
**Origin:** Arabic
**Pronunciation:** shah YAN
**Description:** Shayan is an Arabic male name meaning 'deserving' and 'worthy'.
**Alternative spellings:** Shayaan

## Shaye

See entry in 'Names for Baby Girls A–Z'

## Shayne

See entry in 'Names for Baby Girls A–Z'

## Shea

See entry in 'Names for Baby Girls A–Z'

## Sheikh

**Meaning:** Scholar
**Origin:** Arabic
**Pronunciation:** SHEEK
**Description:** Sheik is an Arabic honorary term referring to a scholar or teacher. It has traditionally been given to the leader of a tribe or wise man. It is rare as a first name.
**Alternative spellings:** Sheek

## Sheldon

**Meaning:** Steep valley
**Origin:** English
**Pronunciation:** SHEL den
**Description:** Sheldon is an English boys' name meaning 'steep valley' or 'flat-topped hill'. It was formerly popular, but its usage has decreased in recent years.
**Alternative spellings:** Shelden, Sheldin

## Shepherd

**Meaning:** Sheep herder
**Origin:** English
**Pronunciation:** shep ERD
**Description:** Shepherd is an old English occupational name and given to those who were sheep herders. Like Taylor and Hunter, these occupational names are taken straight from the English vocabulary word.

## Shiloh

**Meaning:** Sanctuary
**Origin:** Hebrew
**Pronunciation:** SHY lo
**Description:** In the Bible, Shiloh was a sanctuary near Jericho. It is mainly a boys' name, but can also be used for girls.
**Alternative spellings:** Shilo, Shylo, Shyloh

## Shiro

**Meaning:** White
**Origin:** Japanese
**Pronunciation:** shee ROH
**Description:** Shiro is a Japanese character that means 'white'. In some contexts, Shiro can also mean 'castle'.

## Shiv

**Meaning:** Pure
**Origin:** Sanskrit
**Pronunciation:** shiv
**Description:** Shiv is a boys' name and a variant of Shiva, a popular name of Hindi and Sanskrit origin. Shiva is the name of a Hindu god. The cult of Shiva is widespread throughout India and is given prominence in many legends.

**S**

## Shivam

**Meaning:** Pure
**Origin:** Sanskrit
**Pronunciation:** SHIV ah
**Description:** Shivam is a variant of Shiva, the name of a Hindu god and a popular name of Hindi and Sanskrit origin.
**Alternative spellings:** Shivaam

## Sholto

**Meaning:** Fruitfulness; sower of seeds
**Origin:** Scottish
**Pronunciation:** shol TOH
**Description:** Sholto is a Scottish name that has associations with harvesting, as it means 'fruitfulness' or 'sower of seeds'.

## Shyanne

See entry in 'Names for Baby Girls A–Z'

## Sia

**Meaning:** One who brings joy
**Origin:** Persian
**Pronunciation:** SEE ah
**Description:** Sia is an unusual name of uncertain origin. The name was originally masculine but can now be found for girls as well and means 'one who brings joy'.
**Alternative spellings:** Siia

## Sid

**Meaning:** Wide meadow
**Origin:** English
**Pronunciation:** SID
**Description:** Sid is a shortened version of the Old English name Sidney, meaning 'wide meadow'. It was popular in the 19th century but is rarer in recent years.
**Alternative spellings:** Cid, Syd

## Siddharth

**Meaning:** Achieved all wishes
**Origin:** Sanskrit
**Pronunciation:** sid HARTH
**Description:** Siddharth is a variant of the Indian boys' name, Siddhartha, meaning 'one who has achieved all wishes'.
**Alternative spellings:** Siddharthe, Sidharth, Sidharthe

## Sidney

**Meaning:** Wide meadow
**Origin:** English
**Pronunciation:** SID nee
**Description:** Sidney is an old English name meaning 'wide meadow'. It was originally a surname and is now also a unisex given name.
**Alternative spellings:** Cydnee, Cydney, Sidnee, Sydnee, Sydney

## Silas

**Meaning:** Forest dweller
**Origin:** Hebrew
**Pronunciation:** SY lus
**Description:** Silas is a masculine name of Hebrew origin. The name is taken to mean 'forest dweller'.
**Alternative spellings:** Silus, Sylas, Sylus

## Simba

**Meaning:** Lion
**Origin:** Swahili
**Pronunciation:** sim BAH
**Description:** Simba is the Swahili word for 'lion', which is appropriate as it was the main character's name in Disney's *The Lion King*.

## Simon

**Meaning:** Listen
**Origin:** Hebrew

**Pronunciation:** SYE mon
**Description:** Simon is a biblical name meaning 'hearkening' (listening).
**Alternative spellings:** Simeon, Symon

## Siya

Meaning: Unknown
**Origin:** Arabic
**Pronunciation:** SEE ah
**Description:** Siya is a name that can be found used for both boys and girls. It appears to be of Arabic origin and is favoured by Muslim parents.
**Alternative spellings:** Siyah

## Skyler

**Meaning:** Scholar
**Origin:** Dutch
**Pronunciation:** sky LER
**Description:** Skyler is a unisex name that comes from the Dutch surname Schuler, meaning 'scholar'. The name is not used in the Netherlands, however. It is uncertain why, but the name became popular as a first name in America in the 1980s.

## Sohail

**Meaning:** Handsome
**Origin:** Arabic
**Pronunciation:** SU hel
**Description:** Sohail is an Arabic term meaning 'handsome', 'brilliant', 'noble', 'glorious', 'easygoing' and 'peaceful'.
**Alternative spellings:** Sohayle, Suhail

## Sol

**Meaning:** Sun

**Origin:** Spanish
**Pronunciation:** SOL
**Description:** Sol is a name that can be used for both boys and girls. It is of Spanish origin as 'sol' is the Spanish word for the sun.

## Solomon

**Meaning:** Peace
**Origin:** Hebrew
**Pronunciation:** SOL oh mon
**Description:** King Solomon, son of David and Bathsheba, was known for his wisdom. Solomon is mainly a Jewish name, and is derived from the word *'shalom'* for 'peace'.
**Alternative spellings:** Soloman

## Sommer

**Meaning:** Summer
**Origin:** Scandinavian
**Pronunciation:** SOH mer
**Description:** Sommer is a Scandinavian form of the name Summer. It is unisex.
**Alternative spellings:** Summer

## Sonny

**Meaning:** Son
**Origin:** English
**Pronunciation:** SUN ee
**Description:** The name Sonny can trace its origin back to use as a pet name. The name is taken to mean 'son of ours', although the name is actually unisex.
**Alternative spellings:** Sonnie, Sunny

## Soren

**Meaning:** Apart
**Origin:** Danish
**Pronunciation:** SOR en

S

**Description:** Soren is a name of Danish origin, meaning 'apart'. The name may derive from an old Roman family name, Severinus, or also possibly from the Norse god of thunder, Thor.
**Alternative spellings:** Sorenn, Sorun

## Spencer

**Meaning:** Dispenser
**Origin:** French
**Pronunciation:** SPEN sur
**Description:** Spencer comes from the French word for a dispenser of supplies in a manor house. The name is also a common surname.
**Alternative spellings:** Spencur, Spenser

## Spike

**Meaning:** Pointed
**Origin:** English
**Pronunciation:** SPIKE
**Description:** Spike is an uncommon name of English origin. Spike literally means a 'pointed end'.
**Alternative spellings:** Spyke

## Stanley

**Meaning:** Stone clearing
**Origin:** English
**Pronunciation:** STAN lee
**Description:** Stanley, originally a place name to describe a stony field, was adopted as a surname and then as a masculine first name. The name therefore means 'stone clearing'. It was very popular around the turn of the 20th century.
**Alternative spellings:** Stanlee

## Stanislaw

**Meaning:** Someone who achieves glory
**Origin:** Polish
**Pronunciation:** stan ISS law
**Description:** Stanislaw is the Polish version of the name Stanislav, and means 'someone who achieves glory'. The name is formed of the Slavic elements of *'stani'*, meaning 'to become' and *'slava'*, meaning 'glory'.
**Alternative spellings:** Stanislav

## Stefan

**Meaning:** Crown
**Origin:** Scandinavian
**Pronunciation:** STEFF ahn
**Description:** The name Stefan derives from the common name Stephen. There are biblical links to this name and Stefan is a popular name in German- and Polish-speaking countries.
**Alternative spellings:** Steffan, Stephan

## Stephen

**Meaning:** Garland; crown
**Origin:** Greek
**Pronunciation:** STEE vun
**Description:** Stephen comes from the Greek word *'stephanos'*, meaning 'garland; crown'. Stephen is also the name of the first Christian martyr, whose feast is celebrated on December 26th.
**Alternative spellings:** Steven

## Steve

**Meaning:** Garland; crown
**Origin:** Greek
**Pronunciation:** STEEV
**Description:** Steve is a short form of Steven and is a popular name.
**Alternative spellings:** Steev

## Stevie

**Meaning:** Honourable
**Origin:** Greek
**Pronunciation:** STE vee
**Description:** Stevie is a modern pet form of the name Stephen. It can be used for girls or boys.
**Alternative spellings:** Stevee

## Stiles

**Meaning:** To climb
**Origin:** English
**Pronunciation:** styles
**Description:** Stiles is an Old English name taken from the word '*stigan*', which means 'to climb'.

## Storm

**Meaning:** Storm
**Origin:** English
**Pronunciation:** STORM
**Description:** Storm is a rare unisex name that comes from the English word 'storm'.

## Stuart

**Meaning:** Steward
**Origin:** English
**Pronunciation:** STEW ert; STOO ert
**Description:** Stuart comes from the French version of the surname 'Stewart', originally used for someone with the occupation of a steward, or someone who served in a royal manor.
**Alternative spellings:** Stewart

## Subhaan

**Meaning:** Glory
**Origin:** Arabic
**Pronunciation:** soob HAAN
**Description:** Subhaan is an Arabic boys' name and is said to mean 'glory'.
**Alternative spellings:** Subhan

## Sufyan

**Meaning:** Fast walker
**Origin:** Arabic
**Pronunciation:** soof YAN
**Description:** Sufyan is popular in Arabic-speaking countries and in the English-Arabic community.
**Alternative spellings:** Sufian, Sufyaan

## Sufyyan

**Meaning:** Bearing a sword
**Origin:** Persian
**Pronunciation:** soof YAN
**Description:** Sufyaan, also spelt Sufyan or Sufjan, is a masculine name of Persian origin and its meaning is debated but it is generally held to mean 'bearing a sword'.
**Alternative spellings:** Sufjan, Sufyan

## Sulaiman

**Meaning:** Peace
**Origin:** Arabic
**Pronunciation:** su LAY man
**Description:** Sulaiman is a spelling variation of the boys' name Sulayman. Both are Arabic in origin and are said to mean 'peace'. It is found in many similar forms in different countries such as the Turkish Suleiman or English Solomon.
**Alternative spellings:** Sulayman, Suleiman

## Suleman

**Meaning:** Peace
**Origin:** Turkish
**Pronunciation:** SUL ee man
**Description:** Suleman is the Turkish form of Solomon, meaning 'peace'. Suleman the Magnificent

S

was a sultan of the Ottoman Empire in the 16th century.
**Alternative spellings:** Suleiman, Suleyman

## Sullivan
**Meaning:** Dark eyes
**Origin:** Gaelic
**Pronunciation:** SULL li van
**Description:** Sullivan is one of the most common surnames in the English-speaking world. It is not very popular as a given name for boys. The name is of Gaelic origin and the meaning is 'dark eyes'.
**Alternative spellings:** Sullavan, Sullevan

## Sully
**Meaning:** To stain
**Origin:** French
**Pronunciation:** sul LEE
**Description:** Sully is a name taken from the French word '*souiller*' meaning 'to stain' or to make something dirty.

## Sultan
**Meaning:** Ruler
**Origin:** Arabic
**Pronunciation:** SUL tan
**Description:** Sultan is a common title to signify power and leadership, and is often used as a name in Arabic cultures. The word

transliterates as 'ruler', 'emperor' and 'king'.
**Alternative spellings:** Sulten, Sulton, Sultun

## Sutton
**Meaning:** Town in the south
**Origin:** English
**Pronunciation:** SUT ton
**Description:** Sutton is an Old English place name referring to a 'town in the south', composed of the elements of '*suth*' meaning 'south' and 'tun' meaning 'town'. Sutton is also the name of many 'towns' in Britain.

## Sven
**Meaning:** Lad
**Origin:** Norse
**Pronunciation:** SVEN
**Description:** From the Old Norse byname 'Sveinn'.
**Alternative spellings:** Svenn, Svven

## Szymon
**Meaning:** Listen
**Origin:** Hebrew
**Pronunciation:** SHEE mon
**Description:** The name Szymon is a variation of the traditional English name Simon. The Hebrew element of this name comes from the biblical character Simon.
**Alternative spellings:** Szimon

# T

## Tadhg
**Meaning:** Poet; philosopher
**Origin:** Gaelic

**Pronunciation:** TAYg
**Description:** Tadhg is an Irish and Scottish name referring

to 'poet' or 'philosopher'. It was the name of many Irish kings in the 10th and 16th centuries.

## Taha
**Meaning:** Unknown
**Origin:** Arabic
**Pronunciation:** tah HA
**Description:** Taha is an Arabic name that is used in reference to prayers. The name is more common as a surname.
**Alternative spellings:** Tahaa, Tahha, Tahhaa

## Tai
**Meaning:** Great
**Origin:** Chinese
**Pronunciation:** TIE
**Description:** Tai is a Chinese name meaning 'great' or 'extreme'. It might also mean 'from Thai', denoting someone from Thailand.
**Alternative spellings:** Taio, Thai, Ti

## Talha
**Meaning:** Big tree
**Origin:** Arabic
**Pronunciation:** tahl HAH
**Description:** Talhah is an Arabic masculine name meaning 'big tree'. It was the name of one of the prophet Muhammad's most well-known companions (Talha ibn Obaidullah).

## Talon
**Meaning:** Bird claw
**Origin:** English
**Pronunciation:** TAL on
**Description:** This unusual name is taken from the English vocabulary word of the same name, referring to a 'bird's claw'.

## Tamika
See entry in 'Names for Baby Girls A–Z'

## Tanner
**Meaning:** Leather-maker
**Origin:** English
**Pronunciation:** tan NER
**Description:** Tanner is an English occupational name meaning 'leather-maker'. Like Taylor and Hunter, these types of names were given to people who held these jobs but have now become popular names in their own right.

## Taran
**Meaning:** Thunder
**Origin:** Gaelic
**Pronunciation:** TAH ran
**Description:** Taran is a unisex name, and was probably introduced by American writer Lloyd Alexander in his novel *The Chronicles of Prydain*.
**Alternative spellings:** Tarann

## Tariq
**Meaning:** Evening caller
**Origin:** Arabic
**Pronunciation:** TAH rik
**Description:** An Arabic name meaning 'evening caller' and 'nocturnal visitor'.
**Alternative spellings:** Tarek, Tareq, Tarick, Tarik

## Tate
**Meaning:** Colourful
**Origin:** Norse
**Pronunciation:** TAY te

T

**Description:** Tate is a masculine name that originally began life as a surname.
**Alternative spellings:** Tait, Tayt, Tayte

## Taylan
**Meaning:** Tailor
**Origin:** English
**Pronunciation:** tay LAAN
**Description:** This name is Turkish in origin, meaning 'elegant' or 'long and thin person'. It could also derive from Taylor.
**Alternative spellings:** Taylon, Teylan

## Taylor
**Meaning:** Tailor
**Origin:** English
**Pronunciation:** TAY lor
**Description:** Taylor was originally a surname given to those with the occupation of tailor. It is a popular unisex name.
**Alternative spellings:** Tailor, Tayla, Taylah, Tayler, Teyla, Teylah, Teylor

## Ted
**Meaning:** God's gift
**Origin:** Greek
**Pronunciation:** ted
**Description:** Ted is an abbreviated version of Theodore, but can also be shortened from Edward. Theodore means 'God's gift,' but is more commonly shortened to Theo in the UK.

## Teddy
**Meaning:** Gift of god
**Origin:** Greek
**Pronunciation:** TED ee

**Description:** Teddy is a name in its own right, but could be a nickname for someone named Theodore or Edward.
**Alternative spellings:** Teddi, Tedi, Tedy

## Teejay
**Meaning:** Crown
**Origin:** Sanskrit
**Pronunciation:** TEE jay
**Description:** Teejay is a name of Sanskrit and Punjabi origin. It is commonly used as a nickname for boys named Tajinder, which means 'crown'.
**Alternative spellings:** Tijay

## Teo
**Meaning:** Gift of God
**Origin:** Greek
**Pronunciation:** TAY oh
**Description:** Teo is a name of Greek origin, meaning 'gift of God'. It is a shortened version of Teodor, a variant of Theodore. Teo is common in Italy and Spain, where the name is pronounced with an 'ay' sound instead of 'e'.
**Alternative spellings:** Tayo, Teodor, Teyo

## Terence
**Meaning:** Instigator
**Origin:** Gaelic
**Pronunciation:** TEH rense
**Description:** Terence is derived from the Roman name Terentius, but it is also the anglicised form of the Gaelic word 'turlough'.
**Alternative spellings:** Terance, Terrence

## Terry
**Meaning:** Power of the people

**Origin:** German
**Pronunciation:** TEH ree
**Description:** Terry is commonly found as a masculine name, but it can be considered unisex if changed to the alternate spelling, Terri. It is also considered a shortened version of Terence.
**Alternative spellings:** Terrey, Terri, Terrie

## Thatcher

**Meaning:** Person who thatches roofs
**Origin:** English
**Pronunciation:** thatch ER
**Description:** Thatcher is an old occupational name given to those who used to fix or thatch roofs for a living. Like Taylor and Hunter, these occupational names are taken straight from the English vocabulary word.

## Theo

**Meaning:** Gift of God
**Origin:** French
**Pronunciation:** THEE oh
**Description:** Theo is a shortened version of the masculine name Theodore and has become very popular in its own right.
**Alternative spellings:** Theeo

## Theodore

**Meaning:** Gift of God
**Origin:** Greek
**Pronunciation:** THEE a daw
**Description:** Theodore can be abbreviated to Ted or Teddy, but is commonly shortened to Theo in the UK.
**Alternative spellings:** Theodaw

## Theon

**Meaning:** Godly
**Origin:** Greek
**Pronunciation:** thee ON
**Description:** Theon is a Greek boys' name meaning 'Godly'. It was also the name of a famous Greek mathematician.

## Thiago

**Meaning:** Supplanter
**Origin:** Portuguese
**Pronunciation:** chee AH go
**Description:** Thiago is a different spelling of the name Tiago, which in itself is a dimiutive of Santiago. To make things more complicated, Santiago is the Spanish version of the name James. That is why all these names share the same meaning as James, which is 'supplanter'.
**Alternative spellings:** Tiago

## Thierry

**Meaning:** People's ruler
**Origin:** French
**Pronunciation:** tee AIR ee
**Description:** Thierry is a name of French and Old German origin, meaning 'people's ruler'. It is also a variant of the Greek Theodoric, but is commonly used as the French form of the German name Terry.
**Alternative spellings:** Thierri, Thierrie

## Thomas

**Meaning:** Twin
**Origin:** Aramaic
**Pronunciation:** TOM us
**Description:** Thomas is a biblical name, and is the name of one of Christ's 12 apostles. The name is

**T**

popular throughout the Christian world.
**Alternative spellings:** Tomas

## Tiago

**Meaning:** St James
**Origin:** Spanish
**Pronunciation:** tee AY go
**Description:** Tiago is the abbreviated form of the Spanish name Santiago. This name comes from a combination of 'saint' and 'Diego', and the shortened version has become popular in the Iberian peninsula.
**Alternative spellings:** Tiaygo

## Tim

**Meaning:** Honour God
**Origin:** Greek
**Pronunciation:** TIM
**Description:** Tim is an abbreviation of the name 'Timothy'. This shortened version has recently grown in popularity.

## Timothy

**Meaning:** Honour God
**Origin:** Greek
**Pronunciation:** TIM uh thee
**Description:** This name has derived from the Greek name Timotheos. He was a companion of St Paul in the Bible. The name was not used in England before the Reformation, but has risen in popularity ever since.
**Alternative spellings:** Timothee

## Timur

**Meaning:** Iron
**Origin:** Turkish
**Pronunciation:** tim OOR

**Description:** Timur is a Turkish name that means 'iron'. A famous historical figure with this name was Timur, also called Tamerlane, who was a Central Asian ruler in the 14th century.
**Alternative spellings:** Timor

## Titus

**Meaning:** Unknown
**Origin:** Latin
**Pronunciation:** TIE tus
**Description:** Titus is a Latin name of unknown meaning, although it was the name of a Roman military commander who later became emperor. It was also the name of the main character of Shakespeare's play, *Titus Andronicus*.

## Tobey

**Meaning:** God is good
**Origin:** Hebrew
**Pronunciation:** TOW bee
**Description:** Tobey is a variant of the Hebrew name Tobias and a different spelling of the English name Toby. It can be used for both boys and girls.
**Alternative spellings:** Tobee, Tobi, Tobie, Toby

## Tobias

**Meaning:** God is good
**Origin:** Hebrew
**Pronunciation:** toe BY us
**Description:** Tobias is derived from the Hebrew '*Tobiah*', meaning 'God is good'. It is a fairly common name in the Bible, and was popular in the Middle Ages.
**Alternative spellings:** Tobyas

## Todd

**Meaning:** Fox

**Origin:** English
**Pronunciation:** TOD
**Description:** Todd would originally have been a surname, taken from the English dialect word meaning 'fox'. It is more common in the US than the UK.
**Alternative spellings:** Tod

## Tom

**Meaning:** Twin
**Origin:** Aramaic
**Pronunciation:** TOM
**Description:** Tom is a pet form of Thomas, but has become popular as a name in its own right.
**Alternative spellings:** Thom

## Tommy

**Meaning:** Twin
**Origin:** Aramaic
**Pronunciation:** TOM ee
**Description:** Tommy is an abbreviation of the name Thomas, but has become a popular name in its own right.
**Alternative spellings:** Tommey, Tommi, Tommie

## Tommaso

**Meaning:** Twin
**Origin:** Italian
**Pronunciation:** tom MAS oh
**Description:** Tommaso is the Italian version of the traditional boys' name, Thomas. It is classic boys' name and has been popular for years and years. The name was originally borne in the Bible by the Apostle Thomas, who himself was a twin, which is where the meaning comes from. This name was given to Christians in the medieval period as a sign of honour.

## Tony

**Meaning:** Protector
**Origin:** Latin
**Pronunciation:** TOE nee
**Description:** Originally a shortening of Anthony, Tony has now become a name in its own right. Its spelling variants Toni and Tonie are specifically feminine.
**Alternative spellings:** Toni, Tonie

## Torin

**Meaning:** Chief
**Origin:** Gaelic
**Pronunciation:** TOR en
**Description:** Torin is a name often thought to be an anglicised form of the Gaelic name Torfhinn, meaning 'chief', or Toirneach, meaning 'thunder' (and thus linked to Thor, Norse god of thunder).
**Alternative spellings:** Toren, Torrin

## Travis

**Meaning:** Traverser
**Origin:** French
**Pronunciation:** TRAV iss
**Description:** Travis would originally have been a name given to people who were traversers. The name has grown in popularity in recent years.
**Alternative spellings:** Traviss, Travys

## Trent

**Meaning:** Floodwater
**Origin:** English
**Pronunciation:** TRENT
**Description:** The name Trent is taken from the English river of the same name. The river name actually means 'trespasser',

**T**

referring to its frequent flooding.
**Alternative spellings:** Trente

## Trevor
**Meaning:** Large settlement
**Origin:** Welsh
**Pronunciation:** TREV va
**Description:** Trevor was originally a surname given to people from Welsh villages called 'Trefor'. It has risen in popularity across the English-speaking world.
**Alternative spellings:** Trever, Trevur

## Trey
**Meaning:** Three
**Origin:** English
**Pronunciation:** trey
**Description:** Trey is an English name meaning 'three', and was originally a nickname for a son who was the third generation in a family. It is now being used as a given name, however.

## Tristan
**Meaning:** Noise
**Origin:** Gaelic
**Pronunciation:** TRISS tan
**Description:** Tristan is a name of Welsh origin. In Arthurian legend this name belonged to one of the knights of King Arthur's round table, who gave his name to the tragic tale of Tristan and Isolde.
**Alternative spellings:** Tristin, Trystan, Trystin

## Triumph
**Meaning:** To succeed
**Origin:**
**Pronunciation:** try UMPH

**Description:** Triumph is taken from the English vocabulary word of the same spelling and means 'to succeed'.

## Troy
**Meaning:** Descendant of footsoldier
**Origin:** Gaelic
**Pronunciation:** TROI
**Description:** While Troy is a name of Gaelic origin, it is probably more well known for its Greek influence. Troy was a city in Greek legend that was besieged by the Greeks.
**Alternative spellings:** Troi

## Truman
**Meaning:** Trusty man
**Origin:** English
**Pronunciation:** TROO man
**Description:** Truman is an Old English name that is very rare nowadays.
**Alternative spellings:** Trooman,Trueman

## Tucker
**Meaning:** To torment
**Origin:** German
**Pronunciation:** tuck ER
**Description:** Tucker was originally a surname found in many parts of England and Ireland. The name comes from various German verbs meaning 'to torment'. In modern times, Tucker is much more commonly found in the USA than in Britain.

## Tudor
**Meaning:** Ruler of the people
**Origin:** Welsh
**Pronunciation:** too DOOR

**Description:** Tudor is a Welsh name that means 'ruler of the people'. It is the Welsh equivalent of the German name Theodoric, which has the same meaning. The name is from the Germanic elements of '*peudo*' meaning 'people' and '*riks*' meaning 'ruler'.

## Ty

**Meaning:** Unknown
**Origin:** English
**Pronunciation:** TIE
**Description:** While Ty is mainly used to shorten names such as Tyler, Tyson and Tyrone, it has become popular in its own right.
**Alternative spellings:** Tie

## Tyga

**Meaning:** No meaning
**Origin:** American
**Pronunciation:** ty GAH
**Description:** Tyga is a modern invented name and as such, it has no meaning. It owes its popularity to rapper Tyga, who explained that his stage name means 'Thank you God always'.

## Tyler

**Meaning:** Tile-maker
**Origin:** English
**Pronunciation:** TY ler
**Description:** Once a surname, Tyler has morphed into a first name. It can be unisex, but has risen in popularity among boys.
**Alternative spellings:** Tyla, Tylah, Tylar, Tylor

## Tymon

**Meaning:** God's honour
**Origin:** Greek

**Pronunciation:** TY mon; ty MON
**Description:** Tymon is an uncommon name and a variant of Timothy, a Greek name meaning 'God's honour'.
**Alternative spellings:** Timon, Tymonn

## Tymoteusz

**Meaning:** Honour God
**Origin:** Polish
**Pronunciation:** tim OOT ee usz
**Description:** Tymoteusz is the Polish form of the name Timothy, meaning 'Honour God'. The names come from the biblical name Timotheos, with 'time' meaning 'honour' and 'theeos' meaning 'God'.

## Tyrell

**Meaning:** Puller
**Origin:** French
**Pronunciation:** TI rell
**Description:** It is thought that Tyrell derives from the Scandinavian god of battle Tyr.
**Alternative spellings:** Terrell, Tirell, Tyrel, Tyrrell

## Tyrese

**Meaning:** No meaning
**Origin:** American
**Pronunciation:** TIE rees
**Description:** Tyrese is a modern, American invented name that is associated with names such as Terence, Tyree and Tyrone. As such, it has no real meaning.

## Tyrone

**Meaning:** Irish county
**Origin:** Gaelic
**Pronunciation:** TYE rone

T

**Description:** Tyrone is derived from the name of a district in Ireland and has been adopted as a first name.
**Alternative spellings:** Tierone, Tyroan

## Tyson
**Meaning:** High-spirited
**Origin:** French
**Pronunciation:** TY sun
**Description:** Tyson is a name of French origin, meaning 'high-spirited'. It has recently become popular in America.
**Alternative spellings:** Tycen, Tyeson, Tysen

# U

## Ulric
**Meaning:** Wolf power
**Origin:** English
**Pronunciation:** UL rik
**Description:** Ulric was originally coined in the Middle Ages where it meant 'wolf power'. It has become associated with the German name 'Ulrich' in recent times.
**Alternative spellings:** Ulrik

## Ulysses
**Meaning:** Wrathful
**Origin:** Latin
**Pronunciation:** OO ly SEES
**Description:** Ulysses is the Latin form of the Greek name Odysseus. It was made famous by United States president Ulysses S. Grant and James Joyce's novel, *Ulysses*.

## Umair
**Meaning:** Intelligent one
**Origin:** Arabic
**Pronunciation:** OO mare
**Description:** Umair is a popular name across Islamic communities.
**Alternative spellings:** Omair, Umaire

## Umar
**Meaning:** Thriving
**Origin:** Arabic
**Pronunciation:** OO mar
**Description:** Umar is a favourite name across the Arabic world, although it is common in Sunni Muslim, rather than Shia Muslim communities.
**Alternative spellings:** Umer, Umur

## Uri
**Meaning:** Light
**Origin:** Hebrew
**Pronunciation:** your EE
Description: Uri comes from the Hebrew word meaning 'light'. It is linked to 'Uriah' but not 'Yuri', as that name has a completely different meaning.

## Uriah
**Meaning:** God is light
**Origin:** Hebrew
**Pronunciation:** yuh RY ah
**Description:** Uriah is a biblical name. It can be shortened to Uri.
**Alternative spellings:** Youriah

## Usman

**Meaning:** Bustard
**Origin:** Arabic
**Pronunciation:** uss MAHN
**Description:** Usman is an Arabic boys' name meaning 'bustard,' which is a large, heavily-built, swift-running bird breed

## Uzair

**Meaning:** Helpful
**Origin:** Muslim
**Pronunciation:** oo ZAIR
**Description:** Uzair is the Muslim version of the Hebrew name, Ezra. It comes from the Hebrew word for 'helpful' and Ezra was the author of one of the Old Testament books.

# V

## Valentin

**Meaning:** Strong; healthy
**Origin:** Latin
**Pronunciation:** val EN tin
**Description:** Valentin comes from the Latin name Valentinus, meaning 'strong' and 'healthy'.
This name in common in Russia, Ukraine, Scandinavia and France.
**Alternative spellings:** Valentine, Valentino

## Valentino

**Meaning:** Strong
**Origin:** Latin
**Pronunciation:** val en TEE no
**Description:** Valentino is a variant of the Latin boys' name Valentine, meaning 'strong' or 'healthy'. It is a common name in Italy and among Italian-Americans.
**Alternative spellings:** Valenteno, Valentyno

## Vance

**Meaning:** One who lives near marshland
**Origin:** English
**Pronunciation:** vance
**Description:** Vance is an English surname that was given to people who lived near a marshland or a bog. However, the letter 'V' makes this a modern-sounding and edgy baby name.

## Varin

**Meaning:** Rich in gifts
**Origin:** Indian
**Pronunciation:** VAAR in
**Description:** Varin is an Indian boys' name meaning 'rich in gifts'. It can also be found in France as a last name, particularly the members of aristocracy in the Burgundy region.

## Vasco

**Meaning:** Crow
**Origin:** Spanish
**Pronunciation:** vaas COH
**Description:** Vasco is a Spanish name most likely taken from the surname Velázquez, which in turn became Velasco, which means 'crow' in Basque.

## Vaughn

**Meaning:** Small

U

V

257

**Origin:** Welsh
**Pronunciation:** von
**Description:** Vaughn is derived from the Welsh word '*bychan*', meaning 'small'. Although more popular as a surname, it can also be used as a given name.

## Viaan

**Meaning:** Lively
**Origin:** Indian
**Pronunciation:** vee AAHN
**Description:** Viaan is an Indian male name meaning 'lively' or 'full of life and energy'. An alternative spelling of the name is Vian, and has the same meaning as well.
**Alternative spellings:** Vian

## Vicente

**Meaning:** Conquerer
**Origin:** Italian
**Pronunciation:** vee CENT eh
**Description:** Vicente is the Italian, Spanish and Portuguese version of the name Vincent, and as such shares the same meaning of 'conquerer'.

## Veer

**Meaning:** Brave
**Origin:** Sanskrit
**Pronunciation:** VEER
**Description:** Veer seems to have come from the Sanskrit word meaning 'brave'. It is popular among Indian communities.
**Alternative spellings:** Vier

## Victor

**Meaning:** Conqueror
**Origin:** Latin
**Pronunciation:** VIK tor
**Description:** Victor is a Latin name that would have been given to winners in a battle. While the name is uncommon today, it has previously been extremely popular.
**Alternative spellings:** Vicktor, Viktor, Wiktor

## Vihaan

**Meaning:** Dawn; morning
**Origin:** Indian
**Pronunciation:** vee HAAN
**Description:** Vihaan is a male Indian name that comes from the Sanskrit word for 'dawn' or 'morning,' hence the meaning of the name. The female form of this name is Vihana, and that name also has the same meaning.
**Alternative spellings:** Vihan

## Vincent

**Meaning:** Conquering
**Origin:** Latin
**Pronunciation:** VIN sent
**Description:** Vincent is derived from Latin, and has been a popular name across Europe for many years.
**Alternative spellings:** Vinsent

## Vinny

**Meaning:** Friend
**Origin:** English
**Pronunciation:** VIN knee
**Description:** The name Vinny derives from the Old English names Alvina and Elvina. It could also be a shortened version of Vincent.
**Alternative spellings:** Vinni, Vinnie

## Vivaan

**Meaning:** First rays of the sun
**Origin:** Sanskrit

**Pronunciation:** viv AAHN
**Description:** The name Vivaan comes from a Sanskrit word that means 'first rays of the sun'. Vivaan is also one of the names of the Hindu god, Lord Krishna.
**Alternative spellings:** Vivan

## Vlad
**Meaning:** Rule
**Origin:** Russian

**Pronunciation:** vlahd
**Description:** Vlad is a Slavic name that comes from the element of '*vladeti*', meaning 'rule'. Vlad III, known as Vlad the Impaler, was the prince of Wallachia in the 15th century. He was the son of Vlad Dracul and was known as a cruel leader. He famously inspired Bram Stoker's 1897 vampire novel, *Dracula*.

# W

## Wade
**Meaning:** Able to go
**Origin:** English
**Pronunciation:** WAYDE
**Description:** Wade is a popular name of Old English and Scandinavian origin, meaning 'able to go'.
**Alternative spellings:** Waide, Wayde

## Waldo
**Meaning:** Ruler
**Origin:** German
**Pronunciation:** wall DOH
**Description:** Waldo is a German name meaning 'ruler'. It was made famous by the children's books series Where's Waldo? (or as it is known in the UK, Where's Wally?)

## Waleed
**Meaning:** Newborn
**Origin:** Arabic
**Pronunciation:** wah LEED
**Description:** Waleed is an Arabic name meaning 'newborn'. The name is also often spelt

Walid. The name comes from the Arabic word '*walada*' meaning 'to give birth'.
**Alternative spellings:** Walid

## Wali
**Meaning:** Custodian; protector; helper; friend
**Origin:** Arabic
**Pronunciation:** wall EE
**Description:** Wali is an Arabic word that has many meanings, including 'custodian,' 'protector,' 'helper' and 'friend'. This would be an ideal choice for parents looking for something with a variety of wonderful meanings.

## Walter
**Meaning:** Army ruler
**Origin:** German
**Pronunciation:** WAL ter
**Description:** While the constituents of Walter are German, the name is actually Old French. It has recently become rare.
**Alternative spellings:** Wolter
**Alternative spellings:** Wally, Wallie

V

W

## Waris

**Meaning:** Belong to the last one
**Origin:** Arabic
**Pronunciation:** WARE is
**Description:** Waris comes from an Urdu vocabulary word meaning 'belong to the last one', as in being a successor or heir to someone.

## Warren

**Meaning:** Protector
**Origin:** French
**Pronunciation:** WAR run
**Description:** Warren would have been a common name for someone hailing from the French village of La Varrenne. It also has roots in the German language.
**Alternative spellings:** Warran, Warron

## Waverly

**Meaning:** Meadow of quivering aspen
**Origin:** English
**Pronunciation:** wave ERR lee
**Description:** Waverly is a unisex name meaning 'meadow of quivering aspen'. The word 'waver' means to tremble or flicker.

## Waylon

**Meaning:** Land beside the road
**Origin:** English
**Pronunciation:** WAY lon
**Description:** Waylon was originally an English surname meaning 'land beside the road'. The name comes from the Old English *'wieland'*.

## Wayne

**Meaning:** Cartwright
**Origin:** English
**Pronunciation:** WAIN

**Description:** Wayne is a first name derived from a surname that would have been given to a carter or cartwright.
**Alternative spellings:** Wain, Wayn

## Wesley

**Meaning:** West meadow
**Origin:** English
**Pronunciation:** WEZ lee
**Description:** Wesley was originally a surname meaning 'west meadow' but was adopted as a first name in tribute to founders of the Methodist Church Charles and John Wesley.
**Alternative spellings:** Weslee, Wesli, Weslie, Wesly, Wezlee, Wezli, Wezlie, Wezley

## Weston

**Meaning:** Town in the west
**Origin:** English
**Pronunciation:** west TUN
**Description:** Like Easton, it was originally a surname but is now used regularly as a first name. In Old English, it is composed of 'west' meaning the direction and 'ton' meaning town, givings its meaning of 'town in the west'.
**Alternative spellings:** Victor

## Wilberforce

**Meaning:** From Wilberfoss
**Origin:** English
**Pronunciation:** WIL ber forse
**Description:** Wilberforce comes from Old English and was given as the name to someone from Wilberfoss.
**Alternative spellings:** Wilbeforce, Wilburforce

## Wilbur

**Meaning:** Wild boar; resolute; brilliant
**Origin:** English
**Pronunciation:** will BOOR
**Description:** Wilbur is from an English surname meaning 'wild boar'. However, it also has German roots and can mean 'resolute' or 'brilliant'.

## Wilder

**Meaning:** To be wild
**Origin:** English
**Pronunciation:** wild ER
**Description:** Wilder comes from the English vocabulary word of the same spelling, meaning 'to be (even more) wild'. This is part of the trend of taking English words and turning them into names, such as Prince or Maverick.

## Wilf

**Meaning:** Desires peace
**Origin:** English
**Pronunciation:** wilf
**Description:** Wilf is a short form of the name Wilfred, meaning 'desires peace'. Wilfred is a name that first appeared in Old English, and was the name of a saint in the 7th century.

## Wilfred

**Meaning:** Will
**Origin:** English
**Pronunciation:** WIL fred
**Description:** Wilfred is an old-fashioned name of English origin, meaning 'will', 'desire' and 'peace'. It is often shortened to Wilf.
**Alternative spellings:** Wilfrid

## Will

**Meaning:** Protection
**Origin:** German
**Pronunciation:** WILL
**Description:** Will is a shortened form of the name William.
**Alternative spellings:** Wil

## Willem

**Meaning:** Protection
**Origin:** German
**Pronunciation:** WIL lem
**Description:** Willem is a Dutch variant of the popular German name William.
**Alternative spellings:** Wilem, Willum

## William

**Meaning:** Protection
**Origin:** German
**Pronunciation:** WILL yum
**Description:** This name was introduced to England by the Normans, and was in fact the name of the conqueror himself. In the first century after the conquest it was the most common name in all of Britain. It has risen in popularity following the marriage of Prince William and Kate Middleton.
**Alternative spellings:** Wiliam, Willyam

## Willie

**Meaning:** Will, desire; helmet, protection
**Origin:** German
**Pronunciation:** WILL ee
**Description:** Willie is a shortened version of the traditional boys' name, William. It has multiple meanings meaning 'will' and 'desire' and also 'helmet' and 'protection'.
**Alternative spellings:** Willy

## Wilson

**Meaning:** Son of Will

**W**

**Origin:** English
**Pronunciation:** WIL son
**Description:** Wilson is a common surname derived from Old English. It has been a first name for many years, but is fairly uncommon.
**Alternative spellings:** Willson, Wilsun

## Winston

**Meaning:** Joy stone
**Origin:** English
**Pronunciation:** WIN ston
**Description:** The name Winston is taken from the place in Gloucestershire. It has become rare in recent times.
**Alternative spellings:** Whinston, Whynston, Wynston

## Wojciech

**Meaning:** Joy of war; smiling warrior
**Origin:** Polish
**Pronunciation:** voi CHEKH
**Description:** Wojciech is a Polish name formed from two components of archaic Polish: '*woj*' means 'war' or 'warrior' and '*ciech*' means 'joy,' hence the combined meaning of 'joy of war' or 'smiling warrior'.

## Woodrow

**Meaning:** Row of houses by a wood
**Origin:** English
**Pronunciation:** wuhd ROW
**Description:** Woodrow is an English surname that means 'row of houses by a wood'. It was made popular by US president Woodrow Wilson.

## Woody

**Meaning:** Row of houses by a wood
**Origin:** English
**Pronunciation:** WUH dee
**Description:** Woody came about as an abbreviation of such names as Woodrow. It probably came into fashion due to such film stars as Woody Allen.
**Alternative spellings:** Woodie, Woodee

## Wyatt

**Meaning:** Brave
**Origin:** Greek
**Pronunciation:** WY att
**Description:** Wyatt, sometimes a pet form of William, was a medieval surname but has adapted to become a first name. It is popular in America.
**Alternative spellings:** Wyett

# X

## Xander

**Meaning:** Defender of man
**Origin:** Greek
**Pronunciation:** ZAN duh
**Description:** Xander is a shortened form of Alexander but has become a popular name in its own right.

**Alternative spellings:** Sander, Zander

## Xavier

**Meaning:** The new house
**Origin:** Spanish
**Pronunciation:** ZAV ee air

**Description:** Xavier is a Hispanic version of the Basque place name Etcheberria.

**Alternative spellings:** Javier, Savier, Zavier

# Y

## Yaaqub
**Meaning:** Supplanter
**Origin:** Arabic
**Pronunciation:** yack UB
**Description:** Yaaqub is the Arabic version of the Hebrew name Jacob and as such, shares the same meaning of 'supplanter'.
**Alternative spellings:** Yaqub

## Yaasir
**Meaning:** To be rich
**Origin:** Arabic
**Pronunciation:** yaas IR
**Description:** Yaasir is a variation of the more common Yasir, and the name means 'to be rich'. It comes from the Arabic word 'yasira' meaning 'one who makes things easier'.
**Alternative spellings:** Yasir

## Yagiz
**Meaning:** Unknown
**Origin:** Turkish
**Pronunciation:** yaa GEEZ
**Description:** Yagiz is a Turkish boys' name. Because it is quite rare, not much is known about it.

## Yahir
**Meaning:** He shines; he enlightens
**Origin:** Arabic
**Pronunciation:** YAH heer
**Description:** The entymology of Yahir is conflicted but it is most likely an Arabic name derived from the Hebrew name Yair, meaning 'he shines'.

## Yahya
**Meaning:** He lives
**Origin:** Arabic
**Pronunciation:** YUH ya
**Description:** Yahya is a prophet in the Quran, and it is believed that the name means 'he lives' – which means his legacy will continue forever.

## Yair
**Meaning:** He will enlighten
**Origin:** Hebrew
**Pronunciation:** yaah AIR
**Description:** Yair is a Hebrew verb that means 'He will enlighten'. It is found in ancient Jewish texts and is also a name often found in contemporary Israel.
**Alternative spellings:** Jair, Ya'ir

## Yani
**Meaning:** Peace
**Origin:** Aboriginal
**Pronunciation:** yanny
**Description:** Yani is an Australian Aboriginal name meaning 'peace'. It is a unisex name that can be used for both boys and girls.
**Alternative spellings:** Yanny, Yanni

X
Y

## Yanis

**Meaning:** God is gracious
**Origin:** Greek
**Pronunciation:** YAAN iss
**Description:** Yanis is a Greek variation of the common boys' name, John, and as such shares the same meaning with it. Other forms of the name include: Yannis, Yiannis and Giannis, all of them having Greek roots.
**Alternative spellings:** Yannis

## Yaqub

**Meaning:** Held by the heel
**Origin:** Hebrew
**Pronunciation:** YA coob
**Description:** Yaqub is the Hebrew version of the name Jacob, and is mainly found in Muslim and Arabic areas.
**Alternative spellings:** Yacob, Yacoob

## Yaseen

**Meaning:** Refers to a passage in the Quran
**Origin:** Arabic
**Pronunciation:** YAAS iyn
**Description:** Yaseen is a phonetically spelt variant of the Arabic name Yasin. Yasin is formed by combining two Arabic letters from a prolific extract in the Quran, 'Ya' and 'Seen,' and is also used in Egyptian folk-tales. The name is popular in Turkey.
**Alternative spellings:** Yasin

## Yash

**Meaning:** Successful
**Origin:** Sanskrit
**Pronunciation:** YASH
**Description:** Yash is uncommon in the UK but it is common among Indian communities. It is said to mean 'success'.
**Alternative spellings:** Yashe

## Yasir

**Meaning:** Rich
**Origin:** Arabic
**Pronunciation:** yah SEER; YAH sir
**Description:** Yasir is Arabic in origin and is popular throughout the Middle East. It is said to mean 'rich' and is a common name among Muslim families.
**Alternative spellings:** Yahsir, Yaseer

## Yehuda

**Meaning:** Praise
**Origin:** Hebrew
**Pronunciation:** ye hu DA
**Description:** Yehuda is a biblical name that means 'praise', 'gratitude' and 'thanks'.
**Alternative spellings:** Yehudah

## Yoshinobu

**Meaning:** Splendid faith
**Origin:** Japanese
**Pronunciation:** yosh in OO bu
**Description:** Yoshinobu is a common name in Japan and Japanese-speaking communities, but is found across Asia.
**Alternative spellings:** Yosinobu

## Youssef

**Meaning:** The Lord gave more
**Origin:** Hebrew
**Pronunciation:** YOU sef
**Description:** Youssef is a boys' given name of Hebrew origin common in the Arabic world. It is a variant of Joseph.
**Alternative spellings:** Yousef, Youssef, Yousaf, Yousif, Yosef, Yosif, Yusef

## Yu

**Meaning:** Unknown
**Origin:** Chinese
**Pronunciation:** YOO
**Description:** Yu is a unisex name, and has various different meanings due to the 13 different Chinese characters that represent the name.
**Alternative spellings:** Yoo

## Yunus

**Meaning:** Dove
**Origin:** Hebrew
**Pronunciation:** YOU nus
**Description:** Yunus is the Arabic version of the English Jonas.
**Alternative spellings:** Yonus, Younus

## Yuri

**Meaning:** Farmer; earth worker
**Origin:** Russian
**Pronunciation:** YOUR ee

**Description:** Yuri is the Russian translation of George.
**Alternative spellings:** Yury

## Yuvraj

**Meaning:** Crown prince
**Origin:** Sanskrit
**Pronunciation:** yuv RAJH
**Description:** Yuvraj is a name that is popular among Indian communities, and was originally given to the son of one of the ruling maharajahs or chiefs of the various kingdoms in India. It has grown in popularity in the UK in recent years.

## Yves

**Meaning:** Yew
**Origin:** French
**Pronunciation:** EEV
**Description:** Yves is a very rare name in the UK and is French in origin.

# Z

## Zac

**Meaning:** The Lord recalled
**Origin:** Hebrew
**Pronunciation:** ZAK
**Description:** Zac derives from Zachary, and has become a name in its own right. It has become extremely popular in recent years due to film star Zac Efron.
**Alternative spellings:** Zach, Zack, Zak, Zakk

## Zachariah

**Meaning:** The Lord recalled
**Origin:** Hebrew

**Pronunciation:** zak ah RYE ah
**Description:** Zachariah is a biblical name and features 31 times in the Bible. It is popular in the UK.
**Alternative spellings:** Zacarias, Zaccaria, Zakaria

## Zacharias

**Meaning:** The Lord recalled
**Origin:** Hebrew
**Pronunciation:** zak a RYE ass
**Description:** Zacharias is the Greek or northern African spelling of the Hebrew name Zachariah, meaning 'the Lord recalled'.

Y
Z

**Alternative spellings:** Zaccarias, Zacharius

## Zachary
**Meaning:** The Lord recalled
**Origin:** Hebrew
**Pronunciation:** ZAK ah ree
**Description:** This name is a derivative of Zachariah and as such is a Hebrew name.
**Alternative spellings:** Zachari, Zachery, Zackary, Zakary

## Zahir
**Meaning:** Helper; supporter
**Origin:** Arabic
**Pronunciation:** ZAH heer
**Description:** Zahir is an Arabic boys' name meaning 'helper' or 'supporter'. In the Quran and Islamic religion, al-Zahir is one of the 99 names of Allah.

## Zaid
**Meaning:** He who progresses
**Origin:** Arabic
**Pronunciation:** ZADE
**Description:** Zaid is the anglicised variation of the name Zayd, which itself is Arabic.
**Alternative spellings:** Zade, Zayd

## Zaiden
**Meaning:** No meaning
**Origin:** American
**Pronunciation:** ZAY den
**Description:** Zaiden is a variation of the name Zaden, which is a modern invention and has no meaning as such. This would be a great choice for parents looking for something very cool-sounding and unique.
**Alternative spellings:** Zaden, Zayden

## Zain
**Meaning:** Handsome
**Origin:** Arabic
**Pronunciation:** zane
**Description:** Zain is an Islamic name that means 'beauty' or 'handsome'. The name is popular in Muslim communities and there is a Muslim singer and songwriter who shares this name, Zain Bhikha.
**Alternative spellings:** Zayn, Zane, Zayne

## Zak
**Meaning:** Purity
**Origin:** Hebrew
**Pronunciation:** zak
**Description:** Zak spelt in this way can be taken as a name in itself. Its Hebrew meaning is 'purity'. It can however also be the shortened form of Zakaria or Zakarias, both of which have numerous spelling variations originating from both Hebrew and Arabic. The meaning of Zak when considered a shortened version of Zakaria is 'God has remembered'.
**Alternative spellings:** Zach, Zack

## Zaki
**Meaning:** The Lord recalled
**Origin:** Greek
**Pronunciation:** ZAK ee
**Description:** Zaki and similar names have become extremely popular since the fame of film star Zac Efron. It is thought to be of Greek origin.
**Alternative spellings:** Zakki

## Zakir
**Meaning:** The Lord recalled
**Origin:** Arabic
**Pronunciation:** za KEER

**Description:** This name means 'the one who remembers'. It is unusual in Britain but popular across the Arabic world.
**Alternative spellings:** Zahkir, Zakeer

## Zana
**Meaning:** Wise; knowing
**Origin:** Kurdish
**Pronunciation:** zaan AH
**Description:** Zana is a Kurdish boys' name meaning 'wise' or 'knowing' and has connotations of knowledge and learning.
**Alternative spellings:** Zanna, Zanah, Zannah

## Zander
**Meaning:** Defender of man
**Origin:** Greek
**Pronunciation:** ZAN der
**Description:** Zander is a Dutch and Slavic variant of the boys' name Xander, which is a variant of the Greek name Alexander, meaning 'defender of man'. Xander and Zander have both risen greatly in popularity in recent years.
**Alternative spellings:** Sander, Xander

## Zayaan
**Meaning:** Graceful
**Origin:** Arabic
**Pronunciation:** ZAY aan
**Description:** Zayaan is a name and a variant of the Arabic name Zayan. It is common as both a given name and as a surname in the Arabic world.
**Alternative spellings:** Zayain, Zayan

## Zaydan
**Meaning:** Grow; increase

**Origin:** Arabic
**Pronunciation:** zaay DAAN
**Description:** Zaydan is an Arabic boys' name that means 'growth' or 'increase'. It is similar to the name Zayd, which shares the similar meaning of 'abundance' or 'plentiful'. It is both a given name and a surname in Arabic countries.
**Alternative spellings:** Zayden

## Zayer
**Meaning:** Tourist who visits holy places
**Origin:** Arabic
**Pronunciation:** zaay ER
**Description:** Zayer is an Arabic boys' name meaning 'tourist who visits holy places'. It is more commonly found in Muslim/Islamic communities.
**Alternative spellings:** Zayir

## Zebediah
**Meaning:** Gift from God
**Origin:** Hebrew
**Pronunciation:** zeb EH DIE ah
**Description:** Zebediah is a Hebrew name meaning 'gift from God'. It is the name of several characters in the Old Testament.
**Alternative spellings:** Zebedia

## Zeeshan
**Meaning:** Noble
**Origin:** Arabic
**Pronunciation:** ZEE sharn
**Description:** Zeeshan is said to mean 'possessor of high status' and is of Arabic origin. It is commonly used to signify nobility, and is also regularly abbreviated to Shan.
**Alternative spellings:** Zeesharn, Zeshan

**Z**

## Zeke

**Meaning:** God will provide strength
**Origin:** Hebrew
**Pronunciation:** zee-kee
**Description:** Zeke is a shortened form or nickname of the Hebrew name Ezekiel. Ezekiel was the name of a prophet in the Old Testament. It is said to mean 'God will provide strength'.

## Zenith

**Meaning:** Peak; most successful
**Origin:** English
**Pronunciation:** zen ITH
**Description:** Zenith is taken from the English vocabulary word of the same spelling, and it means 'peak' or 'most successful', as in the point at which something reaches its highest.

## Zephaniah

**Meaning:** Yahweh is hidden
**Origin:** Hebrew
**Pronunciation:** zef ahn EYE ah
**Description:** Zephaniah is a biblical name meaning 'Yahweh is hidden'. He is the author of the Book of Zephaniah and one of 12 minor prophets of the Old Testament.
**Alternative spellings:** Zephinia

## Zhi

**Meaning:** Nature
**Origin:** Chinese
**Pronunciation:** JHEE
**Description:** Zhi is a unisex name of Chinese origin, common as both a given name and a surname. It roughly transliterates as 'nature', 'character' or 'quality'.
**Alternative spellings:** Zhee, Zi

## Zia

See entry in 'Names for Baby Girls A–Z'

## Zidane

**Meaning:** Growth; progress; increase
**Origin:** Arabic
**Pronunciation:** zee dan
**Description:** Zidane is an Arabic boys' name, and because it has a 'zyd' root, the name means 'progress,' 'growth' or 'to increase'. It is the name of the famous French footballer and manager, Zinedine Zidane.
**Alternative spellings:** Zidan

## Ziggy

**Meaning:** Victory; peace
**Origin:** English
**Pronunciation:** zig EE
**Description:** Ziggy is a variation of the name Siegfried, a German name that is composed of the elements of '*sig*' meaning 'victory' and '*frithu*' meaning 'peace'. The late David Bowie made the name popular because Ziggy Stardust was his alter ego.

## Zion

**Meaning:** Highest point
**Origin:** Hebrew
**Pronunciation:** ZI on
**Description:** Zion is a masculine name of Hebrew origin. It is an extremely rare name, unlike many other Hebrew names in Britain. It is said to mean the 'highest point' or 'pinnacle'.
**Alternative spellings:** Zyon

## Ziya

**Meaning:** Splendour; light; glow

**Origin:** Arabic
**Pronunciation:** ZEE yah
**Description:** Ziya is a name taken from the Arabic word '*diya*', which means 'splendour', 'light' and 'glow'.
**Alternative spellings:** Zia

## Zohaib

**Meaning:** Leader
**Origin:** Arabic
**Pronunciation:** zo HAYB
**Description:** The name Zohaib comes from an Arabic word that means 'leader', 'king', 'gold' or 'ocean of knowledge'. It is common as both a given name and a surname.
**Alternative spellings:** Zohayb

## Zorawar

**Meaning:** Strong; powerful
**Origin:** Indian
**Pronunciation:** zorah WAR

**Description:** Zorawar is an Indian boys' name meaning 'strong' or 'powerful'.

## Zubair

**Meaning:** Proper name
**Origin:** Arabic
**Pronunciation:** zu BAYR
**Description:** The boys' name Zubair comes from the Arabic word that means 'proper name' or 'superior'. It is sometimes written as Zubayr, which is a city in Iraq. Zubair is also the name of a group of islands in the Red Sea.
**Alternative spellings:** Zubaair, Zubayr

## Zylan

**Meaning:** No meaning
**Origin:** American
**Pronunciation:** zye LAAN
**Description:** Zylan is a modern invented name and as such, has no real meaning.

Z

# Names for Baby Girls A–Z

# Names For Baby Girls A–Z

# A

## Aamna
**Meaning:** Security
**Origin:** Arabic
**Pronunciation:** AHM na
**Description:** Aamna derives from an Arabic word meaning 'security'.
**Alternative spellings:** Amna

## Aarna
**Meaning:** Strong mountain
**Origin:** Hebrew
**Pronunciation:** AHR nah
**Description:** Aarna originates from the longer Hebrew name Arnina, and is the feminine version of the name Aaron.
**Alternative spellings:** Aarrna, Arna

## Aasiyah
**Meaning:** Caring one
**Origin:** Arabic
**Pronunciation:** ah SEE yah
**Description:** As Aasiyah is found in Islamic scriptures the name was initially favoured by Muslim parents, however its use has now spread to Africa.
**Alternative spellings:** Aasiya, Asiya, Asiyah

## Aadya
**Meaning:** First power or the beginning
**Origin:** Hindi
**Pronunciation:** Ah DEE yah
**Description:** Aadya is a Hindu name of Indian origin. The translation is similar in many Eastern languages, meaning 'first power', 'goddess' and 'unequalled'. It is a popular name throughout the Hindu community and variations of the spelling have seen a rise in popularity in mainstream culture.
**Alternative spellings:** Aadyha, Adya

## Aairah
**Meaning:** Noble; honourable; respectful
**Origin:** Urdu
**Pronunciation:** AY rah
**Description:** Aairah is a pretty, feminine name of Urdu origin, that means 'noble' or 'respectful'. Variations of the name include Aaira and Ayra.
**Alternative spellings:** Aaira, Ayra, Ayrah

## Aaliya
**Meaning:** Exalted; ascending
**Origin:** Hebrew
**Pronunciation:** Ah LEE ah
**Description:** Aaliya is a feminine form of the Arabic name, Ali, that translates as 'exulted' or 'ascending'. The name had a huge surge in popularity in the late 90s thanks to Grammy and Academy Award nominated singer and actress, Aaliyah, who tragically died in a plane crash in 2001.
**Alternative spellings:** Aliya, Aaliyah, Aliyah, Alia

## Aamina

**Meaning:** Dependable
**Origin:** Arabic
**Pronunciation:** Ah MEE nah
**Description:** Aamina is a spelling variation of Amina and translates as 'dependable'. It is a widely-used name in the Muslim community as it is understood that 'Āminah bint Wahb (who died in 577AD) was mother of the prophet Muhammad.
**Alternative spellings:** Amina, Ahmina, Aminah, Aaminah

## Aanya

**Meaning:** Limitless
**Origin:** Hindi
**Pronunciation:** AHN yah
**Description:** Aanya is a Hindu name that means 'limitless' or 'resurrection'. The name is also a variation of Anya, a Russian form of Hannah that means 'with grace'.
**Alternative spellings:** Anya

## Aariya

**Meaning:** Lioness
**Origin:** Hebrew
**Pronunciation:** Ah REE ah
**Description:** Aariya is a spelling variation of Arya, an Iranian name of Indian origin. The name received a surge in popularity in Western society thanks to the female character, Arya Stark in popular TV series *Game of Thrones*.
**Alternative spellings:** Aria, Arya, Aarya

## Aasiya

**Meaning:** Healer; one who tends to the sick
**Origin:** Arabic
**Pronunciation:** ah SEE yah
**Description:** Aasiya, a spelling variation of Asiya, is a revered name within the Muslim community. In history, Asiya bint Muzahim was the wife of the Pharoah, who reigned during the time of Moses. She is regarded as one of the four greatest women of all time in Muslim faith, the other three being Mary (mother of Jesus), Khadija (wife of Muhammad) and Fatimah (daughter of Muhammad).
**Alternative spellings:** Asiya, Asija

## Aayat

**Meaning:** Miracles of the Quran
**Origin:** Arabic
**Pronunciation:** AH yat
**Description:** The Islamic translation of Aayat is 'verse of the Quran' or 'miracles of the Quran'. It refers to 'signs' or proof of the validity of the verses of the Quran.
**Alternative spellings:** Ayat

## Abbie

**Meaning:** Father's joy
**Origin:** Hebrew
**Pronunciation:** AB ee
**Description:** The most popular spelling variant of the pet form for Abigail. This name is a name in its own right.
**Alternative spellings:** Abbey, Abbi, Abby, Abi

## Abida

**Meaning:** God's follower
**Origin:** Hebrew
**Pronunciation:** AB ee dah

**Description:** A feminine version of the masculine name Abid, meaning 'God's follower'.
**Alternative spellings:** Abbida, Abeeda

## Abigail
**Meaning:** Father's joy
**Origin:** Hebrew
**Pronunciation:** AB ih gayl
**Description:** Abigail is a biblical Hebrew name meaning 'father in exaltation'.
**Alternative spellings:** Abbigail, Abygail

## Abiha
**Meaning:** Father
**Origin:** Arabic
**Pronunciation:** ah BEE ah
**Description:** Abiha is a name of Arabic origins and it could share a root with the Hebrew name Abigail. In Islamic belief it was a title of one of the daughters of the prophet Muhammad.
**Alternative spellings:** Abbiha, Abeeha

## Abilene
**Meaning:** Grass
**Origin:** Hebrew
**Pronunciation:** AB ih leen
**Description:** Abilene is both the name of a small town in Texas and the translation of a Hebrew word meaning 'grass'. According to the New Testament, Abilene is a region of the Holy Land.
**Alternative spellings:** Abelene, Abileen

## Abir
See entry in 'Names for Baby Boys A–Z'

## Abishag
**Meaning:** Wise; educated
**Origin:** Hebrew
**Pronunciation:** AB ih shag
**Description:** Abishag is a biblical name, borne by a beautiful virgin brought to King David on his death bed in an attempt to restore his vigour and lust for life. It is very rarely seen these days
**Alternative spellings:** Abbishag, Abyshag

## Abital
**Meaning:** Dewy
**Origin:** Hebrew
**Pronunciation:** AB ih tal
**Description:** Abital is a biblical name meaning 'dewy', so this name has connotations with dawn and nature.
**Alternative spellings:** Abbital, Abitel

## Abla
**Meaning:** Woman with a full figure; wild rose
**Origin:** Arabic
**Pronunciation:** AB la
**Description:** The name Abla is thought to have Arabic roots and refers to 'a woman with a full figure'. It could also be Swahili in origin, in which case it could mean 'a wild rose'.
**Alternative spellings:** Ablah

## Acacia
**Meaning:** Point; thorn
**Origin:** Greek
**Pronunciation:** ah KAY shuh; ah KAY see uh
**Description:** This unusual girls' name is also the name of a flower, the acacia, which is the national symbol of Australia. It is suggested

that the flower has the power to ward off evil.
**Alternative spellings:** Akacia, Akaysha, Akeisha

## Ada
**Meaning:** Noble
**Origin:** German
**Pronunciation:** AY da
**Description:** Ada is sometimes used as a pet form of Adele, but is also a name in its own right.
**Alternative spellings:** Adah, Aida

## Adah
**Meaning:** Adornment
**Origin:** Hebrew
**Pronunciation:** AY da
**Description:** Adah is a biblical name meaning 'adornment', or 'enhancement'. Particularly popular in Sweden.
**Alternative spellings:** Ada, Aida

## Adaline
**Meaning:** Noble
**Origin:** Teutonic
**Pronunciation:** AD e lin
**Description:** An unusual spelling variation of Adeline that has risen in popularity in recent years. The name is of German origin, the diminutive of Adèle.
**Alternative spellings:** Adeline, Adelyn, Adaleine, Adalyn

## Adamina
**Meaning:** Red earth
**Origin:** Hebrew
**Pronunciation:** AD ah ME na
**Description:** This name is the feminine form of Adam and shares the same meaning, 'earth'.
**Alternative spellings:** Adamena, Addamina

## Addison
See entry in 'Names for Baby Boys A–Z'

## Adela
**Meaning:** Noble
**Origin:** Teutonic
**Pronunciation:** a DEL a
**Description:** Adela is a further diminutive of the German name Adèle or the masculine form Adel, meaning 'noble'. In history, Saint Adela was a 7th-century Frankish princess who founded a monastery in France. It was also the name of one of William the Conqueror's daughters.
**Alternative spellings:** Adèle, Adele

## Adelaide
**Meaning:** Noble; kind
**Origin:** German
**Pronunciation:** AD ee lade
**Description:** This name of Old German origin means 'full of kindness'.
**Alternative spellings:** Adelade, Adelayde

## Adele
**Meaning:** Noble; kind
**Origin:** German
**Pronunciation:** a DELL
**Description:** Adele is a variant of the Old German name Adeline or Adelaide.
**Alternative spellings:** Adel, Adelle

## Adelina
**Meaning:** Noble; kind; small-winged one
**Origin:** French
**Pronunciation:** A del EE na
**Description:** A popular girls' name that derives from the Old

German names Adelaide and Adeline. It is a name rich with associations and means 'noble', 'kind' and 'small-winged one'.
**Alternative spellings:** Adeleina, Adelena

## Adina
**Meaning:** Slender
**Origin:** Hebrew
**Pronunciation:** a DEE na
**Description:** Adina was formerly a male name and was borne by a soldier in King David's army. Now it is more common with females due to its feminine sound.
**Alternative spellings:** Adeena, Adena

## Aditi
**Meaning:** No boundaries
**Origin:** Sanskrit
**Pronunciation:** ah DEE tah
**Description:** Aditi is a name said to mean 'no boundaries'. It is the name of a Hindu goddess so is popular with Hindu parents.
**Alternative spellings:** Adeeti, Aditie, Adity

## Admete
**Meaning:** Untamed
**Origin:** Greek
**Pronunciation:** ad MEE tee
**Description:** In Greek mythology, Admete's father asked Heracles to acquire for his daughter the belt of the queen of the Amazons.
**Alternative spellings:** Admeete, Admette

## Adrianna
**Meaning:** From Hadria
**Origin:** Latin
**Pronunciation:** ah dre AH nah

**Description:** Adrianna is the feminine form of the masculine Adrian. This refers to a man from Hadria, so Adriana means 'girl from Hadria'.
**Alternative spellings:** Adreana, Adriana, Adrihanna

## Adrianne
**Meaning:** From Hadria
**Origin:** Latin
**Pronunciation:** AY dri ann
**Description:** Another feminine variant of the popular boys' name Adrian.
**Alternative spellings:** Adreanne, Adrienne

## Aeryn
**Meaning:** Ireland
**Origin:** Gaelic
**Pronunciation:** EH rin
**Description:** Aeryn is the American respelling of the Gaelic name Erin. In the 19th century many Irish poets used the name Erin to refer to Ireland or as a feminine personification of the land.
**Alternative spellings:** Aerin, Airin, Eirinn, Erin, Eryn

## Afaf
**Meaning:** Chastity
**Origin:** Arabic
**Pronunciation:** AY faf
**Description:** Afaf is a popular name and has associations with virtue.
**Alternative spellings:** Avaf, Avaff

## Afia
**Meaning:** Born on a Friday
**Origin:** African
**Pronunciation:** ah FEE ah
**Description:** Afia is a feminine form of the name Afua. Both of

277

the names are derived from the Ewe language spoken in Benin, Togo and Ghana in Africa.
**Alternative spellings:** Aafia, Aphia, Afiyah

## Africa
**Meaning:** Africa
**Origin:** English
**Pronunciation:** AF ri ka
**Description:** Africa is a girls' name that first arose in the 18th century. It derives from the continent of the same name and is usually found as a baby name in English-speaking countries.
**Alternative spellings:** Africah, Afrika

## Agatha
**Meaning:** Good
**Origin:** Greek
**Pronunciation:** AG a tha
**Description:** Derived from the Greek word for 'good', *agathos*, the name was also introduced to Britain in the 11th century by the Normans.
**Alternative spellings:** Agetha, Agata

## Agnes
**Meaning:** Purity; lamb
**Origin:** Greek
**Pronunciation:** AG nes
**Description:** Agnes is said to come from the Greek word for 'purity'. It also originates from the Latin word *'agnus'*, which means 'lamb'.
**Alternative spellings:** Agness, Agyness

## Ahlam
**Meaning:** A pleasant dreamer
**Origin:** Arabic
**Pronunciation:** AH lam
**Description:** Ahlam is a popular girls' name that means 'a pleasant dreamer' or 'imaginative dreams'.
**Alternative spellings:** Ahlaam, Arlam

## Ai
**Meaning:** Love
**Origin:** Japanese
**Pronunciation:** AH ee
**Description:** This name is most commonly found within Japanese-speaking communities and is very popular. Although mainly used in a feminine capacity, Ai is actually unisex.

## Aida
**Meaning:** Returning
**Origin:** Arabic
**Pronunciation:** AI ee dah
**Description:** The name is derived from the Arabic name Āyidah, meaning 'returning'. The name entered pop culture in the late 19th century with the release of Guiseppe Verde's opera of the same name.
**Alternative spellings:** Aeeda, Aide, Ayeeda, Ayida

## Aiko
**Meaning:** Child of love
**Origin:** Japanese
**Pronunciation:** AYE koh
**Description:** Aiko is a Japanese name that is comprised of the elements of *'ai'* meaning 'love' and *'ko'* meaning 'child'.
**Alternative spellings:** Ayko

## Aila
**Meaning:** Bird
**Origin:** Gaelic
**Pronunciation:** EYE luh
**Description:** Aila is a name that

can be found in several languages. In Scotland it is the shortened form of Aileen. The ultimate root of the name is thought to be the Latin word *'avis'*, which means 'bird.'
**Alternative spellings:** Ayla, Eila

## Ailsa
**Meaning:** Elizabeth's rock
**Origin:** Gaelic
**Pronunciation:** AYL sah
**Description:** Ailsa comes from the island Ailsa Craig in Scotland, which originally meant Elizabeth's Rock. Although the root name is specifically feminine, many boys were also named Ailsa, after the island.
**Alternative spellings:** Eilsa, Elsa, Else

## Aima
**Meaning:** Leader or ruler
**Origin:** Arabic
**Pronunciation:** aim ah
**Description:** Aima is an unconventional name that translates from Arabic as 'leader' or 'ruler'. It may also be adopted as an exotic form of the French name, Amy, meaning 'beloved'.
**Alternative spellings:** Ayma

## Aimee
**Meaning:** Beloved
**Origin:** French
**Pronunciation:** AIM me
**Description:** A French name from the French verb *'aimer'*, meaning 'to love'.
**Alternative spellings:** Ami, Amie, Amiee, Amy

## Aine
**Meaning:** Brightness
**Origin:** Gaelic
**Pronunciation:** ON ya
**Description:** Aine is the traditional Irish name of the fairy queen in Celtic mythology. It is also considered an Irish equivalent of Anne. Note the interesting pronunciation of this name.
**Alternative spellings:** Aina, Anya, Onya

## Ainsley
**Meaning:** Meadow
**Origin:** Gaelic
**Pronunciation:** AINS lee
**Description:** Ainsley is a unisex Gaelic name that comes from a Scottish place of the same name. The name is derived from an Old English word for 'meadow'.

## Aisha
**Meaning:** Prosperous
**Origin:** Arabic
**Pronunciation:** ah EE sha
**Description:** Aisha is a name of Arabic origin, most often found in Muslim communities. The prophet Muhammad's third wife was named Aisha.
**Alternative spellings:** Aiesha, Aishah, Ayesha, Ayisha, Aysha

## Aisling
**Meaning:** Spirit of Ireland
**Origin:** Gaelic
**Pronunciation:** ASH ling
**Description:** Aisling, a name of Old Gaelic origin, is a mythical maiden who represents the spirit of Ireland. This is a very patriotic Irish name.
**Alternative spellings:** Aishling, Aisleyne, Aislin, Aisling, Aislinn, Aislynn, Ashleen, Ashlyn, Ashlynne, Eislinn and Isleen

## Aiva

**Meaning:** Bird
**Origin:** Latin
**Pronunciation:** AY vuh
**Description:** Aiva is a variant form of the name Ava, which is short for Avalon. The name is derived from the Latin word *'avis'*, which means 'bird'. Very popular in English-speaking countries.
**Alternative spellings:** Aive, Ava, Ayva, Eva

## Aiyana

**Meaning:** Flowering
**Origin:** Native American
**Pronunciation:** ay AHN na
**Description:** In Native American Aiyana means 'flowering'. It is also a variant of the name Ayanna, which originates from an African language.
**Alternative spellings:** Ayana, Ayanha, Ayanna

## Aizah

**Meaning:** Prosperous
**Origin:** Arabic
**Pronunciation:** AY zah
**Description:** A favourite with Muslim parents, Aizah comes from the name Asia, after the continent, and means 'prosperous'. Unsurprisingly, it is most widely found in countries within Asia.
**Alternative spellings:** Aiza, Asia, Asiah, Asya

## Akira

**Meaning:** Bright; intelligent; clear
**Origin:** Japan
**Pronunciation:** AK i rah
**Description:** Akira is predominantly a common Japanese male name but it has also begun to garner popularity as a female name. In Scotland, the name is a female version of the name Acair, meaning 'anchor'. It is also an Indian female name derived from the Sanskrit, meaning 'graceful strength'.
**Alternative spellings:** Akeera

## Akshara

**Meaning:** Unchangeable
**Origin:** Sanskrit
**Pronunciation:** ak SHA rah
**Description:** A unisex name said to mean 'unchangeable'. This versatile name is popular with Indian parents.
**Alternative spellings:** Akhshara, Aksara

## Alaa

**Meaning:** Servant of Allah
**Origin:** Arabic
**Pronunciation:** ah LAH
**Description:** This name can be used for both girls and boys. It is often used as a shortened version of Aladdin and is said to mean 'servant of Allah'. Alaa is often given as a name by Muslim parents.
**Alternative spellings:** Ala, Allaa

## Alaia

**Meaning:** Joyful; happy
**Origin:** Basque
**Pronunciation:** ah LYE ah
**Description:** Alaia is of Arabic, Hebrew and Basque origin and means 'exulted', 'happy' and 'joyful'. This spelling variation has been rising in popularity in recent years as an alternative to similar-sounding names like Aaliyah, Ahalya and Alaya.
**Alternative spellings:** Allayah, Alaya, Alayah

## Alaina

**Meaning:** Rock
**Origin:** Gaelic
**Pronunciation:** ah LANE ah
**Description:** Alaina, a name found mainly in Wales, is a variation of Alana and pronounced slightly differently. Its meaning is the same as Alana.
**Alternative spellings:** Alayna, Alena, Aleyna

## Alana

**Meaning:** Rock
**Origin:** Gaelic
**Pronunciation:** a LAH nuh
**Description:** This is the feminine form of popular masculine name Alan, the name of a river that runs through Wales. The name has Celtic origins.
**Alternative spellings:** Alanah, Alannah, Allana, Allanah, Allannah

## Alanis

**Meaning:** Rock
**Origin:** Gaelic
**Pronunciation:** ah LAN iss
**Description:** This is a Gaelic name meaning 'rock' and is the female version of Alan. Alanis Morissette is a famous Canadian singer with this name. She was named after her father, whose name is Alan.
**Alternative spellings:** Alannis

## Alara

**Meaning:** One who brings brightness and happiness to the soul
**Origin:** Persian
**Pronunciation:** a LAR ah
**Description:** Alara is a popular name in Turkey and means 'the one who brings brightness and happiness to the heart and soul'.

Alara is also the name of a water fairy in Turkish mythology who must remain beside the water to maintain her youth and beauty.
**Alternative spellings:** Allara, Alarah, Elara

## Alarna

**Meaning:** Rock
**Origin:** Gaelic
**Pronunciation:** ah LAR nah
**Description:** Alarna is another variation of the feminine form of Alan. It has a slightly different pronunciation than Alana and is mainly found in Wales thanks to its Celtic origin.
**Alternative spellings:** Alahna, Alarnah

## Alaw

**Meaning:** Melodious river
**Origin:** Welsh
**Pronunciation:** AH low
**Description:** Alaw comes from a Welsh name of a river in Anglesey. The river's name means 'melodious'. The name is not common outside of Wales. It is pronounced like the word 'allow'.
**Alternative spellings:** Allaw, Alow

## Alayna

**Meaning:** Light; torch; bright
**Origin:** Greek
**Pronunciation:** a LAY nah
**Description:** A variation of the name Elaine, a French cognate of the Greek Helenē, meaning light, torch or bright. Alternatively, Alayna can be used as a Scottish feminine form of Alan, meaning 'little rock'.
**Alternative spellings:** Alaina, Alana

## Alba

**Meaning:** White; clear; bright
**Origin:** Latin
**Pronunciation:** al ber
**Description:** Alba is female name from the masculine, Albus or Albinus. Alba is also a prevalent place name (being the Gaelic name for Scotland as well as a poetic name for England). It is also a common surname in Spain.
**Alternative spellings:** Allba

## Albany

**Meaning:** City in New York state
**Origin:** English
**Pronunciation:** al BAAN nee
**Description:** Albany is one of the major cities in the state of New York. Like London and Paris, this name follows the trend of using place names for baby names.

## Alberta

**Meaning:** Noble; bright; famous
**Origin:** German
**Pronunciation:** al BER ta
**Description:** Alberta is the feminine form of Albert and the name of one of Queen Victoria's daughters, and the Canadian province of Alberta was named after her.
**Alternative spellings:** Alburta, Allberta

## Aleah

**Meaning:** Noble
**Origin:** Hebrew
**Pronunciation:** AH lee yah
**Description:** A rare girls' name, Aleah is another variant of the name Aliyah. While Aliyah is popular among Muslim parents, Aleah is a popular baby name with Jewish parents.
**Alternative spellings:** Aaleyah, Aalia, AAliyah, Aaliyah, Aleya, Alia, Aliya, Aliyah, Aliyyah

## Aleena

**Meaning:** Noble
**Origin:** Arabic
**Pronunciation:** ah LEE nah
**Description:** This modern spelling of Alina is found mostly in America.
**Alternative spellings:** Aleenah, Alina

## Aleeza

**Meaning:** Joyful
**Origin:** Hebrew
**Pronunciation:** Ah LEE zah
**Description:** Aleeza is a female Hebrew name that translates as 'joyful' or 'cheerful'. Aleeza can also be a diminutive for the Persian name, Aleezadeh, which means 'offspring of Ali' or 'high-born'.
**Alternative spellings:** Aliza

## Aleisha

**Meaning:** Noble
**Origin:** German
**Pronunciation:** ah LEE sha
**Description:** Aleisha is a variant of the popular name Alisha.
**Alternative spellings:** Aleesha, Alesha, Alicia, Alicja, Aliesha, Alisha, Alysha, Elisha

## Alena

**Meaning:** Light; torch; bright
**Origin:** Greek
**Pronunciation:** a LAY nah
**Description:** A variation of the name Elaine, a French cognate of the Greek Helenē, meaning light,

torch or bright. Alternatively, Alayna can be used as a Scottish feminine form of Alan, meaning 'little rock'.
**Alternative spellings:** Alaina, Alana

## Alessia
**Meaning:** Defender of man
**Origin:** Greek
**Pronunciation:** ah LAY ser ah
**Description:** This popular Italian name is a nice variation of Alicia.
**Alternative spellings:** Alecia, Alicia, Alicja, Alisia, Alissia, Alycia, Alysia, Alyssia, Elicia, Elissia

## Alex
**Meaning:** Defender of man
**Origin:** Greek
**Pronunciation:** AL ix
**Description:** Alex is a shortened form of Alexander, Alexandra and Alexis. It is also a unisex name in its own right.
**Alternative spellings:** Alix

## Alexa
**Meaning:** Defender of man
**Origin:** Greek
**Pronunciation:** ah LEX uh
**Description:** The feminine version of Alex, Alexa derives from the Greek name Alexander.
**Alternative spellings:** Aleksa, Alexah, Alixa

## Alexandra
**Meaning:** Defender of man
**Origin:** Greek
**Pronunciation:** AL eks AHN druh
**Description:** Alexandra is the feminine form of Alexander and became popular in the UK after Alexandra of Denmark's marriage to Edward VII.
**Alternative spellings:** Aleksandra, Alessandra, Alexsandra, Aliksandra, Alisandra, Alissandra, Alixandra, Alyxandra

## Alexandre
See entry in 'Names for Baby Boys A–Z'

## Alexandria
**Meaning:** Defender of man
**Origin:** Greek
**Pronunciation:** ah leks AHN dree ah
**Description:** A variation of the name Alexandra, this is also the name of a major Egyptian city.
**Alternative spellings:** Aleksandria, Alessandria, Alexandrea, Alexsandria, Aliksandria, Alisandria, Alissandria, Alixandria, Alyxandria

## Alexi
**Meaning:** Defender of man
**Origin:** Greek
**Pronunciation:** ah LEX ee
**Description:** Alexi is a shortened form of Alexis but can also be used as a name in its own right. As it derives from the Greek name Alexander it also shares the meaning of 'defender of man'.
**Alternative spellings:** Aleksi, Alexie, Alexsee, Alexy

## Alexia
**Meaning:** Defender of man; helper
**Origin:** Greek
**Pronunciation:** ah LEX ee ah
**Description:** Alexia is a feminine alternative to the unisex name Alexis that derives from Alexander, meaning 'defender of man', or it could come from a Greek word meaning 'helper'.
**Alternative spellings:** Aleksia, Alexiya

## Alexis

**Meaning:** Defender of man; helper
**Origin:** Greek
**Pronunciation:** a LEX iss
**Description:** Derived from Alexander, Alexis was originally a boy's name, but is now more common among girls.
**Alternative spellings:** Aleksis, Alexiss, Alexsis, Alexus

## Ali

See entry in 'Names for Baby Boys A–Z'

## Alice

**Meaning:** Noble
**Origin:** French
**Pronunciation:** AL iss
**Description:** A distinct name in medieval England, Alice enjoyed a surge of popularity in the 19th century and periods of favour ever since.
**Alternative spellings:** Alise, Aliss, Alys

## Alicia

**Meaning:** Noble
**Origin:** French
**Pronunciation:** a LEE sha; a LEE si a
**Description:** A modern form of Alice, with two different pronunciations.
**Alternative spellings:** Alecia, Alessia, Alicja, Alisia, Alissia, Alycia, Alysia, Alyssia, Elicia, Elissia; Aleesha, Aleisha, Alesha, Aliesha, Alisha, Alysha

## Alina

**Meaning:** Noble
**Origin:** French
**Pronunciation:** a LEE nah
**Description:** Commonly found in English-, Italian-, Polish-, Russian- and Spanish-speaking countries, this name is also considered the shortened form of the French name Adelaide.
**Alternative spellings:** Aleena, Alinah

## Alishba

**Meaning:** Favoured by God
**Origin:** Hebrew
**Pronunciation:** ah LISH bah
**Description:** This Hebrew form of the English name Elizabeth is found in the the Old Testament. Alishba was the wife of Aaron, Moses' older brother. The name also has Islamic roots.
**Alternative spellings:** Allishba, Alyshba

## Alison

**Meaning:** Noble; exalted
**Origin:** German
**Pronunciation:** AL iss on
**Description:** Alison is an Old German name that was originally derived from the name Alice. It is commonly shortened to Ali, or Ally.
**Alternative spellings:** Alicen, Alisson, Allison, Allyson, Alycen Alyson, Alysson

## Alissa

**Meaning:** From the flower; alyssum
**Origin:** Greek
**Pronunciation:** ah liss ah
**Description:** A popular feminine name used across the world with origins in Greek, Arabic and Filipino. In Western countries the name is usually derived from the name of the flower, alyssum.

**Alternative spellings**: Alica

## Alivia
**Meaning**: Olive
**Origin**: Latin
**Pronunciation**: ah LI vee ah
**Description**: Alivia is a modern American variation of Olivia, which originates from the Latin for an olive.
**Alternative spellings**: Alivya

## Allegra
**Meaning**: Happy
**Origin**: Italian
**Pronunciation**: a LEG ra
**Description**: Allegra is a name taken from the Italian adjective meaning 'happy', and in music 'allegro' is a tempo meaning 'cheerful' or 'brisk'.
**Alternative spellings**: Allegrah, Allegre

## Alma
**Meaning**: Lift the Spirit
**Origin**: Latin
**Pronunciation**: AHL mah
**Description**: The origin of the name Alma is disputed but was most likely derived from the Latin word, 'almus', which means 'kind' or 'nourishing'. It is a feminine form of Almo.
**Alternative spellings**: Elma

## Aloha
**Meaning**: Love
**Origin**: Polynesian
**Pronunciation**: a LO ha
**Description**: Aloha is a modern name from the Polynesian word meaning 'love', which is often used as a greeting. Its popularity has rapidly increased.
**Alternative spellings**: Alloha

## Alpha
See entry in 'Names for Baby Boys A–Z'

## Althea
**Meaning**: Unknown; derived from Greek mythology
**Origin**: Greek
**Pronunciation**: al THEE uh
**Description**: Derived from the Greek name Althaea, the mother of the hero Meleager in Greek mythology. The name became better known in the late 70s when the Jamaican reggae duo Althea & Donna released their number 1 hit 'Uptown Top Ranking'.
**Alternative spellings**: Althaea, Althaia

## Alya
**Meaning**: Sky; to ascend
**Origin**: Arabic
**Pronunciation**: AH lya
**Description**: Alya is a name used in many countries that originates from Ancient Greek, Hebrew and Arabic. The most common translation of the name refers to sky, heaven or ascent.
**Alternative spellings**: Aalya, Alia

## Alyssa
**Meaning**: Noble
**Origin**: German
**Pronunciation**: ah LIS sah
**Description**: This name is another variation of Alice.
**Alternative spellings**: Alisa, Alissa, Alysa, Elisa, Elissa, Elyssa

## Amaia
**Meaning**: Mother city
**Origin**: Spanish

**Pronunciation:** am EYE ya
**Description:** A given and sur-name of Spanish origins derived from the village of Amaya in Spain. The name is composed of the elements of '*am(ma)*', mean-ing 'mother' and the suffix '*ia*' that is used to form action names, suggesting the meaning of Amaia is 'mother city'.
**Alternative spellings:** Amayah, Ammaya, Amya

## Amanah
**Meaning:** To uphold trust
**Origin:** Arabic
**Pronunciation:** AM an ah
**Description:** Amanah is the closest English translation of the word '*Al-Amanah*', 'The Trust', which refers to the moral responsi-bility of fulfilling one's obligations due to Allah.
**Alternative spellings:** Amana

## Amal
See entry in 'Names for Baby Boys A–Z'

## Amalia
**Meaning:** Hard-working
**Origin:** German
**Pronunciation:** ah MAHL ee ah
**Description:** Amalia is a variation of Amelia. Despite sharing its meaning with Amelia, Amalia is pronounced differently and is popular in Germany.
**Alternative spellings:** Amelia, Amilia, Emelia, Emilia, Emilija

## Amalie
**Meaning:** Hard-working
**Origin:** German
**Pronunciation:** ah ma LEE

**Description:** Another name de-rived from the Old German name Amelia. This name is most widely used in France as a variant spelling of Amelie. This name is rising in popularity in the UK.
**Alternative spellings:** Amelie

## Amana
**Meaning:** Security
**Origin:** Arabic
**Pronunciation:** ah MAN na
**Description:** Amana is an un-usual name that can be found in several languages and its meaning is uncertain. As it is similar to the Arabic name Aman, it could share its meaning of 'security'.
**Alternative spellings:** Ahmana, Amanah

## Amanda
**Meaning:** Loveable
**Origin:** Latin
**Pronunciation:** a MAN duh
**Description:** The name Amanda derives from the Latin '*amabilis*', meaning 'loveable'. When originat-ing from Sanskrit, Amanda is also (rarely) seen as a boys' name.
**Alternative spellings:** Amander

## Amani
**Meaning:** Desires
**Origin:** Arabic
**Pronunciation:** ah MAH ne
**Description:** In Arabic-speaking countries Amani is used as a male name; however in Swahili-speaking countries it is also used for females.
**Alternative spellings:** Ahmani

## Amara
**Meaning:** Unfading
**Origin:** Greek

**Pronunciation:** a MAH ra
**Description:** This name may come from the Greek word *'amarantos'*, which means 'unfading'; however some believe that it derives from the Latin word *'amarus'*, which means bitter.
**Alternative spellings:** Amarah, Ammara

## Amarachi

**Meaning:** God's grace
**Origin:** African
**Pronunciation:** ah MAR ah chi
**Description:** Amarachi comes from the language of the Igbo people who take it to mean 'God's grace'. Amara is the short form.
**Alternative spellings:** Amerachi

## Amari

**Meaning:** Possessor of great strength
**Origin:** Africa
**Pronunciation:** am AR ee
**Description:** Amari is an attractive name of African origin. It translates as 'strength' or 'possessor of great strength'. It is also a feminine forn of the masculine Arabic name, Amar, which translates as 'moon'.
**Alternative spellings:** Amare

## Amaris

**Meaning:** You are loved
**Origin:** Latin
**Pronunciation:** a MER iss
**Description:** Amaris is a Latin word that translates as 'you are loved'. It is popular in Latin America and Spain. It could also be a short form of the name Amarysia, a name that derives from Greek mythology.

## Amaya

**Meaning:** High place
**Origin:** Spanish
**Pronunciation:** a MAY ah
**Description:** Amaya was the name of a heroine in the traditional Basque stories of the knight Teodosio de Goni.
**Alternative spellings:** Amaha, Amaia, Ammaya

## Amba

**Meaning:** Amber; mother
**Origin:** English
**Pronunciation:** AM buh
**Description:** A variant of Amber, this name could also come from the Sanskrit word meaning 'mother'. In this case it is used mainly by Hindu parents.
**Alternative spellings:** Ambah, Amber

## Amber

**Meaning:** Amber
**Origin:** English
**Pronunciation:** AM buh
**Description:** Amber is the word for a fossilised resin, derived from the Arabic word *'ambar'*.
**Alternative spellings:** Amba, Ambah

## Ameena

**Meaning:** Honest; trustworthy
**Origin:** Arabic
**Pronunciation:** ah MEE nah
**Description:** A beautiful female given name originating from the Arabic for 'honest' or 'trustworthy'. It is popular within Muslim communities throughout the world as there are many important Islamic figures who share the name within the Islamic faith.
**Alternative spellings:** Amina, Amna, Aminah

## Ameerah

**Meaning:** Princess
**Origin:** Arabic
**Pronunciation:** ah MEER ah
**Description:** Another spelling variant of the name Amira, found in both Arabic and Swahili-speaking countries.
**Alternative spellings:** Ameera, Amera, Amira, Amirah

## Amelia

**Meaning:** Hard-working
**Origin:** German
**Pronunciation:** ah MEE lee uh
**Description:** One of the most popular girls' names in Britain, Amelia is comprised of the Latin name Emilia and the Germanic name Amalia.
**Alternative spellings:** Amilia, Emelia, Emilia, Emilija

## Amelie

**Meaning:** Hard-working
**Origin:** French
**Pronunciation:** AH meh lee
**Description:** The French equivalent of Amelia, Amelie is used widely across the English-speaking world.
**Alternative spellings:** Amalie

## Amiee

**Meaning:** Beloved
**Origin:** French
**Pronunciation:** AY mee
**Description:** Amiee is a name of French origin and it means 'beloved'. It is the original form of Amy, which is the more common version in Britain.
**Alternative spellings:** Aimee, Ami, Amie, Amy

## Amika

**Meaning:** Loved friend
**Origin:** Latin
**Pronunciation:** AH mik ah
**Description:** Amika is a Latin name meaning 'loved friend'. It can also be related to the English vocabulary word 'amicable'.
**Alternative spellings:** Ammika

## Aminata

**Meaning:** Serenity
**Origin:** Arabic
**Pronunciation:** ah min AH ta
**Description:** Aminata is of Arabic origin; however its use has spread into Swahili. The name can be found across Africa and the Middle East.
**Alternative spellings:** Aminahta

## Amiyah

**Meaning:** Unknown
**Origin:** Arabic
**Pronunciation:** ah MEE yah
**Description:** Amiyah, an unusual name of uncertain origin and meaning, may come from the Arabic language.
**Alternative spellings:** Amiya

## Amiya

**Meaning:** Beloved
**Origin:** Old French
**Pronunciation:** a MEE ah
**Description:** Amiya is a variant of the Old French and Latin name, Amy, meaning 'beloved' or 'to love'. A modern, neater alternative spelling of the name is Amia.
**Alternative spellings:** Amia

## Amrit

**Meaning:** Nectar of immortals
**Origin:** Sanskrit
**Pronunciation:** AM rit
**Description:** Amrit, a unisex name, is of Sanskrit origin and is found in the Hindu Vedic epics to

refer to a physical object that gives immortality.
**Alternative spellings:** Amreet

## Amrita
**Meaning:** Nectar of immortals
**Origin:** Sanskrit
**Pronunciation:** am REE tah
**Description:** Amrita is the feminine version of Amrit and is often favoured by Hindu parents.
**Alternative spellings:** Amreeta

## Ana
**Meaning:** Favoured by God
**Origin:** Hebrew
**Pronunciation:** AH nah
**Description:** A variant of the popular girls' name Anna. This spelling is common in Eastern Europe.
**Alternative spellings:** Anna, Annah

## Anaïs
**Meaning:** Love
**Origin:** Persian
**Pronunciation:** ah NAY ISS
**Description:** Commonly found in French-speaking countries, this name has its origins in Persian and Hebrew and is associated with the Persian goddess of love, Anaitis.
**Alternative spellings:** Anais, Annais

## Anabia
**Meaning:** Turn towards Allah
**Origin:** Arabic
**Pronunciation:** anah BI ya
**Description:** Anabia is a feminine Arabic name meaning 'turn towards Allah.' A variation of this name is Anaba, a Quaranic word meaning 'he/she made repentance and returned to Allah'.

## Anaiya
**Meaning:** God Answers
**Origin:** Hebrew
**Pronunciation:** A nay ah
**Description:** A derivative of the masculine Hebrew name, Anaiah, which means 'Yahweh (God) answers'.
**Alternative spellings:** Anaya, Anaiah, Anayah

## Anam
**Meaning:** A blessing
**Origin:** Arabic
**Pronunciation:** AH nam
**Description:** Anam is an Arabic name used mainly by Muslim parents who feel their child is a blessing from Allah.
**Alternative spellings:** Ahnam

## Ananya
**Meaning:** With no match
**Origin:** Sanskrit
**Pronunciation:** ah NAHN yah
**Description:** Ananya is mainly used in India and is popular with Hindu parents. Sometimes shortened to Anu.
**Alternative spellings:** Ananyah

## Anas
**Meaning:** Friendly
**Origin:** Arabic
**Pronunciation:** Ah Nas
**Description:** A unisex name of Arabic origin. Anas is also a shortened form of names such as Anastasia.
**Alternative spellings:** Annas

## Anastasia
**Meaning:** Resurrection
**Origin:** Russian
**Pronunciation:** a na STAY ZEE ah; a na STAY zhah

**Description:** Anastasia is a Russian name that has enjoyed solid popularity in Eastern Europe. The famous 'lost' Russian princess named Anastasia boosted the name's popularity.
**Alternative spellings:** Anastacia, Anastasja, Anastazia, Anastazja

## Andrea
**Meaning:** Virility
**Origin:** Greek
**Pronunciation:** AN dree ah; an DREY ah
**Description:** This feminine form of the name Andreas or Andrew is derived from *'andreia'*, meaning 'virility'.
**Alternative spellings:** Andria

## Andy
See entry in 'Names for Baby Boys A–Z'

## Aneira
**Meaning:** Gold
**Origin:** Welsh
**Pronunciation:** a NEER ah
**Description:** The origin of this name is not definite but it is believed to come fron the Welsh word *'eur'* meaning gold.
**Alternative spellings:** Aneera, Anira

## Angel
See entry in 'Names for Baby Boys A–Z'

## Angie
**Meaning:** Messenger of God
**Origin:** Latin
**Pronunciation:** an GEE
**Description:** Angie is the short form of the name Angelina and as such, shares the same meaning of 'messenger of God'. Starting out as a nickname, Angie is now a name in its own right.

## Angela
**Meaning:** Messenger of God
**Origin:** Greek
**Pronunciation:** AN gel uh; an GEL uh
**Description:** This feminine form of Angelus is an elaboration of 'angel'.
**Alternative spellings:** Angella

## Angelica
**Meaning:** Messenger of God
**Origin:** Latin
**Pronunciation:** an GEL ih ka
**Description:** Angelica is taken from the Latin word meaning 'angelic'.
**Alternative spellings:** Angellica, Anjelica

## Angelina
**Meaning:** Messenger of God
**Origin:** Latin
**Pronunciation:** AN ja LEE na
**Description:** This variation of Angela is popular, especially in Italy.
**Alternative spellings:** Angeleena, Angelena

## Angharad
**Meaning:** Beloved
**Origin:** Welsh
**Pronunciation:** ang HAH rad
**Description:** Angharad, a popular name in Celtic folklore, is a traditional Welsh name. It is becoming fashionable in other parts of Britain.
**Alternative spellings:** Angherad

## Aniela

**Meaning:** Hard-working
**Origin:** German
**Pronunciation:** ah NEE lee ah
**Description:** Aniela is found mainly in Eastern European countries and is especially popular in Poland. It is thought to be a variant of Amelia.
**Alternative spellings:** Anelia

## Anika

**Meaning:** Grace
**Origin:** Sanskrit
**Pronunciation:** AN i KAH
**Description:** This attractive name is of Sanskrit, Dutch, Hebrew and Japanese origin. In all but Japanese it has a similar meaning, roughly translating as 'grace'. In Japanese the name translates as 'apricot from Nara'.
**Alternative spellings:**

## Anis

**Meaning:** Friendly; pure
**Origin:** Arabic; Greek
**Pronunciation:** Ah nees
**Description:** A popular girls' name in Greece, this is also a boys' name in Tunisia. In Arabic Anis means 'friendly' and in Greek, 'pure' or 'holy'.
**Alternative spellings:** Anais, Anees, Annis

## Anisa

**Meaning:** Good companion
**Origin:** Arabic
**Pronunciation:** a NEE sa
**Description:** With roots in Hebrew and Arabic, this name is fairly popular in Arabic-speaking countries.
**Alternative spellings:** Aneesa, Anisah

## Anisah

**Meaning:** One with no master
**Origin:** Sanskrit
**Pronunciation:** ah NEE sah
**Description:** A variant of Anise, Anisah also has Sanskrit origins.
**Alternative spellings:** Anisa, Aneesa, Anisha

## Anise

**Meaning:** Anise seed
**Origin:** English
**Pronunciation:** uh NIECE
**Description:** Anise comes from the anise seed, a herb that is known for its licorice-like flavor. Like Basil and Rosemary, Anise is part of the trend of using herbs for given names.

## Anita

**Meaning:** Favoured by God
**Origin:** Hebrew
**Pronunciation:** ah NEE tah
**Description:** Anita is one of many variations of Anne, which itself comes from the Hebrew name Hannah.
**Alternative spellings:** Aneeta, Anitah

## Aniya

**Meaning:** Favoured by God; caring
**Origin:** Hebrew
**Pronunciation:** ah NEE yah
**Description:** Aniya is a variant of Ania, a name of Hebrew origin, and is found all over Europe and parts of Asia.
**Alternative spellings:** Aneeya, Aniyah, Anniya, Anniyah

## Anjali

**Meaning:** Gift
**Origin:** Sanskrit
**Pronunciation:** AHN ja lee
**Description:** Anjali is an

uncommon name in English-speaking countries and is favoured more by Indian parents.
**Alternative spellings:** Anjaly, Anjuly

## Annabel
**Meaning:** Loveable
**Origin:** Latin
**Pronunciation:** AN a bell
**Description:** Thought to derive from the Latin *'amabilis'* meaning 'loveable', this name is also a combination of Anne and the French word *'belle'* meaning 'beautiful'. As such, the name could also mean 'beautiful favoured one'.
**Alternative spellings:** Anabel, Anabelle, Annabell, Annabelle

## Annabella
**Meaning:** Loveable
**Origin:** Latin
**Pronunciation:** AH na bel ah
**Description:** Annabella, like Annabel, is derived from the Latin *'amabilis'*.
**Alternative spellings:** Anabela, Anabella, Annabela

## Annalese
**Meaning:** Noble and promised of God; graceful
**Origin:** German
**Pronunciation:** ah nah LEES
**Description:** Annalese is a compound name made up of Anna and Lisa. Its combined meaning is 'noble birth' and 'promised of God', as well as 'graceful'.
**Alternative spellings:** Annaliese, Annalise

## Anne
**Meaning:** Favoured by God
**Origin:** Greek
**Pronunciation:** AN

**Description:** Anne is the English form of the Hebrew name Hannah. It is the name of many English queens, including Anne Boleyn and Anne of Cleves.
**Alternative spellings:** Ann

## Annella
**Meaning:** Grace
**Origin:** Hebrew
**Pronunciation:** ANN ell a
**Description:** Annella is a contemporary variant of the Latin name, Anne, which evolved fom the Hebrew name, Hannah, which means 'favour' or 'grace'.
**Alternative spellings:** Anella, Anela

## Annette
**Meaning:** Favoured by God
**Origin:** French
**Pronunciation:** ann ETTE
**Description:** Annette is a French diminutive of Ann, and as such shares the same meaning of 'favoured by God'.

## Annie
**Meaning:** Favoured by God
**Origin:** Greek
**Pronunciation:** AN nee
**Description:** A pet form of Anne.
**Alternative spellings:** Anney, Anni, Anny

## Annika
**Meaning:** Grace
**Origin:** Hebrew
**Pronunciation:** Ann ee kah
**Description:** A further modernised name from the traditional Latin name, Anne, developed from the Hebrew name, Hannah. The meaning of the name translates as 'grace' or 'grace of God'.

**Alternative spellings:** Anika

## Anniyah
**Meaning:** Caring
**Origin:** Arabic
**Pronunciation:** ah NEE yah
**Description:** This Arabic name is popular with Muslim parents.
**Alternative spellings:** Aneeya, Aniya, Aniyah, Anniya

## Annya
**Meaning:** Inexhaustible
**Origin:** Hebrew, Greek
**Pronunciation:** AHN yah
**Description:** This name, of both Hebrew and Old Greek origin, is pronounced in a similar way to the Russian Anya.
**Alternative spellings:** Annyah

## Anouk
**Meaning:** Favoured by God
**Origin:** Hebrew
**Pronunciation:** AH nook
**Description:** Anouk is a variant of the name Anna and is more popular in French- and Dutch-speaking countries. It is also used in Arabic.
**Alternative spellings:** Anook

## Anoushka
**Meaning:** Grace
**Origin:** Hebrew; Russian
**Pronunciation:** AN oosh kah
**Description:** A Russian diminutive of Anne that translates as 'little Anna'. The traditional name, Anne, means 'grace' or 'grace of God'.
**Alternative spellings:** Annoushka, Anoushkah, Annushka

## Antigone
**Meaning:** The opposite of her forebears

**Origin:** Greek
**Pronunciation:** an TIG oh nee
**Description:** In Greek mythology, Antigone was the daughter of Oedipus and Jocasta.
**Alternative spellings:** Antigon, Antigonos

## Antonia
**Meaning:** Priceless
**Origin:** Latin
**Pronunciation:** an TO nee uh
**Description:** A Latin feminine form of Anthony and a common Roman family name in classical times.
**Alternative spellings:** Antoniah, Antonya

## Antonina
**Meaning:** Protector
**Origin:** Latin
**Pronunciation:** ahn toh NEE nah
**Description:** This fairly unusual variant of Antonia is most commonly found in Eastern Europe and is often shortened to Nina.
**Alternative spellings:** Antoneena, Antonena

## Anum
**Meaning:** Grace; God favours
**Origin:** Arabic
**Pronunciation:** AN oom
**Description:** Anum may be used as a variant of the classic Latin name, Anne. The name is also featured in the Quran and is a popular Muslim name. The Arabic translation is 'blessings of God'.
**Alternative spellings:** Annum

## Anusha
**Meaning:** Beautiful sky
**Origin:** Sanskrit
**Pronunciation:** ah NOO sha

**Description:** Anusha is a unisex name thought to mean 'beautiful sky' or 'beautiful morning'. It is a popular baby name with Indian parents.
**Alternative spellings:** Anoosha

## Anwen
**Meaning:** Very beautiful
**Origin:** Welsh
**Pronunciation:** AN wen
**Description:** Anwen is an attractive female name with a classic Welsh sound pattern. The name translates as 'very beautiful'.
**Alternative spellings:** Arnwen

## Aoife
**Meaning:** Beaming radiance
**Origin:** Gaelic
**Pronunciation:** EE fa
**Description:** Aoife is a name of Gaelic origin, and means 'beaming radiance'. It is especially popular in Ireland.
**Alternative spellings:** Eefa, Efa, Efah

## Aphrodite
**Meaning:** Risen from the foam
**Origin:** Greek
**Pronunciation:** AF ro DYE tee
**Description:** In Greek myth, Aphrodite was the goddess of love and beauty.
**Alternative spellings:** Afrodite, Afrodyte, Aphrodyte

## April
**Meaning:** Blooming flowers
**Origin:** Latin
**Pronunciation:** AY pril
**Description:** The word April, from the Latin *'aprilis'*, meaning 'to open', is associated with spring.
**Alternative spellings:** Aprill

## Aqsa
**Meaning:** Temple
**Origin:** Arabic
**Pronunciation:** AC sah
**Description:** The name Aqsa originates from Al-Aqsa in Jerusalem, the second-oldest mosque in Islam.
**Alternative spellings:** Acksa, Aksa

## Arabella
**Meaning:** Loveable
**Origin:** Latin
**Pronunciation:** AH ra BELL ah
**Description:** With its Latin origins it is thought that the name Arabella either derives from Annabel or Annabella. It is likely that this name first occurred because of a misspelling in the 1600s.
**Alternative spellings:** Arabela, Arrabella

## Araya
**Meaning:** Inspired by the town Araia, Spain
**Origin:** Basque
**Pronunciation:** uh RAY yuh
**Description:** Araia is originally a Basque surname, from the town Araia in Aspárrena, province of Alava, Basque Country. Although rare, it is used in Western countries as a female given name.
**Alternative spellings:** Araia, Arayah

## Arda
See entry in 'Names for Baby Boys A–Z'

## Areeba
**Meaning:** Witty; intelligent
**Origin:** Arabic
**Pronunciation:** ah REE bah
**Description:** Areeba is a name of Arabic origin and means 'witty' or

'intelligent'. It is mainly used in the Middle East and other Muslim countries.
**Alternative spellings:** Areebah, Ariba

## Areesha
**Meaning:** Under an umbrella; peace
**Origin:** Arabic
**Pronunciation:** AR eesh ah
**Description:** Areesha is an obscure name but may be of Arabic origin. Possible translations of the name include 'under an umbrella', 'peace' and 'living'.
**Alternative spellings:** Arisha, Arreesha, Aeresha

## Aren
**Meaning:** Eagle ruler
**Origin:** German
**Pronunciation:** AIR ren
**Description:** Aren is an Old German name meaning 'eagle ruler'. It is also an African name that also means 'eagle'.

## Aretha
**Meaning:** Excellence
**Origin:** Greek
**Pronunciation:** a RI thuh
**Description:** Aretha is intended as a derivative of the Greek word *'arete'* meaning 'excellence'.
**Alternative spellings:** Areetha, Aritha

## Aria
**Meaning:** Lion
**Origin:** Various
**Pronunciation:** AHR ee ah
**Description:** Aria has various origins and meanings. It could come from the Italian word for 'air' and is a musical term. In Hebrew its

meaning is said to be 'lion'. It is a unisex name.
**Alternative spellings:** Arya, Ariya

## Ariadne
**Meaning:** Chaste; Most Holy
**Origin:** Greek
**Pronunciation:** a ree AD nee
**Description:** Ariadne is a popular Greek name composed of the elements of αρι (ari), 'most' and αδνος (adnos). 'holy'. In Greek mythology, Ariadne was the daughter of King Minos.
**Alternative spellings:** Arriadne

## Ariana
**Meaning:** Silver
**Origin:** Welsh
**Pronunciation:** ah ree AH nah
**Description:** This name is chiefly used in Dutch-, German-, French- and Italian-speaking countries.
**Alternative spellings:** Arriana, Arianna, Aryana

## Arianne
**Meaning:** Silver
**Origin:** Welsh
**Pronunciation:** ah ree AN
**Description:** A variant of Ariana and also the feminine form of Arian. This name can be shortened to Ari or Anne.
**Alternative spellings:** Arienne

## Ariel
**Meaning:** God's lion
**Origin:** Hebrew
**Pronunciation:** AR ee el; AIR ee al
**Description:** This unisex name widely increased in popularity after Shakespeare's play *The Tempest*.
**Alternative spellings:** Arial

## Ariella

**Meaning:** God's lion
**Origin:** Hebrew
**Pronunciation:** AR ee el ah
**Description:** Ariella derives from the unisex name Ariel; however, this form is specifically feminine thanks to its use of 'a' at the end of the name.
**Alternative spellings:** Arialla, Ariela

## Arielle

**Meaning:** Lion of God
**Origin:** Hebrew
**Pronunciation:** a REE ell
**Description:** Arielle is the feminine form of the Hebrew *ariel*, which means 'lion of God'. Ariel is also an accepted girls' name, epitomised in the Hans Cristian Andersen story, 'The Little Mermaid', and its Disney adaptation.
**Alternative spellings:** Ariel

## Arina

**Meaning:** Peaceful
**Origin:** Greek
**Pronunciation:** ah REE na
**Description:** Arina is an unusual name. It is a variant of Irina, the Russian equivalent of the name Irene. It is most predominantly found in Russia.
**Alternative spellings:** Irina

## Arissa

**Meaning:** The best
**Origin:** Greek
**Pronunciation:** ah RIS ah
**Description:** The Greek word *'arista'*, meaning 'the best', was used to refer to a healthy ear of corn at harvest. A very popular name in continental Europe.
**Alternative spellings:** Arisa, Arisah, Arissah

## Arla

**Meaning:** Eagle's hill; manly
**Origin:** English
**Pronunciation:** AR lah
**Description:** This is a comtemporary name that may have derived from the masculine name, Arlo or a shortening of the female name, Charlene.
**Alternative spellings:** Ala

## Armani

**Meaning:** Free
**Origin:** Italian
**Pronunciation:** ah MAR nee
**Description:** Armani is an Italian surname that is said to mean 'free'.
**Alternative spellings:** Armaani, Armanie

## Aroush

**Meaning:** Angel from paradise
**Origin:** Arabic
**Pronunciation:** ah ROOSH
**Description:** Aroush, an Arabic name, is used mainly by Muslim parents and means 'angel come from paradise'.
**Alternative spellings:** Aroosh

## Artemis

**Meaning:** Strong-limbed
**Origin:** Greek
**Pronunciation:** AH teh mis
**Description:** In Greek mythology, Artemis was the goddess of the hunt and the twin sister of Apollo.
**Alternative spellings:** Artemus, Artimis, Artimus

## Arwa

**Meaning:** Gracefulness; beauty
**Origin:** Arabic

**Pronunciation:** AR wah
**Description:** Arwa is a lyrical Muslim name that interprets as 'beauty', 'lightness', 'softness'. Arwa was also the name of one of the aunts of the prophet Muhammad, which possibly contributes to the name's popularity.
**Alternative spellings:** Arwaa

## Arwen

**Meaning:** Fair skin
**Origin:** Welsh
**Pronunciation:** AR wen
**Description:** Arwen is a name of Welsh origin and it means 'fair skin'. In Tolkien's *Lord Of The Rings* Arwen is the name of a main Elf character.
**Alternative spellings:** Ahwen

## Aryana

**Meaning:** Chaste; most holy
**Origin:** Greek
**Pronunciation:** a ree ARN ah
**Description:** Arianna is a variant of the classical Greek name Ariadne. The name interprets as 'chaste' or 'most holy'. Ariadne was also a figure in Greek mythology, the daughter of King Minos.
**Alternative spellings:** Ariana, Arianna

## Aseel

**Meaning:** Pure; genuine
**Origin:** Arabic
**Pronunciation:** AS il
**Description:** Aseel is an Arabic name more commonly chosen as a male given name but gaining popularity as a female name. The meaning of the name is 'authentic', 'pure' or 'genuine'. It is also an adjective used to describe people with good moral conduct.

**Alternative spellings:** Asil

## Asha

**Meaning:** Full of aspiration
**Origin:** Greek
**Pronunciation:** AH shah
**Description:** Asha is a fairly uncommon name in Britain but is sometimes used as a variant of Aisha.
**Alternative spellings:** Ashah, Asher

## Ashanti

**Meaning:** Ghanaian
**Origin:** African
**Pronunciation:** a SHAN tee; ah SHARN tee
**Description:** Ashanti is the name of a major ethnic group in Ghana and is also used as a surname by the Akan people of Ghana.
**Alternative spellings:** Ashantie, Ashanty

## Ashlee

**Meaning:** Field of ash
**Origin:** English
**Pronunciation:** ASH lee
**Description:** A specifically feminine variant of the popular name Ashley. The name comes from an English surname that refers to a 'field of ash'.
**Alternative spellings:** Ashleigh, Ashley

## Asma

**Meaning:** Important
**Origin:** Arabic
**Pronunciation:** AHS mah
**Description:** Asma, a popular girls' name among Muslim parents, is the daughter of the brother of Muhammad Abu-Bakr in Islamic belief.
**Alternative spellings:** Asmaa, Asmah

## Aspen

**Meaning:** Aspen tree
**Origin:** English
**Pronunciation:** ASS pen
**Description:** Aspen is a unisex name derived from the aspen tree, known by its delicate leaves and white bark. As a given name, it is common in America.
**Alternative spellings:** Aspun

## Aston

See entry in 'Names for Baby Boys A–Z'

## Astra

**Meaning:** Star
**Origin:** Greek
**Pronunciation:** ASS tra
**Description:** This girls' name meaning 'star' is based on the Greek word *'aster'* or the Latin word *'astrum'*.
**Alternative spellings:** Astrah, Astre

## Astrid

**Meaning:** Beautiful goddess
**Origin:** Norse
**Pronunciation:** ASS trid
**Description:** Astrid is of Old Norse origin and has strong associations with beauty. In Old Norse myth it was the name of a valkyrie.
**Alternative spellings:** Astryd

## Asya

**Meaning:** Resurrection
**Origin:** Greek
**Pronunciation:** AHS ya
**Description:** Asya was originally a pet form of the name Anastasia, but has since become a name in its own right.
**Alternative spellings:** Aiza, Aizah, Asia, Asiah

## Atarah

**Meaning:** Crown
**Origin:** Hebrew
**Pronunciation:** a TAH rah
**Description:** Atarah is a biblical name meaning 'crown'. According to the Bible, it was borne by one of the wives of Jerahmeel. Often shortened to Tara.
**Alternative spellings:** Atara, Attara

## Athena

**Meaning:** Goddess of wisdom and war
**Origin:** Greek
**Pronunciation:** ah THEE nah
**Description:** Athena is the Latin form of the Greek name Athene, who was the goddess of wisdom and war in Greek mythology. Athena and Athene are popular girls' names in Greece.
**Alternative spellings:** Athina

## Aubree

**Meaning:** Unknown
**Origin:** Latin
**Pronunciation:** OR bree
**Description:** A venacular form of the Latin name, Albereda. The etymology of this name is unclear but is different to the male derivation, which translates as 'Leader of the Elves'.
**Alternative spellings:** Aubrey, Aubrée, Aubrie

## Aubrey

See entry in 'Names for Baby Boys A–Z'

## Audra

**Meaning:** Noble strength
**Origin:** English
**Pronunciation:** OR dra
**Description:** Sometimes used as a

**A**

pet form of Audrey, Audra is also a name in its own right.
**Alternative spellings:** Audre

## Audrey
**Meaning:** Noble strength
**Origin:** English
**Pronunciation:** OR dree
**Description:** This Old English name, borne by actress Audrey Hepburn, also has associations with lace.
**Alternative spellings:** Audree, Audrie, Awdrey

## Augusta
**Meaning:** Great; magnificent
**Origin:** Latin
**Pronunciation:** oog GUS tah
**Description:** Augusta is the female version of the Latin name Augustus. It is also used as a title given to empresses of the Roman and Byzantine Empires.

## Aurelia
**Meaning:** Golden
**Origin:** Latin
**Pronunciation:** aw REE lee uh
**Description:** Aurelia has similar Latin roots to the name Aurora, which refers to the dawn. Both names have connotations of light and beauty.
**Alternative spellings:** Aureliah, Aureliya

## Aurora
**Meaning:** Dawn
**Origin:** Latin
**Pronunciation:** aw RO rah
**Description:** Aurora, the Roman goddess of dawn, is also a meteorological term for light displays in the sky.
**Alternative spellings:** Arora, Aurara, Aurorah

## Austeja
**Meaning:** Bee goddess
**Origin:** Lithuania
**Pronunciation:** ow STAY ah
**Description:** Austeja is a popular, contemporary name in Lithuania. It is derived from the name of an ancient Lithuanian bee goddess.
**Alternative spellings:** Austėja, Austeya

## Austin
See entry in 'Names for Baby Boys A–Z'

## Autumn
**Meaning:** Autumn
**Origin:** English
**Pronunciation:** AW tum
**Description:** Like Summer, this is a seasonal name.
**Alternative spellings:** Autum, Ortumn

## Avani
**Meaning:** Earthly
**Origin:** Sanskrit
**Pronunciation:** ah VAH nee
**Description:** Avani is a name used predominantly, although not exclusively, by Hindu families. It comes from a Sanskrit word meaning 'earthly'.
**Alternative spellings:** Ahvani, Avahni, Avanee, Avany

## Avaya
**Meaning:** Gift of God
**Origin:** Sanskrit
**Pronunciation:** avv AY ah
**Description:** An unusual Hindu name that means 'gift of God' or 'first ray of sun'.
**Alternative spellings:** Avayah, Avaia

## Aveline

**Meaning:** Bird; struggle
**Origin:** French
**Pronunciation:** AV er leen
**Description:** The meaning of Aveline, a French name derived from Avis, may stem from the German for 'struggle' or the Latin *'avis'* meaning 'bird'.
**Alternative spellings:** Aveleen, Aveleene, Avelene

## Avery

**Meaning:** Elf ruler
**Origin:** Old French
**Pronunciation:** AY var ee
**Description:** Originally an English surname derived from the Old English words *'aelf'*, meaning 'elf', and *'raed'*, meaning 'counsel'. In recent years the name has increased in popularity as a female given name, possibly as an extension of the name Ava.
**Alternative spellings:** Avary

## Aviana

**Meaning:** Like a bird
**Origin:** Latin
**Pronunciation:** ah vee AH na
**Description:** Aviana translates from Latin as 'like a bird' or 'delicate one'.
**Alternative spellings:** Avianna

## Avleen

**Meaning:** Blessed by God
**Origin:** Hindi
**Pronunciation:** AV leen
**Description:** Avleen is a unisex name of Indian origin. It translates as 'blessed by God' or 'different'.
**Alternative spellings:** Avline

## Avneet

**Meaning:** God is light

**Origin:** Hebrew
**Pronunciation:** AHV neet
**Description:** In Hebrew, Avneet means 'God is light.'
**Alternative spellings:** Avneat

## Avni

**Meaning:** Earth
**Origin:** Hindi
**Pronunciation:** AV nee
**Description:** An attractive girls' name of Indian origin that can be interpreted as 'earth' or 'princess of God'.
**Alternative spellings:** Avnee

## Avril

**Meaning:** April
**Origin:** French
**Pronunciation:** AV ril
**Description:** Avril is the French word for the month of April. It may also be linked to the words 'boar' and 'battle' because of its Old English roots.
**Alternative spellings:** Avrill, Avrille

## Aya

**Meaning:** Design; bird of prey
**Origin:** Japanese, Hebrew
**Pronunciation:** AH yah
**Description:** In Japan Aya is a girls' name and refers to paintings and objects of visual beauty. In Hebrew it is a boys' name, meaning a 'bird of prey'.
**Alternative spellings:** Ayah, Iya

## Ayaan

See entry in 'Names for Baby Boys A–Z'

## Ayah

**Meaning:** Miracle
**Origin:** Arabic
**Pronunciation:** AY yah

**Description:** This variant of Aya has roots in Arabic. It comes from the word for 'miracle' and was first used in the Middle East.
**Alternative spellings:** Aya, Iyah

## Ayana

**Meaning:** Flower of beauty
**Origin:** African
**Pronunciation:** AY an ah
**Description:** Ayana is a popular name with African parents and is also found in Arab countries.
**Alternative spellings:** Ayanna

## Ayda

**Meaning:** Adornment; nobility
**Origin:** Hebrew
**Pronunciation:** AY dah
**Description:** Ayda is a biblical name that means 'adornment' or 'enhancement'. It also traces back to the Germanic element of 'adel', meaning 'nobility'.
**Alternative spellings:** Ada, Aida, Adah

## Aydan

See Ayden in 'Names for Baby Boys A–Z'

## Ayeza

**Meaning:** Noble
**Origin:** Arabic
**Pronunciation:** ay EE zah
**Description:** Ayeza is an Arabic feminine name. The meaning is difficult to determine exactly, but many think that it means 'noble'. It is most likely associated with the name Aiza, which has the same meaning.

## Ayla

**Meaning:** Moonlight
**Origin:** Persian
**Pronunciation:** AY lah
**Description:** Ayla is of Turkish and Old Persian origin. In Turkish the name means 'halo of light around the moon' and in Old Persian it translates as 'moonlight'.
**Alternative spellings:** Isla, Eilah, Aila

## Aylin

**Meaning:** Moon
**Origin:** Persian
**Pronunciation:** AY linn
**Description:** Aylin is a popular Turkish name that derives from the word 'ay', meaning 'moon'. It is a variant of Ayla.
**Alternative spellings:** Ayleen, Ayleene, Aylinn

## Ayomide

**Meaning:** My joy has arrived
**Origin:** African
**Pronunciation:** Ey Aa Mayde
**Description:** Although Ayomide is a unisex name it is more common for girls. Owing to its meaning, the name is often given to children who suffered a traumatic or troublesome birth.
**Alternative spellings:** Ayomaid, Ayomayd

## Aysha

**Meaning:** She who lives or womanly.
**Origin:** Arabic
**Pronunciation:** I eesh a
**Description:** Aysha is a variant spelling of the Arabic name Aisha. Aisha was the name of the last and youngest wife of the Islamic prophet, Muhammad.
**Alternative spellings:** Aisha, Ayeesha

## Ayuka

**Meaning:** Sweetfish
**Origin:** Japanese
**Pronunciation:** a YU ka
**Description:** This name can most commonly be found in Japanese-speaking countries.
**Alternative spellings:** Aiuka, Ayooka

## Ayva

**Meaning:** Bird
**Origin:** German
**Pronunciation:** AY vuh
**Description:** Ayva is a variant spelling of Ava, a popular name of German, Hebrew and Latin origin. It is most likely a derivative of the Latin '*avis*' meaning 'bird'.
**Alternative spellings:** Ava, Avah

## Azalea

**Meaning:** Flower name
**Origin:** English
**Pronunciation:** azz AYE lee ah
**Description:** Azalea comes from the pink and red flower of the same name that is found all over the world. Like Rose and Tulip, Azalea is part of the trend of using flowers as given names.

## Azra

**Meaning:** Helper; young maid
**Origin:** Hebrew
**Pronunciation:** AZ ra
**Description:** Azra may come from the Hebrew, Azara, meaning 'helper', or from Arabic, meaning 'young maid'.
**Alternative spellings:** Asra, Azrah

# B

## Baha

See entry in 'Names for Baby Boys A–Z'

## Bahija

**Meaning:** Joyous
**Origin:** Arabic
**Pronunciation:** ba HE ja
**Description:** Bahija is a name primarily associated with good cheer and happiness. It would be a good name for a very smiley baby girl.
**Alternative spellings:** Bahijah

## Bailey

See entry in 'Names for Baby Boys A–Z'

## Barbara

**Meaning:** Foreign woman
**Origin:** Greek
**Pronunciation:** BAH bah ruh
**Description:** According to Roman Catholic custom, St Barbara is a protector against fire and lightning, as well as the patron saint of architects, stonemasons and fortifications.
**Alternative spellings:** Barbarah, Barbarer

## Baylor

**Meaning:** Horse trainer
**Origin:** English
**Pronunciation:** BAY lor

**Description:** Baylor is an English girls' name meaning 'horse trainer'. It is an unusual name that is not very popular, but it is very unique.
**Alternative spellings:** Bayler

## Bea
**Meaning:** Happy
**Origin:** Latin
**Pronunciation:** BEE
**Description:** Bea originally came about as a pet form of the name Beatrice but is now found as an independent name. Despite its spelling it is pronounced 'bee'.
**Alternative spellings:** Bee

## Beatrice
**Meaning:** Happy
**Origin:** Latin
**Pronunciation:** BE ah triss
**Description:** Derived from the Latin word 'beatus', Beatrice means 'happy'.
**Alternative spellings:** Beatriss, Beatrix, Beatriz

## Becca
**Meaning:** Binding
**Origin:** Hebrew
**Pronunciation:** BEK cuh
**Description:** This modern form of Rebecca, sometimes used as a name in its own right, can be shortened to Bex.
**Alternative spellings:** Beca, Becka

## Becky
**Meaning:** Binding
**Origin:** Hebrew
**Pronunciation:** BEK kee
**Description:** Originally a shortened form of Rebecca and now a name in its own right, Becky was especially popular during the 18th and 19th centuries.
**Alternative spellings:** Beccy, Beci, Becki, Beckie, Beki

## Belinda
**Meaning:** Beautiful
**Origin:** Italian
**Pronunciation:** buh LIN dah
**Description:** Belinda is a name taken from the Italian word 'bella', meaning 'beautiful'. Alternatively, it can also be from the Old German word 'betlinde', meaning 'bright serpent' or 'bright linden tree'.

## Bella
**Meaning:** Beautiful
**Origin:** Hebrew
**Pronunciation:** BEL luh
**Description:** Bella is linked to both the French and Italian words for 'beautiful' and is also a shortened form of Isabella.
**Alternative spellings:** Bela

## Belle
**Meaning:** Beautiful
**Origin:** Latin
**Pronunciation:** BELL
**Description:** Belle is the French word for 'beauty' and can be a pet form of Isabelle or Annabelle.
**Alternative spellings:** Bell

## Bellona
**Meaning:** War
**Origin:** Latin
**Pronunciation:** bel LOH nah
**Description:** In Roman mythology, Bellona was a Roman goddess of war.
**Alternative spellings:** Bellonna, Belona

B

## Bernice

**Meaning:** Bringer of victory
**Origin:** Greek
**Pronunciation:** BER niss
**Description:** This Hebrew name is said to derive from the Macedonian name Berenice.
**Alternative spellings:** Berneice, Bernisse

## Beryl

**Meaning:** Pale green stone
**Origin:** Greek
**Pronunciation:** BEH rill
**Description:** This name of a semi-precious pale green stone peaked in popularity in the UK during the 1930s.
**Alternative spellings:** Beril, Berill, Beryll

## Bessie

**Meaning:** Promised by God
**Origin:** Hebrew
**Pronunciation:** BESS ee
**Description:** Bessie came about as a pet form of the popular name Elizabeth, but is now a name in its own right.
**Alternative spellings:** Bessi, Bessy

## Beth

**Meaning:** Promised by God
**Origin:** Hebrew
**Pronunciation:** BETH
**Description:** The name Beth is of Hebrew origin meaning 'house'. It is also a shortened form of Elizabeth.
**Alternative spellings:** Bethe

## Bethan

**Meaning:** Promised by God
**Origin:** Hebrew
**Pronunciation:** BEH than
**Description:** As well as being a shortened form of Bethany and Elizabeth, the name Bethan can also be seen as a name in its own right.
**Alternative spellings:** Bethane, Bethann

## Bethany

**Meaning:** Village
**Origin:** Hebrew
**Pronunciation:** BETH anny
**Description:** This name first appeared in the New Testament as the name of a village where Jesus stayed before his crucifixion. It could also derive from the name Elizabeth, meaning 'promised by God'.
**Alternative spellings:** Bethani, Bethanie

## Bethel

**Meaning:** House of God
**Origin:** Hebrew
**Pronunciation:** beth ELL
**Description:** Bethel is a Hebrew name that, when translated, means 'house of God'. Although they sound similar, Bethel is not Bethlehem.
**Alternative spellings:** Bethell

## Betsy

**Meaning:** Promised by God
**Origin:** Hebrew
**Pronunciation:** BET see
**Description:** Like Bessie, Betsy came about as a pet form for the name Elizabeth.
**Alternative spellings:** Betsi, Betsie

## Betty

**Meaning:** Promised by God
**Origin:** Hebrew
**Pronunciation:** BET ee
**Description:** Another pet form of the name Elizabeth, Betty rose to popularity in the 1930s.

**Alternative spellings:** Betti, Bettie

## Beverley
**Meaning:** Beaver stream
**Origin:** English
**Pronunciation:** BEV er lee
**Description:** Transferred use of the surname used by those from an East Yorkshire settlement.
**Alternative spellings:** Beverlie, Beverly

## Bianca
**Meaning:** White
**Origin:** Latin
**Pronunciation:** bi AN cuh
**Description:** This name was used by Shakespeare in both *The Taming of the Shrew* and *Othello*. It derives from the French name Blanche.
**Alternative spellings:** Biancah, Bianka

## Bibi
**Meaning:** Lady of the house
**Origin:** Persian
**Pronunciation:** BEE bee
**Description:** This nickname in several languages is also a given name.
**Alternative spellings:** Bebe, Beebi

## Billie
**Meaning:** Seeking protection
**Origin:** German
**Pronunciation:** BIL ee
**Description:** Although the name is unisex, this particular spelling is favoured among girls.
**Alternative spellings:** Billi, Billy

## Binky
**Meaning:** No
**Origin:** English
**Pronunciation:** BINK ee
**Description:** Binky is a modern invention and as such, has no real meaning. It was made popular by Made in Chelsea star Binky Felstead, whose real name is Alexandra.

## Birdy
**Meaning:** Bird
**Origin:** English
**Pronunciation:** bird EE
**Description:** Birdy is a cuter version of the English word 'bird' and is both a nickname and a given name.
**Alternative spellings:** Birdie, Byrdie

## Bisma
**Meaning:** Unknown
**Origin:** Arabic
**Pronunciation:** BIS ma
**Description:** This unusual name is found across Asia and seems to be favoured by Muslim parents.
**Alternative spellings:** Bismah, Bismer

## Blake
**Meaning:** Dark; pale
**Origin:** Old English
**Pronunciation:** bl aike
**Description:** Blake is a contemporary name with two conflicting etymologies. Both from Old English, the first 'a derivative of '*blæc*', meaning 'black' and the second, '*blæac*', meaning 'pale'.
**Alternative spellings:** Blaike

## Blanka
**Meaning:** White
**Origin:** French
**Pronunciation:** BLON kah
**Description:** Blanka, like Bianca, is a pet form of Blanche and is popular in Polish-speaking countries.
**Alternative spellings:** Blanca, Blankah

## Blessing

**Meaning:** God-given treasure; fortunate event
**Origin:** English
**Pronunciation:** BLES ing
**Description:** With its positive meaning, this name is more common in America than in Britain.
**Alternative spellings:** Blesing

## Bliss

**Meaning:** Happiness
**Origin:** English
**Pronunciation:** blyss
**Description:** Bliss is a feminine name that comes from the English vocabulary. The word used today can be traced back to the Old English word '*bliss*' meaning 'happiness'. The name has been used in England since the Middle Ages.

## Blossom

**Meaning:** Flower blossom
**Origin:** English
**Pronunciation:** BLOH sum
**Description:** The name comes from the English word for 'flower' and was originally a term of affection.
**Alternative spellings:** Blosom, Blossum

## Bluebell

**Meaning:** Grateful
**Origin:** English
**Pronunciation:** BLOO bell
**Description:** Bluebell, a wild flower, symbolises gratitude.
**Alternative spellings:** Bloobell, Bluebelle

## Blythe

**Meaning:** Joyful
**Origin:** English

**Pronunciation:** BLYTH
**Description:** A more common variant of the unisex name Blithe. The word appears in Shelley's poem 'To a Skylark'.
**Alternative spellings:** Blithe, Blyth

## Bo

See entry in 'Names for Baby Boys A–Z'

## Bobbi

**Meaning:** Bright fame
**Origin:** German
**Pronunciation:** BOH bee
**Description:** A specifically feminine spelling of the unisex name Bobby and a diminutive of the name Roberta.
**Alternative spellings:** Bobbie, Bobby

## Bobbie

See entry in 'Names for Baby Boys A–Z'

## Bonnie

**Meaning:** Pretty; attractive; good
**Origin:** Scottish
**Pronunciation:** BON ee
**Description:** Bonnie is a direct translation of the Scottish adjective, meaning 'pretty', which traces back to the Latin word '*bonus*', meaning 'good'. The name is also a pet form of Bonita.
**Alternative spellings:** Bonny

## Bow

**Meaning:** Handsome; pretty
**Origin:** French
**Pronunciation:** B oh
**Description:** Bow may be a spelling variant of the French, '*beau*', meaning 'pretty' or 'handsome'. It could

also be from the Old English, '*boga*', meaning 'to bend, bow or arch'.
**Alternative spellings:** Bo, Beau

## Bracken
See entry in 'Names for Baby Boys A–Z'

## Brandy
**Meaning:** Gorse hill
**Origin:** English
**Pronunciation:** BRAN dee
**Description:** The name refers to a type of alcohol but is more likely to be a feminine form of Brandon.
**Alternative spellings:** Brandee, Brandi, Brandie

## Breanna
**Meaning:** The strength of grace
**Origin:** English
**Pronunciation:** bree ANN ah
**Description:** Breanna is a modern American name that combines Bree and Anna.
**Alternative spellings:** Brianna, Bryanna

## Bree
**Meaning:** The exalted one
**Origin:** Gaelic
**Pronunciation:** BREE
**Description:** Bree is an anglicised form of the Irish name Brighe, linked to the Gaelic name Bridget.
**Alternative spellings:** Bri, Brie

## Brenda
**Meaning:** Sword; torch
**Origin:** Nordic
**Pronunciation:** bren DAH
**Description:** Brenda is an Old Norse name. Its roots are found

in the Norse word '*brandr*' meaning 'sword' or 'torch'. It is also considered the female version of Brendan in many countries.

## Brennan
See entry in 'Names for Baby Boys A–Z'

## Bridget
**Meaning:** The exalted one
**Origin:** Gaelic
**Pronunciation:** BRID jet
**Description:** Bridget comes from the Gaelic name Brighid, which was borne by a Celtic goddess.
**Alternative spellings:** Bridjit

## Bridie
**Meaning:** The exalted one
**Origin:** Gaelic
**Pronunciation:** BRI dee
**Description:** This pet form of the Gaelic Brighid is popular in Ireland.
**Alternative spellings:** Bridi, Bridy

## Briella
**Meaning:** Strength from God
**Origin:** Hebrew
**Pronunciation:** BREE el lah
**Description:** Briella is a shortened form of the name Gabriella and as such, shares the same meaning of 'strength from God'.

## Brises
**Meaning:** Mythical queen
**Origin:** Greek
**Pronunciation:** Briss ESS
**Description:** A variant of Briseis, the name of a Trojan widow taken by Achilles in Greek myth.
**Alternative spellings:** Briseis, Brisses, Brissess

## Bristol

**Meaning:** City in England
**Origin:** English
**Pronunciation:** brist OL
**Description:** Bristol is a city in south-west England and, like Camden or Brooklyn, is part of the trend of using place names as baby names.

## Britney

**Meaning:** Brittany
**Origin:** English
**Pronunciation:** BRIT nee
**Description:** A respelling of Brittany made famous by singer Britney Spears.
**Alternative spellings:** Brittany

## Brittany

**Meaning:** Brittany
**Origin:** English
**Pronunciation:** BRIT a nee
**Description:** The name of the region of north-west France. Britannia was a 2nd-century Roman goddess. The name is especially popular in America.
**Alternative spellings:** Britney

## Brogan

See entry in 'Names for Baby Boys A–Z'

## Brontë

**Meaning:** Literary scribe
**Origin:** Gaelic
**Pronunciation:** BRON tay
**Description:** This first name has been adopted from the surname of the English writers Emily, Charlotte and Anne.
**Alternative spellings:** Brontay, Brontie

## Bronwyn

**Meaning:** White breast
**Origin:** Welsh
**Pronunciation:** BRON win
**Description:** Bronwyn is a very popular girls' name in Wales. It is also found in many Welsh legends.
**Alternative spellings:** Bronwen, Bronwin

## Brook

**Meaning:** Stream
**Origin:** English
**Pronunciation:** BRUCK
**Description:** The name comes from the English word for a little stream and was originally a surname. It can also be found as a boys' name.
**Alternative spellings:** Brooke

## Brooklyn

**Meaning:** Stream
**Origin:** English
**Pronunciation:** BRUCK lin
**Description:** An extension of the English name, Brook, meaning 'little stream', with the common suffix -lyn. It has also been used as a name in honour of Brooklyn, the New York City borough.
**Alternative spellings:** Brooklin

## Bryce

**Meaning:** Speckled
**Origin:** English
**Pronunciation:** brice
**Description:** Bryce is most likely a variant of the name Brice, which in term came from the Latin name Bricius, meaning 'speckled'. Bryce Dallas Howard is a famous American actress with this name.
**Alternative spellings:** Brice

## Bryn

See entry in 'Names for Baby Boys A–Z'

## Bryony

**Meaning:** Vine
**Origin:** Greek
**Pronunciation:** BRY o nee
**Description:** This name of a Greek climbing plant has connotations of nature and life.
**Alternative spellings:** Brioni, Brionie, Briony, Bryoni, Bryonie

## Bunny

**Meaning:** Rabbit
**Origin:** English
**Pronunciation:** BUN nee
**Description:** Bunny is a nickname derived from names such as Barbara and Bernice, but is also used as a first name.
**Alternative spellings:** Bunni, Bunnie

## Bushra

**Meaning:** Good omen
**Origin:** Arabic
**Pronunciation:** BUSH ra
**Description:** The name is probably Arabic in origin and supposedly brings good luck to the bearer of the name and to the bearer's family.
**Alternative spellings:** Bushrah

# C

## Cade

See entry in 'Names for Baby Boys A–Z'

## Cadence

**Meaning:** Flowing rhythm
**Origin:** English
**Pronunciation:** KAY dense
**Description:** Cadence is a musical term and its definition is 'the rhythm and movement of tone in sound'.
**Alternative spellings:** Caydence, Kaydence

## Cadi

**Meaning:** Rhythym; flow
**Origin:** English
**Pronunciation:** CAY dee
**Description:** A diminutive of the name Cadence, from an English word meaning 'rhythym, flow'.
**Alternative spellings:** Cady

## Caelan

See entry in 'Names for Baby Boys A–Z'

## Cain

See entry in 'Names for Baby Boys A–Z'

## Caitlyn

**Meaning:** Pure
**Origin:** Greek
**Pronunciation:** KATE lin
**Description:** Caitlyn is an alternative spelling of Caitlin, itself the Irish form of Katharine. Caitlyn is a well-loved name in English-speaking countries and is

especially popular in America.
**Alternative spellings:** Caitlin,
Catelin, Catelyn, Kaitlin, Kaitlyn,
Katelin, Katelyn, Katelynn

## Callie

**Meaning:** Beautiful
**Origin:** Greek
**Pronunciation:** KAH lee
**Description:** Originally the pet
form of the name Caroline, it is
now used as a name in its own
right. 'Cal' comes from the Greek
word for 'beauty'.
**Alternative spellings:** Cali,
Calleigh, Callie, Cally

## Calliope

**Meaning:** Beautiful voice
**Origin:** Greek
**Pronunciation:** kuh LIE o pee
**Description:** Calliope is an
uncommon name of Greek origin
and an alternative spelling of
Kalliope. In Greek mythology,
Kalliope was the eldest of the seven
muses and represented epic poetry.
**Alternative spellings:** Calleope,
Calliopee, Kalliope

## Callisto

**Meaning:** Most beautiful
**Origin:** Greek
**Pronunciation:** kah LISS toe
**Description:** Callisto is an uncommon name of Greek origin. In Greek
mythology, Callisto was a nymph
of Artemis. It is also the name of a
moon, the third-largest in the solar
system, of the planet Jupiter.
**Alternative spellings:** Calisto, Kallisto

## Cameron

See entry in 'Names for Baby Boys
A–Z'

## Camilla

**Meaning:** Sacrifice
**Origin:** Italian
**Pronunciation:** cah MIL ah
**Description:** Camilla originates
from Roman mythology in which
Camilla was the queen of the Volsci.
**Alternative spellings:** Camila,
Kamila, Kamilla

## Camille

**Meaning:** Sacrifice
**Origin:** Italian
**Pronunciation:** kah MEEL
**Description:** The French version
of the name Camilla. Whereas
Camilla is specifically feminine,
Camille is used as a name for both
boys and girls.
**Alternative spellings:** Camill,
Kamile, Kamille

## Campbell

See entry in 'Names for Baby Boys
A–Z'

## Candace

**Meaning:** Queen; mother; clarity
**Origin:** Latin
**Pronunciation:** can DEESE
**Description:** Candace was the
hereditary title of a succession of
Ethiopian queens. It is now a first
name but still carries the meaning of 'queen' or 'mother'. It could
also have come from the Late Latin
word *'candita'*, meaning 'clarity'.
**Alternative spellings:** Candice

## Caoimhe

**Meaning:** Beautiful
**Origin:** Gaelic
**Pronunciation:** KEEV ah
**Description:** Caoimhe is a name
of Gaelic origin that is usually

C

found in England anglicised as Keeva. It comes from the Gaelic word *'caomh'*, which means 'beautiful'.

**Alternative spellings:** Keeva

## Caprice

**Meaning:** Fanciful
**Origin:** Italian
**Pronunciation:** CUH price
**Description:** Caprice is an Italian name that means 'fanciful'. It is the same spelling and meaning as the English word.

## Cara

**Meaning:** Dearest
**Origin:** Italian
**Pronunciation:** KAR ah
**Description:** Cara is a variant spelling of the Italian name Kara.
**Alternative spellings:** Carah, Kara

## Carla

**Meaning:** Free man
**Origin:** English
**Pronunciation:** CAR la
**Description:** Carla is a feminine version of the English name Carl. As such, it means 'free man'. It first came into general use in the 1940s.
**Alternative spellings:** Karla

## Carley

**Meaning:** Free man
**Origin:** German
**Pronunciation:** CAR lee
**Description:** Carley is a spelling variant of the name Carlie. Carlie and Carley originally came about as pet forms of Carlene.
**Alternative spellings:** Carli, Carlie, Carly

## Carmel

**Meaning:** Garden
**Origin:** Hebrew
**Pronunciation:** car MEL
**Description:** Carmel is a unisex name used mainly by Roman Catholics. In the 12th century a monastery was founded in Mount Carmel and the Carmelite order came about from that.
**Alternative spellings:** Karmel

## Carmen

**Meaning:** Garden
**Origin:** Hebrew
**Pronunciation:** CAR mun; CAR men
**Description:** Carmen is the Spanish version of the name Carmel and can most commonly be found in English- and Spanish-speaking countries.
**Alternative spellings:** Carman, Karmen

## Carlotta

**Meaning:** Free Man
**Origin:** Italian
**Pronunciation:** car LOT ah
**Description:** Carlotta is the Italian version of the name Charlotte, which in turn is the feminine version of the name Charles, meaning 'free man'.

## Carolina

**Meaning:** Free man
**Origin:** German
**Pronunciation:** KARE oh lie nah
**Description:** Carolina is the feminine version of Carlo, which is itself the Spanish form of Charles. The names Carlo and Carolina are popular in Latin America. It may be given as a name to girls born in Carolina in America.

**Alternative spellings:** Carolena, Carolyna, Karolena, Karolina, Karolyna

## Caroline
**Meaning:** Free man
**Origin:** German
**Pronunciation:** CA ruh line
**Description:** Caroline comes from the Latin name Carolina. It is thought to have been first borne by Lady Caroline Lamb, the mistress of Lord Byron.
**Alternative spellings:** Carolyne, Karoline

## Carrie
**Meaning:** Free man
**Origin:** German
**Pronunciation:** KA ree
**Description:** A short form of Caroline.
**Alternative spellings:** Cari, Carri

## Carys
**Meaning:** Love
**Origin:** Welsh
**Pronunciation:** CA riss
**Description:** Carys means 'love', deriving from the Welsh word *'caru'*, and is sometimes shortened to Cass.
**Alternative spellings:** Carice, Caris, Karice, Karis, Kariss, Karys

## Casey
See entry in 'Names for Baby Boys A–Z'

## Cassandra
**Meaning:** Entangler of men
**Origin:** Greek
**Pronunciation:** kah SAN dra
**Description:** Cassandra is a name associated with tragedy in Greek myth and legend. In Homer's epic poem *The Iliad*, Cassandra was a Trojan princess who foretold the fall of Troy, but no one believed her. She was considered both blessed and cursed.
**Alternative spellings:** Cassandre, Kassandra

## Cassia
**Meaning:** Spice
**Origin:** Latin
**Pronunciation:** CAS see ah; CASH ah
**Description:** Cassia is a name that can be traced to two separate origins. It can be seen as the feminine form of the name Cassius, which is said to come from a Roman family name. Alternatively, Cassius could be of Greek origin, from the word *'kasia'*, which is the name of a spice.
**Alternative spellings:** Cashia, Cassiah, Cassier

## Cassidy
**Meaning:** Curly
**Origin:** Gaelic
**Pronunciation:** CASS id ee
**Description:** Cassidy comes from the Gaelic surname O'Caiside. It can be seen as both a boys' and a girls' name.
**Alternative spellings:** Cassidey, Cassidi, Cassidie

## Cassie
**Meaning:** Entangler of men
**Origin:** Greek
**Pronunciation:** KASS ee
**Description:** Originally a pet form of Cassandra, Cassie is now a first name in its own right. The name is most commonly used in English-speaking countries.

312

**Alternative spellings:** Cassi, Cassy, Kassey, Kassie

## Cataleya
**Meaning:** Genus of orchids
**Origin:** English
**Pronunciation:** cat a lay ah
**Description:** A contemporary name that may be connected to the Cattleya orchids of Argentina. The flowers were named after English botanist, Wiliam Cattley.
**Alternative spellings:** Katalaya, Cattleya

## Catalina
**Meaning:** Pure
**Origin:** Greek
**Pronunciation:** cat a lee nah
**Description:** Catalina is a Spanish form of Katherine, derived from the Greek name, Katerina, which translates as 'pure'.
**Alternative spellings:** Katalina

## Catherine
**Meaning:** Pure
**Origin:** Greek
**Pronunciation:** CATH er in
**Description:** Catherine is an English name that can be traced back to the Greek name Aikaterina. It is linked to the word 'katharos' meaning 'pure'. The name was introduced to England in the medieval period.
**Alternative spellings:** Catharin, Catharine, Catharyn, Catherin, Catheryn, Cathryn, Katharin, Katharine, Katherin, Katherine, Katheryn, Kathryn

## Catrin
**Meaning:** Pure
**Origin:** Greek
**Pronunciation:** KAT reen
**Description:** Catrin derives from the same roots as Katherine or Catherine. Catrin may have come about as a pet form of Katrina.
**Alternative spellings:** Catrine, Katreen, Katrin

## Catriona
**Meaning:** Pure
**Origin:** Greek
**Pronunciation:** kah tree OH nah
**Description:** Catriona is the Gaelic version of the Greek name Catherine. The name is mostly found in Scotland and Ireland; however Catriona has also spread to other countries.
**Alternative spellings:** Catrionah, Katriona

## Cece
**Meaning:** Blind
**Origin:** Latin
**Pronunciation:** see see
**Description:** Cece is most likely a short form or nickname for the name Cecelia, meaning 'blind'. The name became popular because it was the name of Jim and Pam's baby in the US version of *The Office*.

## Cecilia
**Meaning:** Blind
**Origin:** Latin
**Pronunciation:** seh SEE lee ah
**Description:** Cecilia is derived from the Latin 'caecus', which means 'blind'. It was introduced to the UK in the medieval period and is also a feminine equivalent of the name Cecil.
**Alternative spellings:** Cecelia, Cecillia

## Cecily
**Meaning:** Blind
**Origin:** Latin

**Pronunciation:** SES ih lee
**Description:** Cecily is a variant of the name Cecilia, which is the feminine version of Cecil. Cecil is of Latin origin and it means 'blind'. When first used, Cecil was a name given to girls.
**Alternative spellings:** Ceciley, Cecili, Cecilie, Cicily

## Celia

**Meaning:** Heavenly
**Origin:** Latin
**Pronunciation:** see lee ah
**Description:** Celia is a variant of the Roman family name, Caelius, meaning 'heaven'. It is also a pet form of Cecilia and Celeste.
**Alternative spellings:** Cilia

## Celeste

**Meaning:** Heavenly
**Origin:** French
**Pronunciation:** sell EST
**Description:** Celeste is a French name now seen across the English-speaking world. It comes from the Latin 'caelestis', meaning 'heavenly'. In Greek mythology Celesta is the sister of Hades.
**Alternative spellings:** Celesta, Seleste

## Celine

**Meaning:** Heavenly; follower of Mars
**Origin:** Latin
**Pronunciation:** su LEEN
**Description:** Celine may come from the same root as Celeste, Celina and Celia and mean 'heavenly'. It could also derive from the Roman Marceline, meaning 'follower of Mars'.
**Alternative spellings:** Celeen, Celline, Seline

## Celyn

**Meaning:** Holly
**Origin:** Welsh
**Pronunciation:** KEH lin
**Description:** Celyn, a unisex name from the Celtic for 'holly', is a good name for a child born around Christmas time. It is more common in Wales.
**Alternative spellings:** Kelyn

## Ceri

**Meaning:** Fair, blessed poetry
**Origin:** Welsh
**Pronunciation:** KER ee
**Description:** Ceri is a Welsh name meaning 'fair, blessed poetry'. It is the short form of Ceridwen and Cerise. Note that the name is pronounced different from how it is spelt.

## Cerys

**Meaning:** Love
**Origin:** Welsh
**Pronunciation:** CARE iss
**Description:** Cerys is a variant of the Welsh name Carys. It should be noted that the two names have slightly different pronunciations.
**Alternative spellings:** Carys, Ceriss

## Chana

**Meaning:** Favoured by God
**Origin:** Hebrew
**Pronunciation:** KAH na
**Description:** Chana is a spelling variant of the name Channah, which is itself a variant of the popular Hebrew name Hannah. Chana is a popular name in Israel with Jewish parents.
**Alternative spellings:** Channah

## Chance

See entry in 'Names for Baby Boys A–Z'

## Chanel

**Meaning:** Wine
**Origin:** French
**Pronunciation:** SHA nel
**Description:** Chanel was originally a surname, notably that of French fashion designer Gabrielle Coco Chanel. It was adopted as a first name due to Coco Chanel's success and has since developed connotations of couture and high society.
**Alternative spellings:** Chanelle

## Chantelle

**Meaning:** Stone; song
**Origin:** French
**Pronunciation:** shon TELL; sharn TELL
**Description:** Chantelle was originally a French surname but has been adopted as a first name in France and many Dutch- and English-speaking countries. Derived from the word *'cantal'*, meaning 'stone', it is more commonly associated with the French for 'song'.
**Alternative spellings:** Chantal, Chantel

## Chardonnay

**Meaning:** Chardonnay wine
**Origin:** French
**Pronunciation:** SHAR don ay
**Description:** Chardonnay, a variety of grape, is also a village in the Maconnais region of France. This name was made popular in the UK by the character in the TV show *Footballers' Wives*.

**Alternative spellings:** Chardonay, Shardonnay

## Charis

**Meaning:** Graceful
**Origin:** Greek
**Pronunciation:** KA riss
**Description:** In Greek myth, Charis was a goddess said to have the best qualities of all women. The name came to England around the 17th century.
**Alternative spellings:** Cariss, Carys, Cerys

## Charlee

**Meaning:** Free man
**Origin:** French
**Pronunciation:** CHAR lee; char LEE
**Description:** This is a modern spelling variation of the popular unisex name Charlie, which is short for Charlotte.
**Alternative spellings:** Charleigh, Charley, Charli, Charlie, Charly

## Charlize

**Meaning:** Free Man
**Origin:** English
**Pronunciation:** char LEE ze
**Description:** Charlize is the feminine version of the name Charles, and as such shares the same meaning of 'free man'. The name was made popular by actress Charlize Theron.

## Charlotte

**Meaning:** Free man
**Origin:** French
**Pronunciation:** SHAR lot
**Description:** French feminine diminutive of Charles, used in

England since the 17th century. It owed its popularity in the 18th and 19th centuries to Queen Charlotte and Charlotte Brontë.
**Alternative spellings:** Charlette, Charlott

## Chaya
**Meaning:** Free man
**Origin:** German
**Pronunciation:** CHYE yah
**Description:** Chaya was originally a surname, and the forename version could have derived from that. It may also be a feminine form of Chay, which is itself a pet form of Charles.
**Alternative spellings:** Chayah, Cheya

## Chelsea
**Meaning:** From Chelsea
**Origin:** English
**Pronunciation:** CHEL see
**Description:** Chelsea, introduced as a name from the south-west London district of Chelsea, could have also been influenced by the name Kelsey.
**Alternative spellings:** Chelci, Chelcie, Chelsey, Chelsie, Chelsy

## Cherry
**Meaning:** Charity; fruit
**Origin:** Latin
**Pronunciation:** CHE ree
**Description:** Cherry, a short form of Charity, is now a name in its own right.
**Alternative spellings:** Cheri, Cherri, Cherrie

## Cheryl
**Meaning:** Charity; fruit
**Origin:** Latin
**Pronunciation:** CHEH ral
**Description:** Cheryl is a relatively modern name and was coined in around the 1940s. It is thought to be a variation of the name Cherry, the short form of the name Charity.
**Alternative spellings:** Cheril, Cherrylle

## Chiara
**Meaning:** Bright
**Origin:** Italian
**Pronunciation:** kee AR uh
**Description:** Chiara is a variant of the names Clare and Clara and means 'bright' or 'famous'. It is popular with Italian parents.
**Alternative spellings:** Chiarah, Ciara, Kiara

## Chitose
**Meaning:** Strength of a thousand
**Origin:** Japanese
**Pronunciation:** ch it O see
**Description:** This name can be written by using different Japanese characters, as well as the traditional Japanese alphabet Hiragana. The different characters mean 'thousand', 'to climb or ascend' and 'strength and force'.
**Alternative spellings:** Chetose, Chetosi

## Chloe
**Meaning:** A green shoot
**Origin:** Greek
**Pronunciation:** KLO ee
**Description:** From the Greek name Khloe, this was originally used in the classical period as an epithet of the fertility goddess Demeter.
**Alternative spellings:** Chloë, Chlöe, Chloé, Chloey, Cloe, Cloey, Khloe, Khloë, Kloé, Kloë, Kloey

## Chris

See entry in 'Names for Baby Boys A–Z'

## Christa

**Meaning:** Anointed; chosen one
**Origin:** Greek
**Pronunciation:** kris TAH
Description: Possibly a derivation of the Greek word '*Cristos*', meaning 'anointed' or 'chosen one'. It could also be a pet form of Christine, which translates as 'follower of Christ'.
**Alternative spellings:** Krista, Crista

## Christabel

**Meaning:** Beautiful Christian
**Origin:** Latin
**Pronunciation:** KRIST ah bel
**Description:** This name of Latin and French origin combines Christian, a 'follower of Christianity' and *belle*, 'beauty'. We can take Christabel to mean 'beautiful Christian'.
**Alternative spellings:** Christabelle, Kristabel

## Christian

See entry in 'Names for Baby Boys A–Z'

## Christiana

**Meaning:** Follower of Christ
**Origin:** English
**Pronunciation:** kris tee AH nah
**Description:** Christiana is a variant of the name Christine, which is the feminine version of Christian.

## Christina

**Meaning:** Follower of Christ
**Origin:** Latin
**Pronunciation:** kris TEE nuh
**Description:** A simplified form of the Latin feminine form of Christian.
**Alternative spellings:** Christena, Cristina, Kristina

## Christine

**Meaning:** Follower of Christ
**Origin:** French
**Pronunciation:** kris TEEN
**Description:** Christine is the feminine version of the name Christian, which means 'follower of Christ'. The name is often subject to variation and adaptation – Chris, Chrissy, Kirsty, Kristen and Kristine all bear links to the name Christine.
**Alternative spellings:** Christeen, Christene, Kristine

## Ciara

**Meaning:** Dark-haired; bright
**Origin:** Gaelic
**Pronunciation:** see AIR ah; KEER ah; kee AR ah
**Description:** This feminine form of the Irish name Ciaran means 'dark' or 'black'. Ciara could also be a variant of the Italian Chiara, meaning 'bright'. The 'c' can be soft or hard.
**Alternative spellings:** Chiara, Chiarah, Kiara

## Cienna

**Meaning:** From Siena
**Origin:** Italian
**Pronunciation:** see EN ah
**Description:** Cienna is an alternative spelling for Sienna, derived from the Italian city Siena. It is a fitting name given to baby girls conceived there. The variant form Cienna may have come about as

C

a way of distinguishing the given name from the name of the city.
**Alternative spellings:** Sienna

## Cindy
**Meaning:** From Mount Cynthus
**Origin:** Greek
**Pronunciation:** SIN dee
**Description:** Cindy originally came about as a pet form of names such as Cynthia or Lucinda, but it is now used as a given name. It experienced a popularity boost in the 1960s with the launch of the popular Sindy doll.
**Alternative spellings:** Cindee, Cindi, Cindie, Sindy

## Claire
**Meaning:** Bright
**Origin:** French
**Pronunciation:** KLARE
**Description:** Claire is the French form of the name Clara. It is a popular name in English-speaking countries and was introduced to Britain by the Normans.
**Alternative spellings:** Clare

## Clancy
**Meaning:** Red-haired warrior
**Origin:** Irish
**Pronunciation:** clan SEE
**Description:** Clancy is an Irish name meaning 'red-haired warrior'. Translated directly from the Gaelic, it means 'son of Fhlannchadh', where 'flann' means 'reddish'.

## Clara
**Meaning:** Bright
**Origin:** Latin
**Pronunciation:** CLAH ra
**Description:** Clara derives from the Latin word *'clarus'*,

meaning 'bright'. It is currently one of the top ten girls' names in France.

## Clarice
**Meaning:** Bright
**Origin:** Latin
**Pronunciation:** CLA riss
**Description:** Clarice came about as an elaboration on the Latin name Clara.
**Alternative spellings:** Clarisse, Claryce

## Clarissa
**Meaning:** Bright
**Origin:** Latin
**Pronunciation:** cla RISS a
**Description:** A Latinate form of Clarice. Sometimes shortened to Claire.
**Alternative spellings:** Clairissa, Clarica, Claryssa

## Claudette
**Meaning:** Lame
**Origin:** French
**Pronunciation:** KLO dett
**Description:** Claudette is the French version of the Latin surname Claudius, which in turn is from *'claudus'*, meaning 'lame'. Alternatively it is also the female version of Claude.

## Claudia
**Meaning:** Lame
**Origin:** Latin
**Pronunciation:** CLOR de uh
**Description:** This is a version of the Roman name Claudius. The French unisex form 'Claude' used to be very popular in France.
**Alternative spellings:** Claudier, Klaudia

## Clemency

**Meaning:** Merciful
**Origin:** English
**Pronunciation:** clem EN see
**Description:** Clemency is from the English word of the same spelling and means 'merciful'. It comes from the Latin root 'clemens', which means the same thing

## Clementine

**Meaning:** Mild-mannered
**Origin:** Latin
**Pronunciation:** CLEH men tyne
**Description:** Clementine is the feminine equivalent of the name Clement. It is also associated with the fruit. A popular name in Germany.
**Alternative spellings:** Clementyne, Clemintine, Klementine

## Cleo

**Meaning:** Father's glory
**Origin:** Greek
**Pronunciation:** KLEE oh
**Description:** Cleo is the short form of the name Cleopatra, which is Greek in origin. It was the name of a famous Egyptian queen, so carries connotations of allure and mystery.
**Alternative spellings:** Cleoh, Clio, Kleo

## Cleopatra

**Meaning:** Glory father
**Origin:** Greek
**Pronunciation:** clee OH pat ra
**Description:** The name Cleopatra is famous for being borne by the ruler of Egypt, born 69 BC. She had children with both Caesar and Mark Anthony before dying aged 39 from a snakebite.

## Clover

**Meaning:** Clover plant
**Origin:** English
**Pronunciation:** cloh VER
**Description:** Clover is a type of plant that is found almost all over the world. It is most often used as fodder, as in animal feed. Clovers usually have three leaves. Four-leaf clovers are very rare and therefore considered to be tokens of luck.

## Coco

**Meaning:** Chocolate
**Origin:** French
**Pronunciation:** KO ko
**Description:** Coco was the nickname of the pioneering French fashion designer, Chanel, and is associated with couture and high society.
**Alternative spellings:** Coko, Koco, Koko

## Cody

See entry in 'Names for Baby Boys A–Z.'

## Colette

**Meaning:** Victory of the people
**Origin:** Greek
**Pronunciation:** coll ET
**Description:** Colette is a French feminine form of Colle, the medieval short form of Nicholas. Colette is also a shortened form of the name Nicolette.
**Alternative spellings:** Collette, Kolette

## Connie

**Meaning:** Steadfast
**Origin:** Latin
**Pronunciation:** KOH nee

**Description:** Distinct from the masculine Conny, which is short for Connor, Connie is a pet form of Constance, but has become a name in its own right.
**Alternative spellings:** Conie, Conni, Conny

## Constance
**Meaning:** Steadfast
**Origin:** Latin
**Pronunciation:** KON stanse
**Description:** The name derives from the Latin word for 'constant' or 'steadfast' and was popular in Norman times. It is often shortened to Connie.
**Alternative spellings:** Constanse, Konstance

## Constantine
See entry in 'Names for Baby Boys A–Z'

## Cora
**Meaning:** Maiden
**Origin:** Greek
**Pronunciation:** KORE ah
**Description:** Cora derives from the Greek '*kore*' meaning 'the maiden'. Kore was another name for Persephone, a daughter of Zeus in Greek mythology.
**Alternative spellings:** Corah, Kora

## Coral
**Meaning:** Coral
**Origin:** English
**Pronunciation:** KOH ral
**Description:** Coral, the skeleton of marine animals, became a name once the substance was considered rare and valuable. It has an exotic feel.
**Alternative spellings:** Corelle, Koral

## Coraline
**Meaning:** Coral
**Origin:** Greek
**Pronunciation:** core UH ine
**Description:** It is a variation of the name Coral, referring to the hard, stone-like substance found in the sea.

## Cordelia
**Meaning:** Heart
**Origin:** Latin
**Pronunciation:** kor DEE lee ah
**Description:** Cordelia is a variant of Cordellia. The name is thought to be derived from the Latin word '*cor*', which means 'heart'.
**Alternative spellings:** Cordellia, Kordelia

## Corey
See entry in 'Names for Baby Boys A–Z'

## Corinne
**Meaning:** Beautiful maiden
**Origin:** English
**Pronunciation:** COR inn
**Description:** Corinne is a variation of the name Corina, and as such shares the meaning of 'beautiful maiden'. It has roots in the Greek word '*kore*' meaning 'maiden'.

## Cornelia
**Meaning:** Horn
**Origin:** Latin
**Pronunciation:** kor NEE lee ah
**Description:** Cornelia is the feminine equivalent of Cornelius, a Roman family name thought to have come from the Latin word '*cornu*', meaning 'horn'.
**Alternative spellings:** Kornelia

## Cosima

**Meaning:** Order; decency
**Origin:** Greek
**Pronunciation:** ko SEE ma
**Description:** The girls' name Cosima is derived from the Greek name Kosmas. In the 4th century St Cosmas was martyred along with his brother,
**Alternative spellings:** Cosimah, Kosima

## Courtney

**Meaning:** Domain of Curtius
**Origin:** French
**Pronunciation:** KORT nee
**Description:** Once thought to mean 'short nose', this was a surname for those who lived in places called Courtenay, meaning 'Domain of Curtius'.
**Alternative spellings:** Cortney, Courteney, Kortney, Kourteney, Kourtney

## Cressida

**Meaning:** Golden
**Origin:** Greek
**Pronunciation:** cress EE dah
**Description:** Cressida was created by Shakespeare for his play, *Troilus and Cressida*. He took it from the Greek name Chryseis, meaning 'daughter of Chryses'. All of these have a common Greek root, '*chrysos*' meaning 'golden'.

## Cruz

See entry in 'Names for Baby Boys A–Z'

## Crystal

**Meaning:** Crystal
**Origin:** English
**Pronunciation:** KRIS tall
**Description:** Crystal is derived from the Greek word '*krustallos*' meaning 'ice'. Crystal is suggestive of gemstones.
**Alternative spellings:** Chrystal, Kristel, Krystal

## Cydney

**Meaning:** Wide meadow
**Origin:** English
**Pronunciation:** SID nee
**Description:** Cydney is a specifically feminine variant of the unisex name Sydney.
**Alternative spellings:** Cydnee, Sidnee, Sidney, Sydnee, Sydney

## Cynthia

**Meaning:** From Mount Cynthus
**Origin:** Greek
**Pronunciation:** SIN thee ah
**Description:** Derived from the Greek mountain, this would have originally been the surname of those who lived by or on the mountain. It was also the name of a Greek goddess born there.
**Alternative spellings:** Cinthia, Cynthea, Synthia

# D

## Dahlia

**Meaning:** Dahlia flower; valley
**Origin:** English
**Pronunciation:** DAHL yuh
**Description:** The dahlia is a bushy flower native to Mexico, where it is

considered the national flower. It also means 'valley' in Swedish.
**Alternative spellings:** Dahlya, Dalia, Darlia

## Daisy
**Meaning:** Day's eye
**Origin:** English
**Pronunciation:** DAY zee
**Description:** The yellow centre of the flower of the same name is covered by petals come dusk and was named 'day's eye'. This then became 'daisy' over time.
**Alternative spellings:** Daisi, Daisie, Daysie

## Dalia
**Meaning:** Dahlia flower; grapevine
**Origin:** Arabic
**Pronunciation:** DAHL yuh
**Description:** Dalia is a common name in Arabic and Hebrew and stems from the word 'grapevine'. It is also a spelling variant of Dahlia, derived from the name of the flower.
**Alternative spellings:** Dahlya, Dahlia, Darlia

## Dallas
**Meaning:** City in Texas
**Origin:** English
**Pronunciation:** DALL as
**Description:** Dallas is a city in the American state of Texas. Like London and Paris, this name follows the trend of using place names for baby names.

## Dana
**Meaning:** Fertility; from Denmark
**Origin:** Gaelic
**Pronunciation:** DAY na
**Description:** In Irish myth, Dana

was the name of the goddess of fertility.
**Alternative spellings:** Danah, Dayna

## Danae
**Meaning:** Founder of Ardea
**Origin:** Greek
**Pronunciation:** dah NAY
**Description:** In Greek mythology, Danae was a daughter of King Acrisius of Argos and Queen Eurydice.
**Alternative spellings:** Danaea, Danay

## Dania
**Meaning:** God is my judge
**Origin:** Hebrew
**Pronunciation:** DAN yah
**Description:** Dania is a variation of Danielle, the feminine form of Daniel.
**Alternative spellings:** Daniah, Daniya

## Danica
**Meaning:** From Denmark
**Origin:** Slavic
**Pronunciation:** dah NEE kah
**Description:** Danica, thought to come from the word 'Dane', would have been given as a first name to Danish girls.
**Alternative spellings:** Danicah, Danika

## Daniella
**Meaning:** God is my judge
**Origin:** Hebrew
**Pronunciation:** dan YELL ah
**Description:** The feminine form of the name Daniel. This spelling is mainly used in English-speaking countries.
**Alternative spellings:** Daniela, Daniyella, Danniella

## Danielle

**Meaning:** God is my judge
**Origin:** Hebrew
**Pronunciation:** dan ee ELL; dan YELL
**Description:** A French feminine form of the Hebrew name Daniel and is a popular name in Britain.
**Alternative spellings:** Daniele, Danivelle, Dannielle

## Danni

**Meaning:** God is my judge
**Origin:** Hebrew
**Pronunciation:** DAH nee
**Description:** Danni came about as a pet form of the name Danielle, but is now used as a name in its own right.
**Alternative spellings:** Dani, Dannie

## Daphne

**Meaning:** Laurel tree
**Origin:** Greek
**Pronunciation:** DAF nee
**Description:** In Greek mythology Daphne was a nymph who was pursued by Apollo. When she asked the gods to help they turned her into a laurel tree.
**Alternative spellings:** Daphnee, Daphney

## Darcey

**Meaning:** From Arcy
**Origin:** French
**Pronunciation:** DAR see
**Description:** Darcey is the specifically feminine spelling of the unisex name Darcy. Darcy is a French surname, which means 'person from Arcy'. It is also found as a surname in Ireland.
**Alternative spellings:** Darci, Darcie, Darcy

## Darcy

See entry in 'Names for Baby Boys A–Z'

## Daria

**Meaning:** Guardian
**Origin:** Persian
**Pronunciation:** DAR ee ah
**Description:** Daria is the feminine version of the masculine name Darius, which is of Persian origin and means 'guardian'.
**Alternative spellings:** Dariah, Darya

## Darla

**Meaning:** Darling
**Origin:** English
**Pronunciation:** daar LAH
**Description:** Darla is derived from the Old English '*dearling*', or as it is more commonly known in modern English, 'darling'.

## Davina

**Meaning:** Darling
**Origin:** Hebrew
**Pronunciation:** da VEE nuh
**Description:** Davina, or Davinia, is a Latinate feminine form of David, said to have originated in Scotland.
**Alternative spellings:** Davena, Davinah, Davinia

## Dawn

**Meaning:** Daybreak
**Origin:** English
**Pronunciation:** DORN
**Description:** The name Dawn originates from the English word for the beginning of the day.
**Alternative spellings:** Dawne

## Daya

**Meaning:** Man Destroyer

**D**

**Origin:** Greek
**Pronunciation:** DAY ah
**Description:** A contemporary name that may be a diminutive of the Ancient Greek name, Deianira. Deianira was a figure in Greek mythology whose name translates as 'man-destroyer'.
**Alternative spellings:** Daia, Dayah, Deya, Deia

## Deanna

**Meaning:** Divine
**Origin:** Greek
**Pronunciation:** de AH nah; DEE nah
**Description:** The name Deanna can be seen as a variation on the popular name Diana, meaning 'divine'. It could also be of Old English origin, meaning 'girl from the dean'.
**Alternative spellings:** Deana, Deannah

## Debbie

**Meaning:** Bee
**Origin:** Hebrew
**Pronunciation:** DEB bee
**Description:** Debbie came about as a pet form of the name Deborah, but is now a name in its own right.
**Alternative spellings:** Debbee, Debbi, Debby

## Deborah

**Meaning:** Bee
**Origin:** Hebrew
**Pronunciation:** DEB or ah
**Description:** This biblical name, which was very popular in the 1960s, can often be shortened to Debbie or Bee.
**Alternative spellings:** Debbora, Debborah, Debora

## Dee

**Meaning:** Bee
**Origin:** English
**Pronunciation:** dee
**Description:** Dee is often the pet form of names such as Deborah and Debbie. It can also be used as a pet name for any names beginning with the letter D.
**Alternative spellings:** Dea

## Delia

**Meaning:** Woman from the island of Delos
**Origin:** Greek
**Pronunciation:** Dee lee ah
**Description:** Delia is of Greek origin and generally translates as 'woman from the island of Delos'. It is also a pet form of names such as Cordelia and Odelia.
**Alternative spellings:** Deliah

## Delilah

**Meaning:** Flirtatious
**Origin:** Hebrew
**Pronunciation:** de LYE lah
**Description:** Delilah is the biblical name of the woman who gave Samson up to the Philistines.
**Alternative spellings:** Delila, Delylah

## Delphine

**Meaning:** Of Delphi
**Origin:** French
**Pronunciation:** DEHL feen
**Description:** Delphine is the French form of the name Delphina, which is from the Latin meaning 'of Delphi', which refers to the city in Ancient Greece that was the site of the oracle Apollo.

## Delta

**Meaning:** Fourth born
**Origin:** Greek
**Pronunciation:** del TAH
**Description:** Delta is actually the fourth letter of the Greek alphabet and refers to children who are the fourth born in a family.

## Delyth

**Meaning:** Pretty
**Origin:** Welsh
**Pronunciation:** del ITH
**Description:** Delyth is a Welsh name and is derived from the Welsh word for 'pretty'.

## Demelza

**Meaning:** Place in Cornwall
**Origin:** Cornish
**Pronunciation:** deh MEL zah
**Description:** Demelza is a Cornish place name, specifically a hamlet in St. Wenn, Corwall. It is the name of the heroine in Winston Graham's Poldark series.

## Demeter

**Meaning:** Earth mother
**Origin:** Greek
**Pronunciation:** deh MEE ter
**Description:** In Greek mythology, Demeter was the goddess associated with the fertility of the earth and also protected the sanctity of marriage.
**Alternative spellings:** Demeta, Demetre

## Demi

**Meaning:** Half
**Origin:** French
**Pronunciation:** DEH me
**Description:** Demi is a name coined in modern times. It may also be a pet form of Demetria or Demetrius, making its meaning 'earth'.
**Alternative spellings:** Demie, Demy

## Denisa

**Meaning:** Servant of Dionysus
**Origin:** Greek
**Pronunciation:** deh NEES ah
**Description:** Denisa is a variant of the French name Denise.
**Alternative spellings:** Deneesa, Denisah

## Denise

**Meaning:** Servant of Dionysus
**Origin:** Greek
**Pronunciation:** deh NEECE
**Description:** Like Denisa, Denise is the feminine form of Denis, derived from the name of the Greek god, Dionysus.
**Alternative spellings:** Deneese, Dineese

## Desiree

**Meaning:** Desired
**Origin:** French
**Pronunciation:** DES er RAY
**Description:** An anglicisation of the French name Désirée meaning 'desired'.
**Alternative spellings:** Desirée

## Destiny

**Meaning:** Fate
**Origin:** Latin
**Pronunciation:** DES tih nee
**Description:** Destiny, from the word meaning 'the power of fate', derives from the Latin 'destinare'. It is very popular in the US.
**Alternative spellings:** Destini, Destinie

## Devin

**Meaning:** Fawn
**Origin:** Irish
**Pronunciation:** deh VIN
**Description:** Devin is the anglicised version of the Irish name, Ó Damháin, which is a reference to the given name 'Damán Allaid', meaning 'fawn'.

## Devon

**Meaning:** From Devon
**Origin:** English
**Pronunciation:** DEH vun
**Description:** Devon is a unisex name that derives from the county in south-west England.
**Alternative spellings:** Devone, Devun

## Devora

**Meaning:** Bee
**Origin:** Hebrew
**Pronunciation:** dev OR ah
**Description:** Devora is a Hebrew name meaning 'bee'. In the Torah, Devorah was a prophetess who taught the Jewish nation for forty years.

## Diamond

**Meaning:** Diamond
**Origin:** English
**Pronunciation:** DIE mund
**Description:** The name of one of the most precious stones, Diamond is still fairly rare but is used for girls who are considered very precious.
**Alternative spellings:** Dyamond

## Diana

**Meaning:** Pure
**Origin:** Latin
**Pronunciation:** dy AH nah
**Description:** Diana was the Roman goddess of the moon and virginity. The name increased in popularity after the death of Diana, Princess of Wales.
**Alternative spellings:** Dianah, Dyana

## Didi

**Meaning:** A Pet Name
**Origin:** English
**Pronunciation:** dee dee
**Description:** Didi is a pet name given to people with names such as Diana. However, it can also be a given name on its own as well.

## Dilara

**Meaning:** Heart's desire
**Origin:** Persian
**Pronunciation:** dee LAH rah
**Description:** Dilara is a name of both Persian and Turkish origins. It comes from the Persian word *'dil'*, which means 'heart', and shares a root with *'dilek'*, which means 'desire' in Turkish.
**Alternative spellings:** Delara, Dilarah

## Dima

**Meaning:** Torrential rain
**Origin:** Arabic
**Pronunciation:** DI ma
**Description:** Dima is said to refer to rain; however it could come from the Arabic word meaning 'life'. It could also be a shortened version of the Russian name Dmitri, which means 'of Demeter'.
**Alternative spellings:** Dema, Dimah

## Dina

**Meaning:** Judgement; daytime; valley

326

**Origin:** Hebrew
**Pronunciation:** DEE nah
**Description:** Dina is a name that can be traced back to three separate origins. It could come from a Sanskrit word meaning 'daytime'. Equally, it could derive from a Hebrew word meaning 'judgement' or the name could come from an Old English word meaning 'valley'.
**Alternative spellings:** Deena, Dena, Denah, Dinah

## Dion

**Meaning:** Servant of Dionysus
**Origin:** Greek
**Pronunciation:** DYE on
**Description:** Dion is a unisex name that is derived from the name of the Greek god of revelry, Dionysus. Dione is a specifically feminine form of the name, while Deon is the spelling more often used for boys.
**Alternative spellings:** Deon, Dione, Dionne

## Disha

**Meaning:** Direction
**Origin:** Indian
**Pronunciation:** dee SHAH
**Description:** Disha is an Indian girls' name meaning 'direction'.

## Divine

**Meaning:** Heavenly
**Origin:** Latin
**Pronunciation:** dih VINE
**Description:** Divine is a girls' name that is a variant of Divina. Divine has religious implications and the name means 'heavenly' or 'of heaven'.
**Alternative spellings:** Davine, Devine, Divina, Divinia, Divyne

## Divya

**Meaning:** Divine
**Origin:** Sanskrit
**Pronunciation:** div YAAH
**Description:** Divya comes directly from the Sanskrit word of the same spelling and means 'divine'.

## Dixie

**Meaning:** Southerner
**Origin:** English
**Pronunciation:** DICK see
**Description:** The name Dixie comes from the term used to describe those who lived south of the line drawn up to settle disputes between British colonies in America in the 1700s.
**Alternative spellings:** Dixi, Dixy

## Diya

**Meaning:** Bright
**Origin:** Arabic
**Pronunciation:** DI ya
**Description:** Although Diya was originally a masculine name it is becoming popular as a girls' name.
**Alternative spellings:** Deya, Dia, Diyah

## Dolcie

**Meaning:** Sweet
**Origin:** Italian
**Pronunciation:** Dolt je; Doll see
**Description:** *Dolce*, the Italian word for 'sweet', may refer to: Dolcè, an Italian municipality located in the province of Verona. The name may also be used in honour of luxury fashion house, Dolce & Gabbana.
**Alternative spellings:** Dolce, Dolcè, Dulcie

## Dolly

**Meaning:** Gift of God

D

**Origin:** Greek
**Pronunciation:** DOR oth ee
**Description:** A diminutive of Dorothy, from the Greek, Dorothea, meaning 'God's gift'. The shortening became popular in the 16th century.
**Alternative spellings:** Dollie, Dolley

## Dominica
**Meaning:** Lord
**Origin:** Latin
**Pronunciation:** do me NEE kah
**Description:** Dominica is the less common feminine equivalent of Dominic and is from the Latin *'dominicus'* meaning 'from the Lord' or just 'Lord'.
**Alternative spellings:** Dominika, Dominikah

## Dominique
**Meaning:** Lord
**Origin:** Latin
**Pronunciation:** dom in EEK
**Description:** Dominique is the more usual feminine version of Dominic, although in France and America it is used as a unisex name.
**Alternative spellings:** Domineke

## Donna
**Meaning:** Lady
**Origin:** Italian
**Pronunciation:** DON na
**Description:** The name Donna comes from the Italian word for 'lady' and was first taken up by English speakers in the early 20th century.
**Alternative spellings:** Dona, Donnah

## Dora
**Meaning:** Gift of God

**Origin:** Greek
**Pronunciation:** DOR ah
**Description:** A further diminutive of the Greek, Dorothea, Dora is now a popular name on its own. It is also a shortening of the female name, Theodora.
**Alternative spellings:** Dorah

## Doris
**Meaning:** From Dorian; gift
**Origin:** Greek
**Pronunciation:** DOR riss
**Description:** Doris was originally a name given to women of the Greek Dorian tribe. *'Doron'* means 'gift'.
**Alternative spellings:** Doriss, Dorris

## Dorothy
**Meaning:** God's gift
**Origin:** Greek
**Pronunciation:** DOR oth ee
**Description:** Dorothy, from the Greek Dorothea, is a combination of the words *'doron'* and *'theos'*, meaning 'gift' and 'God' respectively.
**Alternative spellings:** Dorothi, Dorothie

## Dottie
**Meaning:** Gift of God
**Origin:** Greek
**Pronunciation:** DOT ee
**Description:** Dottie is a further shortening of the English name, Dorothy, which in turn derives from the Greek, Dorothea.
**Alternative spellings:** Dotty

## Dream
**Meaning:** To Dream
**Origin:** English
**Pronunciation:** dreem

**Description:** Dream is taken from the English vocabulary word of the same meaning. Like Faith or Grace, this is part of the trend to use English words as baby names.

## Drew

See entry in 'Names for Baby Boys A–Z'

## Dua

**Meaning:** Prayer

**Origin:** Arabic
**Pronunciation:** doo AH
**Description:** Dua derives from the Arabic word that means 'prayer'. It is an unusual name in Britain but is popular in the Middle East.
**Alternative spellings:** Dewa

## Dusty

See entry in 'Names for Baby Boys A–Z'

# E

## Eadie

**Meaning:** Riches; blessed
**Origin:** English
**Pronunciation:** ee dee
**Description:** A sweet variation of the traditional English name, Edith, meaning 'riches' or 'blessed'. Further variations include Ditte and Edyth.
**Alternative spellings:** Edie

## Easha

**Meaning:** She who lives or womanly
**Origin:** Arabic
**Pronunciation:** eesh ah
**Description:** A variant of the popular Islamic name, Aisha. Aisha was the name of the last and youngest wife of the prophet Muhammad.
**Alternative spellings:** Isha

## Ebony

**Meaning:** Dark wood
**Origin:** Latin
**Pronunciation:** EH ben ee
**Description:** This name of an

extremely dark wood is popular with African-Americans. It has Latin, Greek and Egyptian origins.
**Alternative spellings:** Eboni, Ebonie

## Echo

**Meaning:** Echo
**Origin:** Greek
**Pronunciation:** EK oh
**Description:** In Greek myth, Echo was a nymph used by the adulterous Zeus to distract his wife Hera.
**Alternative spellings:** Ecko, Ekho

## Eden

**Meaning:** Paradise
**Origin:** Hebrew
**Pronunciation:** E den
**Description:** Eden may be considered a short form of Edith, but is more likely to be used in relation to the 'garden of Eden' where, according to the Bible, Adam and Eve lived in paradise.
**Alternative spellings:** Edan, Edon

## Eddie
See entry in 'Names for Baby Boys A–Z'

## Edith
**Meaning:** Ambitious
**Origin:** English
**Pronunciation:** EE dith
**Description:** Edith is an Old English name that is made up of the elements of *'ead'*, which means 'riches', and *'gyth'* meaning 'strife'.
**Alternative spellings:** Edithe

## Efa
**Meaning:** Beaming radiance
**Origin:** Hebrew
**Pronunciation:** EE fah
**Description:** Efa is a variant of the name Eva, and is usually found in Wales. It is very similar in pronunciation to the Irish name Aoife.
**Alternative spellings:** Aoife, Eefa, Efah

## Effie
**Meaning:** Beautiful silence
**Origin:** Greek
**Pronunciation:** EH fee
**Description:** Effie, a pet form of Euphemia, is now used as a name in its own right and is especially popular in Scotland.
**Alternative spellings:** Effi, Effy

## Eiko
**Meaning:** Prosperous child
**Origin:** Japanese
**Pronunciation:** ee EE koh
**Description:** Although this name has its roots in Japanese, it is commonly found in many other Asian countries. The character *'ei'* means 'flourish and prosperity' while *'ko'* means 'child'.
**Alternative spellings:** Eheko, Eyko

## Eileen
**Meaning:** Pleasant
**Origin:** Gaelic
**Pronunciation:** eye LEEN
**Description:** This anglicised form of Eibhlin is linked to Helen and Evelyn.
**Alternative spellings:** Aileen, Eyleen

## Eilidh
**Meaning:** Pleasant; bright
**Origin:** Gaelic
**Pronunciation:** AY lee
**Description:** Eilidh is thought to be a Gaelic variant of either Eileen, which means 'pleasant' or Ellie, which means 'bright'.
**Alternative spellings:** Ailidh, Eiledh

## Eira
**Meaning:** Snow
**Origin:** Welsh
**Pronunciation:** AIR ah; AY rah
**Description:** Eira is a name of Welsh origin, and comes from the Welsh word for 'snow'.
**Alternative spellings:** Aira, Eyra

## Ela
**Meaning:** Beautiful; fairy maiden
**Origin:** Greek
**Pronunciation:** ELL ah
**Description:** A modern contraction of Ella, which has many derivations. It is often used as a shortening for names beginning with 'El', including Elizabeth and Eleanor. It is also a pet name for names such as Annabella or Danniella.
**Alternative spellings:** Ella

## Elaina

**Meaning:** Bright
**Origin:** French
**Pronunciation:** eh LAY nah
**Description:** Elaina is a variant of the Greek name Elaine.
**Alternative spellings:** Elana, Elayna, Eliana

## Elaine

**Meaning:** Bright
**Origin:** Greek
**Pronunciation:** eh LANE
**Description:** Elaine is the French form of the Greek name Helen. In English legend, Elaine is the name of a woman who falls in love with Sir Lancelot.
**Alternative spellings:** Elane, Elayne

## Elana

**Meaning:** Bright
**Origin:** Greek
**Pronunciation:** eh LAH nah
**Description:** As well as being a variant of Elaina, Elana is also considered a phonetically spelt variant of Eleanor. It is also found as a Hebrew name in its own right and in this form means 'tree'.
**Alternative spellings:** Elaina, Elanor, Eleana, Eleanor, Elena

## Elara

**Meaning:** One who brings brightness and happiness to the soul
**Origin:** Persian
**Pronunciation:** ell AR ah
**Description:** Elara is a variant spelling of Alara, a popular name in Turkey that means 'the one who brings brightness and happiness to the heart and soul'. Alara is also the name of a water fairy in Turkish mythology who must remain beside the water to maintain her youth and beauty.
**Alternative spellings:** Alara

## Eleanor

**Meaning:** Bright
**Origin:** French
**Pronunciation:** ELL a nor
**Description:** An Old French respelling of the Old Provencal name Aliénor. Introduced to England in the 12th century by Eleanor of Aquitaine, who came from France to wed King Henry II.
**Alternative spellings:** Elana, Elanor, Eleana, Elena, Ellena, Elina

## Eleonora

**Meaning:** Bright
**Origin:** French
**Pronunciation:** ELL ee oh nor
**Description:** A variant spelling of Eleanor, itself a contraction of the traditional French name Aliénor.
**Alternative spellings:** Eleanor, Elanor, Eleanora

## Electra

**Meaning:** Shining
**Origin:** Greek
**Pronunciation:** el LEHK tra
**Description:** Electra is of Greek origin and an alternative spelling to Elektra. It is the name given to one of the nine brightest stars in the Pleiades star cluster, in the constellation of Taurus.
**Alternative spellings:** Elektra

## Elen

**Meaning:** Mischievous
**Origin:** Gaelic
**Pronunciation:** EH len
**Description:** Elen is a Gaelic

**E**

name associated with a nymph and carries with it connotations of mischievousness.
**Alternative spellings:** Elin, Elinn, Ellen

## Eleni
**Meaning:** Bright
**Origin:** Greek
**Pronunciation:** eh LEH ne
**Description:** Like Elaine, Eleni comes from the Greek name Helen and shares its meaning of 'bright'.
**Alternative spellings:** Elene, Elleni

## Eleri
**Meaning:** River
**Origin:** Welsh
**Pronunciation:** EH lee ree
**Description:** This unusual, predominantly Welsh name is likely to have associations with the Welsh river Eleri.
**Alternative spellings:** Elerie, Elery, Elleri

## Elia
**Meaning:** Jehovah is good
**Origin:** Hebrew
**Pronunciation:** EH le ah
**Description:** Elia, a unisex name, comes from the same root as Elijah, which means 'Jehovah is good'.
**Alternative spellings:** Elea, Eliah

## Elif
**Meaning:** Symbol
**Origin:** Arabic
**Pronunciation:** ELL eef
**Description:** The name occurs in the Old Testament, the female form of Aleph. Although not

attributed a meaning, the name is also the name for many powerful symbols in Arabic and Hebrew.
**Alternative spellings:** Alif, Alepph, Eliph

## Elija
**Meaning:** My God is Yaweh
**Origin:** Hebrew
**Pronunciation:** ELL aye ja
**Description:** A variant of Elijah, who was a prophet in Israel in the 9th century BC mentioned in many holy texts. It has been predominantly used as a male name but is now considered unisex.
**Alternative spellings:** Elijah, Elias

## Elin
**Meaning:** Beautiful nymph
**Origin:** Welsh
**Pronunciation:** ELL in
**Description:** Welsh form of Helen, which translates as 'beautiful nymph', or 'intelligent, beautiful'.
**Alternative spellings:** Elyn, Ellin

## Elisa
**Meaning:** Promised by God
**Origin:** Hebrew
**Pronunciation:** eh LEE sah
**Description:** Elisa is a modern variant of the name Eliza, itself a pet form of Elizabeth.
**Alternative spellings:** Alisa, Alissa, Alysa, Alyssa, Elissa, Elyssa

## Elise
**Meaning:** Promised by God
**Origin:** Hebrew
**Pronunciation:** ell EEZ
**Description:** Elise is a pet form of the Hebrew name Elizabeth, and

hence means 'promised by God'. It is the title of Beethoven's piano piece 'Für Elise'.

**Alternative spellings:** Eleese, Elize, Ellisa, Elyse

## Elisha

**Meaning:** Powerful
**Origin:** Hebrew
**Pronunciation:** ell EE sha; ell ISH a
**Description:** This name is thought to derive from the biblical name 'El', which means 'powerful', and 'Sha' which means 'to help and deliver'. It can also be considered a variant of the name Alisha, meaning 'noble'.
**Alternative spellings:** Aleesha, Aleisha, Alesha, Alicia, Alicja, Aliesha, Alisha, Alysha, Eleisha, Elisher

## Elissia

**Meaning:** Noble
**Origin:** German
**Pronunciation:** eh LIS ee ah
**Description:** Elissia is a German variant of the popular name Alicia.
**Alternative spellings:** Alecia, Alessia, Alicia, Alicja, Alisia, Alissia, Alycia, Alysia, Alyssia, Elicia

## Eliza

**Meaning:** Promised by God
**Origin:** Hebrew
**Pronunciation:** ey LYE zah
**Description:** Eliza was originally a pet form of the name Elizabeth.
**Alternative spellings:** Aliza, Alyza, Elyza

## Elizabeth

**Meaning:** Promised by God
**Origin:** Hebrew

**Pronunciation:** eh LIZ a buth
**Description:** From Elisabet, the Greek form of the Hebrew name Elisheva. The name was made popular by Queen Elizabeth I in the 16th century and is still favoured by royals. Lilibet is a variation chosen by Harry and Meghan.
**Alternative spellings:** Elisabeth

## Ella

**Meaning:** All bright
**Origin:** German
**Pronunciation:** ELL lug
**Description:** The name Ella was introduced to Britain by the Normans. It derives from a word meaning 'all' or 'inclusive' but is also a form of Helen, which means 'bright'.
**Alternative spellings:** Ellah

## Elle

**Meaning:** Bright woman
**Origin:** French
**Pronunciation:** ELL
**Description:** Elle is a modern name from the French word for 'she'. It could also be considered a variant of the Greek name Helen, meaning 'bright'.
**Alternative spellings:** Ell

## Ellen

**Meaning:** Bright
**Origin:** Greek
**Pronunciation:** ELL en
**Description:** Ellen is a variant form of the Greek name Helen. It originally came into use in the 16th century.

## Ellia

**Meaning:** Promised by God; bright
**Origin:** Hebrew
**Pronunciation:** ELL ee ah

**Description:** A modern contraction of Ella, which has many deriviations. It is often used as a shortening for names beginning with 'El', including Elizabeth and Eleanor.
**Alternative spellings:** Ellie, Elia

## Elliana
**Meaning:** God has answered; bright
**Origin:** Hebrew
**Pronunciation:** ELL ee arn ah
**Description:** Composed of the Hebrew elements of '*El*', meaning God and '*ana*', meaning '*answered*'. It could also be considered as a variation of the Greek, Helene, meaning 'bright'.
**Alternative spellings:** Eliana, Eleana

## Ellie
**Meaning:** Bright woman
**Origin:** French
**Pronunciation:** ELL lee
**Description:** Ellie is generally a pet name for a variety of names beginning 'El', in particular the name Eleanor.
**Alternative spellings:** Elli, Elly

## Elliot
See entry in 'Names for Baby Boys A–Z'

## Ellis
**Meaning:** Jehovah is good
**Origin:** Hebrew
**Pronunciation:** ELL iss
**Description:** Ellis derives from a medieval version of Elias. Often used as a transferred surname, Ellis has enjoyed popularity as a unisex name.
**Alternative spellings:** Eliss, Elliss

## Ellise
**Meaning:** Promised by God
**Origin:** Hebrew
**Pronunciation:** eh LEECE
**Description:** As well as being a spelling variant of the name Elise, Ellise could also have developed in France as a feminine version of the name Elisee. It shares its meaning of 'promised by God' with Elizabeth.
**Alternative spellings:** Eleese, Elise, Elize, Elyse

## Elodie
**Meaning:** Wealthy
**Origin:** German
**Pronunciation:** ell LOAD ee
**Description:** This name is extremely popular in German- and French-speaking countries and is a variation of the German name Elodia. The element of '*od*' means 'wealth and riches'.
**Alternative spellings:** Elodi, Elody

## Eloisa
**Meaning:** Famed warrior
**Origin:** French
**Pronunciation:** eh loh EE sa
**Description:** Eloisa comes from the same roots as the name Louise, which is popular in Britain. It could also derive from the French Heloise.
**Alternative spellings:** Elloisa, Eloisah, Elouisa

## Eloise
**Meaning:** Sun
**Origin:** French
**Pronunciation:** EH lo eez
**Description:** Eloise is the anglicised form of Heloise. It is seen as

a more unique alternative to the name Louise.

**Alternative spellings:** Elloise, Elouise

## Elora

**Meaning:** Bright
**Origin:** Greek
**Pronunciation:** EH lor ah
**Description:** Elora originally came about as a variation of Eleanor, the French version of the Greek name Helen. It may also be a variation of the name of a group of caves in India.
**Alternative spellings:** Elaura, Ellora, Elorah

## Elowen

**Meaning:** Elm Tree
**Origin:** Cornish
**Pronunciation:** ELL oh wen
**Description:** From the Cornish word, '*elowenn*', meaning 'elm tree'.
**Alternative spellings:** Ellowen

## Elsa

**Meaning:** Promised by God
**Origin:** English
**Pronunciation:** ELL sa
**Description:** Elsa is a girls' name predominantly seen in Sweden, Germany and England. It is derived from the classic name Elizabeth.
**Alternative spellings:** Ailsa, Eilsa, Else

## Elsie

**Meaning:** Promised by God
**Origin:** Hebrew
**Pronunciation:** ELL see
**Description:** The name Elsie is a pet form of Elspeth, which

itself is a Scottish variation of the Hebrew name Elizabeth. Elsie is currently experiencing a surge in popularity.

**Alternative spellings:** Ellsi, Ellsie, Ellsy, Elsi, Elsy

## Elspeth

**Meaning:** Promised by God
**Origin:** Hebrew
**Pronunciation:** ELL speth
**Description:** Elspeth is a Scottish variation of the name Elizabeth. It is gaining popularity and can be found in many places outside of Scotland.
**Alternative spellings:** Ellspeth, Elsbeth

## Elvie

**Meaning:** Bright white
**Origin:** Gaelic
**Pronunciation:** ELL vee
**Description:** Elvie is a variant of the feminine Irish name Elva. It is thought that the original Gaelic name is Ailbhe, which means 'bright white'.
**Alternative spellings:** Elvi, Elvy

## Elysia

**Meaning:** Blissful heaven
**Origin:** Latin
**Pronunciation:** eh LIZ ee ah
**Description:** Elysia is a name that comes from the Latin Elysium, the destination of the blessed after death and equivalent to Christianity's heaven.
**Alternative spellings:** Elisia, Elisya

## Eman

See entry in 'Names for Baby Boys A–Z'

## Emaan

**Meaning:** Belief; faith

E

**Origin:** Arabic
**Pronunciation:** ee MAHN
**Description:** A variation of the name Iman, which can be used as a name for boys and girls. It translates as 'faith' or 'faith in the metaphysical realities of Islam'.
**Alternative spellings:** Eman, Iman

## Ember

**Meaning:** Spark burning low
**Origin:** English
**Pronunciation:** EM burgh
**Description:** Ember is an English noun that describes the smouldering remains of a fire that appear in the form of glowing ashes.
**Alternative spellings:** Unknown

## Emelia

**Meaning:** One who excels; friendly
**Origin:** Latin
**Pronunciation:** em EE lee uh
**Description:** This name derives from the Latin name Emily, and in Greek the name means 'friendly'. It could also come from the Germanic Amelia.
**Alternative spellings:** Amalia, Amelia, Amilia, Emilia, Emilija

## Emersyn

**Meaning:** Son of Emery
**Origin:** English
**Pronunciation:** emer SON
**Description:** Emersyn is a different spelling of the more common Emerson. It is a unisex name that used to be a surname given to those whose father was named Emery.
**Alternative spellings:** Emerson

## Emi

**Meaning:** All-encompassing

**Origin:** German
**Pronunciation:** EH me
**Description:** Emi is a variant form of Emmi, which is a pet form of the popular name Emma. Emi is now found used as a name in its own right. Emi could also be considered a Japanese name, meaning 'blessed with beauty'.
**Alternative spellings:** Emmi, Emmie, Emmy, Emy

## Emilie

**Meaning:** One who excels
**Origin:** French
**Pronunciation:** EH mill ee
**Description:** A modern respelling of the popular name Emily.
**Alternative spellings:** Emilee, Emily

## Emilija

**Meaning:** One who excels
**Origin:** Latin
**Pronunciation:** eh MEE lee ah
**Description:** Emilija is a variant of Emilia, a variation of Emily. The name is Latin in origin, but this spelling is more common in the Baltics.
**Alternative spellings:** Amalia, Amelia, Amilia, Emelia, Emilia

## Emma

**Meaning:** All-encompassing
**Origin:** German
**Pronunciation:** EM muh
**Description:** Originally a Frankish name, Emma was first used as a short form of names such as Ermintrude.
**Alternative spellings:** Ema

## Emmanuella

**Meaning:** God is with us

**Origin:** Hebrew
**Pronunciation:** eh man yu EH lah
**Description:** Emmanuella is a variation on Emanuelle, the feminine version of Emanuel.
**Alternative spellings:** Emmanuela

# Emmanuelle

**Meaning:** God is with us
**Origin:** Hebrew
**Pronunciation:** eh man yu EH lah
**Description:** Emmanuelle is the feminine version of Emanuel.

# Emme

**Meaning:** All-encompassing
**Origin:** German
**Pronunciation:** EH me
**Description:** Emme is a pet form of Emma, a name of Old German origin and one of the most popular girls' names in Britain. Emme is becoming more widely used as a name in its own right.
**Alternative spellings:** Em, Emm

# Emmeline

**Meaning:** One who excels
**Origin:** Latin
**Pronunciation:** EM uh leen
**Description:** This French version of Emily is part of a current British trend for French names.
**Alternative spellings:** Emeline, Emmalene, Emmaline, Emmelene

# Emmylou

**Meaning:** All-encompassing
**Origin:** English
**Pronunciation:** emmi LOO
**Description:** Emmylou is a variant of the name Emma and Emmy, both of which mean 'all-encompassing'. Emmylou Harris is a famous country singer with this name.

# Enid

**Meaning:** Purity or soul
**Origin:** Welsh
**Pronunciation:** EE nid
**Description:** From the Welsh, '*eneit*', meaning 'purity' or 'soul'. The given name of popular British children's writer Enid Blyton.
**Alternative spellings:** Eanid, Enide

# Eniola

**Meaning:** Wealthy
**Origin:** African
**Pronunciation:** eh ne OH lah
**Description:** Eniola is an African name, found predominantly in Nigeria. It is thought to come from the Yoruba language, and means 'wealthy one'.
**Alternative spellings:** Eneola, Eniolah

# Enya

**Meaning:** Kernel
**Origin:** Gaelic
**Pronunciation:** EN yah
**Description:** Enya is a modern variation of the name Eithne, a name found in Irish history, legend and poetry.
**Alternative spellings:** Enyah

# Enyo

**Meaning:** Warlike
**Origin:** Greek
**Pronunciation:** EN yo
**Description:** In Greek mythology, Enyo was an ancient goddess of war, acting as a companion to the war god Ares.
**Alternative spellings:** Ennyo, Enyoh

# Eowyn

**Meaning:** Horse lover
**Origin:** Old English

E

**Pronunciation:** EOO win
**Description:** Eowyin is an Old English name meaning 'horse lover'. It was made famous by J. R. R Tolkein, who named one of his *Lord of the Rings* characters Eowyn.

## Erica
**Meaning:** Eternal ruler; heather
**Origin:** Norse
**Pronunciation:** EH rih kah
**Description:** Erica is the feminine version of the Old Norse name Eric. In this sense it shares its meaning of 'eternal ruler'. However, the name Erica could also have roots in Latin, where it would mean 'heather'.
**Alternative spellings:** Ericka, Erika

## Erin
**Meaning:** Ireland
**Origin:** Gaelic
**Pronunciation:** EH rin
**Description:** This anglicised version of the Irish name Eirinn was used as a poetic name for Ireland for centuries.
**Alternative spellings:** Aerin, Aeryn, Airin, Eirinn, Eryn

## Esa
See entry in 'Names for Baby Boys A–Z'

## Esha
**Meaning:** Desire
**Origin:** Arabic
**Pronunciation:** ISH ah
**Description:** Esha is of Arabic origin and means 'desire'. It is particularly popular with Hindu parents.
**Alternative spellings:** Eesha, Eshah

## Eshal
**Meaning:** Heavenly flower

**Origin:** Arabic
**Pronunciation:** ESH ahl
**Description:** Eshal is a Quranic baby name that translates as 'heavenly flower'. It is derived from the SH-AIN-L root, similar to other Muslim names includung Ashal and Shaalah.
**Alternative spellings:** Eshaal

## Esma
**Meaning:** To esteem
**Origin:** French
**Pronunciation:** EZ mah
**Description:** An unusual variant, most likely a deriviation of Esme, an English name from the French word '*esmer*', meaning 'to esteem'.
**Alternative spellings:** Esme, Esmé, Esmée, Esmae, Esmai

## Esme
**Meaning:** Respected
**Origin:** French
**Pronunciation:** EZ may
**Description:** Esme is a French name, originally unisex but now more commonly given to girls. It is sometimes thought of as a pet form of Esmerelda.
**Alternative spellings:** Esmae, Esmee, Esmie

## Esmerelda
**Meaning:** Emerald
**Origin:** Spanish
**Pronunciation:** EZ mer EL da
**Description:** Deriving from the Spanish for emerald.
**Alternative spellings:** Esmeralda

## Esperanza
**Meaning:** Hope; expectation
**Origin:** Spanish

**Pronunciation:** es per AN zah
**Description:** Esperanza comes from the Spanish vocabulary word for 'hope' or 'expectation'. It has been made popular by jazz singer, Esperanza Spalding.

## Essa

**Meaning:** Salvation
**Origin:** African
**Pronunciation:** ESS ah
**Description:** Essa is a variant of the African unisex name Issa, meaning 'salvation' or 'protection'.
**Alternative spellings:** Essah, Issa

## Estella

**Meaning:** Star
**Origin:** Latin
**Pronunciation:** ESY ell ah
**Description:** A French feminine name, a derivative of the Latin 'stella', meaning 'star'.
**Alternative spellings:** Stella, Estellar

## Estelle

**Meaning:** Star
**Origin:** Latin
**Pronunciation:** eh STEL
**Description:** Estelle is from the French 'estella', which derives from the Latin word for 'star', 'stella'.
**Alternative spellings:** Estell

## Estera

**Meaning:** Star
**Origin:** Persian
**Pronunciation:** ESS tair ah
**Description:** A variant of the Hebrew female name, Esther, based on the name of the Persian goddess, Ishtar, a translation of the word 'star'.

**Alternative spellings:** Esthera, Esther

## Esther

**Meaning:** Star
**Origin:** Persian
**Pronunciation:** ESS ter
**Description:** Esther is the Hebrew variation of the name of the Persian goddess Ishtar, which means star.
**Alternative spellings:** Ester, Estha

## Ethel

**Meaning:** Noble
**Origin:** English
**Pronunciation:** ETH ell
**Description:** Ethel, an Old English name meaning 'noble', was popular in the early 1900s.
**Alternative spellings:** Ethal, Ethelle

## Etta

**Meaning:** Keeper of the hearth
**Origin:** Germanic
**Pronunciation:** ETT ah
**Description:** Etta is a short form of the English name Henrietta, derived from the French Henriette. The female version of Henri, meaning 'home ruler' or 'keeper of the hearth'.
**Alternative spellings:** Eta, Ette

## Ettie

**Meaning:** Keeper of the hearth
**Origin:** Germanic
**Pronunciation:** ETT ee
**Description:** Ettie is a further variant of the English name Henrietta, derived from the French Henriette. It is originally from the Germanic name Heimiric, derive from the word elements, of 'heim' meaning 'home' and 'ric', meaning of 'power'.
**Alternative spellings:** Etty, Hetty

## Eunice

**Meaning:** Good victory
**Origin:** Greek
**Pronunciation:** yoo NIS
**Description:** Eunice is the Latinised form of the Greek name Eunike, meaning 'good victory'. It is made up of the elements of *'eu'* meaning *'good'* and *'nike'*, which means 'victory'.

## Europa

**Meaning:** Wide eyes
**Origin:** Greek
**Pronunciation:** yoo RO pah
**Description:** In Greek mythology, Europa was seduced by Zeus and became the first queen of Crete. It is also the name of the sixth moon of Jupiter.
**Alternative spellings:** Europe, Eurupa

## Eurydice

**Meaning:** Broad justice
**Origin:** Greek
**Pronunciation:** yur ri DIH see
**Description:** In Greek mythology, Eurydice was the wife of Orpheus. The story of Eurydice and Orpheus became a popular theme in Renaissance art.
**Alternative spellings:** Euredice, Euridice

## Eva

**Meaning:** Living
**Origin:** Hebrew
**Pronunciation:** EE vuh
**Description:** The name Eva comes from the Hebrew name Eve, which means 'living' and is the name of the first woman put on the earth in Christian belief.
**Alternative spellings:** Ewa

## Evadne

**Meaning:** Well
**Origin:** Greek
**Pronunciation:** ee VAD nee
**Description:** In Greek mythology, Evadne was the wife of Capaneus of Argos, who committed suicide after the death of her husband.
**Alternative spellings:** Evadnee, Evedne

## Evalyn

**Meaning:** Bird
**Origin:** Latin
**Pronunciation:** EH va lin
**Description:** Closely related to the name Evelyn, both names come from the Latin *'avis'*, which means 'bird'.
**Alternative spellings:** Evelyn

## Evangeline

**Meaning:** Good news
**Origin:** Greek
**Pronunciation:** ee VAN geh lene
**Description:** This name is most often used in English- and French-speaking countries and derives from the word *'evange',* which is a term for the gospels.
**Alternative spellings:** Evangelene, Evangilene, Evangiline

## Evanna

**Meaning:** God is gracious
**Origin:** Welsh
**Pronunciation:** ee VAN uh
**Description:** Evanna is a Welsh name meaning 'God is gracious'. Evanna Lynch is a famous British actress who played Luna in the Harry Potter series.

## Eve

**Meaning:** Life

**Origin:** Hebrew
**Pronunciation:** EVE
**Description:** In the Christian tradition, Eve, from the Hebrew *'havva'*, was the first woman. Eve also means 'animal'.
**Alternative spellings:** Eeve

## Evelina

**Meaning:** Hazelnut
**Origin:** Norman French
**Pronunciation:** EV ah LEEN ah
**Description:** Evelina is a variation of Evelyn, which originated from the Norman French surname, Aveline. The modern French translation of aveline is 'hazelnut'.
**Alternative spellings:** Evelyna, Evelin, Evelyn

## Eveline

**Meaning:** Hazelnut
**Origin:** Norman French
**Pronunciation:** EV eh lin
**Description:** Eveline is a variant spelling of the English given name, Evelyn. The name originated from the Norman French surname, Aveline, that translates as 'hazelnut'.

**Alternative spellings:** Evelyn, Aveline, Evelynn

## Everly

**Meaning:** Grazing meadow
**Origin:** English
**Pronunciation:** EV er lee
**Description:** Everly is a unisex variation on the feminine name Evelyn.
**Alternative spellings:** Everli, Everlie

## Evie

**Meaning:** Life
**Origin:** Hebrew
**Pronunciation:** EE vee
**Description:** Evie originated as a pet form of the names Eve, Eva or Evelyn and is currently extremely popular.
**Alternative spellings:** Evi, Evy

## Evita

**Meaning:** Living one
**Origin:** Hebrew
**Pronunciation:** eh VEE tah
**Description:** Evita is a Hebrew name meaning 'living one'. It has connections to Eve, who was the first woman in the bible.

# F

## Fabienne

**Meaning:** Bean grower
**Origin:** French
**Pronunciation:** fa BEE en
**Description:** Fabienne is a French name meaning 'bean grower'. It is also the feminine version of the name Fabien.

## Fahima

**Meaning:** Chaste
**Origin:** Arabic
**Pronunciation:** fah HEE mah
**Description:** Fahima is a variation of the name Fatima.
**Alternative spellings:** Faatimah, Fatema, Fathima, Fatima, Fatimah

## Fahmida

**Meaning:** Full of knowledge
**Origin:** Arabic
**Pronunciation:** fah ME dah
**Description:** Fahmida is a name of Arabic origins said to mean 'full of knowledge'. It is predominantly used by parents of the Muslim faith.
**Alternative spellings:** Fameda, Famida

## Faith

**Meaning:** Faith
**Origin:** English
**Pronunciation:** FAYTH
**Description:** The name Faith comes directly from the word meaning 'confident belief in the truth or a person or idea'.
**Alternative spellings:** Faithe, Fayth

## Faiza

**Meaning:** Successful
**Origin:** Arabic
**Pronunciation:** FAH ee za
**Description:** Faiza is a name of Arabic origin that means 'successful'. Although uncommon in Britain, Faiza is a popular name in African and Arabic countries.
**Alternative spellings:** Faizah, Fayiza

## Falak

See entry in 'Names for Baby Boys A–Z'

## Fallon

**Meaning:** Chief
**Origin:** Gaelic
**Pronunciation:** FAH lin
**Description:** Fallon is an anglicised version of the Irish surname Fallamhain, which means 'chief'.
**Alternative spellings:** Fallan

## Farah

**Meaning:** Cheerful
**Origin:** Arabic
**Pronunciation:** FAH rah
**Description:** Farah is a name of Arabic origin and means 'cheerful'.
**Alternative spellings:** Fara, Farrah

## Faria

**Meaning:** Happiness; towering
**Origin:** Arabic
**Pronunciation:** FAH ree ah
**Description:** Faria could be of Arabic origin and mean 'towering'. It could also mean 'happiness'.
**Alternative spellings:** Fariah, Farya

## Fariha

**Meaning:** Happiness
**Origin:** Arabic
**Pronunciation:** fah REE ha
**Description:** Fariha comes from an old Arabic word meaning 'happiness'.
**Alternative spellings:** Farihah, Faryha

## Faryal

**Meaning:** Angel
**Origin:** Arabic
**Pronunciation:** far YAAL
**Description:** Faryal is an Arabic feminine name meaning 'angel'. Related names include Faryaal, Farryal and Farryaal.
**Alternative spellings:** Faryaal, Farrya, Farryaal

## Fatma

**Meaning:** Chaste
**Origin:** Arabic
**Pronunciation:** FAT ma
**Description:** Fatma is a Turkish variation of the feminine Arabic

name Fatima. It is a popular name among Muslim parents.
**Alternative spellings:** Fatmah

## Faustina
**Meaning:** Fortunate
**Origin:** Latin
**Pronunciation:** foss TEEN ah
**Description:** Faustina is a Latin name meaning 'fortunate'. It comes from the Latin word *'faustus'*, which gives the name its meaning.

## Favour
See entry in 'Names for Baby Boys A–Z'

## Fay
**Meaning:** Fairy
**Origin:** English
**Pronunciation:** FAY
**Description:** Fay is the traditional word for 'fairy'. It is commonly used as a pet form for Faith.
**Alternative spellings:** Faye

## Felicia
**Meaning:** Happy times
**Origin:** Latin
**Pronunciation:** feh LEE shah; feh LISS eh ah
**Description:** Felicia derives from the Latin phrase *'tempora felicia'* meaning 'happy times'. It is thought to be the feminine equivalent of Felix.
**Alternative spellings:** Felicya, Felisia

## Felicity
**Meaning:** Happy; fortunate
**Origin:** Latin
**Pronunciation:** feh LISS it ee
**Description:** Like Felicia, Felicity derives from the Latin *'felicia'*

meaning 'happy'. It is also the feminine form of Felix, which means good fortune.
**Alternative spellings:** Feliciti, Felicitie

## Fern
**Meaning:** Fern plant
**Origin:** English
**Pronunciation:** fern
**Description:** Fern is a feminine name of English origin and comes from the English word for the fern plant. The variant form Fearne has developed to differentiate the name from the plant, and is becoming the more popular form, aided perhaps by the fame of the English radio and television presenter Fearne Cotton.
**Alternative spellings:** Fearne, Ferne

## Ffion
**Meaning:** Foxglove
**Origin:** Welsh
**Pronunciation:** FEE on
**Description:** Ffion is a name of Welsh origin and is derived from the Welsh name for the foxglove flower.
**Alternative spellings:** Fion, Fionn, Fyon

## Fifi
**Meaning:** The Lord gave more
**Origin:** French
**Pronunciation:** fee fee
**Description:** Fifi is a diminutive of the name Josephine and as such, shares the same meaning of 'the Lord gave more'.

## Fiona
**Meaning:** Fair-haired

343

**Origin:** Gaelic
**Pronunciation:** fee OH na
**Description:** Fiona derives from the Gaelic word *'fionn'* meaning 'fair', and shares this derivation with the masculine names Finn and Finlay.
**Alternative spellings:** Fionah, Fyona

## Fiza

**Meaning:** Breeze
**Origin:** Urdu
**Pronunciation:** FEE zah
**Description:** The name Fiza is most likely of Urdu origin and is popular with Muslim parents.
**Alternative spellings:** Fizah, Fyza

## Fleur

**Meaning:** Flower
**Origin:** French
**Pronunciation:** FLURE
**Description:** Fleur comes from the French word for 'flower'.

## Flick

**Meaning:** Happy; fortunate
**Origin:** Latin
**Pronunciation:** FLIK
**Description:** Flick is a colloquial pet name for a girl named Felicity. It is not often used as a name in its own right.
**Alternative spellings:** Flic, Flik

## Fliss

**Meaning:** Happiness; luck; good fortune
**Origin:** Latin
**Pronunciation:** flyss
**Description:** Fliss is an English name that is related to Felicity and shares the same meaning, 'happiness'. Both names have roots in the Latin word 'felicitas', meaning 'luck' or 'good fortune'.

## Flo

**Meaning:** Flower
**Origin:** Latin
**Pronunciation:** FLO
**Description:** Flo is a short form for Florence or Flora, but is also becoming a name in its own right. Thanks to its meaning of 'flower' the name Flo has connotations of beauty and serenity.
**Alternative spellings:** Flow

## Flora

**Meaning:** Flower
**Origin:** Latin
**Pronunciation:** FLOR ah
**Description:** The name Flora comes from the Latin word *'flos'*, meaning 'flower'. It is also the name of the Roman mythological goddess of flowers and the spring.
**Alternative spellings:** Flaura, Florah

## Florence

**Meaning:** Blossoming
**Origin:** Latin
**Pronunciation:** FLOR ence
**Description:** Florence derives from the Latin male name Florentius.
**Alternative spellings:** Florense, Florenze

## Florentina

**Meaning:** Blooming
**Origin:** Latin
**Pronunciation:** floor EN teen uh
**Description:** Florentina is a Latin name meaning 'blooming'. The Latin root 'flora' means that this name has a strong connotation with flowers and plants.

## Florrie

**Meaning:** Blossoming
**Origin:** Latin
**Pronunciation:** FLOH ree
**Description:** Florrie came about as a pet form of the name Florence, but is now found used as a name in its own right.
**Alternative spellings:** Flori, Florri, Florry

## Flynn

See entry in 'Names for Baby Boys A–Z'

## Fran

**Meaning:** From France
**Origin:** English
**Pronunciation:** FRAN
**Description:** Fran is a short form of names such as Francesca, Francis or Frances. It is sometimes used as a name in its own right.
**Alternative spellings:** Franne

## Frances

**Meaning:** From France
**Origin:** Italian
**Pronunciation:** FRAN sis
**Description:** The feminine equivalent of Francis, an Italian nickname for a man from France.
**Alternative spellings:** Francessc

## Francesca

**Meaning:** From France
**Origin:** Italian
**Pronunciation:** fran CHESS cuh
**Description:** The Italian form of Frances, Francesca originally existed as a word for 'French' and still carries its meaning of 'from France'.
**Alternative spellings:** Franceska, Franchesca

## Francine

**Meaning:** From France
**Origin:** French
**Pronunciation:** fran SEEN
**Description:** Francine is the feminine version of Francis and as such, shares the same meaning of 'from France'.

## Frankie

**Meaning:** Liberated person from France
**Origin:** French
**Pronunciation:** FRAN kee
**Description:** Frankie is a unisex name that means 'he who is free' if taken from the French name Frank, or 'person from France' if taken from the Latin name Francis.
**Alternative spellings:** Franckie, Franki, Franky

## Freida

**Meaning:** Peace
**Origin:** German
**Pronunciation:** FREE dah
**Description:** Freida is a name of German origin and is a shortened variant of Alfreda. It was common in the early 20th century but has since declined in popularity.
**Alternative spellings:** Freda, Frida

## Frenchy

**Meaning:** Nickname
**Origin:** English
**Pronunciation:** fren CHEE
**Description:** Frenchy is a possible nickname for Francine or Francesca, but could stand as a given name on its own. Frenchy is a character from the popular movie, *Grease*.
**Alternative spellings:** Frenchie

## Freya

**Meaning:** Goddess of love
**Origin:** Scandinavian
**Pronunciation:** FRAY yuh
**Description:** Freya was the goddess of love in Scandinavian mythology, whose name was derived from the Germanic word *'frouwa'*, meaning 'lady'.
**Alternative spellings:** Freja, Freyja

## Fujiko

**Meaning:** Wisteria child
**Origin:** Japanese
**Pronunciation:** foo JEE ko
**Description:** This popular Japanese girls' name is made up of the element *'fuji'*, which means 'wisteria', and *'ko'*, which means 'child'.
**Alternative spellings:** Fujeko, Fujico

## Fumiko

**Meaning:** Strong beautiful child
**Origin:** Japanese
**Pronunciation:** foo MEE ko
**Description:** This Japanese girls' name may mean 'child of treasured body' or 'child of abundant beauty'. Parents hope a child with this name will grow to be a strong successful woman.
**Alternative spellings:** Fumeko, Fumico

# G

## Gabriella

**Meaning:** Strength from God
**Origin:** Hebrew
**Pronunciation:** GAB ree EL la
**Description:** Gabriella is an elaboration upon the girls' name Gabrielle, derived from the archangel Gabriel in Christian belief.
**Alternative spellings:** Gabriela

## Gabrielle

**Meaning:** Strength in God
**Origin:** Hebrew
**Pronunciation:** GAB ree ELL
**Description:** Gabrielle is the feminine equivalent of the biblical name Gabriel and means 'strength in God'.
**Alternative spellings:** Gabriele

## Gaby

**Meaning:** Strength from God
**Origin:** French
**Pronunciation:** gah BEE
**Description:** Gaby is a French feminine version of the name Gabriel and as such, shares the same meaning of 'strength from God'.
**Alternative spellings:** Gabby

## Gaia

**Meaning:** Earth mother
**Origin:** Greek
**Pronunciation:** GAY a; GUY a
**Description:** In Greek mythology, Gaia was the goddess of Earth and the great mother of all.
**Alternative spellings:** Gaiaa, Gaiya, Gaya

## Gail

**Meaning:** Father of exaltation
**Origin:** Hebrew
**Pronunciation:** GAYL
**Description:** Gail is a girls' name of Hebrew origin and a shortened variant of Abigail.

**Alternative spellings:** Gael, Gale

## Gemma
**Meaning:** Precious stone
**Origin:** Italian
**Pronunciation:** JEM ma
**Description:** The popular name Gemma comes from an Italian nickname for 'gem', a 'precious stone'.
**Alternative spellings:** Jemma

## Gene
See entry in 'Names for Baby Boys A–Z'

## Genesis
**Meaning:** Birth
**Origin:** Greek
**Pronunciation:** jeh EH sis
**Description:** Genesis is a Greek name meaning 'birth'. It is also one of the most famous books in the Old Testament in the Bible, which tells of the creation of the world and Adam and Eve. Because it is the name of the creation story, the meaning of 'birth' is very appropriate.

## Genevieve
**Meaning:** Woman
**Origin:** German
**Pronunciation:** JEN eh veev
**Description:** Genevieve is a French name of Old German origin. It comes from the words *'geno'* meaning 'people', and *'wefa'* meaning 'woman'. Genevieve is the name of the patron saint of Paris.
**Alternative spellings:** Geneveve, Genevive

## Georgette
**Meaning:** Farmer; earth worker

**Origin:** French
**Pronunciation:** jorge ETTE
**Description:** Georgette is the female version of the name George, and as such shares the same meaning of 'farmer' or 'earth worker'.

## Georgia
**Meaning:** Farmer
**Origin:** Greek
**Pronunciation:** JAW yuh
**Description:** This feminine form of George was borne by a 5th-century saint. Georgia is a country on the east coast of the Black Sea and a US state.
**Alternative spellings:** Georgea, Jorgia, Jorja

## Georgiana
**Meaning:** Farmer
**Origin:** Greek
**Pronunciation:** jor jee AHN ah
**Description:** Georgiana is a feminine version of the Greek name George. Georgiana was popular in the 18th century but now the preferred feminine version is Georgina.
**Alternative spellings:** Georgeana, Jorgiana

## Georgie
See entry in 'Names for Baby Boys A–Z'

## Georgina
**Meaning:** Farmer
**Origin:** Greek
**Pronunciation:** jor JEE na
**Description:** First rising to popularity in Scotland in the 18th century, the name Georgina is the feminine version of the Greek name George, meaning 'farmer'.
**Alternative spellings:** Georgena, Jorgina

347

## Geraldine

**Meaning:** Spear ruler
**Origin:** French
**Pronunciation:** geral DEEN
**Description:** Geraldine is the French and feminine version of the name Gerald and as such, they share the same meaning of 'spear ruler'.

## Gertrude

**Meaning:** Spear strength
**Origin:** German
**Pronunciation:** gert RUDE
**Description:** Gertrude is a German name composed of the elements of '*ger*' meaning 'spear' and '*thrud*' meaning 'strength'.
**Alternative spellings:**

## Gia

**Meaning:** God is gracious
**Origin:** Italian
**Pronunciation:** GEE ah
**Description:** Gia is a pet form of the name Gianna, which itself is a shortened version of the Italian name Giovanna. Gia is now given as a first name in its own right.
**Alternative spellings:** Giah, Jia

## Gigi

**Meaning:** Farmer; earth worker
**Origin:** French
**Pronunciation:** gee gee
**Description:** Gigi is most likely a French diminutive of Georgine, which in turn is the female version of George, meaning 'farmer' or 'earth worker'.

## Gian

See entry in 'Names for Baby Boys A–Z'

## Gianna

**Meaning:** God is gracious
**Origin:** Italian
**Pronunciation:** gee AR na
**Description:** Gianna is a short form of the Italian name Giovanna, the feminine version of Giovanni. The name is popular in Italy and America.
**Alternative spellings:** Geanna, Jianna

## Gilly

**Meaning:** Gillyflower
**Origin:** English
**Pronunciation:** jil EE
**Description:** Gilly was invented for the *Game of Thrones* series, and is named after the gillyflower. She is one of the many daughters of Craster in the story.

## Gina

**Meaning:** Queen; farmer
**Origin:** Italian
**Pronunciation:** JEE na
**Description:** Gina came about as a pet form of the names Regina and Georgina. Regina is an Italian name that means 'queen', while Georgina, like George, means 'farmer'.
**Alternative spellings:** Gena, Jeana

## Ginny

**Meaning:** Of the virgin
**Origin:** Latin
**Pronunciation:** jin EE
**Description:** Ginny is a Latin name meaning 'of the virgin'. Ginny Weasley is a well known character in the Harry Potter series.
**Alternative spellings:** Jinny

## Giovanna

**Meaning:** God is gracious

**Origin:** Italian
**Pronunciation:** GEE oh VAR na
**Description:** Giovanna is the feminine form of the Italian name Giovanni, itself derived from the name John. Giovanna, Giovanni, Gianna and Gio all share the same meaning as the name John, which is 'God is gracious'
**Alternative spellings:** Giovana, Giovannah

## Giselle

**Meaning:** Promised
**Origin:** German
**Pronunciation:** ji ZEL
**Description:** Giselle is of Old German origin, said to mean 'one who was promised'. The spelling Gisele is very popular in France.
**Alternative spellings:** Gisele, Gisell

## Giulia

**Meaning:** Youth
**Origin:** Italian
**Pronunciation:** JOO le ah
**Description:** Guilia is an Italian girls' name. The anglicised version is Julia.
**Alternative spellings:** Jiulia, Julia

## Giuliana

**Meaning:** Youthful; graceful
**Origin:** Italian
**Pronunciation:** giu LEE ana
**Description:** Giuliana is an Italian name derived from the Latin word '*iuliana*' meaning 'youthful' or 'graceful'. Many argue that it is a combination of Julia and Anna.

## Gladys

**Meaning:** Country
**Origin:** Welsh
**Pronunciation:** GLAD iss

**Description:** Gladys is a Welsh girls' name of many possible origins. It could come from the Old Welsh name 'gwladus', which means 'country' or 'nation'. There are also suggestions that the name could stem from '*gwledig*' meaning 'ruler', or even that it might be a Welsh version of Claudia.
**Alternative spellings:** Gladis, Gladiss, Gladyss

## Gloria

**Meaning:** Glory
**Origin:** Latin
**Pronunciation:** GLOR ee ah
**Description:** The name Gloria derives directly from the Latin word for 'glory'.
**Alternative spellings:** Gloriah, Gloriya

## Glory

**Meaning:** High honour
**Origin:** English
**Pronunciation:** gloor EE
**Description:** Glory comes from the English vocabulary word of the same spelling and means 'high honour'.

## Goda

**Meaning:** River Godavari
**Origin:** Sanskrit
**Pronunciation:** GOH da
**Description:** Goda is a very rare and unusual name of uncertain meaning. It seems to have Sanskrit origins and is thought to come from the name of the River Godavari in India.
**Alternative spellings:** Godah

## Grace

**Meaning:** Elegance
**Origin:** Latin

**Pronunciation:** GRAYSE
**Description:** The name Grace, meaning 'elegance', came to prominence in the 1540s and was particularly popular in Scotland and northern England.
**Alternative spellings:** Grayce

## Gracie

**Meaning:** Elegance
**Origin:** Latin
**Pronunciation:** GRAY see
**Description:** Gracie came about as a pet form of the name Grace. It is now a name in its own right and is sometimes given to boys.
**Alternative spellings:** Gracey, Graci

## Greta

**Meaning:** Pearl; light's creation
**Origin:** Latin
**Pronunciation:** GREH ta
**Description:** Greta, an abbreviated form of Margaret, originates from Sweden and means 'light's creation'.
**Alternative spellings:** Gretah, Gretta

## Gretel

**Meaning:** Pearl
**Origin:** German
**Pronunciation:** gret EL
**Description:** Gretel is a diminuitive of Grete, which in turn is the short form of Margaret, meaning 'pearl'. Gretel is one half of Hansel and Gretel, from the famous Brothers Grimm fairytale of a witch trying to eat the siblings.

## Gurleen

**Meaning:** Absorbed in the guru's readings
**Origin:** Sanskrit

**Pronunciation:** GOOR leen
**Description:** Gurleen is a name of Punjabi origin, and it means 'absorbed in the guru's readings'. It is often found in India where it is used mostly by Hindu parents.
**Alternative spellings:** Gerleen, Gurline

## Guadalupe

**Meaning:** From the Guadalupe River
**Origin:** Spanish
**Pronunciation:** GUA de loop eh
**Description:** Guadalupe is a Spanish place name referring to the town that was near the source of the Guadalupe River, which is a pilgrimage site due to the apparition of Our Lady of Guadelupe.

## Gwen

**Meaning:** Fair-haired
**Origin:** Welsh
**Pronunciation:** GWEN
**Description:** Gwen is both an independent name and the shortened form of the names Gwendolen and Gwyneth.
**Alternative spellings:** Gwenn, Gwyn

## Gwendolen

**Meaning:** Fair-haired; white ring
**Origin:** Welsh
**Pronunciation:** GWEN do len
**Description:** Gwendolen was the wife of the mythical Welsh king, Locrine. It is made up of *'gwen'*, meaning 'fair' and *'dolen',* a word for 'eyebrows'.
**Alternative spellings:** Gwendolyn, Gwyndolen

## Gwyneth

**Meaning:** Fair-haired
**Origin:** Welsh
**Pronunciation:** GWIN eth
**Description:** Gwyneth comes from the Welsh name Gwynned, which is derived from the place in North Wales.
**Alternative spellings:** Gweneth, Gwenyth

## Gypsy

**Meaning:** Wanderer
**Origin:** English
**Pronunciation:** gyp SEE
**Description:** Gypsy is derived from the English vocabulary word of the same spelling and means 'wanderer'.

# H

## Haaniya

**Meaning:** Happy; delighted; content
**Origin:** Indian
**Pronunciation:** haa NEE ya
**Description:** Haaniya is an Indian girls' name meaning 'happy,' 'delighted' or 'content'.
**Alternative spellings:** Hanniyah, Haniya, Haniyah

## Habiba

**Meaning:** Beloved one
**Origin:** Arabic
**Pronunciation:** hah BEE bah
**Description:** Habiba is a name of Arabic origin and means 'beloved one'. It is a popular name with parents of Pakistani descent and those following the Islamic religion.
**Alternative spellings:** Habbiba, Habibah

## Hadassah

**Meaning:** Myrtle tree
**Origin:** Hebrew
**Pronunciation:** had AH saah
**Description:** Hadassah is a Hebrew name meaning 'myrtle tree' and was the name of Queen Esther in the Old Testament. The myrtle tree is one of four types of tree that forms the *lulav*, a bouquet made up of palm fronds, willow, citron and myrtle tree branches for the Jewish holiday of Sukkot.
**Alternative spellings:** Hadassa

## Hadia

**Meaning:** Religious guide
**Origin:** Urdu
**Pronunciation:** HAH de ah
**Description:** Hadia is a name of Urdu origin, most commonly found in Pakistan and in Muslim communities across the world. Its meaning refers to a 'guide on the path of righteousness'.
**Alternative spellings:** Hadiah, Hadya

## Hadiya

**Meaning:** Religious guide
**Origin:** Arabic
**Pronunciation:** HAH dee yah
**Description:** Hadiya is the feminine version of the masculine name Hadi,

which is said to come from the Arabic for 'true direction of religion'.
**Alternative spellings:** Hadija, Hadiyah

## Hadley
**Meaning:** Heather meadow
**Origin:** English
**Pronunciation:** HAD ley
**Description:** Hadley is an uncommon given name but a popular surname. It is of Old English origin meaning 'heather meadow'. It is also a unisex name.

## Hafsa
**Meaning:** Lioness
**Origin:** Arabic
**Pronunciation:** HAHF sa
**Description:** Hafsa means 'lioness'. It is the name of one of the wives of the prophet Muhammad who looked after the Quran after Muhammad's death. Hafsa is a popular girls' name within Muslim communities.
**Alternative spellings:** Hafsah, Hafza

## Hajar
**Meaning:** Emigrant
**Origin:** Arabic
**Pronunciation:** hhaa JHAA r
**Description:** Hajar is a feminine Arabic name meaning 'emigrant'. It also has Hebrew roots and can also mean 'flight'.

## Hajra
**Meaning:** Promise of pilgrimage
**Origin:** Arabic
**Pronunciation:** HIJ rah
**Description:** Hajra is a name that comes from 'Hajj', the name of the annual pilgrimage to Mecca made by Muslims. The name signifies a promise of pilgrimage to the newborn.
**Alternative spellings:** Hajrah

## Halia
**Meaning:** Island nymph
**Origin:** Greek
**Pronunciation:** HAY lee ah
**Description:** In Greek mythology, the nymph Halia lived alone on the island that would later be named Rhodes.
**Alternative spellings:** Haliah, Hallia

## Halima
**Meaning:** Gentle-mannered
**Origin:** Arabic
**Pronunciation:** ha LEE mah
**Description:** This Arabic name has some of its roots in the Swahili language and means 'gentle' or 'mild mannered'. It is often shortened to pet forms such as Halma or Hallie.
**Alternative spellings:** Haleema, Haleemah, Halimah

## Hallie
**Meaning:** Ruler of the home
**Origin:** English
**Pronunciation:** HAL lee
**Description:** The name Hallie has Norwegian and German roots, whereas Hayley is of Old English origin.
**Alternative spellings:** Halle, Halli, Hallie, Hally

## Halo
**Meaning:** Circular aura of light
**Origin:** English
**Pronunciation:** Halo comes from the English vocabulary word of the same spelling and refers to the

circle of light often seen on depictions of angels.
**Description:** hay LOH

## Hamna
**Meaning:** Dark-coloured berry
**Origin:** Arabic
**Pronunciation:** HAM na
**Description:** Hamna comes from an Arabic word for a 'dark-coloured berry'. In Islamic belief it was the name of the sister of one of the wives of the prophet Muhammad.
**Alternative spellings:** Hamnah

## Hana
**Meaning:** Blissful
**Origin:** Arabic
**Pronunciation:** HA nah
**Description:** Hana is a name of Arabic origin and its meaning is said to be 'blissful'. It could also be considered a respelling of the popular name Hannah.
**Alternative spellings:** Hanna, Hannah

## Hanan
**Meaning:** Tenderness
**Origin:** Arabic
**Pronunciation:** hah NAN
**Description:** Hanan is a feminine Arabic name with roots meaning 'tenderness'. Other variations of the name include Haneen, Hanin and even the Hebrew name, Hannah, which has a very similar meaning.

## Hania
**Meaning:** Favoured by God; grace; blissful
**Origin:** Hebrew
**Pronunciation:** HAH nee ah
**Description:** Hania is a name that comes from the Middle East and can be found in Hebrew and Arabic languages. It could be from the same origin as the names Anna and Hannah.
**Alternative spellings:** Haniah, Haniya

## Hanifa
**Meaning:** Upholder of Islam
**Origin:** Arabic
**Pronunciation:** hah NEE fah
**Description:** The name Hanifa is the feminine form of the masculine Hanif and is popular with Muslim parents.
**Alternative spellings:** Hanifah, Hanifer

## Hannah
**Meaning:** Favoured by God
**Origin:** Hebrew
**Pronunciation:** HAN nuh
**Description:** A biblical name borne by the mother of the prophet Samuel, from the Hebrew name Hanna. Hannah enjoyed a huge revival in the 1990s.
**Alternative spellings:** Hana, Hanna

## Hari
See entry in 'Names for Baby Boys A–Z'

## Harleen
**Meaning:** Hare and eagle
**Origin:** English
**Pronunciation:** HAR leen
**Description:** Harleen is a feminine variation of the now unisex name Harley. Harleen also shares Harley's meaning of 'hare and eagle'.
**Alternative spellings:** Harlene, Harline

H

## Harley
See entry in 'Names for Baby Boys A–Z'

## Harlow
See entry in 'Names for Baby Boys A–Z'

## Harmonia
**Meaning:** Harmony
**Origin:** Greek
**Pronunciation:** har MOAN ee a
**Description:** In Greek mythology, Harmonia was the immortal goddess of harmony and concord.
**Alternative spellings:** Harmoniai, Harmoniya

## Harmony
**Meaning:** Pleasing musical sound
**Origin:** English
**Pronunciation:** HAR moh nee
**Description:** The name Harmony has been adapted from the English word. Like the name Melody, it is often used by parents who are fans of music.
**Alternative spellings:** Harmoney, Harmoni, Harmonie

## Harper
**Meaning:** Harp-player
**Origin:** English
**Pronunciation:** HAR per
**Description:** Harper was originally a surname used by those who had a history of playing the harp. It is now used as a unisex given name and was made famous in 2011 when David and Victoria Beckham named their first daughter Harper Seven Beckham.
**Alternative spellings:** Harpah, Harpor

## Harriet
**Meaning:** Ruler of the home
**Origin:** German
**Pronunciation:** HA ri et
**Description:** Harriet is an anglicised version of the French name Henriette, the feminine form of Henry. It first appeared in the 17th century then rose in popularity over the next 200 years.
**Alternative spellings:** Hariet, Harriett, Harriette

## Hasna
**Meaning:** Beautiful one
**Origin:** Arabic
**Pronunciation:** HAS nah
**Description:** Hasna is a name of uncertain meaning but it is generally considered to mean 'beautiful one' or 'strong'.
**Alternative spellings:** Hasnah, Hazna

## Hattie
**Meaning:** Ruler of the home
**Origin:** German
**Pronunciation:** HAT ee
**Description:** This pet form of Harriet is now a name in its own right.
**Alternative spellings:** Hatti, Hatty

## Havana
**Meaning:** Capital of Cuba
**Origin:** Spanish
**Pronunciation:** hah VAH nah
**Description:** Havana is the capital city of Cuba, but is also a very popular modern name that is common in Spanish-speaking countries.
**Alternative spellings:** Havanah

## Haven
**Meaning:** Place of safety; shelter

**Origin:** English
**Pronunciation:** HAY ven
**Description:** Haven is directly taken from the English vocabulary word meaning 'place of safety' or 'shelter'. While its literal meaning is a safe place for ships to dock, it has come to take on a general meaning of refuge.

## Hawwa
**Meaning:** Full of life
**Origin:** Arabic
**Pronunciation:** HA wah
**Description:** Like Hawa, Hawwa is the Arabic equivalent to the name Eve, the first woman created by Allah and predominantly used by Muslim parents.
**Alternative spellings:** Hawa, Hawwah

## Haya
**Meaning:** Full of life
**Origin:** Hebrew
**Pronunciation:** HAH yah
**Description:** Haya is a variation of the Hebrew name Chava, which means 'full of life'. The name has long been used in the Middle East but is now spreading into other parts of the world.
**Alternative spellings:** Hayah, Hayar

## Hayden
See entry in 'Names for Baby Boys A–Z'

## Hayley
**Meaning:** Clearing of hay
**Origin:** English
**Pronunciation:** HAY lee
**Description:** The name Hayley comes from the surname adopted by those from Hailey in Oxfordshire. It is also a more modern spelling of the Old English name Hayleigh, which comes from the elements of *'hay'* and *'leigh'*, meaning 'a clearing of land'.
**Alternative spellings:** Hailey, Haylee, Hayleigh, Hayli, Haylie, Hailie

## Hazel
**Meaning:** Hazel tree; light brown
**Origin:** English
**Pronunciation:** HAY zell
**Description:** Hazel, a nut-bearing tree, is also a colour commonly used to describe light-brown eyes.
**Alternative spellings:** Hazelle, Hazile

## Heath
See entry in 'Names for Baby Boys A–Z'

## Heather
**Meaning:** Heather
**Origin:** English
**Pronunciation:** HEH ther
**Description:** The name Heather comes from the moorland plant.
**Alternative spellings:** Heatha, Hether

## Heba
**Meaning:** Gift
**Origin:** Arabic
**Pronunciation:** HE ba
**Description:** From an Arabic word meaning 'gift', Heba is mainly used by Muslim parents and is popular in Africa and the Middle East. It could also be a variation of the Greek name Hebe.
**Alternative spellings:** Heaba, Hebah

H

## Hebe

**Meaning:** Youthful
**Origin:** Greek
**Pronunciation:** HEE bee
**Description:** In Greek myth, Hebe was the name of the goddess of youth. The name could also come from New Zealand, where Hebe is a native plant.
**Alternative spellings:** Heaby, Hebi, Hebie

## Hecate

**Meaning:** Triple-formed
**Origin:** Greek
**Pronunciation:** HEK a tee
**Description:** In Greek mythology, Hecate was an ancient goddess of dark places, often associated with ghosts, witches and sorcery.
**Alternative spellings:** Hecatee, Hekate

## Hecuba

**Meaning:** Worker
**Origin:** Greek
**Pronunciation:** HEK yoo bah
**Description:** In Greek mythology, Hecuba was married to King Priam of Troy, with whom she had 19 children.
**Alternative spellings:** Hecabe, Hecueba, Hekuba

## Heidi

**Meaning:** Noble
**Origin:** German
**Pronunciation:** HI dee
**Description:** Heidi is a Swiss pet form of Adelheid, the German form of Adelaide.
**Alternative spellings:** Heidie, Heidy

## Helen

**Meaning:** Bright
**Origin:** Greek
**Pronunciation:** HEL en
**Description:** The mythical Helen of Troy was known as 'the face which launched a thousand ships'. The name has associations of extreme beauty.
**Alternative spellings:** Hellen

## Helena

**Meaning:** Bright
**Origin:** Greek
**Pronunciation:** HEL eh nuh; hel AY nah
**Description:** A Latinate form of Helen. Helena carries the same associations of beauty as the name Helen.
**Alternative spellings:** Helenah, Helene

## Helice

**Meaning:** She-bear
**Origin:** Greek
**Pronunciation:** HEL ee see
**Description:** In Greek mythology, Helice was beloved by Zeus, but Hera, out of jealousy, metamorphosed her into a she-bear, whereupon Zeus placed her among the stars.
**Alternative spellings:** Helise, Helyce

## Hemera

**Meaning:** Day
**Origin:** Greek
**Pronunciation:** he MEE ra
**Description:** In Greek mythology, Hemera was one of the earliest Greek deities and the personification and goddess of daytime.
**Alternative spellings:** Hemerah, Hemira

## Henley

See entry in 'Names for Baby Boys A–Z'

## Hennessy

**Meaning:** Choice
**Origin:** Irish
**Pronunciation:** hen ESS ee
**Description:** Hennessy is a surname meaning derived from the Irish word '*aonghus*' meaning 'choice.' This follows the contemporary trend of using last names as first names.

## Henrietta

**Meaning:** Ruler of the home
**Origin:** German
**Pronunciation:** hen ree EH tah
**Description:** Henrietta, the feminine equivalent of Henry, was made popular in 17th-century England when Charles I married Henrietta Marie.
**Alternative spellings:** Henriette, Henryetta

## Hera

**Meaning:** Lady
**Origin:** Greek
**Pronunciation:** HEH rah
**Description:** In Greek mythology, Hera was the queen of the ancient Greek pantheon. She was the wife of Zeus and the goddess of marriage, childbirth and the home.
**Alternative spellings:** Heera, Herah

## Hermione

**Meaning:** Travel
**Origin:** Greek
**Pronunciation:** her MY o nee
**Description:** In Greek mythology, Hermione was the daughter of Helen of Troy and Menelaus, King of Sparta.
**Alternative spellings:** Hermioney, Hermioni

## Hero

**Meaning:** Courage
**Origin:** Greek
**Pronunciation:** HERE row
**Description:** In Greek mythology, Hero was a priestess of Aphrodite. In modern English, a hero is a man admired for his courage or noble qualities. Heroine is the female equivalent.
**Alternative spellings:** Hiro

## Hester

**Meaning:** Star
**Origin:** English
**Pronunciation:** hes TAR
**Description:** Hester is the Latin form of the biblical name, Esther. It is a name most commonly found in England but it was also popularised by Nathaniel Hawthorne's book, *The Scarlet Letter*, where the protagonist was called Hester Prynne.

## Hestia

**Meaning:** Home
**Origin:** Greek
**Pronunciation:** HESS tee ah
**Description:** In Greek mythology, Hestia was the virgin goddess of the hearth, the family and the state.
**Alternative spellings:** Hestiaa, Hestya

## Hetty

**Meaning:** Star
**Origin:** Greek
**Pronunciation:** HEH tee
**Description:** Hetty came about as a pet form of the name Hester, but

H

is now used as a name in its own right. Hester is Greek in origin and means 'star'.
**Alternative spellings:** Hetti, Hettie

# Hiba
**Meaning:** Gift
**Origin:** Arabic
**Pronunciation:** HIB ah
**Description:** Hiba is a name of Arabic origin and comes from an Arabic word meaning 'to give' or 'gift'. It is very important in Islamic belief to give charitably and it is from this that the name Hiba has come about.
**Alternative spellings:** Hibah, Hibba

# Hilary
**Meaning:** Cheerful
**Origin:** Latin
**Pronunciation:** HIL uh ree
**Description:** Hilary is from the Latin word *'hilaris'*, which shares the same root as 'hilarious'.
**Alternative spellings:** Hilari, Hilarie, Hillary

# Hilda
**Meaning:** Battle
**Origin:** German
**Pronunciation:** HILL da
**Description:** Hilda is a German girls' name, from the element of *'hild'* meaning 'battle'.
**Alternative spellings:** Hildah

# Himeko
**Meaning:** Princess child
**Origin:** Japanese
**Pronunciation:** HEE meh ko
**Description:** This baby name can be written using a variety of Japanese character combinations. Depending on the characters used it can either mean 'princess child'

or 'sun and rice child'.
**Alternative spellings:** Himekoh

# Hippodamia
**Meaning:** Ladybird
**Origin:** Greek
**Pronunciation:** hee po DAY mee ah
**Description:** In Greek mythology, Hippodamia was the bride of King Pirithous of the Lapiths. It is also the scientific name given to the ladybird.
**Alternative spellings:** Hippodaymia, Hippodaymya

# Hippolyta
**Meaning:** Loosener of horses
**Origin:** Greek
**Pronunciation:** he POL it ah
**Description:** In Greek mythology, Hippolyta was an Amazonian queen who possessed a magical girdle. The male version of the name is Hippolytus.
**Alternative spellings:** Hippolita

# Hira
**Meaning:** Diamond
**Origin:** Sanskrit
**Pronunciation:** HIH rah
**Description:** The name Hira can be unisex, although using different pronunciations. The masculine form is pronounced 'hih-rar' whereas the feminine form is pronounced 'hih-ra'. The name comes from an old Sanskrit word said to mean 'diamond'.
**Alternative spellings:** Hirah, Hirra

# Hiromi
See entry in 'Names for Baby Boys A–Z'

## Holly

**Meaning:** Holly
**Origin:** English
**Pronunciation:** HOLL lee
**Description:** The name Holly comes from the word for the evergreen tree. It was traditionally given to girls born around Christmas.
**Alternative spellings:** Holley, Holli, Hollie

## Honey

**Meaning:** Honey
**Origin:** English
**Pronunciation:** HUN ee
**Description:** The name Honey comes from the word for the sweet substance produced by bees. It is also a term of affection but a rare given name.
**Alternative spellings:** Hunnie, Hunny

## Honor

**Meaning:** Honour
**Origin:** Latin
**Pronunciation:** Hon Or
**Description:** Honor derives from the Latin name Honoria, which also means 'honour'. The name could be considered a variant of the English word for 'personal integrity' or 'fame and glory'.
**Alternative spellings:** Honour

## Hope

**Meaning:** Hope
**Origin:** English
**Pronunciation:** HOPE
**Description:** From the word meaning 'a feeling of desire or expectation for a certain thing to happen.' Hope is considered one of the 'quality names' like Charity and Faith and is often favoured by Christian parents.

## Huda

**Meaning:** Guidance
**Origin:** Arabic
**Pronunciation:** HOO dah
**Description:** Huda, popular among Muslim parents, means 'guidance'
**Alternative spellings:** Hudah, Hudda

## Humaira

**Meaning:** Reddish colour
**Origin:** Arabic
**Pronunciation:** hugh MARE ah
**Description:** The name Humaira means 'reddish colour' in Arabic. In Islamic belief it was the nickname that the prophet Muhammad gave to his wife Aisha due to her rosy red cheeks.
**Alternative spellings:** Humairah, Humera

## Husna

**Meaning:** Kindness
**Origin:** Arabic
**Pronunciation:** HOOS nah
**Description:** Husna means 'kindness' and is a popular name in Pakistan.
**Alternative spellings:** Husnah

## Hyacinth

**Meaning:** Flower
**Origin:** English
**Pronunciation:** high AH synth
**Description:** Hyacinth refers to the flower of the same name and is found throughout the world. Like Rose and Tulip, Hyacinth is part of the trend of using Flowers for given names.

H

# I

## Ianthe
**Meaning:** Violet flower
**Origin:** Greek
**Pronunciation:** eye AN theh
**Description:** From the Greek words *'ion'* and *'anthos'*, meaning 'violet' and 'flower' respectively.
**Alternative spellings:** Ianthie

## Ida
**Meaning:** Hard-working
**Origin:** German
**Pronunciation:** EYE dah
**Description:** The name Ida was brought to Britain by the Normans and was made popular in the 19th century by Lord Alfred Tennyson. It can mean both 'hard-working' and 'princess'.
**Alternative spellings:** Idah, Iyda

## Iga
**Meaning:** Fight
**Origin:** German
**Pronunciation:** EE gah
**Description:** The name Iga originally came about as a pet form of the name Jadwiga, which is itself the Polish variant of the German name Hedwig. Hedwig means 'battle fight' and Iga also shares this meaning.
**Alternative spellings:** Igah, Iyga

## Ikram
See entry in 'Names for Baby Boys A–Z'

## Imaan
**Meaning:** Faith
**Origin:** Arabic
**Pronunciation:** im MAAN
**Description:** Imaan is the feminine version of the name Iman. It comes directly from the Arabic word *'iman'*, which means 'faith' and 'believer'.
**Alternative spellings:** Imarn

## Iman
See entry in 'Names for Baby Boys A–Z'

## Imani
**Meaning:** Faith; dependable
**Origin:** Arabic
**Pronunciation:** ee MAH nee
**Description:** Imani can be seen as the feminine version of the Arabic name Iman, meaning 'faith', or a diminutive form of the name Amina, meaning 'dependable'.
**Alternative spellings:** Imanie

## Imogen
**Meaning:** Maiden
**Origin:** Shakespeare
**Pronunciation:** IHM oh jen
**Description:** This name derives from the Celtic name Innogen, meaning 'maiden'. Imogen features in Shakespeare's play *Cymbeline* where it is the name of a strong heroine.
**Alternative spellings:** Imojen

## Inaaya
**Meaning:** Gift from God
**Origin:** Arabic
**Pronunciation:** ihn AH yah
**Description:** Inaaya is a name of Arabic origin, believed to mean 'gift from God' or 'one to behold'. Of the spelling variations, some

have separate meanings. The short form is Inny or Immy.
**Alternative spellings:** Inaiya, Inaya, Inayah, Inyaih

## Inaya
**Meaning:** Empathy
**Origin:** Arabic
**Pronunciation:** in NY yah
**Description:** Inaya is another spelling variation of the Arabic name Inaaya; however its meaning of 'empathy' is different to Inaaya, which is 'gift from God'.
**Alternative spellings:** Inaaya, Inaiya, Inayah, Inyaih

## India
**Meaning:** India
**Origin:** English
**Pronunciation:** IN dee uh
**Description:** India is a relatively modern name, taken from the name of the Asian country.
**Alternative spellings:** Indiya, Indya

## Indiana
**Meaning:** India
**Origin:** English
**Pronunciation:** in dee AHR nah; in dee ANN ah
**Description:** Indiana is an elaboration on the feminine name India. However, Indiana Jones is the name of the fictional male character from the Indiana Jones franchise.
**Alternative spellings:** Indianah, Indyana

## Indie
**Meaning:** India; blue; independent
**Origin:** English
**Pronunciation:** IN dee

**Description:** Indie seems to have come about as a pet form of the names India and Indigo and its meaning can therefore vary. The name can either mean 'blue' or 'from India'. The word 'indie' is often used in English as a shortened form of the word 'independent'.
**Alternative spellings:** Indi, Indy

## Indigo
**Meaning:** Indian plant
**Origin:** English
**Pronunciation:** IN dih go
**Description:** Indigo, like India, became popular in the 1970s when Indian culture was fashionable and it is the name of an Indian plant. Recently, Indigo has surged in popularity along with other colour names such as Blue and Violet.
**Alternative spellings:** Indygo

## Indira
**Meaning:** Beauty
**Origin:** Sanskrit
**Pronunciation:** In DEER ah
**Description:** A name of Hindu and Sanskrit origin, Indira means 'beauty' or 'splendid'. The name became well known in the 1970s and 80s when Indira Gandhi was India's first female Prime Minister.
**Alternative spellings:** Indeera

## Ines
**Meaning:** Pure
**Origin:** Greek
**Pronunciation:** EE ness
**Description:** Ines is a variant of the name Agnes, which is Greek in origin and means 'pure'. The form Ines is the Spanish version of the name. It is popular in

I

Spanish-speaking countries, especially Mexico.
**Alternative spellings:** Inez

## Ingrid
**Meaning:** Beauty
**Origin:** Norse
**Pronunciation:** IN grid
**Description:** The name Ingrid
comes from the Norse element of
*'ing'* meaning 'beauty'. Ing was
also the name of a Norse god of
fertility. The name is mostly popu-
lar in Scandinavia.
**Alternative spellings:** Engrid,
Ingryd

## Ino
**Meaning:** White goddess
**Origin:** Greek
**Pronunciation:** EYE no
**Description:** In Greek mythology,
Ino was a mortal queen of Thebes
who, after her death, was wor-
shipped as a goddess.
**Alternative spellings:** Eyno, Iyno

## Io
**Meaning:** Heifer
**Origin:** Greek
**Pronunciation:** EYE oh
**Description:** In Greek mythology,
Io was a young maiden who was
loved by Zeus. She was turned into
a heifer – a young female cow – by
Zeus to protect her from Hera.
**Alternative spellings:** Eyo

## Ioana
**Meaning:** God is gracious
**Origin:** Greek
**Pronunciation:** ee OH ah nah
**Description:** Ioana is a variation
of the name Ioanna, which in
turn is a Greek variation of the

name Joanna. The name ultimately
means 'God is gracious,' as the
name has its roots in the biblical
name John. Related names include
the Bulgarian Yoana, as well as the
variant spellings of Joanna.

## Iole
**Meaning:** Violet
**Origin:** Greek
**Pronunciation:** EYE oh lee
**Description:** Iole is an uncom-
mon girls' name of Greek origin.
The name is the transliteration
of the classic Greek word for a
violet.
**Alternative spellings:** Eyole

## Iona
**Meaning:** Island
**Origin:** Norse
**Pronunciation:** Eye Own Ah
**Description:** The name Iona comes
from the Scottish island Ioua,
named as the 'dew-tree island'. It
could also derive from the English
name Ione, which means 'violet'.
**Alternative spellings:** Ionah

## Iqra
**Meaning:** To read
**Origin:** Arabic
**Pronunciation:** ihk RAH
**Description:** The name Iqra
comes from an Islamic word
that refers to the process of
reading, hence its meaning of
'to read'. It is a rare name in
Britain, used mainly in Islamic
communities.
**Alternative spellings:** Ikra, Iqrah

## Irene
**Meaning:** Peace
**Origin:** Greek

**Pronunciation:** eye REEN
**Description:** Irene is a Greek
name meaning 'peace'. Eirene was
the Greek goddess of peace.

## Irina

**Meaning:** Peace
**Origin:** Greek
**Pronunciation:** ee REE nah
**Description:** Irina is a popular
girls' name of Greek origin. The
name is one of the most common
female names in Eastern Europe
and Russia.
**Alternative spellings:** Arina, Irene,
Iryna

## Iris

**Meaning:** Rainbow
**Origin:** Greek
**Pronunciation:** EYE riss
**Description:** The name Iris de-
rives from Greek mythology,
where Iris was a messenger of the
gods and the personification of the
rainbow. It is now linked to the
English flower name.
**Alternative spellings:** Iriss

## Isabella

**Meaning:** Promised by God
**Origin:** Latin
**Pronunciation:** IS uh BELL luh
**Description:** The Latin form of
Isabel and derived from the
name Elizabeth. Along with its
alternate spellings, the name has
surged in popularity recently,
possibly due to the success of the
Twilight franchise, in which Isa-
bella is the full name of the main
character.
**Alternative spellings:** Isabela,
Isobela, Isobella, Izabela, Izabella,
Izzabella

## Isabelle

**Meaning:** Promised by God
**Origin:** French
**Pronunciation:** IS uh BELL
**Description:** This French form of
Isabel is derived from Elizabeth.
Isabelle is the most popular spell-
ing of this name.
**Alternative spellings:** Isabel,
Isabell, Isobel, Isobelle, Izabel,
Izabelle, Izzabelle

## Isadora

**Meaning:** Gift from Isis
**Origin:** Greek
**Pronunciation:** eye sa DOR ah
**Description:** The name Isadora derives from the male name Isadore,
meaning 'gift from Isis', the Egyptian god. It can also be considered
a feminine version of the name
Iadore, which was used in Greece
before and during the Christianisa-
tion of the Roman Empire.
**Alternative spellings:** Isadorah,
Isadorra

## Isha

**Meaning:** Woman; goddess
**Origin:** Sanskrit
**Pronunciation:** EE shaa
**Description:** Isha is a unisex
name and is often found in India.
As a feminine name it means
'woman' and is the name of the
goddess Durga, whereas in the
male form it means 'the Lord'.
**Alternative spellings:** Esha, Ishah

## Isla

**Meaning:** From Islay
**Origin:** English
**Pronunciation:** EYE luh
**Description:** First coined in the
20th century in Scotland, the name

I

Isla originates from the island of Islay in the Hebrides.
**Alternative spellings:** Eila

## Isma
**Meaning:** Protection
**Origin:** Arabic
**Pronunciation:** IS ma
**Description:** Isma is an unusual name in the UK, though is more popular in the Middle East. It is of Arabic origin and means 'protection' or 'safeguarding of the prophets'.
**Alternative spellings:** Ismah

## Ismene
**Meaning:** Knowledgeable
**Origin:** Greek
**Pronunciation:** is MEE nee
**Description:** Ismene is Greek in origin. In Greek mythology, Ismene was a daughter of Oedipus.
**Alternative spellings:** Ismeneh, Ismine

## Isra
**Meaning:** Night journey
**Origin:** Arabic
**Pronunciation:** IS ra
**Description:** Isra is of Arabic origin and means 'night-time journey'. Its meaning refers to the prophet Muhammad's night journey to Jerusalem, where he met Jesus and Moses before returning to Mecca that night.
**Alternative spellings:** Israh

## Israel
See entry in 'Names for Baby Boys A–Z'

## Issa
**Meaning:** Salvation
**Origin:** African
**Pronunciation:** ESS ah

**Description:** Issa is a variant of the African name Essa, meaning 'salvation' or 'protection'. It can be used for both baby boys and girls.
**Alternative spellings:** Essa, Essah

## Ivana
**Meaning:** Gift from God
**Origin:** Russian
**Pronunciation:** EE van na
**Description:** Ivana is the feminine form of the name Ivan, which is the Slavic form of the name John, which is where the meaning 'gift from God' comes from. Related names include Ivanka, Iva and Ivka.
**Alternative spellings:** Ivanah

## Ivie
**Meaning:** Faithfulness
**Origin:** English
**Pronunciation:** i VEE
**Description:** The name Ivy is taken straight from the creeping green plant often seen growing on the site of buildings or gardens. The name was popular at the beginning of the 20th century, though is far less common nowadays.
**Alternative spellings:** Ivy

## Ivory
**Meaning:** White
**Origin:** English
**Pronunciation:** EYE voree
**Description:** Ivory comes from the English vocabulary word of the same name, referring to the white-ish colour. The name also refers to the tusks of animals, especially elephants, which are the same colour.

## Iyla
**Meaning:** Moonlight
**Origin:** Sanskrit

**Pronunciation:** EYE la
**Description:** It is thought that Iyla originates from India and means 'moonlight'. It could also be considered a variant of the Persian name Lyla.
**Alternative spellings:** Eila, Ila

## Iylah

**Meaning:** Scottish island
**Origin:** Scottish
**Pronunciation:** ie LAH
**Description:** Iylah is a variation of the Scottish name Isla and that in turn is a variation of the name Islay, referring to the island off the west coast of Scotland.

**Alternative spellings:** Iyla, Isla

## Izzy

**Meaning:** Promised by God
**Origin:** Hebrew
**Pronunciation:** IH zee
**Description:** Izzy originally came about as a shortened form of the name Elizabeth or Isabelle. Izzy is a relatively modern name in its own right and is especially popular in Britain. Izzy can also be found as a boys' name; however it is rare and does not come from the name Elizabeth.
**Alternative spellings:** Izzi, Izzie

# J

## Jacinta

**Meaning:** Hyacinth
**Origin:** Spanish
**Pronunciation:** jah SIN tah
**Description:** Jacinta is the Spanish name for the flower, hyacinth. It ultimately comes from the Greek word 'hyakinthos'.
**Alternative spellings:** Jacintah

## Jacqueline

**Meaning:** Supplanter
**Origin:** Hebrew
**Pronunciation:** JAK eh lin; JAK eh leen
**Description:** Jacqueline is the feminine diminutive form of Jacques, the French version of James.
**Alternative spellings:** Jacquelean, Jacqueleen, Jacquelyn

## Jada

**Meaning:** Green stone; precious
**Origin:** English
**Pronunciation:** JAY dah
**Description:** Jada is a relatively modern name and can be seen as a development of Jade.
**Alternative spellings:** Jaida, Jayda

## Jade

**Meaning:** Green stone; precious
**Origin:** English
**Pronunciation:** JAYD
**Description:** Jade comes from the Spanish name for the precious stone. The word can be literally translated as 'stone of the bowels', and jade was believed to offer protection against intestinal disorders. The name also means 'precious'.
**Alternative spellings:** Jaide, Jayde

## Jagoda

**Meaning:** Berry
**Origin:** German
**Pronunciation:** yah GOW dah
**Description:** Jagoda is an unusual name that comes from a Slavic word meaning 'berry'. It is often found in Croatia and Poland.
**Alternative spellings:** Jagodah

## Jaime

**Meaning:** Supplanter; love
**Origin:** Hebrew
**Pronunciation:** JAY me
**Description:** A variation of the unisex name Jamie. The verb *'aimer'* means 'to love' in the French language, which gives this name a double meaning.
**Alternative spellings:** Jaimy, Jamie

## Jamila

**Meaning:** Beautiful
**Origin:** African
**Pronunciation:** jah MEEL ah
**Description:** Jamila is the feminine version of Jamil or Jamal. The names mean 'handsome' so we can take the feminine meaning to be 'beautiful'.
**Alternative spellings:** Jameela, Jamela, Jamilah

## Jana

**Meaning:** God is gracious
**Origin:** Hebrew
**Pronunciation:** JAH nah
**Description:** Jana is a variant of the name Jane, itself a version of the masculine name John.
**Alternative spellings:** Janah

## Jane

**Meaning:** God is gracious
**Origin:** Hebrew
**Pronunciation:** JAYN
**Description:** Jane was originally a feminine form of John, but is now a given name in its own right.
**Alternative spellings:** Jaine, Jayne

## Janelle

**Meaning:** God is gracious
**Origin:** English
**Pronunciation:** je NEL
**Description:** Janelle is a modern version of the name Jane and has only been used since the 20th century. It is ultimately derived from the name John, meaning 'God is gracious'.

## Janet

**Meaning:** God is gracious
**Origin:** Hebrew
**Pronunciation:** JAN et
**Description:** The name Janet is a diminutive of the name Jane. It also derives from the French Jeanette.
**Alternative spellings:** Janett, Janette, Jannet

## Jannah

**Meaning:** Garden of heaven
**Origin:** Arabic
**Pronunciation:** JAH nah
**Description:** The Arabic name Jannah refers to the Islamic paradise or 'garden of heaven' and is a popular name with Muslim parents.
**Alternative spellings:** Janah, Janna

## Jannat

**Meaning:** Heaven
**Origin:** Persian
**Pronunciation:** ja NAT

**Description:** Jannat is a name of Persian origin, which has become popular in India too. It is said to mean 'heaven'. Jannat is also the name of a famous Bollywood film.
**Alternative spellings:** Janat

## Jasleen
**Meaning:** Jasmine flower
**Origin:** Persian
**Pronunciation:** JAZ leen
**Description:** Jasleen is a modern variant form of the name Jasmine. Often shortened to Jas or Jaz.
**Alternative spellings:** Jaslene, Jasline

## Jasmin
**Meaning:** Jasmine flower
**Origin:** Persian
**Pronunciation:** JAZ min; YAZ min
**Description:** The name Jasmin is of Persian origin and can also be found in its original form: Yasmin. The flower is used in Thailand as a symbol for 'mother'.
**Alternative spellings:** Jasmine, Jazmin, Jazmine, Yasmin

## Javeria
**Meaning:** Bringer of happiness
**Origin:** Arabic
**Pronunciation:** jah VEER ah
**Description:** In Islamic belief, Javeria is the name of one of the wives of the prophet Muhammad.
**Alternative spellings:** Javeriah, Javeriya

## Jay
See entry in 'Names for Baby Boys A–Z'

## Jaya
See entry in 'Names for Baby Boys A–Z'

## Jayda
**Meaning:** Precious
**Origin:** English
**Pronunciation:** jay DAH
**Description:** Jayda is likely to be a development of Jade, and is a relatively modern name. Jade is a feminine name that comes from the English noun referring to the precious stone, similar to the name Ruby. In this way its meaning is 'precious'.

## Jayla
**Meaning:** Unknown
**Origin:** English
**Pronunciation:** JAY la
**Description:** Jayla is a relatively modern name created from the names Kayla and Jay. Jayla is part of a trend to form new names that have no specific meaning but are phonetically pleasing.
**Alternative spellings:** Jaila, Jaylah

## Jaylan
See entry in 'Names for Baby Boys A–Z'

## Jean
**Meaning:** God is gracious
**Origin:** Hebrew
**Pronunciation:** JEEN; ZHAHN
**Description:** Jean is a unisex name most often found on girls. As a male name it derives from the Hebrew name John, as a feminine name it comes from Jane.
**Alternative spellings:** Gene, Gine

## Jeanette
**Meaning:** God is gracious

**J**

**Origin:** French
**Pronunciation:** jean ETT
**Description:** Jeanette is a French name meaning 'God is gracious' and is a variation of the name Jeanne. It is also related to Janet and Janette.

## Jeanne

**Meaning:** God is gracious
**Origin:** French
**Pronunciation:** jee ANNE
**Description:** Jeanne is a French, feminine version of the name John and as such, shares the same meaning of 'God is gracious'.

## Jemima

**Meaning:** Handsome
**Origin:** Hebrew
**Pronunciation:** je MYE ma
**Description:** In the Old Testament, Jemima was the eldest daughter of Job. Although its peak of popularity was in the 19th century, it is still used today.
**Alternative spellings:** Gemima, Jemimah

## Jemma

**Meaning:** Precious stone
**Origin:** Italian
**Pronunciation:** JEM ah
**Description:** Jemma is a version of the Italian name Gemma.
**Alternative spellings:** Gemma

## Jenna

**Meaning:** White-haired
**Origin:** Gaelic
**Pronunciation:** JEN na
**Description:** Originally a shortened form of Jennifer, but can now be found as a name in its own right.
**Alternative spellings:** Jena, Jenah

## Jennifer

**Meaning:** White-haired
**Origin:** Gaelic
**Pronunciation:** JEN ih fur
**Description:** Jennifer, a very popular baby name in the UK, derives from the Welsh name Guinevere, which is the name of the legendary King Arthur's wife.
**Alternative spellings:** Jenifer

## Jenny

**Meaning:** White-haired
**Origin:** Welsh
**Pronunciation:** JEH ne
**Description:** Jenny came about as a pet form of the name Jennifer, but can now be seen as a name in its own right.
**Alternative spellings:** Jeni, Jenney, Jenni, Jennie

## Jermaine

**Meaning:** Of Germany
**Origin:** German
**Pronunciation:** JER mane
**Description:** Jermaine is an alternative spelling for the more usual Germaine, and is thought to mean 'from Germany'.
**Alternative spellings:** Germaine, Germane, Jermane

## Jerry

See entry in 'Names for Baby Boys A–Z'

## Jersey

**Meaning:** From Jersey
**Origin:** Norse
**Pronunciation:** JER zee
**Description:** Jersey, the name of the largest of the Channel Islands, is also an American state. The

name has Norse origins and means 'grassy island'.
**Alternative spellings:** Jersie, Jersy

## Jess
**Meaning:** Gift
**Origin:** Hebrew
**Pronunciation:** JESS
**Description:** Jess originally came about as a shortened form of the girls' names Jessie or Jessica but is now found as a unisex name in its own right.
**Alternative spellings:** Jesse

## Jessa
**Meaning:** Gift
**Origin:** Hebrew
**Pronunciation:** jess AH
**Description:** Jessa is a short form of the name Jessica, and shares the same meaning of 'gift'.

## Jessica
**Meaning:** Gift
**Origin:** Hebrew
**Pronunciation:** JESS ikker
**Description:** This name is thought to have been created by Shakespeare in his play *The Merchant of Venice*. It could also be a name of Hebrew origin.
**Alternative spellings:** Jessicah, Jessicka, Jessika

## Jessie
**Meaning:** Gift
**Origin:** Hebrew
**Pronunciation:** JESS ee
**Description:** Jessie is often used as a pet form of the names Jessica and Jess and is often seen as a unisex name in its own right.
**Alternative spellings:** Jesse, Jessi, Jessy

## Jia
**Meaning:** Champion
**Origin:** Sanskrit
**Pronunciation:** jay
**Description:** Jai could be the short form of several names but it is also a name in its own right. It is also spelt Jay, is of Sanskrit origin and in this form is usually masculine but is found used for both boys and girls. It is said to mean 'champion'. When used as a short form of any name starting with a 'Jay' sound it was originally given as a nickname meaning 'chatty,' in reference to the jay bird.

## Jiay
**Meaning:** Sweet heart
**Origin:** Sanskrit
**Pronunciation:** jee YA
**Description:** Jiya is a name popular among Hindus and other religious groups in India. It is said to mean 'sweet heart'. It is not very common in the UK but is slowly gaining in popularity.

## Jo
**Meaning:** God is gracious
**Origin:** Hebrew
**Pronunciation:** JO
**Description:** Jo may be the shortened form of any girls' name beginning with 'Jo—', such as Joanna or Jolene.
**Alternative spellings:** Joe

## Joan
**Meaning:** God is gracious
**Origin:** Hebrew
**Pronunciation:** JONE
**Description:** One of the more old-fashioned female variants of 'John'. Predominantly a female name, this

**J**

can occasionally be found as a male name.

## Joanna
**Meaning:** God is gracious
**Origin:** Hebrew
**Pronunciation:** jo AN nuh
**Description:** Joanna is a variation of the name Joanne, itself a feminine version of the masculine name John.
**Alternative spellings:** Joana, Joannah

## Joanne
**Meaning:** God is gracious
**Origin:** Hebrew
**Pronunciation:** jo AN
**Description:** Joanne is one of a few feminine versions of the Hebrew name John. In France the name started as Johan, before coming to Britain in the 12th century and developing into Joanna and Joanne.
**Alternative spellings:** Johanne

## Jocelyn
**Meaning:** Lord
**Origin:** English
**Pronunciation:** JOSS sa lin
**Description:** It is thought that the name Jocelyn is a mixture of the feminine names Joyce and Lynn. While Joyce is of Latin origin and means 'Lord', Lynn comes from an Old English surname meaning 'water pool'.
**Alternative spellings:** Jocelin, Josslin, Josslyn

## Jodie
**Meaning:** From Judea
**Origin:** English
**Pronunciation:** JO dee

**Description:** Jodie is a feminine spelling of the unisex name Jody.
**Alternative spellings:** Jodi, Jody

## Jody
See entry in 'Names for Baby Boys A–Z'

## Joelle
**Meaning:** One true God
**Origin:** French
**Pronunciation:** jo ELLE
**Description:** Joelle is the feminine version of the name Joel, and as such shares the same meaning of 'one true God'.

## Joely
**Meaning:** Pretty
**Origin:** French
**Pronunciation:** jo LEE
**Description:** Joely has its roots in French and is most likely a variation of the word '*jolie*' meaning 'pretty'. Joely Richardson is a famous British actress with this name.

## Johanna
**Meaning:** God is gracious
**Origin:** Hebrew
**Pronunciation:** yoh HAN nah
**Description:** Johanna is a continental variant of the name Joanna. Both of the names are ultimately of Hebrew origin and mean 'God has given'. Note the difference in pronunciation.
**Alternative spellings:** Johannah, Yohanna

## Jojo
**Meaning:** Nickname
**Origin:** English
**Pronunciation:** jojo

**Description:** Jojo is a nickname for names such as Jolene and Josephine, but can also stand as a given name on its own. Jojo is a famous American singer with this name.

## Jolene

**Meaning:** No meaning
**Origin:** English
**Pronunciation:** jo LEEN
**Description:** Jolene is a modern, invented name combining 'jo' with the suffix 'lene'. As such, it has no meaning.

## Jolie

**Meaning:** Pretty
**Origin:** French
**Pronunciation:** jo LEE
**Description:** Jolie comes from the French word for 'pretty' and has recently been adopted into a girls' given name.
**Alternative spellings:** Joley, Joli

## Joni

**Meaning:** God is gracious
**Origin:** Hebrew
**Pronunciation:** JONE ee
**Description:** A modern spelling variant of the name Joanie.
**Alternative spellings:** Joanie, Joany, Jonie

## Jordan

**Meaning:** Flowing down
**Origin:** Hebrew
**Pronunciation:** JOR den
**Description:** The name Jordan was originally given to children baptised using the holy water from the River Jordan. It is also the name of a country.
**Alternative spellings:** Jorden, Jordon, Jordun, Jordyn

## Jorgie

**Meaning:** Farmer
**Origin:** Greek
**Pronunciation:** jorge EE
**Description:** Jorgie is an alternative spelling of the name Georgie, which itself is a pet name of names such as Georgina. While Jorgie is a more modern construction, Georgina and similar names are heavily featured in legendary stories.
**Alternative spellings:** Georgie

## Jorja

**Meaning:** Farmer
**Origin:** Latin
**Pronunciation:** JORJ aah
**Description:** Jorja is a fairly modern variation of the English name Georgia. The meaning derives from the Greek word *'georgos'*, which means 'farmer'.
**Alternative spellings:** Georga, Jorga

## Josephina

**Meaning:** The Lord gave more
**Origin:** German
**Pronunciation:** JO zeh FEE nuh
**Description:** Josephina is a variant of the Hebrew name Josephine.
**Alternative spellings:** Josefina, Josephena

## Josephine

**Meaning:** The Lord gave more
**Origin:** Hebrew
**Pronunciation:** JO zeh feen
**Description:** The name Josephine is one of the feminine versions of the biblical name Joseph and shares its meaning of 'God will give more'.
**Alternative spellings:** Josefine, Josephene

J

## Josie

**Meaning:** The Lord gave more
**Origin:** Hebrew
**Pronunciation:** JO see
**Description:** Although Josie started as a pet name for the name Josephine, it is a first name in its own right.
**Alternative spellings:** Josey, Josi, Josy

## Josslyn

**Meaning:** Member of German tribe
**Origin:** German
**Pronunciation:** JAWS lin
**Description:** Josslyn is a variation of the more common Joselyn and comes from the French name Gautzelin, which is a name for a member of an old German tribe called the Gauts.
**Alternative spellings:** Joselyn

## Joy

**Meaning:** Joy
**Origin:** Latin
**Pronunciation:** JOY
**Description:** The name Joy comes from the word meaning 'extreme happiness'. It may also be considered a pet form of Joyce.

## Joyce

**Meaning:** Lord; joy
**Origin:** Breton
**Pronunciation:** JOYS
**Description:** Joyce originally comes from the Breton name 'Iodoc', meaning 'Lord'. It was first adapted to Jodocus, then to the male name Josce. Joyce disappeared as a male name in the 14th century.
**Alternative spellings:** Joyse

## Judith

**Meaning:** Of Judea
**Origin:** Hebrew
**Pronunciation:** JOO dith
**Description:** Judith is a biblical name borne by a Jewish heroine and beautiful widow who delivered her people from invading Assyrians. Judith can be taken to mean 'from Judea'.
**Alternative spellings:** Judithe, Judyth

## Judy

**Meaning:** Of Judea
**Origin:** Hebrew
**Pronunciation:** JOO dee
**Description:** Judy is a Hebrew name that is closely related to Judith, meaning 'of Judea'. Judith is a biblical name borne by a Jewish herione.
**Alternative spellings:** Judi, Judie

## Jules

**Meaning:** Bearded youth
**Origin:** Latin
**Pronunciation:** JOOLZ
**Description:** Jules is a unisex baby name of Latin origin, meaning 'down-bearded youth'. It is found in both English- and French-speaking countries. The name is the French form of Julius. In English, as a girls' name, it is often used as a pet form of Julia.
**Alternative spellings:** Jools

## Julia

**Meaning:** Youth
**Origin:** Latin
**Pronunciation:** JOO lee ah
**Description:** Julia is a feminine form of the Roman family name

Julius, famously shared by Julius Caesar.
**Alternative spellings:** Guilia, Juliah

## Julianna
**Meaning:** Youth
**Origin:** Latin
**Pronunciation:** JOO lee AN uh
**Description:** The name Julianna is a modern combination of Julia and Anna. It could also be considered as a spelling variant of the Latin name Juliana, which is the feminine form of Julian.
**Alternative spellings:** Juliana, Juliannah, Julyanna

## Julianne
**Meaning:** Youth
**Origin:** Latin
**Pronunciation:** JOO lee AN
**Description:** The feminine form of the male name Julian. Or it is often considered to be a modern combination of the names Julia and Anne.
**Alternative spellings:** Juliane, Julyanne

## Julie
**Meaning:** Youth
**Origin:** Greek
**Pronunciation:** JOO lee
**Description:** Julie is the French form of Julia, but is also used as a pet form of Juliana and Juliette. All of these names stem from the masculine name Julius, which is of Latin origin.
**Alternative spellings:** Juley, Juli

## Juliet
**Meaning:** Youth
**Origin:** Latin

**Pronunciation:** JOO lee et
**Description:** Juliet is a form of the Latin name Julia, made famous by the lead female character in Shakespeare's play *Romeo and Juliet*. Juliette is the French version of this name.
**Alternative spellings:** Juliett, Juliette

## June
**Meaning:** Month of June
**Origin:** English
**Pronunciation:** JOON
**Description:** June is a name coined from the English word for the summer month, and is popular with babies either born or conceived at this time of year. Interestingly, the month of June was named after the Roman goddess Juno.
**Alternative spellings:** Gune

## Juniper
**Meaning:** Juniper tree
**Origin:** English
**Pronunciation:** JOON ip er
**Description:** The name Juniper comes from the type of tree of the same name, which has evergreen-like needles and a distinctive type of berry that is used in a variety of culinary dishes and is a primary flavouring in gin. Juniper is one of a long line of flower-and-plant-related names.

## Juno
**Meaning:** Queen of heaven
**Origin:** Latin
**Pronunciation:** JOO no
**Description:** Juno is a name of Latin origin. In Roman mythology it was the name of the queen of the

J

gods; the equivalent of the Greek goddess Hera.
**Alternative spellings:** Junoh

## Justina
**Meaning:** Fair; just
**Origin:** Latin
**Pronunciation:** JUST een ah
**Description:** Justina is the anglicised version of Latin name Iustina and the female version of the name Justin. Both names are related to the word 'justice' and as such, mean 'fair' or 'just'.

## Justine
**Meaning:** Fair; just
**Origin:** Latin
**Pronunciation:** jus TEEN
**Description:** Justine is the feminine form of the name Justin, which is of Latin origins.
**Alternative spellings:** Justeen, Justene

# K

## Kacey
**Meaning:** From Cayce
**Origin:** English
**Pronunciation:** kay CEE
**Description:** Kacey is a modern alternative spelling of the name Casey. It is more commonly given as a female name but could be also given as a boys' name. Casey was a name given to Casey Jones as he hailed from a town called Cayce. This name could also be given to someone with the initials K.C.
**Alternative spellings:** Kaci, Kacie, Casey

## Kadie
**Meaning:** Pure
**Origin:** Greek
**Pronunciation:** KAY dee
**Description:** Kadie is a modern name that has come about as an elongated version of the name Kay or a variation of the popular name Katie. Most of these names come from the Greek name Kathoros, which means 'pure'.

**Alternative spellings:** Kadi, Kady

## Kaede
**Meaning:** Maple
**Origin:** Japanese
**Pronunciation:** kah eh DH
**Description:** This unisex Japanese name is written using only one character. It is an unusual character also used for the word 'maple'. The name could also be considered a spelling variation of the name Kayda.
**Alternative spellings:** Kaeida, Kaeide

## Kaelan
See entry in 'Names for Baby Boys A–Z'

## Kai
See entry in 'Names for Baby Boys A–Z'

## Kaia
**Meaning:** Pure

**Origin:** Greek
**Pronunciation:** KAY ah
**Description:** The name Kaia is thought to be an elongated version of Kay, which is a pet form for many names starting with the letter K. It could also be a unisex name meaning 'restful place'.
**Alternative spellings:** Kaiya, Kaja, Kaya

## Kaira

**Meaning:** Dark-haired
**Origin:** Gaelic
**Pronunciation:** KARE ah
**Description:** Kaira is a variant of the more commonly found Keera, or Keira. These names are all feminine versions of the masculine name Kieran, meaning 'dark one'.
**Alternative spellings:** Kaera, Kayra

## Kaitlin

**Meaning:** Pure
**Origin:** Greek
**Pronunciation:** KATE lin
**Description:** It is believed that this name derives from the Old Greek name Catherine and is a spelling variant of the Irish name Caitlin. Like Katherine, it is often shortened to Kate.
**Alternative spellings:** Caitlin, Caitlyn, Catelin, Catelyn, Kaitlyn, Katelin, Katelyn, Katelynn

## Kaja

**Meaning:** No meaning
**Origin:** English
**Pronunciation:** kye AH
**Description:** Kaja is a feminine name, thought to be an elongated version of the name Kay. Kay originated as a pet form for many

names starting with a K such as Katherine. It later became a name in its own right and since the variations Kaja and Kaya have formed.

## Kali

**Meaning:** The dark one
**Origin:** Sanskrit
**Pronunciation:** KAH lee
**Description:** Kali is the name of the Hindu goddess of time. It derives from a Sanskrit word meaning 'the dark one'. Kali is thought of as the bringer of death, but depending on the beliefs of the individual she can also been seen as a benevolent god.
**Alternative spellings:** Cali, Kalli

## Kamila

**Meaning:** Sacrifice
**Origin:** Latin
**Pronunciation:** cah MIL ah
**Description:** Kamila is a variant of Camilla, a name that originates from Roman mythology. It was the name for the queen of the Volsci, who was known for being a fast runner and a great warrior. This spelling is usually found in Poland.
**Alternative spellings:** Camila, Camilla, Kamilla

## Kamile

See entry in 'Names for Baby Boys A–Z'

## Kaori

**Meaning:** Fragrant fabric
**Origin:** Japanese
**Pronunciation:** kah O ree
**Description:** This Japanese name is considered one of the prettiest

K

for girls in Japan. This name is often spelt using the character of *'kao'* meaning 'incense' or 'perfume' together with the character *'ri',* which stands for 'fabric' or 'to weave'.
**Alternative spellings:** Kaorhi, Kaorie

## Kaoru
See entry in 'Names for Baby Boys A–Z'

## Kara
**Meaning:** Dearest
**Origin:** Italian
**Pronunciation:** KAR ah
**Description:** Kara is a spelling variant of the name Cara, which is of Italian origin and means 'dearest'.
**Alternative spellings:** Cara, Carah

## Karen
**Meaning:** Pure
**Origin:** Greek
**Pronunciation:** KA ren
**Description:** A Danish equivalent of Katherine introduced to America by Scandinavian settlers.
**Alternative spellings:** Caren, Karin, Karren

## Karina
**Meaning:** Loved one
**Origin:** Italian
**Pronunciation:** ka REE nah
**Description:** Karina derives from an Italian word for 'dearest one'. A spelling variant can be found in the Italian phrase *'che carina',* meaning 'how lovely'. It is a relatively modern name also often found in northern Europe.

**Alternative spellings:** Careena, Carina, Kareena

## Karis
**Meaning:** Graceful
**Origin:** Greek
**Pronunciation:** KARE iss
**Description:** Karis is a Greek name that has spread throughout Europe.
**Alternative spellings:** Carice, Caris, Carys, Karice, Kariss, Karys

## Karla
**Meaning:** Free man
**Origin:** German
**Pronunciation:** KAR lah
**Description:** Karla is the feminine version of the name Karl. This spelling is more common in continental Europe.
**Alternative spellings:** Carla

## Karlie
**Meaning:** Free man
**Origin:** English
**Pronunciation:** KAR lee
**Description:** Karlie is a variation of the name Carly, which in turn is the feminised version of the name Carl, meaning 'free man'. Karlie Kloss is a famous supermodel.
**Alternative spellings:** Carlie, Carly

## Karolina
**Meaning:** Free man
**Origin:** German
**Pronunciation:** ka ro LINE a
**Description:** The name Karolina ultimately derives from the masculine name Charles, which means 'free man'. It is a spelling variant of Carolina and can be most

commonly found in English- and Polish-speaking countries.
**Alternative spellings:** Carolina, Carolyna

## Kasey

See entry in 'Names for Baby Boys A–Z'

## Katarina

**Meaning:** Pure
**Origin:** Greek
**Pronunciation:** kah tah REE nah
**Description:** Katarina is a variant of the popular name Katherine. Although ultimately Greek in origin, Katarina is most likely to be found in Eastern European countries.
**Alternative spellings:** Catarena, Catarina, Caterena, Caterina, Katarena, Katerena, Katerina

## Katarzyna

**Meaning:** Pure
**Origin:** Greek
**Pronunciation:** kat ar ZEE nah
**Description:** Katarzyna is a variant of the Greek name Catherine and is one of the most popular names in Poland at this time. The name comes from the Greek word *'katharos',* meaning 'pure'.
**Alternative spellings:** Katarzena, Katarzina

## Kate

**Meaning:** Pure
**Origin:** Greek
**Pronunciation:** KAYT
**Description:** Kate is a short form of Katherine, and shares the meaning of 'pure'.
**Alternative spellings:** Cate, Kaite

## Katherine

**Meaning:** Pure
**Origin:** Greek
**Pronunciation:** KATH er in
**Description:** Katherine is another form of the name Catherine. The name has many variants but all of them derive from the Greek word *'katharos',* which means 'pure'.
**Alternative spellings:** Catharin, Catharine, Catharyn, Catherin, Catherine, Catheryn, Cathryn, Katharin, Katharine, Katherin, Katheryn, Kathryn

## Kathleen

**Meaning:** Pure
**Origin:** Greek
**Pronunciation:** kath LEEN
**Description:** Kathleen is one of the many variants based on the name Katherine. Kathleen seems to have come from Ireland, where it is most popular.
**Alternative spellings:** Cathleen, Cathlene, Kathlene

## Kathy

**Meaning:** Pure
**Origin:** English
**Pronunciation:** KATH ee
**Description:** Kathy is a shortened version of the name Katherine and both names mean 'pure'. Kathy is often a nickname of Katherine but can stand as a name in its own right as well.
**Alternative spellings:** Cathy

## Katie

**Meaning:** Pure
**Origin:** Greek
**Pronunciation:** KAY tee
**Description:** The name Katie

started as a pet form of Katherine but is now a first name in its own right.

**Alternative spellings:** Kaity, Katey, Kati, Katy

## Katrina

**Meaning:** Pure
**Origin:** Greek
**Pronunciation:** cah TREE nah
**Description:** Katrina is one of the many variants of the name Katherine and shares its meaning of 'pure'.

**Alternative spellings:** Catrina

## Katya

**Meaning:** Promised by God
**Origin:** Russian
**Pronunciation:** kat YAH
**Description:** Katya is a shortened version of the Russian name Yekaterina and Ekaterina, meaning 'pure'. All of these names are the Russian version of the Hebrew name Elizabeth and share the meaning 'promised by God'.

**Alternative spellings:** Katja

## Kay

**Meaning:** Pure
**Origin:** English
**Pronunciation:** KAY
**Description:** Kay is a pet form of any name beginning with the letter K, but also a name in its own right.

**Alternative spellings:** Kae

## Kaya

**Meaning:** Pure
**Origin:** English
**Pronunciation:** KAY ah
**Description:** Kaya is thought to be an elongated version of the name Kay.

**Alternative spellings:** Kaia, Kaiya, Kaja

## Kaya

**Meaning:** Restful place
**Origin:** Japanese
**Pronunciation:** KAY ah
**Description:** Kaya is an unusual unisex name. Its origins are Japanese, Zulu, Turkish, Hopi and Hindi, and other meanings are 'yew tree', 'forgiveness', 'home' and 'wise child'.

**Alternative spellings:** Kaia, Kaiya, Kaja

## Kaycee

**Meaning:** Vigilant guard
**Origin:** Gaelic
**Pronunciation:** KAY see
**Description:** A phonetically spelt variant of the unisex Casey and Kasey.

**Alternative spellings:** Casey, Casie, Cayce, Caycie, Caysie, Kacey, Kaci, Kacie, Kacy, Kasey, Kasie, Kaycie, Kaysie

## Kayd

See entry in 'Names for Baby Boys A–Z'

## Kaydee

**Meaning:** Pure
**Origin:** Greek
**Pronunciation:** KAY dee
**Description:** Kaydee is a phonetic spelling of Kady, and both are likely to be a modern variant of Katie.

**Alternative spellings:** Kadi, Kadie, Kady, Kaydey, Kaydi, Kaydie

## Kaydence

**Meaning:** Rhythm
**Origin:** English

**Pronunciation:** KAY dense
**Description:** Kaydence, derived from cadence, follows the trend for phonetically spelt names. It has risen in popularity in recent years.
**Alternative spellings:** Cadence, Kadence

## Kayla
**Meaning:** Who is like God?
**Origin:** Hebrew
**Pronunciation:** KAY lah
**Description:** Probably a pet form of the name Michaela, this relatively modern name is popular in the US.
**Alternative spellings:** Kaela, Kaylah

## Kaylee
**Meaning:** Slender
**Origin:** Gaelic
**Pronunciation:** KAY lee
**Description:** Although the origin of Kaylee is uncertain, some speculate that it is a variant of Kayla. Both names could come from the Gaelic name Caoilainn, meaning 'slender' or from the name Michaela meaning 'who is like God?'.
**Alternative spellings:** Kayleigh, Kayley

## Kaysha
**Meaning:** Fruit tree
**Origin:** Hebrew
**Pronunciation:** KAY shuh
**Description:** Kaysha is a name of uncertain origin. It is possible it is a Hebrew name that means 'fruit tree'. However, it could also derive from the modern name Keisha.
**Alternative spellings:** Caysha, Kaesha, Kaisha

## Kazumi
See entry in 'Names for Baby Boys A–Z'

## Keavy
**Meaning:** Precious
**Origin:** Gaelic
**Pronunciation:** KEE vee
**Description:** The name Keavy is a variant of the anglicised form of the Gaelic name Caoimhe, which is pronounced 'keeva'. The names come from the Old Gaelic word *'caomh'* meaning 'precious'.
**Alternative spellings:** Keavi, Keavie, Keevy

## Keeva
**Meaning:** Beautiful; gentle; kind
**Origin:** Gaelic
**Pronunciation:** kee VAH
**Description:** Keeva is the phonetic spelling of the Irish name, Caoimhe. In Gaelic, the name comes from the word 'caomh,' meaning 'beautiful,' 'gentle' and 'kind'. The male version of the name is Caomhin – or Kevin, in English.

## Keelan
See entry in 'Names for Baby Boys A–Z'

## Keeley
**Meaning:** White; slender
**Origin:** Gaelic
**Pronunciation:** KEE lee
**Description:** Keeley is most likely to be derived from the Irish name 'Caoilfhionn' and is possibly the Gaelic version of Kelly. It could also come from 'Caoilinn', meaning 'slender'.
**Alternative spellings:** Keeli, Keelie, Keely

K

## Kei
See entry in 'Names for Baby Boys A–Z'

## Keiko
**Meaning:** Blessed child
**Origin:** Japanese
**Pronunciation:** KAY koh
**Description:** This name has its roots in the Japanese language and is one of the most popular Japanese names ending in 'ko'. Depending on the characters used to spell this name the meaning can vary from 'joyful child' to 'respectful child'.
**Alternative spellings:** Kaiko

## Keira
**Meaning:** Dark-haired
**Origin:** Gaelic
**Pronunciation:** KEER uh
**Description:** Keira is a variant of the Gaelic name Ciara. Like Kiera, it is also the feminine form of Kieran.
**Alternative spellings:** Keirah, Kiera, Kira, Kyra

## Keisha
**Meaning:** Prosperous
**Origin:** Arabic
**Pronunciation:** KEE sha
**Description:** The name Keisha became popular in the 1980s. It is probably a variation of the Arabic Aisha.
**Alternative spellings:** Keesha, Keysha

## Kelis
**Meaning:** Unknown
**Origin:** American
**Pronunciation:** keh LEES
**Description:** As Kelis is most likely a recently created name, its meaning is uncertain.
**Alternative spellings:** Keliss, Kellis

## Kelly
**Meaning:** Bright-headed
**Origin:** Gaelic
**Pronunciation:** KEL lee
**Description:** Kelly is most commonly found as a girls' name despite originating from the Irish male name Ceallach.
**Alternative spellings:** Kelli, Kellie

## Kelsea
**Meaning:** Victorious ship
**Origin:** English
**Pronunciation:** KEL see
**Description:** Kelsea is a variant of the unisex name Kelsey, most commonly used for girls. The names are thought to derive from the Old English word *'ceolsige'*, which means 'victorious ship'.
**Alternative spellings:** Kelsey, Kelsi, Kelsie, Kelsy

## Kelsey
See entry in 'Names for Baby Boys A–Z'

## Kendra
**Meaning:** Keen power
**Origin:** English
**Pronunciation:** KEN dra
**Description:** Kendra is the feminine version of the English surname Kendrick and it shares its meaning of 'keen power'.
**Alternative spellings:** Kendrah

## Kennedy
See entry in 'Names for Baby Boys A–Z'

## Kenza

**Meaning:** The fairest
**Origin:** Gaelic
**Pronunciation:** KEN zah
**Description:** Kenza is the feminine variant of the name Kenzie, which derives from the Gaelic surname McKenzie – itself part of a group of surnames now popular as first names. Both Kenzie and Kenza share the surname's meaning of 'the fairest'.
**Alternative spellings:** Kensa, Kenzah

## Kenzie

**Meaning:** Fair one
**Origin:** Gaelic
**Pronunciation:** ken ZEE
**Description:** When anglicised, Kenzie becomes Kenneth. Kenzie is usually adopted in the USA as a shortened form of Mackenzie. The meaning of Mackenzie varies between 'fair one' for a girl, or 'son of the fair one' for a boy.

## Kerem

See entry in 'Names for Baby Boys A–Z'

## Keren

**Meaning:** Ray of power
**Origin:** Hebrew
**Pronunciation:** KARE en
**Description:** Keren is a name of biblical origins. It means 'ray of power'. In the Bible Keren was the name of one of the three daughters of Job. It could also be considered a variant of the name Karen.
**Alternative spellings:** Kerin, Kerren

## Kerry

**Meaning:** Descendants of Ciar
**Origin:** Gaelic
**Pronunciation:** KEH ree
**Description:** Kerry was originally a surname, from the Irish county of the same name. Kerry means 'descendants of Ciar' and the original Gaelic spelling is Chiarrai. The name is unisex, but is more commonly given to girls.
**Alternative spellings:** Kerrey, Kerri, Kerrie

## Keya

**Meaning:** Flower
**Origin:** Sanskrit
**Pronunciation:** KAY ah
**Description:** The name Keya comes from the Bengali word for 'flower'. In Hindu scripture the god Brahma uses the name of the flower in a story called 'The Cursed Flower'.
**Alternative spellings:** Keeya

## Kezia

**Meaning:** Cassia spice
**Origin:** Hebrew
**Pronunciation:** key ZYE ah
**Description:** Kezia comes from the Hebrew name for 'cassia spice', which is a general term for spices such as cinnamon. In the Bible it was the name of the second daughter of Job.
**Alternative spellings:** Keziah, Kezzia, Kezziah

## Khadija

**Meaning:** Early child
**Origin:** Arabic
**Pronunciation:** ka DEE ja
**Description:** Khadija is an Arabic name meaning 'early baby' and

**K**

is traditionally given to babies born earlier than expected. In the Quran it is the name of one of the wives of the prophet Muhammad. The spelling variants of this name are all popular names.

**Alternative spellings:** Khadeeja, Khadeejah, Khadijah

## Khaleesi

**Meaning:** Queen
**Origin:** English
**Pronunciation:** KA lee see
**Description:** A name derived from George. R. R. Martin's popular series, Game of Thrones, Khaleesi means 'queen' in Dothraki, a language invented for the series.

## Khloe

**Meaning:** Greenery
**Origin:** Greek
**Pronunciation:** klowh EE
**Description:** Khloe is a variant spelling of Chloe, and is a modern form of the name that has appeared along with many other 'C' names that have been replaced by 'K,' which is a very modern trend. Chloe is of Greek origin and is said to mean 'greenery'; it was another name given to the Greek goddess Demeter, who was the protector of fields of greenery.

**Alternative spellings:** Chloe

## Khushi

**Meaning:** Happiness
**Origin:** Sanskrit
**Pronunciation:** KUSH ee
**Description:** Khushi may have come about as a short form of the masculine name Khushiram, however the form Khushi is only seen

on girls. The name is often found in India and its meaning is thought to relate to happiness.

**Alternative spellings:** Kushee, Kushi, Khushy

## Kia

**Meaning:** Go well
**Origin:** English
**Pronunciation:** KEE ah
**Description:** The name Kia is thought to originate from New Zealand, where the phrase 'kia ora' is used as a greeting to wish someone well.

**Alternative spellings:** Kiah

## Kiana

**Meaning:** Ancient
**Origin:** English
**Pronunciation:** kee AHN ah
**Description:** The name Kiana may derive from the Gaelic name Cian, which means 'ancient'.

**Alternative spellings:** Chiana, Ciana, Kianah, Kianna

## Kiara

**Meaning:** Bright
**Origin:** Latin
**Pronunciation:** kee AH ra; KEER ah
**Description:** The name Kiara is mainly used in English-speaking countries, especially England and America. It is thought that this name derives from the Italian name Chiara, which was borne by Saint Chiara of Assisi.

**Alternative spellings:** Chiara, Chiarah, Ciara

## Kiki

**Meaning:** No meaning
**Origin:** French
**Pronunciation:** kee kee

**Description:** Kiki is a French name was originally a nickname at the turn of the last century. As such, it has no meaning as it is a nickname that has slipped into the mainstream as a given name.

## Kim
**Meaning:** Wood clearing
**Origin:** English
**Pronunciation:** KIM
**Description:** Kim is a short form of Kimberley, but also an independent given name for both boys and girls.
**Alternative spellings:** Kimm

## Kimberley
**Meaning:** Wood clearing
**Origin:** English
**Pronunciation:** KIM ber lee
**Description:** Kimberley is the name of a South African town named after a Lord Kimberley, whose surname originates from England. The name is unisex but most often found on girls in the UK.
**Alternative spellings:** Kimberlee, Kimberleigh, Kimberly

## Kimmy
**Meaning:** Wood clearing
**Origin:** English
**Pronunciation:** kim EE
**Description:** Kimmy is a diminutive of the name Kimberley and as such, means 'wood clearing'.
**Alternative spellings:** Kimmi, Kimmie

## Kimora
**Meaning:** Unknown
**Origin:** English
**Pronunciation:** ki MOH rah
**Description:** Kimora is a modern name thought to have evolved from the name Kimberley.
**Alternative spellings:** Kimmora, Kimorah

## Kinga
**Meaning:** Brave in war
**Origin:** German
**Pronunciation:** KIN gah
**Description:** Kinga is the pet form of the Old German name Kunegunda, meaning 'brave in war'. The name is often found in Germany, Poland and Hungary; however, its use is unusual in the UK.
**Alternative spellings:** Kingah

## Kinsley
**Meaning:** King's woods
**Origin:** English
**Pronunciation:** kins LEE
**Description:** Kinsley is an English surname derived from the elements of '*cyne*' meaning 'kingly' and '*lëah*' meaning 'wood'. As a given name, it was first used in America.

## Kinza
**Meaning:** Hidden treasure
**Origin:** Arabic
**Pronunciation:** KIN za
**Description:** The name Kinza comes from the Arabic word '*kinz*', meaning 'hidden treasure'. The name has extreme associations with wealth.
**Alternative spellings:** Kinsa, Kinzah

## Kiran
See entry in 'Names for Baby Boys A–Z'

## Kirika
**Meaning:** Natural beauty
**Origin:** Japanese
**Pronunciation:** ki ri KA

K

**Description:** Kirika is written using the Japanese characters of *'kiri'*, meaning 'plant' and *'ka'*, meaning 'summer flower'. Therefore the name has lots of associations with nature and plant life.
**Alternative spellings:** Kirikah, Kiryka

## Kirsten

**Meaning:** Follower of Christ
**Origin:** Latin
**Pronunciation:** KUR sten
**Description:** Kirsten is the Scandinavian form of the Latin name Christine.
**Alternative spellings:** Kirstenne, Kirstin

## Kirsty

**Meaning:** Follower of Christ
**Origin:** Gaelic
**Pronunciation:** KUR stee
**Description:** Kirsty is a diminutive of the name Christine or Kirsten, but now a popular name in its own right.
**Alternative spellings:** Kirstey, Kirsti, Kirstie

## Kitty

**Meaning:** Pure
**Origin:** Greek
**Pronunciation:** KIT ee
**Description:** Originally a short form of Katherine but now used as a name in its own right.
**Alternative spellings:** Kitti, Kittie

## Kiva

**Meaning:** Protected
**Origin:** Hebrew
**Pronunciation:** KEY va
**Description:** The name Kiva is closely related to the Hebrew name Akiva, meaning 'protector'.

Though typically considered a girls' name, it is in fact unisex.
**Alternative spellings:** Keeva, Kivah

## Kiya

**Meaning:** Unknown
**Origin:** Arabic
**Pronunciation:** KYE ah
**Description:** The name Kiya can be traced back to Egyptian history as the name of the wife of the Pharaoh Akhenaten. It is generally considered to have roots in the Arabic language but has an uncertain meaning.
**Alternative spellings:** Kiyah

## Kizzy

**Meaning:** Spice
**Origin:** African
**Pronunciation:** KEE zee
**Description:** Kizzy is a name of uncertain origin, but possibly a pet form of Kezia, which could carry the same meaning of 'spice' as Cassia.
**Alternative spellings:** Kizzi, Kizzie

## Klara

**Meaning:** Clarity
**Origin:** Latin
**Pronunciation:** KLAH ra
**Description:** Klara is an alternate spelling of Clara, meaning 'clarity'. This spelling is often found in Eastern Europe.
**Alternative spellings:** Clara

## Klaudia

**Meaning:** Lame
**Origin:** Italian
**Pronunciation:** claw de AH
**Description:** Klaudia is a spelling variation of the name Claudia. It is popular to modernise names by

replacing 'c' with 'k'. Claudia is a feminine name of Roman origin and like its masculine equivalent, Claud, it comes from the Roman name Claudius, which is said to mean 'lame'.
**Alternative spellings:** Claudia

## Kodi
See entry in 'Names for Baby Boys A–Z'

## Korey
See entry in 'Names for Baby Boys A–Z'

## Kornelia
**Meaning:** Horn
**Origin:** Latin
**Pronunciation:** kor nee lee AH
**Description:** Kornelia, more usually spelt Cornelia, is the feminine equivalent of the masculine name Cornelius. Cornelius was a Roman family name thought to have come from the Latin word 'cornu' meaning 'horn'.
**Alternative spellings:** Cornelia

## Kristen
**Meaning:** Follower of Christ
**Origin:** Latin
**Pronunciation:** KRIS ten
**Description:** Kristen is a variant of the name Christine, meaning 'follower of Christ'. Kristen is found more in Eastern Europe where 'K' often replaces 'C' at the beginning of names.
**Alternative spellings:** Christen, Cristen, Kristenne, Kristin

## Kristian
See entry in 'Names for Baby Boys A–Z'

## Kristina
**Meaning:** Christian
**Origin:** English
**Pronunciation:** kris TEE nah
**Description:** Kristina is a feminine name that is derived from the name Christine, the feminine equivalent of the masculine Christian and used for the same purpose. It comes from the English word 'Christian' and refers to a follower of Christianity.
**Alternative spellings:** Cristina, Christina

## Krystal
**Meaning:** Christian; precious
**Origin:** German
**Pronunciation:** KIRS tul
**Description:** Krystal is a modern spelling variation of Crystal. Crystal is a feminine name that can come from two sources. It could be from the English noun referring to the precious stone, similar to the name Jade. In this way its meaning is seen as 'precious'. However, it is also found as a variation of the German name Christel, which is itself a variation of Christine. Christine is the feminine version of Christian, and means literally 'Christian'.
**Alternative spellings:** Crystal

## Kya
**Meaning:** Unknown
**Origin:** English
**Pronunciation:** KYE ah
**Description:** The name Kya is especially popular with African-American parents. It is thought to be a variation of the names Kyla or Kai, given for its phonetically pleasing sound.
**Alternative spellings:** Kyah

K

## Kyla

**Meaning:** Beautiful or narrow spit of land
**Origin:** Gaelic
**Pronunciation:** kye LAH
**Description:** Kyla is a Gaelic name, which may have two meanings. It could be a derivative of the name Cadhla, which means 'beautiful', or it may be the feminine version of the name Kyle, which means 'narrow spit of land'.
**Alternative spellings:** Kylah

## Kylie

**Meaning:** Boomerang
**Origin:** Australian
**Pronunciation:** KY lee
**Description:** An Australian name said to mean 'boomerang'. Kylie could also be of Irish origin and mean 'graceful'.
**Alternative spellings:** Kiley, Kyley, Kyli

## Kyoko

**Meaning:** Respectful child
**Origin:** Japanese
**Pronunciation:** kyo KOH
**Description:** This name derives from the Japanese name Kyouko, which is pronounced with a longer 'o' sound.
**Alternative spellings:** Kioko, Kyokoh

# L

## Laaibah

**Meaning:** Most beautiful from heaven
**Origin:** Arabic
**Pronunciation:** LAY bah
**Description:** Laaibah is a popular Arabic girls' name. It means 'most beautiful from heaven' and has connotations with beauty and religion.
**Alternative spellings:** Laaiba, Laiba, Laibah, Layba, Laybah

## Lacey

**Meaning:** Laced
**Origin:** English
**Pronunciation:** LAY see
**Description:** Lacey is a unisex name, taken from the surname Lassy. It could also derive from the fabric lace.
**Alternative spellings:** Laci, Lacie, Lacy, Laicee, Laicey, Laycie

## Laila

**Meaning:** Dark-haired
**Origin:** Persian
**Pronunciation:** LAY la
**Description:** Laila is a variant of the Persian name Leila, meaning 'dark-haired'.
**Alternative spellings:** Lailah, Layla, Laylah, Leila, Leilah, Leyla

## Lainey

**Meaning:** Bright
**Origin:** Greek
**Pronunciation:** LAYN ee
**Description:** Lainey is the pet form of the name Elaine, a French variant of the name Helen. The name carries

connotations of beauty and brightness.
**Alternative spellings:** Lainey, Laini, Lainie, Lainy, Laney, Lanie, Lany, Laynee, Laynie, Leni

## Lana
**Meaning:** Little rock
**Origin:** Gaelic
**Pronunciation:** lahn AH
**Description:** Lana is likely to be a Gaelic name meaning 'little rock,' although it could also be a shortened version of the German name Alana.

## Laney
**Meaning:** Bright
**Origin:** French
**Pronunciation:** LAY nee
**Description:** As well as being a spelling variant of Lainey, meaning 'bright', the name Laney also derives from the French surname Delaney. A unisex name most commonly found on girls.
**Alternative spellings:** Lainey, Laini, Lainie, Lainy, Lanie, Lany, Laynee, Laynie, Leni

## Lara
**Meaning:** From Larissa; cheerful
**Origin:** Russian
**Pronunciation:** LA ra
**Description:** Lara is a shortened Russian form of the name Larissa, and it first ventured into the English-speaking world in the early 20th century. It is considered a name in its own right.
**Alternative spellings:** Larah, Larrah

## Laraib
**Meaning:** Undoubting

**Origin:** Urdu
**Pronunciation:** lah RAYB
**Description:** Laraib is a name of Urdu origin, from a word meaning 'undoubting'. It is often favoured by parents following the Islamic faith.
**Alternative spellings:** Laraaib, Larayb

## Larissa
**Meaning:** From Larissa; cheerful
**Origin:** Greek
**Pronunciation:** lah RISS ah
**Description:** Larissa originates from Greece where it is the name of a city. It may have originally been used for girls born there, but could also come from the Latin *'hilaris'*, meaning 'cheerful'.
**Alternative spellings:** Larisa, Larissah

## Larna
**Meaning:** River; rock
**Origin:** Welsh
**Pronunciation:** LAHR na
**Description:** Larna is a variant of the Celtic name Lana. Both names derive from Alana, the feminine form of Alan.
**Alternative spellings:** Lahna, Lana

## Latifah
**Meaning:** Gentle
**Origin:** African
**Pronunciation:** lah TEE fah
**Description:** The name Latifah comes from a Swahili word meaning 'gentle'. The name is found mainly in Africa.
**Alternative spellings:** Latefah, Latifa

## Latisha
**Meaning:** Happy

L

**Origin:** Latin
**Pronunciation:** lah TEE sha
**Description:** Latisha is a variant of the Latin Laetitia, the Roman goddess associated with joy.
**Alternative spellings:** Laetitia, Latishah, Leticia

## Latoya

**Meaning:** Victorious One
**Origin:** Latin
**Pronunciation:** la TOY ah
**Description:** Latoya is a Latin name meaning 'victorious one'. It originates from the Spanish Toya, which is a nickname for Victoria.

## Laura

**Meaning:** Laurel
**Origin:** Latin
**Pronunciation:** LAW ruh
**Description:** Laura is the feminine form of the Latin name Laurus, meaning 'laurel'. The name was popularised in part by Italian poet Petrarch, who wrote love poems to a woman named Laura.
**Alternative spellings:** Laurah, Lora

## Laurel

**Meaning:** Laurel
**Origin:** English
**Pronunciation:** LOH rul
**Description:** Originally Laurel was a feminine name, deriving from the Old English laurel tree.
**Alternative spellings:** Loral

## Lauren

**Meaning:** From Laurentum
**Origin:** Latin
**Pronunciation:** LOR ren
**Description:** This feminine version of Laurence comes from the Roman name Laurentia.

**Alternative spellings:** Laurin, Lauryn, Lawren, Lorenne

## Laurence

See entry in 'Names for Baby Boys A–Z'

## Laurie

**Meaning:** Victory
**Origin:** Latin
**Pronunciation:** LAW ree
**Description:** Originally a shortened version of the names Laura and Laurence, this unisex name is now used in its own right and means 'victory'.
**Alternative spellings:** Lauri, Laury, Lawrie, Lowry

## Lavender

**Meaning:** Flower name
**Origin:** English
**Pronunciation:** lav EN dur
**Description:** Lavender is derived from the name of the purple, strong-scented flower. Like Rose and Tulip, Lavender is part of the trend of using flowers as given names.

## Lavinia

**Meaning:** Mother of Rome
**Origin:** Latin
**Pronunciation:** lah VEE ne ah
**Description:** The name of the mythical mother of Rome.
**Alternative spellings:** Laviniah, Lavinja, Lavinya

## Layan

**Meaning:** Soft; gentle
**Origin:** Arabic
**Pronunciation:** lie YAAN
**Description:** Layan is a feminine Arabic name meaning 'soft'

and 'gentle'. It is a popular name given to newborn girls in the Arab world, and is related to names such as Lina, Leena and Lena, all of which have the same meaning.

## Leah
**Meaning:** Spiritless
**Origin:** Hebrew
**Pronunciation:** LEE uh
**Description:** Leah, a biblical name, has grown in popularity since the 1990s and is now a favourite in Britain.
**Alternative spellings:** Lea, Leia, Leigha, Lia

## Leanna
**Meaning:** Bright
**Origin:** Greek
**Pronunciation:** lee AHN ah
**Description:** A modern name, created by combining the names Lee and Anna, Leanna could also derive from Helen, meaning 'bright'.
**Alternative spellings:** Leana, Lianna

## Leanne
**Meaning:** Bright
**Origin:** Greek
**Pronunciation:** lee AN
**Description:** Leanne is a variant of Leanna and a combination of the names Lee and Anne. It could also derive from the Greek name Helen.
**Alternative spellings:** LeAnn, Leann, Lianne

## Lee
**Meaning:** Wood; clearing
**Origin:** English
**Pronunciation:** LEE
**Description:** From the Old

English word *'lea'* meaning 'clearing' or 'meadow', this is a unisex name.
**Alternative spellings:** Lei. Leigh

## Leela
**Meaning:** Dark-haired
**Origin:** Persian
**Pronunciation:** LEE lah
**Description:** A phonetically spelt variation of the Persian name Leila, and most commonly pronounced 'lie-la', whereas Leela is pronounced 'lee-la'.
**Alternative spellings:** Leelah, Leila, Leilah, Lila

## Leen
**Meaning:** Bright
**Origin:** Greek
**Pronunciation:** LEEN
**Description:** Leen is a Greek name, mainly found in Dutch-speaking countries. It derives as a pet name of the Dutch version of Helen, which is Helena, pronounced 'heh-leen a'.
**Alternative spellings:** Lean, Lene

## Leena
**Meaning:** Palm tree
**Origin:** Arabic
**Pronunciation:** LEE nah
**Description:** In origin, an elongation of the Greek name Leen or a variant of the name Lina.
**Alternative spellings:** Leenah, Lena, Lenah, Lina, Linah

## Leja
**Meaning:** Weary
**Origin:** Lithuanian
**Pronunciation:** lee YA
**Description:** Leja is an alternative spelling of the Lithuanian name Leah.

L

The name ultimately comes from the Hebrew word '*le'ah*', meaning 'weary'.
**Alternative spellings:** Leah

## Leilani
**Meaning:** Heavenly lei
**Origin:** Hawaiian
**Pronunciation:** lay LAH nee
**Description:** This Hawaiian name is uncommon in Britain but gaining popularity in America. Lei is the Hawaiian name for flowers in a garland around the neck, which symbolise love, so Leilani may mean 'heavenly love'.
**Alternative spellings:** Lailani, Laylani, Leilanee

## Leland
See entry in 'Names for Baby Boys A–Z'

## Lena
**Meaning:** Bright
**Origin:** Greek
**Pronunciation:** LAY nah
**Description:** Lena is a shortened name of the Greek name Helena, or the Greek name Magdalena. It could also be a spelling variant of the name Lina.
**Alternative spellings:** Leena, Leenah, Lenah, Lina, Linah

## Leni
**Meaning:** Bright
**Origin:** Greek
**Pronunciation:** LAY nee
**Description:** Leni is one of many pet forms of the name Helen and a variation on Laney, from the name Helena.
**Alternative spellings:** Lainey, Laini, Lainie, Lainy, Laney, Lanie, Lany, Laynee, Laynie

## Leona
**Meaning:** Lion
**Origin:** Latin
**Pronunciation:** LEE oh na
**Description:** Leona is a Latinate feminine form of the masculine name Leo, meaning 'lion'.
**Alternative spellings:** Leonah, Liona

## Leoni
**Meaning:** Courageous
**Origin:** Latin
**Pronunciation:** lee OH ne
**Description:** Leoni is a feminine version of the Latin name Leo, meaning 'lion' and was probably given as a virtuous name, meaning 'courageous'.
**Alternative spellings:** Leonie, Leony, Lioni, Lionie, Liony

## Leonie
**Meaning:** Courageous
**Origin:** Latin
**Pronunciation:** LAY oh ne
**Description:** This name is a spelling variation of Leoni.
**Alternative spellings:** Leoni, Leony, Lioni, Lionie, Liony

## Leslie
See entry in 'Names for Baby Boys A–Z'

## Leticia
**Meaning:** Happy
**Origin:** Latin
**Pronunciation:** leh TEE shah
**Description:** Leticia is a variant of the Latin name Laetitia, the Roman goddess associated with joy.
**Alternative spellings:** Laetitia, Laticia, Latisha, Latishah

## Lettie

**Meaning:** Joy; Happiness
**Origin:** English
**Pronunciation:** let EE
**Description:** Lettie is the English diminutive of Letitia, a Latin name meaning 'joy' and 'happiness'. Lettie can also be spelt Letty, and all three names have a traditional feel ꜰꜰꜰ ꜰꜰꜰ ꜰꜰꜰ
**Alternative spellings:** Letty

## Levi

See entry in 'Names for Baby Boys A–Z'

## Lexi

**Meaning:** Defender of man
**Origin:** Greek
**Pronunciation:** LEK see
**Description:** The name Lexi originated as a pet form of the names Alexandra, Alexa or Alexis, all feminine forms of the Greek name Alexander, meaning 'man's defender'.
**Alternative spellings:** Leksi, Leksy, Lexie, Lexy

## Lexus

See entry in 'Names for Baby Boys A–Z'

## Leya

**Meaning:** Always with God; law
**Origin:** Hebrew
**Pronunciation:** LEEY ah
**Description:** As well as being a variant of the Hebrew name Leeya, meaning 'always with God', Leya could also be considered a Spanish name, meaning 'law'.
**Alternative spellings:** Leeya, Liya

## Liana

**Meaning:** Captivating
**Origin:** French
**Pronunciation:** lee AH nah
**Description:** Liana is a French given name as well as a name for a vine which is often found in the rainforest. These factors imply that the meaning of the given name is along the lines of 'ensnaring' or 'captivating'.
**Alternative spellings:** Leana, Lianah, Liyana

## Libby

**Meaning:** Promised by God
**Origin:** Hebrew
**Pronunciation:** LIB ee
**Description:** Libby originally came about as the pet form of Elizabeth, meaning 'promised by God'. It is now a name in its own right, possibly based on a child's attempt to say 'Elizabeth'.
**Alternative spellings:** Libbi, Libbie

## Liberty

**Meaning:** Freedom
**Origin:** Latin
**Pronunciation:** LIB er tee
**Description:** Liberty derives from the Latin word *'libertas'*, meaning 'free'. The name has strong links to America due to the Statue of Liberty.
**Alternative spellings:** Liberti, Libertie

## Lila

**Meaning:** Dark-haired
**Origin:** Persian
**Pronunciation:** LEE lah; LYE la
**Description:** Lila is a phonetically spelt variation of the name Leila, which is of Persian origin and means 'dark-haired'.

L

**Alternative spellings:** Leela, Leelah, Leila, Leilah, Lilah, Lilla, Lillah

## Lili

**Meaning:** Bright one; God is perfection
**Origin:** Welsh
**Pronunciation:** lil LEE
**Description:** This name has become very popular in English-speaking countries in recent years due to current trends. This name has roots in the Old Greek language, meaning 'bright one', and Old Hebrew, where it means 'God is perfection'. It was once that this name was a pet form of the name Elizabeth; however it is now considered a forename in its own right.
**Alternative spellings:** Lily, Lillie, Lilly

## Lilia

**Meaning:** Lilies
**Origin:** Latin
**Pronunciation:** LIL ee ah
**Description:** The name Lilia comes from the Latin word *'lilia'*, meaning 'lilies'. Lily is a very popular name choice at the moment and Lilia could make a nice alternative.
**Alternative spellings:** Lilah, Lillia, Lilliah

## Lilian

**Meaning:** Lily flower
**Origin:** Latin
**Pronunciation:** lil ee An
**Description:** Lilian is an elaboration upon the Latin name Lily, itself coming from the commonly white flower. As with the name Lily,

it can also be spelt with two Ls.
**Alternative spellings:** Lillian

## Lilianna

**Meaning:** Peace and grace
**Origin:** Hebrew
**Pronunciation:** LIH lee AH nah
**Description:** Lilianna is thought to be a relatively new name, created by combining Lily and Anna. The lily is a Christian symbol of peace and Anna means 'grace', so Lilianna could mean 'graceful flower' or 'peace and grace'.
**Alternative spellings:** Liliana, Lilliana, Lillianna

## Lilibeth

**Meaning:** Flower; promised by God
**Origin:** English
**Pronunciation:** lili BETH
**Description:** Lilibeth is a combination of Lily, the flower and Beth, from Elizabeth meaning 'promised by God'. As such, it has a combined meaning from both names.

## Lilith

**Meaning:** Of the night
**Origin:** Assyrian
**Pronunciation:** lil ITH
**Description:** Lilith is the name of a demon in ancient Assyrian myths, and the name itself means 'of the night' in Akkadian. In Jewish tradition, she was Adam's first wife before she was cast out of Eden for not being submissive to him.

## Lilla

**Meaning:** Peace
**Origin:** English
**Pronunciation:** LIH lee

**:** English
**nciation:** lo EN na
**ption:** Lowenna is a rare
n name, specifically deriving
e county of Cornwall. It is
s a place name in many
f the world. It means 'joy'
n also be found spelt with a
n'
**tive spellings:** Lowena,
n

**g:** Crown of laurels
Latin
**ciation:** LAUW ree
**tion:** Lowri is the Welsh
nt of the name Laura,
derived from the Latin
'laurel'. It is quite a
wn name in Wales.
**ive spellings:** Lauri,
ury, Lawrie

**:** Moon
atin
**ation:** LOO ah
**on:** Lua is an uncom-
name of Latin origin
ant of the name Luna,
vord for moon and the
e Roman goddess of

**e spellings:** Looa,

**avoured warrior
nch
**tion:** loo AHN ah
**n:** Luana is thought to
nation of the names
Anna. Louise is of
in, meaning 'famous

**Description:** Lilla has come about as a variant of the extremely popular name Lily. Lily could be taken as a shortened form of Elizabeth or from the flower name.
**Alternative spellings:** Lila, Lilah, Lillah

## Lillian
**Meaning:** Promised by God
**Origin:** Hebrew
**Pronunciation:** LIL ee an
**Description:** Lillian is an elaboration upon the Latin name Lily, which comes from the name of the white flower. It can be spelt so that there is an emphasis on the 'anne' element of the name.
**Alternative spellings:** Lilian, Lilianne, Lillianne

## Lilo
**Meaning:** Generous one
**Origin:** Hawaiian
**Pronunciation:** lee LOH
**Description:** Lilo is a Hawaiian name meaning 'generous one'. It was made famous by the Disney animated film, *Lilo and Stitch*.

## Lily
**Meaning:** White flower; purity
**Origin:** Latin
**Pronunciation:** LILL lee
**Description:** The name Lily comes from the English word for the flower. It is regarded in many cultures as a symbol of purity and in Christian belief it is a symbol of peace. The name has recently enjoyed a huge popularity boost and is very popular in the UK and US.
**Alternative spellings:** Lili, Lilli, Lillie, Lilly

## Lina
**Meaning:** Palm tree
**Origin:** Arabic
**Pronunciation:** LEE nah
**Description:** Lina originally came about as a shortened form of Carolina and Avelina. It is now a given name in its own right and may originate from the Arabic for 'palm tree'.
**Alternative spellings:** Leena, Leenah, Lena, Lenah, Linah

## Linda
**Meaning:** Pretty; neat; snake
**Origin:** English
**Pronunciation:** LIN da
**Description:** The popular name Linda may have originally developed as a shortened form of Belinda. The word *'linda'* also means 'pretty' in Spanish, 'neat' in Italian and 'snake' in German.
**Alternative spellings:** Lynda

## Lindsay
**Meaning:** Lincoln island
**Origin:** English
**Pronunciation:** LIN zee
**Description:** Originally, Lindsay was a Scottish surname, but it is now a forename found worldwide. Sometimes seen as a boys' name in Scotland and Australia, it is usually a female name.
**Alternative spellings:** Lindsee, Lindsey, Lindsi, Lindsie, Linsay, Linsee, Linsey, Linsi, Linsie, Lyndsay, Lyndsey, Lynsay, Lynsey

## Lisa
**Meaning:** Promised by God
**Origin:** Hebrew
**Pronunciation:** LEE suh
**Description:** Lisa is a variant of

L

the less popular name Liza, itself a shortened form of Elizabeth. It may also be considered a shortening of the spelling Elisabeth.
**Alternative spellings:** Leesa, Lissa

## Lissa
**Meaning:** Honey bee
**Origin:** Greek
**Pronunciation:** LEE sah
**Description:** Lissa, once a short version of Melissa, is now a name in its own right. It can also be considered a variant of the name Lisa.
**Alternative spellings:** Leesa, Lisa

## Livia
**Meaning:** Peace; olive
**Origin:** Latin
**Pronunciation:** LIV ee uh
**Description:** Livia is considered the shortened form of Olive, a tree that symbolises peace in Christian tradition. It is thought to have derived from the Roman family name Livius, meaning 'blue'. It is often shortened to Liv.
**Alternative spellings:** Liviah, Livja, Lyvia

## Livvy
**Meaning:** Peace; olive
**Origin:** Latin
**Pronunciation:** LIV ee
**Description:** Livvy could be the pet form of the names Olivia, Olive or Livia. All of these names are of Latin origin and mean 'olive' or 'olive tree'.
**Alternative spellings:** Livi, Livie, Livvi, Livvi, Livvie, Livy

## Liyana
**Meaning:** Captivating
**Origin:** French

**Pronunciation:** lee AH
**Description:** Liyana is a variant form of Liana a feminine name of Fr and it is said to refer around. It is the name rainforest vine. These that the meaning of t along the lines of 'en 'captivating'.
**Alternative spelling** Liana

## Liz
**Meaning:** Promised
**Origin:** Hebrew
**Pronunciation:** LIZ
**Description:** Origi form of Elizabeth, 'promised from Gc name in its own ri
**Alternative spelli**

## Liza
**Meaning:** Promis
**Origin:** Hebrew
**Pronunciation:** L
**Description:** Liz form of Eliza, wh the name Elizabe times seen as an name Lisa.
**Alternative spe** Lyza

## Lizzie
**Meaning:** Prom
**Origin:** Hebrev
**Pronunciation:**
**Description:** L of the popular it is also foun own right.
**Alternative s|** Lizzy

modern name that combines the names Louise and Helen. Louise is of French origin and means 'famed warrior', while Ella derives from the Greek Helen meaning 'bright' and associated with beauty. We can therefore take the meaning to be 'beautiful warrior'.
**Alternative spellings:** Loella, Louela, Luella

## Louisa
**Meaning:** Famed warrior
**Origin:** Latin
**Pronunciation:** loo EE zah
**Description:** Louisa is the feminine form of the French name Louis, originally derived from Latin.
**Alternative spellings:** Louesa, Louiza, Luisa

## Louise
**Meaning:** Famed warrior
**Origin:** French
**Pronunciation:** LOO ease
**Description:** Louise is the primary feminine version of the French name Louis and is a popular name in Britain.
**Alternative spellings:** Louize, Luise

## Lourdes
**Meaning:** Craggy slope
**Origin:** Basque
**Pronunciation:** lords
**Description:** Lourdes is a Basque name meaning 'craggy slope'. It was made popular because Madonna named her daughter Lourdes.
**Alternative spellings:** Lords, Lordes

## Lowenna
**Meaning:** Joy

**Origi**
**Pronu**
**Descr**
English from t found parts o and ca single 'Alterna Lowena

## Lowri
**Meanin**
**Origin:**
**Pronun**
**Descrip** equivale which is word for well-kno
**Alternat** Laurie, L

## Lua
**Meaning**
**Origin:** L
**Pronunci**
**Descripti** mon girls and a vari the Latin name of t the moon.
**Alternativ** Luah

## Luana
**Meaning:**
**Origin:** Fr
**Pronuncia**
**Descriptic** be a comb Louise and French origi

warrior', while Anna is of Hebrew origin, meaning 'grace' and 'God favours'.
**Alternative spellings:** Louana, Louanna, Luanna

## Lucia
**Meaning:** Light
**Origin:** Latin
**Pronunciation:** loo CHEE ah
**Description:** St Lucia, a popular saint in northern Europe, represents light and is celebrated on 13 December, when light is scarce.
**Alternative spellings:** Loucia, Lucya

## Lucinda
**Meaning:** Light
**Origin:** Latin
**Pronunciation:** loo SIN dah
**Description:** Lucinda came about as an embellished version of the name Lucy, meaning 'light'. Traditionally the Romans used to give the name to baby girls born at dawn.
**Alternative spellings:** Loucinda, Lucindah, Lucynda

## Lucy
**Meaning:** Light
**Origin:** French
**Pronunciation:** LOO see
**Description:** Lucy comes from the Old French name Lucie, derived from the Latin word *'lux'*, meaning 'light'. It was in fairly widespread use back in the Middle Ages, increasing greatly in popularity in the 1990s.
**Alternative spellings:** Luci, Lucie

## Luella
**Meaning:** Famed warrior

**Origin:** French
**Pronunciation:** loo EH la
**Description:** Luella is a variant of Louella, a feminine name of relatively modern coinage. The name is a compound of the two favourite feminine names, Louise and Ella. Louise is of ultimately French origin and comes from the masculine Louis meaning 'famed warrior'. Ella is the pet form of the French Eleanor, which is itself the French variant of the Greek Helen. Although both the root names are French in origin, Luella is thought to have been invented in English-speaking countries.
**Alternative spellings:** Louella

## Lula
**Meaning:** No meaning
**Origin:** English
**Pronunciation:** loo LAH
**Description:** Lula is a diminutive of Louise and another other name that starts with Lu. It is also a nickname that is similar to Lulu, Lula or Lou.

## Lulu
**Meaning:** Light; famed warrior
**Origin:** German
**Pronunciation:** LOO loo
**Description:** Lulu came about as a pet form of the names Lucy and Louise, but is now often found as a name in its own right.
**Alternative spellings:** Loulou

## Luna
**Meaning:** Moon
**Origin:** Latin
**Pronunciation:** LOO nah
**Description:** The name Luna

L

comes from the Latin word for the moon. Best known as a character in the Harry Potter series.
**Alternative spellings:** Loona, Louna, Lunah

## Lydia
**Meaning:** Woman from Lydia
**Origin:** Greek
**Pronunciation:** LID ee uh
**Description:** Lydia was originally a place name for an area in Asia. In the New Testament, Lydia was converted by St Paul to Christianity.
**Alternative spellings:** Lidia, Lidiya, Lidya

## Lyla
**Meaning:** Dark-haired
**Origin:** Persian
**Pronunciation:** LYE lah
**Description:** Lyla can be seen as a spelling variant of the names Leila and Lila. Unlike these names, there is only one common pronunciation of Lyla.

**Alternative spellings:** Leila, Leilah, Lila, Lilah, Lylah

## Lynn
**Meaning:** Pretty
**Origin:** English
**Pronunciation:** LIN
**Description:** Lynn is a name of uncertain origin. It is thought to be a shortened form of Linda, in which case it would mean 'pretty'. It could also be a Gaelic surname related to water.
**Alternative spellings:** Lyn, Lynne

## Lyra
**Meaning:** Lyre
**Origin:** Latin
**Pronunciation:** LY ra
**Description:** Lyra is a modern name derived from the Latin for 'lyre', a stringed instrument. Lyra is also the name of a star constellation and so has connotations of brightness.
**Alternative spellings:** Lyrah

# M

## Maame
**Meaning:** Mother; pearl
**Origin:** African
**Pronunciation:** MAYM
**Description:** The name Maame could derive from an African word meaning 'mother' or it could be a form of the pet name Mame, from Margaret. In this case it would mean 'pearl'.
**Alternative spellings:** Mayme

## Mabel
**Meaning:** Loveable
**Origin:** Latin
**Pronunciation:** MAY bell
**Description:** Mabel is a short form of the Latin name Amabel, itself thought to be related to the name Annabel.
**Alternative spellings:** Mabelle, Maybel

## Mabli
**Meaning:** Loveable

**Origin:** Welsh
**Pronunciation:** mahb LEE
**Description:** Mabli is the Welsh form of the name Mabel, meaning 'loveable'. It was made popular by C.M Yonge's novel *The Heir of Redclyffe* (1854), which featured a character called Mabel.

## Macie

**Meaning:** Estate of Marcius
**Origin:** French
**Pronunciation:** may SEE
**Description:** Macie is a form of the feminine Macy, which comes from the French surname that means 'the Estate of Marcius'. The surname is thought of as masculine; however as a first name Macy is only used for girls. It is especially popular in America, famous because of Macy's department store.
**Alternative spellings:** Macy, Maci, Macey

## Mackenzie

**Meaning:** The fairest
**Origin:** Gaelic
**Pronunciation:** ma KEN zee
**Description:** Mackenzie derives from the Gaelic surname McKenzie, originally MacCoinneach. The meaning of the name varies. For a girl it is said to mean 'the fairest' yet as a boy's name it means 'handsome one'.
**Alternative spellings:** Mackenzi, Mackenzy, Makenzie, Mckenzi, Mckenzie, Mckenzy

## Maddie

**Meaning:** Relative of Maud
**Origin:** English
**Pronunciation:** mad DEE
**Description:** The female name Maddie is actually the shortened version of the name Madison, but has now become a forename in its own right. Beginning life as a unisex name, it quickly became more common to be used for females. This name is most commonly found in English-speaking countries.
**Alternative spellings:** Maddy

## Maddison

**Meaning:** Matthew's son
**Origin:** English
**Pronunciation:** mad ISSON
**Description:** Maddison is a variation of the more common Madison, meaning 'Matthew's son'. Maddison can also be a boys' name.
**Alternative spellings:** Madison

## Madeline

**Meaning:** From Magdala
**Origin:** Hebrew
**Pronunciation:** MAD uh line
**Description:** Madeline derives from the French form of Magdalene, which means 'from Magdala'. Magdala was the birthplace of Mary Magdalene, found in the Bible. The name was brought over from France in the 12th century.
**Alternative spellings:** Madeleine, Madelene, Madelyn

## Madiha

**Meaning:** Praiseworthy
**Origin:** Arabic
**Pronunciation:** mah DEE hah
**Description:** Madiha is a popular name in the Middle East and Swahili-speaking countries.
**Alternative spellings:** Madeeha

**M**

## Madina

**Meaning:** City of Islam
**Origin:** Arabic
**Pronunciation:** meh DEE nah
**Description:** Madina is a spelling variation of the name Medina, deriving from the city in the Middle East. Medina was the first city that the prophet Muhammad introduced Islam to, so it has great importance in that religion.
**Alternative spellings:** Madeena, Medeena, Medina

## Madison

See entry in 'Names for Baby Boys A–Z'

## Madonna

**Meaning:** My lady
**Origin:** Italian
**Pronunciation:** ma DON na
**Description:** Madonna comes from the Italian title of the Virgin Mary and means 'my lady'.
**Alternative spellings:** Madona, Madonnah

## Mae

**Meaning:** Star of the sea
**Origin:** Hebrew
**Pronunciation:** may
**Description:** Unlike May, the name Mae does not possess a link to the calendar month. However, the two names do share meaning. Both are pet forms of Mary, hence meaning 'star of the sea'.
**Alternative spellings:** May

## Maeve

**Meaning:** Intoxicating
**Origin:** Gaelic
**Pronunciation:** MAYV
**Description:** Maeve is a phonetically spelt variation of the Irish name Meadhbh. Maeve is the name of a powerful figure in Irish mythology.
**Alternative spellings:** Maieve, Mayeve

## Mafalda

**Meaning:** Mighty in battle
**Origin:** Italian
**Pronunciation:** ma FAL dah
**Description:** Mafalda is the Italian version of the German name Matilda and as such, shares the same meaning of 'mighty in battle'.

## Magdalena

**Meaning:** From Magdala
**Origin:** Hebrew
**Pronunciation:** mag dah LAY nah
**Description:** Magdalena derives from the name Magdalene, meaning 'from Magdala'.
**Alternative spellings:** Magdalina

## Maggie

**Meaning:** Pearl; light's creation
**Origin:** Latin
**Pronunciation:** MA gee
**Description:** Maggie came about as a pet name of Margaret, meaning 'pearl'. It has now become a name in its own right.
**Alternative spellings:** Maggey, Maggi, Maggy

## Magnolia

**Meaning:** Flower
**Origin:** English
**Pronunciation:** ma NO lee ah
**Description:** Magnolia comes from the white and pink flowers of the same name. Like Rose and Tulip, Magnolia is part of the

trend of using flowers as given names.

## Maha

**Meaning:** Great
**Origin:** Sanskrit
**Pronunciation:** MAH ha
**Description:** Maha derives from the Sanskrit word meaning 'great'. It is used in many titles in Hinduism, such as *maharaj*, meaning 'great king' and *mahashi,* which means 'great saint'.
**Alternative spellings:** Mahar

## Mahdiya

**Meaning:** Guided by Allah
**Origin:** Arabic
**Pronunciation:** MAH dee ah
**Description:** Mahdiya is the feminine version of the name Mahdi. Both are Arabic in origin and are favoured by Muslim parents due to their meaning.
**Alternative spellings:** Madiya, Madiyah, Mahdiyah

## Maheen

**Meaning:** Moonlight
**Origin:** Arabic
**Pronunciation:** mah HEEN
**Description:** The name Maheen derives from an Arabic word referring to the moon. It is quite a rare name.
**Alternative spellings:** Mahene, Mahine

## Mahi

**Meaning:** Goddess
**Origin:** Sanskrit
**Pronunciation:** muh HEE
**Description:** In Indian mythology Mahi is the name of an earth goddess. Mahi is also the name of

a village in India, and in several languages it means 'fish'.
**Alternative spellings:** Mahee

## Mahima

**Meaning:** Great one
**Origin:** Sanskrit
**Pronunciation:** mah HEE mah
**Description:** Mahima derives from a Sanskrit word meaning 'great one' and is often favoured by Hindu parents.
**Alternative spellings:** Maheema, Mahema, Mahimah

## Mahira

**Meaning:** Talented
**Origin:** Arabic
**Pronunciation:** meh HEER ah
**Description:** Mahira is the feminine version of the name Mahir and found mainly in the Middle East. Its origins are probably either Hebrew or Arabic.
**Alternative spellings:** Maheera, Mahirah

## Mahnoor

**Meaning:** Moonlight
**Origin:** Arabic
**Pronunciation:** MAH noor
**Description:** Mahnoor is a phonetically soft name with the beautiful meaning of 'moonlight'.
**Alternative spellings:** Mahnor

## Maia

**Meaning:** Mother; illusion
**Origin:** Greek
**Pronunciation:** MAY ah
**Description:** Maia is found in Greek and Roman mythology, where it is the name of the goddess of spring and the mother of the god Hermes. Maia is also a

**M**

variation of the name Maya, which means 'illusion' and is often found in Hindu philosophy.
**Alternative spellings:** Maiya, Maja, Maya, Mya, Myah

## Maira
**Meaning:** Sea dew
**Origin:** Hebrew
**Pronunciation:** MAY rah
**Description:** Maira is the Irish equivalent of the name Mary. The Maira is also the name of an Italian river, and the name is used in Italy.
**Alternative spellings:** Mairah, Mayra

## Maisha
**Meaning:** Prosperous
**Origin:** Arabic
**Pronunciation:** mah EE sha
**Description:** Maisha is a popular variant of the name Aisha. Aisha was the name of the third wife of the prophet Muhammad.
**Alternative spellings:** Maesha, Maishah

## Maisy
**Meaning:** Pearl; light's creation
**Origin:** Latin
**Pronunciation:** MAY zee
**Description:** This very popular name may have come about as a pet name for Margaret or the Gaelic Mairead. Both names come from the Latin *'margarita'*, meaning 'pearl'.
**Alternative spellings:** Maisee, Maisey, Maisie, Maizie, Maysie, Mazie

## Makayla
**Meaning:** Who is like God?
**Origin:** Hebrew
**Pronunciation:** mee KAY lah

**Description:** Makayla is a fairly modern name, created as a phonetically spelt version of Michaela. It is often shortened to Kayla.
**Alternative spellings:** Michaela

## Malaika
**Meaning:** Angel
**Origin:** Arabic
**Pronunciation:** mah lah EE kah; mah LIE kah
**Description:** Malaika is the female form of the Arabic name Malak, meaning 'angel'. It is often shortened to Mal.
**Alternative spellings:** Malaikah, Malayka

## Malak
See entry in 'Names for Baby Boys A–Z'

## Malala
**Meaning:** Grief-stricken
**Origin:** Afghan
**Pronunciation:** ma LA LA
**Description:** Malala is an Afghan name meaning 'grief-stricken'. Malala Yousafzai is a Pakistani activist and the world's youngest Nobel Prize laureate.

## Maleeha
**Meaning:** Beautiful one
**Origin:** Sanskrit
**Pronunciation:** MAH lee ah
**Description:** Maleeha is a variant of Maliha, which is a feminine name that originates from a Sanskrit word meaning 'beautiful one'. It is quite a popular name with Muslim parents and is found used mostly in the Middle East and Africa.
**Alternative spellings:** Maliha

## Mali

**Meaning:** Star of the sea
**Origin:** Welsh
**Pronunciation:** mal LEE
**Description:** Mali is a popular Welsh name, derived from the English name Molly, which is itself a pet form of Mary, meaning 'star of the sea'. It could also refer to the African country of the same name, or the Thai name Mali, which means 'flower'.

## Malia

**Meaning:** Sea dew
**Origin:** Hebrew
**Pronunciation:** mah LEE ah
**Description:** Malia is a variant of the name Mary, and is popular in Hawaii.
**Alternative spellings:** Maliah, Maliya

## Malika

**Meaning:** Nobility
**Origin:** Arabic
**Pronunciation:** MAH lee kah
**Description:** Malika is the feminine equivalent of Malik. It is sometimes used in Pakistan for the title of lady, which gives it the meaning of 'nobility'.
**Alternative spellings:** Maleeka, Malikah

## Malina

**Meaning:** Raspberry
**Origin:** Russian
**Pronunciation:** ma LEE nah
**Description:** Malina, when directly translated from Russian, means 'raspberry'. It could also be a variation of the name Melina.

## Maliyah

**Meaning:** Bitter
**Origin:** Hawaiian
**Pronunciation:** MAH lee yah
**Description:** Maliyah is the Hawaiian version of the name Mary, and shares the same meaning of 'bitter'.
**Alternative spellings:** Maliya

## Malka

**Meaning:** Queen
**Origin:** Hebrew
**Pronunciation:** MAHL kah
**Description:** Malka derives from the Hebrew word meaning 'queen'.
**Alternative spellings:** Malca, Malcah, Malkah

## Mallory

**Meaning:** Unfortunate
**Origin:** French
**Pronunciation:** mal OR ee
**Description:** Mallory is a name derived from the French word 'maloret,' which means 'unfortunate'. Despite the meaning, it would still make a lovely baby name for a girl.
**Alternative spellings:** Malory

## Mamie

**Meaning:** Sea dew
**Origin:** English
**Pronunciation:** maim EE
**Description:** Mamie is a nickname for the name Mary, but can also be used as a given name on its own. As such, it shares the same meaning of 'sea dew'. Mamie Gummer is an American actress and daughter of Meryl Streep.

## Mamrie

**Meaning:** No meaning
**Origin:** English

**Pronunciation:** maim REE
**Description:** Mamrie is a modern invented name and as such, has no real meaning. It is associated with YouTube personality, Mamrie Hart, whose great-grandmother's middle name was Mamrie.

## Manahil
**Meaning:** Atmosphere of paradise
**Origin:** Urdu
**Pronunciation:** MAH na hil
**Description:** Manahil is a variant of the name Minahil, which is of Urdu origin. Some sources claim the name means 'atmosphere of paradise'.
**Alternative spellings:** Manahill

## Manal
**Meaning:** One who attains
**Origin:** Arabic
**Pronunciation:** MAH nal
**Description:** Manal is a unisex name; however it is most often found used for girls. As well as having Arabic roots, it is also thought to derive from a Sanskrit word meaning 'bird'.
**Alternative spellings:** Manel, Mannal

## Mandy
**Meaning:** Loveable
**Origin:** Latin
**Pronunciation:** MAN dee
**Description:** Mandy is a pet form of the Latin name Amanda, and therefore means 'loveable'. It is now a name in its own right.
**Alternative spellings:** Mandi, Mandie

## Manha
**Meaning:** Gift from Allah; morning

**Origin:** Arabic
**Pronunciation:** man HA
**Description:** Manha is often favoured by those of the Muslim faith and is currently quite a popular name for girls. In Portuguese it means 'morning'.
**Alternative spellings:** Manhah

## Mannat
**Meaning:** Special prayer
**Origin:** Sanskrit
**Pronunciation:** MAN nat
**Description:** Mannat is quite an unusual name in Britain but when found it is mainly favoured by Sikh parents. It is quite a popular name in India, and can often be found in the UK as a surname.
**Alternative spellings:** Manat, Mannatt

## Manon
**Meaning:** Sea dew
**Origin:** French
**Pronunciation:** mah NON
**Description:** Manon came about as a French pet form of the Hebrew name Mary.
**Alternative spellings:** Mannon

## Mara
**Meaning:** Sea dew
**Origin:** Hebrew
**Pronunciation:** MAHR ah
**Description:** Mara was once a pet name of Mary, but is now a name in its own right. It could also be considered the pet form of longer names such as Tamara or Samara, in which case it would carry their meaning.
**Alternative spellings:** Marah, Marar

## Marcelina
**Meaning:** From the god Mars

**Origin:** Latin
**Pronunciation:** mar suh LEE nah
**Description:** Marcelina is a feminine version of the name Marcel, derived from the name of the Roman god of war, Mars.
**Alternative spellings:** Marceleena, Marcelena, Marcelinah

## Marcella

**Meaning:** From the god Mars
**Origin:** Italian
**Pronunciation:** mar SELL uh
**Description:** Marcella is the Italian, feminine version of the name Mark and as such, shares the same meaning of 'from the god Mars'.

## Marcheline

**Meaning:** From the god Mars
**Origin:** Latin
**Pronunciation:** MAR shuh LEEN
**Description:** Marcheline is a variation of the French name Marceline, ultimately derived from the name of the Roman god of war, Mars. It could also be seen as a name taken from the month of March.
**Alternative spellings:** Marchaline, Marchalyne, Marchelyne, Marsheline

## Marcia

**Meaning:** From the god Mars
**Origin:** Latin
**Pronunciation:** MAR sha; MAR cee a
**Description:** Marcia comes from the same roots as Marcella and Marcelina. These are feminine versions of the Latin name Marcel, derived from the name of the Roman god of war, Mars.
**Alternative spellings:** Marciah, Marcya

## Marcie

**Meaning:** From the god Mars
**Origin:** Italian
**Pronunciation:** MAR see
**Description:** Marcie was originally the pet form of Latin names such as Marcella and Marcia, but is also found used as a name in its own right.
**Alternative spellings:** Marci, Marcy

## Margaret

**Meaning:** Pearl; light's creation
**Origin:** Greek
**Pronunciation:** MAR gah ret
**Description:** Margaret has been an enduringly popular name ever since the Middle Ages. It is derived from the Greek word *'margaron'* meaning 'pearl'.
**Alternative spellings:** Margeret, Margret

## Margo

**Meaning:** Pearl
**Origin:** Latin
**Pronunciation:** mar GO
**Description:** Margo is a variation of the name Margot, meaning 'pearl'. It is also likely influenced by the wine-making French town. Both names are also connected to Margaret, which also has the same meaning.
**Alternative spellings:** Margaux, Margot

## Marguerite

**Meaning:** Pearl
**Origin:** French
**Pronunciation:** marg ARR eet
**Description:** Marguerite is the French version of the name Margaret and shares the same meaning of 'pearl'.

**M**

## Marhaw

**Meaning:** Plant
**Origin:** Arabic
**Pronunciation:** MAR wah
**Description:** Marhaw is thought to be of Arabic origin, although its meaning is debated. It is thought to come from the Arabic name of a plant.
**Alternative spellings:** Marhow

## Maria

**Meaning:** Sea dew
**Origin:** Latin
**Pronunciation:** ma REE ah; ma RYE ah
**Description:** Maria is the Latin form of Mary. It is especially popular in Spain. The name has religious connotations in Christian belief as it is the name of the mother of Christ.
**Alternative spellings:** Maariya, Maariyah, Mariah, Mariya, Mariyah

## Mariam

**Meaning:** Uncertain
**Origin:** Arabic
**Pronunciation:** MAR ee um
**Description:** Mariam is an Arabic girls' name and a variant of Miryam, the Arabic alternative form of Mary, the mother of Jesus. It is an uncommon name for girls, meaning 'uncertain'.
**Alternative spellings:** Marian, Marium, Mariyam, Maryam

## Mariama

**Meaning:** Sea dew
**Origin:** Hebrew
**Pronunciation:** mah ree AH ma
**Description:** Mariama is a more modern variation of the name Miriam, which is the original

form of Mary. Its first appearance is as the name of the sister of Moses. However, some argue that its origins lie further back in ancient Egypt and its meaning is debated.
**Alternative spellings:** Mariamah, Maryama

## Mariana

**Meaning:** Sea dew
**Origin:** Hebrew
**Pronunciation:** mah ree AH nah
**Description:** Mariana is a variant of Marian, which comes from the same source as the name Mary. The variant Mariana is popular in Spanish-speaking countries.
**Alternative spellings:** Marianah, Marianna

## Marianna

**Meaning:** No Meaning
**Origin:** English
**Pronunciation:** mer EE an ah
**Description:** Marianna is a combination of the names Maria and Anna. It should not be confused with the name Mariana, which is Roman in origin. Marianna is also sometimes the Latinised form of the name Marianne.

## Marianne

**Meaning:** Sea dew
**Origin:** Hebrew
**Pronunciation:** MAH ree an
**Description:** Marianne is a variant of Marian, which comes from the same source as the name Mary.
**Alternative spellings:** Marian, Mariane

## Marie

**Meaning:** Sea dew
**Origin:** Hebrew
**Pronunciation:** muh REE
**Description:** Marie, the French form of Maria, can also be considered a spelling variant of the biblical name Mary.
**Alternative spellings:** Mari, Mary

## Mariella

**Meaning:** Sea dew
**Origin:** Hebrew
**Pronunciation:** mah re EH lah
**Description:** Mariella is an elaborated version of the popular name Mary.
**Alternative spellings:** Mariela, Mariellah, Maryella

## Marigold

**Meaning:** Flower
**Origin:** English
**Pronunciation:** mary GOLD
**Description:** Marigold comes from the bright yellow-orange flower of the same name. Like Rose and Tulip, Marigold is part of the trend of using flowers as given names.

## Marilyn

**Meaning:** No meaning
**Origin:** English
**Pronunciation:** mer LIN
**Description:** Marilyn is a combination of Mary and Lynn, and thus has no real meaning. Perhaps the most famous bearer of this name is Marilyn Monroe. Other names related to Marilyn are Maralyn, Marie, Mary, Marylyn and Merrilyn.

## Marina

**Meaning:** Sea dew

**Origin:** Latin
**Pronunciation:** ma REE nah
**Description:** Marina derives from the Latin name Marino, meaning 'man of the sea'. Shakespeare introduced many to the name in his play *Pericles, Prince Of Tyre*.
**Alternative spellings:** Marinah, Maryna

## Marion

**Meaning:** Sea dew
**Origin:** French
**Pronunciation:** mary ON
**Description:** Marion is the French version of the name Marie, which in turn comes from the Hebrew Miryam. All of these names mean 'sea dew'.

## Marisa

**Meaning:** Sea dew
**Origin:** Hebrew
**Pronunciation:** mar EES ah
**Description:** Marisa is a spelling variant of the name Marissa and pronounced 'mar EES ah', whereas Marissa is usually pronounced 'ma RIS ah'.
**Alternative spellings:** Marisah, Marissa, Marissah

## Marisol

**Meaning:** Mary of the solitude
**Origin:** Spanish
**Pronunciation:** mary SOL
**Description:** Marisol is the Spanish title given to the Virgin Mary. It is a shortened form of María de la Soledad, meaning 'Mary of the solitude'.

## Marjorie

**Meaning:** Pearl
**Origin:** Latin

**M**

**Pronunciation:** mar JOOR ee
**Description:** Marjorie is a variation of the name Margaret, and both names come from the Latin word '*margarita*' meaning 'pearl'. It is also said that Marjorie is influenced by marjoram, a type of herb.

## Marla

**Meaning:** No meaning
**Origin:** German
**Pronunciation:** MAAR lah
**Description:** Marla is the German version of Marlene. The name is a combination of Mary and Magdalen, and as such has no meaning.

## Marley

See entry in 'Names for Baby Boys A–Z'

## Marlie

**Meaning:** Forest of joy
**Origin:** English
**Pronunciation:**
**Description:** Marlie is a variation of Marley, which is from Old English words meaning 'forest' and 'pleasure'. The name Marley can be seen to mean 'forest of joy'. Adopted as a first name in fairly modern English, Marley can be both a masculine and feminine name.
**Alternative spellings:** Marley

## Marlon

See entry in 'Names for Baby Boys A–Z'

## Marlowe

**Meaning:** Driftwood
**Origin:** English
**Pronunciation:** mar LOW
**Description:** Marlowe is an English girls' name meaning

'driftwood'. It is attributed to the 16th-century poet and playwright, Christopher Marlowe.
**Alternative spellings:** Marlow

## Marnie

**Meaning:** Sea dew
**Origin:** Latin
**Pronunciation:** MAR nee
**Description:** Marnie is a name that is derived from Marina, meaning 'from the sea'. Marnie has become a name in its own right and is especially popular in English-speaking countries.
**Alternative spellings:** Marney, Marni, Marny

## Marta

**Meaning:** Lady
**Origin:** Hebrew
**Pronunciation:** MAR tah
**Description:** Marta is a name seen as a variation of Martha, meaning 'lady'. Marta is a popular name on the continent.
**Alternative spellings:** Martah

## Martha

**Meaning:** Lady
**Origin:** Aramaic
**Pronunciation:** MAR tha
**Description:** In the New Testament, Martha was the sister of Lazarus. Due to this character's life, the name Martha is associated with hard domestic work.
**Alternative spellings:** Marther

## Martina

**Meaning:** From the god Mars
**Origin:** Latin
**Pronunciation:** mar TEE nah
**Description:** Martina, a common girls' name of Latin origin, is the

female form of Martin. It is popular in English-, German-, Italian-, Romanian- and Spanish-speaking countries. The variation Martyna may come from Wales, where the male name is Martyn.
**Alternative spellings:** Martinah, Martyna

## Marwa
**Meaning:** Flower
**Origin:** Arabic
**Pronunciation:** MAR wah
**Description:** Marwa derives from the Arabic name for a species of flower. It is also the name of a mountain in Saudi Arabia, Al-Marwa. The name is popular in the Middle East.
**Alternative spellings:** Marwah

## Mary
**Meaning:** Sea dew
**Origin:** Hebrew
**Pronunciation:** MAIR ee
**Description:** Mary is a Middle English form of the Hebrew name Miriam. Mary was the name of the Mother of Christ, the Virgin Mary. As a result the name was very popular among early Christians. The name was popular until the 1960s, when it declined.
**Alternative spellings:** Mari, Marie

## Maryam
**Meaning:** Sea dew
**Origin:** Hebrew
**Pronunciation:** MAH ree AM
**Description:** Maryam is a variant of the more common Mariama, a variant form of names such as Miriam and Marianna. All of the names are closely linked to the Hebrew name Mary, meaning 'sea dew'.
**Alternative spellings:** Mariama, Mariamma, Maryaa

## Marzia
**Meaning:** Mars
**Origin:** Italian
**Pronunciation:** MAR tsya
**Description:** Marzia is the Italian form of the name Marcia, and the two share the meaning of 'Mars' or the Roman God of War. These names all come from the same root as the similar feminine name Marcella and the masculine name Marcus.

## Masha
**Meaning:** Sea dew
**Origin:** Russian
**Pronunciation:** mah SHA
**Description:** Masha is the Russian form of the name Marie and as such, shares the same meaning of 'sea dew'. It is often used as a nickname for women named Marie or Maria.

## Mason
See entry in 'Names for Baby Boys A–Z'

## Matilda
**Meaning:** Mighty in battle
**Origin:** German
**Pronunciation:** muh TIL duh
**Description:** Matilda, the name of an early German queen, derives from the Old German words *'macht'* and *'hiltja'* meaning 'mighty' and 'battle' respectively. In recent times, the book by Roald Dahl and subsequent Hollywood film have kept this name in the spotlight.
**Alternative spellings:** Mathilda, Matildah, Matylda, Matilde

**M**

## Maude

**Meaning:** Powerful battler
**Origin:** German
**Pronunciation:** maude
**Description:** Maude is an Old German name meaning 'powerful battler'. It is also seen as a variant of the name Matilda, so the two have very similar meanings.

## Maureen

**Meaning:** Sea Dew
**Origin:** Irish
**Pronunciation:** more EEN
**Description:** Maureen is the Irish version of Mary and Miryam, and as such shares the same meaning of 'sea dew'. It is also the feminine version of Maurice.

## Mavis

**Meaning:** Type of Bird
**Origin:** English
**Pronunciation:** MAY vis
**Description:** Mavis is actually a type of bird, more specifically the song thrush. It was used as a given name in Marie Corelli's 19th-century novel, *The Sorrows of Satan*.

## May

**Meaning:** Month of May
**Origin:** English
**Pronunciation:** MAY
**Description:** A pet form of Margaret, Mary or Mabel, May also exists as an independent given name from the month of May. It is often chosen as a name for a girl born in May.
**Alternative spellings:** Mae, Mai

## Maya

**Meaning:** Mother; illusion
**Origin:** Greek Pronunciation:** MAY ah
**Description:** Maya is found in Greek and Roman mythology, where it is the name of the goddess of spring and the mother of the god Hermes. See also Maia.
**Alternative spellings:** Maiya, Maja, Maia, Mya, Myah

## Maysa

**Meaning:** Graceful
**Origin:** Arabic
**Pronunciation:** MAY sah
**Description:** Although of Arabic origins, Maysa could also be a variant of the name Maisy. Maisy has become an extremely popular name recently and Maysa could be a nice alternative.
**Alternative spellings:** Maisa, Maysah

## Meadow

**Meaning:** Meadow
**Origin:** English
**Pronunciation:** MED oh
**Description:** Although it has connotations of beauty and freedom, Meadow is a name that comes from the English word for a grassy field, and has no other meaning.
**Alternative spellings:** Medow

## Medea

**Meaning:** Cunning
**Origin:** Greek
**Pronunciation:** meh DEE ah
**Description:** In Greek mythology, Medea was a sorceress who took revenge on her husband Jason of the Argonauts after being betrayed by him. She became a common antagonist of ancient playwrights.
**Alternative spellings:** Medeia, Media

## Meera

**Meaning:** Prosperous
**Origin:** Sanskrit
**Pronunciation:** mee RAH
**Description:** Meera is an Indian name, meaning 'prosperous' in Sanskrit. Meera Bai was a popular Hindu mystical poet and her writings are well known in India. She was a 15th-century Indian princess whose poems were devoted to the Indian god Krishna.

## Meerab

**Meaning:** Unknown
**Origin:** Urdu
**Pronunciation:** MEE rab
**Description:** Meerab, an unusual name whose meaning is uncertain, seems likely to be of Urdu origin. It is often favoured by Muslim parents.
**Alternative spellings:** Merab

## Megan

**Meaning:** Pearl; light's creation
**Origin:** Welsh
**Pronunciation:** MEG uhn
**Description:** Megan is a longer version of Meg, a pet name for Margaret. It is a very popular name in Britain, although Meghan is the more common spelling in America and Australia.
**Alternative spellings:** Meghan

## Mehek

**Meaning:** Sweet smell
**Origin:** Arabic
**Pronunciation:** meh HEK
**Description:** Mehek is a variant of Mehak, a name of Arabic origins. It is quite rare in Britain but has more popularity in the Middle East.
**Alternative spellings:** Mehak

## Mehreen

**Meaning:** Bright
**Origin:** Arabic
**Pronunciation:** mah REEN
**Description:** Mehreen is an Arabic girls' name often found in Pakistan.
**Alternative spellings:** Mehrene, Mehrine

## Meisha

**Meaning:** Alive
**Origin:** Arabic
**Pronunciation:** MAY shah
**Description:** Meisha is an uncommon name of Arabic origin and a variant of Aisha, who was the third and favoured wife of the prophet Muhammad.
**Alternative spellings:** Mischa, Misha, Mysha

## Melania

**Meaning:** Black; dark
**Origin:** Greek
**Pronunciation:** mee LAN ee ah
**Description:** Melania is actually a Greek word meaning 'black' or 'dark'. It was the name of two Roman saints who were known for their charity to the poor.

## Melanie

**Meaning:** Dark-haired
**Origin:** Greek
**Pronunciation:** MELL ann ee
**Description:** Melanie derives from the Greek adjective *'melas'*, meaning 'black' or 'dark'. Melanie was the name of two 5th-century Roman saints, a grandmother and granddaughter. The name was introduced to England from France in the Middle Ages and became popular in the late 20th century.

**M**

**Alternative spellings:** Melaney, Melani, Melany

## Melantho
**Meaning:** Dark flower
**Origin:** Greek
**Pronunciation:** mel AN tho
**Description:** In Greek mythology, Melantho appeared in Homer's epic poem *The Odyssey* as an unfaithful maid.
**Alternative spellings:** Melanthios, Melanthus

## Melia
**Meaning:** Ash tree
**Origin:** Greek
**Pronunciation:** ME lee ya
**Description:** Melia is an uncommon girls' name of Greek origin and a variant of Amelia. The name means 'ash tree' in Greek and it is also the name of a nymph in Greek mythology.
**Alternative spellings:** Meliah, Melya

## Melina
**Meaning:** Dark-haired
**Origin:** Greek
**Pronunciation:** meh LEE nah
**Description:** Melina is a name of ultimately Greek origin and may derive from *'meli'* (honey), *'melon'* (apple) or *'melas'* (dark). It is similar to the name Melanie, so could be seen as holding the same meaning of 'dark-haired'.
**Alternative spellings:** Meleena, Melena

## Melinda
**Meaning:** No meaning
**Origin:** English
**Pronunciation:** meh LIN dah
**Description:** Melinda is thought to have been invented in the 18th century from the elements 'mel' and the suffix 'inda'. As such, it has no real meaning.

## Melissa
**Meaning:** Honey bee
**Origin:** Greek
**Pronunciation:** meh LIS sa
**Description:** Melissa comes from the Greek word meaning 'honey bee'.
**Alternative spellings:** Melisa, Melisah

## Melody
**Meaning:** A song
**Origin:** Greek
**Pronunciation:** MEL oh dee
**Description:** Melody comes from the Greek word *'melodia'*, meaning 'to sing'. According to the English dictionary, a melody is a pleasing arrangement of musical notes. Like Harmony, Melody has become a popular given name.
**Alternative spellings:** Melodey, Melodi, Melodie

## Melrose
**Meaning:** Scottish town
**Origin:** Gaelic
**Pronunciation:** MEL roze
**Description:** Melrose is a name taken from the small Scottish town of the same name. It can be found as both a first name and a surname.
**Alternative spellings:** Mellrose, Melroze

## Memphis
**Meaning:** Place in Tennessee
**Origin:** English
**Pronunciation:** mem FISS
**Description:** Memphis is a city in the American state of Tennessee.

Like London and Paris, this name follows the trend of using place names for baby names.

## Menna

**Meaning:** Unknown
**Origin:** Welsh
**Pronunciation:** MEH na
**Description:** The name Menna is found in several languages and therefore has an uncertain origin and meaning. It is a male ancient Egyptian name, as well as a modern Welsh girls' name.
**Alternative spellings:** Menah, Mennah

## Mercedes

**Meaning:** Merciful
**Origin:** Spanish
**Pronunciation:** mer SAY dees
**Description:** The name Mercedes comes from a Spanish title for the Virgin Mary, 'our lady of the mercies', and has long been popular in that country. Its popularity may have been increased in the UK owing to the luxury car.
**Alternative spellings:** Merceydes, Mersaydes

## Mercy

**Meaning:** Merciful
**Origin:** English
**Pronunciation:** MER see
**Description:** Mercy is from the English word for the virtue. It is used in the same way as Hope and both seem to be popular with Christian parents.
**Alternative spellings:** Mercey, Merci, Mercie

## Meredith

**Meaning:** Great lord

**Origin:** Welsh
**Pronunciation:** ME re dith
**Description:** Meredith is the English form of the Old Welsh male name Maredudd. The name is well established in the US.
**Alternative spellings:** Meridith, Merredith

## Merida

**Meaning:** One who has achieved a high honour
**Origin:** Latin
**Pronunciation:** mer ID ah
**Description:** Merida is a Latin name meaning 'one who has achieved a high honour'. It is the name of the main character from Disney's 2012 animated film, *Brave*.

## Merryn

**Meaning:** Joyful
**Origin:** English
**Pronunciation:** MEH rin
**Description:** Merryn is a name of either Cornish or Old English origin, said to mean 'joyful'. St Merryn is the name of a village in Cornwall and the name may have originally been given to girls born here.
**Alternative spellings:** Merrin, Merin

## Meryem

**Meaning:** Bitter
**Origin:** Turkish
**Pronunciation:** MERY am
**Description:** Meryem is the Turkish version of the Hebrew name Miriam, which in turn is a variation of the name Mary, meaning 'bitter'. Related names include Maryam and Maryann.
**Alternative spellings:** Mariam, Maryam

M

## Meryl

**Meaning:** Bright; sea
**Origin:** Celtic
**Pronunciation:** mer RYL
**Description:** Meryl is the feminine version of the name Muriel. The name is composed of '*muir*' meaning 'sea,' and '*gheal*' meaning 'bright'. Meryl Streep is a famous American actress with this name.

## Mia

**Meaning:** Sea dew
**Origin:** Danish
**Pronunciation:** MEE uh
**Description:** Mia is thought to be the Danish and Swedish form of Maria. The name enjoyed a sharp rise in popularity in the late 1990s and has since gained even more popularity. The name could have also come about as a pet form of names ending in 'mia', such as Hermia.
**Alternative spellings:** Mea, Miah

## Miami

**Meaning:** Big water
**Origin:** Native American
**Pronunciation:** my AM ee
**Description:** Miami is a city in the south-eastern corner of Florida. The city was named for the nearby Miami River, derived from the Native American word *mayaimi* (meaning 'big water'), who were the people who lived around Lake Mayaimi.

## Michaela

**Meaning:** Who is like God?
**Origin:** Hebrew
**Pronunciation:** me KAY lah
**Description:** Michaela is the feminine version of Michael, often shortened to Kayla. It is popular in English-, German- and Italian-speaking countries.
**Alternative spellings:** Makayla, Mikayla

## Michalina

**Meaning:** Who is like God?
**Origin:** Hebrew
**Pronunciation:** me ka LEE nah
**Description:** Michalina is a variant of the masculine name Michael and it is found used mainly by Polish parents.
**Alternative spellings:** Michaelina, Michalena, Michalinah

## Michelle

**Meaning:** Who is like God?
**Origin:** Hebrew
**Pronunciation:** MICH ell
**Description:** Michelle is the French feminine form of Michael, and soared in popularity during the 1970s and 80s. It is sometimes shortened to Shelley.
**Alternative spellings:** Michele, Mishelle

## Mila

**Meaning:** Pleasant
**Origin:** Latin
**Pronunciation:** MEE lah
**Description:** Mila is used as a pet form for many Eastern European names, but is also a name in its own right, meaning 'pleasant'.
**Alternative spellings:** Melah, Milla

## Milan

See entry in 'Names for Baby Boys A–Z'

## Milana

**Meaning:** Favoured; from Milan
**Origin:** Slavic

**Pronunciation:** mee LAN ah
**Description:** Milana is a popular name in Slavic countries, and is an alternative spelling of the name Milena. It could also be an Italian name, meaning someone who comes from Milan.
See entry in 'Names for Baby Boys A–Z.'

## Mildred
**Meaning:** Gentle strength
**Origin:** English
**Pronunciation:** mill DRED
**Description:** Mildred is an Old English name composed of the elements of '*milde*' meaning 'gentle' and '*dryd*' meaning 'strength'.

## Miley
**Meaning:** Smiley
**Origin:** Hawaiian
**Pronunciation:** MY lee
**Description:** Miley is a phonetic spelling of the feminine Hawaiian name Maile. It has gained popularity owing to the teenage star Miley Cyrus and has taken on the meaning 'smiley'.
**Alternative spellings:** Mylee, Myley, Myli, Mylie

## Millicent
**Meaning:** Hard-working
**Origin:** German
**Pronunciation:** MEE lee sent
**Description:** Millicent comes from an Old German word referring to having a strong work ethic. It was a popular name in France in the 12th century in the form Melisent, yet it has since returned to its original form. It is not a common name in Britain at the moment, although its pet form Millie is very popular.

**Alternative spellings:** Milicent, Milisent, Millisent

## Millie
**Meaning:** Hard-working
**Origin:** German
**Pronunciation:** MILL lee
**Description:** Millie was originally used as the pet form of Millicent, but is now a first name in its own right.
**Alternative spellings:** Milli, Milly

## Mimi
**Meaning:** Sea dew
**Origin:** Hebrew
**Pronunciation:** ME me
**Description:** Mimi is a pet form of the name Mary, a biblical name of Hebrew origin that means 'sea dew'.
**Alternative spellings:** Mimie, Mimy

## Mina
**Meaning:** Love
**Origin:** German
**Pronunciation:** MEE nah
**Description:** It is thought that Mina first came about as a pet form of names ending in 'mina', such as Wilhelmina. Now as a name in its own right, it means 'love'. It could also be a variant of the Arabic Meena, meaning 'fish'.
**Alternative spellings:** Meena, Mena, Minah

## Minahil
**Meaning:** Atmosphere of paradise
**Origin:** Urdu
**Pronunciation:** MIH na hil
**Description:** It is difficult to ascertain the precise origin and

M

meaning of Minahil, although a few sources claim it means 'atmosphere of paradise'.
**Alternative spellings:** Minahill

## Minako
**Meaning:** Child of the beautiful Nara
**Origin:** Japanese
**Pronunciation:** Min A Ko
**Description:** Although Japanese, this name can be found right across Asia. The character *'mi'* means 'beautiful' and *'ko'* means 'child'.
**Alternative spellings:** Minakoh

## Minami
**Meaning:** South
**Origin:** Japanese
**Pronunciation:** MEE nah mee
**Description:** Minami is most commonly found in Japan and only requires one Japanese character to be written, which means 'south'.
**Alternative spellings:** Miname, Minamie, Minamy

## Mindy
**Meaning:** No meaning
**Origin:** English
**Pronunciation:** min DEE
**Description:** Mindy is a diminutive of the name Melinda. As Melinda is an 18th century invented name, neither names have any real meaning.

## Minerva
**Meaning:** Intellect
**Origin:** Latin
**Pronunciation:** min ER vah
**Description:** Minerva is derived from the Latin word *'mens'* meaning 'intellect'. Minerva was the Roman goddess of wisdom and war. Minerva McGonagall is a character in the Harry Potter series.

## Minnie
**Meaning:** Seeking protection
**Origin:** German
**Pronunciation:** MIH nee
**Description:** Minnie is a name that came about as the pet form of Wilma and Wilhelmina. Both of these names are feminine variants of the name William, meaning 'seeking protection'.
**Alternative spellings:** Minni, Minny

## Mira
**Meaning:** Famed one; surprise
**Origin:** Latin
**Pronunciation:** MEER ah
**Description:** The name Mira is said to come from a Latin word used to express surprise. However, it is also used in Slavic languages to mean 'famed one'.
**Alternative spellings:** Mirah, Mirra

## Mirabelle
**Meaning:** Wondrous
**Origin:** Latin
**Pronunciation:** mira BELLE
**Description:** Mirabelle is a Latin name meaning 'wondrous'. It stems from the Latin word *'mirabilis'*, giving the name its meaning.

## Miracle
**Meaning:** Miracle
**Origin:** English
**Pronunciation:** MIH rih cul
**Description:** The name Miracle comes from the English word for an extraordinary event that surpasses all known human and natural powers. These virtues

names are often favoured by Christian parents.

**Alternative spellings:** Miracel, Miricle

## Miranda

**Meaning:** Worthy of admiration
**Origin:** Latin
**Pronunciation:** mih RAN dah
**Description:** This name was supposedly invented by William Shakespeare for a character in his play *The Tempest*. He may have been inspired by the Latin name Mirabel, meaning 'admirable'.
**Alternative spellings:** Mirandah, Myranda

## Miri

**Meaning:** Sea dew
**Origin:** Hebrew
**Pronunciation:** mi REE
**Description:** Miri is a diminutive of the name Miriam and both names are Hebrew in origin. The names mean 'sea dew'.

## Miriam

**Meaning:** Sea dew
**Origin:** Hebrew
**Pronunciation:** MARE ee um
**Description:** This name was also spelt as Maryam and is an old version of the name Mary. It is thought to derive from the Hebrew *'harim'* meaning 'to raise'. It could also have the same meaning as Mary, which is 'sea dew'.
**Alternative spellings:** Miryam

## Mischa

**Meaning:** Who is like God?
**Origin:** Hebrew
**Pronunciation:** ME sha

**Description:** Mischa derives from the masculine name Michael and so technically is a boys' name. However, due to its feminine sound the name has become popular as a girls' name.
**Alternative spellings:** Meisha, Misha, Mysha

## Misty

**Meaning:** Thin fog
**Origin:** English
**Pronunciation:** MISS tee
**Description:** The name Misty derives from the English word 'mist' and may have started out as a nickname.
**Alternative spellings:** Misti, Mistie

## Mitsuko

**Meaning:** Child of light
**Origin:** Japanese
**Pronunciation:** MEE tsoo koh
**Description:** This female name can be found throughout Asia, although it is most popular in Japan. It is written using two Japanese characters, *'mitsu'*, meaning 'light', and *'ko'*, meaning 'child'.
**Alternative spellings:** Mitsukoh

## Miya

**Meaning:** The sacred house
**Origin:** Japanese
**Pronunciation:** mee YAH
**Description:** Miya could be an alternative spelling of the popular name Mia, although it is also a girls' name from Japan. It is said to mean 'temple' or 'sacred house'.

## Miyuki

**Meaning:** Beautiful fortune
**Origin:** Japanese
**Pronunciation:** MEE yoo kee
**Description:** Miyuki is a Japanese

**M**

417

name of multiple meanings. It can be taken to mean 'beautiful fortune' or 'deep snow'. The pet form is Yuki.
**Alternative spellings:** Meyuki, Miyukie

## Miyumi
**Meaning:** True bow; reasonable beauty
**Origin:** Japanese
**Pronunciation:** MEE yu mee
**Description:** Using traditional Japanese characters, Miyumi would mean 'true bow'. However, it can also be written using the character *'yu'*, meaning 'reason' and *'mi'*, meaning 'beauty'.
**Alternative spellings:** Meyumi, Miyumih

## Moana
**Meaning:** Large body of water
**Origin:** Hawaiian
**Pronunciation:** mo ANNA
**Description:** Moana is a Hawaiian/Maori name meaning 'large body of water'. It was the name of the main character in the 2016 Disney animated film, *Moana*.

## Molly
**Meaning:** Sea dew
**Origin:** English
**Pronunciation:** MOLL lee
**Description:** Molly first came about as a pet form of the name Mary and was coined in the 18th century. It is now a name in its own right.
**Alternative spellings:** Molli, Mollie

## Momina
**Meaning:** Unknown
**Origin:** Arabic

**Pronunciation:** moh MEE nah
**Description:** There is not much in the way of documentation on the name Momina; however it is known that it is used in Persian and Urdu.
**Alternative spellings:** Mominah, Momyna

## Mona
**Meaning:** Moon
**Origin:** English
**Pronunciation:** MOH na
**Description:** Mona, a unisex name though more usually feminine, is found in various forms in many languages and does not have a distinct origin. In Old English it means 'moon'.
**Alternative spellings:** Monah

## Monica
**Meaning:** One with good advice
**Origin:** Latin
**Pronunciation:** MOH ni ka
**Description:** The name Monica is said to come from the Latin word *'monere'*, which refers to the giving of advice.
**Alternative spellings:** Monika

## Monique
**Meaning:** One with good advice
**Origin:** Latin
**Pronunciation:** moh NEEK
**Description:** Monique is a variant of the Latin name Monica, meaning 'one with good advice'. The variant Monique is quite popular across Europe.
**Alternative spellings:** Moneke, Moneque, Monike

## Monroe
**Meaning:** From the mouth of the

River Roe
**Origin:** Scottish
**Pronunciation:** mon ROW
**Description:** Monroe is a Scottish surname meaning 'from the mouth of the River Roe', the River Roe being a river in Ireland. This follows the contemporary trend of using last names as first names.

## Montana
**Meaning:** State in the United States
**Origin:** English
**Pronunciation:** mon TAN uh
**Description:** Montana is the name of a state in the northwestern United States. Like London and Paris, this name follows the trend of using place names for baby names.

## Morgan
**Meaning:** Great circle
**Origin:** Welsh
**Pronunciation:** MOR gun
**Description:** The name Morgan derives from the Old Welsh masculine name Morcant, which can mean 'bright' or 'great sea' or 'great circle'.
**Alternative spellings:** Morgann, Morganne

## Morgana
**Meaning:** Sea; circle; bright
**Origin:** Welsh
**Pronunciation:** mor GAN uh
**Description:** Morgana is a Welsh name composed of the elements of '*môr*' meaning 'sea', '*cant*' meaning 'circle' or '*can*' meaning 'bright'.

## Morwenna
**Meaning:** Maiden

**Origin:** Latin; Welsh
**Pronunciation:** mor WHEN nah; mor WEEN nah;
**Description:** Daughter of the Welsh King Brychan in the 12th century. Morwenna later became the patron saint of Morwenstow, a parish in Cornwall. Her name is thought to have derived from the Welsh word '*morwyn*' meaning 'maiden'.

## Munira
**Meaning:** A wish
**Origin:** Arabic
**Pronunciation:** mu NEER ah
**Description:** Munira is a variant of the Arabic name Mouna, meaning 'a wish', and is popular in the Middle East.
**Alternative spellings:** Muneera, Munirah

## Muskaan
**Meaning:** Smiling
**Origin:** Sanskrit
**Pronunciation:** mus KAHN
**Description:** Muskaan is a name often found used by Punjabi-speaking parents. It is said to come from a word meaning 'smiling'.
**Alternative spellings:** Muskan

## Myla
**Meaning:** Mild and merciful
**Origin:** Latin
**Pronunciation:** MYA lah
**Description:** Myla is the feminine equivalent of the masculine name Miles, which is thought to derive from the Latin name Milo. It could also have come into usage as a shortened form of Michael.
**Alternative spellings:** Milah, Mylah

**M**

419

## Myra

**Meaning:** Myrrh
**Origin:** Latin
**Pronunciation:** MY rah
**Description:** It is said that the name Myra was invented by the poet Fulke Greville and is based on the Latin noun *'myrrh'*. In Christian belief myrrh was given to Jesus upon his birth.
**Alternative spellings:** Myrah

## Mysha

**Meaning:** Alive
**Origin:** Arabic
**Pronunciation:** ME sha
**Description:** As well as being a variant for the Arabic name Meisha, meaning 'alive', Mysha could also be considered a variant of the Hebrew name Mischa, meaning 'who is like God?'.
**Alternative spellings:** Meisha, Mischa, Misha

# N

## Nabila

**Meaning:** Noble
**Origin:** Arabic
**Pronunciation:** nah BEE lah
**Description:** Nabila is the feminine version of the name Nabil and shares its meaning. It is a popular name in the Middle East.
**Alternative spellings:** Nabeela, Nabilla

## Nada

**Meaning:** Dew
**Origin:** Arabic
**Pronunciation:** nah DAH
**Description:** Nada is a feminine Arabic name meaning 'dew', as in the small water droplets that form on cool surfaces during the night. It is also the Spanish word for 'nothing'.

## Nadia

**Meaning:** Hope
**Origin:** Russian
**Pronunciation:** NAR dee ah
**Description:** Nadia is the English form of the Russian name Nadya, short for Nadezhda, which means 'hope'.
**Alternative spellings:** Nadiah, Nadya

## Nadine

**Meaning:** Hope
**Origin:** Russian
**Pronunciation:** NAY deen; nuh DEEN
**Description:** Nadine shares its roots with the name Nadia as they both derive from the Russian name Nadezhda.
**Alternative spellings:** Nadeene, Naydine

## Nafisa

**Meaning:** Delicate and valuable
**Origin:** Arabic
**Pronunciation:** nah FEE sah
**Description:** Nafisa is uncommon in Britain but found throughout Arabic- and Swahili-speaking countries.
**Alternative spellings:** Nafeesa, Nafisah

## Nahla

**Meaning:** To drink water
**Origin:** Arabic
**Pronunciation:** NAH lah
**Description:** Nahla is a name of Arabic origin; however, there are many similar names found in neighbouring languages such as Nala, which means 'gift' in Swahili.
**Alternative spellings:** Nala

## Naila

**Meaning:** One who accomplishes
**Origin:** Arabic
**Pronunciation:** nah EEL ah
**Description:** In the history of the Islamic Empire, Naila was the name of the wife of Uthman, a caliph. The name is more popular with Muslim parents.
**Alternative spellings:** Nahlia, Naliah

## Naima

**Meaning:** Content
**Origin:** Arabic
**Pronunciation:** nah EE mah
**Description:** Naima is an uncommon name in the UK but is more frequently found in Africa and America.
**Alternative spellings:** Naema, Naemah, Naimah

## Naina

**Meaning:** Content
**Origin:** Arabic
**Pronunciation:** na AY na
**Description:** Naina is a variant of the name Naima, meaning 'content'.
**Alternative spellings:** Nainah, Nayana

## Naira

**Meaning:** Shining; glittering
**Origin:** Indian
**Pronunciation:** NAI rah
**Description:** Naira is an Indian girls' name meaning 'shining' or 'glittering'.
**Alternative spellings:** Nairah

## Naiya

**Meaning:** Vessel
**Origin:** Sanskrit
**Pronunciation:** NAY ah
**Description:** Naiya is of Sanskrit origin and probably means 'a vessel'. Names ending in 'ya' are becoming popular.
**Alternative spellings:** Naiyah, Naya

## Najma

**Meaning:** Star
**Origin:** Arabic
**Pronunciation:** NAHJ mah
**Description:** Najma seems to be mostly found in the Middle East and in parts of Africa, and so is presumably of either Arabic or Swahili origin. The meaning of the name is also uncertain, but is generally accepted to mean 'star'.
**Alternative spellings:** Najmah

## Nala

**Meaning:** Unknown
**Origin:** African
**Pronunciation:** nah LAH
**Description:** Nala is an African name that is commonly used throughout the Middle East, but the meaning is unknown. The name was made famous in the Disney film *The Lion King*, where she was Simba's wife.
**Alternative spellings:** Nalah

**N**

## Nana

**Meaning:** Springtime
**Origin:** Hawaiian
**Pronunciation:** NAH na
**Description:** Nana comes from the springtime Hawaiian month of Nana. The name has spread somewhat in America; however it is not particularly popular in Britain because the title Nana is often used as an affectionate name for a grandmother.
**Alternative spellings:** Nanah, Nanna

## Nana

**Meaning:** Various
**Origin:** Japanese; Greek; Ghanaian
**Pronunciation:** Na na
**Description:** Nana is a unisex name. In Japan and Korea it is a girls' name, as well as in Georgia where it is the fifth most popular girls' name. In Ghana, among the Akans, Nana is the title of a king or a queen, signifying royalty.
**Alternative spellings:** Naana, Nanah, Nanna

## Nancy

**Meaning:** Favoured by God
**Origin:** Greek
**Pronunciation:** NAN see
**Description:** Nancy was originally a pet form of the Latin name Ann, but is now a name in its own right.
**Alternative spellings:** Nancey, Nanci, Nancie

## Naomi

**Meaning:** Pleasantness
**Origin:** Hebrew
**Pronunciation:** nay OH mee
**Description:** Naomi means 'pleasantness' in Hebrew. In Christian belief Naomi was the mother-in-law of Ruth, an ancestor of Jesus.
**Alternative spellings:** Naomie, Naomy

## Nat

**Meaning:** Birthday of Christ
**Origin:** Italian
**Pronunciation:** NAT
**Description:** Nat is a pet form of a number of names, such as Natalie, Natasha and Nathaniel. It is most often seen in a feminine context and is still rare as a given name in its own right.
**Alternative spellings:** Natt

## Natalia

**Meaning:** Birthday of Christ
**Origin:** Italian
**Pronunciation:** na TAH lia; na TAR lia
**Description:** Natalia derives from the Italian word *'natale'*, meaning 'birthday' – especially that of Christ. It is therefore often given to children born around Christmas. St Natalia is regarded as a Christian saint.
**Alternative spellings:** Natalya

## Natalie

**Meaning:** Birthday of Christ
**Origin:** Italian
**Pronunciation:** NAT a li
**Description:** Natalie is the French form of the Italian name Natalia. It appeared in the early 20th century, possibly as a result of the touring Ballets Russes, which was established in 1909.
**Alternative spellings:** Nataley, Natali, Nataly, Nathalie

## Natasha

**Meaning:** Birthday of Christ
**Origin:** Russian
**Pronunciation:** na TA shuh
**Description:** Natasha is the Russian pet form of Natalia, but now exists as a well-adopted name worldwide.
**Alternative spellings:** Natacha, Natascha, Natassja

## Nausicaa

**Meaning:** Excelling in ships
**Origin:** Greek
**Pronunciation:** NAW sik e a
**Description:** In Greek mythology, Nausicaa appeared in Homer's epic poem *Odyssey* as a young and beautiful princess who aids the shipwrecked Odysseus.
**Alternative spellings:** Nausica, Nausika

## Nawal

**Meaning:** Gift
**Origin:** Arabic
**Pronunciation:** nah WAHL
**Description:** Nawal is an Arabic girls' name meaning 'gift'. Other names related to Nawal are Munal, Nawal, Nawl and Nawlaa.

## Naya

**Meaning:** Resolve
**Origin:** Swahili
**Pronunciation:** nah YA
**Description:** Naya is an alternative spelling of the Swahili name Nia, meaning 'resolve'. It is one of the days of Kwanzaa, the African-American cultural holiday that is celebrated at the end of December and early January.

## Neda

**Meaning:** Born on Sunday
**Origin:** Greek
**Pronunciation:** NEE dah
**Description:** In Greek mythology, Neda was a nymph who nurtured Zeus as a child. A river and a town were named after her.
**Alternative spellings:** Needa, Neyda

## Neel

See entry in 'Names for Baby Boys A–Z'

## Neha

**Meaning:** Raindrop
**Origin:** Sanskrit
**Pronunciation:** NEY ha
**Description:** The name Neha derives from the Sanskrit word *'nehal'*, meaning 'rain'. It is quite a popular name in India.
**Alternative spellings:** Nehah, Neyha

## Nehir

**Meaning:** Unknown
**Origin:** Arabic
**Pronunciation:** neh HIR
**Description:** Nehir is an unusual name of uncertain origin and meaning. It is thought the name may be Turkish.
**Alternative spellings:** Nehire

## Nela

**Meaning:** Horned
**Origin:** Latin
**Pronunciation:** NEE lah
**Description:** Nela originally came about as a pet form of Cornelia, meaning 'horned'. Although uncommon, it is now a name in its own right.
**Alternative spellings:** Neela, Nelah

N

## Nell

**Meaning:** Ray of sunshine
**Origin:** Latin
**Pronunciation:** NELL
**Description:** The name Nell has roots in Old English, Latin, Greek and Arabic; however, its meaning is always associated with light. Nell was originally a shortened form for names such as Helen, Eleanor and Danielle.
**Alternative spellings:** Nel

## Nella

**Meaning:** Bright one; light
**Origin:** English
**Pronunciation:** nehl AA
**Description:** The origins of Nella are very mixed; it and is often said to be the short form of several different names, including: Antonella, Cornelia and Fenella. However, in Old Greek, the word Nella means 'bright one' or 'light'.

## Nellie

**Meaning:** Various
**Origin:** English
**Pronunciation:** NEL lee
**Description:** Nellie is a spelling variant of Nelly, the shortened form of Helen or Eleanor.
**Alternative spellings:** Nelli, Nelly

## Nephele

**Meaning:** Cloudy
**Origin:** Greek
**Pronunciation:** NEH fel leh
**Description:** Nephele is an uncommon girls' name of Greek origin. In Greek mythology, Nephele was a goddess formed out of the clouds in the shape of the goddess Hera, by Zeus.
**Alternative spellings:** Nefele, Nephelee

## Neriah

**Meaning:** Lamp of Yaweh
**Origin:** Hebrew
**Pronunciation:** ni RIE ya
**Description:** A unisex name meaning 'lamp of Yahweh' in Hebrew, Neriah was also the name of the father of Baruch in the Old Testament.

## Nevaeh

**Meaning:** Heaven
**Origin:** English
**Pronunciation:** neh VAY ah
**Description:** Nevaeh is an alternative spelling of the popular modern name Neveah, which is 'heaven' spelt backwards. This is a relatively modern creation.

## Nia

**Meaning:** Purpose
**Origin:** Gaelic
**Pronunciation:**
**Description:** Although this female name has mainly Gaelic origins it is also influenced by African-Swahili languages, in which it means 'purpose'. It is thought that Nia derives from the Welsh name Niamh, pronounced Neev, who was a goddess in Irish mythology and a queen in the land of eternal youth.

## Niah

**Meaning:** Intended
**Origin:** Sanskrit
**Pronunciation:** NEE ah
**Description:** As well as being a spelling variant of the name Nia, Niah is also a name of Sanskrit

origins.
**Alternative spellings:** Nea, Nia, Nya, Nyah

## Niamh
**Meaning:** Radiant
**Origin:** Gaelic
**Pronunciation:** NEEV
**Description:** Niamh is a popular name in Ireland. It first appears in Irish mythology where Niamh was the princess daughter of a sea god.
**Alternative spellings:** Neave, Neive, Neve

## Nicol
See entry in 'Names for Baby Boys A–Z'

## Nicola
**Meaning:** Victory of the people
**Origin:** Greek
**Pronunciation:** NIK olla
**Description:** Nicola is the Latinate feminine form of the masculine name Nicholas. The spelling Nikola can sometimes be used for boys.
**Alternative spellings:** Nickola, Nikola

## Nicole
**Meaning:** Victory of the people
**Origin:** Greek
**Pronunciation:** NI cole
**Description:** Nicole is the French feminine form of Nicholas, meaning 'victory of the people'.
**Alternative spellings:** Nichole, Nikole

## Nicolette
**Meaning:** Victory of the people
**Origin:** Greek
**Pronunciation:** NIC oll ETT
**Description:** Nicolette is a French

variation on the name Nicola, the feminine version of Nicholas.
**Alternative spellings:** Nicollette, Nikolette

## Nicky
**Meaning:** Victory of the people
**Origin:** Greek
**Pronunciation:** NIK ee
**Description:** Nicky is a unisex name of Greek and English origin. It is a shortened variant of the Greek Nicholas.
**Alternative spellings:** Nickee, Nicki, Nickie

## Nida
**Meaning:** Voice
**Origin:** Arabic
**Pronunciation:** nee DAH
**Description:** Nida is a feminine name of Arabic origins and because much documentation on the name is scarce in English translation it is difficult to give reliable information. It is used mainly by Muslim parents. The name is said to come from an Arabic word meaning 'voice'.

## Nieve
**Meaning:** Snow
**Origin:** Spanish
**Pronunciation:** ne AY vay
**Description:** Nieve derives from the Spanish for 'snow' and is not common outside Spain. Names with a soft 'v' sound are, however, currently becoming more popular in Britain.
**Alternative spellings:** Niave, Niayva

## Nihal
See entry in 'Names for Baby Boys A–Z'

N

## Nika

**Meaning:** Good
**Origin:** Persian
**Pronunciation:** nee KAH
**Description:** Nika has Persian origins and the name means 'good'. However, it has other roots as well; in Greek, it means 'victory' and in Croatia and Slovenia it is the female variation of Nikola or Nikolaj.

## Nikita

**Meaning:** Undefeated
**Origin:** Russian
**Pronunciation:** nee KEE ath
**Description:** In its original Russian form Nikita is a masculine name said to mean 'undefeated'. It has since been found in many languages used as a unisex or a feminine name.
**Alternative spellings:** Nichita, Nicita, Nikitah

## Nikki

**Meaning:** Victory of the people
**Origin:** Greek
**Pronunciation:** NIK kee
**Description:** Nikki came about as a pet form of Nicola, but is now found as a given name in its own right.
**Alternative spellings:** Nicki, Nickie, Nicky, Nikkie, Nikky

## Nikola

**Meaning:** People of victory
**Origin:** Greek
**Pronunciation:** nik O la
**Description:** There are many spelling variations of this female name including Nicola and Nickola and it is mainly used in English- and Italian-speaking countries. The name comes from the Greek '*nike*'

meaning 'victory' and 'loas' meaning 'people'. The name developed into this feminine form from the male form Nickolas and has been used in the English tongue since the 12th century.
**Alternative spellings:** Nicola

## Nimra

**Meaning:** Cheetah
**Origin:** Arabic
**Pronunciation:** nim RAH
**Description:** Nimra is a name that is found used by Muslim parents, although its meaning is uncertain. It could derive from the word '*nimravidae*', meaning 'cheetah', or the Punjabi word '*nimrata*', meaning 'humility'.
**Alternative spellings:** Nimrah, Nymra

## Nina

**Meaning:** Unknown
**Origin:** Russian
**Pronunciation:** NEE na
**Description:** The name Nina originated as the pet form of many Russian names ending in 'nina' such as Antonina and Tatynina. As such it does not have a specific meaning of its own.
**Alternative spellings:** Neena, Niina

## Niobe

**Meaning:** Fern
**Origin:** Greek
**Pronunciation:** NEE o bee
**Description:** In Greek mythology, Niobe was a boastful queen of Thebes whose children were killed by Apollo as a reprimand for her arrogance.
**Alternative spellings:** Niobee, Niobi, Niobie, Nioby

## Nisa

**Meaning:** Follower of Dionysus
**Origin:** Greek
**Pronunciation:** NEES ah
**Description:** Nisa is a pet form of the name Denisa, which derives from the Greek name Dennis, a follower of the Greek god Dionysus.
**Alternative spellings:** Neesa, Nisah

## Nisha

**Meaning:** Night-time
**Origin:** Sanskrit
**Pronunciation:** NEE sha
**Description:** The name Nisha is often found in India and might be appropriate for a baby born during the night.
**Alternative spellings:** Neesha, Nichsa, Nishah

## Niya

**Meaning:** Intended; caring
**Origin:** Arabic
**Pronunciation:** NEE ah
**Description:** In Arabic the name means 'intended', but in Ireland and Wales the name is thought to derive from Gaelic and could mean 'bright'. Niya could also be a pet form of the Arabic Anniyah, meaning 'caring'.
**Alternative spellings:** Neeya, Niyah

## Noa

**Meaning:** Motion
**Origin:** Hebrew
**Pronunciation:** NOH ah
**Description:** Noa is an uncommon girls' name of Hebrew origin, meaning 'motion' and 'movement'. In the Old Testament, Noa was a daughter of Zelophehad.
**Alternative spellings:** Noah, Nua

## Noel

See entry in 'Names for Baby Boys A–Z'

## Noelle

**Meaning:** Christmas
**Origin:** English
**Pronunciation:** no EL
**Description:** Noelle is the feminine version of the name Noel. Noel comes from a French word meaning 'birthday' and is associated with the day of Christ's birth, Christmas Day. Noel is the original spelling but the variation Nowell can be found in Britain.
**Alternative spellings:** Nowell

## Noemi

**Meaning:** Pleasant
**Origin:** Hebrew
**Pronunciation:** no EE mi
**Description:** Noemi is a variant of the Hebrew name Naomi, who was the mother-in-law of Ruth in the Bible.
**Alternative spellings:** Noemie, Noemy

## Nola

**Meaning:** Charming; pale shoulders
**Origin:** German
**Pronunciation:** NOH la
**Description:** Nola could have come about as the pet form of several names. It could be short for the German name Winola, meaning 'charming', or derive from the Gaelic name Fionnuala, meaning 'pale shoulders'.
**Alternative spellings:** Nolah

## Noor

**Meaning:** Light

**N**

**Origin:** Arabic
**Pronunciation:** NOOR
**Description:** This name is a variation of the Arabic name Nura, borne by the former queen of Jordan. Noor can most commonly be found in Malaysian-, Arabic- and Indian-speaking countries.
**Alternative spellings:** Nore, Nour, Nur, Nure

## Nora

**Meaning:** Honour; pale shoulders
**Origin:** Latin
**Pronunciation:** NOR ra
**Description:** Nora is most probably a pet form of the Latin name Honora, meaning 'honour'. It is also thought of as a variant of the Irish name Fionnuala, meaning 'pale shoulders'.
**Alternative spellings:** Norah

## Nova

**Meaning:** New
**Origin:** English
**Pronunciation:** no VAH
**Description:** Nova comes from the Latin word '*novus*,' meaning 'new'. It was first used as a name during the 19th century.

## Nuala

**Meaning:** Fair-haired; pale shoulders
**Origin:** Gaelic
**Pronunciation:** NOO lah
**Description:** Nuala is a shortened form of the Gaelic name Fionnuala, which appears in Irish mythology and means 'pale shoulders'. For a baby, we can probably take Nuala to mean 'fair-haired'.
**Alternative spellings:** Nualah

## Nuha

**Meaning:** Sun god
**Origin:** Arabic
**Pronunciation:** NOO hah
**Description:** Before the advent of Islam, northern tribes in Arabia worshipped three deities: Ruda, Nuha and Atarsamain. The goddess Nuha was associated with the sun.
**Alternative spellings:** Nuhah

## Nusaybah

**Meaning:** Noble bloodline
**Origin:** Arabic
**Pronunciation:** noo SAY ba
**Description:** The name Nusaybah was originally given to a baby of a noble bloodline. Nusaybah Bint Ka'ab was a companion of Muhammad and the first woman to fight for the cause of Islam.
**Alternative spellings:** Nusayba, Nusaybaa

## Nyah

**Meaning:** Lustrous
**Origin:** Gaelic
**Pronunciation:** nee AH
**Description:** Nyah is a spelling variation of the feminine name Nia, which can be traced to Gaelic origins where it is said to mean 'lustrous'. However it is also found used as a pet form of names ending in 'nia' such as Antonia, whereby its meaning would differ. The form Nyah was probably invented to give the name more credit as an independent name.

## Nyla

**Meaning:** Champion
**Origin:** Gaelic
**Pronunciation:** NYE lah

**Description:** Nyla could be a feminine form of Nyles, deriving from the Irish name Neil, meaning 'champion'. The name could also be Hebrew or Arabic, come from the name of the river Nile.
**Alternative spellings:** Nilah, Nylah

## Nylah
**Meaning:** Cloud
**Origin:** Gaelic
**Pronunciation:** nye LAH
**Description:** Nylah is a feminine name of uncertain origin and meaning. It seems it could come from Gaelic origins, where it is said its meaning is 'cloud'.

However some also trace it back to Egyptian origins, where it is thought to stem from the name of the River Nile, and is thought to be the feminine version of the masculine name Nile.

## Nyx
**Meaning:** Night
**Origin:** Greek
**Pronunciation:** Nyks
**Description:** In Greek mythology, Nyx is the goddess of the night. She was found only in the shadows of the world and only ever seen in glimpses.
**Alternative spellings:** Naix, Niks, Nix

# O

## Ocean
**Meaning:** The ocean
**Origin:** English
**Pronunciation:** oh SHUN
**Description:** Ocean is a name that comes from the noun in the English language. It is found used for both boys and girls. It is an uncommon name but mostly used in English-speaking countries.

## Octavia
**Meaning:** Eighth
**Origin:** Latin
**Pronunciation:** ok TAY vee uh
**Description:** Octavia is a Latin female name derived from the Roman family name Octavius.
**Alternative spellings:** Octayvia

## Ola
**Meaning:** Descendant of an ancestor
**Origin:** Norse
**Pronunciation:** OH la
**Description:** Ola is a unisex variant of the Old Norse masculine name Olaf, meaning 'descendant of an ancestor'. It is most often found in Germany.
**Alternative spellings:** Olah, Olla

## Olga
**Meaning:** Holy
**Origin:** Norse
**Pronunciation:** ol GAH
**Description:** Olga is a variant of the Old Norse feminine name Helga, which is mainly found in Russia. Saint Olga was a Russian

saint and many take the name after her. The name in its various forms has long been popular across Scandinavia. The Old Norse name is said to mean 'holy'.

## Olive
**Meaning:** Olive
**Origin:** Latin
**Pronunciation:** OL iv
**Description:** Olive refers to the Mediterranean fruit and the olive branch is considered a symbol of peace.
**Alternative spellings:** Olife

## Olivia
**Meaning:** Olive
**Origin:** Latin
**Pronunciation:** oh LIVY uh
**Description:** Olivia was first used by Shakespeare in his play *Twelfth Night*. Shakespeare may have taken it as a feminine form of Oliver or he may have derived it from the Latin for 'olive'.
**Alternative spellings:** Oliviah, Oliwia

## Ollie
See entry in 'Names for Baby Boys A–Z'

## Omari
See entry in 'Names for Baby Boys A–Z'

## Ondine
**Meaning:** Little wave
**Origin:** Latin
**Pronunciation:** on DINE
**Description:** Ondine is a Latin name meaning 'little wave'. Ondines are mythical beings associated with water and are found throughout classical literature.

## Onyx
**Meaning:** Gemstone
**Origin:** Greek
**Pronunciation:** on ICKS
**Description:** Onyx is the name of a gemstone that is usually jet-black in colour. Like Opal and Ruby, this follows the trend of using gemstone names as given names.

## Opal
**Meaning:** Precious stone
**Origin:** English
**Pronunciation:** opal
**Description:** Opal is taken from the precious stone of the same name. Like Ruby and Sapphire, these gemstone names are a popular trend for baby naming.

## Ophelia
**Meaning:** Help; serpent
**Origin:** Greek
**Pronunciation:** o FEE lee a
**Description:** Ophelia, the name of the tragic female character in *Hamlet*, was made famous by Shakespeare. It is thought that the name either derives from the Greek *'ophelos'*, meaning 'help', or *'ophis'*, meaning 'serpent'.
**Alternative spellings:** Ofelia, Ofeliah, Opheliah

## Oprah
**Meaning:** Fawn
**Origin:** Hebrew
**Pronunciation:** OH pruh

**Description:** Oprah is a spelling variant of the name Ophrah. It has been popularised by the success of US chat show hostess Oprah Winfrey.
**Alternative spellings:** Ophrah

## Oreoluwa
**Meaning:** A gift from God
**Origin:** African
**Pronunciation:** oh REE oh LOO wa
**Description:** Oreoluwa originates from the Yoruba tribe in Nigeria and means 'a gift from God'. It is an uncommon name outside Africa.
**Alternative spellings:** Oreoluwah, Orioluwa

## Oriana
**Meaning:** Golden sunrise
**Origin:** Greek
**Pronunciation:** or ree AN ah
**Description:** The exact origin of Oriana is uncertain. It could have derived from the Latin name Aurara, meaning 'sunrise' or 'dawn'. It could also have roots in Gaelic, where it would mean 'golden'.
**Alternative spellings:** Orianah, Oryana

## Orla
**Meaning:** Golden princess
**Origin:** Gaelic
**Pronunciation:** OR lah
**Description:** Orla is a Gaelic name derived from the original Irish spelling Orlaith, meaning 'golden princess'. Orla and Orliath are popular in Ireland, with Orla also becoming popular elsewhere.
**Alternative spellings:** Orlagh, Orlah, Orlaith

## Orlagh
**Meaning:** Precious princess
**Origin:** Gaelic
**Pronunciation:** or LAH
**Description:** Orlagh is a feminine name of Gaelic origin, and is said to mean 'precious princess'. Its original Irish spelling is Orlaith and although not often found in England, both the original and the modern form are popular in Ireland. This is one of the anglicised spellings of Órfhlaith, others being Órlaith and Órla.

## Orleanna
**Meaning:** Golden
**Origin:** English
**Pronunciation:** or LEE anna
**Description:** Orleanna is an English name that is related to the Latin name Aurelius and French name Orlina, both of which mean 'golden' or have something to do with gold.

## Ottilie
**Meaning:** Rich
**Origin:** German
**Pronunciation:** OTT eh lee
**Description:** The name Ottilie derives from the German masculine name Otto, which means 'rich'. Ottilie is mainly found in Germany.
**Alternative spellings:** Otili, Otilie, Otily, Ottili, Ottily

## Ottoline
**Meaning:** Wealth
**Origin:** English
**Pronunciation:** otto LINE
**Description:** Ottoline is a diminutive of the name Ottilie, which in turn was the German version of the name Odilia, meaning 'wealth'.

O

# P

## Padme

**Meaning:** No meaning
**Origin:** English
**Pronunciation:** pad MA
**Description:** Padme is a modern, invented name and as such has no meaning. It was made for Padme Amidala, a character in the Star Wars franchise.

## Paige

**Meaning:** Page
**Origin:** English
**Pronunciation:** PAYJ
**Description:** Paige was originally a surname given to those who served as pages to the lord. Paige then became a popular given name in the US during the 20th century and is usually found on girls.
**Alternative spellings:** Page, Payge

## Paisley

**Meaning:** Persian pattern
**Origin:** Gaelic
**Pronunciation:** PAYZ lee
**Description:** Paisley is the name of a town in Scotland famous for its weaving. The name could have come about as a surname for those who lived there before it transferred to a girls' name.
**Alternative spellings:** Paislee, Paisleigh, Paislie, Payslee, Paysleigh, Paysley, Payslie

## Paloma

**Meaning:** Dove
**Origin:** Latin
**Pronunciation:** Puh LOH muh

**Description:** Popular in other European countries, particularly in Spain and Italy, Paloma derives from the Latin word '*palumbus*' meaning a pigeon, or a dove.

## Pamela

**Meaning:** Honey bread
**Origin:** English
**Pronunciation:** PAM eh la; pah MEH la
**Description:** This name was invented by the Elizabethan poet Sir Philip Sidney, who may have combined the Greek words '*pan*' and '*meli*'. At this time, the emphasis was on the second syllable.
**Alternative spellings:** Pamelah, Pamella

## Pandora

**Meaning:** All gifts
**Origin:** Greek
**Pronunciation:** pan DAWR ya
**Description:** Pandora was a famous figure from Greek mythology. She was the first mortal woman and Zeus gave her a jar containing all the troubles and ills of mankind, telling her not to open it. She did, however, and unleashed the evil spirits into the world. The name is a combination of '*pan*' (all) and '*doron*' (gift).

## Paris

**Meaning:** Paris
**Origin:** Greek
**Pronunciation:** PA riss
**Description:** Paris, the capital city of France, was a name often given

to boys in the Middle Ages. In Greek legend Paris carries Helen from Sparta to Troy, causing the Trojan War.
**Alternative spellings:** Pariss, Parys

## Patience
**Meaning:** Endure suffering
**Origin:** Latin
**Pronunciation:** PAY shunce
**Description:** This name derives from the English word, which itself comes from the Latin *'pati'*, meaning 'to suffer'. Patience is a name often favoured by Christian parents.

## Patricia
**Meaning:** Noble
**Origin:** Latin
**Pronunciation:** pa TRISH ah
**Description:** Patricia is the feminine version of the Gaelic name Patrick. Both names derive from the Latin *'patricius'*, a title given to a nobleman, so the name means 'noble'.
**Alternative spellings:** Patricjia, Patricya, Patrycia, Patrycja

## Paula
**Meaning:** Modest
**Origin:** Latin
**Pronunciation:** PAW luh
**Description:** Paula is the Latin feminine form of Paul, meaning 'small' or 'modest', and is the name of various early saints.
**Alternative spellings:** Paulah, Paulla

## Paulina
**Meaning:** Modest
**Origin:** Latin
**Pronunciation:** pall LEE nah
**Description:** Paulina is the Spanish feminine version of the popular name Paul, from the Latin name Paulus meaning 'small' or 'modest'. Paulina is especially popular in Poland and Italy.
**Alternative spellings:** Paulinah, Paullina

## Pauline
**Meaning:** Modest
**Origin:** Latin
**Pronunciation:** pall LEEN
**Description:** Pauline is the French feminine version of the popular name Paul, from the Latin name Paulus meaning 'small' or 'modest'.
**Alternative spellings:** None

## Pavani
**Meaning:** Purifying
**Origin:** Sanskrit
**Pronunciation:** pah VAN ee
**Description:** Pavani is a Sanskrit girls' name meaning 'purifying'. It has connotations of holiness and purity.

## Payton
See entry in 'Names for Baby Boys A–Z'

## Peaches
**Meaning:** Fruit name
**Origin:** English
**Pronunciation:** peech ES
**Description:** Peaches is taken directly from the fruit name. It was made famous by the late British socialite, Peaches Geldof.

## Pearl
**Meaning:** Light's creation
**Origin:** English
**Pronunciation:** PERL
**Description:** The name Pearl comes from the English word

**P**

for the valuable gemstone and the name carries connotations of beauty. Pearl is also the birthstone for June.
**Alternative spellings:** Pearle, Pearll

## Peggy
**Meaning:** Pearl; light's creation
**Origin:** Latin
**Pronunciation:** PEG ee
**Description:** Peggy was originally a pet form of the name Margaret but is now often found as a name in its own right.
**Alternative spellings:** Peggi, Peggie

## Penelope
**Meaning:** Weaver
**Origin:** Greek
**Pronunciation:** pen EL lo pe
**Description:** In Greek mythology Penelope was the wife of Odysseus, who waited for him to return home for 20 years. The name therefore has associations with faithfulness.
**Alternative spellings:** Penelopi, Penelopie, Penelopy

## Penny
**Meaning:** Weaver
**Origin:** Greek
**Pronunciation:** PEN ee
**Description:** Penny is a pet form of the name Penelope and has become a name in its own right.
**Alternative spellings:** Penni, Pennie

## Peony
**Meaning:** Flower name
**Origin:** English
**Pronunciation:** pee ON ee

**Description:** Peony comes from the pink flowers of the same name. Like Rose and Tulip, Peony is part of the trend of using flowers as given names.

## Perdita
**Meaning:** Lost
**Origin:** Latin
**Pronunciation:** per DEE tah
**Description:** Perdita is the Latin word for 'lost'. This was the name of the heroine in Shakespeare's play, *The Winter's Tale*.

## Perrie
**Meaning:** Pear tree
**Origin:** French
**Pronunciation:** pe RIE
**Description:** Perrie is a French name meaning 'pear tree'. Perrie is actually a unisex name, although there are more girls with this name than boys. It is also an alternative spelling of the French boys' name, Perry, which has the same meaning.
**Alternative spellings:** Perry

## Perry
See entry in 'Names for Baby Boys A–Z'

## Persephone
**Meaning:** To Destroy; murder
**Origin:** Greek
**Pronunciation:** per SEF e nee
**Description:** Persephone is the name of Demeter and Zeus' daughter in Greek mythology. She was famously abducted by Hades, god of the Underworld, and made to be his bride. She is allowed to return to the surface for part of the year, and her movements helped explain the changing of the seasons.

## Petal

**Meaning:** Flower petal
**Origin:** English
**Pronunciation:** pet ALL
**Description:** Petal comes from the English vocabulary word of the same spelling, referring to the petals on a flower. It is also often used as a nickname as well as a given name

## Petra

**Meaning:** Rock
**Origin:** Greek
**Pronunciation:** PET ra
**Description:** Petra is the feminine form of Peter, meaning 'rock'. It is a fairly uncommon name in Britain.
**Alternative spellings:** Peitra, Pettra

## Peyton

**Meaning:** Farm of Paege
**Origin:** English
**Pronunciation:** PAY ton
**Description:** The name Peyton is actually a unisex name and so can be used for both boys and girls. There is a different spelling variation, which is Payton, and the Farm of Paege was often referred to as peacock town. The name derives from two elements of '*pawa*' meaning 'peacock' and '*tun*' meaning 'town'.
**Alternative spellings:** Payton

## Phaedra

**Meaning:** Bright
**Origin:** Greek
**Pronunciation:** fay DRAH
**Description:** Phaedra is derived from the Greek word '*phaidros*', meaning 'bright'. She was the daughter of King Minos and wife of Theseus in Greek mythology.

## Pheobe

**Meaning:** One who glows
**Origin:** Greek
**Pronunciation:** FEE be
**Description:** Pheobe is a variant spelling of the name Phoebe, which is a feminine name of Greek origin and is said to mean 'one who glows'. It is also sometimes found as a pet form of the Greek name Euphemia, which means 'beautiful silence'. This name is extremely rare in Britain; however its variant Phoebe is currently a popular name for girls.
**Alternative spellings:** Phoebe

## Phil

See entry in 'Names for Baby Boys A–Z'

## Philippa

**Meaning:** Lover of horses
**Origin:** Greek
**Pronunciation:** FILL ih puh
**Description:** Philippa is the feminine form of Philip. It is often shortened to Pippa or Pip.
**Alternative spellings:** Philipa, Philipah, Phillipa, Phillippa

## Phoebe

**Meaning:** Bright
**Origin:** Greek
**Pronunciation:** FEE bee
**Description:** Phoebe is the feminine version of Phoebus, from the Greek name for the god of light. Phoebe is also an irregular satellite of Saturn. The name has experienced a boost since its use in hit TV sitcom *Friends*.

P

**Alternative spellings:** Febe, Phebe, Phoebee, Phoebie, Phoeby

## Phoenix
See entry in 'Names for Baby Boys A–Z'

## Phyllis
**Meaning:** Green bough
**Origin:** Greek
**Pronunciation:** fill US
**Description:** Phyllis is a Greek name meaning 'green bough'. In Greek mythology, she is the daughter of a Thracian king and wife of Demophon.

## Pia
**Meaning:** Devout
**Origin:** Latin
**Pronunciation:** PEE ah
**Description:** Pia is the feminine version of the Latin name Pius, which shares the same root as the word 'pious', meaning 'devout'.
**Alternative spellings:** Pea, Piah

## Piper
**Meaning:** Pipe player
**Origin:** English
**Pronunciation:** PIPE er
**Description:** Piper, originally a surname for families whose father played the pipe, is now a unisex name.
**Alternative spellings:** Pypa, Pyper

## Pippa
**Meaning:** Lover of horses
**Origin:** Greek
**Pronunciation:** PIP pah
**Description:** Pippa originally came about as a shortened female version of the name Philip. Now it is

seen as the short form of the name Philippa or a given name in its own right.
**Alternative spellings:** Pipa, Pippah

## Pixie
**Meaning:** Mischievous fairy
**Origin:** English
**Pronunciation:** PIX ee
**Description:** Pixie comes from the word for the sprite-like creature. Its origin is uncertain since many fairy tales are shared between cultures. The name became more popular when Bob Geldof gave it to his daughter.
**Alternative spellings:** Pixey, Pixi, Pixy

## Pocahontas
**Meaning:** Playful one
**Origin:** Native American
**Pronunciation:** poh CAH hon tas
**Description:** While Pocahontas was a real-life Native American figure, many most likely know her through Disney's 1995 film *Pocahontas*. She was the daughter of Chief Powhatan, of the Powhatan Indian tribe in Virginia. The name Pocahontas is most likely a childhood nickname that referred to her spirited nature, and also why it means 'playful one'.

## Pola
**Meaning:** Poppy
**Origin:** Arabic
**Pronunciation:** POH la
**Description:** Pola is the pet form of the Arabic name Amapola, meaning 'poppy'. It is now seen as a name in its own right and has associations with beauty.

**Alternative spellings:** Polah, Polar

## Polly
**Meaning:** Sea dew
**Origin:** Gaelic
**Pronunciation:** POL lee
**Description:** Polly actually derives from the name Molly, as in the Middle Ages it was commonplace to replace 'M' with 'P' to form a pet name.
**Alternative spellings:** Polley, Polli, Pollie

## Pollyanna
**Meaning:** Optimistic
**Origin:** Hebrew
**Pronunciation:** POH lee AH na
**Description:** Pollyanna was originally a double-barrelled name. Owing to the use of the name in E.H. Porter's children's novel *Pollyanna*, the name is associated with optimism and bravery.
**Alternative spellings:** Poliana, Polianna, Polliana, Pollianna, Pollyana, Polyana, Polyanna

## Pooja
**Meaning:** Prayer; worship
**Origin:** Indian
**Pronunciation:** poo JAH
**Description:** Pooja is a popular Indian girls' name meaning 'prayer' or 'worship'.

## Poppy
**Meaning:** Poppy flower
**Origin:** English
**Pronunciation:** POP ee
**Description:** Poppy is the name of a flower and often given to girls born on Remembrance Sunday. Poppies are seen as symbols of remembrance owing to their link with World War I.
**Alternative spellings:** Poppey, Poppi, Poppie

## Posey
**Meaning:** Flower bouquet
**Origin:** English
**Pronunciation:** poh ZEE
**Description:** Posey comes from the English vocabulary word of the same spelling, referring to a small, decorative flower bouquet usually tied with ribbon.

## Precious
**Meaning:** Precious
**Origin:** English
**Pronunciation:** PREH shus
**Description:** Precious is a name that comes directly from the English word, which means 'of high value'. It is often used as a term of affection and is now a name in its own right.

## Primrose
**Meaning:** Flower
**Origin:** English
**Pronunciation:** PRIM rose
**Description:** Primrose comes directly from the name of the flower. The name means 'first rose' because it is one of the first flowers to bloom in the spring.
**Alternative spellings:** Primroze, Prymrose, Prymroze

## Princess
**Meaning:** Royalty
**Origin:** English
**Pronunciation:** PRIN sess
**Description:** This name was originally only used as a title for particular members of the royal

P

family; however in recent years it seems to have transferred into a popular forename.
**Alternative spellings:** Pryncess

## Priscilla
**Meaning:** Long life
**Origin:** Latin
**Pronunciation:** pre SIL ah
**Description:** Priscilla is an elongated version of the Roman name Pricsa, which derives from the Latin word *'pricus'*, meaning 'old'. It is thought the name would have been given to wish long life on the bearer.
**Alternative spellings:** Priscila, Pryscilla

## Prisha
**Meaning:** Gift
**Origin:** Arabic
**Pronunciation:** PREE sha
**Description:** Prisha is a unisex name often favoured by Hindu parents and is most commonly found in India.
**Alternative spellings:** Preesha, Prishah

## Priya
**Meaning:** Beloved
**Origin:** Sanskrit
**Pronunciation:** PREE yah
**Description:** The translation of Priya is 'beloved'. In Hindu texts the name is often used to denote a romantic lover or a wife. Priya was a daughter of Daksha, the creator god.
**Alternative spellings:** Preeya, Priyah

## Priyal
**Meaning:** Beloved
**Origin:** Indian

**Pronunciation:** pee YAL
**Description:** Priyal is an Indian girls' name meaning 'beloved'. The name is directly translated from the Sanskrit word.

## Priyanka
**Meaning:** Symbol of love; beloved symbol
**Origin:** Sanskrit
**Pronunciation:** pre YANK ah
**Description:** Priyanka comes from the Sanskrit words *'priya'*, meaning 'beloved' and *'anka'*, meaning 'symbol'. We can take the name to mean either 'symbol of love' or 'beloved symbol'.
**Alternative spellings:** Preeyanka, Priyankah

## Pru
**Meaning:** Good judgement
**Origin:** English
**Pronunciation:** proo
**Description:** Pru is the shortened version of the name Prudence, meaning 'good judgement'. Although it is a nickname, it can also be used as a given name.
**Alternative spellings:** Prue

## Prudence
**Meaning:** Good judgement
**Origin:** English
**Pronunciation:** proo DENCE
**Description:** Prudence is an English name from the word of the same meaning. The name means 'good judgement,' and in England it was used during the Middle Ages and revived in the 17th century by the Puritans.

## Purdy
**Meaning:** For God

438

**Origin:** French
**Pronunciation:** pure DEE
**Description:** Purdy is a French surname translated from the words 'pour Dieu,' meaning 'for God'. This follows the contemporary trend of using last names as first names.
**Alternative spellings:** Purdie

## Purity

**Meaning:** Pure
**Origin:** English
**Pronunciation:** pure IT ee
**Description:** Purity comes from the English vocabulary word of the same name and means 'pure'. Like Charity and Grace, Purity is a virtue name.

# Q

## Queenie

**Meaning:** Queen
**Origin:** English
**Pronunciation:** KWEE nee
**Description:** The name Queenie derives from the English word 'queen' and comes from the Old English *'cwen'*, meaning 'woman'.

Queenie was also used as a pet name for Queen Victoria.
**Alternative spellings:** Queeney, Queeni, Queeny

## Quinn

See entry in 'Names for Baby Boys A–Z'

# R

## Rabia

**Meaning:** Garden in flower
**Origin:** Arabic
**Pronunciation:** RAH bee ah
**Description:** Rabia, the name of an Islamic saint, is popular with Muslim parents. Rabia is also the name of a small town in Iraq.
**Alternative spellings:** Rabbia, Rabiya

## Rachel

**Meaning:** Ewe
**Origin:** Hebrew
**Pronunciation:** RAY chul
**Description:** This biblical name means 'ewe' in Hebrew. Rachel was the wife of Jacob and mother of Joseph.
**Alternative spellings:** Rachael, Rachelle

## Rachelle

**Meaning:** Ewe
**Origin:** Hebrew
**Pronunciation:** rash EL
**Description:** Rachelle is an elaboration upon Rachel with a French influence.

439

**Alternative spellings:** Rachel, Rachael

## Rae
**Meaning:** Ewe
**Origin:** Hebrew
**Pronunciation:** ray
**Description:** Rae is a pet form of the name Rachael which is originally a Hebrew name meaning 'ewe'. It could also be the feminine form of Ray, but this is less common.
**Alternative spellings:** Ray

## Rahma
**Meaning:** Compassion
**Origin:** Swahili
**Pronunciation:** rah MAH
**Description:** Rahma is a name that has its origin in Africa, and most likely among Swahili-speaking people. It is a name that means 'compassion'.
**Alternative spellings:** Rahmah

## Rain
**Meaning:** Rain fall
**Origin:** English
**Pronunciation:** rain
**Description:** Rain comes from the English vocabulary word of the same spelling referring to the type of weather.

## Raina
**Meaning:** Queen
**Origin:** Slavic
**Pronunciation:** rain AH
**Description:** Raina is a Slavic name meaning 'queen' and likely has the same roots as the English vocabulary word 'reign'. Therefore, the name refers to a ruler or leader.
**Alternative spellings:** Rayna

## Rainbow
**Meaning:** Rainbow
**Origin:** English
**Pronunciation:** RAYN bo
**Description:** The name Rainbow comes from the English word. It was popularised as a name during the 'flower power' movement of the 1960s.
**Alternative spellings:** Rainbo, Raynbow

## Raisa
**Meaning:** Rose
**Origin:** Yiddish
**Pronunciation:** rai SAH
**Description:** Raisa is a Yiddish name meaning 'rose'. Another name that is similar to Raisa is Raisel, and is the male variation to the name.

## Raja
**Meaning:** Optimism
**Origin:** Arabic
**Pronunciation:** rah-JAH
**Description:** Although the Arabic name Raja is considered unisex, the feminine and masculine forms are often pronounced differently. For boys the pronunciation is 'rah-juh'.
**Alternative spellings:** Raija, Raijah, Rajah

## Ramla
**Meaning:** Seer
**Origin:** African
**Pronunciation:** RAM lah
**Description:** The name Ramla is found across several African languages and its exact origin is unclear. However, it generally translates to mean 'seer', which means a person who has the gift to see into the future.

**Alternative spellings:** Ramlah, Ramlla

# Ramona
**Meaning:** Wise protector
**Origin:** Spanish
**Pronunciation:** rah mo NAH
**Description:** Ramona is the female version of the name Ramon and it means 'wise protector'. It became popular in English-speaking regions after the publication of Helen Hunt Jackson's novel, *Ramona*, in 1884.

# Rana
**Meaning:** Mesmerising
**Origin:** Arabic
**Pronunciation:** RAH nah
**Description:** Rana is a unisex Arabic name; however it is more commonly found on girls due to the feminine 'a' sound.
**Alternative spellings:** Raina, Ranah, Rayna

# Rania
**Meaning:** Singing queen
**Origin:** Sanskrit
**Pronunciation:** RAN yah
**Description:** Rania is a variant of the Sanskrit name Rani, meaning 'singing queen'. It has increased in popularity by association with Queen Rania of Jordan.
**Alternative spellings:** Raniah, Raniya

# Rashida
**Meaning:** Righteous; wise
**Origin:** Arabic
**Pronunciation:** ra SHEE dah
**Description:** Rashida is an Arabic word that means 'righteous' or 'wise', and has connotations of someone who knows their way. Rashida Jones is a famous American actress with this name.

# Raven
**Meaning:** A black bird
**Origin:** English
**Pronunciation:** ray VEN
**Description:** Raven comes from the black bird that shares the same name. Raven Symoné is a famous actress who has this name, and was the star of the Disney show, also called *That's So Raven*.

# Rawan
**Meaning:** River that feeds
**Origin:** Arabic
**Pronunciation:** rah WAN
**Description:** Rawan derives from the Arabic verb *'rawi'*, meaning 'to feed with water'. A popular girls' name, it is also the name of a river that flows through heaven in Islamic belief.
**Alternative spellings:** Rawanne

# Raya
**Meaning:** Friend to all
**Origin:** Arabic
**Pronunciation:** RAY ah
**Description:** The name Raya appears in many languages and is likely to have derived as a shortened form of a longer name such as Rayan. It is believed to be Arabic in origin.
**Alternative spellings:** Raiya, Rayah

# Rayaan
**Meaning:** Young maid
**Origin:** English
**Pronunciation:** ray AN
**Description:** Rayaan is a variation

**R**

of the name Rayann, which in itself is an unusual name of uncertain origin and meaning. It is found used in several different languages. It sounds similar to a group of Welsh names including Rhianna, which are said to mean 'young maid'. Rihana is another similar name, this time from Arabic origins, and is said to refer to a kind of herb. Rayann could also have come about as a compound of the two names Ray and Ann.

## Rayah

**Meaning:** Friend
**Origin:** Arabic
**Pronunciation:** RAY ah
**Description:** Rayah is an Arabic Muslim girls' name meaning 'friend,' and would be a good choice for parents looking for something with a sweet meaning.
**Alternative spellings:** Raya, Reaya

## Rayan

See entry in 'Names for Baby Boys A–Z'

## Rayann

**Meaning:** Great goddess
**Origin:** English
**Pronunciation:** ray AN; RAY an
**Description:** As well as being a spelling variant of the Sanskrit name Rayan, Rayann could derive from a group of Welsh names, including Rhianna, which mean 'great goddess'. It may also be a combination of the names Ray and Ann.
**Alternative spellings:** Raiyan, Rayan, Rayanne

## Reba

**Meaning:** Binding

**Origin:** English
**Pronunciation:** ree BAH
**Description:** Reba was originally a shortened form of the name Rebecca and as such, shares the same meaning of 'binding'. However, it is not established as a given name in its own right. Reba McEntire is a famous American country singer and actress.
**Alternative spellings:** Reeba

## Rebecca

**Meaning:** Binding
**Origin:** Hebrew
**Pronunciation:** REH beh cuh
**Description:** In the Bible, Rebecca was the wife of Isaac. It derives from a Hebrew word meaning to tie or constrict and its meaning is 'binding'.
**Alternative spellings:** Rebeca, Rebeka, Rebekah

## Reem

**Meaning:** Little deer
**Origin:** Arabic
**Pronunciation:** REEM
**Description:** From the Arabic word for a 'little deer', Reem is popular across the Middle East and Africa.
**Alternative spellings:** Ream, Reeme

## Reese

**Meaning:** Enthusiastic
**Origin:** Welsh
**Pronunciation:** REECE
**Description:** Reese is another anglicised version of the Welsh name Rhys. It is unisex and especially popular with girls in America.
**Alternative spellings:** Reece, Rhys

## Reeva

**Meaning:** Shore, riverbank; the sacred Narmada River
**Origin:** French
**Pronunciation:** ree VAH
**Description:** Reeva has both French and Sanskrit roots, meaning 'shore' and 'riverbank' in the former, and 'the sacred Narmada River' in the latter
**Alternative spellings:** Riva

## Regan

**Meaning:** Royalty
**Origin:** Gaelic
**Pronunciation:** RAY gen; REE gan
**Description:** Regan is a unisex Gaelic name first featuring in Shakespeare's play *King Lear*. The name has associations with the word 'regal'.
**Alternative spellings:** Raegan, Reagan, Reagun, Reegan

## Regina

**Meaning:** Queen
**Origin:** Latin
**Pronunciation:** reh GEEN ah
**Description:** Regina comes directly from the Latin word of the same spelling, meaning 'queen'. It is also the feminine version of the name Reginald.

## Reiko

**Meaning:** Courteous child; thankful child
**Origin:** Japanese
**Pronunciation:** REH eh ko
**Description:** The name Reiko is traditionally written using the Japanese characters *'rei'*, meaning 'thanks' or 'salute', and *'ko'*, meaning 'child'. This gives the name the meaning 'courteous child' or 'thankful child'.
**Alternative spellings:** Rehiko, Reikoh

## Remi

**Meaning:** From Rheims
**Origin:** French
**Pronunciation:** REH me
**Description:** The name Remi derives from the French town Rheims and would have originally been given to those who lived in the town. There was also a French saint who bore the name Remi.
**Alternative spellings:** Remy

## Remy

See entry in 'Names for Baby Boys A–Z'

## Renee

**Meaning:** Reborn
**Origin:** French
**Pronunciation:** REH nay
**Description:** Like many French names, Renee is often spelt using an accent. The name comes from the Latin word *'renatus'*, meaning 'reborn'.
**Alternative spellings:** Renae, Rene, Rennee

## Reya

**Meaning:** Singer
**Origin:** Sanskrit
**Pronunciation:** RAY ah
**Description:** Reya is a feminine Sanskrit Indian name that comes from the word 'riya,' meaning 'singer'. Other related names include Rea, Reeya, Rheeya, Ria and Riyah.
**Alternative spellings:** Rhia, Riya, Rhea

R

## Rhia

**Meaning:** Flowing water
**Origin:** Greek
**Pronunciation:** ree AH
**Description:** Rhia is a variation of Rhea, a feminine name of Greek origin. The Greek meaning is said to refer to flowing water. The name is widely used in Welsh and probably comes from the same origin, as it is the name of a river that flows through Wales as well as being a popular girls' name. In Greek mythology Rhea was the name of the mother of the influential gods Zeus, Poseidon, Demeter and Hera. Like many Greek gods, Rhea is also found in Roman mythology.
**Alternative spellings:** Rhea, Reya, Riya

## Rhian

**Meaning:** Great goddess
**Origin:** Welsh
**Pronunciation:** REE an
**Description:** Rhian is the shortened form of the Welsh name Rhiannon, meaning 'great goddess' or 'young maid'.
**Alternative spellings:** Reeanne, Rhiann, Rhianne

## Rhianna

**Meaning:** Great goddess
**Origin:** Welsh
**Pronunciation:** ree AHN aah
**Description:** Rhianna is a combination of the Welsh name Rhiannon and the Irish name Riane.
**Alternative spellings:** Reeana, Reeanna, Rhiana, Rhiannah, Rianna, Rihana, Rihanna

## Rhiannon

**Meaning:** Great goddess

**Origin:** Gaelic
**Pronunciation:** ree ANN on
**Description:** The name derives from the Welsh 'rigantona', meaning 'great queen'. In the *Mabinogion*, a collection of stories from Welsh mythology, Rhiannon was the horse goddess.
**Alternative spellings:** Reeannon, Reeanon, Rhianon, Riannon, Rianon

## Ria

**Meaning:** Sea dew
**Origin:** Hebrew
**Pronunciation:** REE ah
**Description:** This name is a spelling variant of the Greek name Rhea. It can also be considered the shortened and more unusual form of the name Maria.
**Alternative spellings:** Rhea, Rhia, Rea, Reah, Riah

## Ricky

See entry in 'Names for Baby Boys A–Z'.

## Rida

**Meaning:** Right
**Origin:** Sanskrit
**Pronunciation:** REE dah
**Description:** Rida is a pet form of the name Afrida, said to come from a Sanskrit word meaning 'right'. Rida is now a given name in its own right.
**Alternative spellings:** Reeda, Ridah

## Rihanna

**Meaning:** Basil
**Origin:** Arabic
**Pronunciation:** ree AN nah

**Description:** Rihanna is a spelling variant of the Arabic name Rihana, meaning 'basil', as well as being a variant of the Welsh name Rhianna, meaning 'great goddess'. The name has become extremely popular recently, no doubt due to the fame of singer Rihanna.
**Alternative spellings:** Reeana, Reeanna, Rhiana, Rhiannah, Rianna, Rihana

## Riley
See entry in 'Names for Baby Boys A–Z'

## Rio
See entry in 'Names for Baby Boys A–Z'

## Rita
**Meaning:** Virtuous; pearl
**Origin:** Sanskrit
**Pronunciation:** REE tah
**Description:** Rita is used by Hindu parents and comes from a Sanskrit name meaning 'virtuous'. However, it has also been found for centuries throughout Europe as a pet form of Margarita, meaning 'pearl'.
**Alternative spellings:** Reeta, Ritah

## River
**Meaning:** River
**Origin:** English
**Pronunciation:** RIH vuh
**Description:** River is a fairly modern name, borne out of the so-called 'flower power' era in the 1960s. It is considered unisex.
**Alternative spellings:** Riva, Ryver

## Rivka
**Meaning:** Young calf
**Origin:** Hebrew
**Pronunciation:** riv KAH
**Description:** Rivka is a variation of the name Rivkah, which is the traditional Hebrew form of Rebecca. The name itself means 'young calf'.
**Alternative spellings:** Rivkah

## Roberta
**Meaning:** Bright fame
**Origin:** German
**Pronunciation:** roh BER tah
**Description:** The feminine form of Robert, meaning 'bright fame'. Roberta is most popular in continental Europe.
**Alternative spellings:** Roburta

## Robin
See entry in 'Names for Baby Boys A–Z'

## Robyn
**Meaning:** Bright fame
**Origin:** German
**Pronunciation:** ROB in
**Description:** A popular feminine spelling of the name Robin, especially common in the US. It shares the same meaning as Robin, meaning 'bright fame'.
**Alternative spellings:** Robin

## Rochelle
**Meaning:** Rock
**Origin:** French
**Pronunciation:** roh SHELL
**Description:** The name Rochelle derives from the place name of La Rochelle in France. It comes from the French word *'roche'*, meaning 'rock', and would have been given

R

as a surname to those from La Rochelle.
**Alternative spellings:** Rochell, Roshelle

## Roisin
**Meaning:** Little rose
**Origin:** Latin
**Pronunciation:** ro SHEEN
**Description:** This name can most commonly be found in Irish- and English-speaking communities. It comes from the Irish name Rois, meaning 'rose'.
**Alternative spellings:** Roisheen, Rosheen

## Roksana
**Meaning:** Star
**Origin:** Persian
**Pronunciation:** rok SAH nah
**Description:** Roksana is the Polish variant of the name Roxanna. It ultimately derives from the Persian name Roshan, meaning 'star'. Although Roshan is unisex, Roksana is specifically feminine.
**Alternative spellings:** Roksanna, Roxana, Roxanna

## Roma
**Meaning:** City of Rome
**Origin:** Latin
**Pronunciation:** ROH ma
**Description:** Roma is the Latin word for the city of Rome. It has transferred into a unisex given name.
**Alternative spellings:** Romah

## Romana
**Meaning:** Citizen of Rome
**Origin:** Latin
**Pronunciation:** roh MA na
**Description:** Romana is the specifically feminine version of the unisex name Roman, derived from the Latin word for citizens of Rome.
**Alternative spellings:** Romanah, Romona

## Romilly
**Meaning:** Rosemary herb
**Origin:** Latin
**Pronunciation:** RO mil ee
**Description:** Romilly is believed to be an elaboration of the name Romy, itself a pet form of the name Rosemary, which is a herb. Romilly seems to be rising in popularity as a baby name.
**Alternative spellings:** Romilley, Romilli, Romillie

## Romola
**Meaning:** From Rome
**Origin:** Latin
**Pronunciation:** rom OH lah
**Description:** Romola is the feminine version of Romulus, meaning 'from Rome'. It was the titular character of George Eliot's 1862 book. Romola Garai is a British actress with this name.

## Romy
**Meaning:** Sea dew
**Origin:** Latin
**Pronunciation:** RO mee
**Description:** Romy is a pet form of the name Rosemary, which comes from the English noun for the herb.
**Alternative spellings:** Romey, Romi, Romie

## Ronit
**Meaning:** Song
**Origin:** Hebrew
**Pronunciation:** ron IT
**Description:** Ronit is a Hebrew

name and the feminine version of the name Ron, meaning 'song'.

## Ronni
**Meaning:** Bringer of victory
**Origin:** Greek
**Pronunciation:** ROH ni
**Description:** Ronni could be either a pet form of the Greek name Veronica, meaning 'bringer of victory', or a feminine version of Ronny, meaning 'open-minded'.
**Alternative spellings:** Ronnie, Ronny

## Ronnie
**Meaning:** Open-minded
**Origin:** Norse
**Pronunciation:** RON ee
**Description:** Ronnie is a spelling variant of the feminine name Ronni or the masculine name Ronny. It is unisex.
**Alternative spellings:** Ronni, Ronny

## Rory
See entry in 'Names for Baby Boys A–Z'

## Rosa
**Meaning:** Rose
**Origin:** Latin
**Pronunciation:** ROH za
**Description:** Rosa is the Latin word for the flower and also the Italian version of the name. Rosa could also be the shortened form of the German name Rosalind, meaning 'gentle horse'.
**Alternative spellings:** Roza

## Rosabelle
**Meaning:** Beautiful rose
**Origin:** Latin

**Pronunciation:** rosa BEL
**Description:** Rosabelle is a combination of two elements, '*rosa*' meaning 'rose' and '*belle*' meaning 'beautiful'.

## Rosalie
**Meaning:** Rose
**Origin:** French
**Pronunciation:** roh ZAH lee
**Description:** Rosalie is a French variation on the Italian Rosalia. It has gained in popularity over recent years due to the character in the Twilight series of books with the same name.
**Alternative spellings:** Rosalia

## Rosalind
**Meaning:** Gentle horse
**Origin:** German
**Pronunciation:** ROZ a lind
**Description:** The name Rosalind was originally popularised in England by Shakespeare in his play *As You Like It*.
**Alternative spellings:** Rosalynd, Rozalind, Rozalynd

## Rosalyn
**Meaning:** Beautiful rose
**Origin:** Latin
**Pronunciation:** ROZ ah lin
**Description:** Rosalyn could be a variant of the German name Rosalind, meaning 'gentle horse', or a combination of the names 'Rose' and 'Lyn' to mean 'beautiful rose'.
**Alternative spellings:** Rosalin, Rosalynn, Rosalynne, Rozalin, Rozalyn

## Rosamund
**Meaning:** Horse protection
**Origin:** German
**Pronunciation:** rosa MUND

R

447

**Description:** Rosamund is a German name composed of the elements of '*hros*', meaning 'horse', and '*mund*', meaning 'protection'. Rosamund Pike is a famous British actress with this name.

## Rosanna
**Meaning:** Flower of grace
**Origin:** English
**Pronunciation:** roh ZAN ah
**Description:** Rosanna is a combination of the names Rose and Anna, and consequently it has the meaning 'flower of grace'. It has become increasingly popular in recent years as double-barrelled and combined names are sought.
**Alternative spellings:** Roseanna

## Rosanne
**Meaning:** Rose
**Origin:** Latin
**Pronunciation:** ROZE an
**Description:** Rosanne, which is of Latin origin, was initially a compound name, combining Rose and Anne, but has since become a name in its own right.
**Alternative spellings:** Rosann, Roseann, Roseanne

## Rosario
**Meaning:** Rosary
**Origin:** Spanish
**Pronunciation:** row SAR ee oh
**Description:** Rosario is a Spanish name that means 'rosary'. It is taken from the title for the Virgin Mary, Nuestra Señora del Rosario, meaning 'Our Lady of the Rosary.'

## Rose
**Meaning:** Rose

**Origin:** English
**Pronunciation:** ROZE
**Description:** Rose is an elegant name for a girl, taken directly from the English name of the flower. It is considered a traditionally English name, taken from the phrase 'an English rose'.
**Alternative spellings:** Roze

## Rosemary
**Meaning:** Rosemary herb; sea dew
**Origin:** Latin
**Pronunciation:** ROZE ma ree
**Description:** The name Rosemary was coined in the 19th century. Rosemary is a fragrant herb; however the girls' name was derived from the Latin words '*ros marinus*', meaning 'sea dew'. The name carries both of these meanings.
**Alternative spellings:** Rosemarey, Rosemari, Rosemarie, Rozemari, Rozemarie, Rozemary

## Rosetta
**Meaning:** Rose
**Origin:** Italian
**Pronunciation:** roze ET tah
**Description:** Rosetta is the Italian version of the common name Rose, which refers to the flower of the same name.

## Roshan
**Meaning:** Star
**Origin:** Persian
**Pronunciation:** roh SHAHN
**Description:** Roshan is a unisex name meaning 'star' in reference to fame and luminosity. The name is very popular in India. It is also a variant of the anglicised form Roxanne, which is specifically a feminine name.

**Alternative spellings:** Roshann, Roshanne

## Roshni
**Meaning:** Light
**Origin:** Sanskrit
**Pronunciation:** rosh NI
**Description:** Roshni is a feminine name of Indian origins and because much documentation on the name is scarce in English translation it is difficult to give reliable information. The exact origin is uncertain and the name seems to be used by both Muslim and Hindu parents. It seems to be agreed that the name means 'light'.

## Rosie
**Meaning:** Rose
**Origin:** English
**Pronunciation:** RO zee
**Description:** Rosie came about as a pet name for the English name Rose, taken from the name of the flower. Now it is seen as a name in its own right.
**Alternative spellings:** Rosi, Rosy, Rozi, Rozie, Rozy

## Rosina
**Meaning:** Rose
**Origin:** Latin
**Pronunciation:** roh ZEE nah; roh SEE nah
**Description:** The name Rosina is an elaboration of the Latin name Rosa, meaning 'rose', and is most commonly found in Italy and Spain.
**Alternative spellings:** Rosinah, Rosyna, Rozina

## Rosita
**Meaning:** Rose
**Origin:** Spanish
**Pronunciation:** roze EE tah
**Description:** Rosita is the Spanish version of the common name Rose, which refers to the flower of the same name.

## Rowan
See entry in 'Names for Baby Boys A–Z'

## Rowena
**Meaning:** Fame; bliss
**Origin:** German
**Pronunciation:** row EEN ah
**Description:** The meaning of Rowena is uncertain, but it is composed of the Germanic elements of 'hrod' meaning 'fame' and 'wunn' meaning 'bliss'. It was made famous by Sir Walter Scott's novel, *Ivanhoe*, which featured a character called Lady Rowena.

## Roxanna
**Meaning:** Star
**Origin:** Persian
**Pronunciation:** rox AN ah
**Description:** Roxanna is a variant of Roxanne, which is itself an anglicised version of the Persian name Roshan.
**Alternative spellings:** Roksana, Roksanna, Roxana

## Roxanne
**Meaning:** Star
**Origin:** Persian
**Pronunciation:** ROKS an
**Description:** Roxanne is an anglicised version of the Persian name Roshan. Its popularity may have been increased by the song 'Roxanne', a big hit in the 1980s.
**Alternative spellings:** Roksanne, Roxane, Roxann

R

## Roxie

**Meaning:** Star
**Origin:** Persian
**Pronunciation:** ROK see
**Description:** Roxy is the pet form of Roxanne and from the Persian name Roshan, meaning 'star'. The name has associations with independence.
**Alternative spellings:** Roksi, Roksie, Roksy, Roxi, Roxy

## Ruby

**Meaning:** Precious
**Origin:** English
**Pronunciation:** ROO bee
**Description:** The name Ruby comes from the precious red gemstone. Common in the late 19th and mid-20th century, the name is enjoying a partial revival in English-speaking regions. Ruby is also the birthstone for July.
**Alternative spellings:** Rubee, Rubey, Rubi, Rubie

## Ruhi

**Meaning:** Spiritual
**Origin:** Indian
**Pronunciation:** rue HEE
**Description:** Ruhi has Indian origins and means 'spiritual'. The name also has Muslim and Hindu roots, and can also mean 'soul'. Similar names are Rahi, Raha and Rhea.
**Alternative spellings:** Ruhee

## Rumaisa

**Meaning:** Unknown
**Origin:** Arabic
**Pronunciation:** roo MAY sa
**Description:** Rumaisa is an unusual name of uncertain meaning and origin. The name is likely to be Arabic and is used mainly by Muslim parents.
**Alternative spellings:** Rumaysa

## Rumi

**Meaning:** Name of a poet
**Origin:** Persian
**Pronunciation:** ROO mi
**Description:** It is speculated that Rumi comes from the 13th-century Persian poet of the same name, Jalāl ad-Dīn Muhammad Rumi. In Japanese, the name Rumi also means 'beauty,' 'current,' 'flow', and 'water'. Beyoncé and Jay-Z named one of their newborn twins Rumi.
**Alternative spellings:** Roomi

## Ruqayyah

**Meaning:** Delicate
**Origin:** Arabic
**Pronunciation:** ruh QUAI ah
**Description:** Ruqayyah is a name of Arabic origin, which means 'delicate'. This name is popular with Muslim parents and was the name of the second daughter of the prophet Muhammad.
**Alternative spellings:** Ruquaiah

## Ruth

**Meaning:** Companion
**Origin:** Hebrew
**Pronunciation:** ROOTH
**Description:** The name Ruth is derived from the Hebrew meaning 'companion' or 'friend'. It also means 'compassion' in English.
**Alternative spellings:** Rooth, Ruthe

## Ryan

See entry in 'Names for Baby Boys A–Z'

## Rylee

**Meaning:** No meaning
**Origin:** Gaelic
**Pronunciation:** ry LEE
**Description:** The meaning of this name is unknown, although it can be traced back as an Irish surname. It has become a popular name in modern times, especially in America, for both girls and boys in its variously spelt forms. However, the version spelt Rylee is that usually given to a girl, along with Ryleigh.
**Alternative spellings:** Rilee, Riley

## Ryleigh

**Meaning:** Courageous
**Origin:** English
**Pronunciation:** RI lee
**Description:** Ryleigh is a unisex name of Old English origin, meaning 'rye clearing' or 'courageous'. The name is a variant of the boys' name Ryley, and the girls' names Rylee and Rylie. Ryleigh is more commonly seen as a girls' name.
**Alternative spellings:** Reilley, Reilly, Rielly, Riley, Ryley

## Ryoko

**Meaning:** Refreshing child
**Origin:** Japanese
**Pronunciation:** ree OH ko
**Description:** The name Ryoko originates from Japan and means 'refreshing or good child'.
**Alternative spellings:** Rioko

# S

## Saanvi

**Meaning:** One who follows
**Origin:** Sanskrit
**Pronunciation:** SAHN vee
**Description:** Saanvi is a name that comes from Sanskrit origins; the name means 'one who follows'. It is mainly used by Hindu families.
**Alternative spellings:** Saanvee

## Sabah

**Meaning:** Dawn sunrise
**Origin:** Arabic
**Pronunciation:** sah BAH
**Description:** Sabah is a name of Arabic origin and it is said to come from an Arabic word for a 'dawn sunrise'. It is popular in Arab-speaking countries.
**Alternative spellings:** Saba

## Sabiha

**Meaning:** Beautiful
**Origin:** Arabic
**Pronunciation:** sah BI ha
**Description:** Sabiha is a name that is quite popular in Africa. It is thought to be originally of Muslim origin, from the Arabic word meaning 'beautiful'. Its use has spread into Swahili.
**Alternative spellings:** Saabiha

## Sabina

**Meaning:** Sabine

R
S

**Origin:** Latin
**Pronunciation:** sah BEE nah
**Description:** Sabina comes from Latin origin of the name Sabine, which is a region in Italy and the name of a saint.
**Alternative spellings:** Sabbina

## Sabrina

**Meaning:** River Sabrina
**Origin:** Gaelic
**Pronunciation:** sah BREE nah
**Description:** Sabrina comes from the name of a legendary Celtic character whose name was lent to the River Severn.
**Alternative spellings:** Sabbrina, Sabreena

## Sade

**Meaning:** Honoured one
**Origin:** African
**Pronunciation:** shah DAY
**Description:** Sade, a name of African origin, came about as a pet form of Folasade. This name means 'honoured'.
**Alternative spellings:** Saide

## Sadia

**Meaning:** Honoured one
**Origin:** African
**Pronunciation:** sah DAY ah
**Description:** Sadia is a relatively rare name in Britain. The name is a variant of the name Sade and in Portuguese means 'healthy'.
**Alternative spellings:** Saddia, Sahdia

## Sadie

**Meaning:** Princess
**Origin:** Hebrew
**Pronunciation:** SAY dee
**Description:** Sadie was originally a pet form of the name Sarah.
**Alternative spellings:** Saidie, Saydie

## Safa

**Meaning:** Pure
**Origin:** Arabic
**Pronunciation:** SAH fah
**Description:** Safa is a name of Arabic origin and it means 'pure'. It is popular in Middle Eastern countries and is also a name given to a park in Dubai.
**Alternative spellings:** Safah

## Safaa

**Meaning:** Large rock
**Origin:** Arabic
**Pronunciation:** suh FAH
**Description:** Safaa is a name that comes directly from the Quran. It is a hill in Mecca and is of importance during the Hajj proceedings every year.
**Alternative spellings:** Safa

## Saffron

**Meaning:** Yellow
**Origin:** French
**Pronunciation:** SAF fron
**Description:** Saffron is an English name that is also the name of a rare and highly sought after yellow spice.
**Alternative spellings:** Saphron

## Safiya

**Meaning:** Purity
**Origin:** Arabic
**Pronunciation:** sah FEE yah
**Description:** Safiya is a name said to mean 'purity' or 'sincere friend'. It is popular in Britain mainly among Muslim and African-American parents.

**Alternative spellings:** Safia, Safi-yah, Safiyyah

## Sage
**Meaning:** Herb
**Origin:** English
**Pronunciation:** sage
**Description:** Sage is a type of herb often used in cooking. Like Rosemary, it is part of the trend to use plants and flowers as baby names.

## Sahana
**Meaning:** Melody
**Origin:** Sanskrit
**Pronunciation:** sah HA na
**Description:** Sahana is an Indian name and can mean 'melody' as it is the name of a raga, which is a melodic mode in Indian music.
**Alternative spellings:** Sahaana

## Sahar
See entry in 'Names for Baby Boys A–Z'

## Sahara
**Meaning:** Desert
**Origin:** African
**Pronunciation:** sah HAHR rah
**Description:** While the name Sahara is most commonly associated with the desert, it is also the feminine version of the masculine name Sahar and it is the Arabic name for 'desert'.
**Alternative spellings:** Sahaara

## Sahra
**Meaning:** Desert
**Origin:** Arabic
**Pronunciation:** SAH ru
**Description:** Sahra is a variant

of the name Sahara. This name is popular in the Middle East and Saharan regions.
**Alternative spellings:** Sahraa

## Sakina
**Meaning:** Peace
**Origin:** Arabic
**Pronunciation:** sak KEE nah
**Description:** Sakina, which is Arabic in origin, comes from the word *'sakun'*, which means 'peace'. In the Quran, Sukaina is the name given to a spirit who brings peace to the prophet Muhammad.
**Alternative spellings:** Sakinah

## Salina
**Meaning:** Moon
**Origin:** Greek
**Pronunciation:** sah LEE na
**Description:** Salina is a name of ultimately Greek origins. It is a variant form of the name Celina, which is derived from a Greek word referring to the moon. Salina is also a name of an island off the coast of Italy.
**Alternative spellings:** Salinah

## Sally
**Meaning:** Princess
**Origin:** Hebrew
**Pronunciation:** SAL ee
**Description:** Sally, like Sadie, was originally a form of the name Sarah. Now the name stands alone.
**Alternative spellings:** Sallee, Salley, Sallie

## Salma
**Meaning:** Whole
**Origin:** Arabic
**Pronunciation:** SAL mah
**Description:** This name is most

common in African, Arabic- and Swahili-speaking countries. It originates from the female name Salima.
**Alternative spellings:** Salmah

## Salome
**Meaning:** Peace
**Origin:** Hebrew
**Pronunciation:** salom EH
**Description:** Salome is derived from the Hebrew word *'shalom'*, meaning 'peace'. It was also the name of the daughter of Herodias and enemy of John the Baptist.

## Sam
See entry in 'Names for Baby Boys A–Z'

## Sama
**Meaning:** Sky
**Origin:** Arabic
**Pronunciation:** SAH ma
**Description:** Sama, from the Arabic for 'sky', is mainly used in the Middle East and popular with Muslim parents.
**Alternative spellings:** Samah

## Samanta
**Meaning:** God listens
**Origin:** Hebrew
**Pronunciation:** sah MAN tah
**Description:** Samanta is a variant of the name Samantha, the feminine version of the masculine name Samuel. Samuel is a popular name of Hebrew origins and means 'God listens'. The version Samanta is most common in Italy, France and Germany.
**Alternative spellings:** Samannta

## Samantha
**Meaning:** God listens
**Origin:** Hebrew
**Pronunciation:** sa MAN thah
**Description:** Samantha consists of a shortened form of Samuel, which means 'God listens', and the suffix 'antha', which means 'flower'.
**Alternative spellings:** Samanther, Sammantha

## Samara
**Meaning:** Lively in conversation
**Origin:** Arabic
**Pronunciation:** sah MAYR ah
**Description:** Samara is a feminine variant of the masculine name Samir, which is Arabic in origin and is said to mean 'lively in conversation'.
**Alternative spellings:** Samarah

## Sameeha
**Meaning:** Blessing from Allah
**Origin:** Arabic
**Pronunciation:** sah MEE hah
**Description:** Sameeha is an unusual name of Arabic origin and although its exact meaning and origin are uncertain, it may mean 'blessing from Allah'.
**Alternative spellings:** Sameehah

## Sameera
**Meaning:** Lively in conversation
**Origin:** Arabic
**Pronunciation:** sah MEER ah
**Description:** Sameera is the feminine version of the masculine name Samir, which is of Arabic origins and is popular with Muslim parents. The name means 'lively in conversation'.
**Alternative spellings:** Samira, Samirah

## Samia

**Meaning:** Lofty
**Origin:** Arabic
**Pronunciation:** sah MEE ah
**Description:** Samia is a name of Arabic origin and means 'lofty'. This name is mostly used in Pakistan.
**Alternative spellings:** Samiha, Samiya, Samiyah

## Sammy

See entry in 'Names for Baby Boys A–Z'

## Sana

**Meaning:** Dazzling; to shine
**Origin:** Arabic
**Pronunciation:** SAH nah
**Description:** Sana is a name of Arabic origin and means 'dazzling' or 'to shine'. It is found mainly in Arabic-speaking countries.
**Alternative spellings:** Sanaa, Sanah

## Sanae

**Meaning:** Rice seedlings
**Origin:** Japanese
**Pronunciation:** sa NA eh
**Description:** This name is not often found outside Japanese-speaking countries. Although it uses the same Japanese characters required to write 'rice seedlings', the name may mean 'sand together' or 'seedling'.
**Alternative spellings:** Sahnae

## Sanaya

**Meaning:** Noble
**Origin:** Arabic
**Pronunciation:** saan AH ya
**Description:** Sanaya is an Arabic name that means 'noble,' 'admirable' or 'praiseworthy'. Other related names include Sanayah Saniyya and Sonya.

**Alternative spellings:** Sanayah

## Sandra

**Meaning:** Defender of man
**Origin:** Greek
**Pronunciation:** SAHN dra
**Description:** Sandra is a short form of Alessandra, the Italian form of Alexandra.
**Alternative spellings:** Sandraa

## Sandy

**Meaning:** Defender of man
**Origin:** Greek
**Pronunciation:** SAN dee
**Description:** Sandy is a unisex name and pet form of either 'Alexander' or 'Alexandra'.
**Alternative spellings:** Sandie

## Saniya

**Meaning:** Shining brilliance
**Origin:** Arabic
**Pronunciation:** sah NEE yah
**Description:** Saniya is a name of Arabic origin and it is said to come from the word 'sana', which means to shine. Saniya is a popular name with Muslim parents.
**Alternative spellings:** Saniyah

## Sanjiana

**Meaning:** Gentle
**Origin:** Sanskrit
**Pronunciation:** san JAH nah
**Description:** Sanjiana is a name favoured by Hindu parents. Like many names with Sanskrit or Urdu origins, there is little translated documentation about its meaning. It may mean 'gentle'.
**Alternative spellings:** Sanjianah

## Saoirse

**Meaning:** Freedom

S

**Origin:** Gaelic
**Pronunciation:** SEER sha
**Description:** Saoirse is a name of Irish origin and its meaning is said to be 'freedom'. It is the name of an Irish Republican newspaper and as such the name has patriotic connotations.

## Sapphire
**Meaning:** Blue gemstone
**Origin:** English
**Pronunciation:** SA fire
**Description:** The name Sapphire comes from the name of the blue gemstone. This stone is also the birthstone for September.
**Alternative spellings:** Saphire

## Sarah
**Meaning:** Princess
**Origin:** Hebrew
**Pronunciation:** SAIR uh
**Description:** Sarah, the biblical wife of Abraham and mother of Isaac, was originally named Sarai, which may mean 'contentious' in Hebrew. Her name changed to Sarah, which means 'princess'.
**Alternative spellings:** Saira, Sara, Saora

## Sariah
**Meaning:** Princess
**Origin:** Hebrew
**Pronunciation:** sa RYE ah
**Description:** Sariah is a name of Hebrew origin from the same source as the name Sarah, and means 'princess'. The name is one of the original ancestors of the Mormon people in America.
**Alternative spellings:** Saryah

## Sarina
**Meaning:** Princess
**Origin:** Hebrew
**Pronunciation:** sa REE nah
**Description:** Sarina is a modern variation of the name Sarah. Sarah is of Hebrew origin and means 'princess'.
**Alternative spellings:** Sarinah, Serena

## Sasha
See entry in 'Names for Baby Boys A–Z'

## Saskia
**Meaning:** Unknown
**Origin:** Dutch
**Pronunciation:** SASS kee uh
**Description:** Saskia is a name of Dutch origin. Its meaning is unknown but it does carry a phonetically pleasing sound.
**Alternative spellings:** Saskiah

## Satin
**Meaning:** Satin
**Origin:** English
**Pronunciation:** SAT in
**Description:** Satin is a luxurious fabric and is now a name.

## Savannah
**Meaning:** Treeless plain
**Origin:** Spanish
**Pronunciation:** sav AN nah
**Description:** Savannah is the name of two US cities in Georgia and South Carolina. They are linked to the local Savannah River, possibly derived from the word *'savanna'* meaning 'treeless plain'.
**Alternative spellings:** Savanna

## Saya

**Meaning:** Quick arrow
**Origin:** Japanese
**Pronunciation:** say YAH
**Description:** Saya is a feminine name of Asian origins and because much documentation on the name is scarce in English translation, it is difficult to give reliable information. The name seems to come from a Japanese word and is said to mean 'quick arrow'.
**Alternative spellings:** Sayah

## Scarlett

**Meaning:** Scarlet
**Origin:** French
**Pronunciation:** SCAR let
**Description:** Scarlett is a name of English origin and refers to a shade of red. Scarlett O'Hara is a character from the novel and film *Gone With The Wind*.
**Alternative spellings:** Scarlet, Scarlette

## Seerat

**Meaning:** Inner beauty; fame; brightness
**Origin:** Indian
**Pronunciation:** see RAAT
**Description:** An Indian name meaning 'inner beauty,' 'fame' and 'brightness'. Seerat is a tradional girls' name used in the Hindu and Sikh religions. Some other related names are Sarat, Sarit and Soorat.

## Sehar

**Meaning:** Early morning
**Origin:** Persian
**Pronunciation:** seh HAJ
**Description:** Sehar is an unusual name; it is thought to be of Persian origin and means 'early morning'.
**Alternative spellings:** Seher
See entry in 'Names for Baby Boys A–Z'

## Selby

See entry in 'Names for Baby Boys A–Z'

## Selena

**Meaning:** Goddess of the moon
**Origin:** Greek
**Pronunciation:** seh LEE na
**Description:** Selena is of Greek origin and means 'goddess of the moon'.
**Alternative spellings:** Celena, Selina

## Selin

**Meaning:** Moon
**Origin:** Greek
**Pronunciation:** SEH lin
**Description:** Selin is an unusual name thought to come from the name Selina, meaning 'moon'.
**Alternative spellings:** Celin

## Selma

**Meaning:** Beautiful
**Origin:** Gaelic
**Pronunciation:** SEL ma
**Description:** Selma is a name of Gaelic origin; it means 'beautiful'.
**Alternative spellings:** Selmah

## Seraphina

**Meaning:** Burning ones
**Origin:** Hebrew
**Pronunciation:** SEH ra FEE na
**Description:** Seraphina is a Hebrew name, which means 'burning'. The Hebrew word that

S

it comes from is *'seraphim'*, which refers to an order of angels.
**Alternative spellings:** Serafina, Serrafina, Serraphina

## Seren
**Meaning:** Star
**Origin:** Welsh
**Pronunciation:** SEH ren
**Description:** Seren is given to both males and females and means 'star', but is uncommon in the UK outside of Wales.
**Alternative spellings:** Sehren

## Serena
**Meaning:** Calm; serene
**Origin:** Latin
**Pronunciation:** seh REE na
**Description:** Serena is a modern variation of the name Sarah. Serena comes from the Latin word *'serenus'*, meaning 'serene'.
**Alternative spellings:** Sarina

## Serenity
**Meaning:** Peaceful
**Origin:** English
**Pronunciation:** seh REH nih tee
**Description:** Serenity is a name taken from the English word for 'calm'. Like Charity or Hope, it is a virtue name and is of English and French origin.
**Alternative spellings:** Serenitee, Sereniti, Serenitie

## Setsuko
**Meaning:** Season child
**Origin:** Japanese
**Pronunciation:** SET su ko
**Description:** Setsuko is popular in Japanese-speaking countries. It means 'season child'.
**Alternative spellings:** Setsukoh

## Shaan
**Meaning:** God is gracious
**Origin:** Welsh
**Pronunciation:** sha AN; SHARN
**Description:** Shaan (pronounced sha AN) is of feminine origin The name is of Punjabi origin that means 'respected one'. The name is a variant of the spelling 'Sian', which is of Celtic origin.
**Alternative spellings:** Sian

## Shakira
**Meaning:** Thankful
**Origin:** Arabic
**Pronunciation:** sha KEER ah
**Description:** Shakira is a name of Arabic origin, which means 'thankful'.
**Alternative spellings:** Shakeera, Shakeira

## Shalom
**Meaning:** Go in peace
**Origin:** Hebrew
**Pronunciation:** sha LOM
**Description:** Shalom is a name of Hebrew origin. The word can be used as a greeting and a farewell, and means 'go in peace'.

## Shanae
**Meaning:** God is gracious
**Origin:** Gaelic
**Pronunciation:** sha NAY
**Description:** Shanae is a name of modern coinage that started in America. It is thought that the name is based on the Irish name Sinead.
**Alternative spellings:** Shanay, Shanea, Shannea, Shenae

## Shania
**Meaning:** I am coming

**Origin:** American
**Pronunciation:** sha NEE yah
**Description:** Shania is an extremely popular American name. It is thought to be inspired by a Native American word from the Ojibwa language meaning 'I am coming'.
**Alternative spellings:** Shaniia, Shaniya

## Shanice

**Meaning:** God is gracious
**Origin:** Hebrew
**Pronunciation:** sha NEECE
**Description:** Shanice is a modern name that was first used in America as a combination of the name Janice and the fashionable prefix 'sha'.
**Alternative spellings:** Shannice

## Shannon

**Meaning:** Old river
**Origin:** Gaelic
**Pronunciation:** SHAN nun
**Description:** The increasingly popular name Shannon refers to the Irish river. The Gaelic for 'old river' is *'seanan'*.
**Alternative spellings:** Shanon

## Sharon

**Meaning:** Forest
**Origin:** Hebrew
**Pronunciation:** SHA ron
**Description:** The name Sharon is a Hebrew name and refers to a fertile plain near the coast of Israel. The name is given to the rose of Sharon, a flowering plant of yellow and purple.
**Alternative spellings:** Sharron

## Shaun

See entry in 'Names for Baby Boys A–Z'

## Shauna

**Meaning:** God is gracious
**Origin:** Hebrew
**Pronunciation:** SHON ah; SHAW na
**Description:** Shauna is the name that comes from Sean, the Irish variant of the masculine name John.
**Alternative spellings:** Shawna

## Shaye

**Meaning:** Admirable
**Origin:** Gaelic
**Pronunciation:** SHAY
**Description:** Shaye is a unisex name suitable for boys and girls. It is a variant of the Gaelic name Shea, which means 'admirable'.
**Alternative spellings:** Shae, Shai, Shay

## Shayla

**Meaning:** Blind
**Origin:** Latin
**Pronunciation:** SHAY lah
**Description:** Shayla is a name that has developed in America as a variant of the Irish name Sheila. It is a relatively popular name in both America and Ireland and means 'from the fairy palace'.
**Alternative spellings:** Shaylah, Sheylah

## Shayleigh

**Meaning:** Full of majesty in the woods
**Origin:** Gaelic
**Pronunciation:** shay LEE
**Description:** Shayleigh is a name of relatively modern coinage. It is a compound of the two names Shay and Leigh.

S

**Alternative spellings:** Shaelee, Shaeleigh, Shaylee

# Shayna
**Meaning:** Beautiful
**Origin:** Hebrew
**Pronunciation:** SHAY nuh
**Description:** Shayna is a name taken from the Yiddish meaning 'beautiful'. It is a very unusual name in the UK.
**Alternative spellings:** Shaina, Shainah, Shaynah

# Shayne
**Meaning:** God is gracious
**Origin:** Hebrew
**Pronunciation:** SHAY n
**Description:** This is the female variation of the common male name Shane, but can also be a variant of the name for boys. It has become popular only in recent years.
**Alternative spellings:** Chayne, Sheyn

# Shea
**Meaning:** Descendant of the fortunate
**Origin:** English
**Pronunciation:** SHAY
**Description:** Shea is a unisex name originally used as an Irish surname. It means 'descendant of the fortunate' and may have become more common across the UK since the arrival of shea butter in many cosmetic stores.
**Alternative spellings:** Shae, Shay, Shey

# Sheila
**Meaning:** Blind
**Origin:** Irish

**Pronunciation:** shee LAH
**Description:** Sheila is an Irish name, believed to be taken from the Irish Sile, which is a Gaelic form of Cecilia. As such, they all share the same meaning of 'blind'.

# Shelby
**Meaning:** Area of willow trees
**Origin:** English
**Pronunciation:** SHEL bee
**Description:** Shelby would have originally been given to someone who lived in an 'area of willow trees'. It has since evolved into a first name.
**Alternative spellings:** Shelbee, Shelbie

# Shelley
**Meaning:** Wood beside cliff
**Origin:** English
**Pronunciation:** SHEL lee
**Description:** Shelley is a transferred surname used by those in Essex, Suffolk and Yorkshire. It has become a name in its own right.
**Alternative spellings:** Shellie, Shelly

# Sheri
**Meaning:** The plains
**Origin:** Greek
**Pronunciation:** SHER ee
**Description:** Sheri is a name of Hebrew origin now found in English-speaking countries. It means 'the plains'.
**Alternative spellings:** Sherie, Sherii, Sherry

# Shifa
**Meaning:** Healer

**Origin:** Hebrew
**Pronunciation:** SHE fa
**Description:** It is uncertain whether the name Shifa is Arabic or Hebrew in origin as it is used by both Muslim and Jewish parents. The meaning is thought to be 'healer' or 'abundance'.
**Alternative spellings:** Sheefa

## Shiloh

See entry in 'Names for Baby Boys A–Z'

## Shion

**Meaning:** Sound of the water
**Origin:** Japanese
**Pronunciation:** SHEE on
**Description:** This feminine Japanese name is used throughout Asia. 'Shio' means 'tide' or 'water', and 'ne' means 'sound', so the name means 'sound of the water'. It is an uncommon name across the UK.
**Alternative spellings:** Shione

## Shira

**Meaning:** Song
**Origin:** Hebrew
**Pronunciation:** SHEER ah
**Description:** Shira is thought to come from a Hebrew word meaning 'song'. The name is favoured by Jewish parents. It is a rare name in the UK.
**Alternative spellings:** Shirah, Shyra, Shyrah

## Shirley

**Meaning:** Bright wood
**Origin:** English
**Pronunciation:** shir LEE
**Description:** Shirley is composed of the Old English elements of

'scīr' meaning 'bright' and 'lēah' meaning 'wood'. Shirley Temple was a famous American child star.

## Shivani

**Meaning:** Mother of all
**Origin:** Sanskrit
**Pronunciation:** shih VAR nee
**Description:** Shivani, which means 'mother of all', is a name of Sanskrit origin. The name is mostly used by Hindu parents, as in Hindu belief it is the name of the wife of the god Shiva.
**Alternative spellings:** Shivanee, Shivarnee, Shivarni

## Shona

**Meaning:** God is gracious
**Origin:** Hebrew
**Pronunciation:** SHO nah
**Description:** Shona is the Irish form of the name Joan, which is itself the feminine version of the masculine John.
**Alternative spellings:** Shonah

## Shreya

**Meaning:** Fortunate one
**Origin:** Sanskrit
**Pronunciation:** SHREE yah
**Description:** Shreya, which means 'fortunate one', is an extremely popular name with Indian parents and is fairly popular in Britain.
**Alternative spellings:** Shreeya, Shriya

## Shyanne

**Meaning:** Worthy
**Origin:** American
**Pronunciation:** shi AN
**Description:** The name Shyanne is thought to have originated as

S

a phonetic spelling of the name Cheyenne, a Native American place name. It became popular as a boys' name; however, Shyanne is a feminine name.
**Alternative spellings:** Shyenne

## Shyla
**Meaning:** Goddess
**Origin:** Sanskrit
**Pronunciation:** SHY lah
**Description:** Shyla is a name of Sanskrit origin that is particularly popular among Hindu families. It is one of the names of the Hindu goddess Parvati.

## Sia
See entry in 'Names for Baby Boys A–Z'

## Siân
**Meaning:** God has given
**Origin:** Welsh
**Pronunciation:** SHARN
**Description:** Siân is the Welsh version of the name Jane, used since the 1940s. The name means 'God has given'.
**Alternative spellings:** Shaan

## Sianna
**Meaning:** God is gracious
**Origin:**
**Pronunciation:**
**Description:** Sianna is a Hebrew name meaning 'God is gracious'. It is also a variation on the English name Seanna, and also the Welsh name Siân. Sianna was also the daughter of the Faerie Queen in Marion Zimmer Bradley's *Lady of Avalon*.
**Alternative spellings:** Siana, Seanna

## Sidney
See entry in 'Names for Baby Boys A–Z'

## Sidra
**Meaning:** Born from a star
**Origin:** Latin
**Pronunciation:** SID rah
**Description:** The name Sidra comes from the Latin meaning 'born from a star'. It is also a place name in Poland.
**Alternative spellings:** Sidrah, Sydra, Sydrah

## Sienna
**Meaning:** Brownish orange
**Origin:** Italian
**Pronunciation:** si EH nuh
**Description:** Sienna, a name of Italian origin, is associated with the city Siena.
**Alternative spellings:** Siena

## Sierra
**Meaning:** Jagged mountains
**Origin:** Spanish
**Pronunciation:** see AIR uh
**Description:** Sierra is a feminine Spanish name that literally means 'saw' and also refers to mountain ranges.

## Siham
**Meaning:** Arrow
**Origin:** Arabic
**Pronunciation:** see HAM
**Description:** The name Siham appears across the Middle East and parts of Africa. The Arabic meaning is 'arrow'.
**Alternative spellings:** Siiham

## Simona
**Meaning:** Listen

462

**Origin:** Hebrew
**Pronunciation:** sih MOH nah
**Description:** Simona, a variant of Simone, is found in Eastern Europe.
**Alternative spellings:** Simonah

## Simone

**Meaning:** Listen
**Origin:** Hebrew
**Pronunciation:** si MONE; see MOHN
**Description:** This is a feminine version of the masculine name Simon, which is of Hebrew origin and means 'hark'.
**Alternative spellings:** Semone

## Simrah

**Meaning:** Heaven
**Origin:** Arabic
**Pronunciation:** SIM rah
**Description:** This name is used by Muslim parents and comes from an Arabic word meaning 'heaven'.
**Alternative spellings:** Simra

## Simran

**Meaning:** Meditation
**Origin:** Sanskrit
**Pronunciation:** sim RAN
**Description:** Simran is a unisex name that is popular among Hindu communities. It means 'meditation,' and while it is more commonly given to girls the Sikh community often chooses it as a name for boys too.

## Sinead

**Meaning:** God is gracious
**Origin:** Hebrew
**Pronunciation:** shan AID
**Description:** Sinead, a feminine Irish name, has its roots in Jane,

which is itself the feminine version of John. The name means 'God is gracious'.
**Alternative spellings:** Shinead

## Siobhan

**Meaning:** God is gracious
**Origin:** Gaelic
**Pronunciation:** shiv ORN
**Description:** Siobhan is the Gaelic version of the Hebrew name 'Joan'.
**Alternative spellings:** Sioban, Siobain, Siobhain

## Siya

**Meaning:** Unknown
**Origin:** Arabic
**Pronunciation:** SEE ah
**Description:** Siya, a unisex name, appears to be of Arabic origin and is favoured by Muslim parents.
**Alternative spellings:** Siyah

## Siyana

**Meaning:** Protection
**Origin:** Muslim
**Pronunciation:** see YAN ah
**Description:** Siyana is a feminine Muslim name meaning 'protection'. Related names include Siya, Siyah and Siyanna.
**Alternative spellings:** Siyanna

## Skye

**Meaning:** Cloud
**Origin:** Norse
**Pronunciation:** SKY
**Description:** The name Skye comes from the Old Norse word for 'cloud'. It rose to prominence during the 1960s.
**Alternative spellings:** Sky

## Skyla

**Meaning:** Fugitive

**S**

**Origin:** Dutch
**Pronunciation:** sky LA
**Description:** Although the name Skyla is thought to derive from the Dutch name Schuyler, it is most commonly found within England and America. The masculine version is spelt Skyler.
**Alternative spellings:** Skila, Skylar, Skyler

## Skylah
**Meaning:** Scholar
**Origin:** Dutch
**Pronunciation:** SKY lah
**Description:** The name Skylah has Dutch origins and means 'scholar' in the langauage. It is also an alternative spelling of the more mainstream Skyler or Skyla, and could also be a variation of the name Kayla.
**Alternative spellings:** Skylar, Skyler

## Sofia
**Meaning:** Wisdom
**Origin:** Greek
**Pronunciation:** so FEE uh
**Description:** Sofia is a variant of Sophia, the capital city of Bulgaria. The name is Greek and means 'wisdom'.
**Alternative spellings:** Sofiya, Sofiyah, Sophia

## Sol
See entry in 'Names for Baby Boys A–Z'

## Soleil
**Meaning:** Sun
**Origin:** French
**Pronunciation:** so LAY
**Description:** Translated directly from the French, Soleil means 'sun'. Note that the pronounciation of the name does not include the last 'L'.

## Sommer
**Meaning:** Summer
**Origin:** Scandinavian
**Pronunciation:** SOH mer
**Description:** Sommer is a unisex name and a Scandinavian term for summer.
**Alternative spellings:** Summer

## Sonia
**Meaning:** Wisdom
**Origin:** Greek
**Pronunciation:** SOHN yuh
**Description:** Sonia is a variant of the Greek name 'Sophia', meaning 'wisdom'.
**Alternative spellings:** Soniah, Sonya, Sonyah

## Sophie
**Meaning:** Wisdom
**Origin:** Greek
**Pronunciation:** SO fee
**Description:** This popular name is of Greek origin and it means 'wisdom'.
**Alternative spellings:** Sofi, Sofie, Sofy, Sophi, Sophy

## Soraya
**Meaning:** Princess
**Origin:** Persian
**Pronunciation:** sor RYE ah
**Description:** Soraya is a name of Persian origin and it means 'princess'. It is popular in the Middle East and in Spain.
**Alternative spellings:** Sorayaa, Sorayah

## Stacey

**Meaning:** Fruitful
**Origin:** Greek
**Pronunciation:** STAY see
**Description:** Stacey is the feminine variant of the unisex name Stacy, derived from the Greek name Eustace.
**Alternative spellings:** Stacee, Stacy, Stayce

## Star

**Meaning:** Bright
**Origin:** English
**Pronunciation:** STAR
**Description:** Star is a name that has associations with brightness and fame. The name is not common in Britain but it is used in other English-speaking countries.
**Alternative spellings:** Starr

## Stefania

**Meaning:** Garland; crown
**Origin:** Greek
**Pronunciation:** ste fan NYAH
**Description:** Stefania is a Greek name meaning 'garland' or 'crown'. It is also the Greek version of the name Stephanie, which is a feminine variation of the male name Stephen. The Greek word for 'crown' is Stephanos.
**Alternative spellings:** Stephania

## Stella

**Meaning:** Star
**Origin:** Latin
**Pronunciation:** STEH luh
**Description:** Stella is the Latin word for 'star'. In Catholic tradition, the Virgin Mary was given the title 'Stella Maris', meaning 'star of the sea'.
**Alternative spellings:** Stellah, Stellar

## Steph

**Meaning:** Garland; crown
**Origin:** Greek
**Pronunciation:** STEFF
**Description:** Steph, a shortened version of Stephanie, is popular as a name in its own right across the English-speaking world.
**Alternative spellings:** Stef

## Stephanie

**Meaning:** Garland; crown
**Origin:** Greek
**Pronunciation:** STEH fah nee
**Description:** Stephanie comes from the same derivative as Stephen and means 'garland' or 'crown'.
**Alternative spellings:** Stefanee, Stefanie, Stephanee

## Storm

**Meaning:** Storm
**Origin:** English
**Pronunciation:** STORM
**Description:** Storm is a unisex name and means violent weather. It is a fairly unusual name.

## Sue

**Meaning:** Lily
**Origin:** English
**Pronunciation:** SOO
**Description:** Sue is a short form of Susan, and, less commonly, of Susanna and Suzanne. The name means 'lily'.
**Alternative spellings:** Su

## Suha

**Meaning:** Forgotten one
**Origin:** Arabic
**Pronunciation:** soo HA
**Description:** Suha is a name that comes from the Arabic word

S

for 'forgotten one' and also the Arabic for a star in the Great Bear constellation.
**Alternative spellings:** Suhar

## Suhana
**Meaning:** Pleasing
**Origin:** Urdu
**Pronunciation:** soo HAH nah
**Description:** Suhana is a name of Urdu origin and can be found in Hindu, Sikh and Punjabi communities. Its Urdu meaning is said to be 'pleasing'.
**Alternative spellings:** Suehana, Suehanah, Suhanah

## Sukhmani
**Meaning:** Bringing peace
**Origin:** Sanskrit
**Pronunciation:** sook MANI
**Description:** Sukhmani is an Indian name meaning 'bringing peace'. This name appears to be a more modern Indian girls' name and perhaps was not used as much throughout history.

## Suki
**Meaning:** To love
**Origin:** Japanese
**Pronunciation:** SOO ki
**Description:** Suki is a name of Japanese origin; however, in Japan it is not used as a given name. It comes from a Japanese verb meaning 'to love'.
**Alternative spellings:** Sukii

## Sumaiya
**Meaning:** Sacrifice
**Origin:** Arabic
**Pronunciation:** soo MAH ee YAH

**Description:** Sumaiya is a variant of the feminine name Sumayyah, which is of Arabic origin and was the name of the first martyr of Islam. This has given the name connotations of 'sacrifice'. It is a popular name with Muslim parents.
**Alternative spellings:** Sumayyah, Sumaya, Sumayah

## Summa
**Meaning:** From Somma
**Origin:** Italian
**Pronunciation:** SOO mah
**Description:** Summa is a variant of the name Suma. The name may have come from Italy where it was the surname given to people from Somma.
**Alternative spellings:** Suma

## Summer
**Meaning:** Summer
**Origin:** English
**Pronunciation:** SUM muh
**Description:** The name Summer comes from the English word for the season.
**Alternative spellings:** Sommer

## Sunny
**Meaning:** Bright and cheerful
**Origin:** English
**Pronunciation:** SUH nee
**Description:** Sunny is a relatively modern name, taken from the adjective describing a person with a bright and cheerful disposition.
**Alternative spellings:** Sonni, Sonnie, Sonny, Sunni, Sunnie

## Suraya
**Meaning:** Star constellation

**Origin:** Arabic
**Pronunciation:** su RAY ah
**Description:** Suraya is a variant of the name Soraya, which is found mostly in the Middle East. Both the names come originally from the Arabic name Thurayya. Thurayya is the Arabic name of the Seven Sisters constellation.
**Alternative spellings:** Suraaya

## Suri
**Meaning:** Red
**Origin:** Persian
**Pronunciation:** SUR ee
**Description:** Made famous by Suri Cruise, daughter of Tom Cruise and Katie Holmes, the meaning of the name has been the subject of some debate. Tom and Katie originally stated that it was Hebrew and meant 'princess' but there is little evidence to support this.
**Alternative spellings:** Soori

## Susan
**Meaning:** Lily
**Origin:** Hebrew
**Pronunciation:** SOO san
**Description:** Susan is a popular Hebrew name. Its original form was Susanna.
**Alternative spellings:** Susanne, Suzanne

## Susanna
**Meaning:** Lily
**Origin:** Hebrew
**Pronunciation:** soo SAH na
**Description:** Susanna is the New Testament form of Shoshana, from the word meaning 'lily', which in modern Hebrew also means 'rose'. It carries connotations of purity and as the lily is a Christian symbol this name is popular with Christian parents.
**Alternative spellings:** Susannah, Suzanna, Suzannah

## Suzie
**Meaning:** Lily; rose
**Origin:** Hebrew
**Pronunciation:** SOO zee
**Description:** Both Suzie and its variant Susie came about as pet forms of Susan or Susanna, which both mean 'lily' or 'rose'. The name is mostly found in Eastern Europe and the Netherlands.
**Alternative spellings:** Susie, Susy, Suzy

## Sydney
**Meaning:** Wide meadow
**Origin:** English
**Pronunciation:** sid NEE
**Description:** Sydney, as well as being a major Australian city, is a unisex name meaning 'wide meadow'. It was introduced as a boys' name, but has now been overtaken by the female given name.
**Alternative spellings:** Sidney

## Syeda
**Meaning:** Noble
**Origin:** Arabic
**Pronunciation:** SIGH yed ah
**Description:** Syeda is a name of Arabic origin, which is equivalent to the popular masculine Muslim name Syed. The meaning of the word is said to be 'noble'.
**Alternative spellings:** Sayyida

## Sylvia
**Meaning:** Woodland woman

S

**Origin:** Latin
**Pronunciation:** SIL vee ah
**Description:** Sylvia is a name that comes from a Latin word meaning 'lives in the woods'. It was a popular name in Roman times because it was the name of the mother of Romulus and Remus, founders of Rome.
**Alternative spellings:** Silvia

## Sylvie
**Meaning:** Woodland woman
**Origin:** Latin
**Pronunciation:** SIL vee
**Description:** Sylvie is a diminutive form of the name Sylvia. It is popular across the English-speaking world.
**Alternative spellings:** Silvie, Silvy, Sylvi

# T

## Tabitha
**Meaning:** Gazelle
**Origin:** Aramaic
**Pronunciation:** TA bi tha
**Description:** Tabitha is said to come from the word for a gazelle, which carries connotations of gracefulness. The name is found in the New Testament.
**Alternative spellings:** Tabbitha, Tabbytha, Tabytha

## Tahani
**Meaning:** Best wishes
**Origin:** Arabic
**Pronunciation:** ta HAN ee
**Description:** Tahani is an Arabic name meaning 'best wishes' and is associated with congratulations or happy greetings.

## Tahira
**Meaning:** Pure
**Origin:** Arabic
**Pronunciation:** tah HE rah
**Description:** Tahira is the feminine version of the Arabic masculine name Tahir. The name means 'pure' and

is often favoured by Muslim parents.
**Alternative spellings:** Taheera, Taheerah

## Tahiya
**Meaning:** Security
**Origin:** Arabic
**Pronunciation:** tah HI ya
**Description:** Tahiya is an unusual name, which comes from around the Middle East and into Africa. It can be found in several languages around this area. Some speculate that the meaning of the name is 'security'.
**Alternative spellings:** Tahiyah

## Tahlia
**Meaning:** Lamb
**Origin:** Hebrew
**Pronunciation:** TAL yah
**Description:** Tahlia can be seen as a variant of the Hebrew name Talya, which means 'lamb'; it is also the pet name of Natalie. Tahlia is a popular name with Jewish parents.
**Alternative spellings:** Tahliah, Talia, Taliah, Taliyah

## Taiba

**Meaning:** Refrains from evil doings
**Origin:** Arabic
**Pronunciation:** tah IB ah
**Description:** Taiba, which is of Arabic origin, is the feminine form of the masculine Taib. This name is very rare in the UK, and would suit families looking for a unique baby name.
**Alternative spellings:** Taibah

## Tala

**Meaning:** Christmas
**Origin:** Italian
**Pronunciation:** TAHL ah
**Description:** Tala is a pet form of Natalia, which comes from an Italian word meaning 'birthday', specifically that of Christ. It can be found in the Italian phrase *'buon natale'* meaning 'merry Christmas'.
**Alternative spellings:** Talah

## Talia

**Meaning:** Dew of God
**Origin:** Hebrew
**Pronunciation:** tal EE ya
**Description:** This female name is mainly used in English and Hebrew-speaking countries and can also be spelt as Talya. The name derives from the Arabic word *'Tal'* meaning 'dew,' but is also thought to have roots in Old Greek.
**Alternative spellings:** Thalia, Taliah, Talya

## Tallulah

**Meaning:** Leaping water
**Origin:** Gaelic
**Pronunciation:** TAHL oo lah
**Description:** Tallulah is an alternative spelling of the Gaelic name Tallula, which was a name borne by two Irish saints. It could also derive from the Native American Choctaws.
**Alternative spellings:** Tallula

## Tamar

**Meaning:** Date
**Origin:** Hebrew
**Pronunciation:** tah MAR
**Description:** Especially popular in Israel, Tamar and its variant Tamara are names of Hebrew origin and are found in the Bible. They come from the Hebrew word for a palm tree.
**Alternative spellings:** Tahma, Tahmar, Tamah

## Tamara

**Meaning:** Palm tree
**Origin:** Hebrew
**Pronunciation:** tah MAR ah
**Description:** The name Tamara has two separate roots. It can come from the Hebrew biblical name Tamar, which means 'palm tree'. It is also found in Indian languages originating from a Sanskrit word meaning 'spice'.
**Alternative spellings:** Tamarah

## Tamia

**Meaning:** Spice
**Origin:** American
**Pronunciation:** tah ME ah
**Description:** Tamia is a relatively modern name that may be a compound of popular female names such as Tammy and Mia. It is very popular among African-American parents.
**Alternative spellings:** Tahmia, Tamea

T

## Tamika

**Meaning:** Unknown
**Origin:** American
**Pronunciation:** tah MEE kah
**Description:** Tamika is a unisex name of uncertain meaning found across the English-speaking world.
**Alternative spellings:** Tameeka, Tamica

## Tammy

**Meaning:** Twin
**Origin:** English
**Pronunciation:** tam EE
**Description:** Tammy is a nickname for names such as Tamsin and Thomasima, which in turn are the feminine version of the name Thomas. All of these names mean 'twin'.

## Tamsin

**Meaning:** Twin
**Origin:** Aramaic
**Pronunciation:** TAM zin
**Description:** Tamsin is the feminine equivalent of the masculine name Thomas. It has become a very popular name in the UK over recent years.
**Alternative spellings:** Tamzin

## Tanisha

**Meaning:** Born on Monday
**Origin:** African
**Pronunciation:** tan EE sha
**Description:** The origins of this name lie in the West African language Hausa, where it is the name for babies born on a Monday. Tani is the short form.
**Alternative spellings:** Taneesha, Taneisha, Tanishah

## Tanvi

**Meaning:** Feminine one
**Origin:** Sanskrit
**Pronunciation:** tan vee
**Description:** Tanvi is a feminine name that comes from Sanskrit origins. The meaning of the name is said to be 'feminine one'. The name is mostly found used in India and Iran and is particularly popular with Hindu parents.
**Alternative spellings:** Tanvee

## Tanya

**Meaning:** Roman name
**Origin:** Latin
**Pronunciation:** TARN yah
**Description:** Tanya is a very popular pet form of the name Tatiana.
**Alternative spellings:** Tania, Taniah, Tanyah

## Tara

**Meaning:** Hill
**Origin:** Gaelic
**Pronunciation:** TAH ra
**Description:** Tara is a name that is common across all English-speaking countries and derives from a word that means 'hill'.
**Alternative spellings:** Tarah

## Taran

See entry in 'Names for Baby Boys A–Z'

## Taryn

**Meaning:** Unknown
**Origin:** Gaelic
**Pronunciation:** TAH rin
**Description:** Taryn is an unusual name of uncertain origin, and is found across many languages in various forms. It is now becoming popular across the UK.
**Alternative spellings:** Tarin, Tarynn

## Tasha

**Meaning:** Birthday of Christ
**Origin:** Latin
**Pronunciation:** TASH ah
**Description:** Tasha began as a pet form of the name Natasha, but is now a name in its own right. It would originally have been given to girls born around Christmas time.
**Alternative spellings:** Tasher

## Tasneem

**Meaning:** A spring in paradise
**Origin:** Arabic
**Pronunciation:** TAHS meen
**Description:** Tasneem is a variation of the Arabic name Tasnim, meaning 'a spring in paradise'.
**Alternative spellings:** Tasnim

## Tatiana

**Meaning:** Unknown
**Origin:** Latin
**Pronunciation:** taht ee AHN ah
**Description:** Tatiana is a name of Latin origin said to come from the Roman family name Tatius. It is popular in continental Europe.
**Alternative spellings:** Tatianna, Tatyana

## Taya

**Meaning:** Favourite
**Origin:** Russian
**Pronunciation:** TAY uh
**Description:** Taya is a pet form of the name Taisiya. It is very popular in Russia and means 'favourite'.
**Alternative spellings:** Tayah

## Tayla

**Meaning:** Tailor
**Origin:** English
**Pronunciation:** TAY lah
**Description:** Tayla is a phonetically spelt variation of the name Taylor. Taylor is a unisex name that comes from an Old English surname, which denoted someone who was a tailor by trade. The variation Tayla is a specifically feminine name.
**Alternative spellings:** Taylah

## Taylor

**Meaning:** Tailor
**Origin:** English
**Pronunciation:** TAY lor
**Description:** Taylor was originally a surname given to those with this occupation. Its popularity as a unisex name has risen in recent years.
**Alternative spellings:** Tailor, Tayla, Taylah, Tayler, Teyla, Teylah, Teylor

## Teagan

**Meaning:** Beautiful thing
**Origin:** English
**Pronunciation:** tee GAN
**Description:** Teagan is a variation of Tegan, which is a feminine name of English origin and comes from a Cornish word for something pretty and ornamental. 'Teg' a Welsh and Cornish word meaning 'pretty'.
**Alternative spellings:** Teigan, Tegan

## Tehya

**Meaning:** Precious
**Origin:** American
**Pronunciation:** TAY ah
**Description:** Tehya is a name of Native American origin and means 'precious'. It could also be a variant of the name Taya and is rare in the UK.
**Alternative spellings:** Taya, Thaya

## Temperance

**Meaning:** Moderation
**Origin:** English
**Pronunciation:** temp ER rance
**Description:** Temperance comes from the English vocabulary word of the same spelling, meaning `moderation'. Like Chastity or Faith, this is a virtue name.

## Teresa

**Meaning:** Summertime
**Origin:** Greek
**Pronunciation:** teh REES ah
**Description:** Teresa is a variant of Theresa. Mother Teresa was a Christian missionary who was awarded the Nobel Peace Prize.
**Alternative spellings:** Tereza, Theresa

## Terese

**Meaning:** Summertime
**Origin:** Greek
**Pronunciation:** teh REES ah
**Description:** Terese is a variant of the name Theresa, which is Greek in origin.
**Alternative spellings:** Tereza, Theresa

## Terry

See entry in 'Names for Baby Boys A–Z'

## Tess

**Meaning:** Summertime
**Origin:** Greek
**Pronunciation:** TES
**Description:** While Tess is a shortened version of Teresa, it has become a very popular name in its own right.
**Alternative spellings:** Tes

## Tessa

**Meaning:** Summertime
**Origin:** Greek
**Pronunciation:** TESS ah
**Description:** Tessa is a shortened version of the name Teresa, but it has become a popular name in its own right. Tessa Sanderson was a British Olympic javelin thrower.
**Alternative spellings:** Tessah, Tesza

## Thalia

**Meaning:** Blooming
**Origin:** Greek
**Pronunciation:** TAHl ee ah
**Description:** Thalia is a feminine name of Greek origin and is said to mean 'blooming'. In Greek mythology, it was the name of one of the three graces along with her sisters, all daughters of Zeus. Thalia is an uncommon name in English-speaking countries and is mainly found used in Greece and its surrounding countries.
**Alternative spellings:** Talia, Taliah, Talya

## Thandie

**Meaning:** Loving one
**Origin:** South African
**Pronunciation:** thaan DEE
**Description:** Thandie is a name from South Africa that means 'loving one'. Thandie Newton is a British actress with this name.

## Thea

**Meaning:** Unknown; derived from Greek mythology
**Origin:** Greek
**Pronunciation:** THEE uh
**Description:** A shortened version of the given name Althea.

**Alternative spellings:** Thaea, Thaia

## Theia
**Meaning:** Goddess
**Origin:** Greek
**Pronunciation:** the YA
**Description:** With origins from the Greek word meaning 'goddess,' this was the name of a Titan goddess of sight, glittering and glory. She was the wife of Hyperion and the mother of the sun god Helios, the moon goddess Selene and the dawn goddess Eos.

## Thelma
**Meaning:** Will; volition
**Origin:** Greek
**Pronunciation:** thel MAH
**Description:** Thelma is a Greek name meaning 'will' and 'volition'. Thelma is one half of the famous female duo "Thelma and Louise" from the movie of the same name.

## Theodora
**Meaning:** Gift of God
**Origin:** Greek
**Pronunciation:** thee ah DOR ah
**Description:** Theodora is the feminine version of the masculine Theodore. It means 'gift of God' and has become rare in the UK in recent years.
**Alternative spellings:** Theodorah

## Thomasina
**Meaning:** Twin
**Origin:** English
**Pronunciation:** thoma SEE nah
**Description:** Thomasina is the feminine version of the name Thomas, and both names mean 'twin'.

## Tia
**Meaning:** Aunt
**Origin:** English
**Pronunciation:** TEE uh
**Description:** Tia is a name that has recently become popular, but its origins are uncertain. It could come from the Spanish word for 'aunt', or derive from the Greek god of light Theia.
**Alternative spellings:** Tiah

## Tiana
**Meaning:** Princess
**Origin:** Greek
**Pronunciation:** ti AH na
**Description:** This name is most popular in English-speaking countries such as the United States and Canada. It may have been a shortened version of Christiana or even Diana.
**Alternative spellings:** Tianna, Tiarna

## Tiara
**Meaning:** Jewelled headdress
**Origin:** Latin
**Pronunciation:** tee ARH ah
**Description:** Tiara is a feminine name that comes from Latin origins. It comes from the Latin word for a 'jewelled headdress', which is still found today in the English language.

## Tierney
**Meaning:** Lord
**Origin:** Gaelic
**Pronunciation:** TEER ney
**Description:** Tierney is a unisex

T

given name of Gaelic origin. It would originally have been a surname, O'Tiarnaigh.
**Alternative spellings:** Tearney, Teerney,

## Tiffany
**Meaning:** Appearance of God
**Origin:** Greek
**Pronunciation:** tiff AN ee
**Description:** This girls' name derives from the word 'epiphany,' which was given to the appearance of Jesus to the three wise men. It is commonly associated with fashion brand Tiffany and Co.
**Alternative spellings:** Tiffani

## Tigerlily
**Meaning:** Flower name
**Origin:** English
**Pronunciation:** tiger LILY
**Description:** Tigerlily comes from the bright orange flower of the same name. Like Rose and Tulip, Tigerlily is part of the trend of using flowers as given names.

## Tilda
**Meaning:** Strength in battle
**Origin:** German
**Pronunciation:** till DAH
**Description:** Tilda is a shortened form of the name Matilda, which is a German name meaning 'strength in battle'. Tilda Swinton is a famous British actress with this name.

## Tilly
**Meaning:** Mighty in battle
**Origin:** German
**Pronunciation:** TIL lee
**Description:** Tilly is the pet form of the name Matilda, but it has become popular as a name in its

own right.
**Alternative spellings:** Tillee, Tilley, Tilli, Tillie

## Tina
**Meaning:** Follower of Christ
**Origin:** Latin
**Pronunciation:** TEE na
**Description:** Tina was originally the short form of any girls' name that ended in 'tina', although it is now also seen as a name in its own right.
**Alternative spellings:** Teena

## Tisha
**Meaning:** Joy
**Origin:** American
**Pronunciation:** tish AH
**Description:** Tisha is an American name meaning 'joy'. It could also be seen as a shortened version of Letitia.

## Tobey
See entry in 'Names for Baby Boys A–Z'

## Tomoko
**Meaning:** Wise child
**Origin:** Japanese
**Pronunciation:** to MO ko
**Description:** This unusual name is most commonly found in Japan.
**Alternative spellings:** Tomokoh

## Toni
**Meaning:** Protector
**Origin:** Latin
**Pronunciation:** TOE nee
**Description:** Toni is the feminine form of the male name Tony, and it could also be a shortened version of Antonia.

**Alternative spellings:** Toney, Tonie

## Tonia
**Meaning:** Protector
**Origin:** Latin
**Pronunciation:** TOE nee ah
**Description:** Tonia was originally the short form of the name Antonia, but it is now a name in its own right.
**Alternative spellings:** Toniah, Tonya, Tonyah

## Topaz
**Meaning:** Topaz
**Origin:** English
**Pronunciation:** TOE paz
**Description:** Topaz is a gemstone and the birthstone for those born in November. It is a fairly uncommon name.
**Alternative spellings:** Topazz

## Tori
**Meaning:** Victory
**Origin:** Latin
**Pronunciation:** TOR ee
**Description:** Tori is a name with unisex roots in the United States. It is usually a pet form of the name Victoria, and it shares the same meaning.
**Alternative spellings:** Toree, Tori, Torie, Tory

## Tracey
**Meaning:** French place name
**Origin:** French
**Pronunciation:** TRAY see
**Description:** A popular name in the 60s and 70s. There are several places in France named 'Tracy' but 'Tracey' is the slightly more popular spelling variation in the UK.
**Alternative spellings:** Tracy

## Trinity
**Meaning:** Three
**Origin:** Latin
**Pronunciation:** TRIN it ee
**Description:** Trinity is a popular name with Christian parents owing to its associations with the Holy Trinity.
**Alternative spellings:** Trinitee, Trinitey, Trinitie, Trinti

## Trudie
**Meaning:** Spear strength
**Origin:** English
**Pronunciation:** troo DEE
**Description:** Trudie is a diminutive of the name Gertrude, which is a German name composed of the elements of '*ger*' meaning 'spear' and '*thrud*' meaning 'strength'. Trudie has also become a name in its own right.
**Alternative spellings:** Trudy

## Tulip
**Meaning:** Tulip flower
**Origin:** Turkish
**Pronunciation:** TOO lip
**Description:** Tulip comes from the Turkish and Persian flower of the same name. This name is part of the popular flower name trend, such as Rose and Violet.

## Tulisa
**Meaning:** No meaning
**Origin:** English
**Pronunciation:** too LEE sah
**Description:** Tulisa is a name that has only come to popularity in recent years, owing to Tulisa Contostavlos, who is a singer and

T

TV personality. It is a modern construction so it has no meaning.
**Alternative spellings:** Tulisah

## Tulsi
**Meaning:** Basil
**Origin:** Indian
**Pronunciation:** tul SEE
**Description:** Tulsi is an Indian/Hindu girls' name meaning 'basil'.

## Twiggy
**Meaning:** Name of supermodel
**Origin:** English
**Pronunciation:** twig EE
**Description:** Twiggy was made famous by the mod supermodel, Lesley Lawson. She changed her name to Twiggy based on her childhood nickname, Twigs.

## Tyler
See entry in 'Names for Baby Boys A–Z'

## Tyra
**Meaning:** Irish county
**Origin:** Gaelic
**Pronunciation:** TYE ra
**Description:** Tyra is the female equivalent of the masculine name Tyrone.
**Alternative spellings:** Tyrah

# U

## Ulrica
**Meaning:** Wolf power
**Origin:** Scandinavian
**Pronunciation:** ul REE kah
**Description:** Ulrica is derived from the German male name Ulric, and first gained popularity in Scandinavia.
**Alternative spellings:** Ulreka, Ulrika, Ullrika

## Uma
**Meaning:** Tranquillity; splendour; fame; night
**Origin:** Sanskrit
**Pronunciation:** oo MAH
**Description:** Uma is a feminine Sanskrit name that has multiple meanings, including 'tranquillity', 'splendour', 'fame' and 'night'. It is also another name for the Hindu goddess Parvati. American actress Uma Thurman has this name.
**Alternative spellings:** Umma, Umah

## Umaiza
**Meaning:** Beautiful and bright
**Origin:** Arabic
**Pronunciation:** oo MAY za
**Description:** Umaiza is a name that is found most often in Arabic countries, and is very popular among Muslim parents. It is rare in the UK and far more popular in the Middle East.
**Alternative spellings:** Umaizah

## Umaymah
**Meaning:** Young mother

**Origin:** Arabic
**Pronunciation:** oo MAY mah
**Description:** Umaymah is a rare name of Arabic origins and a character in the Arabic book of folk tales *One Thousand and One Nights*.
**Alternative spellings:** Oomaymah

## Una

**Meaning:** One
**Origin:** Latin
**Pronunciation:** OO nah
**Description:** Una comes from the Latin for the number one, and was traditionally given to the first-born child.
**Alternative spellings:** Unah

## Ursula

**Meaning:** Girl bear cub
**Origin:** Scandinavian

**Pronunciation:** UR suh lah
**Description:** Ursula is a name found across Europe, although it is Scandinavian in origin. It is the name of a Christian saint and its popularity in Britain may stem from Shakespeare's play *Much Ado About Nothing*.
**Alternative spellings:** Ersula, Ursala

## Urte

**Meaning:** God's gift
**Origin:** Slavic
**Pronunciation:** ur TEH
**Description:** Urte is a feminine name of uncertain origin and meaning. It is thought that the name may have come from Baltic origins, and may be a Baltic version of the feminine name Dorothy and as such shares the same meaning of 'God's gift'.

# V

## Valencia

**Meaning:** Brave
**Origin:** Spanish
**Pronunciation:** vall EN see ah
**Description:** Valencia is a Spanish name meaning 'brave'. It is also the name of a city in Spain.

## Valentina

**Meaning:** Good health
**Origin:** Latin
**Pronunciation:** vah len TEE nah
**Description:** Valentina is the feminine version of the masculine name Valentine. It carries connotations of romance owing to Valentine's Day.
**Alternative spellings:** Valentena

## Valeria

**Meaning:** Brave
**Origin:** Spanish
**Pronunciation:** vah leh REE yah
**Description:** Valeria is a Spanish name that is a variation of Valerius, which comes from the Latin word *valere*, meaning 'to be strong' or 'brave'. The name Valeria was the name of a 2nd-century saint.

U
V

## Valerie

**Meaning:** Healthy
**Origin:** Latin
**Pronunciation:** VAL er ee
**Description:** This French form of the name Valeria was originally masculine but is now almost exclusively female.
**Alternative spellings:** Valarie, Valary, Valery

## Vanessa

**Meaning:** Star
**Origin:** English
**Pronunciation:** van ESS er
**Description:** The name Vanessa was invented by 18th-century poet Jonathan Swift. It has remained popular in English-speaking communities.
**Alternative spellings:** Vanesa

## Venus

**Meaning:** Love
**Origin:** Latin
**Pronunciation:** veen US
**Description:** Venus, in Roman mythology, was the goddess of love. It is also the name of the second planet from the sun as well as Venus Williams, the tennis champion.

## Vera

**Meaning:** Truth
**Origin:** Greek
**Pronunciation:** VEER ra
**Description:** Vera is a Russian name, but also has similarities to the Latin *'veritas'* meaning truth. Although the name peaked in the UK in the 1920s, it is associated with singer Vera Lynn and a *Coronation Street* character.
**Alternative spellings:** Veera, Viera

## Verity

**Meaning:** Truth
**Origin:** Latin
**Pronunciation:** VEH ri tee
**Description:** Verity comes from the abstract noun meaning 'truth' and, although once popular, it is currently fairly rare in the UK.
**Alternative spellings:** Veritee, Veritey Veriti, Veritie

## Verona

**Meaning:** Italian city
**Origin:** Italian
**Pronunciation:** ver OWN ah
**Description:** Verona is a city in northern Italy. It is famous for being the city in which Shakespeare's *Romeo and Juliet* is set.

## Veronica

**Meaning:** Truth
**Origin:** Latin
**Pronunciation:** vuh RON ih ka
**Description:** Veronica is a name derived from Latin, which became popular due to the saint of the same name who is said to have wiped sweat from Jesus's face.
**Alternative spellings:** Veronika

## Vesper

**Meaning:** Evening star
**Origin:** Latin
**Pronunciation:** VES per
**Description:** Vesper is a Latin name meaning 'evening star'. It is also the name of a popular scooter brand as well as a main character in the James Bond novel, *Casino Royale*.

## Vicky

**Meaning:** Victory

**Origin:** Latin
**Pronunciation:** VIK ee
**Description:** Vicky is the short form of Victoria. This shorter version has become a popular name in its own right.
**Alternative spellings:** Vickie, Vikki

## Victoria

**Meaning:** Victory
**Origin:** Latin
**Pronunciation:** vik TOR ee ah
**Description:** Victoria is the feminine form of Victor. It would have arrived in the UK from Germany and its most famous bearer was Queen Victoria, England's longest-reigning monarch.
**Alternative spellings:** Victoriah, Viktoria

## Vida

**Meaning:** Life
**Origin:** Latin
**Pronunciation:** VEE da
**Description:** Vida is a name believed to derive from the Latin word that means 'life'.
**Alternative spellings:** Veda, Veeda

## Vienna

**Meaning:** White; city of dreams
**Origin:** Latin
**Pronunciation:** vee EN ah
**Description:** Vienna is the name of the capital city of Austria. The name, which spread through Europe owing to the city's power, is now fairly rare.
**Alternative spellings:** Viena

## Vilte

**Meaning:** Hope; people; nation

**Origin:** Lithuanian
**Pronunciation:** vil TE
**Description:** Vilte is a feminine Lithuanian name that is traced all the way back to the masculine name Viltautas. Both names have the Baltic elements of '*vil*' meaning hope and '*tauta*' meaning people or nation.

## Viola

**Meaning:** Violet
**Origin:** Latin
**Pronunciation:** vee OH la
**Description:** Viola is one of the characters in Shakespeare's *Twelfth Night*. A shipwrecked orphan who has no one to protect her, Viola is a practical and resourceful character. Viola is a feminine name that is mainly found in Italy. It comes from the Latin word '*violet*', which is a shade of the colour purple. *Twelfth Night* introduced the name into England.

## Violet

**Meaning:** Violet
**Origin:** Latin
**Pronunciation:** VI oh let
**Description:** Violet is the name of a flower and also one of the colours that make up a rainbow.
**Alternative spellings:** Violette

## Virginia

**Meaning:** Virgin
**Origin:** Latin
**Pronunciation:** VER gin ee ah
**Description:** Virginia is a name that comes from the Latin word '*virgo*', meaning 'virgin'. It is also the name of a state in the United States of America.

## Vivienne

**Meaning:** Alive

V

**Origin:** Latin
**Pronunciation:** VIV ee en
**Description:** Vivienne has gone out of fashion recently but it

is derived from the French for 'living'.
**Alternative spellings:** Vivian, Vivien Viviene

# W

## Wanda
**Meaning:** Wanderer
**Origin:** Polish
**Pronunciation:** WAN dah
**Description:** Wanda is a Polish name meaning 'wanderer,' and is probably derived from the name of the Wends tribe. It is a popular name in Poland due to the legend of Princess Wanda, who was queen of the Poles.

## Wendy
**Meaning:** Friend
**Origin:** English
**Pronunciation:** WEN dee
**Description:** Wendy, the name coined by J.M. Barrie in the novel *Peter Pan*, comes from a childhood nickname he was given. The name peaked in the 1960s and has declined in recent years.
**Alternative spellings:** Wendee, Wendi Wendie

## Whitney
**Meaning:** White island
**Origin:** English
**Pronunciation:** WIT nee
**Description:** Whitney is most commonly found in North America and means 'white island'.
**Alternative spellings:** Whitni, Whitnie, Whitny, Witnee

## Willa
**Meaning:** Will, desire; helmet, protection
**Origin:** English
**Pronunciation:** will AH
**Description:** Willa is the feminine version of the name William, meaning 'will,' or 'desire,' and 'helmet,' or protection'. Willa can also be a short form of the name Wilhelmina, and is a popular modern name.
**Alternative spellings:** Willah

## Willow
**Meaning:** Willow tree
**Origin:** English
**Pronunciation:** WIL low
**Description:** Willow trees are known for their grace and flexibility. It has been a popular name for many years.
**Alternative spellings:** Willo, Wilow

## Winifred
**Meaning:** Fair; blessed
**Origin:** Welsh
**Pronunciation:** WIN ee fred
**Description:** An English variation on the Welsh name Gwenfrewi. Winifred was a 7th-century saint.
**Alternative spellings:** Wynifred, Wynyfred

## Winnie

**Meaning:** Blessed with peace
**Origin:** Welsh
**Pronunciation:** win EE
**Description:** Winnie is the pet form of the name Winifred, but is now found used independently as a name in its own right. Winifred is an Anglicisation of the old Celtic Welsh name Gwenfrewi, which is said to mean 'blessed with peace'. Winifred is used as a name for both boys and girls, although nowadays Winnie is found mainly as a feminine name. An increase in popularity may be due to A.A. Milne's loveable bear, Winnie-the-Pooh.
**Alternative spellings:** Winny

## Winona

**Meaning:** Firstborn daughter
**Origin:** Native American
**Pronunciation:** win OWN ah
**Description:** Winona is the English version of the Dakota word '*winúŋna*', meaning 'first-born daughter'. Winona Ryder is a famous American actress with this name.

## Winter

**Meaning:** Cold season
**Origin:** English
**Pronunciation:** WIN ter
**Description:** Winter comes from the English word of the same meaning, referring to the cold season during the year.
**Alternative spellings:** Wynter

## Wren

**Meaning:** Small bird
**Origin:** English
**Pronunciation:** REN
**Description:** Wren, which is Old English in origin, is associated with the small bird and is an uncommon name.
**Alternative spellings:** Ren

# X

## Xanthe

**Meaning:** Yellow; bright
**Origin:** Greek
**Pronunciation:** ZAN thee
**Description:** Xanthe is an unusual name and was one of the Oceanids in Greek mythology as well as an Amazon.
**Alternative spellings:** Zanthe, Zanthi

## Xena

**Meaning:** Stranger; foreigner
**Origin:** Greek
**Pronunciation:** zina
**Description:** Xena is a Greek name meaning 'stranger' or 'foreigner'. It was made popular by the television series, *Xena: Warrior Princess*.
**Alternative spellings:** Zena

## Xenia

**Meaning:** Hospitality

W
X

**Origin:** Greek
**Pronunciation:** ZEE nee uh
**Description:** While this name is mainly used in Russia and Greece, it has spread in popularity. It is now more common across Europe, especially Spain.
**Alternative spellings:** Zenia

## Xin

**Meaning:** Beautiful
**Origin:** Chinese
**Pronunciation:** SHIN
**Description:** Xin is a name of a Chinese dynasty that ran between AD 9–23. It was then passed down as a surname and first name throughout generations.

# Y

## Yana

**Meaning:** He answers
**Origin:** Slavic
**Pronunciation:** YAE nah
**Description:** Yana is a Slavic girls' name meaning 'He (God) answers'. The name is a variation of the similar name Jana, but has a different meaning.
**Alternative spellings:** Yanna, Yanah, Yannah

## Yara

**Meaning:** Butterfly
**Origin:** Arabic
**Pronunciation:** YAH rah
**Description:** Yara means 'butterfly' and is popular across the Arabic world. As the name of a Brazilian goddess, it is also popular in South America.
**Alternative spellings:** Yahrah, Yarah

## Yasmin

**Meaning:** Jasmine flower
**Origin:** Persian
**Pronunciation:** YAH smin
**Description:** Yasmin is a variant on the name Jasmine. It has become very popular in the UK over recent years.
**Alternative spellings:** Yasmine, Yazmin

## Yayoi

**Meaning:** Full life
**Origin:** Japanese
**Pronunciation:** yah YO ee
**Description:** While this name is uncommon in the UK it is popular across Asia and Japan. It is the name of one of the most important eras in Japanese history, the Yayoi Period.
**Alternative spellings:** Yahyoi, Yayoe

## Yi

**Meaning:** Righteous
**Origin:** Chinese
**Pronunciation:** YE
**Description:** Yi is a name from Eastern Asia and associated with historical Chinese rulers.
**Alternative spellings:** Ye

## Yoko

**Meaning:** Honoured child

**Origin:** Japanese
**Pronunciation:** yo KO
**Description:** Yoko is a variation on the Japanese name Youko and is popular across Japan and Asia.
**Alternative spellings:** Youko

## Yolanda

**Meaning:** Violet
**Origin:** Greek
**Pronunciation:** yo LAN dah
**Description:** Yolanda comes from the Greek word '*iolanthe*' meaning 'violet', as in the purple flower. In many European countries, this name is spelt with a 'J'.

## Yu

**Meaning:** Unknown
**Origin:** Chinese
**Pronunciation:** YOO
**Description:** Yu is unisex and its meanings depend on the 13 Chinese characters that make up the name.
**Alternative spellings:** Yoo

## Yuka

**Meaning:** Fragrant
**Origin:** Japanese
**Pronunciation:** yoo KAH
**Description:** Yuka is a name found across Asia, but more commonly in Japan and Japanese-speaking communities. It means 'fragrant'.
**Alternative spellings:** Uka, Yooka

## Yuki

**Meaning:** Snow; happiness
**Origin:** Japanese
**Pronunciation:** yoo KEE
**Description:** Depending on the kanji character used, Yuki can mean either 'snow' or 'happiness'.

## Yumiko

**Meaning:** Helpful beautiful child
**Origin:** Japanese
**Pronunciation:** yu MI ko
**Description:** Yumiko is common across Asia, but is most popular among Japanese communities. Yumiko Abe is a Japanese professional wrestler.
**Alternative spellings:** Yumikoh

## Yumna

**Meaning:** Lucky
**Origin:** Arabic
**Pronunciation:** YUHM na
**Description:** Yumna is an Arabic name that means 'lucky'. It has spread throughout the Middle East and into Africa, but is favoured mainly by Muslim parents.
**Alternative spellings:** Yummna

## Yuriko

**Meaning:** Lily child
**Origin:** Japanese
**Pronunciation:** yur EE ko
**Description:** Yuriko is a common name across Asia and is most popular in Japan. It is said to mean 'lily child'.
**Alternative spellings:** Yureko

## Yvette

**Meaning:** Yew
**Origin:** French
**Pronunciation:** ee VET
**Description:** Yvette is a common name in France. It means 'yew'.
**Alternative spellings:** Ivette

## Yvie

**Meaning:** Full of life
**Origin:** Hebrew
**Pronunciation:** EE vee

Y

**Description:** Although Yvie could be seen as an alternative to Evie, it is also derived from the name Yvonne. It has grown in popularity in recent years.

**Alternative spellings:** Evee, Evie, Yvee

# Z

## Zadie
**Meaning:** Princess
**Origin:** English
**Pronunciation:** zay DEE
**Description:** Zadie is a variation of the name Sadie, which was originally a pet form of Sarah. All of these names mean 'princess'.

## Zahara
**Meaning:** She will flourish
**Origin:** Arabic
**Pronunciation:** za HAR ah
**Description:** This name has become popular because of its similarity to Sahara. For Muslims, Zahara is the name of the prophet Muhammad's mother.
**Alternative spellings:** Zahaara

## Zahra
**Meaning:** In flower
**Origin:** Arabic
**Pronunciation:** ZAH rah
**Description:** Zahra is a spelling variation of the feminine name Zara, which is of Arabic origin and is said to mean 'in flower,' as in to flourish. In Islamic belief it was the surname of the prophet Muhammad's mother, and is a popular name with Muslim parents, who use it in tribute to her.

**Alternative spellings:** Zahraa, Zarah, Zara

## Zainab
**Meaning:** Fragrant
**Origin:** Arabic
**Pronunciation:** zay NAB
**Description:** Zainab is another way of spelling Zaynab, a feminine name of Arabic origin that is popular amongt Muslims. Its meaning is uncertain, although it is sometimes held to mean 'fragrant'. It is found in Islamic belief as the name for several members of the prophet Muhammad's family.
**Alternative spellings:** Zaynab

## Zayna
**Meaning:** Beauty
**Origin:** Persian
**Pronunciation:** ZAY nah
**Description:** Zayna is a phonetic spelling of Zaina, the feminine equivalent of the masculine name, Zain, which is an Islamic name that means 'beauty' or 'handsome'. It does, however, also have a separate origin to this and can be traced to the Greek name, Xenia, which is said to mean 'stranger'.
**Alternative spellings:** Zaynah, Zaina

**BabyNames**.co.uk

The UK's most popular baby names website

Babynames.co.uk is the UK's favourite baby names website. If you want to extend your search online there couldn't be a better place to start. With a strong community of over 30,000 members providing help and advice, as well as entertainment, you can be sure that any question you have will be answered. Babynames.co.uk also offers a baby names generator for inspiration and quizzes to keep you entertained while you decide on your baby's name.

## Zofia

**Meaning:** Wisdom
**Origin:** Greek
**Pronunciation:** zi FEE ah
**Description:** Zofia is a name that derives from the more common Greek name Sophia. It is common in Polish- and English-speaking communities.
**Alternative spellings:** Zophia

## Zoha

**Meaning:** Morning light
**Origin:** Arabic
**Pronunciation:** ZOH ha
**Description:** Zoha is a name which is extremely popular among Muslim parents, and means 'morning light'.
**Alternative spellings:** Zohah

## Zohra

**Meaning:** Flower blossom
**Origin:** Arabic
**Pronunciation:** ZOR ah
**Description:** Zohra means 'flower blossom'. There is a Hebrew city of the same name in the Bible.
**Alternative spellings:** Sora, Zora, Zorah

## Zoya

**Meaning:** Life
**Origin:** Greek
**Pronunciation:** ZOI ya
**Description:** Zoya is derived from the Greek Zoe. It is extremely popular in Russia, where it is spelt Zoia. It means 'life and subsistence'.
**Alternative spellings:** Zoia

## Zunaira

**Meaning:** Guiding light
**Origin:** Arabic
**Pronunciation:** zun AIR ah
**Description:** Zunaira is an Arabic feminine name meaning 'guiding light'. Zunairah al-Rumiya was a Muslim figure who was tortured until she became blind and her sight was restored by a miracle from Allah.
**Alternative spellings:** Zunairah

## Zunairah

**Meaning:** A flower of paradise
**Origin:** Arabic
**Pronunciation:** zoo NAIR ah
**Description:** Zunairah is an unusual name of Arabic origin. It may mean 'flower of paradise'.
**Alternative spellings:** Zunaira

## Zuri

**Meaning:** Good; beautiful
**Origin:** Swahili
**Pronunciation:** ZUR ee
**Description:** Zuri is a girls' name meaning 'good' and 'beautiful' in Swahili. It is often found in African-American communities to celebrate their heritage.

## Zuzanna

**Meaning:** Lily
**Origin:** Slavic
**Pronunciation:** zoo ZAN ah
**Description:** Zuzanna is an alternative spelling of the name Susannah and it would have originated from the Slavic regions of Europe. It means 'lily,' referring to the flower, which is a popular Christian symbol.
**Alternative spellings:** Susanna, Susannah

## Zeenat

**Meaning:** Decoration
**Origin:** Sanskrit
**Pronunciation:** ZEE nat
**Description:** Zeenat is a name of Urdu origin that means 'decoration'. It is common among Hindu families.
**Alternative spellings:** Zinat

## Zelda

**Meaning:** Dark battle
**Origin:** Germanic
**Pronunciation:** ZEHL dah
**Description:** This is a shortened version of Griselda, a German name meaning 'dark battle'. It can also be the feminine form of the Yiddish name Selig, meaning 'happy' or 'blessed'.

## Zena

**Meaning:** Zeus's life
**Origin:** Greek
**Pronunciation:** ZEE na
**Description:** Said to derive from Zenobia, meaning 'Zeus's life', Zena is popular in English-speaking countries.
**Alternative spellings:** Xena

## Zendaya

**Meaning:** Give thanks
**Origin:** African
**Pronunciation:** zen DAY ah
**Description:** Zendaya is an African name meaning 'give thanks'. Zendaya is also the name of a famous American actress and singer.

## Zeynep

**Meaning:** Father's jewellery
**Origin:** Arabic
**Pronunciation:** ZEY nep
**Description:** Zeynep is a name of Arabic origin and is extremely popular in Turkey. It means 'father's jewellery' and is the name of one of the daughters of the prophet Muhammad.
**Alternative spellings:** Zeynip

## Zhi

**Meaning:** Nature
**Origin:** Chinese
**Pronunciation:** JHEE
**Description:** Zhi is a unisex name of Chinese origin, common as both a given name and a surname.
**Alternative spellings:** Zhee, Zi

## Zia

**Meaning:** Light; splendour
**Origin:** Arabic
**Pronunciation:** ZEE ah
**Description:** Zia, derived from the Arabic name Ziva, is usually given to girls. It is said to mean 'light', but also means 'aunt' in Italian.
**Alternative spellings:** Ziah

## Ziva

**Meaning:** Light of God
**Origin:** Hebrew
**Pronunciation:** ZEE vah
**Description:** Ziva, derived from the Hebrew Ziv, means 'light of God'.
**Alternative spellings:** Zivah

## Zoe

**Meaning:** Life
**Origin:** Greek
**Pronunciation:** ZO ee
**Description:** Zoe is a Greek name that was extremely popular during the classical period of Rome. It means 'life'.
**Alternative spellings:** Zoë, Zoé, Zoey, Zooey

Z